Baseball A

DIRECTORY

Baseball America
DIRECTORY

Editors
Kegan Lowe, Josh Norris

Assistant Editors
Justin Coleman, Carlos Collazo,
J.J. Cooper, Teddy Cahill,
Kyle Glaser, Ben Badler

Contributing
Paul Trap

Database & Application Development
Brent Lewis

Photo Editor
Brendan Nolan

Cover Photo
Ed Wolfstein

Design & Production
James Alworth,
Sara Hiatt McDaniel,
Linwood Webb

Programming & Technical Development
Brent Lewis

No portion of this book may be reprinted or reproduced without the written consent of the publisher. For additional copies, visit our Website at BaseballAmerica.com or call 1-800-845-2726 to order. Cost is US $31.95, plus shipping and handling per order. Expedited shipping available.

Distributed by Simon & Schuster ISBN-13: 978-1-932391-83-1

Printed in Canada

Baseball America

BASEBALL... IT'S IN OUR DNA
LIVE LOOK-INS AND ANALYSIS ON MLB TONIGHT™
PLUS 5 LIVE GAMES EACH WEEK

10 MLB NETWORK YEARS™

OUR NATIONAL PASTIME
ALL THE TIME®

TABLE OF CONTENTS

ED WOLFSTEIN

ANDREW WOOLLEY

TRIPLE-A
Classification Change: San Antonio moves from Double-A (Texas) to Triple-A (Pacific Coast). Colorado Springs moves from Triple-A (Pacific Coast) to Rookie-level (Pioneer).
Affiliation Changes: Syracuse (International) from Nationals to Mets
Las Vegas (Pacific Coast) from Mets to Athletics
San Antonio (Pacific Coast) from Padres to Brewers
Fresno (Pacific Coast) from Astros to Nationals
Nashville (Pacific Coast) from Athletics to Rangers
Round Rock (Pacific Coast) from Rangers to Astros

DOUBLE-A
Classification Addition: Amarillo joins Texas League, affiliates with Padres, is named Sod Poodles.
Affiliation Changes: Pensacola (Southern) from Reds to Twins
Chattanooga (Southern) from Twins to Reds

HIGH CLASS A
Affiliation Relocation: Buies Creek (Carolina) moves to Fayetteville, renames as Woodpeckers.

LOW CLASS A
Affiliation Changes: Clinton (Midwest) from Mariners to Marlins
Greensboro (South Atlantic) from Marlins to Pirates
West Virginia (South Atlantic) from Pirates to Mariners

ROOKIE
Affiliation Additions: Athletics, Brewers, Cubs, Dodgers add a second Arizona League team
Affiliation Subtraction: Helena (Pioneer) ceases operations
Classification Change: Colorado Springs moves from Triple-A (Pacific Coast) to Rookie-level (Pioneer), changes its name to Rocky Mountain Vibes.

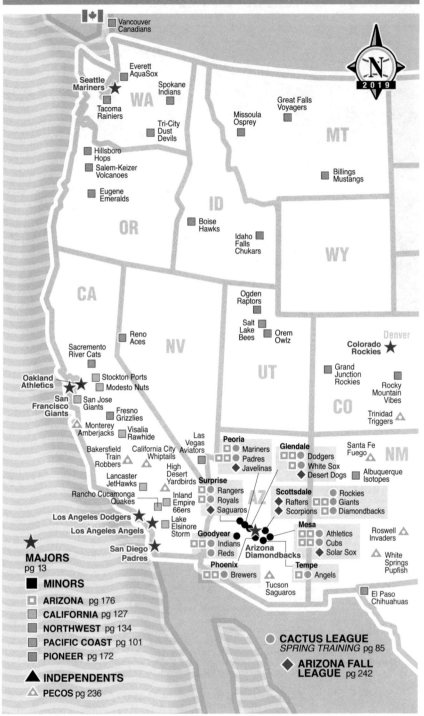

Map illustrations by Paul Trap

N 2019

Vancouver Canadians

Everett AquaSox

Seattle Mariners

Spokane Indians

WA

Tacoma Rainiers

Great Falls Voyagers

Missoula Osprey

MT

Tri-City Dust Devils

Hillsboro Hops

Salem-Keizer Volcanoes

Billings Mustangs

Eugene Emeralds

ID

Boise Hawks

OR

Idaho Falls Chukars

WY

CA

Ogden Raptors

Reno Aces

Salt Lake Bees

Orem Owlz

Denver

NV

Colorado Rockies

Sacramento River Cats

UT

Grand Junction Rockies

Rocky Mountain Vibes

Oakland Athletics

Stockton Ports

Modesto Nuts

CO

Trinidad Triggers

San Francisco Giants

San Jose Giants

Fresno Grizzlies

Las Vegas Aviators

Peoria
- Mariners
- Padres
- Javelinas

Glendale
- Dodgers
- White Sox
- Desert Dogs

Santa Fe Fuego

NM

Monterey Amberjacks

Visalia Rawhide

Albuquerque Isotopes

Bakersfield Train Robbers

California City Whiptails

Surprise
- Rangers
- Royals
- Saguaros

AZ

Scottsdale
- Rafters
- Scorpions

- Rockies
- Giants
- Diamondbacks

High Desert Yardbirds

Lancaster JetHawks

Rancho Cucamonga Quakes

Inland Empire 66ers

Mesa
- Athletics
- Cubs
- Solar Sox

Roswell Invaders

Los Angeles Dodgers

Los Angeles Angels

Lake Elsinore Storm

Goodyear
- Indians
- Reds

Arizona Diamondbacks

White Springs Pupfish

San Diego Padres

Phoenix
- Brewers

Tempe
- Angels

Tucson Saguaros

El Paso Chihuahuas

★ **MAJORS**
pg 13

■ **MINORS**

□ **ARIZONA** pg 176

■ **CALIFORNIA** pg 127

■ **NORTHWEST** pg 134

■ **PACIFIC COAST** pg 101

■ **PIONEER** pg 172

▲ **INDEPENDENTS**

△ **PECOS** pg 236

● **CACTUS LEAGUE**
SPRING TRAINING pg 85

◆ **ARIZONA FALL LEAGUE** pg 242

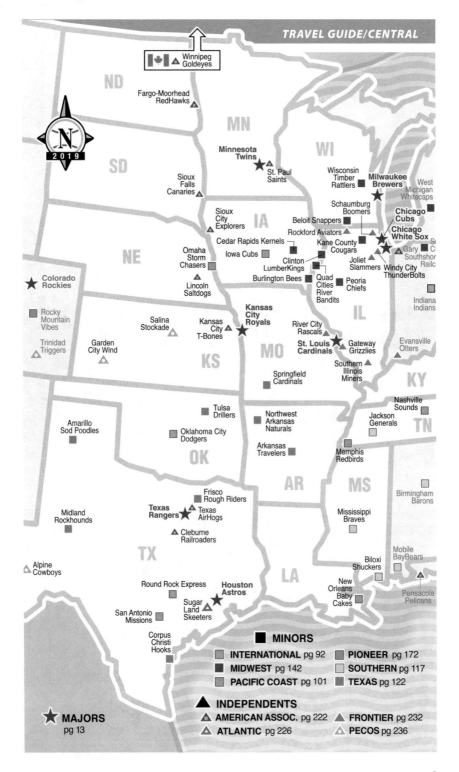

Winnipeg Goldeyes

ND

Fargo-Moorhead RedHawks

N 2019

MN

WI

SD

Minnesota Twins

St. Paul Saints

Wisconsin Timber Rattlers

Milwaukee Brewers

West Michigan Whitecaps

Sioux Falls Canaries

Sioux City Explorers

IA

Schaumburg Boomers

Beloit Snappers

Chicago Cubs

Rockford Aviators

Chicago White Sox

Cedar Rapids Kernels

Kane County Cougars

Gary Southshore Railc

NE

Omaha Storm Chasers

Iowa Cubs

Clinton LumberKings

Joliet Slammers

Windy City ThunderBolts

Burlington Bees

Quad Cities River Bandits

Peoria Chiefs

Colorado Rockies

Lincoln Saltdogs

IL

Indiana Indians

Rocky Mountain Vibes

Salina Stockade

Kansas City T-Bones

Kansas City Royals

River City Rascals

Evansville Otters

Trinidad Triggers

Garden City Wind

St. Louis Cardinals

Gateway Grizzlies

KY

KS

MO

Southern Illinois Miners

Springfield Cardinals

Nashville Sounds

Tulsa Drillers

Northwest Arkansas Naturals

Jackson Generals

TN

Amarillo Sod Poodles

Oklahoma City Dodgers

Arkansas Travelers

OK

Memphis Redbirds

AR

MS

Birmingham Barons

Frisco Rough Riders

Midland Rockhounds

Texas Rangers

Texas AirHogs

Mississippi Braves

Cleburne Railroaders

TX

Mobile BayBears

Alpine Cowboys

LA

Biloxi Shuckers

Round Rock Express

Houston Astros

New Orleans Baby Cakes

Pensacola Pelicans

San Antonio Missions

Sugar Land Skeeters

Corpus Christi Hooks

■ MINORS

■ INTERNATIONAL pg 92   ■ PIONEER pg 172
■ MIDWEST pg 142   □ SOUTHERN pg 117
■ PACIFIC COAST pg 101   ■ TEXAS pg 122

▲ INDEPENDENTS

▲ AMERICAN ASSOC. pg 222   ▲ FRONTIER pg 232
△ ATLANTIC pg 226   △ PECOS pg 236

★ MAJORS
pg 13

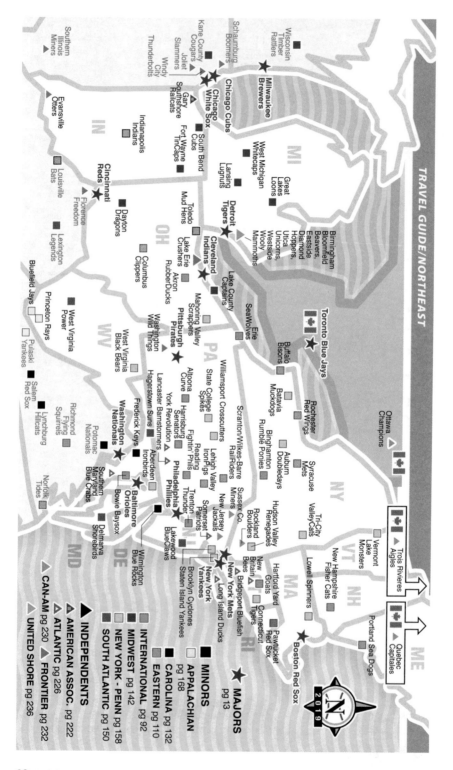

Southern Illinois Miners
Schaumburg Boomers
Kane County Cougars
Joliet Slammers
Windy City Thunderbolts
Evansville Otters
Wisconsin Timber Rattlers
Gary Southshore Railcats
Chicago Cubs
Chicago White Sox
Milwaukee Brewers
Indianapolis Indians
Fort Wayne TinCaps
South Bend Cubs
West Michigan Whitecaps
Lansing Lugnuts
Great Lakes Loons
Louisville Bats
Cincinnati Reds
Florence Freedom
Dayton Dragons
Lexington Legends
Toledo Mud Hens
Lake Erie Crushers
Akron RubberDucks
Cleveland Indians
Columbus Clippers
Detroit Tigers
Birmingham Bloomfield Beavers, Eastside Diamond Hoppers, Utica Unicorns, Westside Woolly Mammoths
Lake County Captains
Erie SeaWolves
Bluefield Jays
Princeton Rays
West Virginia Power
West Virginia Black Bears
Washington Wild Things
Pittsburgh Pirates
Mahoning Valley Scrappers
Williamsport Crosscutters
State College Spikes
Altoona Curve
Buffalo Bisons
Batavia Muckdogs
Rochester Red Wings
Toronto Blue Jays
Ottawa Champions
Salem Red Sox
Lynchburg Hillcats
Richmond Flying Squirrels
Potomac Nationals
Washington Nationals
Frederick Keys
Hagerstown Suns
Lancaster Barnstormers
York Revolution
Harrisburg Senators
Fightin Phils
Reading
Scranton/Wilkes-Barre RailRiders
Binghamton Rumble Ponies
Auburn Doubledays
Syracuse Mets
Pulaski Yankees
Norfolk Tides
Delmarva Shorebirds
Southern Maryland Blue Crabs
Bowie Baysox
Baltimore Orioles
Aberdeen Ironbirds
Wilmington Blue Rocks
Philadelphia Phillies
Trenton Thunder
Somerset Patriots
Lehigh Valley IronPigs
New Jersey Jackals
Sussex Co. Miners
Tri-City ValleyCats
Hudson Valley Renegades
Rockland Boulders
Lakewood BlueClaws
New York Yankees
Long Island Ducks
Brooklyn Cyclones
Staten Island Yankees
New York Mets
New Britain Bees
Bridgeport Bluefish
Connecticut Tigers
Hartford Yard Goats
Pawtucket Red Sox
New Hampshire Fisher Cats
Vermont Lake Monsters
Lowell Spinners
Portland Sea Dogs
Boston Red Sox

Trois Rivieres Aigles
Quebec Capitales

MAJORS pg 13

MINORS
APPALACHIAN pg 168
INTERNATIONAL pg 92
MIDWEST pg 142
NEW YORK - PENN pg 158
SOUTH ATLANTIC pg 150
EASTERN pg 110
CAROLINA pg 132

INDEPENDENTS
AMERICAN ASSOC. pg 222
ATLANTIC pg 226
CAN-AM pg 230
FRONTIER pg 232
UNITED SHORE pg 236

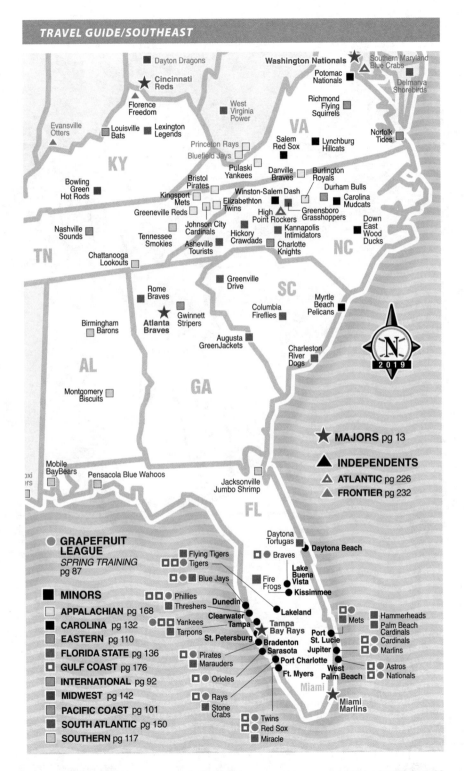

MAJORS pg 13
INDEPENDENTS
ATLANTIC pg 226
FRONTIER pg 232

GRAPEFRUIT LEAGUE
SPRING TRAINING pg 87

MINORS
APPALACHIAN pg 168
CAROLINA pg 132
EASTERN pg 110
FLORIDA STATE pg 136
GULF COAST pg 176
INTERNATIONAL pg 92
MIDWEST pg 142
PACIFIC COAST pg 101
SOUTH ATLANTIC pg 150
SOUTHERN pg 117

MAJOR
LEAGUES

MAJOR LEAGUE BASEBALL

Mailing Address: 245 Park Ave. New York, NY 10167.
Telephone: (212) 931-7800. **Website:** www.mlb.com.
Commissioner of Baseball: Rob Manfred.
Deputy Commissioner, Baseball Administration and Chief Legal Officer: Dan Halem.
Deputy Commissioner, Business & Media: Tony Petitti. **Chief Communications Officer:** Pat
Courtney. **Chief Baseball Officer:** Joe Torre. **Chief Financial Officer/Sr. Advisor:** Bob Starkey.
Executive Vice President, Strategy, Technology/Innovation: Chris Marinak. **Executive Vice
President, Commerce:** Noah Garden. **Chief Technology Officer:** Jason Gaedtke.

Rob Manfred

ON-FIELD OPERATIONS

Senior VP, On-Field Operations & Umpiring: Peter Woodfork. **VP, On-Field Operations,
Initiatives & Strategy:** Chris Young. **Senior Director, Umpire Operations:** Matt McKendry.
Senior Director, Instant Replay: Justin Klemm. **Director, Minor League Operations:**
Fred Seymour. **Director, Major League Umpiring:** Randy Marsh. **Director, Umpiring
Development:** Rich Rieker. **Director, Umpire Medical Services:** Mark Letendre. **Senior Video
Coordinator:** Freddie Hernandez. **Manager, Instant Replay:** Jeffrey Moody. **Manager, Umpire Operations:** Raquel
Wagner. **Senior Coordinator, On-Field Operations:** Michael Sansarran. **Coordinator, Umpire Operations:** Alejandro
Bermudez. **Analyst, Baseball Operations:** Josh Keen. **Executive Assistant, Baseball Operations:** Chris Romanello.
Umpiring Supervisors: Cris Jones, Tom Lepperd, Chuck Meriwether, Ed Montague, Ed Rapuano, Charlie Reliford, Larry
Young.

LABOR RELATIONS

Senior Vice President, Deputy General Counsel, Labor Relations: Patrick Houlihan. **Vice President, Deputy
General Counsel, Labor Relations & Player Programs:** Paul Mifsud. **Vice President, Drug, Health & Safety
Programs:** Jon Coyles. **Director, Labor Relations & Player Programs:** Yenifer Fauche. **Senior Manager, Labor
Relations & Player Programs:** Ricardhy Grandoit. **Senior Manager, MLB Drug, Health & Safety Program:** Lindsey
Ingraham. **Senior Counsel:** Kasey Sanossian. **Counsel:** Vanish Grover.

LEAGUE ECONOMICS & OPERATIONS

Senior Vice President, League Economics & Operations: Morgan Sword. **Senior Director, League Operations:**
Roy Krasik. **Senior Director, League Operations:** Jeff Pfeifer. **Senior Director, League Economics:** John D'Angelo.
Senior Director, League Economics: Reed MacPhail. **Manager, International Operations:** Rebecca Seesel. **Senior
Coordinator, League Operations:** Gina Liento. **Senior Coordinator, League Operations:** Garrett Horan. **Senior
Coordinator, League Economics:** Cameron Barwick. **Coordinator, League Economics:** Travis Buck, Jalen Phillips.
Coordinator, International Operations: Patrick Nathanson. **Coordinator, Medical Administration:** Kevin Ma.
Coordinator, Amateur Administration: Diego Delgado.

BASEBALL & SOFTBALL DEVELOPMENT

Executive Vice President, Baseball & Softball Development: Tony Reagins. **Senior Vice President, Baseball
Operations & International Development:** Kim Ng. **Vice President, Baseball & Softball Development:** David James.
Vice President, Youth & Facility Development: Darrell Miller. **Senior Director, Baseball & Softball Development:**
Chris Haydock. **Senior Director, Baseball & Softball Development:** Bill Bavasi. **Senior Director, Baseball
Development:** Del Matthews. **Senior Manager, Baseball & Softball Development:** Chuck Fox. **Senior Manager,
Latin American Game Development:** Joel Araujo. **Senior Manager, Play Ball & RBI:** Bennett Shields. **Senior
Coordinator, International Baseball Operations:** Max Thomas. **Manager, International Baseball Operations:** Shane
Barclay. **Manager, Baseball & Softball Development:** Henry Gonzalez. **Senior Coordinator, Baseball Development:**
Kindu Jones. **Coordinator, Youth Softball:** Koely Kempisty. **Coordinator, Youth Programs:** Kenneth Landreaux.
Coordinator, Softball: Bryana Simpson. **Coordinator, Youth Programs, RBI, Play Ball:** Steven Smiegocki. **Senior
Administrative Assistant:** Rose Aparicio.

COMMUNICATIONS

Telephone: (212) 931-7878. **Fax:** (212) 949-5654.
Chief Communications Officer: Pat Courtney. **Vice President, Communications:** John Blundell, Mike Teevan.
Vice President, Business Communications: Matt Bourne. **Vice President, Corporate Communications:** Matt
Gould. **Senior Director, Business Communications & Youth Engagement:** Steve Arocho. **Senior Director,
Business Communications:** Ileana Peña. **Director, Communications:** Donald Muller. **Manager, Communications:**
Lydia Devlin. **Specialist, Business Communications:** David Hochman. **Coordinator, Communications:** Yolayna
Alvarez, Paul Koehler. **Coordinator, Business Communications:** Kerline Batista, Troy Watson. **Executive Assistant,
Communications:** Ginger Dillon. **Senior Administrative Assistant, Communications:** Lisa Teitelbaum. **Official
Historian:** John Thorn.

AMERICAN LEAGUE

Year League Founded: 1901.
2019 Opening Date: March 28. **Closing Date:** Sept. 29.
Regular Season: 162 games.
Division Structure: East—Baltimore, Boston, New York, Tampa Bay, Toronto.
Central—Chicago, Cleveland, Detroit, Kansas City, Minnesota. **West**—Houston, Los Angeles, Oakland, Seattle, Texas.

Playoff Format: Two non-division winners with best records meet in one-game wild card. Wild card winner and three division champions meet in two best-of-five Division Series. Winners meet in best-of-seven Championship Series.

All-Star Game: July 9, Progressive Field, Cleveland (American League vs. National League).

Roster Limit: 25, through Aug. 31, when rosters expand to 40. **Brand of Baseball:** Rawlings.

Statistician: MLB Advanced Media, 75 Ninth Ave., 5th Floor, New York, NY 10011.

STADIUM INFORMATION

Team	Stadium	Dimensions			Capacity	2018 Att.
		LF	CF	RF		
Baltimore	Oriole Park at Camden Yards	333	410	318	45,971	1,564,192
Boston	Fenway Park	310	390	302	37,673	2,895,575
Chicago	Guaranteed Rate Field	330	400	335	40,615	1,608,817
Cleveland	Progressive Field	325	405	325	37,675	1,926,701
Detroit	Comerica Park	345	420	330	41,782	1,856,970
Houston	Minute Maid Park	315	435	326	40,976	2,980,549
Kansas City	Kauffman Stadium	330	410	330	37,903	1,665,107
Los Angeles	Angel Stadium	333	404	333	45,050	3,020,216
Minnesota	Target Field	339	404	328	39,504	2,051,279
New York	Yankee Stadium	318	408	314	50,291	1,959,197
Oakland	Oakland Coliseum	330	400	367	35,067	1,573,616
Seattle	T-Mobile Park	331	401	326	47,447	2,299,489
Tampa Bay	Tropicana Field	315	404	322	41,315	1,154,973
Texas	Globe Life Park in Arlington	332	400	325	48,114	2,107,107
Toronto	Rogers Centre	328	400	328	50,598	2,325,281

NATIONAL LEAGUE

Year League Founded: 1876.
2019 Opening Date: March 28. **Closing Date:** Sept. 29.
Regular Season: 162 games.
Division Structure: East—Atlanta, Miami, New York, Philadelphia, Washington.
Central—Chicago, Cincinnati, Milwaukee, Pittsburgh, St. Louis. **West**—Arizona, Colorado, Los Angeles, San Diego, San Francisco.
Playoff Format: Two non-division winners with best records meet in one-game wild card. Wild card winner and three division champions meet in two best-of-five Division Series. Winners meet in best-of-seven Championship Series.

All-Star Game: July 9, Progressive Field, Cleveland (American League vs. National League).

Roster Limit: 25, through Aug. 31 when rosters expand to 40. **Brand of Baseball:** Rawlings.

Statistician: MLB Advanced Media, 75 Ninth Ave., 5th Floor, New York, NY 10011.

STADIUM INFORMATION

Team	Stadium	Dimensions			Capacity	2018 Att.
		LF	CF	RF		
Arizona	Chase Field	330	407	334	49,033	2,242,695
Atlanta	SunTrust Park	335	400	325	41,500	2,555,781
Chicago	Wrigley Field	355	400	353	41,160	3,156,185
Cincinnati	Great American Ball Park	328	404	325	42,319	1,629,356
Colorado	Coors Field	347	415	350	50,499	3,015,880
Los Angeles	Dodger Stadium	330	395	330	56,000	3,857,500
Miami	Marlins Park	344	407	335	36,742	811,104
Milwaukee	Miller Park	344	400	345	41,900	2,850,875
New York	Citi Field	335	408	330	42,200	2,224,995
Philadelphia	Citizens Bank Park	329	401	330	43,647	2,158,124
Pittsburgh	PNC Park	325	399	320	38,496	1,465,316
St. Louis	Busch Stadium	336	400	335	46,681	3,403,587
San Diego	Petco Park	336	396	322	42,685	2,168,536
San Francisco	Oracle Park	339	399	309	41,503	3,156,185
Washington	Nationals Park	336	402	335	41,888	2,529,604

ARIZONA DIAMONDBACKS

Office Address: Chase Field, 401 E. Jefferson St, Phoenix, AZ 85004.
Mailing Address: P.O. Box 2095, Phoenix, AZ 85001.
Telephone: (602) 462-6500. **Fax:** (602) 462-6599. **Website:** www.dbacks.com

OWNERSHIP
Managing General Partner: Ken Kendrick. **General Partners:** Mike Chipman, Jeff Royer.

BUSINESS OPERATIONS
President/CEO: Derrick Hall. **Executive Vice President, Business Operations/Chief Revenue Officer:** Cullen Maxey. **Executive Vice President/Chief Financial Officer:** Tom Harris. **Senior Advisor, President/CEO:** Luis Gonzalez. **Special Assistants, President/CEO:** Roland Hemond, Randy Johnson, J.J. Putz, Willie Bloomquist. **Special Advisor on Mexico, President/CEO:** Erubiel Durazo. **Executive Assistant, President/CEO:** Brooke Mitchell. **Executive Assistant, Managing General Partner & CFO:** Sandy Cox. **Executive Assistant, CRO:** Katy Bernham. **Executive Office Administrative Assistant:** Nicki Adair.

Ken Kendrick

BROADCASTING
VP, Broadcasting: Scott Geyer. **VP, Game Operations/DBTV Productions:** Rob Weinheimer.

CORPORATE PARTNERSHIPS/MARKETING
VP, Corporate Partnerships: Judd Norris. **Senior Director, Corporate Partnership Services:** Kerri White. **VP, Marketing/Analytics:** Kenny Farrell. **Director, Marketing:** Rayme Lofgren. **Senior Manager, Hispanic Marketing:** Jerry Romo.

FINANCE/LEGAL
VP, Finance: Craig Bradley. **Director, Financial Management and Purchasing:** Jeff Jacobs. **Director, Accounting:** Jeffrey Barnes. **General Counsel:** Caleb Jay. **Associate General Counsel**: Maacah Scott.

COMMUNITY AFFAIRS
VP, Corporate/Community Impact: Debbie Castaldo. **Director, Community Events:** Robert Itzkowitz. **Senior Manager, Community/Foundation Operations:** Tara Trzinski. **Senior Manager, Community Initiatives/Partner Programs:** Dustin Payne.

COMMUNICATIONS/MEDIA RELATIONS
Senior VP, Content/Communications: Josh Rawitch. **Senior Director, Player/Media Relations:** Casey Wilcox. **Senior Manager, Player/Media Relations:** Patrick O'Connell. **Manager, Player/Media Relations:** Patrick Kurish. **Senior Manager, Corporate Communications:** Katie Krause.

SPECIAL PROJECTS/FAN EXPERIENCE
VP, Special Projects: Graham Rossini. **Director, Special Projects/Brand Development:** Matt Helmeid. **Director, Baseball Outreach/Development:** Jeff Rodin. **General Manager, Salt River Fields:** David Dunne.

2019 SCHEDULE
Standard Game Times: 6:40 p.m.; Sun. 1:10.

MARCH	6-8 . . . . at Tampa Bay	24-26 . . . Los Angeles (NL)
28-31 . at Los Angeles (NL)	9-12 . . . . Atlanta	27-30 . . . at San Francisco
	13-15 . . . . Pittsburgh	
APRIL	17-19 . . . . . San Francisco	**JULY**
1-3 . . . . . . at San Diego	20-22 . . . . at San Diego	2-3 . . . at Los Angeles (NL)
5-7 . . . . Boston	24-26 . . . at San Francisco	5-7 . . . . Colorado
9-10 . . . . Texas	27-30 . . . . . at Colorado	12-14 . . . . .at St. Louis
11-14 . . . . . . San Diego	31 . . . . . . .New York (NL)	16-17 . . . . .at Texas
16-18 . . . . at Atlanta		18-21 . . . . . .Milwaukee
19-21 . . . .at Chicago (NL)	**JUNE**	22-24 . . . . . . Baltimore
22-25 . . . . . at Pittsburgh	1-2 . . . . . .New York (NL)	26-29 . . . . . . at Miami
26-28 . . . . . Chicago (NL)	3-5 . . . . Los Angeles (NL)	30-31 . . at New York (AL)
30 . . . . . . .New York (AL)	7-9 . . . . at Toronto	
	10-12 . . . . at Philadelphia	**AUGUST**
MAY	13-16 . . . . at Washington	2-4 . . . . Washington
1 . . . . . .New York (AL)	18-20 . . . . .Colorado	5-7 . . . . .Philadelphia
3-5 . . . . at Colorado	21-23 . . . . . San Francisco	9-11 . . at Los Angeles (NL)
		12-14 . . . . . . at Colorado
		15-18 . . . . . San Francisco
		19-21 . . . . .Colorado
		23-25 . . . . . at Milwaukee
		26-27 . . . at San Francisco
		29-31 . . .Los Angeles (NL)
		SEPTEMBER
		1 . . . . . .Los Angeles (NL)
		2-4 . . . . San Diego
		6-8 . . . . .at Cincinnati
		9-12 . . . .at New York (NL)
		13-15 . . . . Cincinnati
		16-18 . . . . .Miami
		20-22 . . . . . at San Diego
		23-25 . . . . St. Louis
		27-29 . . . . . . San Diego

GENERAL INFORMATION
Stadium (year opened): Chase Field (1998). **Home Dugout:** Third Base.
Team Colors: Sedona Red, Sonoran Sand and Black. **Playing Surface:** Grass.

TICKET SALES

Telephone: (602) 514-8400. **Fax:** (602) 462-4141. **Senior VP, Ticket Sales/Marketing:** John Fisher. **VP, Ticket Sales/Events:** Ryan Holmstedt. **Senior Director, Ticket Operations:** Josh Simon. **Director, Business Analytics:** Brandon Buser. **Director, Season Ticket Sales/Inside Sales:** Mike Dellosa. **Director, Season Ticket Services:** Jamie Roberts. **Director, Group Events and Hospitality:** Anthony Synegal

BASEBALL OPERATIONS

Mike Hazen

Executive Vice President/General Manager: Mike Hazen. **Senior VP/Assistant GMs:** Jared Porter, Amiel Sawdaye. **VP, Latin Operations:** Junior Noboa. **Special Assistants to GM:** Burke Badenhop, Craig Shipley. **Director, Baseball Operations:** Sam Eaton. **Director, Research & Development:** Michael Fitzgerald. **Coordinator, Amateur Scouting & Baseball Administration:** Kristyn Pierce. **Assistant, Baseball Operations:** Connor Shannon. **Baseball Operations Fellow:** Alex Lorenzo. **Baseball Systems Lead Architect:** John Krazit. **Baseball Systems Developer:** Thomas Johnson. **Jr. Developer, Baseball Systems:** Gavin Sweeny. **Mathematical Modeler, Baseball Analytics:** Cody Callahan. **Quantitative Researcher, Baseball Analytics:** Max Glick. **Research and Development Analysts:** Max Phillips, Taylor Chloe, Micah Daley-Harris. **Pitching Strategist:** Dan Haren. **Pitching Analyst:** Ross Seaton. **Coordinators, Run Production:** Alex Cultice, Drew Hedman. **Coordinator, Mental Skills:** Zach Brandon.

MAJOR LEAGUE STAFF

Manager: Torey Lovullo. **Coaches: Bench**—Jerry Narron, **Pitching**—Mike Butcher, **Hitting**—Darnell Coles, **First Base**—Dave McKay, **Third Base**—Tony Perezchica, **Bullpen**—Mike Fetters, **Assistant Hitting Coach**—Eric Hinske, **Quality Control/Catching**—Robby Hammock, **Major League**—Luis Urueta. **Bullpen Catcher**—Dan Butler, Humberto Quintero.

MEDICAL/TRAINING

Club Physician: Dr. Gary Waslewski. **Director, Sports Medicine & Performance:** Ken Crenshaw. **Head Trainer:** Ryan DiPanfilo. **Strength & Conditioning Coordinator:** Nate Shaw. **Assistant Strength & Conditioning Coordinator:** Matt Tenney. **Physical Therapist:** Ben Hagar. **Analyst, Sports Medicine:** Patrick Sellas.

PLAYER DEVELOPMENT

VP, Player Development: Mike Bell. **Assistant Director, Player Development:** Josh Barfield. **Senior Manager, Player Development:** Shawn Marette. **Assistant, Player Development:** Peter Bransfield. **Assistant, Latin American Baseball Operations:** Mariana Patraca

FARM SYSTEM

Class	Club (League)	Manager	Hitting Coach	Pitching Coach
Triple-A	Reno (PCL)	Chris Cron	Jason Camilli	Jeff Bajenaru
Double-A	Jackson (SL)	Blake Lalli	Rick Short	Doug Drabek
High A	Visalia (CAL)	Shawn Roof	Travis Denker	Shane Loux
Low A	Kane County (MWL)	Vince Harrison	Micah Franklin	Mike Parrott
Short-season	Hillsboro (NWL)	Javier Colina	Franklin Stubbs	Barry Enright
Rookie	Missoula (PIO)	Juan Francia	KC Judge	Manny Garcia
Rookie	Diamondbacks (AZL)	Wellington Cepeda	Jose Amado	Rich Sauveur

SCOUTING

Telephone: (602) 462-6500. **Fax:** (602) 462-6425.

Director, Amateur Scouting: Deric Ladnier. **Coordinator, Amateur Scouting:** Ian Rebhan. **Director, Pro Scouting:** Jason Parks. **Coordinator, Pro Scouting:** Cory Hahn. **Director, Latin American Scouting:** Cesar Geronimo. **Assistant Director, International Scouting:** Peter Wardell. **Director, Pacific Rim Operations:** Mack Hayashi. **Special Assistant, Pacific Rim Operations:** Jim Marshall. **National Crosscheckers:** Greg Lonigro (Connellsville, PA), James Merriweather III (Glendale, AZ). **National Pitching Supervisor:** Jeff Mousser (Gilbert, AZ). **National Junior College Supervisor:** Clark Crist (Phoenix, AZ). **Regional Supervisors:** Steve Connelly (Emerald Isle, NC), Frank Damas (Miami Lakes, FL), Steve McAllister (Chillicothe, IL), Doyle Wilson (Queen Creek, AZ). **Area Scouts:** Hudson Belinsky (Smyrna, GA), Nathan Birtwell (St. Louis, MO), Eric Cruz (Pembroke Pines, FL), Orsino Hill (Elk Grove, CA), Kerry Jenkins (Nashville, TN), Jeremy Kehrt (Avon, IN), Jeremiah Luster (Oceanside, CA), Rick Matsko (Davidsville, PA), Matt Mercurio (Indialantic, FL), Rusty Pendergrass (Missouri City, MO), Dan Ramsay (Spokane, WA), Mark Ross (Tucson, AZ), JR Salinas (Roanoke, TX), Dennis Sheehan (Glasco, NY), George Swain (Wilmington, NC), Garry Templeton (San Marcos, CA), Jake Williams (Kansas City, MO). **Part-Time Scouts:** Pedro Hernandez (Vega Baja, PR), Hal Kurtzman (Lake Balboa, CA), Doug Mathieson (Aldergrove, BC), Jerry Nyman (Stevensville, MT), Luke Wrenn (Lakeland, FL). **Special Assignment Scouts:** Todd Greene (Alpharetta, GA), Danny Haas (Madeira, OH), Alex Jacobs (Lakeland, FL), Mark Snipp (The Woodlands, TX), Tim Wilken (Dunedin, FL). **Major League Scouts:** Bill Bryk (Schererville, IN), Bill Gayton (San Diego, CA), Mike Piatnik (Winter Haven, FL). **Professional Scouts:** Tucker Blair (Estero, FL), Mike Brown (Naples, FL), Chris Carminucci (Scottsdale, AZ), Jacob Frisaro (Scottsdale, AZ), Jeff Gardner (Costa Mesa, CA), Jack Goin (Eagan, MN), Matt Hahn (Tampa, FL), Brad Kelley (Scottsdale, AZ), Rob Leary (Melbourne, FL), Tom Romenesko (Santee, CA), Chris Slivka (Scottsdale, AZ), Scipio Spinks (Sugarland, TX), Brett West (Palm Harbor, FL). **International Crosschecker:** Mike Cadahia (Miami Springs, FL). **Crosschecker, Latin America:** Francisco Cartaya (Collierville, TN). **Supervisor, Venezuela:** Antonio Caballero. **Coordinator, Dominican Republic:** Omar Rogers. **International Scouts:** Jose Ortiz, Ronald Rivas, Johan Maya, Diego Bordas (Dominican Republic); Alfonzo Mora, Didimo Bracho, Kristians Pereira, David Chicarelli, Gregory Blanco (Venezuela); Luis Gonzalez Arteaga (Colombia); Julio Sanchez (Ncaragua); Bradley Stuart (Curacao); Kyle Lee (Korea); TY Wei (Taiwan).

ATLANTA BRAVES

Office Address: 755 Battery Avenue, SE Atlanta, GA 30339-3017.
Mailing Address: PO Box 723009, Atlanta, GA 31139-2704.
Telephone: (404) 522-7630. **Website:** www.braves.com.

OWNERSHIP

Operated/Owned By: Liberty Media. **Chairman:** Terry McGuirk. **Chairman Emeritus:** Bill Bartholomay. **Vice Chairman Emeritus:** John Schuerholz. **Senior Vice President:** Henry Aaron.

BUSINESS OPERATIONS

President/CEO: Derek Schiller. **Executive VP/Chief Legal Officer:** Greg Heller.

MARKETING/SALES

Senior VP, Marketing: Adam Zimmerman. **Senior VP, Ticket Sales:** Paul Adams. **Senior VP, Corporate & Premium Partnerships:** Jim Allen. **Senior VP, Human Resources:** DeRetta Rhodes.

Terry McGuirk

FINANCE

Executive VP, Chief Financial Officer: Jill Robinson.

COMMUNICATIONS

Telephone: (404) 522-7630.
Vice President, Communications: Beth Marshall. **Manager, Baseball Communications:** Jonathan Kerber. **Senior Coordinator, Baseball Communications:** Jared Burleyson. **Bilingual Media Coordinator, Baseball Communications:** Franco García. **Manager, Corporate Communications:** Caroline Burleson.

STADIUM OPERATIONS

Senior Vice President, Facility Operations: Eric Perestuk. **Field Director:** Ed Mangan. **VP, Fan Experience:** Scott Cunningham. **PA Announcer:** Casey Motter. **Official Scorers:** Richard Musterer, Mike Stamus.

TICKETING

Telephone: (404) 577-9100. **Email:** ticketsales@braves.com.
VP, Ticket Operations: Anthony Esposito.

TRAVEL/CLUBHOUSE

Director of Team Travel: Jim Lovell. **Director, Equipment & Clubhouse Service:** John Holland.
Visiting Clubhouse Manager: Fred Stone.

2019 SCHEDULE

Standard Game Times: 7:35; Sat. 4:10; Sun. 1:35.

MARCH	6-8 . . . at Los Angeles (NL)	24-27 . . . .at Chicago (NL)	13-15 . . . . .New York (NL)
28-31 . . . . at Philadelphia	9-12 . . . . at Arizona	28-30 . . . at New York (NL)	16-18 . . . Los Angeles (NL)
	14-16 . . . . St. Louis		20-22 . . . . .Miami
APRIL	17-19 . . . . . .Milwaukee	**JULY**	23-25 . . . at New York (NL)
1-4 . . . . Chicago (NL)	20-23 . . . at San Francisco	2-4 . . . . .Philadelphia	27-28 . . . . at Toronto
5-7 . . . . .Miami	24-26 . . . . . . .at St. Louis	5-7 . . . . .Miami	30-31 . . . . . Chicago (AL)
8-10 . . . . . . at Colorado	28-29 . . . . . Washington	12-14 . . . . at San Diego	
11-14 . . . . .New York (NL)	31 . . . . Detroit	15-17 . . . . at Milwaukee	**SEPTEMBER**
16-18 . . . . Arizona		18-21 . . . . .Washington	1 . . . . Chicago (AL)
19-21 . . . .at Cleveland	**JUNE**	23-24 . . . . . Kansas City	2-3 . . . . .Toronto
23-25 . . . .at Cincinnati	1-2 . . . . Detroit	26-28 . . . at Philadelphia	5-8 . . . . Washington
26-28 . . . . . . .Colorado	4-6 . . . . . . at Pittsburgh	29-31 . . . . at Washington	9-12 . . . . .at Philadelphia
29-30 . . . . . . San Diego	7-9 . . . . at Miami		13-15 . . . . at Washington
	10-13 . . . . . . Pittsburgh	**AUGUST**	17-19 . . . .Philadelphia
MAY	14-16 . . . . .Philadelphia	1-4 . . . . Cincinnati	20-22 . . . . . San Francisco
1-2 . . . . San Diego	17-19 . . . .New York (NL)	5-7 . . . . . . at Minnesota	24-25 . . . .at Kansas City
3-5 . . . . at Miami	21-23 . . . . at Washington	8-11 . . . . at Miami	27-29 . . . at New York (NL)

GENERAL INFORMATION

Stadium (year opened):
SunTrust Park (2017).
Team Colors: Red, white and blue.

Home Dugout: First Base.
Playing Surface: Grass.

BASEBALL OPERATIONS

Telephone: (404) 522-7630. **Fax:** (404) 614-3308.

Executive Vice President/General Manager: Alex Anthopoulos. **Sr. Vice President of Baseball Operations/Assistant GM:** Perry Minasian. **Assistant GM/Research & Development:** Jason Paré. **Assistant GM/Major League Operations:** Alex Tamin. **VP, Scouting:** Dana Brown. **Special Assistant to the GM:** Mike Fast. **Director, Baseball Administration:** Dixie Keller. **Manager, Baseball Video Operations:** Rob Smith. **Executive Assistant:** Elizabeth Teran. **Manager, Baseball Systems:** Garrett Wilson. **Data Architect & Systems Developer:** Mike Copeland. **Manager, Major League Operations:** Noah Woodward. **Coordinator, Major League Operations:** Doug Wachter. **Analysts, Major League Operations:** Caelan Collins, Nick Coppola, & Adam Sonabend. **Analysts, Research & Development:** Michael Lord, Josh Malek, Scott Rapponotti, Kyle Sargent, Ronit Shah.

Alex Anthopoulos

MAJOR LEAGUE STAFF

Manager: Brian Snitker. **Coaches: Bench**—Walt Weiss, **Pitching**—Rick Kranitz, **Hitting**—Kevin Seitzer, **Assistant Hitting Coach**—Jose Castro, **First Base**—Eric Young, **Third Base**—Ron Washington. **Bullpen Coach:** Marty Reed. **Bullpen Catchers:** Jimmy Leo, Jose Yepez. **Batting Practice Pitcher:** Tomas Perez. **Catching Coach:** Sal Fasano.

MEDICAL/TRAINING

Director, Player Health/Head Trainer: George C. Poulis. **Head Team Physician:** Dr. Gary M. Lourie. **Senior Advisor, Athletic Trainer:** Jeff Porter. **Assistant Trainer:** Mike Frostad. **Head Sports Performance Coach:** Bradford Scott. **Performance Therapist:** Jordan Wolf. **Physical Therapist:** Pete Cicinelli. **Assistant Physical Therapist:** Nick Valencia. **Massage Therapist:** Yoshi Nishio

PLAYER DEVELOPMENT

Telephone: (404) 522-7630. **Fax:** (404) 614-1350.

Director, Player Development: Dom Chiti. **Special Assistants to Baseball Operations:** Chipper Jones (Roswell, GA) & Andruw Jones (Duluth, GA). **Assistant Director of Player Development—Operations:** Ron Knight. **Assistant Director of Player Development—Personnel:** A.J. Scola. **Assistant, Player Development:** Dylan Quantz. **Director of Pitching:** Dave Wallace. **Field Coordinator:** Doug Mansolino. **Pitching Coordinator:** Derrick Lewis. **Hitting Coordinator:** Mike Brumley. **Roving Coordinators:** Jeff Datz (catching), Adam Everett (infield), Nick Flynn (medical), Mike Schofield (strength & conditioning), Ryan Driscoll (assistant strength & conditioning), Kyle Clements (video), John Shelby (outfield/baserunning) Fernando Pineres (cultural development). **Coordinator, Florida Operations:** Jeff Pink. **Rehabilitation Pitching Coordinator:** David Chavarria. **Physical Therapist:** Ben Cuddy. **Baseball Operations Assistant:** Phil Guica.

FARM SYSTEM

Class	Club (League)	Manager	Hitting Coach	Pitching Coach
Triple-A	Gwinnett (IL)	Damon Berryhill	Bobby Magallanes	Mike Maroth
Double-A	Mississippi (SL)	Chris Maloney	Carlos Mendez	Dennis Lewallyn
High A	Florida (FSL)	Barrett Kleinknecht	Doug DeVore	Dan Meyer
Low A	Rome (SAL)	Matt Tuiasosopo	Bobby Moore	Kanekoa Texeira
Rookie	Danville (APP)	Anthony Nunez	Danny Santiesteban	Jason Stanford
Rookie	Braves (GCL)	Nestor Perez Jr.	B.Garbey/R. Albert	Elvin Nina
Rookie	Braves (DSL)	J. Romero	O. Rosario/E. De La Cruz	J. Rodriguez

SCOUTING

Telephone: (404) 522-7630. **Fax:** (404) 614-1350.

Special Assistants to Baseball Operations: Fred McGriff, Greg Walker. **Assistant Director, Pro Scouting:** Jonathan Schuerholz. **Professional Scouts:** Billy Ryan, Tom Giordano. Dave Holliday (Bixby, OK), Matt Kinzer, Rick Ragazzo, Ted Simmons, Terry R. Tripp, Rick Williams, Jason Dunn, Rod Gilbreath, Devlin McConnell, Trenton Mozes, Patrick Lowery, Alan Butts. **Assistant Director, Amateur Scouting Operations:** Matt Grabowski. **Coordinator, Scouting:** Chris Lionetti. **Senior Advisor to Scouting:** Tom Davis, Bryan Lambe. **National Crosscheckers:** Joe Jordan, Gary Rajsich, Ron Marigny, Deron Rombach. **Regional Crosscheckers: East**—Reed Dunn (Nashville, TN), **Midwest**—Terry C Tripp (Norris, IL), **West**—Brett Evert (Salem, OR). **Area Scouts:** Kevin Barry (Kinmundy, IL), Billy Best (Holly Spings, NC), Ray Corbett (College Station, TX), Dan Cox (Huntington Beach, CA), Kirk Fredriksson (Gainesville, GA), Ralph Garr (Richmond, TX), Kevin Martin (Los Angeles, CA), Lou Sanchez (Miami, FL), Darin Vaughan (Kingwood, TX), Ricky Wilson (Buckeye, AZ), Alan Sandberg (Ringwood, NJ), Smoke Laval (Reserve, LA), JD French (Kennett, MO) Cody Martin (Vancouver, WA), Ted Lekas (Brewster, MA), Freddy Perez (Denver, CO), Jon Bunnel (Tampa, FL). **Video Coordinators:** Anthony Flora, Bryce Mosier, Trey McNickle. **Coordinator, Latin American Operations:** Jonathan Cruz. **Manager, Dominican Republic Administration** & **Operations:** Lothar Schott. **Manager, International Scouting Administration:** Gerald Milanes. **Administrative Assistant:** Ruth Peguero. **Coordinator:** Chris Roque (Central America). **International Scouts:** Carlos Garcia (Colombia), Luis Santos (Dominican Republic).Carlos Sequera (Venezuela), Renny Villalobos (Venezuela), Raphachel Colatosti (Venezuela). **Video Coordinator:** Jaime Gil.

BALTIMORE ORIOLES

Office Address: 333 W Camden St., Baltimore, MD 21201.
Telephone: (888) 848-BIRD. **Fax:** (410) 547-6272.
E-mail Address: birdmail@orioles.com. **Website:** www.orioles.com.

OWNERSHIP
Operated By: The Baltimore Orioles Limited Partnership Inc.
Chairman/CEO: Peter Angelos. **Executive Vice President:** John Angelos. **Ownership Representative:** Louis Angelos.

BUSINESS OPERATIONS
Chief Operating Officer, Business Operations: John Vidalin. **Executive Vice President, Planning & Development:** Michael Shapiro. **VP/Special Liaison to Chairman:** Lou Kousouris.

FINANCE
Chief Financial Officer: Ed Kabernagel. **Vice President, Finance:** Michael D. Hoppes, CPA. **Director, Finance:** Carole Bohon.

PUBLIC RELATIONS/COMMUNICATIONS
Telephone: (410) 547-6150. **Fax:** (410) 547-6272.
VP, Communications/Marketing: Greg Bader. **Director, Public Relations:** Kristen Hudak. **Manager, Media Relations:** Jim Misudek. **Coordinator, Public Relations:** Kailey Adams. **Coordinator, Baseball Information:** Adam Esselman. **Public Relations Assistant:** Jackie Harig. **Director, Community Relations/Promotions:** Kristen Schultz. **Director, Advertising:** Jason Snapkoski. **PA Announcer:** Ryan Wagner. **Official Scorers:** Jim Henneman, Marc Jacobson, Ryan Eigenbrode.

Peter Angelos

DIGITAL
Vice President, Digital Marketing & Content: Tyler Hoffberger. **Coordinator, Digital Communications:** Amanda Sarver.

BALLPARK OPERATIONS
Vice President, Ballpark Operations: Troy Scott. **Director, Ballpark Operations:** Kevin Cummings. **Director, Food Services:** Tom Orszulak. **Head Groundskeeper:** Nicole Sherry.

TICKETING
Telephone: (888) 848-BIRD. **Fax:** (410) 547-6270.
Vice President, Ticket Sales, Service & Operations: Neil Aloise. **Director, Ticket Sales:** Mark Hromalik. **Director, Ticket Operations/Fan Services:** Scott Rosier.

CORPORATE PARTNERSHIPS
Vice President, Corporate Partnerships: Marco A. Gentile.

2019 SCHEDULE
Standard Game Times: 7:05 p.m; Sun. 1:35

MARCH	6-8 . . . . Boston	25-26 . . . . . . San Diego	12-14 . . . at New York (AL)
28-31 . . . at New York (AL)	10-12 . . . Los Angeles (AL)	28-30 . . . . Cleveland	16-18 . . . . .at Boston
	13-15 . . . at New York (AL)		19-21 . . . . . . Kansas City
APRIL	16-19 . . . . . .at Cleveland	**JULY**	22-25 . . . . . .Tampa Bay
1-3 . . . . at Toronto	20-23 . . . . .New York (AL)	1-3 . . . . . . at Tampa Bay	27-28 . . . at Washington
4-7 . . . . . .New York (AL)	24-26 . . . . . at Colorado	5-7 . . . . at Toronto	30-31 . . . . .at Kansas City
8-11 . . . . Oakland	27-29 . . . . Detroit	12-14 . . . . . .Tampa Bay	
12-15 . . . . . .at Boston	31 . . . . . . San Francisco	16-17 . . . . . Washington	**SEPTEMBER**
16-18 . . . . . at Tampa Bay		19-21 . . . . Boston	1 . . . . . . .at Kansas City
19-21 . . . . . .Minnesota	**JUNE**	22-24 . . . . . . at Arizona	2-4 . . . . . . at Tampa Bay
22-24 . . . . Chicago (AL)	1-2 . . . . . . San Francisco	25-28 . at Los Angeles (AL)	5-8 . . . . Texas
26-28 . . . at Minnesota	4-6 . . . . .at Texas	29-30 . . . . at San Diego	10-12 . . Los Angeles (NL)
29-30 . . . .at Chicago (AL)	7-9 . . . . .at Houston		13-16 . . . . .at Detroit
	11-13 . . . . . . .Toronto	**AUGUST**	17-19 . . . . .Toronto
MAY	14-16 . . . . Boston	1-4 . . . . .Toronto	20-22 . . . . Seattle
1 . . . . . . .at Chicago (AL)	17-19 . . . . . .at Oakland	5-7 . . . . . .New York (AL)	23-25 . . . . . . at Toronto
3-5 . . . . .Tampa Bay	20-23 . . . . .at Seattle	9-11 . . . . Houston	27-29 . . . . .at Boston

GENERAL INFORMATION
Stadium (year opened): Oriole Park at Camden Yards (1992).
Team Colors: Orange, black and white.
Home Dugout: First Base.
Playing Surface: Grass.

HUMAN RESOURCES
Vice President, Human Resources: Lisa Tolson.

STRATEGY & ANALYTICS
Vice President, Strategy & Analytics: Scott Lewis.

TRAVEL/CLUBHOUSE
Director, Team Travel: Kevin Buck.
Equipment Manager (Home): Chris Guth. **Equipment Manager (Road):** Fred Tyler.

BASEBALL OPERATIONS

Telephone: (410) 547-6107. **Fax:** (410) 547-6271.
Executive Vice President and General Manager: Mike Elias.
Vice President, Baseball Operations: Brady Anderson. **Assistant General Manager, Analytics:** Sig Mejdal. **Director, Baseball Operations:** Tripp Norton. **Director, Team Travel:** Kevin Buck. **Manager, Major League Video Operations:** Mike Silverman. **Manager, Advance Scouting Operations:** Bill Wilkes. **Coordinator, Major League Video/Advance Scouting:** Ben Sussman-Hyde. **Assistant, Major League Video/Advance Scouting:** Ryan Klimek. **Developer, Baseball Systems:** Di Zou. **Spanish Translator, Baseball Operations Assistant:** Ramon Alarcon.

Mike Elias

MAJOR LEAGUE STAFF
Manager: Brandon Hyde.
Coaches: Bench—Tim Cossins, **Pitching**—Doug Brocail, **Hitting**—Don Long, **Assistant Hitting**—Howie Clark, **First Base**—Arnie Beyeler, **Third Base**—José Flores, **Bullpen**—John Wasdin, **Coach**—José Hernández.

MEDICAL/TRAINING
Head Athletic Trainer: Brian Ebel. **Assistant Athletic Trainer:** Mark Shires, Pat Wesley. **Strength and Conditioning Coach:** Joseph Hogarty. **Strength and Conditioning Coach:** Ryosuke Naito. **Rehab Coordinator:** Kyle Corrick. **Team Masseuse:** Adrian Pettaway. **Team Physician:** Dr. Sean Curtin. **Orthopedist:** Dr. Michael Jacobs. **Dentist:** Dr. Gus Livaditis. **Optometrist:** Dr. Elliott Myrowitz.

PLAYER DEVELOPMENT
Telephone: (410) 547-6120. **Fax:** (410) 547-6298.
Director, Minor League Operations: Kent Qualls. **Director, Dominican Republic Academy:** Felipe Rojas Alou Jr. **Coordinator, Minor League Pitching:** Chris Holt. **Special Assignment Pitching Instructor:** Ramon Martinez. **Coordinator, Minor League Hitting:** Jeff Manto. **Manager, Minor League Administration:** Maria Arellano. **Instructor, Special Assignment:** B.J. Surhoff. **Coordinator, Minor League Infield:** Dave Anderson. **Coordinator, Minor League Catching:** Don Werner. **Coordinator, Outfield/Baserunning:** Carlos Tosca. **Coordinator, Florida and Latin America Pitching:** Dave Schmidt. **Dominican Republic Field Coordinator:** Miguel Jabalera. **Coordinator, Pitching Rehabilitation:** Scott McGregor. **Minor League Medical Coordinator:** Dave Walker. **Latin American Medical Coordinator:** Manny Lopez. **Administrator, Dominican Republic Academy:** Jorge Perozo. **Minor League Equipment Manager:** Jake Parker. **Dominican Republic Equipment Manager:** Franklin Fajardo.

FARM SYSTEM

Class	Club (League)	Manager	Hitting Coach	Pitching Coach
Triple-A	Norfolk (IL)	Gary Kendall	Butch Davis	Mike Griffin
Double-A	Bowie (EL)	Buck Britton	Keith Bodie	Kennie Steenstra
High A	Frederick (CL)	Ryan Minor	Bobby Rose	Justin Lord
Low A	Delmarva (SAL)	Kyle Moore	TBA	Justin Ramsey
Short-season	Aberdeen (NYP)	Kevin Bradshaw	TBA	Robbie Aviles
Rookie	Orioles (GCL)	Alan Mills	Milt May	Wilson Alvarez
Rookie	Orioles (DSL)	Elvis Morel	Ramon Caballo	Dionis Pascual

SCOUTING
Telephone: (410) 547-6212. **Fax:** 410-547-6928.
Senior Director, International Scouting: Koby Perez. **Director, Pacific Rim Operations & Baseball Development:** Mike Snyder. **Assistant Director, Scouting:** Brad Ciolek. **Administrator, Scouting:** Hendrik Herz. **Major League Scouts:** Dave Engle, Jim Howard. **Special Assignment Scout:** Doug Witt. **Professional Scout:** Dave Machemer. **International Scouts, Latin America:** Calvin Maduro.
West Coast Supervisor: David Blume (Elk Grove, CA). **Lower Midwest Supervisor:** Jim Richardson (Marlow, OK). **Upper Midwest Supervisor:** Ernie Jacobs (Wichita, KS). **Mid-Atlantic Executive Scout:** Dean Albany (Baltimore, MD). **Area Scouts:** Adrian Dorsey (Nashville, TN), Thom Dreier (The Woodlands, TX), Dan Durst (Rockford, IL), John Gillette (Gilbert, AZ), Ken Guthrie (Sanger, TX), David Jennings (Daphne, AL), Arthur McConnehead (Atlanta, GA), Mark Ralston (Carlsbad, CA), Scott Thomas (Town & Country, MO), Frankie Thon (Miami, FL). Brandon Verley (West Linn, OR), Scott Walter (Manhattan Beach, CA). **Special Assignment Scout:** Rich Amaral (Huntington Beach, CA).

BOSTON RED SOX

Office Address: Fenway Park, 4 Yawkey Way, Boston, MA 02215.
Telephone: (617) 226-6000. **Fax:** (617) 226-6416. **Website:** www.redsox.com

OWNERSHIP

Principal Owner: John Henry. **Chairman:** Thomas C. Werner. **President/CEO:** Sam Kennedy. **President/CEO Emeritus:** Larry Lucchino.

BUSINESS OPERATIONS

EVP/ FSG Corporate Strategy & General Counsel: Ed Weiss. **EVP/COO:** Jonathan Gilula. **EVP/Partnerships:** Troup Parkinson. **EVP/Chief Financial Officer:** Tim Zue. **EVP/Chief Strategy Officer:** Dave Beeston.

Sam Kennedy

BALLPARK OPERATIONS

SVP/Ballpark Operations: Peter Nesbit. **SVP/Fan Services & Entertainment:** Sarah McKenna. **VP/Fenway Park Tours:** Marcita Thompson.

FINANCE/STRATEGY/ANALYTICS

VP/Finance: Ryan Oremus. **Financial Advisor to the President:** Jeff White.

HUMAN RESOURCES/INFORMATION TECHNOLOGY

EVP/Chief Human Resources Officer: Amy Waryas. **VP/Information Technology:** Brian Shield.

LEGAL

SVP/Government Affairs & Special Counsel: David Friedman. **VP/Club Counsel:** Elaine Weddington Steward.

MARKETING/COMMUNICATIONS

EVP/Chief Marketing Officer: Adam Grossman. **VP/Corporate Communications:** Zineb Curran. **VP/Marketing & Broadcasting:** Colin Burch. **VP/Media Relations:** Kevin Gregg.

PARTNERSHIPS/CLIENT SERVICES

SVP/Client Services: Marcell Bhangoo. **VP/Community, Alumni & Player Relations:** Pam Kenn.

TICKETING/SALES/EVENTS

EVP/Ticketing, Concerts, & Events: Ron Bumgarner. **SVP/Fenway Concerts & Entertainment:** Larry Cancro. **SVP/Ticketing:** Richard Beaton. **VP/Ticketing Services & Operations:** Naomi Calder. **VP/Ticket Sales:** William Droste. **VP/Fenway Park Events:** Carrie Campbell.

RED SOX FOUNDATION

Honorary Chairman: Tim Wakefield. **Executive Director:** Rebekah Salwasser.

2019 SCHEDULE

Standard Game Times: 7:10 p.m.; Sun. 1:35

MARCH
28-31 . . . . .at Seattle

APRIL
1-4 . . . . .at Oakland
5-7 . . . . at Arizona
9-11 . . . . .Toronto
12-15 . . . . Baltimore
16-17 . . . at New York (AL)
19-21 . . . . . at Tampa Bay
22-25 . . . . Detroit
26-28 . . . . .Tampa Bay
29-30 . . . . Oakland

MAY
1 . . . . Oakland
2-5 . . . . . . .at Chicago (AL)
6-8 . . . . .at Baltimore

10-12 . . . . Seattle
14-15 . . . . .Colorado
17-19 . . . . Houston
20-23 . . . . . . at Toronto
24-26 . . . . . . .at Houston
27-29 . . . . . . Cleveland
30-31 . . . at New York (AL)

JUNE
1-2 . . . . . at New York (AL)
4-6 . . . . . . .at Kansas City
7-9 . . . . .Tampa Bay
10-13 . . . . Texas
14-16 . . . . . .at Baltimore
17-19 . . . . at Minnesota
21-23 . . . . .Toronto
24-26 . . . . . Chicago (AL)

29-30 . . . . .New York (AL)

JULY
2-4 . . . . at Toronto
5-7 . . . . .at Detroit
12-14 . . . Los Angeles (NL)
15-18 . . . . .Toronto
19-21 . . . . .at Baltimore
22-24 . . . . . at Tampa Bay
25-28 . . . . .New York (AL)
30-31 . . . . . . .Tampa Bay

AUGUST
1 . . . . .Tampa Bay
2-4 . . . . . at New York (AL)
5-7 . . . . Kansas City
8-11 . . . .Los Angeles (AL)
12-14 . . . . . .at Cleveland

16-18 . . . . . . Baltimore
20-21 . . . . .Philadelphia
23-25 . . . . . at San Diego
27-28 . . . . . . at Colorado
30-31 . at Los Angeles (AL)

SEPTEMBER
1 . . . . at Los Angeles (AL)
3-5 . . . . .Minnesota
6-9 . . . . . . .New York (AL)
10-12 . . . . at Toronto
14-15 . . . at Philadelphia
17-19 . . . . .San Francisco
20-23 . . . . . at Tampa Bay
24-26 . . . . .at Texas
27-29 . . . . Baltimore

GENERAL INFORMATION

Stadium (year opened):
Fenway Park (1912).
Team Colors: Navy blue, red and white.

Home Dugout: First Base.
Playing Surface: Grass.

BASEBALL OPERATIONS

President, Baseball Operations: Dave Dombrowski.
EVP/Assistant GM: Brian O'Halloran, Eddie Romero. **SVP/Assistant General Manager:** Zack Scott. **SVP/Major and Minor League Operations:** Raquel Ferreira. **SVP/ Player Personnel:** Frank Wren. **VP/Special Asst. to the President of Baseball Operations:** Tony La Russa. **Senior Director, Team Travel:** Jack McCormick. **Assistant Director, Team Travel:** Mark Cacciatore. **Director, Baseball Administration & Special Projects:** Mike Regan. **Coordinator Major League Operations:** Alex Gimenez. **Executive Assistant:** Erin Cox. **Director, Baseball Analytics:** Joe McDonald. **Sr. Analyst, Baseball Analytics:** Greg Rybarczyk. **Analysts, Baseball Analytics:** Spencer Bingol, Dan Meyer, Brad Alberts, Dave Miller. **Analyst, Major League Clubhouse:** Jeb Clarke. **Assistant, Baseball Analytics:** Kayla Mei. **Director, Baseball Systems:** Mike Ganley. **Sr. Developer, Baseball Systems:** Eric Edvalson, Fred Hubert. **Data Architect, Baseball Systems:** Bill Letson **Developer, Baseball Systems:** Connor McCann. **Assistant Director, Baseball Systems:** Ethan Faggett. **Special Assistants to GM:** Pedro Martinez, Jason Varitek.

Dave Dombrowski

MAJOR LEAGUE STAFF

Manager: Alex Cora. **Coaches: Bench**—Ron Roenicke; **Pitching**—Dana Levangie; **Assistant Pitching Coach**—Brian Bannister; **Bullpen**—Craig Bjornson; **Hitting**—Tim Hyers; **Assistant Hitting Coach**—Andy Barkett; **First Base**—Tom Goodwin; **Third Base**—Carlos Febles; **Major League Coach**—Ramon Vazquez.

SPORTS MEDICINE SERVICE

Director, Sports Medicine Service/Head Athletic Trainer: Brad Pearson. **Medical Director:** Dr. Larry Ronan. **Head Team Orthopedist:** Dr. Peter Asnis. **Senior Physical Therapist/Clinical Specialist:** Jamie Creps. **Assistant Athletic Trainers:** Paul Buchheit, Masai Takahashi, Jon Jochim, Brandon Henry. **Head Strength/Conditioning Coach:** Kiyoshi Momose.

PLAYER DEVELOPMENT

Vice President, Player Development: Ben Crockett. **Director, Minor League Operations:** Brian Abraham. **Minor League Field Coordinator:** Ryan Jackson. **Assistant Field Coordinator/Infield Coordinator:** Andy Fox. **Hitting Coordinator:** Greg Norton. **Catching Coordinator:** Chad Epperson. **Outfield/Baserunning Coordinator:** Darren Fenster. **Pitching Coordinator, Logistics:** Ralph Treuel. **Pitching Coordinator, Performance:** Dave Bush. **Latin American Pitching Coordinator/Rehab Coordinator:** Walter Miranda. **Latin American Field Coordinator:** Jose Zapata. **Latin American Pitching Advisor:** Goose Gregson. **Pitching Performance Coach:** Shawn Haviland. **Minor League Strength/Conditioning Coordinator:** Edgar Barreto. **Coordinator, Florida BBOPS/ML League Video:** Patrick McLaughlin. **Coach/Interpreter:** Mickey Jiang. **ATC Coordinator:** Eric Velazquez. **GCL ATC/Assistant ATC Coordinator:** Joel Harris. **Minor League Physical Therapist:** Kevin Avilla.

FARM SYSTEM

Class	Club (League)	Manager	Hitting Coach	Pitching Coach	Position Coach
Triple-A	Pawtucket (IL)	Billy McMillon	Rich Gedman	Kevin Walker	Bruce Crabbe
Double-A	Portland (EL)	Joseph Oliver	Lee May Jr.	Paul Abbott	
High A	Salem (CAR)	Corey Wimberly	Lance Zawadzki	Lance Carter	
Low A	Greenville (SAL)	Iggy Suarez	Nelson Paulino	Bob Kipper	
Short-season	Lowell (NYP)	Luke Montz	Nate Spears	Nick Green	
Rookie	Red Sox (GCL)	Tom Kotchman	Junior Zamora	Miguel Bonilla	Angel Berroa
Rookie	Red Sox (DSL)	Ozzie Chavez	Carlos Adolfo	Oscar Lira	
Rookie	Red Sox (DSL)	Fernando Tatis	Eider Torres	Humberto Sanchez	

SCOUTING

VP/ Professional Scouting: Gus Quattlebaum. **VP/Amateur Scouting:** Mike Rikard. **Director, Professional Scouting:** Harrison Slutsky. **Assistant Director, Amateur Scouting:** Paul Toboni. **Manager, Advance Scouting:** Steve Langone. **Coordinator, Player Personnel:** Marcus Cuellar. **Assistant, International Scouting:** James Kang. **Assistant, Amateur Scouting:** Devin Pearson. **Advance Scouting Assistant:** JT Watkins. **Special Assignment Scouts:** Eddie Bane, Steve Peck, Brad Sloan. **Special Assistant, Player Personnel:** Mark Wasinger. **Global Crosschecker:** Paul Fryer.
Major League Scouts: Jaymie Bane, Nate Field, Bob Hamelin, Blair Henry, Tim Huff, Gary Hughes, John Lombardo, Matt Mahoney, Joe McDonald, David Scrivines, Anthony Turco. **Crosscheckers:** John Booher, Quincy Boyd, Dan Madsen, Fred Petersen, Jim Robinson, Chris Mears, Tom Kotchman, Justin Horowitz. **Area Scouts:** Brandon Agamennone, JJ Altobelli, Tim Collinsworth, Matt Davis, Lane Decker, Raymond Fagnant, Todd Gold, Reed Gragnani, Stephen Hargett, Josh Labandeira, Brian Moehler, Carl Moesche, Edgar Perez, Pat Portugal, Willie Romay, Danny Watkins, Vaughn Williams, Jim Woodward. **Part Time Scouts:** Rob English, Tim Martin, Greg Morhardt, Jay Oliver, Dick Sorkin, Terry Sullivan.
Co-Director, International Scouting: Todd Claus, Ronaldo Pino. **Special Assistant, International Scouting:** Chris Becerra. **International Crosschecker:** Mike Silvestri. **Coordinator, Pacific Rim Operations:** Brett Ward. **Ambassador to the Red Sox in the DR:** Jesus Alou. **Assistant Director, DR Academy:** Javier Hernandez. **Assistant, DR Academy:** Martin Rodriguez. **Assistant, Latin American Operations:** Alberto Mejia. **Supervisor, Dominican Republic:** Manny Nanita. **Assistant Supervisor, Dominican Republic:** Jonathan Cruz. **International Scouts: Aruba/Curacao:** Dennis Neuman. **Australia:** Steve Fish. **Bahamas:** Aneko Knowles. **Brazil:** Rafael Motooka. **Colombia:** Alfredo Castellon. **Dominican Republic:** Domingo Brito, Michel DeJesus, Esau Medina. **Europe:** Rene Saggiadi. **Korea:** Kim Kim. **Mexico:** Sotero Torres. **Nicaragua:** Rafael Mendoza. **Panama:** Cris Garibaldo. **South Africa:** Darryn Smith. **Venezuela:** Angel Escobar, Ernesto Gomez, Wilder Lobo, Ramon Mora, Alex Requena, Lenin Rodriguez. **Taiwan:** Louie Lin. **Pro Scout:** Won Lee.

CHICAGO CUBS

Office Address: Wrigley Field, 1060 W. Addison St., Chicago, IL 60613.
Telephone: (773) 404-2827. **Website:** www.cubs.com.

OWNERSHIP

Chairman: Tom Ricketts. **Board of Directors:** Laura Ricketts, Pete Ricketts and Todd Ricketts. **Executive Assistant, Chairman:** Lorraine Swiatly.

BUSINESS OPERATIONS

President, Business Operations: Crane Kenney. **Senior Vice President, Chief Financial Officer:** Jon Greifenkamp. **Vice President, Wrigley Field Restoration & Expansion:** Carl Rice. **Executive Assistant, President Business Operations:** Michele Dietz. **Coordinator, Associate Events & Wellness:** Becky Rasor. **Associate, Chairman's Office:** Robin Lestina-Cikanek.

BALLPARK/EVENT OPERATIONS

Senior Vice President, Strategy & Ballpark Operations: Alex Sugarman. **Senior Vice President, Operations:** David Cromwell. **Assistant Director, Event Operations & Security:** Morgan Bucciferro. **Assistant Director, Guest Services:** Vanessa Ward. **Vice President, Facility & Supply Chain Operations:** Patrick Meenan. **Assistant Director, Grounds:** Roger Baird. **Assistant Director, Facilities:** Ryan Egan.

Tom Ricketts

MARKETING/COMMUNICATIONS

Senior Vice President, Sales & Marketing: Colin Faulkner. **Vice President, Marketing:** Lauren Fritts. **Vice President, Communications & Community Affairs:** Julian Green. **Director, Marketing & Fan Insights:** Kelly Linstroth. **Director, Communications:** Lindsay Bago. **Director, Brand Activation:** John Morrison.

LEGAL

EVP, Community & Gov't Affairs, Chief Legal Officer: Michael Lufrano. **Vice President, General Counsel:** Brett Scharback. **Counsel:** Amy Timm. **Counsel:** Shameeka Quallo.

TICKET SALES/SALES & PARTNERSHIPS

Senior Vice President, Sales & Marketing: Colin Faulkner. **Senior Vice President, Marquee Sports & Entertainment:** Cale Vennum. **Vice President, Corporate Partnerships:** Alex Seyferth. **Director, Corporate Partnership Development:** Ashley Facchini. **Vice President, New Business:** Andy Blackburn. **Director, Account Management:** Ryan Balogh. **Assistant Director, Ticket Sales:** Chris Weddige. **Director, Corporate Partnership Activation:** Carrie Collins.

MEDIA RELATIONS

Director, Media Relations: Peter Chase. **Assistant Director, Media Relations:** Jason Carr. **Coordinator, Media Relations:** Alex Wilcox.

2019 SCHEDULE

Standard Game Times: Mon.-Sat., 7:05 pm; Sun. 1:20 pm.

MARCH		
28-31 . . . . .at Texas		

APRIL
1-4 . . . . at Atlanta
5-7 . . . . at Milwaukee
8-11 . . . . Pittsburgh
12-14 . . . Los Angeles (AL)
15-17 . . . . at Miami
19-21 . . . . Arizona
23-25 . . . Los Angeles (NL)
26-28 . . . . . . at Arizona
30 . . . . .at Seattle

MAY
1 . . . . .at Seattle
3-5 . . . . St. Louis
6-9 . . . . Miami

10-12 . . . . . . .Milwaukee
14-16 . . . . . .at Cincinnati
17-19 . . . at Washington
20-23 . . . . . .Philadelphia
24-26 . . . . Cincinnati
27-29 . . . . . .at Houston
31 . . . . .at St. Louis

JUNE
1-2 . . . . .at St. Louis
4-6 . . . . Colorado
7-9 . . . . St. Louis
10-12 . . . . . at Colorado
13-16 . at Los Angeles (NL)
18-19 . . . . Chicago (AL)
20-23 . . . .New York (NL)
24-27 . . . . Atlanta
28-30 . . . . . at Cincinnati

JULY
1-4 . . . . . . at Pittsburgh
6-7 . . . . .at Chicago (AL)
12-14 . . . . Pittsburgh
15-17 . . . . . . Cincinnati
19-21 . . . . . . San Diego
22-24 . . . at San Francisco
26-28 . . . . at Milwaukee
30-31 . . . . . .at St. Louis

AUGUST
1 . . . . .at St. Louis
2-4 . . . . .Milwaukee
5-7 . . . . Oakland
8-11 . . . . . .at Cincinnati
13-15 . . . . at Philadelphia
16-18 . . . . . at Pittsburgh

20-22 . . . . . San Francisco
23-25 . . . . . . Washington
27-29 . . . at New York (NL)
30-31 . . . . . . .Milwaukee

SEPTEMBER
1 . . . . .Milwaukee
2-3 . . . . Seattle
5-8 . . . . . at Milwaukee
9-12 . . . . . at San Diego
13-15 . . . . . . Pittsburgh
16-18 . . . . . . Cincinnati
19-22 . . . . . . St. Louis
24-26 . . . . . at Pittsburgh
27-29 . . . . . .at St. Louis

GENERAL INFORMATION

Stadium (year opened):
Wrigley Field (1914).
Team Colors: Royal blue, red and white.

Home Dugout: Third Base.
Playing Surface: Grass.

BASEBALL OPERATIONS

Telephone: (773) 404-2827. **Fax:** (773) 404-4147.
President, Baseball Operations: Theo Epstein. **Executive VP/General Manager:** Jed Hoyer. **Assistant GMs:** Randy Bush, Scott Harris. **Director of Pro Scouting and Baseball Operations:** Jeff Greenberg. **Director, Research & Development:** Chris Moore. **Assistant Director, Minor League Operations:** Bobby Basham. **Senior Advisor:** Billy Williams. **Special Assistants, President/GM:** Kerry Wood.
Senior Director, Player Personnel: Kyle Evans. **Manager, Baseball Operations Administration and Executive Assistant:** Meghan Jones. **Traveling Secretary:** Vijay Tekchanadani. **Baseball Systems Architect:** Ryan Kruse. **Assistant Director, Research & Development:** Jeremy Greenhouse. **Analysts, Research & Development:** Sean Ahmed, Chris Jones, Bryan Cole. **Developer, Research & Development:** Albert Lyu. **Developer, Baseball Systems:** Rishi Chopra.

Theo Epstein

MAJOR LEAGUE STAFF

Manager: Joe Maddon. **Coaches: Bench**—Brandon Hyde, **Pitching**—Tommy Hottovy, **Hitting**—Anthony Iapoce, **Assistant Hitting**—Terrmel Sledge, **First Base**—Will Venable, **Third Base**—Brian Butterfield, **Catching**—Mike Borzello, **Bullpen**—Lester Strode. **Quality Assurance Coach:** Chris Denorfia. **Staff Assistants:** Juan Cabreja, Franklin Font. **Bullpen Catcher**— Chad Noble.

MEDICAL/TRAINING

Team Physician: Dr. Stephen Adams. **Team Orthopaedist:** Dr. Stephen Gryzio. **Orthopaedic Consultant:** Dr. Michael Schafer. **Director, Medical Administration:** Mark O'Neal. **Major League Athletic Trainer:** P.J. Mainville.

PLAYER DEVELOPMENT

Telephone: (773) 404-4035. **Fax:** (773) 404-4147.
Senior Vice President, Player Development & Amateur Scouting: Jason McLeod. **Director, Player Development:** Jaron Madison. **Equipment Manager:** Dana Noeltner. **Manager, Mesa Administration:** Gil Passarella. **Major League Rehab Coordinator:** Jonathan Fierro. **Director, Mental Skills Program:** Josh Lifrak. **Latin America Coordinator, Mental Skills Program:** Rey Fuentes. **Mental Skills Program Coordinator:** Darnell McDonald. **Mental Skills Coordinator:** John Baker. **Minor League Coordinators:** Tim Cossins (field & catching), Jacob Cruz (hitting), Brendan Sagara (pitching), Tom Beyers (assistant hitting), Mike Mason, Steve Merriman (assistant pitching), Jeremy Farrell (infield), Doug Dascenzo (outfield & baserunning). **Latin America Field Coordinator:** Dave Keller. **Minor League Athletic Coordinator:** Chuck Baughman. **Minor League Strength & Conditioning Coordinator:** Doug Jarrow. **Minor League Rehab Pitching Coordinator:** Ron Villone.

FARM SYSTEM

Class	Club (League)	Manager	Hitting Coach	Pitching Coach
Triple-A	Iowa (PCL)	Marty Pevey	D. Wilson/K. De Renne	Rod Nichols
Double-A	Tennessee (SL)	Mark Johnson	Chad Allen	Terry Clark
High A	Myrtle Beach (CL)	Jimmy Gonzalez	R. Medina/O. Melendez	Brian Lawrence
Low A	South Bend (MWL)	Buddy Bailey	Paul McAnulty	Jamie Vermilyea
Short-season	Eugene (NWL)	Steven Lerud	Ty Wright	Armando Gabino
Rookie	Cubs 1 (AZL)	Carmelo Martinez	Michael Carter	Anderson Tavarez
Rookie	Cubs 2 (AZL)	Lance Rymel	Claudio Almonte	Manny Olivera
Rookie	Cubs 1 (DSL)	Leo Perez	D'Angelo Jimenez	Jose Cueto
Rookie	Cubs 2 (DSL)	Carlos Ramirez	Enrique Wilson	Luis Hernandez

SCOUTING

Senior Director, Player Personnel: Kyle Evans. **Director, Professional Scouting & Baseball Operations:** Jeff Greenberg. **Assistant Director, Professional Scouting:** Andrew Bassett. **Special Assignment Scouts:** Jason Cooper, Dave Klipstein, Spike Lundberg, David Howard. **Special Assignment Scout/Supervisor, Pacific Rim Scouting:** Min Kyu Sung. **Major League Scouts:** Terry Kennedy, Jake Ciarrachi, Joe Nelson, Steve Boros. **Pro Scouts:** Billy Blitzer, Willie Fraser, Nic Jackson, Mark Kiefer, Kyle Phillips, Thad Weber, Adam Wogan, Aaron Sele. **Part-Time Professional Scouts:** Robert Lofrano, Mark Servais. **Director, Amateur Scouting:** Matt Dorey. **Assistant Director, Amateur Scouting:** Lukas McKnight. **Assistant, Amateur Scouting:** Adam Unes. **National Supervisors:** Sam Hughes, Ron Tostenson. **Crosscheckers: Midwest/Northeast**—Tim Adkins (Huntington, WV), **Central**—Daniel Carte (McKinney, TX), **West**— Shane Farell (Phoenix, AZ), **Southeast**—Bobby Filotei (Mobile, AL), **Canada**—Gabe Sandy (Gresham, OR). **Area Scouts:** Tom Clark (Lake City, FL), Chris Clemons (Robinson, TX), Trey Forkerway (Houston, TX), Edwards Guzman (Toa Baja, PR), John Koronka (Clermont, FL), Keith Lockhart (Dacula, GA), Alex Lontayo (Murrietta, CA), Alex McClure (Memphis, TN), Steve McFarland (Scottsdale, AZ), Tom Myers (Santa Barbara, CA), Ty Nichols (Broken Arrow, OK), John Pedrotty (Chicago, IL), Steve Riha (Houston, TX), Gabe Sandy (Gresham, OR), Matt Sherman (Kingston, MA), Billy Swoope (Norfolk, VA), Jacob Williams (Lexington, KY), Gabe Zappin (Walnut Creek, CA). **Part-Time Area Scouts:** Eric Servais (Minneapolis, MN), Keronn Walker (Chicago, IL), Zach Zielinski (Chicago, IL), Korey Kier (Vancouver, WA). **Director, International Scouting:** Louie Elijaua. **Director, International Pro Scouting:** Alex Suarez. **Coordinator, International Scouting:** Kenny Socorro. **Latin America Crosschecker/Venezuela Scouting Supervisor:** Hector Ortega. **International Crosschecker:** Gian Guzman. **Coordinator, Dominican Republic Scouting:** Miguel Diaz. **Scouting Supervisor, Mexico:** Sergio Hernandez. **Coordinator, Colombian Operations:** Manny Esquivia. **International Scouts:** Hansel Izquierdo, Jamie McFarland, Brent Phelan. **Latin America Scouts: Dominican Republic**—Alejandro Pena, Carlos Reyes, Marino Encarnacion, Valerio Heredia, **Venezuela**—Julio Figueroa, Manuel Pestana, Rafael Jimenez, Carlos Figueroa, **Panama**—Cirilo Cumberbatch, **Mexico**—Salvador Hernandez.

CHICAGO WHITE SOX

Office Address: Guaranteed Rate Field, 333 W. 35th St., Chicago, IL 60616.
Telephone: (312) 674-1000. **Fax:** (312) 674-5116.
Website: whitesox.com, loswhitesox.com.

OWNERSHIP
Chairman: Jerry Reinsdorf.
Board of Directors: Robert Judelson, Judd Malkin, Allan Muchin, Jay Pinsky, Lee Stern, Burton Ury, Charles Walsh.
Special Assistant to Chairman: Dennis Gilbert. **Assistant to Chairman:** Barb Reincke. **Coordinator, Administration/Investor Relations:** Katie Hermle.

BUSINESS OPERATIONS
Senior Executive Vice President: Howard Pizer. **Senior Director, Information Services:** Don Brown. **Vice President, Human Resources:** Moira Foy. **Senior Coordinator, Human Resources:** Leslie Gaggiano.

Jerry Reinsdorf

FINANCE
Senior VP, Administration/Finance: Tim Buzard. **VP, Finance:** Bill Waters. **Director of Accounting:** Mallory Penn.

MARKETING/SALES
Senior VP, Sales/Marketing: Brooks Boyer. **Senior Director, Business Development/Broadcasting:** Bob Grim. **Director, Game Presentation:** Cris Quintana. **Sr. Manager, Scoreboard Operations/Production:** Jeff Szynal. **Sr. Manager, Game Operations:** Dan Mielke. **Sr. Director, Corporate Partnerships Sales Development:** George McDoniel. **Sr. Director, Corporate Partnerships Activation:** Gail Tucker. **Sr. Manager, Corporate Partnerships Development:** Jeff Floerke. **Coordinators/Managers, Corporate Partnership Activation:** Adam Delgado, Ashley Sorenson, Kat Claeys. **VP of Sales and Service:** Jim Willits. **Sr. Manager, Ticket Sales:** Rich Kuchar.

MEDIA RELATIONS/PUBLIC RELATIONS
Telephone: (312) 674-5300. **Fax:** (312) 674-5116.
Senior VP, Communications: Scott Reifert. **Senior Director, Media Relations:** Bob Beghtol. **Director, Public Relations:** Sheena Quinn. **Assistant Director, Media Relations:** Ray Garcia. **Senior Coordinator, Public Relations:** Julianne Bartosz. **Coordinators, Media Relations/Services:** Joe Roti, Hannah Sundwall. **VP, Community Relations/Executive Director/CWS Charities:** Christine O'Reilly. **Director, Community Relations:** Sarah Marten, Lindsey Jordan. **Manager, Youth Baseball Initiatives:** Anthony Olivo. **Director, Digital Communications:** Brad Boron. **Director, Design Services:** Matt Peterson. **Manager, Online Communications:** Dakin Dugaw.

STADIUM OPERATIONS
Senior VP, Stadium Operations: Terry Savarise. **Senior Director, Park Operations:** Jonathan Vasquez.
Senior Director, Guest Services/Diamond Suite Operations: Julie Taylor. **Head Groundskeeper:** Roger Bossard. **PA Announcer:** Gene Honda. **Official Scorers:** Bob Rosenberg, Don Friske, Allan Spear.

2019 SCHEDULE
Standard Game Times: Mon.-Sat., 7:15 p.m.; Sun. 1:10 pm.

MARCH
28-31 . . . . .at Kansas City

APRIL
1-3 . . . . .at Cleveland
4-7 . . . . Seattle
8-10 . . . . .Tampa Bay
12-14 . . . at New York (AL)
15-17 . . . . . Kansas City
18-21 . . . . . . .at Detroit
22-24 . . . . . .at Baltimore
26-28 . . . . Detroit
29-30 . . . . Baltimore

MAY
1 . . . . Baltimore
2-5. . . . . Boston
6-9 . . . . . . .at Cleveland

10-12 . . . . at Toronto
13-14 . . . . . . Cleveland
16-19 . . . . .Toronto
20-23 . . . . . .at Houston
24-26 . . . at Minnesota
27-29 . . . . . Kansas City
30-31 . . . . Cleveland

JUNE
1-2 . . . . Cleveland
4-5 . . . . . at Washington
7-9 . . . . . .at Kansas City
10-11 . . . . . Washington
13-16 . . . .New York (AL)
18-19 . . .at Chicago (NL)
21-23 . . . . .at Texas
24-26 . . . . . . .at Boston

28-30 . . . . . . Minnesota

JULY
2-4. . . . . Detroit
6-7 . . . . . . Chicago (NL)
12-14 . . . . . .at Oakland
15-18 . . . .at Kansas City
19-21 . . . at Tampa Bay
22-24 . . . . .Miami
25-28 . . . . . Minnesota
30-31 . . . .New York (NL)

AUGUST
1 . . . . . . .New York (NL)
2-4. . . . . at Philadelphia
5-7. . . . . .at Detroit
9-11 . . . . Oakland

12-14 . . . . Houston
15-18 . at Los Angeles (AL)
19-21 . . . . at Minnesota
22-25 . . . . Texas
27-29 . . . . . .Minnesota
30-31 . . . . . . at Atlanta

SEPTEMBER
1 . . . . at Atlanta
2-5. . . . . . . .at Cleveland
6-8. . . . . Los Angeles (AL)
10-12 . . . . . Kansas City
13-15 . . . . .at Seattle
16-18 . . . . at Minnesota
20-22 . . . . .at Detroit
24-26 . . . . . . Cleveland
27-29 . . . . Detroit

GENERAL INFORMATION
Stadium (year opened):
Guaranteed Rate Field (1991).
Team Colors: Black, white and silver.

Home Dugout: Third Base.
Playing Surface: Grass.

TICKETING

Senior Director, Ticket Operations: Mike Mazza. **Manager, Ticket Operations:** Pete Catizone.

TRAVEL/CLUBHOUSE

Director, Team Travel: Ed Cassin. **Manager, White Sox Clubhouse:** Rob Warren. **Manager, Visiting Clubhouse:** Jason Gilliam. **Manager, Umpires Clubhouse:** Joe McNamara Jr.

BASEBALL OPERATIONS

Executive Vice President: Ken Williams. **Senior VP/General Manager:** Rick Hahn. **Assistant GM:** Jeremy Haber. **Special Assistants:** Bill Scherrer, Dave Yoakum, Marco Paddy, Jim Thome, Jose Contreras. **Major League Advance Scout:** Bryan Little. **Executive Assistant to GM:** Nancy Nesnidal. **Senior Director, Baseball Operations:** Dan Fabian. **Director, Baseball Operations:** Daniel Zien. **Special Assignment, Baseball Operations:** Kenny Williams, Jr. **Manager Baseball Operations:** Jeff Lachman. **Coordinator Baseball Information:** Devin Pickett. **Director Baseball Analytics:** Matt Koenig. **Analyst, Baseball Operations:** Emily Blad.

Rick Hahn

MAJOR LEAGUE STAFF

Manager: Rick Renteria. **Coaches: Bench**—Joe McEwing, **Pitching**—Don Cooper, **Hitting**—Todd Steverson, **First Base**—Daryl Boston, **Third Base**—Nick Capra, **Bullpen**—Curt Hasler, **Assistant Hitting Coach**—Greg Sparks. **Bullpen Catcher:** Miguel Gonzalez, Luis Sierra. **Manager of Cultural Development:** Luis Sierra.

MEDICAL/TRAINING

Senior Team Physician: Dr. Nikhil Verma. **Head Athletic Trainer Emeritus:** Herm Schneider. **Head Athletic Trainer:** Brian Ball. **Assistant Athletic Trainer/Physical Therapist:** Brett Walker. **Assistant Athletic Trainer:** James Kruk. **Director, Strength & Conditioning:** Allen Thomas. **Assistant Director, Strength & Conditioning:** Ibrahim Rivera.

PLAYER DEVELOPMENT

Director, Player Development: Chris Getz. **Senior Director, Minor League Operations:** Grace Guerrero-Zwit. **Senior Coordinator, Minor League Administration:** Kathy Potoski. **Senior Coordinator, Latin American & Minor League Operations:** Arturo Perez. **Field Coordinator:** Doug Sisson. **Director, Minor League Pitching Instruction:** Kirk Champion. **Assistant Pitching Coordinator:** Everett Teaford. **Assistant Pitching Coordinator:** J.R. Perdew. **Hitting Coordinator:** Mike Gellinger. **Hitting Analytics Instructor:** Matt Lisle. **Catching Coordinator:** John Orton. **Outfield/Baserunning Coordinator:** Aaron Rowand. **Leadership and Development Coordinator:** Ben Broussard. **Strength & Conditioning Coordinator:** Dale Torborg. **Medical Coordinator:** Scott Takao. **Physical Therapist/Rehab Coordinator:** Derek Garris. **Assistant, Player Development:** Rafael Santana. **Assistant, Player Development:** Tommy Thompson. **Assistant, Player Development:** Rod Larson. **Assistant, Player Development:** Graham Harboe. **Rehab Pitching Coach:** Brian Drahman. **Education Coordinator:** Erin Santana. **Latin/Cultural Development Coordinator:** Anthony Santiago. **Arizona Operations—Facility Manager:** Joe Lachcik. **Minor League Clubhouse and Equipment Manager:** Dan Flood. **Assistant Minor League Clubhouse Manager:** Bryant Biasotti. **Latin Education Assistant:** Grant Flick.

FARM SYSTEM

Class	Club (League)	Manager	Hitting Coach	Pitching Coach
Triple-A	Charlotte (IL)	Mark Grudzielanek	Frank Menechino	Steve McCatty
Double-A	Birmingham (SL)	Omar Vizquel	Charlie Poe	Richard Dotson
High A	Winston-Salem (CL)	Justin Jirschele	Jamie Dismuke	Matt Zaleski
Low A	Kannapolis (SAL)	Ryan Newman	Cole Armstrong	Jose Bautista
Rookie	Great Falls (PIO)	Tim Esmay	Cam Seitzer	John Ely
Rookie	White Sox (AZL)	Ever Magallanes	Gary Ward	Felipe Lira
Rookie	White Sox (DSL)	Angel Rosario	Angel Gonzalez	Leo Hernandez

SCOUTING

Telephone: (312) 674-1000. **Fax:** (312) 674-5105.

Pro Scouts: Bruce Benedict (Atlanta, GA), Joe Butler (Long Beach, CA), Toney Howell (Darien, IL), Chris Lein (Jacksonville, FL), Alan Regier (Gilbert, AZ), Daraka Shaheed (Vallejo, CA), Joe Siers (Wesley Chapel, FL) Keith Staab (College Station, TX), Bill Young (Scottsdale, AZ). **Director, Amateur Scouting:** Nick Hostetler (Hebron, KY). **Senior Advisor, Scouting Operations:** Doug Laumann. **Assistant Director, Amateur Scouting:** Garrett Guest. **Assistant Director, Amateur Scouting:** Mike Shirley. **National Crosschecker:** Nathan Durst (Sycamore, IL), Ed Pebley (Brigham City, UT). **Regional Crosschecker: East**—Tim Bittner (Mechanicsville, PA), **West**—Derek Valenzuela (Temecula, CA), **Southeast**—Juan Alvarez (Miami, FL). **Advisor to Baseball Department:** Larry Monroe (Schaumburg, IL). **Area Scouts:** Mike Baker (Santa Ana, CA), Kevin Burrell (Sharpsburg, GA), Robbie Cummings (Kansas City, MO), Ryan Dorsey (Dallas, TX), Abe Fernandez (Ft. Mill, SC), Mike Gagne (Portland, OR), Joel Grampietro (Revere, MA), Phil Gulley (Morehead, KY), Warren Hughes (Mobile, AL), JJ Lally (Denison, IA), George Kachigian (Coronado, CA), John Kazanas (Phoenix, AZ), Steve Nichols (Mount Dora, FL), Jose Ortega (Fort Lauderdale, FL), Steve Payne (Barrington, RI), Noah St. Urbain (Stockton, CA), Adam Virchis (Modesto, CA), Chris Walker (Houston, TX), Justin Wechsler (Niles, MI). **Supervisor, Latin America:** Ruddy Moreta (Santo Domingo, Dominican Republic). **International Scouts:** Amador Arias (Maracay, Venezuela), Marino DeLeon (Yamasa, Dominican Republic), Robinson Garces (Maracaibo, Venezuela), Tomas Herrera (Saltillo, Mexico), Reydel Hernandez (Puerto La Cruz, Venezuela) Miguel Peguero (Santo Domingo, Dominican Republic), Guillermo Peralta (Santiago, Dominican Republic), Omar Sanchez (Valencia, Venezuela), Fermin Ubri (Bani, Dominican Republic), Oliver Dominguez (Higuey, Dominican Republic).

CINCINNATI REDS

Office Address: 100 Joe Nuxhall Way, Cincinnati, OH 45202.
Telephone: (513) 765-7000. **Fax:** (513) 765-7342. **Website:** www.reds.com.

OWNERSHIP
Operated by: The Cincinnati Reds LLC. **Chief Executive Officer:** Robert H. Castellini. **Chairman:** W. Joseph Williams Jr. **Vice Chairman:** Thomas L. Williams. **President & Chief Operating Officer:** Phillip J. Castellini. **Executive Operations Manager:** Shellie Petrey. **Executive Advisor to the CEO:** Walt Jocketty. **Secretary & Treasurer:** Christopher L. Fister. **Senior Vice President, Finance & CFO:** Doug Healy. **Chief Legal Officer:** James A. Marx.

BUSINESS OPERATIONS
Senior Vice President, Business Operations: Karen Forgus. **Business Operations Assistant:** Teddy Siegel. **Business Operations, Assistant/Speakers Bureau:** Emily Mahle.

FINANCE/ADMINISTRATION
Sr. Vice President of Finance and CFO: Doug Healy. **Chief Legal Counsel:** James A. Marx. **Assistant to CFO/CLO:** Teena Schweier. **Vice President of Finance, Controller:** Bentley Viator. **Accounting Manager:** Jill Niemeyer. **Sr. Accountant:** Cathy Brakers. **Director, Financial Reporting/Payroll:** Leanna Weiss. **Payroll Accountant:** Ayanna Goddard.

TICKETING/BUSINESS DEVELOPMENT
VP, Ticketing & Business Development: Aaron Eisel. **Sr. Director, Ticket Sales & Service:** Mark Schueler. **Director, Ticketing New Business:** Patrick Motague. **Director, Season Ticket Membership:** Shelley Volpenhein. **Season Sales Manager:** Chris Herrell. **Senior Account Executive, Retention & Sales:** Eric Keller. **Account Executive, Retention & Sales:** Jimmy Dollard, Angel Gonzalez, Logan Grapenthien, Tyler Wade. **Director, Premium Sales & Service:** Chris Baussano. **Premium Sales Manager:** Ryan Rizzo. **Director of Group Sales:** Carmen Alberini.

Bob Castellini

MEDIA RELATIONS
Vice President, Media Relations: Rob Butcher. **Director, Media Relations:** Larry Herms. **Director, Media Relations/Digital Content:** Jamie Ramsey.

COMMUNICATIONS/MARKETING
Vice President of Communications & Marketing: Ralph Mitchell. **Director of Digitial Media:** Lisa Braun. **Director of Marketing:** Audra Sordyl. **Director of Communications & Web Content:** Jarrod Rollins. **Public Relations Manager:** Michael Anderson. **Promotional Purchasing/Broadcasting Admin.:** Lori Watt. **Communications Manager:** Brendan Hader. **Social Media Manager:** Chadwick Fischer. **Director of Creative Operations:** Jansen Dell. **Creative Services Manager:** Amy Calo. **Senior Designer:** Michael King, Sara Treash. **Junior Graphic Designer:** Brandon Cafferky.

COMMUNITY RELATIONS
Director, Community Relations: Lindsey Dingeldein. **Diversity Relations Coordinator:** Natalya Herndon. **Executive Director, Community Fund:** Charley Frank. **Assistant Director, Community Fund:** Matthew Wagner.

2019 SCHEDULE
Standard Game Times: 7:10 p.m.; Sun. 1:10

MARCH	
28-31	Pittsburgh

APRIL	
1-3	Milwaukee
4-7	at Pittsburgh
9-11	Miami
13-14	St. Louis
15-17	at Los Angeles (NL)
18-21	at San Diego
23-25	Atlanta
26-28	at St. Louis
29-30 . . .	at New York (NL)

MAY	
1-2	at New York (NL)
3-6	San Francisco

7-9	at Oakland
10-12 . .	at San Francisco
14-16	Chicago (NL)
17-19 . .	Los Angeles (NL)
21-22	at Milwaukee
24-26 . .	at Chicago (NL)
27-29	Pittsburgh
31	Washington

JUNE	
1-2	Washington
4-6	at St. Louis
7-9	at Philadelphia
11-12	at Cleveland
14-16	Texas
17-19	Houston
20-23	at Milwaukee

25-26 .	at Los Angeles (AL)
28-30	Chicago (NL)

JULY	
1-4	Milwaukee
6-7	Cleveland
12-14	at Colorado
15-17 . .	at Chicago (NL)
18-21	St. Louis
22-24 . . .	at Milwaukee
26-28	Colorado
29-31	Pittsburgh

AUGUST	
1-4	at Atlanta
5-6 . .	Los Angeles (AL)
8-11	Chicago (NL)

12-14 . . .	at Washington
15-18	St. Louis
19-21	San Diego
23-25	at Pittsburgh
26-29	at Miami
30-31	at St. Louis

SEPTEMBER	
1	at St. Louis
2-5	Philadelphia
6-8	Arizona
10-12 . . .	at Seattle
13-15	at Arizona
16-18 . .	at Chicago (NL)
20-22 . . .	New York (NL)
24-26 . . .	Milwaukee
27-29 . . .	at Pittsburgh

GENERAL INFORMATION
Stadium (year opened): Great American Ball Park (2003). **Team Colors:** Red, white and black.
Home Dugout: First Base.
Playing Surface: Grass.

BALLPARK OPERATIONS

Vice President, Ballpark Operations: Tim O'Connell. **Senior Director, Ballpark Operations:** Sean Brown. **Director, Ballpark Administration:** Colleen Rodenberg. **Ballpark Operations Superintendent:** Bob Harrison. **Senior Manager, Guest & Event Ops.:** Jan Koshover. **Ballpark Administrative Services Manager:** Jen Clemens. **Ballpark Operations Coordinator:** Chase Vogel. **Head Groundskeeper:** Stephen Lord. **Assistant Head Groundskeeper:** Derrik Grubbs. **Director, Security & Public Safety:** John Cordova.

BASEBALL OPERATIONS

President of Baseball Operations: Dick Williams. **Vice President & General Manager:** Nick Krall. **Executive Assistant to Pres. of Baseball Ops/GM:** Sarah Vedder. **Vice President, Assistant General Manager:** Sam Grossman. **Vice President, Senior Advisor to Pres. of Baseball Ops/GM:** Buddy Bell. **Vice President, Player Personnel:** Chris Buckley. **Senior Director, Player Personnel:** Jeff Graupe. **Senior Advisor to Baseball Operations:** Joe Morgan. **Coordinator, Baseball Operations:** Mark Edwards. **Director, Sports Science Initiatives:** Charles Leddon. **Manager, Baseball Systems Development:** Brett Elkins. **Manager, Baseball Analytics:** Michael Schatz. **Data Scientist:** Kevin Corby, Stuart Wallace, Nick Wan. **Data Major League Analyst:** James Brand. **Baseball Analytics Developer:** Samantha Rack. **Baseball Systems Developer:** Joe Delia. **Manager, Advance Scouting:** Bo Thompson. **Baseball Operations Assistant & Spanish Translator:** Julio Monilo.

Dick Williams

MEDICAL/TRAINING

Director, Athletic Training: Patrick Serbus. **Administrator, Athletic Training:** Erika Sperl. **Director of Physical Therapy/Rehab:** Brad Epstein. **Rehabilitation Coach:** James Baldwin. **Physical Therapist:** Marcus Ahrens, Josh Bickel. **Coordinator, Strength & Conditioning:** Morgan Gregory. **Assistant Strength & Conditioning, Latin America:** Alex Soria. **Assistant Strength & Conditioning, Rehab:** Nate Tamargo. **Minor League Nutrition Coordinator:** Ashley Meuser. **Coordinator, Wellness:** Becky Schnakenberg.

MAJOR LEAGUE STAFF

Manager: David Bell. **Coaches: Bench**—Freddie Benavides, **Hitting**—Turner Ward, **Pitching**— Derek Johnson, **First Base**—Delino DeShields, **Third Base/Catching**—J.R. House, **Assistant Hitting**—Donnie Ecker, **Bullpen**—Lee Tunnell, **Game Planning/Outfield**—Jeff Pickler.

PLAYER DEVELOPMENT

Vice President, Player Development: Shawn Pender. **Senior Director, Player Development:** Eric Lee. **Special Assistant, Player Performance:** Eric Davis, Bill Doran, Barry Larkin, Mario Soto. **Director, Sports Science Initiatives:** Charles Leddon. **Coordinator, Player Development:** Mark Heil. **Coordinator, Baseball Administration:** Melissa Hill. **Coordinator, Minor League Video:** Gary Hall. **Player Development Assistant:** Charlie Rodriguez. **Manager, Arizona Operations:** Mike Saverino. **Arizona Operations Assistant:** Branden Croteau. **Manager, Minor League Equipment:** Jon Snyder. **Minor League Clubhouse Assistant:** John Bryk. **Field Coordinator:** Chris Tremie. **Pitching Coordinator:** Tony Fossas. **Outfield/Baserunning Coordintor:** Billy Hatcher. **Catching Coordinator:** Corky Miller. **Hitting Coordinator:** Milt Thompson. **Mental Skills Coach:** Frank Pfister. **Hitting Assessment/Run Production Coach:** Cody Atkinson. **Video Coordinator:** Tyler Gibbons, Brandon Marr.

FARM SYSTEM

Class	Club (League)	Manager	Hitting Coach	Pitching Coach
Triple-A	Louisville (IL)	Jody Davis	Leon Durham	Jeff Fassero
Double-A	Chattanooga (SL)	Pat Kelly	Daryle Ward	Danny Darwin
High A	Daytona (FSL)	Ricky Gutierrez	Alex Pelaez	Tom Brown
Low A	Dayton (MWL)	Luis Bolivar	Mike Devereaux	Seth Etherton
Rookie	Greeneville (APP)	Gookie Dawkins	Luis Terrero	Derrin Ebert
Rookie	Billings (PIO)	Ray Martinez	Darryl Brinkley	Chris Booker
Rookie	Reds (AZL)	Jose Nieves	Todd Takayoshi	Elmer Dessens
Rookie	Reds (DSL)	Luis Saturria	C. Rodriguez/J. Castro	L. Andujar/L. Montano

SCOUTING

Director, Professional Scouting: Rob Coughlin. **Special Assistant to GM, Player Personnel:** Cam Bonifay, Terry Reynolds. **Special Assistants to the General Manager:** "J" Harrison, Marty Maier, John Morris, Jeff Schugel. **Pro Scouts:** Gary Glover, Joe Jocketty, Bruce Manno, Mick Mattaliano, Jeff Morris, Steve Roadcap. **Director, Amateur Scouting:** Brad Meador. **Assistant Director, Amateur Scouting:** Paul Pierson, Joe Katuska. **National Crosschecker:** Jerry Flowers, Mark McKnight. **Regional Crosschecker: East Coast/Canada**—Bill Byckowski, **West Coast**—Rex De La Nuez, **Midwest**—Will Harford, **Southeast**—Greg Zunino. **Scouting Supervisors:** Charlie Aliano, Tony Arias, Rich Bordi, Jeff Brookens, Sean Buckley, John Ceprini, Nick Christiani, Dan Cholowsky, Rick Jacques, Ben Jones, Mike Keenan, Mike Misuraca, Jim Moran, Hector Otero, John Poloni, Jonathan Reynolds, Paul Scott, Lee Seras, Andy Stack. **Scouts:** Larry Barton, Jamie Bodaly, Kevin Buckley, Ed Daub, Rob Gorrell, Jim Grief, Bill Killian, Denny Nagel, Lou Snipp, Mike Steed, Marlon Styles, Mike Wallace **Director, International Scouting:** Trey Hendricks. **Assistant Director, International Scouting:** Greg McMillin. **Director, Latin America Scouting:** Richard Jimenez. **Crosschecker, Global Scouting:** Bob Engle. **Crosschecker, International Scouting:** Miguel Machado. **Coordinator, Dominican Republic:** Enmanuel Cartagena. **Coordinator, South America:** Richard Castro. **Manager, Pacific Rim Scouting:** Rob Fidler. **Scouts, Pacific Rim:** Jamey Storvick. **International Scouts:** Geronimo Blanco, Jose Valdelamar (Columbia), Edward Bens, Edgar Melo, Victor Nova, Carlos Pellerano, Felix Romero, Samuel Pimentel (Dominican Republic), Alex Ahumada (Mexico), Gustavo Martinez (Nicaragua), Anibal Reluz (Panama), Jean Paul Conde, Aguido Gonzalez, Victor Oramas, Ricardo Quintero (Venezuela).

CLEVELAND INDIANS

Office Address: Progressive Field, 2401 Ontario St., Cleveland, OH 44115.
Telephone: (216) 420-4200. **Fax:** (216) 420-4396.
Website: www.indians.com.

OWNERSHIP

Owner: Larry Dolan. **Chairman/Chief Executive Officer:** Paul Dolan. **Vice Chairman:** John Sherman.

BUSINESS OPERATIONS

President, Business Operations: Brian Barren. **Executive VP, Business:** Dennis Lehman.
Senior Vice President, Marketing/Strategy: Alex King. **Executive Administrative Assistant,
Ownership and Business Operations:** Dru Kosik.

CORPORATE PARTNERSHIPS/FINANCE

Senior Director, Corporate Partnership: Ted Baugh. **Director, Corporate Partnership
& Premium Hospitality:** Dom Polito. **Director, Premium Hospitality:** Ryan Robbins. **Senior
Sales Manager, Corporate Partnerships:** Bryan Hoffart. **Administrative Assistant:** Kim Scott.
VP/General Counsel: Joe Znidarsic. **Vice President, Finance:** Rich Dorffer. **Controller:** Erica
Chambers. **Manager, Accounting:** Karen Menzing. **Manager, Payroll Accounting/Services:**
Mary Forkapa. **Concessions Accounting Manager:** Diane Turner.

Larry Dolan

HUMAN RESOURCES

VP, Human Resources/Chief Diversity Officer: Sara Lehrke. **Director, Human Resources
Operations:** Jennifer Gibson. **Assistant Director, Talent Acquisition:** Mailynh Vu. **Manager, Talent Acquisition:**
Valencia Kimbrough. **Manager, Talent Development:** Nate Daymut. **Coordinator, Talent Development:** John Shand.

MARKETING

VP, Marketing/Brand Management: Nicole Schmidt. **Director, Brand Management:** Jason Wiedemann. **Manager,
Advertising/Promotions:** Anne Madzelan.

COMMUNICATIONS/BASEBALL INFORMATION

Telephone: (216) 420-4380. **Fax:** (216) 420-4430.
Senior VP, Public Affairs: Bob DiBiasio. **Senior Director, Communications:** Curtis Danburg. **Director, Baseball
Information & Player Relations:** Bart Swain. **Director, Communications & Player Relations:** Court Berry-Tripp.
Manager, Communications: Austin Controulis. **Coordinator, Player Engagement & Family Relations:** Megan Ganser.
Team Photographer: Dan Mendlik. **Coordinator, Communications & Team Historian:** Jeremy Feador.

BALLPARK OPERATIONS

VP, Ballpark Operations: Jim Folk. **Senior Director, Ballpark Operations:** Jerry Crabb. **Senior Director, Facility
Operations:** Seth Cooper. **Head Groundskeeper:** Brandon Koehnke. **Director, Facility Maintenance:** Ron Miller.
Manager, Game Day Staff: Renee VanLaningham. **Manager, Ballpark Operations:** Steve Walters. **Manager, Ballpark**

2019 SCHEDULE

Standard Game Times: Mon.-Sat., 7:10 pm; Sun. 1:10 pm.

MARCH	10-12 . . . . . . .at Oakland	28-30 . . . . . .at Baltimore	12-14 . . . . Boston
28-31 . . . . . at Minnesota	13-14 . . . .at Chicago (AL)	**JULY**	15-18 . . . at New York (AL)
	16-19 . . . . . . Baltimore	2-4. . . . . . .at Kansas City	20-22 . . . at New York (NL)
APRIL	20-22 . . . . Oakland	6-7. . . . . . .at Cincinnati	23-25 . . . . . . Kansas City
1-3. . . . . . . Chicago (AL)	23-26 . . . . . .Tampa Bay	12-14 . . . . . . Minnesota	27-29 . . . . .at Detroit
4-7. . . . . .Toronto	27-29 . . . . . . .at Boston	15-18 . . . . Detroit	30-31 . . . at Tampa Bay
9-11 . . . . .at Detroit	30-31 . . . .at Chicago (AL)	19-21 . . . . . Kansas City	
12-14 . . . .at Kansas City		22-24 . . . . . . at Toronto	**SEPTEMBER**
15-17 . . . . . . .at Seattle	**JUNE**	25-28 . . . .at Kansas City	1 . . . . at Tampa Bay
19-21 . . . . Atlanta	1-2. . . . . .at Chicago (AL)	30-31 . . . . Houston	2-5. . . . . . . Chicago (AL)
23-24 . . . . .Miami	4-6. . . . . .Minnesota		6-8. . . . . . . at Minnesota
25-28 . . . . .at Houston	7-9. . . . . .New York (AL)	**AUGUST**	9-11 . . at Los Angeles (AL)
30 . . . . at Miami	11-12 . . . . . . Cincinnati	1 . . . . Houston	13-15 . . . . . . .Minnesota
	14-16 . . . . . . .at Detroit	2-4. . . . Los Angeles (AL)	17-19 . . . . Detroit
MAY	17-20 . . . . .at Texas	5-7. . . . . Texas	20-22 . . . .Philadelphia
1 . . . . at Miami	21-23 . . . . Detroit	8-11 . . . . . at Minnesota	24-26 . . .at Chicago (AL)
3-5. . . . . Seattle	24-26 . . . . . Kansas City		27-29 . . . at Washington
6-9. . . . . . Chicago (AL)			

GENERAL INFORMATION

Stadium (year opened):
Progressive Field (1994).
Team Colors: Navy blue, red and silver.

Home Dugout: Third Base.
Playing Surface: Grass.

Operations: Tyler Cochran. **Manager, Facility Operations:** Andy Finn. **Manager, Ballpark Operations Coordinator:** Vince DiGennaro.

TICKETING

Telephone: (216) 420-4487. **Fax:** (216) 420-4481.
Director, Ticket Services: Matt Coppo. **Ticket Services Manager:** Shedrick Taylor. **Manager, Ticket Operations:** Seth Fuller. **Ticket Services Coordinator:** Paige Selle.

TEAM OPERATIONS/CLUBHOUSE

Director, Team Travel: Mike Seghi. **Home Clubhouse Manager:** Tony Amato. **Assistant Home Clubhouse Manager:** Brandon Biller. **Director, Video Operations:** Bob Chester.

BASEBALL OPERATIONS

President, Baseball Operations: Chris Antonetti. **General Manager:** Mike Chernoff. **Assistant GM:** Matt Forman, Carter Hawkins. **Vice President, Baseball Operations—Strategy/Administration:** Brad Grant. **Vice President, Baseball Operations:** Eric Binder. **VP, Research and Development:** Sky Andrecheck. **Director, Baseball Operations:** Alex Merberg. **Assistant Director, Baseball Research/Development:** Kevin Tenenbaum. **Principal Data Scientist:** Keith Woolner. **Baseball Analyst:** Max Marchi. **Director, Baseball Administration:** Wendy Hoppel. **Executive Administrative Assistant:** Marlene Lehky. **Assistant Director, Baseball Operations:** Sam Giller. **Assistant, Baseball Operations:** Zach Morton.

MAJOR LEAGUE STAFF

Manager: Terry Francona. **Coaches: Bench**—Brad Mills, **Pitching**—Carl Willis, **Hitting**—Ty Van Burkleo, **First Base**—Sandy Alomar Jr., **Third Base**—Mike Sarbaugh, **Bullpen**—Scott Atchison, **Assistant Hitting Coach**—Victor Rodriguez, **Assistant Coach**—Brian Sweeney. **Assistants, Major League Staff:** Mike Barnett, Armando Camacaro, Ricky Pacione.

Chris Antonetti

MEDICAL/TRAINING

Vice President, Medical Services: Lonnie Soloff. **Head Team Physician:** Dr. Mark Schickendantz. **Head Athletic Trainer:** James Quinlan. **Assistant Athletic Trainers:** Jeff Desjardins, Chad Wolfe. **Sports Psychologist & Director of Psychological Services:** Dr. Charles Maher. **Performance Coach (Triple-A/Major League):** Ceci Clark.

PLAYER DEVELOPMENT

Director, Player Development: James Harris. **Special Assistant to GM:** Tom Wiedenbauer. **Assistant Directors, Player Development:** Matt Blake, Alex Eckelman. **Assistant, Player Development:** Rob Cerfolio. **Director, Administration:** Wendy Hoppel. **Advisor, Player Development:** Minnie Mendoza, Tim Tolman, Johnny Goryl. **Special Assistants:** Dave Wallace, Travis Fryman. **Administrative Assistant:** Nilda Taffanelli. **Assistant Field Coordinator:** Anthony Medrano. **Coordinators:** Kevin Howard (hitting), Pete Lauritson (short-season hitting), Ruben Niebla (pitching), John McDonald (defense), Cody Buckel (pitching resource), Kai Correa (short-season defense). **Analyst, Player Development:** Todd Kubacki. **Education & Language Coordinator:** Anna Bolton. **Mental Performance Coach:** Oscar Gutierrez. **Mental Performance Coordinator:** Brian Miles. **Performance Coordinator:** Ryan Faer (Arizona), Hasani Torres (Dominican Republic).

FARM SYSTEM

Class	Club	Manager	Hitting Coach	Pitching Coach
Triple-A	Columbus (IL)	Tony Mansolino	Andy Tracy	Rigo Beltran
Double-A	Akron (EL)	Rouglas Odor	Justin Toole	Tony Arnold
High A	Lynchburg (CL)	Jim Pankovits	Johnny Narron	Joe Torres
Low A	Lake County (MWL)	Luke Carlin	Jason Esposito	Owen Dew
Short-season	Mahoning Valley (NYP)	Dennis Malave	Grant Fink	Jason Blanton
Rookie	Indians 1 (AZL)	Larry Day	Jordan Becker	Joel Mangrum
Rookie	Indians 2 (AZL)	Jerry Owens	Junior Betances	Mike Steele
Rookie	Indians (DSL)	Jesus Taverez	Chris Smith	Jesus Sanchez

SCOUTING

Senior Director, Scouting Operations: John Mirabelli. **Special Assistants to the GM:** Steve Lubratich, Dave Malpass, Don Poplin. **Director, Amateur Scouting:** Scott Barnsby. **Assistant Director, Amateur Scouting:** Clint Longenecker. **Assistant, Amateur Scouting:** Will Clements. **Coordinators, Amateur Scouting:** Kevin Cullen (Frisco, TX), Jon Heuerman (Chandler, AZ), Scott Meaney (Holly Springs, NC). **Underclass Coordinator:** Brad Tyler (Bishop, GA). **Area Scouts:** Kyle Bamberger (Kansas City, MO), CT Bradford (Pensacola, FL), Garrick Chaffee (Dallas, TX), David Compton (Newport Beach, CA), Aaron Etchison (Dexter, MI), Conor Glassey (Bothell, WA), Mike Kanen (Hoboken, NJ), Andrew Krause (Lexington, KY), Jhonathan Leyba (Seminole, FL), Pete Loizzo (Durham, NC), Don Lyle (Sacramento, CA), Bob Mayer (Somerset, PA), Carlos Muniz (San Pedro, CA), Ryan Perry (Phoenix, AZ), Ethan Purser (Dallas, GA), Steffan Segui (Tampa, FL), Kyle Van Hook (Brenham, TX). **Part-Time Scouts:** Trent Friedrich, Bob Malkmus, John Stott, Jose Trujillo. **Director, Pro Scouting:** Victor Wang. **Coordinator, Pro Scouting:** Dan Budreika (Phoenix, AZ). **Special Assignment Scouts:** Doug Carpenter (North Palm Beach, FL), Bo Hughes (Sherman Oaks, CA), Dave Miller (Wilmington, NC). **Pro Scouts:** Chris Calcaino (Milton, DE) Jim Rickon (Cleveland, OH). **Senior Director, International Scouting:** Paul Gillispie. **Assistant Directors, International Scouting:** Richard Conway, Chris Gale. **Coordinator, International Scouting:** Junie Melendez (Avon, OH). **International Crosschecker:** Jason Lynn.

COLORADO ROCKIES

Office Address: 2001 Blake St., Denver, CO 80205.
Telephone: (303) 292-0200. **Fax:** (303) 312-2116.
Website: www.coloradorockies.com.

OWNERSHIP

Operated by: Colorado Rockies Baseball Club Ltd. **Owner/General Partner:** Charles K. Monfort. **Owner/Chairman/ Chief Executive Officer:** Richard L. Monfort. **Executive Assistant to the Owner/Chairman/Chief Executive Officer:** Terry Douglass.

BUSINESS OPERATIONS

Executive Vice President/Chief Operating Officer: Greg Feasel. **Assistant to Executive VP/Chief Operating Officer:** Kim Olson. **VP, Human Resources:** Elizabeth Stecklein.

FINANCE

Executive VP of Colorado Baseball 1993: Hal Roth. **VP/CFO:** Michael Kent. **VP/General Counsel:** Brian Gaffney. **Senior Director, Purchasing:** Gary Lawrence. **Coordinator, Purchasing:** Gloria Giraldi. **Senior Director, Accounting:** Phil Emerson. **Accountants:** Joel Binfet, Laine Campbell. **Payroll Administrator:** Juli Daedelow.

SALES

VP, Corporate Partnerships: Walker Monfort. **Assistant to VP, Corporate Partnerships:** Nicole Ortiz. **Sr. Director – Client Services & Events:** Kari Anderson. **Assistant Director:** Nate VanderWal. **Account Executives:** Sam Porter, Chris Zumbrennen. **VP, Community/Retail Operations:** James P. Kellogg. **Sr. Director, Retail Operations:** Aaron Heinrich. **Sr. Director, In-Game Entertainment & Broadcasting:** Kent Krosbakken.

MARKETING/COMMUNICATIONS

Telephone: (303) 312-2325. **Fax:** (303) 312-2319.
VP, Marketing/Communications: Jill Campbell. Supervisor, **Advertising/Marketing:** Sarah Topf. **Assistant Director, Digital Media & Publications:** Julian Valentin. **Coordinator - Marketing:** Lauren Jacaruso. **Sr. Director, Communications:** Warren Miller. **Supervisor, Communications:** Cory Little. **Coordinators, Communications:** Nick Parson. **Coordinator, Spanish Translator/ Communications:** Abby Thayer. **Assistant – Social Media:** Nicole Morris.

BALLPARK OPERATIONS

VP, Ballpark Operations: Kevin Kahn. **Senior Director, Food Service Operations/Development:** Albert Valdes. **Senior Director, Guest Services:** Steven Burke. **Head Groundskeeper:** Mark Razum. **Assistant Head Groundskeeper:** Doug Zabinsky. **Senior Director, Engineering/Facilities:** Allyson Gutierrez. **Director, Engineering:** Randy Carlill. **Senior Director, Information Systems:** Michael Bush. **Official Scorers:** Dave Einspahr, Dave Plati. **Public Address Announcer:** Reed Saunders.

Richard Monfort

2019 SCHEDULE

Standard Game Times: Mon.-Fri., 6:40 pm; Sat., 6:10 pm; Sun., 1:10 pm.

MARCH		JULY	SEPTEMBER
28-31 . . . . at Miami	7-9 . . . . San Francisco	24-26 . . . at San Francisco	12-14 . . . . .Arizona
	10-12 . . . . San Diego	27-30 . . . Los Angeles (NL)	16-18 . . . . .Miami
APRIL	14-15 . . . . .at Boston		19-21 . . . . . . at Arizona
1-3 . . . . at Tampa Bay	17-19 . . . at Philadelphia	JULY	22-25 . . . . . .at St. Louis
5-7 . . . . Los Angeles (NL)	21-23 . . . . at Pittsburgh	2-3 . . . . Houston	27-28 . . . . Boston
8-10 . . . . Atlanta	24-26 . . . . . . Baltimore	5-7 . . . . at Arizona	29-31 . . . . . . .Pittsburgh
11-14 . . . at San Francisco	27-30 . . . . Arizona	12-14 . . . . . . Cincinnati	
15-16 . . . . . at San Diego	31 . . . . .Toronto	15-17 . . . . . San Francisco	SEPTEMBER
18-21 . . . . .Philadelphia		19-21 . . at New York (AL)	1 . . . . Pittsburgh
22-24 . . . . . . Washington	JUNE	22-25 . . . . at Washington	2-4 . . at Los Angeles (NL)
26-28 . . . . at Atlanta	1-2 . . . . .Toronto	26-28 . . . . . .at Cincinnati	6-8 . . . . . . at San Diego
29-30 . . . . . at Milwaukee	4-6 . . . . . .at Chicago (NL)	29-31 . . . Los Angeles (NL)	10-12 . . . . St. Louis
	7-9 . . . . . at New York (NL)		13-15 . . . . San Diego
MAY	10-12 . . . . . Chicago (NL)	AUGUST	16-18 . . . . .New York (NL)
1-2 . . . . at Milwaukee	13-16 . . . . . . San Diego	2-4 . . . . San Francisco	20-22 . at Los Angeles (NL)
3-5 . . . . Arizona	18-20 . . . . . at Arizona	6-7 . . . . .at Houston	24-26 . . . at San Francisco
	21-23 . at Los Angeles (NL)	8-11 . . . . . . at San Diego	27-29 . . . . . . .Milwaukee

GENERAL INFORMATION

Stadium (year opened): Coors Field (1995). **Playing Surface:** Grass.
Team Colors: Purple, black and silver.
Home Dugout: First Base.

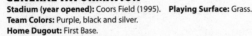

TICKETING

Telephone: (303) 762-5437, (800) 388-7625. **Fax:** (303) 312-2115.

VP, Ticket Operations/Sales/Services: Sue Ann McClaren. **Senior Director, Ticket Services/Finance/Technology:** Kent Hakes. **Assistant Director, Ticket Operations:** Kevin Flood. **Senior Director, Season Tickets/Renewals/Business Strategy:** Jeff Benner. **Assistant Director, Season Tickets:** Farrah Magee. **Senior Director, Groups/Suites/Outbound Sales:** Matt Haddad. **Assistant Director, Suites/Party Facilities:** Traci Abeyta. **Senior Account Executive, Outbound Sales:** Todd Thomas. **Supervisor, Inside Sales:** Justin Bennett.

TRAVEL/CLUBHOUSE

Sr. Director, Major League Operations: Paul Egins. **Manager, Major League Clubhouse:** Mike Pontarelli.

BASEBALL OPERATIONS

Executive VP/General Manager: Jeff Bridich. **Assistant to Executive VP/GM:** Irma Castañeda. **Assistant GM, Baseball Operations/Assistant General Counsel:** Zack Rosenthal. **Assistant GM/Player Personnel:** Jon Weil. **Assistant GM/Player Development:** Zach Wilson. **Director, Baseball Operations:** Domenic Di Ricco. **Coordinator, Baseball Operations/ Staff Counsel:** Matt Obernauer. **Director, Baseball Research & Development:** Trevor Patch. **Manager, Baseball Research & Development:** Jamie Hollowell. **Special Assistant to the GM:** Danny Montgomery.

Jeff Bridich

MAJOR LEAGUE STAFF

Manager: Bud Black. **Coaches: Bench**—Mike Redmond, **Pitching**—Steve Foster, **Hitting**— Dave Magadan, **Assistant Hitting Coach**—Jeff Salazar, **Third Base**—Stu Cole, **First Base**— Ron Gideon, **Bullpen**—Darren Holmes, **Bullpen Catcher**—Aaron Munoz, **Director, Physical Performance**—Gabe Bauer, **Video**—Brian Jones.

MEDICAL/TRAINING

Senior Director, Medical Operations/Special Projects: Tom Probst. **Medical Director:** Dr. Thomas Noonan. **Club Physicians:** Dr. Allen Schreiber, Dr. Douglas Wyland. **Head Trainer:** Keith Dugger. **Assistant Athletic Trainer:** Scott Gehret.

PLAYER DEVELOPMENT

Director, Pitching Operations: Mark Wiley. **Pitching Coordinator:** Doug Linton, Darryl Scott. **Catching Coordinator:** Mark Strittmatter. **Hitting Coordinator:** Darin Everson. **Outfield and Baserunning Coordinator:** Anthony Sanders. **Rehab Coordinator:** Scott Murayama. **Assistant Rehab Coordinator, Scottsdale:** Andy Stover. **Physical Performance Coordinator:** Trevor Swartz. **Mental Skills Coordinator:** Doug Chadwick. **Assistant Mental Skills Coordinator:** Jerry Amador. **Minor League Video Coordinator:** Jeff Nelson. **Supervisor, Cultural Development:** Josh Rosenthal. **Cultural Development Coordinator, DSL:** Angel Amparo. **Latin America Field Coordinator:** Edison Lora. **Equipment Manager:** Ricky Dominguez. **Special Instructor, Player Development (PT):** Bob Apodaca. **Special Instructor, Player Development/Scouting Advisor (PT):** Jerry Weinstein.

FARM SYSTEM

Class	Club (League)	Manager	Hitting Coach	Pitching Coach
Triple-A	Albuquerque (PCL)	Glenallen Hill	Tim Doherty	Brandon Emanuel
Double-A	Hartford (EL)	Warren Schaeffer	Lee Stevens	Steve Merrinam
High A	Lancaster (CAL)	Scott Little	Tom Sutaris	Dave Burba
Low A	Asheville (SAL)	Robinson Cancel	Paco Martin	Mark Brewer
Short-season	Boise (NWL)	Steve Soliz	Cesar Galvez	Ryan Kibler
Rookie	Grand Junction (PIO)	Jake Opitz	Zach Osborne	Blake Beatty
Rookie	Rockies 1 (DSL)	Mauricio Gonzalez	Eugenio Jose	Florentino Nunez
Rookie	Rockies 2 (DSL)	Julio Campos	Michael Ramirez	Helmis Rodriguez

SCOUTING

VP, Scouting: Danny Montgomery. **Assistant Scouting Director:** Damon Iannelli. **Special Assistant, Scouting:** Rick Mathews. **Assistant Director, Scouting Operations:** Sterling Monfort. **Advance Scouts:** Chris Warren, Joe Little. **Special Assistant, Player Personnel:** Ty Coslow (Louisville, KY). **Major League Scouts:** Steve Fleming (Louisa, VA), Will George (Milford, DE), Jack Gillis (Sarasota, FL), Mark Germann (Denver, CO), Joe Housey (Hollywood, FL), Mike Paul (Tucson, AZ), John Corbin (Savannah, GA). **Professional Scout:** Doug Bernier (Littlejohn, CO). **National Crosscheckers:** Mike Ericson (Phoenix, AZ), Jay Matthews (Concord, NC). **Area Scouts:** Scott Alves (Phoenix, AZ), Brett Baldwin (Kansas City, MO), Julio Campos (Guaynabo, PR) John Cedarburg (Fort Myers, FL), Scott Corman (Lexington, KY), Jordan Czarniecki (Greenville, SC), Jeff Edwards (Fresno, TX), Sean Gamble (Atlanta, GA), Mike Garlatti (Edison, NJ), Matt Hattabaugh (Westminster, CA), Darin Holcomb (Woodland, CA), Jon Lukens (Dana Point, CA), Matt Pignataro (Seattle, WA), Jesse Retzlaff (Dallas, TX), Rafael Reyes (Miami, FL), Ed Santa (Powell, OH), Zack Zulli (Hammond, LA). **Part-Time Scouts:** Norm DeBriyn (Fayetteville, AR), Dave McQueen (Bossier City, LA), Greg Pullia (Plymouth, MA). **VP, International Scouting/Player Development:** Rolando Fernandez. **Supervisor, Venezuelan Scouting:** Orlando Medina. **International Scouts:** Phil Allen (Australia), Martin Cabrera (Dominican Republic), Carlos Gomez (Venezuela), Raul Gomez (International), Alving Mejias (International), Frank Roa (Dominican Republic), Jossher Suarez (Venezuela). **Part-Time International Scouts:** Rogers Figueroa (Colombia), Marius Loupadiere (Panama).

DETROIT TIGERS

Office Address: 2100 Woodward Ave, Detroit, MI 48201.
Telephone: (313) 471-2000. **Fax:** (313) 471-2138. **Website:** www.tigers.com

OWNERSHIP
Operated By: Detroit Tigers Inc. **President & CEO, Ilitch Holdings, Inc./Chairman & CEO, Detroit Tigers:** Christopher Ilitch. **Group President, Sports & Entertainment, Ilitch Holdings, Inc.:** Chris Granger.

BUSINESS OPERATIONS
Executive Vice President, Business Operations: Duane McLean.
Executive Assistant to Executive VP, Business Operations: Peggy Thompson.

FINANCE/ADMINISTRATION
VP, Finance/Administration/CFO: Stephen Quinn. **Senior Director, Finance:** Kelli Kollman. **Accounting Manager/Treasury Analyst:** Sheila Robine. **Financial Analyst:** Kristin Jorgensen. **Accounts Payable Coordinator:** Debra Sword. **Accounts Receivable Coordinator:** Monica Basil. **Senior Director, Human Resources:** Karen Gruca. **Human Resources Coordinator:** Kelsey Shuck. **Human Resources & Recruiting Coordinator:** Nicole Nimeth. **Internal Audit Manager:** Candice Lentz. **Payroll Administrator:** Mark Cebelak. **Director, Authentics:** Marc Himelstein. **Authentics Coordinator:** Ashley Baughman. **Administrative/Accounting Assistant:** Tina Sidney.

Chris Ilitch

PUBLIC/COMMUNITY AFFAIRS
VP, Community/Public Affairs: Elaine Lewis. **Director, Player Relations & Detroit Tigers Foundation:** Jordan Field. **Youth Programs & Player Relations Manager:** Ashley Robinson. **Community Affairs Manager:** Courtney Kaplan. **Community Affairs Coordinator:** Brandon Scherzer. **Administrative Assistant:** Donna Bernardo.

SALES/MARKETING
VP, Corporate Partnerships: Steve Harms. **Corporate Partnerships Sales Directors:** Kurt Tiesman, John Wolski. **Corporate Partnership Sales Managers:** Dan D'Alessandro, Corey Thomas. **Corporate Partnerships Account Executive, Digital:** Jordan Bagley. **Director, Partnership Services:** Kaitlin Knutson. **CRM & Partnership Services Manager:** Jazmine Robinson. **Partnership Services Coordinator:** Jessica Langolf. **VP, Ticket/Suite Sales:** Scot Pett. **Director, Ticket Sales:** Steve Fox. **Director, Group Sales:** Mike McAdams. **Director, Business Analytics:** Jeff Lutz. **Manager, Suite Sales/Service:** Dan Griesbaum. **Suite Sales/Services Manager:** Kelsey Decker. **Suite Sales Account Executives:** Jessica Chesley, Bret Price. **Suite Sales Coordinator:** Rachel Barnett VP, **Marketing:** Ellen Hill Zeringue. **Digital/Social Media Manager:** Mac Slavin. **Content Producer:** Brent Brevak. **Social Media Coordinator:** Mikaela Higgins. **Graphic Designer:** Courtney Foyt. **Manager, Promotions/Special Events:** Haley Kolff. **Promotions/Special Events Coordinators:** Evan Novak, Taylor Olson.

MEDIA RELATIONS/COMMUNICATIONS
Telephone: (313) 471-2227. **Fax:** (313) 471-2138.

2019 SCHEDULE
Standard Game Times: Mon-Sat., 7:10 pm; Sun.,1:10 pm.

MARCH		
28-31 . . . . at Toronto	7-9. . . . . Los Angeles (AL)	25-27 . . . . Texas	13-15 . . . . Seattle
	10-12 . . . . . at Minnesota	28-30 . . . . . Washington	16-18 . . . . . at Tampa Bay
APRIL	13-15 . . . . Houston		19-22 . . . . . . .at Houston
1-3. . . . . at New York (AL)	16-19 . . . . Oakland	**JULY**	23-25 . . . . at Minnesota
4-7. . . . . Kansas City	21-23 . . . . .Miami	2-4. . . . . .at Chicago (AL)	27-29 . . . . Cleveland
9-11 . . . . Cleveland	24-26 . . . at New York (NL)	5-7. . . . . Boston	30-31 . . . . . . .Minnesota
12-14 . . . . . at Minnesota	27-29 . . . . .at Baltimore	12-14 . . . . .at Kansas City	
16-17 . . . . . . Pittsburgh	31 . . . . at Atlanta	15-18 . . . . . .at Cleveland	**SEPTEMBER**
18-21 . . . . . Chicago (AL)		19-21 . . . . .Toronto	1-2. . . . . Minnesota
22-25 . . . . . . .at Boston	**JUNE**	23-24 . . . . .Philadelphia	3-5. . . . . .at Kansas City
26-28 . . . .at Chicago (AL)	1-2. . . . . at Atlanta	25-28 . . . . . .at Seattle	6-8. . . . . . . .at Oakland
30 . . . . . at Philadelphia	4-6. . . . . . . .Tampa Bay	29-31 . at Los Angeles (AL)	10-12 . . . .New York (AL)
	7-9. . . . . Minnesota		13-16 . . . . . . Baltimore
MAY	11-13 . . . .at Kansas City	**AUGUST**	17-19 . . . .at Cleveland
1 . . . . at Philadelphia	14-16 . . . . . Cleveland	2-4. . . . . . . .at Texas	20-22 . . . . Chicago (AL)
3-5. . . . . Kansas City	18-19 . . . . . at Pittsburgh	5-7. . . . . . Chicago (AL)	24-26 . . . . . .Minnesota
	21-23 . . . . .at Cleveland	8-11 . . . . . . Kansas City	27-29 . . . .at Chicago (AL)

GENERAL INFORMATION

Stadium (year opened):
Comerica Park (2000).
Team Colors: Navy blue, orange and white.

Home Dugout: Third Base.
Playing Surface: Grass.

VP, Communications: Ron Colangelo. **Director, Baseball Media Relations:** Chad Crunk. **Coordinators, Media Relations:** Ben Fidelman, Michele Wysocki. **Director, Broadcasting/In-Game Entertainment:** Stan Fracker.

BASEBALL OPERATIONS

Telephone: (313) 471-2000. **Fax:** (313) 471-2099.

Executive Vice President, Baseball Operations/General Manager: Al Avila. **Special Assistants to the GM:** Kirk Gibson, Willie Horton, Al Kaline, Jim Leyland, Alan Trammell. **VP/ Assistant GM:** David Chadd. **VP, Player Personnel:** Scott Bream. **VP/Player Development:** Dave Littlefield. **Senior Advisor:** John Westhoff. **Senior Director, Baseball Analytics/ Operations:** Jay Sartori. **Director, Baseball Operations/Professional Scouting:** Sam Menzin. **Director, Baseball Analytics:** Jim Logue. **Director, Team Travel:** Brian Britten. **Associate Counsel, Baseball Operations:** Alan Avila. **Executive Assistant to the Executive Vice President, Baseball Operations/General Manager:** Marty Lyon.

Al Avila

MAJOR LEAGUE STAFF

Manager: Ron Gardenhire. **Coaches: Pitching**—Rick Anderson, **Hitting** —Lloyd McClendon, **First Base**—Ramon Santiago, **Third Base**—Dave Clark, **Bullpen**—Jeff Pico, **Bench**—Steve Liddle, **Assistant Hitting**—Phil Clark, **Quality Control**—Joe Vavra.

MEDICAL/TRAINING

Senior Director, Medical Services: Kevin Rand. **Head Athletic Trainer:** Doug Teter. **Assistant Athletic Trainer:** Matt Rankin. **Physical Therapist:** Robbie Williams. **Strength & Conditioning Coach:** Chris Walter. **Assistant Strength & Conditioning Coach:** Yousef Zamat. **Team Physicians:** Dr. Michael Workings, Dr. Stephen Lemos, Dr. Louis Saco (Florida). **Coordinator, Medical Services:** Gwen Keating.

PLAYER DEVELOPMENT

VP, Player Development: Dave Littlefield. **Director, Minor League Operations:** Dan Lunetta. **Director, Player Development:** Dave Owen. **Director, Minor League/Scouting Administration:** Cheryl Evans. **Player Development Coordinators:** David Allende, Jim McKew. **Minor League Field Coordinator:** Bill Dancy. **Roving Instructors:** Jeff Branson (hitting), Scott Fletcher (hitting), A.J. Sager (pitching), Joe DePastino (catching), Jose Valentin (Infield), Gene Roof (outfield/baserunning), Jaime Garcia (assistant pitching), Dr. Spencer Wood (performance and mental skills coach), Brian Peterson (performance enhancement instructor), Josman Robles (Latin American performance coach). **Minor League Strength & Conditioning Coordinator:** Steve Chase. **Medical & Rehab Coordinator:** Corey Tremble.

FARM SYSTEM

Class	Club	Manager	Hitting Coach	Pitching Coach
Triple-A	Toledo (IL)	Doug Mientkiewicz	Mike Hessman	Juan Nieves
Double-A	Erie(EL)	Mike Rabelo	Brian Harper	Mark Johnson
High A	Lakeland (FSL)	Andrew Graham	Tim Garland	Jorge Cordova
Low A	West Michigan (MWL)	Lance Parrish	John Vander Wal	Willie Blair
Short-season	Connecticut (NYP)	Brayan Pena	Bill Springman	Carlos Bohorquez
Rookie	Tigers West (GCL)	Gary Cathcart	John Murrian	Mike Alvarez
Rookie	Tigers East (GCL)	Luis Lopez	Rafael Gil	Jose Parra
Rookie	DSL Tigers (DSL)	Ramon Zapata	Jose Ovalles	Willians Moreno
Rookie	DSL Tigers 2 (DSL)	Marcos Yepez	Kely Ramos	Luis Marte

SCOUTING

VP, Assistant General Manager: David Chadd. **VP, Player Personnel:** Scott Bream. **Director, Baseball Operations/ Professional Scouting:** Sam Menzin. **Director, Amateur Scouting:** Scott Pleis. **Assistant Director, Amateur Scouting:** Eric Nieto. **Amateur Scouting Video Coordinator:** Sam Nasci. **Amateur Scouting Interns:** Jacob Girard, Logan Schuemann, Johnny Stevenson. **Major League Scouts:** Ray Crone, Jim Elliott, Kevin Ellis, Joe Ferrone, Randy Johnson, PJ Jones, Paul Mirocke, Yadalla Mufdi, Jim Olander, Gary Pellant, Jim Rough, John Stockstill, Bruce Tanner, Josh Wilson. **Senior Advisors:** Scott Reid, Murray Cook. **Special Assistants to the GM:** Dick Egan, Mike Russell. **National Crosscheckers:** Tim Hallgren, Steve Hinton. **Regional Crosscheckers: East**—James Orr, **Central**—Justin Henry, **Midwest**—Tim Grieve, **West**—Dave Lottsfeldt. **Area Scouts:** Nick Avila (South FL, PR, VI), Bryson Barber (GA, FL panhandle), Taylor Black (NC, SC), Jim Bretz (CT, MA, ME, NH, RI, VT, Eastern Canada), RJ Burgess (North/Central FL), Scott Cerny (Northern CA, Northern NV), Dave Dangler (AK, ID, MT, OR, WA, WY, Western Canada), Mike Hankins (Southern TX, MO), Ryan Johnson (KS, NE, ND, SD, IA, MN), Jeff Kunkel (MI, WI, OH, Northern IN, Northern IL), Joey Lothrop (AZ, UT, NM, CO, TX (El Paso)), Tim McWilliam (Southern CA, HI), Steve Pack (Southern CA, Southern NV), Mike Smith (AL, MS, LA), Steve Taylor (Northern TX, OK, AR), Matt Zmuda (VA, MD, WV, DC, DE, PA), Harold Zonder (KY, TN, Southern IL, Southern IN). **Part-Time Scouts:** German Geigel (PR), Deryl Horton (MI), Mark Monahan (MI), Clyde Weir (MI). **Director, International Operations:** Tom Moore. **Director, Latin American Scouting:** Miguel Garcia. **Directors, Latin American Player Development:** Manny Crespo, Rafael Martinez. **Director, Dominican Republic Operations:** Ramon Perez. **International Operations Coordinator:** Rafael Gonzalez. **Coordinator, International Player Programs:** Sharon Lockwood. **International Crosscheckers:** Alejandro Rodriguez, Jeff Wetherby. **Coordinator, Pacific Rim:** Kevin Hooker. **Dominican Scouting Supervisor:** Aldo Perez. **Venezuelan Scouting Supervisor:** Jesus Mendoza. **Venezuelan Academy Administrator/Area Scout:** Oscar Garcia. **International Operations Intern:** Jean Martinez. **Special Assignment Scout, Dominican Republic:** Oliver Arias. **International Area Scouts:** Michael Hsieh (Taiwan), Ho-Kyun Im (Korea), Raul Leiva (Venezuela), Luis Molina (Panama), Delvis Pacheco (Venezuela), Rodolfo Penalo (Dominican Republic), Miguel Rodriguez (Dominican Republic), Carlos Santana (Dominican Republic), Yas Sato (Japan), Glenn Williams (Australia).

HOUSTON ASTROS

Office Address: Minute Maid Park, Union Station, 501 Crawford, Suite 400, Houston, TX 77002.
Mailing Address: PO Box 288, Houston, TX 77001. **Telephone:** (713) 259-8000. **Fax:** (713) 259-8981.
Email Address: fanfeedback@astros.mlb.com. **Website:** www.astros.com.

OWNERSHIP
Owner/Chairman: Jim Crane.

BUSINESS OPERATIONS

Jim Crane

President, Business Operations: Reid Ryan. **Executive Advisor:** Nolan Ryan. **Executive Assistant:** Eileen Colgin. **Executive Assistant:** Brenda Schiro. **Senior VP, Business Operations:** Marcel Braithwaite. **Senior VP, Corporate Partnerships:** Matt Brand. **Senior VP, Community Relations/Executive Director, Astros Foundation:** Twila Carter. **Senior VP, Ticket Sales/Service:** Jason Howard. **Senior VP/ General Counsel:** Giles Kibbe. **Senior VP, Marketing/Communications:** Anita Sehgal. **Chief Financial Officer:** Michael Slaughter. **VP, Tax:** Vito Ciminello. **VP, Communications:** Gene Dias. **VP, Strategy/Analytics:** Michael Dillon. **VP, Stadium Operations:** Bobby Forrest. **VP, Information Technology:** Chris Hanz. **VP, Foundation Development:** Marian Harper. **VP, Merchandising/Retail Operations:** Tom Jennings. **VP, Human Resources:** Vivian Mora. **VP, Finance:** Doug Seckel. **VP, Event Sales/ Operations:** Stephanie Stegall. **VP, Marketing:** Jason Wooden. **Senior Director, Business Operations:** Dan O'Neill.

COMMUNICATIONS/COMMUNITY RELATIONS
Senior Manager, Communications: Steve Grande. **Manager, Communications:** Chris Peixoto. **Manager, Business Communications:** Sarah Kincart. **Coordinator, Communications:** Alexandra Noboa. **Manager, Broadcasting:** Ginny Gotcher Grande. **Director, Astros Youth Academy:** Daryl Wade. **Manager, Astros Youth Academy:** Duane Stelly. **Coordinators, Community Relations/Astros Foundation:** Rachel Bubier, Andrew Remson. **Coordinator, Astros Youth Academy:** Megan Hays.

MARKETING/ANALYTICS
Senior Director, Marketing Operations and Insights: Craig Swaisgood. **Senior Director, Ballpark Entertainment:** Chris E. Garcia. **Senior Director, Business Strategy/Analytics:** Jay Verrill. **Director, Creative Services:** Chris David Garcia. **Senior Managers, Marketing Entertainment:** Kyle Hamsher, Richard Tapia. **Director, Promotions and Events:** Brianna Hughes. **Manager, Social Media:** Danny Farris.

CORPORATE PARTNERSHIPS
Senior Director, Corporate Partnerships: Creighton Kahoalii. **Senior Director, Corporate Partnerships/Special Event Sales:** Jeff Stewart. **Director, Sales/Corporate Sponsorships:** Keshia Henderson. **Sales Managers, Corporate Partnerships:** Enrique Cruz, Matt Richardson. **Senior Account Managers, Corporate Partnerships:** Melissa Hahn, Andrew Shipp. **Account Managers, Corporate Partnerships:** Lauren Antosik, Everett Wolf.

2019 SCHEDULE
Standard Game Times: Mon.-Sat., 7:10 pm; Sun. 1:10 pm.

MARCH	9-12 . . . . Texas	28-30 . . . . Seattle	15-18 . . . . . .at Oakland
28-31 . . . . . at Tampa Bay	13-15 . . . . . . .at Detroit	**JULY**	19-22 . . . . Detroit
APRIL	17-19 . . . . . .at Boston	2-3 . . . . at Colorado	23-25 . . . Los Angeles (AL)
1-3 . . . . .at Texas	20-23 . . . . . Chicago (AL)	5-7 . . . . . Los Angeles (AL)	27-29 . . . . . . .Tampa Bay
5-7 . . . . Oakland	24-26 . . . . Boston	11-14 . . . . .at Texas	30-31 . . . . at Toronto
8-10 . . . . . New York (AL)	27-29 . . . . Chicago (NL)	15-18 . at Los Angeles (AL)	
12-14 . . . . . . .at Seattle	31 . . . . .at Oakland	19-21 . . . . Texas	**SEPTEMBER**
16-17 . . . . . .at Oakland	**JUNE**	22-24 . . . . Oakland	1 . . . . at Toronto
19-21 . . . . .at Texas	1-2 . . . . .at Oakland	26-28 . . . . . .at St. Louis	2-3 . . . . . . at Milwaukee
22-24 . . . . . Minnesota	3-6 . . . . .at Seattle	30-31 . . . . . .at Cleveland	5-8 . . . . Seattle
25-28 . . . . . Cleveland	7-9 . . . . Baltimore	**AUGUST**	9-12 . . . . Oakland
29-30 . . . . . at Minnesota	11-12 . . . . . .Milwaukee	1 . . . . .at Cleveland	13-15 . . . . .at Kansas City
MAY	14-16 . . . . .Toronto	2-4 . . . . Seattle	17-18 . . . . Texas
1-2 . . . . . . at Minnesota	17-19 . . . .at Cincinnati	6-7 . . . . .Colorado	20-22 . . Los Angeles (AL)
4-5 . . at Los Angeles (AL)	20-23 . . at New York (AL)	9-11 . . . . . .at Baltimore	24-25 . . . . .at Seattle
6-8 . . . . Kansas City	25-27 . . . . . . Pittsburgh	12-14 . . . .at Chicago (AL)	26-29 . at Los Angeles (AL)

GENERAL INFORMATION
Stadium (year opened): Minute Maid Park (2000).
Team Colors: Navy and orange.
Home Dugout: First Base.
Playing Surface: Grass.

STADIUM OPERATIONS

Senior Director, Stadium Operations: Thomas Bell. **Director, Audio/Visual:** Lowell Matheny. **Director, Engineering:** Jonovon Rogers. **Director, Security/Parking:** Ben Williams. **Manager, Parking:** Gary Rowberry. **Manager, Engineering:** Michael Seighman. **Head Groundskeeper:** Izzy Hinojsa. **First Assistant Groundskeeper:** Chris Wolfe.

TICKETING

Senior Director, Ticket Sales: P.J. Keene. **Senior Director, Premium Sales/Service:** Clay Kowalski. **Director, Box Office Operations:** Bill Cannon. Director, **Season Ticket Service:** Jeff Close. **Director, Ticket Operations:** Mark Cole. **Director, Season Ticket Sales:** Andre Luck.

BASEBALL OPERATIONS

General Manager: Jeff Luhnow. **Assistant GM:** Brandon Taubman. **Special Assistant to the GM, Player Personnel:** Kevin Goldstein. **Special Assistant to the GM, Baseball Operations:** Oz Ocampo. **Special Assistants:** Craig Biggio, Roger Clemens, Enos Cabell. **Director, Research/ Development:** Ehsan Bokhari. **Director, Latin American Operations:** Caridad Cabrera. **Director, Florida Operations and Minor League Travel:** Jay Edmiston. **Director, Advance Information:** Tom Koch-Weser. **Director, Sports Medicine and Performance:** Bill Firkus.

Jeff Luhnow

MAJOR LEAGUE STAFF

Manager: A.J. Hinch.
Coaches: Bench—Joe Espada, **Pitching**—Brent Strom, **Hitting**— Alex Cintron. **Second Hitting**—Troy Snitker. **First Base**—Don Kelly. **Third Base**—Gary Pettis, **Bullpen**—Josh Miller

TEAM OPERATIONS/CLUBHOUSE

Senior Manager, Team Operations: Derek Vigoa. **Coordinator, Major League Advance Information:** Tommy Kawamura. **Coordinator, MLB Video/Advance Information:** Antonio Padilla. **Clubhouse Manager:** Carl Schneider. **Visiting Clubhouse Manager:** Steve Perry.

MEDICAL/TRAINING

Director, Sports Medicine/Performance: Bill Firkus. **Head Team Physician:** Dr. David Lintner. **Team Physicians:** Dr. Thomas Mehlhoff, Dr. James Muntz, Dr. Pat McCulloch. **Head Athletic Trainer:** Jeremiah Randall. **Team Physical Therapist:** Sam Bell. **Massage Therapist:** Katsumi Oka. **Head Strength/ Conditioning Coach:** Dan Howells. **Assistant Major League Strength/Conditioning Coach:** Brendan Verner.

PLAYER DEVELOPMENT

Director, Player Development: Pete Putila. **Director, Minor League Operations:** Armando Velasco. **Minor League Coordinators:** Bill Murphy (pitching), Jeremy Barnes (hitting), Jason Bell (fundamentals), Mark Bailey (catching).

FARM SYSTEM

Class	Club	Manager	Hitting Coach	Pitching Coach
Triple-A	Round Rock (PCL)	Mickey Storey	Ben Rosenthal	Drew French
Double-A	Corpus Christi (TL)	Omar Lopez	Tim LaMonte	Graham Johnson
High A	Fayetteville (CAR)	Nate Shaver	Jason Kanzler	Thomas Whitsett
Low A	Quad Cities (SAL)	Ray Hernandez	Rafael Pena	Erick Abreu
Short-season	Tri-City (NYP)	Ozney Guillen	Sean Godfrey	John Kovalik
Rookie	Astros (GCL)	Wladimir Sutil	Rene Rojas	Jose Rada
Rookie	Astros 1 (DSL)	Carlos Lugo	Ernesto Irizarry	Rick Aponte

SCOUTING

Special Asst to the GM, Baseball Operations: Oz Ocampo. **Senior Scouting Advisor:** Charlie Gonzalez. **National Scouting Supervisor:** Kris Gross. **Domestic Crosscheckers:** Ralph Bratton (Austin, TX), Evan Brannon (St. Petersburg, FL), Gavin Dickey (Atlanta, GA). **Domestic Scouts:** Travis Coleman (Birmingham, AL), Tim Costic (Los Angeles, CA), Ryan Leake (San Diego, CA), Bobby St. Pierre (Atlanta, GA), Jim Stevenson (Tulsa, OK), Joey Sola (San Juan, PR). **Manager, Amateur Scouting Analysis:** Charles Cook.

Manager, Pro Scouting Analysis: Matt Hogan. **Scouting Analysts:** Aaron DelGiudice, Will Sharp. **Manager, International Scouting:** Eve Rosenbaum. **Assistant Director, International Scouting:** Roman Ocumarez. **Supervisor, DR Scouting:** Alfredo Ulloa. **International Scouts/Venezuela:** Daniel Acuna, Enrique Brito, Jose Palacios. **Panama:** Carlos Gonzalez. **Dominican Republic/Nicaragua:** Leocadio Guevara. **Dominican Republic:** Jose Lima, Johan Maya, Francis Mojica. **Mexico:** Miguel Pintor.

VIDEO & TECHNOLOGY

Coordinator, International Technology: Hassan Wessin. **Assistant, Dominican Scouting:** Francisco Navarro. **Assistant, Dominican Scouting:** Carlos Vasquez. **Assistant, Venezuela Scouting:** Carlos Freites. **Amateur Video Technicians:** Aaron DelGuidice, Cam Pendino.

KANSAS CITY ROYALS

Office Address: One Royal Way, Kansas City, MO 64129.
Mailing Address: PO Box 419969, Kansas City, MO 64141.
Telephone: (816) 921-8000. **Fax:** (816) 924-0347. **Website:** www.royals.com.

OWNERSHIP

Operated By: Kansas City Royals Baseball Club, Inc. **Chairman/CEO:** David Glass. **President:** Dan Glass.
Board of Directors: Ruth Glass, Don Glass, Dayna Martz, Julia Irene Kauffman.
Executive Assistant to the President: Lora Woolever.

BUSINESS OPERATIONS

Senior Vice President, Business Operations: Kevin Uhlich. **Executive Administrative Assistant:** Cindy Hamilton. **Director, Royals Hall of Fame:** Curt Nelson. **Manager, Authentic Merchandise Sales:** Ashley Ficken.

FINANCE/ADMINISTRATION

VP, Finance/Administration: David Laverentz. **Director, Finance:** Whitney Beaver.
Director, Human Resources: Miriam Maiden. **Director, Accounting/Risk Management:** Patrick Fleischmann. **Director, Payroll:** Jodi Parsons. **Sr. Director, Information Systems:** Brian Himstedt. **Sr. Director, Ticket Operations:** Anthony Blue. **Director, Ticket Ops:** Chris Darr.

COMMUNICATIONS/BROADCASTING

VP, Communications/Broadcasting: Mike Swanson. **Assistant Director, Media Relations:** Mike Cummings. **Manager, Media Relations/Alumni:** Dina Blevins. **Coordinator, Communications/Broadcasting:** Nick Kappel.

David Glass

PUBLICITY/COMMUNITY RELATIONS

VP, Publicity: Toby Cook. **Director, Publicity:** Amanda Turk. **VP, Community Relations:** Ben Aken. **Director, Charities:** Amanda Grosdidier. **Director, Community Outreach:** Betty Kaegel. **Director, Community Relations:** Katie McMullen.

BALLPARK OPERATIONS

Sr. Director, Ballpark Operations: Isaac Riffel. **Sr. Director, Landscaping:** Trevor Vance. **Sr. Director, Stadium Engineering:** Todd Burrow. **Director, Ballpark Services:** Johnny Williams. **Director, Guest Services:** Travis Bryant.

MARKETING/BUSINESS DEVELOPMENT

VP, Marketing/Business Development: Michael Bucek. **Senior Director, Event Presentation/Production:** Don Costante. **Director, Event Presentation/Production:** Steven Funke. **Director, Event Presentation:** Nicole Averso. **Senior Director, Marketing/Advertising:** Brad Zollars. **Senior Director, Digital/Social Media:** Erin Sleddens. **Senior Director, Corporate Partnerships/Broadcast Sales:** Jason Booker. **Senior Director, Client Services:** Michele Kammerer. **Director, Corporate Partnership Sales:** Jason Kramer. **Director, Partnership Marketing & Bus. Strategy:** Ben Christian. **Senior Director, Sales/Service:** Steve Shiffman. **Director, Sales/Service:** Scott Wadsworth.

2019 SCHEDULE

Standard Game Times: Mon.-Sat., 7:15 pm; Sun., 1:15 pm.

MARCH		JULY	
28-31 . . . . . Chicago (AL)	10-12 . . . . . Philadelphia	28-30 . . . . at Toronto	16-18 . . . . . New York (NL)
	14-16 . . . . Texas		19-21 . . . . . . at Baltimore
APRIL	17-19 . at Los Angeles (AL)	**JULY**	23-25 . . . . at Cleveland
2-3 . . . . Minnesota	21-22 . . . . . . at St. Louis	1 . . . . at Toronto	26-29 . . . . Oakland
4-7 . . . . at Detroit	24-26 . . . . New York (AL)	2-4 . . . . Cleveland	30-31 . . . . Baltimore
8-11 . . . . Seattle	27-29 . . . at Chicago (AL)	5-7 . . . . . at Washington	
12-14 . . . . Cleveland	30-31 . . . . at Texas	12-14 . . . . Detroit	**SEPTEMBER**
15-17 . . . at Chicago (AL)		15-18 . . . . Chicago (AL)	1 . . . . Baltimore
18-21 . . . at New York (AL)	**JUNE**	19-21 . . . . at Cleveland	3-5 . . . . Detroit
22-24 . . . . at Tampa Bay	1-2 . . . . at Texas	23-24 . . . . . . at Atlanta	6-8 . . . . at Miami
26-28 . . . Los Angeles (AL)	4-6 . . . . Boston	25-28 . . . . . . Cleveland	10-12 . . . at Chicago (AL)
29-30 . . . . Tampa Bay	7-9 . . . . . . Chicago (AL)	29-31 . . . . Toronto	13-15 . . . . Houston
	11-13 . . . . Detroit		16-18 . . . . . . at Oakland
MAY	14-16 . . . . . at Minnesota	**AUGUST**	19-22 . . . at Minnesota
1-2 . . . . Tampa Bay	17-19 . . . . . at Seattle	2-4 . . . . . . at Minnesota	24-25 . . . . Atlanta
3-5 . . . . at Detroit	20-23 . . . . . Minnesota	5-7 . . . . at Boston	27-29 . . . . . . Minnesota
6-8 . . . . at Houston	24-26 . . . . at Cleveland	8-11 . . . . at Detroit	
		13-14 . . . . St. Louis	

GENERAL INFORMATION

Stadium (year opened): Ewing M. Kauffman Stadium (1973). **Team Colors:** Royal blue and white.

Home Dugout: First Base. **Playing Surface:** Grass.

BASEBALL OPERATIONS

Telephone: (816) 921-8000. **Fax:** (816) 924-0347.

Sr. VP, Baseball Operations/General Manager: Dayton Moore. **VP/Asst. GM, Major League/International Operations:** Rene Francisco. **VP/Assistant GM, Player Personnel:** J.J. Picollo. **VP/Assistant GM:** Scott Sharp. **Asst. GM, Baseball Administration:** Jin Wong. **Asst. GM, Research & Development:** Dr. Daniel Mack. **Special Asst. to the GM/Quality Control:** Rusty Kuntz. **Special Asst. to Baseball Ops:** Blaine Boyer, Mike Matheny, Reggie Sanders, Mike Sweeney. **Sr. Director, Baseball Ops/Administration:** Kyle Vena. **Sr. Director, Research & Development:** Guy Stevens. **Director, Behavioral Science:** Ryan Maid. **Director, Leadership Development:** Matt Marasco. **Director, Pro Development:** Jeff Diskin. **Coordinator, Sports Science:** Austin Driggers. **Sr. Developer:** Paul Turner. **Developer:** Joseph San Diego. **Executive Asst. to the GM:** Emily Penning. **Analysts:** Pravin Santhanam, Daniel Schoenfeld. **Baseball Ops Asst.:** Kevin Kuntz, Kristin Lock, Kyle Martz.

Dayton Moore

TRAVEL/CLUBHOUSE

Sr. Director, Clubhouse Operations/Team Travel: Jeff Davenport. **Sr. Director, Clubhouse Operations:** Chuck Hawke. **Sr. Manager, Clubhouse Operations/Team Travel:** Nick Richie. **Manager, Equipment:** Patrick Gorman. **Manager, Clubhouse and Umpire Services:** Tom Walsh.

MAJOR LEAGUE STAFF

Manager: Ned Yost. **Coaches: Bench**—Dale Sveum, **Pitching**—Cal Eldred, **Hitting**—Terry Bradshaw, **First Base**—Mitch Maier, **Third Base**—Mike Jirschele, **Bullpen**—Vance Wilson, **Quality Control/Catching**—Pedro Grifol. **Replay/Advance Scouting Coordinator:** Bill Duplissea. **Bullpen Catcher:** Ryan Eigsti.

MEDICAL/TRAINING

Team Physician: Dr. Vincent Key. **Head Athletic Trainer:** Nick Kenney. **Asst. Athletic Trainers:** Kyle Turner, Chris Delucia. **Strength & Conditioning:** Ryan Stoneberg. **Asst. Strength & Conditioning:** Luis Perez. **Physical Therapist:** Jeff Blum. **Registered Sports Dietitian:** Erika Sharp.

PLAYER DEVELOPMENT

Director, Baseball Ops/Player Development & Scouting: Alec Zumwalt. **Asst. to Player Development/Video Coordinator:** Nick Relic. **Sr. Coordinator:** Chino Cadahia. **Field Coordinator:** Eddie Rodriguez, Victor Baez. **Special Asst., Player Development:** John Wathan, Harry Spilman. **Coordinators:** Larry Carter (pitching), Jason Simontacchi, Jeff Suppan (asst. pitching), Rafael Belliard (infield), J.C. Boscan (catching), Carlos Reyes, Justin Hahn (rehab), Damon Hollins (outfield), David Iannicca, Tony Medina (medical), John Wagle (strength/conditioning), Jarret Abell (asst. strength/conditioning), Will Simon (equipment), Monica Ramirez (Latin American Initiatives), Tim Bavester (asst. video).

FARM SYSTEM

Class	Club (League)	Manager	Hitting Coach	Pitching Coach
Triple-A	Omaha (PCL)	Brian Poldberg	Brian Buchanan	Andy Hawkins
Double-A	Northwest Arkansas (TL)	Darryl Kennedy	Abraham Nunez	Doug Henry
High A	Wilmington (CL)	Scott Thorman	Larry Sutton	Steve Luebber
Low A	Lexington (SAL)	Brooks Conrad	Jesus Azuaje	Mitch Stetter
Rookie	Idaho Falls (PIO)	Omar Ramirez	Damon Hollins	Clayton Mortensen
Rookie	Burlington (APP)	Chris Widger	Andy LaRoche	Carlos Martinez
Rookie	Royals (AZL)	Tony Pena Jr.	R. Castro/W. Aikens	M. Davis/J. Pimentel
Rookie	Royals (DSL)	O. Joseph/R. Martinez	E. Lantigua/W. Betemit	R. Feliz/J. Duran

SCOUTING

Telephone: (816) 921-8000. **Fax:** (816) 924-0347. **Assistant GM/Amateur Scouting:** Lonnie Goldberg. **Sr. Director, Pro Scouting/Assistant to the GM:** Gene Watson. **Director, Pro Scouting:** Michael Cifuentes. **Assistant Director, Amateur Scouting:** Dan Ontiveros. **Coordinator, Scouting Operations:** Jack Monahan. **Sr. Advisors:** Mike Arbuckle, Art Stewart, Donnie Williams, Gene Lamont. **Special Assistant:** Louie Medina, Pat Jones, Mike Pazik, Jim Fregosi, Jr., Tim Conroy, Paul Gibson. **Special Assignment Scout:** Mitch Webster. **Pro Scouts:** Dennis Cardoza (Munds Park, AZ), Mark Leavitt (DeLand, FL), Dave Oliver (Surprise, AZ), Mike Pazik (Bethesda, MD), Jon Williams (Imperial, MO). **Part-Time Pro Scouts:** Rene Lachemann (Scottsdale, AZ). **Advance Scout:** Cody Clark (Maumelle, AR), Tony Tijerina (Newark Valley, NY). **National Supervisor:** Gregg Kilby (Tampa, FL). **Regional Supervisors: Midwest**—Gregg Miller, **Southeast**—Sean Gibbs, **West**—Gary Wilson, **Northeast**—Keith Connolly. **Area Supervisors:** Joe Barbera (Durham, NC), Jim Buckley (Tampa, FL), Travis Ezi (Gulfport, MS), Casey Fahy (Mullica Hill, NJ), Jim Farr (Williamsburg, VA), Mike Farrell (Indianapolis, IN), Sean Gallagher (Cedar Park, TX), Colin Gonzales (Dana Point, CA), Josh Hallgren (Walnut Creek, CA), Nick Hamilton (Atlanta, GA), Will Howard (Columbus, GA), Chad Lee (McKinney, TX), Scott Melvin (Quincy, IL), Alex Mesa (Miami, FL), Ken Munoz (Scottsdale, AZ), Matt Price (Overland Park, KS), Joe Ross (Kirkland, WA), Bobby Shore (Los Angeles, CA). **Part-Time Scouts:** Kirk Barclay (Wyoming, ON), Eric Briggs (Bolivar, MO), Rick Clendenin (Clendenin, WV), Louis Collier (Chicago, IL), Corey Eckstein (Abbotsford, BC), Jeremy Jones (Overland Park, KS), Jerry Lafferty (Kansas City, MO), Brittan Motley (Blue Springs, MO), Chad Raley (Baton Rouge, LA), Johnny Ramos (Carolina, PR), Lloyd Simmons (Shawnee, OK). **Asst. GM/Int'l Operations:** Albert Gonzalez. **Latin America Supervisor:** Orlando Estevez. **Manager, International Ops:** Fabio Herrera. **Asst. to International Ops:** Daniel Guerrero. **International Scouts:** Luis Ortiz (Texas), Phil Dale (Australia), Neil Burke (Australia), Jose Figuera (Venezuela), Edgarluis Fuentes (Venezuela), Alberto Garcia (Venezuela), Jose Gualdron (Venezuela), Joelvis Gonzalez (Venezuela), Djionny Joubert (Curacao), Edson Kelly (Aruba), Juan Lopez (Nicaragua), Nathan Miller (Taiwan), Rafael Miranda (Colombia), Fausto Morel (Dominican Republic), Ricardo Ortiz (Panama), Edis Perez (Dominican Republic), Rafael Vasquez (Dominican Republic), Ramon Pena (Dominican Republic), Manabu Kuramochi (Tokyo, Japan), Hiroyuki Oya (Japan), Hyun-sung Kim (S. Korea).

LOS ANGELES ANGELS

Office Address: 2000 Gene Autry Way, Anaheim, CA 92806.
Mailing Address: 2000 Gene Autry Way, Anaheim, CA 92803.
Telephone: (714) 940-2000. **Fax:** (714) 940-2205. **Website:** www.angels.com.

OWNERSHIP

Owner: Arte Moreno. **Chairman:** Dennis Kuhl. **President:** John Carpino.

BUSINESS OPERATIONS

Chief Financial Officer: Bill Beverage. **Senior Vice President, Finance/Administration:** Molly Jolly. **Director, Legal Affairs/Risk Management:** Alex Winsberg. **Associate Legal Counsel:** Jen Tedmori. **Controller:** Sue Bassett. **Director, Finance:** Doug Mylowe. **Benefits Manager:** Cecilia Schneider. **Payroll Manager:** Lorelei Schlitz. **Accountants:** Kylie McManus, Jennifer Whynott, Matt Asato. **Payroll Assistant:** Alison Kelso. **Accounts Payable Specialist:** Sarah Talamonte. **Financial Operations Manager:** Jennifer Jeanblanc. **Director, Human Resources:** Deborah Johnston. **Human Resources Manager:** Mayra Castro. **Human Resources Coordinator:** Erika Paz. **Director, Information Services:** Al Castro. **Senior Network Engineer:** Neil Fariss. **Senior Desktop Support Analyst:** David Yun. **Technology Integration Specialist:** Paramjit Singh. **Network Administrator:** James Sheu.

Arte Moreno

CORPORATE SALES

VP, Sales: Neil Viserto. **Senior Director, Business Development:** Mike Fach. **Director, Corporate Sponsorship:** Bob McCauley. **Senior Account Executive, National Accounts:** Rick Turner. **Senior Corporate Account Executive:** Lesli Koontz, Drew Zinser. **Director, Partner Services:** Bobby Kowan. **Senior Manager, Corporate Partnerships:** Matt Gamewell. **Account Managers, Sponsorship Services:** Ashley Fleck, Andie Mitsuda, Adam Overgaard, Ryan Vitelli.

MARKETING/ENTERTAINMENT

Director, Ticket Marketing: Ryan Vance. **Senior Marketing Managers:** Alex Tinyo, Vanessa Vega. **Graphic Designers:** Tricia Kami, Dominic Mitrano. **Manager, Social Media & Digital Marketing:** Kevin Vu. **Digital and Promotions Coordinator:** Hannah Stange. **Business Analyst:** Julius Evans. **CRM Data Coordinator:** Seth Arias. **Director, Entertainment/Production:** Peter Bull. **Manager, Video Production:** Jordan Esswein. **Producer, Video and Scoreboard Ops:** David Tsuruda. **Entertainment Coordinator:** Mandi Ortiz. **Team Photographer:** Blaine Ohigashi.

PUBLIC/MEDIA RELATIONS/COMMUNICATIONS

Telephone: (714) 940-2014. **Fax:** (714) 940-2205.
VP, Communications: Tim Mead. **Director, Communications:** Eric Kay. **Senior Manager, Communications:** Adam Chodzko. **Manager, Communications:** Matt Birch. **Sr. Advisor to Sr. Manager, Communications:** Grace McNamee.

COMMUNITY RELATIONS

Director, Community Partnerships: Nicole Provansal. **Manager, Foundation and Community Initiatives:** Adam

2019 SCHEDULE

Standard Game Times: Mon.-Sat., 7:07 pm; Sun., 12:37 pm.

MARCH			
28-31 . . . . . . .at Oakland	7-9 . . . . .at Detroit	25-26 . . . . . . Cincinnati	12-14 . . . . Pittsburgh
	10-12 . . . . . .at Baltimore	27-30 . . . . Oakland	15-18 . . . . . Chicago (AL)
APRIL	13-15 . . . . . at Minnesota		19-21 . . . . .at Texas
1-2 . . . . .at Seattle	17-19 . . . . . Kansas City	**JULY**	23-25 . . . . . . .at Houston
4-7 . . . . Texas	20-22 . . . . . . Minnesota	1-4 . . . . .at Texas	27-28 . . . . Texas
8-10 . . . . . . .Milwaukee	24-26 . . . . Texas	5-7 . . . . .at Houston	30-31 . . . . Boston
12-14 . . .at Chicago (NL)	27-29 . . . . . .at Oakland	12-14 . . . . Seattle	
15-17 . . . . .at Texas	30-31 . . . . . .at Seattle	15-18 . . . . Houston	**SEPTEMBER**
18-21 . . . . Seattle		19-21 . . . . . . .at Seattle	1 . . . . Boston
22-25 . . . . .New York (AL)	**JUNE**	23-24 . at Los Angeles (NL)	3-5 . . . . .at Oakland
26-28 . . . . .at Kansas City	1-2 . . . . .at Seattle	25-28 . . . . . . Baltimore	6-8 . . . . .at Chicago (AL)
30 . . . . .Toronto	4-6 . . . . Oakland	29-31 . . . . Detroit	9-11 . . . . Cleveland
	7-9 . . . . Seattle		13-15 . . . . . . .Tampa Bay
MAY	10-11 . . . Los Angeles (NL)	**AUGUST**	17-19 . . . at New York (AL)
1-2 . . . . .Toronto	13-16 . . . . at Tampa Bay	2-4 . . . . .at Cleveland	20-22 . . . . . . .at Houston
4-5 . . . . Houston	17-20 . . . . . . at Toronto	5-6 . . . . .at Cincinnati	24-25 . . . . Oakland
	21-23 . . . . . .at St. Louis	8-11 . . . . .at Boston	26-29 . . . . Houston

GENERAL INFORMATION

Stadium (year opened): Angel Stadium of Anaheim (1966). **Playing Surface:** Grass.
Team Colors: Red, dark red, blue and silver.
Home Dugout: Third Base.

Cali. **Scholarship Programs and Marketing Coordinator:** Lillea Acasio.

BALLPARK OPERATIONS/FACILITIES

Senior Director, Ballpark Operations: Brian Sanders. **Director, Ballpark Operations:** Sam Maida. **Director, Stadium Operations:** Calvin Ching. **Guest Experience Manager:** Chris Warden. **Senior Manager, Stadium Operations:** Nathan Bautista. **Manager, Stadium Operations:** Carlos Campos, Kelsey Hayes. **Security Manager:** Mark Macias. **Director, Special Events:** Courtney Wallace. **Special Events Coordinator:** Veronica Lee, Kelly Williams. **Custodial Supervisors:** Pedro Del Castillo, Ray Nells. **Scheduling Coordinator:** Tatum Lockett.

TICKETING

Director, Ticket Sales: Jim Panetta. **Senior Manager, Ticket Operations:** Sheila Brazelton. **Ticketing Supervisor:** Armando Reyna. **Director, Ticket Operations/Service:** Tom DeTemple. **Director, Premium Sales/Service:** Kyle Haygood. **Senior Business Development Account Executive:** Jeff Leuenberger.

TRAVEL/CLUBHOUSE

Traveling Secretary: Tom Taylor. **Clubhouse Manager:** Keith Tarter. **Assistant Clubhouse Manager:** Shane Demmitt. **Visiting Clubhouse Manager:** Brian "Bubba" Harkins. **Senior Video Coordinator:** Adam Hunt. **Video Coordinator:** Ruben Montano.

BASEBALL OPERATIONS

Billy Eppler

General Manager: Billy Eppler.
Assistant GMs: Jonathan Strangio, Steve Martone. **Special Advisor:** Bill Stoneman. **Special Assistants to GM:** Eric Chavez. **Director, Baseball Operations:** Andrew Ball. **Director, Quantitative Analysis:** Kevin Ferris. **Coordinator, Baseball Administration:** Peggy Berroa-Morales. **Assistant Director, Quantitative Analysis:** Richard Anderson. **Manager, Baseball Operations:** Andrew Mack. **Analyst, Baseball Operations:** Walter King. **Baseball Operations Assistant:** Andrea LaPointe, Brooke Wakenhut. **Assistant, Quantitative Analysis:** Kevin Brice, Bryce Rogan.

MAJOR LEAGUE STAFF

Manager: Brad Ausmus. **Coaches: Bench**—Josh Paul, **Pitching**—Doug White, **Hitting**—Jeremy Reed, **First Base**—Jesus Feliciano, **Third Base**—Mike Gallego, **Bullpen**—Andrew Bailey, **Assistant Hitting**— Shawn Wooten, **Hitting Instructor**— Paul Sorrento, **Catching**—Jose Molina. **Manager, Video Operations**—Adam Hunt.

MEDICAL/TRAINING

Team Physician: Dr. Craig Milhouse. **Team Orthopedists:** Dr. Steve Yoon, Dr. Ronald Kvitne, Dr. Brian Schulz. **Director, Sport Science/Performance:** Bernard Li. **Head Athletic Trainer:** Adam Nevala. **Assistant Athletic Trainer:** Rick Smith. **Strength/Conditioning Coach:** Lee Fiocchi. **Assistant Strength/Conditioning Coach:** Sean Johnson.

PLAYER DEVELOPMENT

Director, Minor League Operations: Mike LaCassa. **Coordinator, Minor League Operations:** Chris Mosch. **Field Coordinator:** Chad Tracy. **Minor League Equipment Manager (AZ):** Brett Crane. **Video Coordinator:** Ryan Dundee. **Roving Instructors:** Damon Mashore (hitting), Ryan Parker (hitting analysis), Matt Wise (pitching), Buddy Carlyle (assistant pitching), Jordan Oseguera (pitching analyst), Eddy Rodriguez (catching), Bill Lachemann (catching/special assignment), Chris Constantine (outfield/baserunning), Hainley Statia (infield), Kernan Ronan (rehab pitching), Andrew Hawkins (rehab), Geoff Hostetter (training coordinator), Danny Escobar (strength/conditioning), Dylan Cintula (rehab).

FARM SYSTEM

Class	Club	Manager	Hitting Coach	Pitching Coach
Triple-A	Salt Lake (PCL)	Lou Marson	Brian Betancourth	Pat Rice
Double-A	Mobile (SL)	David Newhan	Matt Spring	Jairo Cuevas
High A	Inland Empire (CAL)	Ryan Barba	Derek Florko	Michael Wuertz
Low A	Burlington (MWL)	Jack Howell	Will Bradley	Jonathan Van Eaton
Rookie	Orem (PIO)	Jack Santora,	Ryan Sebra	J. Watson/B. Garman
Rookie	Angels (AZL)	David Stapleton	T. Jeske/D. Ortega	T. Anderson/TBD
Rookie	Angels (DSL)	Hector De La Cruz	R. Gomez/A. De Los Santos	Jose Marte

SCOUTING

Director, Pro Scouting: Nate Horowitz. **Assistant., Pro and International Scouting:** Nick Lampe. **Major League/Special Assignment Scout:** Ric Wilson. **Professional Scouts:** Jeff Cirillo, Buck Coats, Ben Francisco, Phil Geisler, Brendan Harris, Nick McCoy, Jim Miller, Jayson Nix, Roman Rodriguez, Travis Ice, Tim McIntosh, Andrew Schmidt, Ken Stauffer, Bobby Williams. **Director, Amateur Scouting:** Matt Swanson. **Assistant, Amateur Scouting:** Aidan Donovan. **National Crosscheckers:** Jeremy Schied, Jason Smith, Steffan Wilson. **Regional Supervisors: East**—Jason Baker. **South**—Brandon McArthur. **Southeast**—Nick Gorneault. **Northwest**—Scott Richardson. **Southwest**—Jayson Durocher. **Hitting Crosschecker:** Jason Ellison. **Area Scouts:** Don Archer, John Burden, Tim Corcoran, Christopher Cruz, Ben Diggins, Drew Dominguez, Chad Hermansen, Steve Hernandez, Todd Hogan, Kennard Jones, Ryan Leahy, Billy Lipari,, Chris McAlpin, Joel Murrie, Ralph Reyes, Omar Rodriguez, Brett Smith, Brian Tripp, Mark Tucker, Rudy Vasquez, J.T. Zink. **Director, International Scouting:** Carlos Gomez. **Asst. Director, International Scouting:** Giovanni Hernandez. **Administrator, International Scouting:** Grace Mercedes. **International Scouting Supervisor:** Marlon Urdaneta. **International Scouts:** Jochy Cabrera, Rusbell Cabrera, Joel Chicarelli, Andres Garcia, Domingo Garcia, Ender Gonzalez, Raul Gonzalez, Aneudi Mercado, Rubylin Nicasia, Francisco Tejeda.

LOS ANGELES DODGERS

Office Address: 1000 Vin Scully Ave., Los Angeles, CA 90012.
Telephone: (323) 224-1500. **Fax:** (323) 224-1269. **Website:** www.dodgers.com.

OWNERSHIP/EXECUTIVE OFFICE

Chairman: Mark Walter. **Partners:** Earvin 'Magic' Johnson, Peter Guber, Todd Boehly, Robert 'Bobby' Patton, Jr.
President/CEO: Stan Kasten. **Special Advisors to Chairman:** Tommy Lasorda, Don Newcombe.

BUSINESS OPERATIONS

Executive Vice President: Bob Wolfe. **Executive VP/Chief Marketing Officer:** Lon Rosen.
Managing Director, Guggenheim Baseball Management: Tucker Kain. **Executive VP/
General Counsel:** Sam Fernandez. **Senior VP, Planning/ Development:** Janet Marie Smith.
Senior VP, Corporate Partnerships: Michael Wandell. **VP, Ticket Sales/Premium Sales/
Services:** Antonio Morici. **Senior Director, Partnership Administration:** Jenny Oh. **Senior
VP, Corporate Partnerships:** Jim Tucker.

FINANCE

VP, Finance: Eric Hernandez. **Sr. Director, Financial Planning/Analysis:** Gregory
Buonaccorsi. **VP, Business Development/Analytics:** Royce Cohen.

MARKETING/BROADCASTING

Sr. VP, Marketing/Broadcasting Communications: Erik Braverman. **Sr. Director,
Advertising/Promotions:** Shelley Wagner. **Executive Producer, Production:** Greg Taylor.
Sr. Director, Graphic Design: Ross Yoshida. **Sr. Director, Broadcast Engineering:** Tom Darin.

Mark Walter

HUMAN RESOURCES/LEGAL

Sr. Director, Human Resources: Leonor Romero. **Senior Counsel:** Chad Gunderson.

COMMUNICATIONS/COMMUNITY AFFAIRS

VP, External Affairs/Community Relations: Naomi Rodriguez. **Senior Director, Public Relations:** Joe Jareck.
Assistant Director, Public Relations: Jon Chapper. **Manager, Public Relations:** Jesus Quinonez. Coordinator, **Public
Relations:** Lauren Douglas.

INFORMATION TECHNOLOGY/STADIUM OPERATIONS/SECURITY/MERCHANDISE

VP, Information Technology: Ralph Esquibel. **IT, Infrastructure Architect:** Debra Jorgensen. **VP, Security/ Guest
Services:** Shahram Ariane. **Director, Facilities:** David Edford. **Assistant Director, Grounds:** Jordan Lorenz.
VP, Merchandise: Allister Annear. **Director, Retail Operations:** Veronica Huerta.

TICKETING

Telephone: (323) 224-1471. **Fax:** (323) 224-2609.
VP, Ticket Operations: Seth Bluman. **Director, Ticket Operations:** Aaron Dubner. **Managers, Ticket Operations:**
Dan Gilmore. Steven Zymkowitz.

2019 SCHEDULE

Standard Game Times: 7:10 p.m.; Sun. 1:10

MARCH
28-31 . . . . .Arizona

APRIL
1-3 . . . . . . San Francisco
5-7 . . . . at Colorado
8-11 . . . . . . .at St. Louis
12-14 . . . . . .Milwaukee
15-17 . . . . . . Cincinnati
18-21 . . . at Milwaukee
23-25 . . .at Chicago (NL)
26-28 . . . . . . Pittsburgh
29-30 . . . at San Francisco

MAY
1 . . . . . at San Francisco
3-5 . . . . . . at San Diego

6-8 . . . . .Atlanta
9-12 . . . . .Washington
14-15 . . . . . . San Diego
17-19 . . . . .at Cincinnati
21-22 . . . at Tampa Bay
24-26 . . . . . at Pittsburgh
27-30 . . . . .New York (NL)
31 . . . . . . .Philadelphia

JUNE
1-2 . . . . . . .Philadelphia
3-5 . . . . at Arizona
7-9 . . . . at San Francisco
10-11 . at Los Angeles (AL)
13-16 . . . . . Chicago (NL)
17-20 . . . . . San Francisco
21-23 . . . . .Colorado

24-26 . . . . . . at Arizona
27-30 . . . . . at Colorado

JULY
2-3 . . . . .Arizona
4-7 . . . . San Diego
12-14 . . . . .at Boston
15-18 . . . at Philadelphia
19-21 . . . . .Miami
23-24 . . . Los Angeles (AL)
26-28 . . . . at Washington
29-31 . . . . at Colorado

AUGUST
1-4 . . . . San Diego
5-7 . . . . St. Louis
9-11 . . . . .Arizona

13-15 . . . . at Miami
16-18 . . . . at Atlanta
20-22 . . . . .Toronto
23-25 . . . .New York (AL)
26-28 . . . . . at San Diego
29-31 . . . . at Arizona

SEPTEMBER
1 . . . . at Arizona
2-4 . . . . .Colorado
6-8 . . . . . . San Francisco
10-12 . . .at Baltimore
13-15 . . . at New York (NL)
17-18 . . . . . . .Tampa Bay
20-22 . . . . .Colorado
24-26 . . . . . at San Diego
27-29 . . . at San Francisco

GENERAL INFORMATION

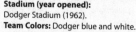

Stadium (year opened):
Dodger Stadium (1962).
Team Colors: Dodger blue and white.

Home Dugout: Third Base.
Playing Surface: Grass

BASEBALL OPERATIONS

Telephone: (323) 224-1500. **Fax:** (323) 224-1463.
President, Baseball Operations: Andrew Friedman. **Senior VP, Baseball Operations:** Josh Byrnes. **Director, Baseball Administration:** Ellen Harrigan. **Director, Team Travel:** Scott Akasaki. **Senior Advisor, Baseball Operations:** Gerry Hunsicker. **Special Assistants:** Pat Corrales, Raul Ibañez.

Andrew Friedman

MAJOR LEAGUE STAFF

Manager: Dave Roberts.
Coaches: Bench—Bob Geren, **Pitching**—Rick Honeycutt, **Hitting**—Robert Van Scoyoc, **First Base**—George Lombard, **Third Base**—Dino Ebel, **Bullpen**—Mark Prior, **Assistant Hitting Coach**—Aaron Bates, **Bullpen Catcher**—Steve Cilladi. **Hitting Strategist:** Brant Brown. **Game Planning Coach:** Chris Gimenez. **Major League Video Coordinator:** John Pratt. **Director of Player Health:** Ron Porterfield, **Head Athletic Trainer:** Neil Rampe. **Assistant Athletic Trainer:** Andrew Hauser. **Assistant Athletic Trainer:** Thomas Albert. **Strength & Conditioning Coach:** Brandon McDaniel. **Assistant Strength & Conditioning Coach:** Travis Smith. **MLB Physical Therapist:** Johnathan Erb. **Assistant Athletic Trainer, Soft Tissue Specialist:** Yosuke Nakajima.

PLAYER DEVELOPMENT

Telephone: (323) 224-1500. **Fax:** (323) 224-1359.
Director, Player Development: Brandon Gomes.
Senior Advisor to Player Development: Charlie Hough. **Field Coordinator:** Clayton McCullough. **Coordinators:** Don Alexander (pitching logistics), Tarrik Brock (outfield/ baserunning), Chris Fetter (pitching integration), Paco Figueroa (hitting), Travis Barbary (catching), Shaun Larkin (skills development), Kremlin Martinez (assistant pitching), Ryan Sienko (assistant catching), Aaron Bates (assistant hitting). **Special Assistant, Infield:** Jose Vizcaino. **Instructor:** Maury Wills. **Rehab Coordinator:** Greg Sabat.

CAMPO LOS PALMAS

Latin American Pitching Coordinator: Kremlin Martinez. **Latin American Defensive Coordinator:** Pedro Mega. **Latin American Field Coordinator:** Carson Vitale. **Latin American Hitting Coordinator:** Humberto Miranda.

CAMELBACK RANCH

Senior Manager, Player Development: Matt McGrath. **Manager, Baseball Operations-Glendale:** Juan Rodriguez.

FARM SYSTEM

Class	Club (League)	Manager	Hitting Coach	Pitching Coach
Triple-A	Oklahoma City (PCL)	Travis Barbary	Scott Coolbaugh	Bill Simas
Double-A	Tulsa (TL)	Scott Hennessey	Adam Melhuse	Dave Borkowski
High A	Rancho Cucamonga (CAL)	Mark Kertenian	Dustin Kelly	Connor McGuiness
Low A	Great Lakes (MWL)	John Shoemaker	Justin Viele	Luis Meza
Rookie	Ogden (PIO)	Austin Chubb	Seth Connor	Dean Stiles
Rookie	Dodgers (AZL)	Jair Fernandez	Jarek Cunningham	Stephanos Stroop
Rookie	Dodgers (DSL)	K. Collado/F. Ishibashi	J.Chavez/S.Mendez	R. Giron/R. Troncoso

SCOUTING

VP, Amateur/International Scouting: David Finley. **Director, Amateur Scouting:** Billy Gasparino. **Assistant Director, Amateur Scouting:** Zach Fitzpatrick. **Coordinator, Amateur Scouting:** Kevin Walsh. **Advisor, Amateur Scouting:** Gary Nickels. **Special Advisor, Amateur Scouting:** Paul Cogan. **National Crosscheckers:** John Green, Brian Stephenson. **Northeast Regional Crosschecker:** Jon Adkins. **Southeast Regional Crosschecker:** Alan Matthews. **Midwest Regional Crosschecker:** Rob St. Julien. **Pitching Crosschecker:** Jack Cressend. **Coordinator, Video Scouting:** Trey Magunson. **Area Scouts:** Garrett Ball (GA, AL), Clint Bowers (Southern TX), Brian Compton (AZ, UT, CO, NM), Kelvin Colon (Southern FL/Puerto Rico), Stephen Head (NE, KS, IA, MO), Heath Holliday (Northern TX, OK, AR), Lon Joyce (NC, SC), Tom Kunis (Northern CA, Northern NV), Brian Kraft (NE TX, Eastern OK, Eastern KS, Western MO, Southern and Western AR), Marty Lamb (IN, KY, OH, TN), Benny Latino (LA, MS, AL, Western FL), Brent Mayne (Southern CA), Dennis Moeller (Central and Southern CA), Paul Murphy (PA, NJ, VA, WV, MD, DE, DC), John Pyle (New England/Eastern Canada/ JC Crosschecker), Jonah Rosenthal (NC, SC), Wes Sargent (North Florida), Jeffrey Stevens (Pacific Northwest/Western Canada). **Part-Time Scout:** Luis Faccio. **Director, Player Personnel:** Galen Carr. **Director, Baseball Development/ Scouting:** Alex Slater. **Professional Scouts:** Peter Bergeron, Greg Booker, DJ Carrasco, Franco Frias, Scott Groot, Bill Latham, Tydus Meadows, Steve Pope, Tim Schmidt, Chris Smith, Chris Stasio, Phillip Stringer, Lee Tackett, Les Walrond, Yogo Suzuki. **Special Assignment Scouts:** Vance Lovelace, Jeff McAvoy, Matt Smith. **Coordinator, Pro Scouting:** Lucas Geoghegan. **VP, International Scouting:** Ismael Cruz. **Senior Advisor, International Scouting:** Ralph Avila. **International Crosscheckers:** Roman Barinas, Brian Parker. **Director, Pacific Rim:** Jon Deeble. **Assistant Director, Pacific Rim:** San-Tai Lin. **Coordinator, International Scouting:** Javier Camps. **Latin American Scouting Supervisor:** Luis Marquez. **Venezuela & Central America Supervisor:** Clifford Nuitter. **Coordinatio, Dominican Republic:** Laiky Uribe. **Special Assignment Scout, Latin America:** Mike Tosar. **Coordinator, International Analytics:** Matthew Doppelt. **International Scouts:** Moises Alou, Jonathan Genao, Elvio Jimenez, Manelik Pimentel, Domingo Toribio, Felvil Veloz, Dunior Zerpa (Dominican Republic); Rafael Arcila, Paul Brazon, Jose Briceno, Leon Jackson Canelon, Jean Castro, Cristian Guzman, Oswaldo Villalobos (Venezuela); Mike Brito, Juvenal Soto (Mexico); Rolando Chirino (Curacao); Carlos Gonzalez (Panama); Seungyun Kim (Korea); Miguel Orozco (Colombia); Nestor Perez (Europe); Andres Simancas (Mexico/Nicaragua). **Associate International Scout:** Dawlyn Lantigua.

MIAMI MARLINS

Office Address: Marlins Park, 501 Marlins Way, Miami, FL 33125
Telephone: (305) 480-1300. **Fax:** (305) 480-3012.
Website: www.marlins.com.

OWNERSHIP
Chairman & Principal Owner: Bruce Sherman.

BUSINESS OPERATIONS

Derek Jeter

Chief Executive Officer: Derek Jeter.
President of Business Operations: Chip Bowers. **Senior Vice President, Strategy & Development:** Adam Jones. **Senior Vice President/Chief of Staff:** Caroline O'Connor. **Executive Assistant to CEO:** Nicolette Lawrence. **Executive Assistant to President of Business Operations:** Kristen Keane. **Coordinator, Chief of Staff:** Karen De Leon.

ADMINISTRATION
VP, Human Resources: Ana Hernandez. **Manager, Human Resources:** Giselle Lopez. **Coordinator, Human Resources:** Alex Vigil, Kaitlyn Stoltzenberg. **Lead Recruiter:** Francisco De Leon. **Director, Risk Management:** Fred Espinoza. **Coordinator, Risk Management:** Claudia Avila.

FINANCE
Executive Vice President & Chief Financial Officer: Michel Bussiere. **Senior Vice President, Finance:** Susan Jaison. **Administrator, Payroll:** Carolina Calderon. **Assistant Payroll Administrator:** Edgar Perez. **Director, Accounting:** John Valdes. **Supervisor, Accounts Payable:** Anthony Paneque. **Staff Accountant:** David Villa. **Coordinator, Accounts Payable:** Brian Weeks. **Coordinators, Finance:** Felix Anderson, Alexander Perera.

MARKETING
SVP, Marketing and Community Relations: Elisa Padilla. **Director, Marketing:** Stacy Pagán. **Director, Events/Promotions:** Juan Martinez. **Director, Game Presentation:** Matthew Mendez. **Manager, Game Presentation:** Sergio Xiques. **Supervisor, Promotions:** Rafael Capdevila. **Coordinators, Marketing:** Karry Pomes, Mariah Monahan.

LEGAL
Vice President and General Counsel: Ashwin Krishnan. **Associate General Counsel:** Stephanie Galvin.

SALES/TICKETING
Vice President, Ticket Sales & Service: Travis Apple. **Senior Director, Sales:** Joseph Schiavi. **Director, Premium Sales & Service:** Ryan Sember. **Suite Service Executive:** Paige Fisher. **Coordinator, Member Benefits & Events:** Jessica Lee. **Director, Inside Sales:** David Campbell. **Senior Premium Sales Executive:** Chema Sanchez. **Director, Membership Experience:** Brian Jemison. **Manager, Member Benefits:** Jillian Gustin. **Senior Membership Experience Executive:** Jason Liss. **Membership Experience Executive:** Samantha MacIntosh. **Director, Membership Sales:** Evans Adonis. **Membership Sales Executives:** Heberto Arauz, Isaac Paladino, Ryan Plasencia, Eric Sutcliffe, Jonathan Williams. **Coordinator, Sales & Service:** Patty Lora. **Director, Ticket Operations:** Mardi Dilger.

2019 SCHEDULE
Standard Game Times: Mon.-Sat., 7:10 pm; Sun., 1:10 pm.

MARCH
28-31 . . . . .Colorado

APRIL
1-3 . . . . . .New York (NL)
5-7. . . . . at Atlanta
9-11 . . . . . .at Cincinnati
12-14 . . . . .Philadelphia
15-17 . . . . . Chicago (NL)
19-21 . . . . . Washington
23-24 . . . . .at Cleveland
25-28 . . . . at Philadelphia
30 . . . . Cleveland

MAY
1 . . . . Cleveland
3-5. . . . . Atlanta
6-9. . . . . .at Chicago (NL)

10-12 . . . at New York (NL)
14-15 . . . . . . .Tampa Bay
17-19 . . . .New York (NL)
21-23 . . . . . . .at Detroit
24-27 . . . . at Washington
28-30 . . . . . San Francisco
31 . . . . . . at San Diego

JUNE
1-2. . . . . at San Diego
4-6. . . . . . . at Milwaukee
7-9. . . . . Atlanta
10-12 . . . . St. Louis
14-16 . . . . . . .Pittsburgh
17-20 . . . . . .at St. Louis
21-23 . . . . at Philadelphia
25-27 . . . . . .Washington

28-30 . . . . . .Philadelphia

JULY
2-4. . . . . . at Washington
5-7. . . . . at Atlanta
12-14 . . . . .New York (NL)
16-18 . . . . San Diego
19-21 . at Los Angeles (NL)
22-24 . . . .at Chicago (AL)
26-29 . . . . Arizona
30-31 . . . . . . .Minnesota

AUGUST
1 . . . . .Minnesota
3-4. . . . . . at Tampa Bay
5-7. . . .at New York (NL)
8-11 . . . . Atlanta
13-15 . . . Los Angeles (NL)

16-18 . . . . . . at Colorado
20-22 . . . . at Atlanta
23-25 . . . . .Philadelphia
26-29 . . . . . . Cincinnati
30-31 . . . . . at Washington

SEPTEMBER
1 . . . . at Washington
3-5. . . . . . . at Pittsburgh
6-8. . . . . Kansas City
9-12 . . . . .Milwaukee
13-15 . . . at San Francisco
16-18 . . . . at Arizona
20-22 . . . . . Washington
23-26 . . .at New York (NL)
27-29 . . . . at Philadelphia

GENERAL INFORMATION

Stadium (year opened): Marlins Park (2012). **Playing Surface:** Grass.
Team Colors: Caliente Red, Miami Blue, Midnight Black and Slate Grey
Home Dugout: Third Base.

COMMUNICATIONS/MEDIA RELATIONS

Senior VP, Communications & Broadcasting: Jason Latimer. **Manager, Baseball Communications & Publications:** Joe Vieira. **Manager, Business Communications & Spanish Media:** Jon Erik Alvarez. **Coordinator, Communications:** Maria Armella. **Player Relations & Spanish Media Liaison:** Luis Dorante. **Manager, Broadcasting:** Kyle Sielaff. **Coordinator, Social Media:** Sarah Penalver.

TRAVEL/CLUBHOUSE

Director, Team Travel: Manny Colon. **Equipment Manager:** John Silverman. **Visiting Clubhouse Manager:** Rock Hughes. **Assistant Clubhouse Manager:** MIchael Diaz.

BASEBALL OPERATIONS

Telephone: (305) 480-1300. **Fax:** (305) 480-3032.
President, Baseball Operations: Michael Hill. **Assistant General Manager:** Brian Chattin.
Director, Player Personnel: Dan Greenlee. **Director, Team Travel:** Manny Colon. **Major League Video Coordinator:** Joseph Nero. **Executive Assistant to President of Baseball Operations:** Amanda Guevara. **Special Advisor, Pres. of Baseball Operations:** Stan Meek.

Michael Hill

MAJOR LEAGUE STAFF

Manager: Don Mattingly.
Pitching Coach: Mel Stottlemyre Jr. **Hitting Coach:** Mike Pagliarulo. **Assistant Hitting Coach:** Jeff Livesey. **Bench Coach:** Tim Wallach. **First Base Coach:** Trey Hillman. **Third Base Coach:** Fredi Gonzalez. **Bullpen Coordinator:** Robert Flippo. **Catching Coach:** Brian Schneider. **Infield/Baserunning Coach:** Gene Glynn.

MEDICAL/TRAINING

Medical Director: Dr. Lee Kaplan. **Head Athletic Trainer:** Dusin Luepker. **Strength & Conditioning Coach:** Kevin Barr. **Athletic Trainers:** Mike Kozak, Gene Basham. **Equipment Managers, Home Clubhouse:** Dominec Camarda, John Silverman. **Visting Clubhouse Manager:** Michael Rock Hughes. **Director, Sports Performance:** Derick Anderson.

PLAYER DEVELOPMENT

Vice President, Player Development & Scouting: Gary Denbo. **Director, Player Development:** Dick Scott. **Director, Player Personnel:** Dan Greenlee. **Special Assistant, Scouting/BBOPS:** Adrian Lorenzo. **Director, International Operations:** Fernando Seguignol. **Director, Amateur Scouting:** DJ Svihlik. **Director, Sports Development:** Derick Anderson. **Manager, Player Development & Scouting:** Geoff Degroot. **Assistant Director, Player Development:** Hector Crespo. **Analyst, Player Development:** Ryan Powers. **Intern, Player Development:** Danny Henriquez. **Pitching Coordinator:** Chris Michalak. **Pitching Consultant:** Dane Johnson. **Hitting Coordinator:** Eric Duncan. **Infield & Baserunning Coordinator:** Gene Glynn. **Catching Coordinator:** Jamie Quirk. **Outfield Coordinator:** Juan Pierre. **Assistant Strength & Conditioning Coordinator:** Spencer Clevenger. **Rehab Strength & Conditioning Coordinator:** Lee Tressel. **Athletic Training Coordinator:** Richard Stark. **Video Coordinator:** Austin Lamkey. **Rehab Coordinator:** Steve Carlin. **Rehab Pitching Coach:** Dave Laroche. **Rehab Position Player Coach:** Cam Kneeland. **Minor League Clubhouse/Equipment Coordinator:** Mark Brown. **Coordinator, Player Development & International Operations:** Jake Jola. **Intern, International Operations:** David Hernandez-Beayne.

FARM SYSTEM

Class	Club (League)	Manager	Hitting Coach	Pitching Coach
Triple-A	New Orleans (PCL)	Keith Johnson	Justin Mashore	Jeremy Powell
Double-A	Jacksonville (SL)	Kevin Randel	Sean Berry	Bruce Walton
High A	Jupiter (FSL)	Todd Pratt	Kevin Witt	Reid Cornelius
Low A	Clinton (MWL)	Mike Jacobs	Frank Moore	Mark DiFelice
Short-season	Batavia (NYP)	Jorge Hernandez	Jesus Merchan	Jason Erickson
Rookie	Marlins (GCL)	John Pachot	Rigoberto Silverio	Manny Olivera
Rookie	Marlins (DSL)	Angel Espada	R. Peralta/E. Linares	I. Arteaga/F. Arias

SCOUTING

Director, Amateur Scouting: DJ Svihlik.
Senior Advisor, Amateur Scouting: Marti Wolever. **National Crosschecker:** Eric Valent. **Special Assignment Scout:** T.R. Lewis. **West Coast Regional Supervisor:** Scott Goldby. **Midwest Regional Supervisor:** Ryan Wardinsky. **South Regional Supervisor:** Carmen Carcone. **East Coast Regional Supervisor:** Mike Soper. **Area Scouts:** Eric Brock, John Hughes, Tim McDonnell, Scott Stanley, Scott Fairbanks, Joe Dunigan, Chris Joblin, Nick Zumsande, Christian Castorri, Mark Willoughby, Nate Adcock, Blake Newsome, Hanke LaRue, Adrian Puig, Alex Smith, Dana Duquette, Josh Kapiloff. **Director, International Scouting:** Fernando Seguignol. **Special Assistant, Baseball Operations & Scouting:** Adrian Lorenzo. **Coordinator, Player Development & International Operations:** Jacob Jola. **Special Assignment Scout, International Operations:** Rich Arena. **International Crosschecker:** Carlos Herazo. **Coordinator, Pacific Rim:** Jalal Leach. **Supervisor, Latin America:** Henry Sandoval. **Supervisor, Dominican Republic:** Rigoberto De Los Santos. **Scouts, Dominican Republic:** Hugo Aguero, Domingo Ortega, Felix Munoz, Angel Izquierdo. **Scouts, Venezuela:** Robin Ordonez, Tibaldo Hernandez. **Scout, Panama:** Luis Cordoba. **Scout, Colombia:** Alvaro Julio. **Scout, Mexico:** Andres Guzman. **Manager, Dominican Operations:** Humberto Reginato. **Video Coordinator, Dominican Republic:** Shamir Arias. **Intern, International Operations:** David Hernandez Beayne. **Professional Scouting Coordinator:** Jared Barnes. **Professional Scouting Analyst:** Alexandria Rigoli. **Professional Scouts:** Joseph Caro, Joe Lisewski, David Espinosa, David Crowson, Matt Gaski, Clint Robinson, Kevin Bootay, Tony Russo, Phil Rossi, Pierre Arsenault, Leon Wurth, Marty Esposito, Paul Ricciarini, John Eshleman.

MILWAUKEE BREWERS

Office Address: Miller Park, One Brewers Way, Milwaukee, WI 53214.
Telephone: (414) 902-4400. **Fax:** (414) 902-4053. **Website:** www.brewers.com.

OWNERSHIP
Operated By: Milwaukee Brewers Baseball Club.
Chairman/Principal Owner: Mark Attanasio.

BUSINESS OPERATIONS
President, Business Operations: Rick Schlesinger. **Senior Vice President, Communications & Affiliate Operations:** Tyler Barnes. **Senior Vice President, Stadium Operations:** Steve Ethier. **Chief Financial Officer:** Daniel Fumai. **Chief Revenue Officer:** Jason Hartlund. **Senior Vice President, Marketing & Fan Experience:** Teddy Werner. **General Counsel & Senior Vice President, Administration:** Marti Wronski. **Executive Assistant, Ownership Group:** Samantha Ernest. **Executive Assistant, General Manager:** Nichole Kinateder. **Executive Assistant, Paralegal:** Kate Rock. **Executive Assistant:** Adela Reeve. **Executive Assistant:** Kate Stempski. **Executive Assistant:** Sonya Martinez.

Mark Attanasio

FINANCE/ACCOUNTING
VP, Finance/Accounting: Jamie Norton. **Accounting Director:** Vicki Wise. **Disbursements Director:** Erica Umbach. **Senior Payroll Administrator:** Corrine Wolff. **Financial Analysts:** Cory Loppnow, Jackie Bauer, Mike Anheuser, Kristin Hahn. **Staff Accountant:** Samantha Berg. **Senior Accounts Payable Specialist:** Taikana Bentley. **Payroll Clerk:** Rita Flores. **VP, Human Resources:** Cas Castro. **Director, Human Resources:** Brenda Best.

MARKETING
VP, Marketing: Sharon McNally. **Senior Director, Marketing:** Kathy Schwab. **Director, Creative Design & Strategy:** Jeff Harding. **Director, Video Production:** Kelley Sibley. **Director, New Media:** Caitlin Moyer. **Senior Coordinator, Marketing Projects:** Brittany Luznicky. **Coordinator, New Media:** Aaron Oberley.

BUSINESS STRATEGY
VP, Strategy & Analytics: Mike Schwartz. **Director, Consumer Insights & Strategy:** Marla Grossberg. **Senior Manager, Data Science:** Michael Dairyko. **Senior Manager, Strategy/Analytics:** Maxwell Stejskal. **Business Analyst:** Sara Halloran. **Coordinator, Business Intelligence:** Danny Henken.

MEDIA RELATIONS/PUBLICATIONS
Senior Director, Media Relations: Mike Vassallo. **Senior Manager, Media Relations:** Ken Spindler. **Coordinator, Media Relations:** Matt Stein. **Coordinator, Communications/Mini-Marathon:** Bryn Winter. **Publications Assistant:** Robbin Barnes.

MILLER PARK OPERATIONS
Senior Director, Security: Randy Olewinski. **Senior Director, Event Services:** Matt Lehmann.

2019 SCHEDULE
Standard Game Times: Mon.-Sat., 7:10 pm; Sun., 1:10 pm.

MARCH		
28-31 . . . . St. Louis	10-12 . . . . at Chicago (NL)	28-30 . . . . Pittsburgh
APRIL	13-16 . . . . at Philadelphia	**JULY**
1-3 . . . . .at Cincinnati	17-19 . . . . at Atlanta	1-4 . . . . . .at Cincinnati
5-7 . . . . Chicago (NL)	21-22 . . . . Cincinnati	5-7 . . . . . . at Pittsburgh
8-10 . . at Los Angeles (AL)	24-26 . . . . .Philadelphia	12-14 . . . . San Francisco
12-14 . at Los Angeles (NL)	27-28 . . . . at Minnesota	15-17 . . . . Atlanta
15-17 . . . . St. Louis	30-31 . . . . . at Pittsburgh	18-21 . . . . . at Arizona
18-21 . . Los Angeles (NL)	**JUNE**	22-24 . . . . . . Cincinnati
22-24 . . . . . .at St. Louis	1-2 . . . . at Pittsburgh	26-28 . . . . Chicago (NL)
26-28 . . at New York (NL)	4-6 . . . . .Miami	30-31 . . . .at Oakland
29-30 . . . . .Colorado	7-9 . . . . Pittsburgh	**AUGUST**
MAY	11-12 . . . . . . .at Houston	1 . . . . .at Oakland
1-2 . . . . .Colorado	14-16 . . . at San Francisco	2-4 . . . . . .at Chicago (NL)
3-5 . . . . . .New York (NL)	17-19 . . . . at San Diego	5-7 . . . . . . at Pittsburgh
6-8 . . . . Washington	20-23 . . . . Cincinnati	9-11 . . . . Texas
	25-27 . . . . Seattle	13-14 . . . . Minnesota

16-18 . . . . at Washington		
19-21 . . . . . . .at St. Louis		
23-25 . . . . .Arizona		
26-28 . . . . St. Louis		
30-31 . . . .at Chicago (NL)		
SEPTEMBER		
1 . . . . . . .at Chicago (NL)		
2-3 . . . . Houston		
5-8 . . . . . . Chicago (NL)		
9-12 . . . . at Miami		
13-15 . . . . . . .at St. Louis		
16-19 . . . . San Diego		
20-22 . . . . Pittsburgh		
24-26 . . . . .at Cincinnati		
27-29 . . . . . . at Colorado		

GENERAL INFORMATION
Stadium (year opened):
Miller Park (2001).
Team Colors: Navy blue, gold and white.

Home Dugout: First Base.
Playing Surface: Grass.

Senior Director, Facility Services: Mike Brockman. Director, Grounds: Michael Boettcher. Manager, Event Services: Scott Quade. Manager, Guest Services: Kari Dawson. Manager, Grounds: Zak Peterson. Manager, Landscape: Josh Ruplinger. Manager, Fields: Tom Henke. Manager, Warehouse: John Weyer.

TICKET SALES

Telephone: (414) 902-4000. Fax: (414) 902-4056.

VP, Ticket Sales: Jim Bathey. Sr. Director, Ticket Sales: Billy Friess. Sr. Director, Ticket Services & Technology: Jessica Brown. Director, Group Sales: Chris Kimball. Director, Inside Sales: Jason Fry. Director, Suite Sales: Chris Rothwell. Director, Suite Services: Kristin Miller.

BASEBALL OPERATIONS

David Stearns

Telephone: (414) 902-4400. Fax: (414) 902-4515.

President, Baseball Operations & General Manager: David Stearns. VP/Assistant GM: Matt Arnold. Senior Advisor: Doug Melvin. VP, Baseball Projects: Gord Ash. Vice President, Player Personnel: Karl Mueller. Special Advisor, Baseball Operations/Player Development: Carlos Villanueva. Special Assistant, General Manager/Pro Scouting/Player Personnel: Dick Groch. Special Assistant, Baseball Strategy: Shawn Hoffman. Director, Baseball Operations: Matt Kleine. Director, Baseball Systems: Will Hudgins. Director, Baseball Research & Development: Dan Turkenkopf. Assistant, Baseball Operations/Spanish Translator: Carlos Brizuela. Manager, Baseball Research & Quantitative Analysis: Nick Davis. Manager, Video Operations: Matt Kerls. Senior Analyst, Baseball Research & Development: Andrew Fox. Analyst, Baseball Research & Development: Ethan Bein.

MAJOR LEAGUE STAFF

Manager: Craig Counsell. Coaches: Bench—Pat Murphy, Pitching—Chris Hook, Hitting—Andy Haines, First Base—Carlos Subero, Third Base—Ed Sedar, Bullpen—Steve Karsay. Assistant Coach: Jason Lane. Bullpen Catchers: Marcus Hanel, Robinson Diaz.

MEDICAL/TRAINING

Director, Medical Operations: Roger Caplinger. Head Team Physician: Dr. William Raasch. Team Physicians: Dr. Mark Niedfeldt, Dr. Craig Young. Director, Psychological Services: Matt Krug. Head Athletic Trainer: Scott Barringer. Asst. Athletic Trainers: Rafael Freitas, Dave Yeager. Director, Integrative Sports Performance: Bryson Nakamura. Strength & Conditioning Specialists: Josh Seligman, Jason Meredith. Rehab Coordinator: Blair Bundy. Coordinator, Sports Performance: Sara Goodrum. EAP Provider, Sports Psychology Professional: Blake Pindyck. Consulting Orthopedic Physician, Phoenix: Dr. Evan Lederman. Consulting Team Physician, Phoenix: Dr. Carlton Richie.

PLAYER DEVELOPMENT

Farm Director: Tom Flanagan. Asst. Farm Director: Eduardo Brizuela. Asst. Director, Outfield & Baserunning Coordinator: Tony Diggs. Roving Outfield/Baserunning Coordinator: Quintin Berry. Sr. Manager, Baseball Administration: Mark Mueller. Hitting Coordinator: Kenny Graham. Field Coordinator & Catching Instructor: Charlie Greene. Roving Infield Coordinator: Bob Miscik. Athletic Training Coordinator: Frank Neville. Pitching Coordinator: Mark Dewey. Pitching Coordinator/Skill Acquisition: Jake McKinley. Phoenix Clubhouse Manager: Travis Voss.

FARM SYSTEM

Class	Club (League)	Manager	Hitting Coach	Pitching Coach
Triple-A	San Antonio (PCL)	Rick Sweet	Al LeBoeuf	Fred Dabney
Double-A	Biloxi (SL)	Mike Guerrero	Danny Santin	Bob Milacki
High A	Carolina (CAR)	Joe Ayrault	Bobby Bell	Cam Castro
Low A	Wisconsin (MWL)	Matt Erickson	Dave Joppie	Jim Henderson
Rookie	Rocky Mountain (PIO)	Nestor Corredor	Nick Stanley	Unavailable
Rookie	Brewers Blue (AZL)	Rafael Neda	Brenton Del Chiaro	Hiram Burgos
Rookie	Brewers Gold (AZL)	Liu Rodriguez	Bobby Spain	Steve Cline
Rookie	Brewers (DSL)	Victor Estevez	Luis De Los Santos	Victor Moreno
Rookie	Brewers/Indians (DSL)	Alcides Melendez	Jose Pena	Jesus Hernandez

SCOUTING

Telephone: (414) 902-4400. Fax: (414) 902-4059.

VP, Scouting: Ray Montgomery. Senior Advisor, Scouting: Marv Thompson. Special Assignment Scout: Scott Campbell. Director, Amateur Scouting: Tod Johnson. Director, International Scouting: Mike Groopman. Assistant Director, Amateur Scouting: Tim McIlvaine. Manager, Advance Scouting: Brian Powalish. Coordinator, Advance Scouting: Walker McKinven. Coordinator, Scouting Operations: Oscar Garcia, Adam Hayes. Supervisor, Pro Scouting: Bryan Gale, Taylor Green. Pro Scouting Crosschecker: Ben McDonough, Ryan Thompson, Derek Watson. Professional/Amateur Scouts: Pete Orr, Ross Pruitt, Bryan Bullington. Pro Scouts: Lary Aaron, Mike Berger, Jeff Bianchi, Pete Vuckovich Jr. National Amateur Supervisor: Doug Reynolds. Regional Amateur Supervisors: Corey Rodriguez, Drew Anderson, Josh Belovsky, Dan Nellum, Brian Sankey, Mike Serbalik. Amateur Scouts: Riley Bandelow, Ty Blankmeyer, Mike Burns, James Fisher, Taylor Frederick, Joe Graham, KJ Hendricks, Dan Huston, Harvey Kuenn Jr., Lazaro Llanes, Mark Muzzi, Scott Nichols, Wynn Pelzer, Jeff Scholzen, Jeff Simpson, Craig Smajstrla, Steve Smith, Shawn Whalen. Latin America, Crosschecker: Esteban Castillo, Fernando Veracierto. Latin America, Supervisor: Jairo Castillo, Rodolfo Rosario. Assistant Director, International Scouting: Luis Perez. International Scouts: Jose Barraza, Teofilo Gutierrez, Julio De La Cruz, Jonas Lantigua, Jose Morales, Jean Carlos Reynoso, Luis Rosario, Martin Arvizu, Salvador Ayestas, Trino Aguilar, Javier Castillo, Diego Flores, Kenji Galavis, Reinaldo, Hidalgo, Javier Meza, Jose Rodriguez.

MINNESOTA TWINS

Office Address: Target Field, 1 Twins Way, Minneapolis, MN 55403.
Telephone: (612) 659-3400. **Fax:** 612-659-4025. **Website:** www.twinsbaseball.com.

OWNERSHIP

Operated By: The Minnesota Twins. **Executive Chair:** Jim Pohlad. **Executive Board:** Jim Pohlad, Bob Pohlad, Bill Pohlad, Dave St. Peter.

BUSINESS OPERATIONS

President/Chief Executive Officer, Minnesota Twins: Dave St. Peter. **Executive Vice President/Chief Business Officer, Business Development:** Laura Day. **Executive VP/Chief Administrative Officer/CFO:** Kip Elliott. **Director, Ballpark Development/Planning:** Dan Starkey.

Jim Pohlad

HUMAN RESOURCES/FINANCE/TECHNOLOGY

Sr. Director, Human Resources: Leticia Silva. **Director, Payroll:** Lori Beasley. **Human Resources Generalist:** Holly Corbin. **Coordinator, Payroll/Benefits:** Molly Partyka. **Coordinator, Human Resources:** Maria Salazar.

MARKETING

Senior Director, Marketing/Content: Chris Iles. **Director, Twins Productions:** Sam Henschen. **Senior Manager, Advertising:** Will Delaney. **Manager, Digital Content:** Brea Hinegardner. **Manager, Video:** Jim Diehl. **Manager, Marketing/Promotions:** Mitch Retelny. **Manager, Marketing/Communications:** Beth Vail Palm.

CORPORATE PARTNERSHIPS

Senior Director, Corporate Partnership: Jeff Jurgella. **Managers, Corporate Partnerships:** Doug Beck, Karen Cleary, Chad Jackson. **Director, Partnership Strategy/Development:** Jordan Woodcroft. **Manager, Broadcast Traffic/Administration:** Amy Johnson. **Project Manager:** Joe Morin.

COMMUNICATIONS

Telephone: (612) 659-3471. **Fax:** (612) 659-4029.
Senior Director, Communications: Dustin Morse. **Senior Manager, Communications:** Mitch Hestad. **Manager, Communications:** Matt Hodson. **Coordinator, Communications:** Cori Frankenberg. **Coordinator, Team Photographer and Publications:** Brace Hemmelgarn. **Communications Assistant/Translator:** Elvis Martinez.

COMMUNITY RELATIONS

Senior Manager, Community Relations: Stephanie Johnson. **Manager, Community Programs:** Josh Ortiz. **Senior Coordinator, Community Relations:** Sondra Ciesielski.

TICKETING/EVENTS

Telephone: 1-800-33-TWINS. **Fax:** (612) 659-4030.

2019 SCHEDULE

Standard Game Times: Mon.-Sat., 7:10 pm; Sun., 1:10 pm.

MARCH		
28-31 . . . . Cleveland		

APRIL
2-3. . . . . . .at Kansas City
5-7. . . . . at Philadelphia
9-10 . . . . at New York (NL)
12-14 . . . . Detroit
15-18 . . . . .Toronto
19-21 . . . . . .at Baltimore
22-24 . . . . . . .at Houston
26-28 . . . . Baltimore
29-30 . . . . Houston

MAY
1-2. . . . . Houston
3-5. . . . . at New York (AL)
6-8. . . . . at Toronto

10-12 . . . . Detroit
13-15 . . . Los Angeles (AL)
16-19 . . . . . . .at Seattle
20-22 . at Los Angeles (AL)
24-26 . . . . Chicago (AL)
27-28 . . . . . . .Milwaukee
30-31 . . . . . at Tampa Bay

JUNE
1-2. . . . . at Tampa Bay
4-6. . . . . . .at Cleveland
7-9. . . . . .at Detroit
11-13 . . . . Seattle
14-16 . . . . . . Kansas City
17-19 . . . . Boston
20-23 . . . . .at Kansas City
25-27 . . . . . .Tampa Bay

28-30 . . . .at Chicago (AL)

JULY
2-4. . . . . . . .at Oakland
5-7. . . . . Texas
12-14 . . . . .at Cleveland
16-17 . . . .New York (NL)
18-21 . . . . Oakland
22-24 . . . .New York (AL)
25-28 . . .at Chicago (AL)
30-31 . . . . at Miami

AUGUST
1 . . . . at Miami
2-4. . . . . . . Kansas City
5-7. . . . . Atlanta
8-11 . . . . Cleveland
13-14 . . . . . at Milwaukee

15-18 . . . . .at Texas
19-21 . . . . . Chicago (AL)
23-25 . . . . Detroit
27-29 . . . .at Chicago (AL)
30-31 . . . . . . .at Detroit

SEPTEMBER
1-2. . . . . .at Detroit
3-5. . . . . .at Boston
6-8. . . . . Cleveland
10-12 . . . . . Washington
13-15 . . . . .at Cleveland
16-18 . . .. . Chicago (AL)
19-22 . . . . . Kansas City
24-26 . . . . . .at Detroit
27-29 . . . . .at Kansas City

GENERAL INFORMATION

Stadium (year opened): Target Field (2010). **Playing Surface:** Grass.
Team Colors: Red, navy blue and white.
Home Dugout: First Base.

Senior Director, Box Office: Mike Stiles. Manager, Box Office: Ashley Geldert. Manager, Call Center: Mark Engstrom. Supervisor, Box Office: Colleen Seeker. Coordinator, Call Center Operations: Chris Frogge. Coordinator, Ticket Operations/Special Events: Kelton Splett. Coordinator, Ticket Operations: Colin Sheehan.

BALLPARK OPERATIONS
Senior Vice President, Operations: Matt Hoy. Senior Director, Ballpark Operations: Dave Horsman. Manager, Ballpark Operations: Jase Miller. Senior Director, Facilities: Gary Glawe. Senior Director, Guest Experience: Patrick Forsland. Security Director: Jeff Beahen. Sr. Manager, Guest Services: Katie Rock. Head Groundskeeper: Larry DiVito. Manager, Grounds: Al Kuehner. Manager, Security: Scott Larson. Coordinator, Office Services: Josh Fallin. Ballpark Operations Assistant: Chelsey Falzone. Manager, Retail Sales: Venika Streeter. Assistant, Front Office: Tina Flowers.

BASEBALL OPERATIONS

Derek Falvey

Executive VP/Chief Baseball Officer: Derek Falvey. Senior VP/General Manager: Thad Levine. VP, Player Personnel: Mike Radcliff. VP/Assistant GM: Rob Antony. Director, Baseball Administration: Kate Townley. Director, Baseball Operations: Daniel Adler. Assistant Director, Baseball Operations: Nick Beauchamp. Director, Pro Scouting: Brad Steil. Special Assistants: Michael Cuddyer, LaTroy Hawkins, Torii Hunter, Justin Morneau. Coordinator, Pro Scouting R&D: Zane MacPhee. Analyst, R&D: Heather Hunt, Andrew Ettel. Analyst, Player Development: Rachel Heacock. Coordinator, Amateur Scouting R&D: Ezra Wise. Director, Team Travel: Mike Herman. Senior Data Engineer: Jerad Parish. Developer, Baseball Systems: Nick Rogers, Hans Van Slooten. Manager, Baseball Systems: Jeremy Raadt.

MAJOR LEAGUE STAFF
Manager: Rocco Baldelli. Coaches: Bench—Derek Shelton, Pitching—Wes Johnson, Hitting—James Rowson, Catching—Bill Evers, First Base—Tommy Watkins, Third Base— Tony Diaz, Assistant Pitching—Jeremy Hefner, Assistant Hitting—Rudy Hernandez. Equipment Manager: Rod McCormick. Assistant Home Clubhouse Manager: Tim Burke. Assistant, Home Clubhouse: Frank Hanzlik. Visitors' Clubhouse Manager: Marcus McKenzie. Coordinator, Major League Video: David Jeffrey.

MEDICAL/TRAINING
Director, Medical Services: Dr. John Steubs. Club Physicians: Dr. Rahul Kapur, Dr. David Olson, Dr. Corey Wulf, Dr. Diane Dahm, Dr. Amy Beacom, Dr. Rick Aberman. Head Trainer: Tony Leo. Assistant Trainers: Masamichi Abe, Matt Biancuzzo. Physical Therapist: Jeff Lahti. Head Dietician: Rasa Troup. Strength & Conditioning Coach: Ian Kadish. Motion Coach: Martijn Verhoeve.

PLAYER DEVELOPMENT
Telephone: (612) 659-3480. Fax: (612) 659-4026.
Director, Minor League Operations: Jeremy Zoll. Assistant Director, Minor League Operations: Alex Hassan. Senior Advisor, Player Development: Sam Perlozzo. Senior Manager, Minor League Administration: Brian Maloney. Assistant, Florida Operations: Victor Gonzalez. Assistant, Florida & International Operations: Brad McKenny. Minor League Coordinators: Edgar Varela (field), Peter Fatse (hitting), Billy Boyer (infield/baserunning), Mike Quade (outfield), Tanner Swanson (catching), Pete Maki (pitching), JP Martinez (assistant pitching) David Rak (strength & conditioning), Jose Marzan (Latin America), Chad Jackson (rehab), Tyler Schmitz (video).

FARM SYSTEM

Class	Club (League)	Manager	Hitting Coach	Pitching Coach
Triple-A	Rochester (IL)	Joel Skinner	Javier Valentin	Stu Cliburn
Double-A	Pensacola (SL)	Ramon Borrego	Steve Singleton	Cibney Bello
High A	Fort Myers (FSL)	Toby Gardenhire	Matt Borgschulte	Luis Ramirez
Low A	Cedar Rapids (MWL)	Brian Dinkelman	Ryan Smith	Virgil Vasquez
Rookie	Elizabethton (APP)	Ray Smith	Jeff Reed	Richard Salazar
Rookie	Twins (GCL)	Robbie Robinson	M. Thomas/N. Rasmussen	Zach Bove
Rookie	Twins (DSL)	Seth Feldman	L. Bonilla/C. Abney	Kevin Rodriguez

SCOUTING
Director, Amateur Scouting: Sean Johnson. Coordinator, Pro Scouting: Vern Followell. Director, Latin American Scouting & US Integration Assistant Scouting Director: Tim O'Neil. Senior Advisor, Scouting: Deron Johnson. Senior Manager, Scouting/International Administration: Amanda Daley. Coordinator, Amateur Scouting: Brit Minder. Scouting Supervisors: Southeast—Billy Corrigan, West Coast—Elliott Strankman, East Coast—Mark Quimuyog, Midwest—Mike Ruth. Area Scouts: Andrew Ayers (AZ, CO, NM, UT, WY, So. NV), Joe Bisenius (IA, MN, NE, ND, SD, WI) Kyle Blackwell (WA, OR, ID, MT, AK), Trevor Brown (TX, No. LA), Walt Burrows (Canada), J.R. DiMercurio (AR, KS, MO, OK), Brett Dowdy (FL), Derrick Dunbar (KY, MS, TN), John Leavitt (HI, CA), Seth Moir (CA), Jeff Pohl (MI, IN, IL & Pitching Crosschecker), Jack Powell (GA, AL), Michael Quesada (NV, CA), Freddie Thon (FL, PR & International Crosschecker), Nick Venuto (OH, WV, PA, NY), Matt Williams (NC, SC, VA), Greg Runser (TX, LA & Pitching Crosschecker), John Wilson (CT, NJ, NY, MA, VA, MD, VT, RI, ME, NH, DE, DC). Junior College Scout: Ty Dawson. Professional Scouts: Ken Compton, Earl Frishman, Bob Hegman, John Manuel, Billy Milos, Rafael Yanez, Keith Stohr, Earl Winn, Wesley Wright. Scouts: Glenn Godwin, Mike Larson. Dominican Republic: Luis Lajara, Manuel Luciano, Eury Luis, Eduardo Soriano. Coordinator, Venezuela Scouting: Jose Leon. Venezuela: Marlon Nava, Oswaldo Troconis. Pacific Rim: David Kim. Part-Time Scouts: Hector Barrios (Panama), John Cortese (Italy), Kenny Su (Taiwan), Koji Takahashi (Japan), Lester Victoria (Curacao) Juan Padilla, Franklin Parra, Pablo Torres (Venezuela).

NEW YORK METS

Office Address: Citi Field, 126th Street, Flushing, NY 11368.
Telephone: (718) 507-6387. **Fax:** (718) 507-6395.
Website: www.mets.com. **Twitter:** @mets.

OWNERSHIP

Operated By: Sterling Mets LP. **Chairman/Chief Executive Officer:** Fred Wilpon. **President:** Saul B. Katz. **Chief Operating Officer:** Jeff Wilpon.

BUSINESS OPERATIONS

Executive VP/Chief Revenue Officer: Lou DePaoli. **Senior VP, Senior Strategy Officer:** John Ricco. **Executive Director, Business Intelligence/Analytics:** John Morris.

LEGAL/HUMAN RESOURCES

Executive VP/Chief Legal Officer: David Cohen. **VP/Deputy General Counsel:** Neal Kaplan. **Senior Counsel:** James Denniston. **Senior Counsel:** Jessica Villanella. **Senior VP, Human Resources & Diversity:** Holly Lindvall.

FINANCE

CFO: Mark Peskin. **VP, Controller:** Len Labita. **VP, Financial Planning & Analysis:** Peter Woll. **Senior Director, Assistant Controller:** John Ventimiglia.

MARKETING/COMMUNICATIONS/SALES

Fred Wilpon

Executive Producer, Entertainment, Marketing & Productions: Joe DeVito. **Executive Director, Marketing:** Mark Fine. **Executive Director, Broadcasting/Special Events:** Lorraine Hamilton. **VP, Alumni Public Relations & Team Historian:** Jay Horwitz. **Senior Director, Social Media:** Will Carafello. **Senior Director, Entertainment Marketing & Productions:** Vito Vitiello. **Vice President, External Affairs & Community Engagement:** Haeda Mihaltses. **Executive Director, External Affairs & Community Engagement:** Danielle Parillo. **Director, Player Relations & Community Engagement:** Donovan Mitchell.

MEDIA RELATIONS

Telephone: (718) 565-4330. **Fax:** (718) 639-3619.
VP, Communications: Harold Kaufman. **Director, Communications:** Ethan Wilson. **Manager, Communications,** Zach Weber. **Coordinator, Communications:** Kristin Wojcik. **Assistant, Communications/Translator:** Alan Suriel. **Assistant, Communications:** Zack Becker.

TRAVEL/CLUBHOUSE

Equipment Manager: Kevin Kierst. **Assistant Clubhouse Manager:** Dave Berni. **Visiting Clubhouse Manager:** Tony Carullo. Director, **Team Travel:** Brian Small.

2019 SCHEDULE

Standard Game Times: 7:10 p.m.; Sun. 1:10.

MARCH	10-12 . . . . .Miami	28-30 . . . . Atlanta
28-31 . . . . at Washington	14-16 . . . . at Washington	
	17-19 . . . . at Miami	**JULY**
APRIL	20-23 . . . . . Washington	2-3 . . . . . . .New York (AL)
1-3 . . . . at Miami	24-26 . . . . Detroit	5-7 . . . . . . .Philadelphia
4-7 . . . . Washington	27-30 . at Los Angeles (NL)	12-14 . . . . at Miami
9-10 . . . . . . .Minnesota	31 . . . . at Arizona	16-17 . . . . . at Minnesota
11-14 . . . . at Atlanta		18-21 . . . at San Francisco
15-17 . . . at Philadelphia	**JUNE**	23-25 . . . . San Diego
19-21 . . . . . .at St. Louis	1-2 . . . . at Arizona	26-28 . . . . Pittsburgh
22-24 . . . . . .Philadelphia	4-6 . . . . . San Francisco	30-31 . . .at Chicago (AL)
26-28 . . . . . . .Milwaukee	7-9 . . . . .Colorado	
29-30 . . . . Cincinnati	10-11 . . . at New York (AL)	**AUGUST**
	13-16 . . . . St. Louis	1 . . . . . . .at Chicago (AL)
MAY	17-19 . . . . . . at Atlanta	2-4 . . . . . . at Pittsburgh
1-2 . . . . Cincinnati	20-23 . . . .at Chicago (NL)	5-7 . . . . .Miami
3-5 . . . . . . at Milwaukee	24-27 . . . . at Philadelphia	9-11 . . . . . . .Washington
6-8 . . . . at San Diego		13-15 . . . . at Atlanta

16-18 . . . . .at Kansas City
20-22 . . . . Cleveland
23-25 . . . . Atlanta
27-29 . . . . . Chicago (NL)
30-31 . . . . at Philadelphia
SEPTEMBER
1 . . . . at Philadelphia
2-4 . . . . . at Washington
6-8 . . . . . . .Philadelphia
9-12 . . . . .Arizona
13-15 . . . Los Angeles (NL)
16-18 . . . . . . at Colorado
20-22 . . . .at Cincinnati
23-26 . . . . .Miami
27-29 . . . . Atlanta

GENERAL INFORMATION

Stadium (year opened): Citi Field (2009).
Team Colors: Blue and orange.
Home Dugout: First Base.
Playing Surface: Grass.

BASEBALL OPERATIONS

Telephone: (718) 803-4013, (718) 565-4339. **Fax:** (718) 507-6391.

Executive Vice President & General Manager: Brodie Van Wagenen. **Vice President, Assistant General Manager, Scouting & Player Development:** Allard Baird. **Special Assistant to the General Manager:** Omar Minaya. **Assistant General Manager, Systematic Development:** Adam Guttridge. **Vice President, International & Amateur Scouting:** Tommy Tanous. **Senior Director, Baseball Operations:** Ian Levin. **Special Assistants to the General Manager:** Ruben Amaro Jr., Terry Collins. **Special Advisor to Mets COO & General Manager:** David Wright. **Director, Baseball Research & Development:** T.J. Barra. **Manager, Baseball Systems & Development:** Joe Lefkowitz. **Manager, Baseball Administration:** June Napoli. **Manager, Video Operations:** Joe Scarola. **Senior Coordinator, Video Operations:** Sean Haggans. **Coordinator, Baseball Operations:** Jeff Lebow. **Coordinator, Advance Scouting & Video Replay:** Michael Wickham. **Analyst, Pitching Research & Development:** David Lang. **Administrative Assistant, Baseball Operations:** Janine Laboy-Gonzalez. **Senior Advisors:** Guy Conti, Bobby Floyd, Lamar Johnson, Ozzie Virgil, Sr.

Brodie Van Wagenen

MAJOR LEAGUE STAFF

Manager: Mickey Callaway. **Coaches: Bench**—Jim Riggleman. **Hitting**—Chili Davis. **Assistant Hitting**—Tom Slater. **Pitching**—Dave Eiland. **First Base**—Glenn Sherlock. **Third Base**—Gary DiSarcina. **Bullpen**—Chuck Hernandez. **Quality Control Coach**—Luis Rojas. **Bullpen Catchers**—Dave Racaniello, Eric Langill.

MEDICAL/TRAINING

Medical Coordinator: Matt Hunter. **Performance Coordinator:** Michael Main. **Strength and Conditioning Coordinator:** Luke Passman. **Rehabilitation & Physical Therapy Coordinator:** David Pearson. **Short-Season Mental Skills Coordinator:** Ruben Aybar. **Minor League Education Coordinator:** Kathleen Dillon. **Dominican Republic Physical Therapist:** Jhomelger Garcia. **Dominican Republic Strength & Conditioning Coordinator:** Angel Ponce. **Latin American Strength & Conditioning Coordinator/GCL Strength & Conditioning Coach:** Alex Tavarez.

PLAYER DEVELOPMENT

Telephone: (718) 565-4302. **Fax:** (718) 205-7920.

Executive Director, Player Development: Jared Banner. **Minor League Field Coordinator:** Kevin Morgan. **Director, Minor League Operations:** Ronny Reyes. **Director, Latin American Operations:** Juan Henderson. **Minor League Information Coordinator:** Colin Schwarz. **Assistant, Player Development:** Troy Rooney. **Assistant, Minor League Operations:** Amy Ross. **Pitching Coordinator:** Jeremy Accardo. **Outfield/Baserunning Coordinator:** Marlon Anderson. **Rehabilitation Pitching Coordinator:** Jon Debus. **Hitting Coordinator:** Ryan Ellis. **International Field Coordinator:** Rafael Landestoy. **Catching Coordinator:** Bob Natal. **Assistant Pitching Coordinator:** Phil Regan. **Infield Coordinator:** Tim Teufel. **Equipment/Operations Manager:** John Mullin. **Assistant Clubhouse Manager:** Drew Dunton. **Senior Advisors:** Guy Conti, Bobby Floyd, Lamar Johnson, Ozzie Virgil, Sr.

FARM SYSTEM

Class	Club	Manager	Hitting Coach	Pitching Coach
Triple-A	Las Vegas (PCL)	Tony DeFrancesco	Joel Chimelis	Glenn Abbott
Double-A	Binghamton (EL)	Kevin Boles	Tony Jaramillo	Jonathan Hurst
High A	St. Lucie (FSL)	Chad Kreuter	TBD	Ricky Bones
Low A	Columbia (SAL)	Pedro Lopez	Luis Rivera	Royce Ring
Short-season	Brooklyn (NYP)	Edgardo Alfonzo	Delwyn Young	Josue Matos
Rookie	Kingsport (APP)	Rich Donnelly	Rafael Fernandez	Jerome Williams
Rookie	Mets (GCL)	David Davalillo	Joel Fuentes	Ariel Prieto
Rookie	Mets 1 (DSL)	Manny Martinez	Leo Hernandez	Francis Martinez
Rookie	Mets 2 (DSL)	Yucarybert De La Cruz	TBD	B. Marte/R. Roque

SCOUTING

Telephone: (718) 565-4311. **Fax:** (718) 205-7920.

Vice President, Amateur Scouting: Thomas Tanous. **Director, Amateur Scouting:** Marc Tramuta. **Senior Coordinator, Amateur Scouting & International Scouting:** Bryan Hayes. **Assistant, Amateur & International Scouting:** Andrew Christie. **National Crosschecker:** Doug Thurman. **Global Crosschecker:** Steve Barningham. **Pitching Crosschecker:** Chris Hervey. **Southeast Supervisor/National Crosschecker:** Mike Ledna. **Northeast:** Marlin McPhail. **Regional Supervisor, Midwest:** Mac Seibert. **Regional Supervisor, West:** Drew Toussaint. Miami, FL. **Area Scouts:** Cesar Aranguren, (So. FL), Nathan Beuster, (KS, OK, NE, MO, ND, SD, IA), Gary Brown, (No. TX), Jet Butler, (LA, MS, AR), Daniel Coles, (NC, SC, So. VA), Jarrett England, (KY, So. OH, TN), Chris Heidt, (IL, IA, IN, MN, WI, MI, No.OH), Tyler Holmes, (No./Cent. CA, No. NV, HI), Tommy Jackson, (FL, GA, AL), John Kosciak, (MA, CT, ME, RI, NH, VT, NY), Jason McLaughlin, (So. CA), Claude Pelletier, (Canada), Jim Reeves, (W. Canada, AK, WA, OR, ID, WY, MT), Brian Reid, (AZ, CO, NM, UT, Las Vegas), Harry Shelton, (So. TX), Jim Thompson, (DE, PA, MD, WV, NJ, No. VA, Washington, D.C.), Jon Updike (Cent. FL), Glenn Walker (So. CA). **Senior Director, Professional Scouting:** Jim D'Aloia. **Assistant Director, Professional Scouting:** Bryn Alderson. **Pro Scouts:** Conor Brooks, Tom Clark, Tim Fortugno, David Keller, Jim Kelly, Joseph Kowal, Ash Lawson, Shaun McNamara, Andy Pratt, Roy Smith, Rudy Terrasas. **Director, International Operations:** Rafael Perez. **Director, International Scouting:** Luis Marquez. **Supervisor, Latin American Scouting:** Moises de la Mota. **Coordinators, Latin American Scouting:** Gerardo Cabrera, Hector Rincones, Harold Herrera. **Supervisors, Venezuela:** Ismael Perez, Manny Batista. **Scouts, Dominican Republic:** Kelvin Dominguez, Fernando Encarnacion, Wilson Peralta, Miguel Vasquez. **Scout, Mexico:** Fred Mazuca. **Scouts, Venezuela:** Robert Espejo, Nestor Moreno, Carlos Perez, Andres Nunez. **Scout, Asia:** Bon Kim. **Tryout Coaches, Dominican Republic:** Carlos Capellan, Samuel Taveras.

NEW YORK YANKEES

Office Address: Yankee Stadium, One East 161st St., Bronx, NY 10451.
Telephone: (718) 293-4300.
Website: www.yankees.com, www.yankeesbeisbol.com.
Twitter: @Yankees, @YankeesPR, @LosYankees, @LosYankeesPR.

OWNERSHIP
Managing General Partner/Co-Chairperson: Harold Z. (Hal) Steinbrenner. **General Partner/Co-Chairperson:** Hank Steinbrenner. **General Partner/Vice Chairperson:** Jennifer Steinbrenner Swindal. **General Partner/Vice Chairperson:** Jessica Steinbrenner.

BUSINESS OPERATIONS
President: Randy Levine, Esq.
Chief Operating Officer/General Counsel: Lonn A. Trost, Esq.
Senior VP, Strategic Ventures: Marty Greenspun. **Senior VP, Chief Security Officer:** Sonny Hight. **Senior VP, Yankee Global Enterprises/Chief Financial Officer:** Anthony Bruno. **Chief Financial Officer/Senior VP, Financial Operations:** Scott M. Krug. **Senior VP, Corporate/Community Relations:** Brian E. Smith. **Senior VP, Partnerships:** Michael J. Tusiani. **Senior VP, Marketing:** Deborah A. Tymon. **Senior VP, Stadium Operations:** Doug Behar. **VP/Chief Financial Officer, Accounting:** Robert B. Brown. **Deputy General Counsel/VP, Legal Affairs:** Alan Chang. **VP, Chief Information Officer:** Mike Lane.

COMMUNICATIONS/MEDIA RELATIONS
Telephone: (718) 579-4460. **Email:** media@yankees.com.
Vice President, Communications/Media Relations: Jason Zillo. **Director, Baseball Information/Public Communications:** Michael Margolis. **Assistant Director, Baseball Information:** Lauren Moran. **Manager, Media Services:** Alexandra Trochanowski. **Sr. Coordinator, Communications/Media Relations:** Rob Morse. **Coordinator, Communications/Media Relations:** Kaitlyn Brennan. **Assistant, Communications/Media Relations:** Andrew Kivette. **Administrative Assistant, Communications/Media Relations:** Germania-Dolores Hernandez. **Bilingual Media Relations Coodinator:** Marlon Abreu. **Japanese Media Advisor:** Yoshiki Sato.

Harold Z.
Steinbrenner

TICKET OPERATIONS
Telephone: (718) 293-6000.
VP, Ticket Sales/Service/Operations: Kevin Dart.

2019 SCHEDULE
Standard Game Times: Mon.-Fri., 7:05 pm; Sat.-Sun., 1:05 pm.

MARCH		JULY	SEPTEMBER
28, 30-31 . . . . . Baltimore	6-9 . . . . Seattle	24-26 . . . . .Toronto	12-14 . . . . . . Baltimore
	10-12 . . . . . at Tampa Bay	29-30 . at Boston (London)	15-18 . . . . Cleveland
APRIL	13-15 . . . . Baltimore		20-22 . . . . . . .at Oakland
1-3 . . . . Detroit	17-19 . . . . . . .Tampa Bay	JULY	23-25 . at Los Angeles (NL)
4, 6-7 . . . . . .at Baltimore	20-23 . . . . . .at Baltimore	2-3 . . . . at New York (NL)	26-28 . . . . .at Seattle
8-10 . . . . .at Houston	24-26 . . . . .at Kansas City	4-7 . . . . . . at Tampa Bay	30-31 . . . . Oakland
12-14 . . . . . Chicago (AL)	27-29 . . . . San Diego	12-14 . . . . .Toronto	
16-17 . . . . Boston	30-31 . . . . Boston	15-18 . . . . . . Tampa Bay	SEPTEMBER
18-21 . . . . . Kansas City		19-21 . . . . . . .Colorado	1 . . . . Oakland
22-25 . at Los Angeles (AL)	JUNE	22-24 . . . . . at Minnesota	2-4 . . . . Texas
26-28 . . . at San Francisco	1-2 . . . . Boston	25-28 . . . . . . .at Boston	6-9 . . . . .at Boston
30 . . . . at Arizona	4-6 . . . . at Toronto	30-31 . . . . Arizona	10-12 . . . . . . .at Detroit
	7-9 . . . . . . .at Cleveland		13-15 . . . . . . at Toronto
MAY	10-11 . . . .New York (NL)	AUGUST	17-19 . . . Los Angeles (AL)
1 . . . . at Arizona	13-16 . . . .at Chicago (AL)	2-4 . . . . Boston	20-22 . . . . .Toronto
3-5 . . . . .Minnesota	17-19 . . . . . . .Tampa Bay	5-7 . . . . . . .at Baltimore	24-25 . . . . at Tampa Bay
	20-23 . . . . Houston	8-11 . . . . at Toronto	27-29 . . . . .at Texas

GENERAL INFORMATION
Stadium (year opened): Yankee Stadium (2009). **Team Colors:** Navy blue and white.
Home Dugout: First Base. **Playing Surface:** Grass.

BASEBALL OPERATIONS

Senior VP/General Manager: Brian Cashman.
Senior VP/Assistant GM: Jean Afterman, Esq. **VP/Assistant GM:** Michael Fishman. **VP, Baseball Operations:** Tim Naehring. **Special Advisors:** Carlos Beltran, Reggie Jackson, Hideki Matsui, Andy Pettitte, Alex Rodriguez, Nick Swisher.

Director, Team Travel & Player Services: Ben Tuliebitz. **Director, Quantitative Analysis:** David Grabiner. **Director, Baseball Operations:** Matt Ferry. **Director, Mental Conditioning:** Chad Bohling. **Director, Advance Scouting:** Brett Weber. **Director, Baseball Systems:** Brian Nicosia. **Senior Web Developer:** Nick Eby. **Senior iOS Developer:** Michael Traverso. **Senior Analyst, Quantitative Analysis:** Christopher Fonnesbeck. **Analysts, Quantitative Analysis:** Theodore Feder, John Morris, Christopher Pang, Justin Sims, Sam Waters. **Database Engineer, Baseball Operations:** Jesse Bradford. **Nutritional Consultant:** Cynthia Sass.

Brian Cashman

MAJOR LEAGUE STAFF

Manager: Aaron Boone.
Coaches: Bench—Josh Bard, **Pitching**—Larry Rothschild, **Hitting**—Marcus Thames, **Assistant Hitting**—P.J. Pilittere, **First Base**—Reggie Willits, **Third Base**—Phil Nevin, **Catching**— Jason Brown, **Infield/Quality Control**— Carlos Mendoza, **Bullpen**—Mike Harkey, **Bullpen Catcher**—Radley Haddad.

MEDICAL/TRAINING

Team Physician, New York: Dr. Christopher Ahmad. **Head Team Internist:** Paul Lee, M.D., M.P.H. **Team Internist:** William Turner, M.D. **Senior Advisor, Orthopedics:** Stuart Hershon, M.D. **Head Athletic Trainer:** Steve Donohue. **Physical Therapist/Assistant Athletic Trainer:** Michael Schuk. **Assistant Athletic Trainer:** Tim Lentych. **Massage Therapist:** Doug Cecil. **Director, Strength/Conditioning:** Matthew Krause.

PLAYER DEVELOPMENT

Senior Director, Player Development: Kevin Reese.
Director, Player Development: Eric Schmitt. **Director, Minor League Operations:** Hadi Raad. **Director, Performance Science:** John Kremer. **Assistant Director, Player Development:** Stephen Swindal Jr. **Enterprise Solutions Engineer:** Rob Owens. **Field Coordinator:** Jody Reed. **Coordinator, Instruction:** Pat McMahon. **Hitting Coordinators:** Dillon Lawson, Edwar Gonzalez. **Pitching Coordinators:** Scott Aldred, Danny Borrell. **Catching Coordinator:** JD Closser. **Infield Coordinator:** Miguel Cairo. **Outfield/Baserunning/Bunting Coordinator:** Jose Javier. **Rehab Pitching Instructor:** Greg Pavlick. **Player Development Consultants:** Marc Bombard, Tino Martinez. **Manager, Pitch Development:** Desi Druschel. **Manager, International Operations:** Vic Roldan. **Medical Coordinator, Preventative and Performance Programs:** Mike Wickland. **Medical Coordinator:** Mark Littlefield. **Assistant Strength & Conditioning Coordinator:** Rigo Febles. **Strength & Rehab Coordinator:** Mike Kicia.

FARM SYSTEM

Class	Club (League)	Manager	Hitting Coach	Pitching Coach
Triple-A	Scranton/WB (IL)	Jay Bell	Phil Plantier	Tommy Phelps
Double-A	Trenton (EL)	Pat Osborn	Ty Hawkins	Tim Norton
High A	Tampa (FSL)	Aaron Holbert	Joe Migliaccio	Jose Rosado
Low A	Charleston (SAL)	Julio Mosquera	Greg Colbrunn	Gabe Luckert
Short-season	Staten Island (NYP)	David Adams	Ken Joyce	Travis Phelps
Rookie	Pulaski (APP)	Luis Dorante	Scott Seabol	Gerardo Casadiego
Rookie	Yankees West (GCL)	Nick Ortiz	Jake Hirst	Justin Pope
Rookie	Yankees East (GCL)	Dan Fiorito	TBD	Gabriel Tatis
Rookie	Yankees (DSL)	Caonabo Cosme	Aaron Leanhardt	Edwin Moreno

SCOUTING

Telephone: (813) 875-7569. **Fax:** (813) 873-2302.
VP, Domestic Scouting: Damon Oppenheimer. **Asst. Director, Domestic Scouting:** Ben McIntyre. **Director, Professional Scouting:** Dan Giese. **Asst. Director, Amateur Scouting—Analytics:** Scott Benecke. **Assistant Director, Pro Scouting:** Matt Daley. **National Crosscheckers:** Brian Barber, Tim Kelly, Steve Kmetko, Jeff Patterson, Mike Wagner. **Pitching Analyst, Amateur Scouting:** Scott Lovekamp. **Draft Medical Coordinator:** Justin Sharpe. **Pro Scouts:** Kendall Carter, Jay Darnell, Brad Del Barba, Marc DelPiano, Jonathan Diaz, Brandon Duckworth, Bill Emslie, Tyler Greene, Kevin Hart, Shawn Hill, Cory Melvin, Pat Murtaugh, James Stokes, JT Stotts, Alex Sunderland, Dennis Twombley, Donnie Veal, Aron Weston, Tom Wilson. **Special Assignment Scout:** Jim Hendry. **Area Scouts:** Troy Afenir, Tim Alexander, Chuck Bartlett, Denis Boucher, Andy Campbell, Jeff Deardorff, Bobby DeJardin, Mike Gibbons, Billy Godwin, Matt Hyde, David Keith, Steve Lemke, Mike Leuzinger, Ronnie Merrill, Darryl Monroe, Nick Ortiz, Bill Pintard, Cesar Presbott, Matt Ranson, Brian Rhees, Tyler Robertson, Kelly Rodman, Mike Thurman. **Director, International Scouting:** Donny Rowland. **Asst. Director, International Scouting:** Brady LaRuffa. **Asst. to Director, Latin America:** Edgar Mateo. **Crosscheckers, International Scouting:** Steve Wilson, Dennis Woody, Ricardo Finol. **Supervisor, Dominican Republic:** Juan Rosario. **Crosscheckers, Latin America:** Miguel Benitez, Victor Mata. **Supervisor, Venezuela:** Jose Gavidia. **Coordinator, Latin America:** Raymon Sanchez. **Video Coordinator, International Scouting:** Ethan Sander. **Video Assistant, Dominican Republic:** Luis Rodriguez. **Technology/Data Analyst:** Vianco Martinez. **Technology/Data Analyst, Venezuela:** Victor Deyan. **Amateur Research, Data Analysis:** Cary Broder. **International Scouts:** Doug Skiles, John Wadsworth, Borman Landaeta, Luis Sierra, Esdras Abreu, Luis Brito, R. Arturo Pena, Juan Piron, Jose Ravelo, Jose Sabino, Troy Williams, Rudy Gomez, Lee Sigman, Raul Gonzalez, Edgar Rodriguez, Carlos Levy, Chi Lee, Peng Pu Lee, Alan Atacho, Darwin Bracho, Roney Calderon, Cesar Suarez, Jesus Taico, Luis Tinoco.

OAKLAND ATHLETICS

Office Address: 7000 Coliseum Way, Oakland, CA 94621.
Telephone: (510) 638-4900. **Fax:** (510) 562-1633. **Website:** www.oaklandathletics.com.

OWNERSHIP

Managing Partner: John Fisher. **Chariman Emeritus:** Lew Wolff. **Board Members:** Sandy Dean, Bill Gurtin, Keith Wolff.

BUSINESS OPERATIONS

President: David Kaval. **Chief Operating Officer:** Chris Giles. **Executive Assistant:** Kai Glass. **General Counsel:** Neil Kraetsch. **Assistant General Counsel:** D'Lonra Ellis.

David Kaval

FINANCE/ADMINISTRATION

VP, Finance: Adam Buckfielder. **Senior Director, Finance:** Kasey Jarcik. **Director, Accounting** John Anki. **Payroll Manager:** Rose Dancil. **Senior Accountant, Accounts Payable:** Isabelle Mahaffey. **Accounting Manager:** Nick Cukar. **Senior Accountants:** Danna Mouat, Paul Basillo. **GL Accountant:** Stephen Curry. **Director, Human Resources:** Andre Chambers. **Human Resources Manager:** Elizabeth Espinoza. **Human Resources Assistant:** Katie Strehlow. **Vice President, Technology:** Vince Vengapally. **Senior Manager, IT:** David Frieberg. **Manager, Technology Innovation:** Dylan Webster.

SALES/MARKETING

VP, Marketing: Troy Smith. **Director, Marketing:** Travis LoDolce. **Marketing Coordinator:** Elizabeth Staub. **Marketing Manager:** Charlie Hunts. **Creative Director:** Ben Mayberry. **Creative Services Manager:** Mike Ono. **Team Photographer:** Michael Zagaris. **Senior Manager, Ballpark Events:** Heather Rajeski.

PUBLIC RELATIONS/COMMUNICATIONS

VP, Communications/Community: Catherine Aker. **Baseball Information Manager:** Mike Selleck. **Media Relations/Broadcasting Coordinator:** Mark Ling. **Director, Alumni/Family Relations:** Detra Paige. **Senior Coordinator, Alumni/Family Relations:** Melissa Guzman. **Senior Director, Engineering/Multimedia Services:** David Don. **Public Address Announcer:** Dick Callahan.

STADIUM OPERATIONS

VP, Stadium Operations: David Rinetti. **Senior Director, Stadium Operations:** Paul La Veau. **Senior Manager, Stadium Operations Events:** Kristy Ledbetter. **Stadium Services Manager:** Randy Duran. **Guest Services Manager:** Elisabeth Aydelotte. **Stadium Operations Manager:** Matt Van Norton. **Stadium Operations Coordinator:** Jason Silva. **Head Groundskeeper:** Clay Wood.

TICKET SALES/OPERATIONS/SERVICES

Director, Ticket Operations: David Adame. **Senior Director, Service/Retention:** Josh Ziegenbusch. **Ticket Operations Manager:** Austin Redman. **Box Office Coordinator:** Patricia Heagy.

2019 SCHEDULE

Standard Game Times: Mon.-Sat., 7:05 pm; Sun. 1:05 pm.

MARCH	7-9 . . . . Cincinnati	27-30 . at Los Angeles (AL)
20-21 . . . . Seattle	10-12 . . . . . . Cleveland	
28-31 . . . Los Angeles (AL)	13-14 . . . . .at Seattle	**JULY**
	16-19 . . . . . . .at Detroit	2-4 . . . . .Minnesota
APRIL	20-22 . . . . . .at Cleveland	5-7 . . . . .at Seattle
1-4 . . . . Boston	24-26 . . . . Seattle	12-14 . . . . . Chicago (AL)
5-7 . . . . .at Houston	27-29 . . . Los Angeles (AL)	16-17 . . . . Seattle
8-11 . . . . .at Baltimore	31 . . . . Houston	18-21 . . . . at Minnesota
12-14 . . . . .at Texas		22-24 . . . . . .at Houston
16-17 . . . . Houston	**JUNE**	25-28 . . . . Texas
19-21 . . . . .Toronto	1-2 . . . . Houston	30-31 . . . . . .Milwaukee
22-24 . . . . Texas	4-6 . . . at Los Angeles (AL)	
26-28 . . . . . . at Toronto	7-9 . . . . .at Texas	**AUGUST**
29-30 . . . . .at Boston	10-12 . . . . at Tampa Bay	1 . . . . .Milwaukee
	14-16 . . . . Seattle	3-4 . . . . St. Louis
MAY	17-19 . . . . . . Baltimore	5-7 . . . .at Chicago (NL)
1 . . . . .at Boston	20-23 . . . . . .Tampa Bay	9-11 . . . .at Chicago (AL)
3-5 . . . . at Pittsburgh	25-26 . . . . . .at St. Louis	13-14 . . . at San Francisco

15-18 . . . . Houston
20-22 . . . . .New York (AL)
24-25 . . . . San Francisco
26-29 . . . . .at Kansas City
30-31 . . . at New York (AL)
SEPTEMBER
1 . . . . . . at New York (AL)
3-5 . . . . .Los Angeles (AL)
6-8 . . . . Detroit
9-12 . . . . .at Houston
13-15 . . . . .at Texas
16-18 . . . . . . Kansas City
20-22 . . . . Texas
24-25 . at Los Angeles (AL)
26-29 . . . . .at Seattle

GENERAL INFORMATION

Stadium (year opened):
O.co Coliseum (1968).
Team Colors: Kelly green and gold.

Home Dugout: Third Base.
Playing Surface: Grass.

TRAVEL/CLUBHOUSE

Director, Team Travel: Mickey Morabito. **Equipment Manager:** Steve Vucinich. **Visiting Clubhouse Manager:** Mike Thalblum. **Assistant Equipment Manager:** Brian Davis. **Umpire/Clubhouse Assistant:** Matt Weiss. **Arizona Senior Facility Manager:** James Gibson. **Arizona Clubhouse Manager:** Chad Yaconetti.

BASEBALL OPERATIONS

Executive VP, Baseball Operations: Billy Beane.
General Manager: David Forst. **Assistant GM, Major League & International Operations:** Dan Feinstein. **Assistant GM:** Dan Kantrovitz. **Assistant GM/Director, Player Personnel:** Billy Owens. **Director, Baseball Systems:** Rob Naberhaus. **Special Assistants to GM:** Grady Fuson, Chris Pittaro. **Executive Assistant:** Betty Shinoda. **Director, Baseball Administration:** Pamela Pitts. **Video Coordinator:** Adam Rhoden. **Special Assistant to Baseball Operations:** Scott Hatteberg. **Research Scientist:** David Jackson-Hanen. **Baseball Operations Analyst:** Pike Goldschmidt. **Baseball Operations Analyst:** Ben Lowry.

Billy Beane

MAJOR LEAGUE STAFF

Manager: Bob Melvin.
Coaches: Bench—Ryan Christenson; **Pitching**— Scott Emerson; **Batting**—Darren Bush; **First Base**—Al Pedrique; **Third Base**—Matt Williams; **Bullpen**—Marcus Jensen; **Assistant Hitting Coach**— Mike Aldrete; **Quality Control Coach**—Mark Kotsay; **Bullpen Catcher**—Phil Pohl; **Bullpen Catcher**—Jeremy Dowdy.

MEDICAL/TRAINING

Head Athletic Trainer: Nick Paparesta. **Assistant Athletic Trainers:** Jeff Collins, Brian Schulman. **Strength/Conditioning Coach:** Josh Cuffe. **Asst. Strength/Conditioning Coach:** Terence Brannic. **Major League Massage Therapist:** Ozzie Lyles. **Team Physicians:** Dr. Allan Pont, Dr. Elliott Schwartz. **Team Orthopedist:** Dr. Jon Dickinson. **Associate Team Orthopedist:** Dr. Will Workman. **Arizona Team Physicians:** Dr. Fred Dicke, Dr. Doug Freedberg.

PLAYER DEVELOPMENT

Telephone: (510) 638-4900. **Fax:** (510) 563-2376.
Director, Player Development: Keith Lieppman. **Director, Minor League Operations:** Zak Basch. **Assistant Director of Player Development & Coordinator of On-Field Analytics:** Ed Sprague. **Coordinator, Player Development:** Nancy Moriuchi. **Coordinator, Minor League Merchandise & Equipment:** Thomas Miller. **Minor League Roving Instructors:** Juan Navarrete (infield), Steve Scarsone (infield), Gil Patterson (pitching), Jim Eppard (hitting). **Supervisor, Minor Leagues:** Rick Magnante. **Minor League Medical Coordinator:** Nate Brooks. **Coordinator, Medical Services:** Larry Davis. **Latin American Medical Coordinator:** Javier Alvidrez. **Minor League Strength/Conditioning Coordinator:** A.J. Seeliger. **Minor League Assistant Strength/Conditioning Coordinator:** Matt Rutledge. **Latin America Strength/Conditioning Coordinator:** J.D. Howell. **Special Instructor, Pitching/Rehabilitation:** Craig Lefferts. **Minor League Instructor:** Hiram Bocachica. **Minor League Rehabilitation Coordinator:** Travis Tims. **Manager, Minor League Technology & Development:** Ed Gitlick.

FARM SYSTEM

Class	Club (League)	Manager	Hitting Coach	Pitching Coach
Triple-A	Las Vegas (PCL)	Fran Riordan	Eric Martins	Rick Rodriguez
Double-A	Midland (TL)	Scott Steinmann	Tommy Everidge	Steve Connelly
High A	Stockton (CAL)	Webster Garrison	Brian McArn	Chris Smith
Low A	Beloit (MWL)	Lloyd Turner	Juan Dilone	Don Schulze
Short-season	Vermont (NYP)	Aaron Nieckula	Kevin Kouzmanoff	Carlos Chavez
Rookie	Athletics Grn (AZL)	Eddie Menchaca	Francisco Santana	Gabriel Ozuna
Rookie	Athletics Gld (AZL)	Hiram Bocachica	Ruben Escalera	Bryan Corey
Rookie	Athletics (DSL)	Carlos Casimiro	Rahdames Mota	David Brito

SCOUTING

Director, Scouting: Eric Kubota (Rocklin, CA). **Assistant Director, Scouting:** Sean Rooney (Apex, NC). **Scouting Coordinator:** Haley Alvarez (San Francisco, CA). **Scouting Assistant:** Greg Ledford (Oakland, CA). **West Coast Supervisor:** Scott Kidd (Folsom, CA). **Midwest Supervisor:** Mark Adair (University City, MO). **Midwest Supervisor:** Armann Brown (Austin, TX). **East Coast Supervisor:** Marc Sauer (Tampa, FL). **Pro Scouts:** Shooty Babitt (Richmond, CA), Jeff Bittiger (Saylorsburg, PA), Grant Brittain (Hickory, NC), Dan Freed (Lexington, IL), Trevor Ryan (San Jose, CA), Will Schock (Oakland, CA), Tom Thomas (Phoenix, AZ), Mike Ziegler (Orlando, FL). **Area Scouts:** Steve Abney (Lawrence, KS), Anthony Aliotti (Lake Forest, CA), Anthony Aloisi (Nashville, TN), Neil Avent (Charlotte, NC), Jim Coffman (Portland, OR), Steve Cohen (Spring, TX), Scott Cousins (Scottsdale, AZ), Ruben Escalera (Carolina, PR), Tripp Faulk (Richmond, VA), Julio Franco, (Weston, FL), Matt Higginson (Grimsby, ON), Derek Lee (Frankfort, IL), Kevin Mello (El Cerrito, CA), Kelcey Mucker (Denham Springs, LA), Chris Reilly (Rockwall, TX), Trevor Schaffer (Belleair, FL), Rich Sparks (Macomb, MI), Jemel Spearman (Cumming, GA), Dillon Tung (Los Angeles, CA), Ron Vaughn (Windsor, CT). **Special Assistant to Professional and International Scouting:** Steve Sharpe (Olathe, KS). **Director, Latin American Operations:** Raymond Abreu (Santo Domingo, DR). **International Scouts:** Yendri Bachelor (Dominican Republic), Ruben Barradas (Venezuela), Dan Brown (Australia), Juan Carlos De La Cruz (Dominican Republic), Angel Eusebio (Dominican Republic), Andri Garcia (Venezuela), Adam Hislop (Taiwan), Lewis Kim (South Korea), Wilfredo Magallanes (Dominican Republic), Juan Mosquera (Panama/Nicaragua), Argenis Paez (Venezuela), Tito Quintero (Colombia), Amaurys Reyes (Dominican Republic), Toshiyuki Tomizuka (Japan), Daniel Tovar (Venezuela), Oswaldo Troconis (Venezuela), Juan Carlos Villanueva (Venezuela).

PHILADELPHIA PHILLIES

Office Address: Citizens Bank Park, One Citizens Bank Way, Philadelphia, PA 19148.
Telephone: (215) 463-6000. **Website:** www.phillies.com.

OWNERSHIP
Operated By: The Phillies. **Managing Partner:** John Middleton. **President:** Andy MacPhail. **Chairman:** David Montgomery. **Chairman Emeritus:** Bill Giles.

BUSINESS OPERATIONS
VP/General Counsel: Rick Strouse. **VP, Administration:** Kathy Killian.
Director, Ballpark Enterprises/Business Development: Joe Giles.
Director, Human Resources/Benefits: JoAnn Marano.

BALLPARK OPERATIONS
Executive VP: David Buck. **VP, Business Affairs:** Howard Smith. **Director, Operations/Facility:** Mike DiMuzio. **Director, Operations/Events:** Eric Tobin. **Director, Operations/Security:** Sal DeAngelis. **Director, Field Operations:** Mike Boekholder. **Director, Landscaping & Site Work Operations:** Pam Hall. **PA Announcer:** Dan Baker. **Official Scorers:** Mark Gola, Mike Maconi, Dick Shute.

COMMUNICATIONS
Telephone: (215) 463-6000. **Fax:** (215) 389-3050
VP, Communications: Bonnie Clark. **Director, Communications:** Greg Casterioto.

David Montgomery

FINANCE
Sr. VP/CFO: John Nickolas. **Director, Payroll Services:** Karen Wright. **Director, Business Intelligence:** Josh Barbieri. **Director, Finance:** John Fetsick. **Director, Finance:** Shannon Snellman.

BROADCAST/VIDEO SERVICES
Director, Broadcasting/Video Services: Mark DiNardo. **Director, Video Production:** Dan Stephenson. **Director, Video Coaching Services:** Kevin Camiscioli. **Chief Technical Engineer:** Dave Abramson.

MARKETING/PROMOTIONS
VP, Partnership Sales and Corporate Marketing: Jackie Cuddeback. **VP, Marketing Programs/Events:** Kurt Funk. **VP, Marketing/New Media:** Michael Harris. **Manager, Client Services/Alumni Relations:** Debbie Nocito. **Director, Corporate Partnerships:** Rob MacPherson. **Director, Advertising Sales:** Brian Mahoney. **Director, Corporate Sales:** Scott Nickle. **Director, Marketing Services/Events:** James Trout. **Director, Entertainment:** Chris Long.

SALES/TICKETS
Telephone: (215) 463-1000. **Fax:** (215) 463-9878.
Sr. VP, Sales/Ticket Operations/Projects: John Weber. **Director, Ticket Technology/Development:** Chris Pohl.

2019 SCHEDULE
Standard Game Times: Mon.-Sat., 7:05 pm; Sun. 1:35 pm.

MARCH
28-31 . . . . Atlanta

APRIL
2-3 . . . . . . at Washington
5-7 . . . . Minnesota
8-10 . . . . . . Washington
12-14 . . . . . . at Miami
15-17 . . . . New York (NL)
18-21 . . . . . at Colorado
22-24 . . . at New York (NL)
25-28 . . . . Miami
30 . . . . Detroit

MAY
1 . . . . Detroit
3-5 . . . . Washington
6-8 . . . . at St. Louis

10-12 . . . . .at Kansas City
13-16 . . . . . . Milwaukee
17-19 . . . . Colorado
20-23 . . . .at Chicago (NL)
24-26 . . . . at Milwaukee
28-30 . . . . St. Louis
31 . . . at Los Angeles (NL)

JUNE
1-2 . . at Los Angeles (NL)
3-5 . . . . . . at San Diego
7-9 . . . . Cincinnati
10-12 . . . . Arizona
14-16 . . . . . . at Atlanta
17-20 . . . at Washington
21-23 . . . . Miami
24-27 . . . .New York (NL)

28-30 . . . . at Miami

JULY
2-4 . . . . at Atlanta
5-7 . . . . at New York (NL)
12-14 . . . . . . Washington
15-18 . . . Los Angeles (NL)
19-21 . . . . at Pittsburgh
23-24 . . . . . . .at Detroit
26-28 . . . . Atlanta
30-31 . . . . . San Francisco

AUGUST
1 . . . . San Francisco
2-4 . . . . . . Chicago (AL)
5-7 . . . . at Arizona
8-11 . . . . at San Francisco
13-15 . . . . . Chicago (NL)

16-18 . . . . . . San Diego
20-21 . . . . . . .at Boston
23-25 . . . . . . at Miami
26-28 . . . . . . Pittsburgh
30-31 . . . .New York (NL)

SEPTEMBER
1 . . . . .New York (NL)
2-5 . . . . . . .at Cincinnati
6-8 . . . . at New York (NL)
9-12 . . . . Atlanta
14-15 . . . . Boston
17-19 . . . . . . at Atlanta
20-22 . . . .at Cleveland
23-26 . . . . at Washington
27-29 . . . . Miami

GENERAL INFORMATION
Stadium (year opened): Citizens Bank Park (2004). **Team Colors:** Red, white and blue.
Home Dugout: First Base. **Playing Surface:** Natural Grass.

Director, Sales: Derek Schuster. **Director, Suite Sales/Client Services:** Kevin Beale. **Director, Group Sales:** Vanessa Mapson. **Director, Ticket Services/Intern Program:** Phil Feather. **Director, Season Ticket Services:** Mike Holdren. **Director, Premium Sales/Services:** Matt Kessler. **Director, Ticket Operations:** Ken Duffy.

TRAVEL/CLUBHOUSE

Manager, Visiting Clubhouse: Kevin Steinhour. **Manager, Clubhouse Services:** Phil Sheridan. **Manager, Equipment/Umpire Services:** Dan O'Rourke. **Coordinator, Team Travel:** Jameson Hall.

BASEBALL OPERATIONS

VP/General Manager: Matt Klentak. **Assistant GM:** Bryan Minniti. **Assistant GM:** Scott Proefrock. **Assistant GM:** Ned Rice. **Senior Advisors to the President/GM:** Pat Gillick. **Senior Advisors, GM:** Larry Bowa, Charlie Manuel. **Special Assistants, GM:** Bart Braun, Pete Mackanin, Jorge Velandia. **Director, International Scouting:** Sal Agostinelli. **Director, Amateur Scouting:** Johnny Almaraz. **Director, Baseball Research & Development:** Andy Galdi. **Director, Amateur Scouting Administration:** Rob Holiday. **Director, Player Development:** Josh Bonifay. **Director, Minor League Operations:** Lee McDaniel. **Director, Professional Scouting:** Mike Ondo.

MAJOR LEAGUE STAFF

Manager: Gabe Kapler. **Coaches: Bench**—Rob Thomson, **Pitching**—Chris Young, **Hitting**—John Mallee, **First Base**—Paco Figueroa, **Third Base**—Dusty Wathan, **Assistant Pitching**—Dave Lundquist, **Infield**—Bobby Dickerson, **Bullpen**—Jim Gott, **Bullpen Catcher/ Receiving**—Craig Driver, **Bullpen Catcher/Catching**—Bob Stumpo. **Manager, Advance Scouting:** Mike Calitri. **Major League Player Information Coordinator:** Sam Fuld.

Matt Klentak

MEDICAL/TRAINING

Director, Medical Services: Dr. Michael Ciccotti. **Head Athletic Trainer:** Scott Sheridan. **Assistant Athletic Trainers:** Shawn Fcasni, Chris Mudd. **Major League Strength & Conditioning Coach:** Paul Fournier. **Assistant Strength & Conditioning Coach:** Dong Lien.

PLAYER DEVELOPMENT

Director, Player Development: Josh Bonifay. **Director, Minor League Operations:** Lee McDaniel. **Special Assistant, Player Development:** Steve Noworyta. **Director, Florida Operations/GM, Clearwater Threshers:** John Timberlake. **Assistant Director, Minor League Operations/Florida:** Joe Cynar. **Assistant Director, International Operations:** Ray Robles. **Field Coordinator:** Chris Truby. **Outfield Coordinator:** Andy Abad. **Hitting Coordinator:** Jason Ochart. **Assistant Hitting:** Russ Steinhorn. **Director, Pitching Development:** Rafael Chaves. **Baserunning Coordinator:** Rob Ducey. **Roving Pitching Coach:** Carlos Arroyo. **Infield Coordinator:** Juan Castro. **Catching Coordinator:** Ernie Whitt. **Minor League Player Information Coordinator:** Ben Werthan. **Minor League Video Coordinator:** Josh Lipman. **Strength and Conditioning Coordinator:** Furey Leva. **Athletic Trainer/Rehab Coordinator:** Joe Rauch.

FARM SYSTEM

Class	Club (League)	Manager	Hitting Coach	Pitching Coach
Triple-A	Lehigh Valley (IL)	Gary Jones	Darryl Robinson	Steve Schrenk
Double-A	Reading (EL)	Shawn Williams	Kevin Riggs	Aaron Fultz
High A	Clearwater (FSL)	Marty Malloy	Tyler Henson	Brad Bergesen
Low A	Lakewood (SAL)	Unavailable	Christian Marrero	Matt Hockenberry
Short-season	Williamsport (NYP)	Pat Borders	Joel McKeithan	Hector Berrios
Rookie	Phillies West (GCL)	Milver Reyes	Chris Heintz	Bruce Billings
Rookie	Phillies East (GCL)	Roly deArmas	Rafael DeLima	Hector Mercado
Rookie	Phillies-1 (DSL)	Waner Santana	Samuel Hiciano	Alex Concepcion
Rookie	Phillies-2 (DSL)	Orlando Munoz	Homy Ovalles	Les Straker

SCOUTING

Director, Amateur Scouting: Johnny Almaraz. **Director, Amateur Scouting Administration:** Rob Holiday. **Assistant Director, Scouting:** Greg Schilz. **National Scouting Coordinators:** Bill Moore, Darrell Conner. **Regional Supervisors:** Shane Bowers, Buddy Hernandez, Brad Holland, Brian Kohlscheen, Stewart Smothers. **Area Scouts:** Alex Agostino, Connor Betbeze, Will Brunson, Joey Davis, Chris Duffy, Zach Friedman, Mike Garcia, Ralph Garr Jr., Aaron Jersild, Chris Knabenshue, Kellan McKeon, Timi Moni, Justin Morgenstern, Justin Munson, Demerius Pittman, Luis Raffan, Mike Stauffer, Jeff Zona Jr. **Director, International Scouting:** Sal Agostinelli. **International Coordinator:** Jesús Méndez. **Latin American Coordinator:** Carlos Salas. **International Scouts:** Rafael Alvarez (Venezuela), Roberto Aquino (Dominican Republic), Oneri Fleita (Mexico), Ubaldo Heredia (Latin America), Howard Norsetter (Pacific Rim), Norman Anciani (Panama), Alvaro Blanco (Colombia), Alex Choi (South Korea), Derrick Chung, Juan Feliciano de Castro (Dominican Republic), Franklin Felida (Dominican Republic), Elvis García (Venezuela), Luis García (Dominican Republic), Charlie Gastelum (Mexico), Gene Grimaldi (Antilles), Andrés Hiraldo (Dominican Republic), Dargello Lodowica (Curacao), William Mota (Venezuela), Isao O'Jimi (Japan), Romulo Oliveros (Venezuela), Bernardo Pérez (Dominican Republic), Philip Riccobono (Korea), Franklin Rojas (Venezuela), Claudio Scerrato, Ebert Velásquez, Youngster Wang. **Special Assignment Scouts:** Craig Colbert, Howie Freiling, Dave Hollins, Charley Kerfeld, Mike Koplove, Terry Ryan, Dan Wright. **Director, Professional Scouting:** Mike Ondo. **Professional Scouts:** Erick Dalton, Todd Donovan, Jeff Harris, Steve Jongewaard, Jesse Levis, Jon Mercurio, Roy Tanner.

PITTSBURGH PIRATES

Office Address: PNC Park at North Shore, 115 Federal St., Pittsburgh, PA, 15212.
Mailing Address: PO Box 7000, Pittsburgh, PA 15212.
Telephone: (412) 323-5000. **Fax:** (412) 325-4412.
Website: www.pirates.com. **Twitter:** @Pirates.

OWNERSHIP
Chairman of the Board: Robert Nutting.
Board of Directors: Donald Beaver, Eric Mauck, G. Ogden Nutting, Robert Nutting, William Nutting, Duane Wittman.

BUSINESS OPERATIONS
President: Frank Coonelly. **Executive Vice President & Chief Financial Officer:** Jim Plake.
Senior VP, Business Affairs/General Counsel: Bryan Stroh.

COMMUNICATIONS
VP, Communications/Broadcasting: Brian Warecki. **Director, Baseball Communications:**
Jim Trdinich. **Director, Broadcasting:** Marc Garda. **Director, Media Relations:** Dan Hart.
Manager, Business Communications/Social Media: Terry Rodgers.

Frank Coonelly

COMMUNITY RELATIONS
Senior VP, Community/Public Affairs: Patty Salerno. **Director, Pirates Charities:** Jackie
Hunter. **Manager, Youth Baseball Initiatives:** Chris Ganter.

MARKETING/CORPORATE SPONSORSHIPS
Senior Vice President, Revenue: Brian Colbert. **Senior Director, Marketing/Advertising:**
Brian Chiera. **Director, Alumni Affairs/Promotions/Licensing:** Joe Billetdeaux. **Director,
Advertising/Creative Services:** Kiley Cauvel. **Director, Special Events:** Christine Serkoch. **Director, PNC Park Events:**
Ann Elder. **Manager, Advertising/Digital Marketing:** Haley Artayet. **Manager, Special Events:** Jason Koval. **Manager,
Promotions/Licensing/Authentics:** Megan Vizzini. **Manager, Entertainment Media:** Paul Denillo. **Manager, Game
Presentation:** Jon Cofer. **Manager, Corporate Partnerships:** Chris Stevens. **Manager, Client Services:** Brittany Hudzik.
Senior Account Manager, Corporate Partnerships: Dave Shinsky.

STADIUM OPERATIONS
Executive VP/General Manager, PNC Park/Facilities: Dennis DaPra. **Vice President, Ballpark Operations:** Chris
Hunter. **Senior Director, Florida Operations:** Jeff Podobnik. **Director, Field Operations:** Matt Brown. **Director,
Guest Experience:** Chuck Miller. **Manager, Cleaning Operations:** Sissy Burkhart. **Manager, Ballpark Operations:** J.J.
McGraw.

2019 SCHEDULE
Standard Game Times: Mon.-Sat., 7:05 pm; Sun.,1:35 pm.

MARCH			
28-31 . . . . . .at Cincinnati	7-8. . . . . Texas	25-27 . . . . . .at Houston	12-14 . at Los Angeles (AL)
	9-12. . . . . . . .at St. Louis	28-30 . . . . . at Milwaukee	16-18 . . . . . Chicago (NL)
APRIL	13-15 . . . . at Arizona		19-22 . . . . . . Washington
1-3. . . . . St. Louis	16-19 . . . . . at San Diego	**JULY**	23-25 . . . . Cincinnati
4-7. . . . . Cincinnati	21-23 . . . . .Colorado	1-4. . . . . . . Chicago (NL)	26-28 . . . . at Philadelphia
8-11 . . . .at Chicago (NL)	24-26 . . . Los Angeles (NL)	5-7. . . . . .Milwaukee	29-31 . . . . . . at Colorado
12-14 . . . . at Washington	27-29 . . . . . .at Cincinnati	12-14 . . .at Chicago (NL)	
16-17 . . . . . . .at Detroit	30-31 . . . . .Milwaukee	15-17 . . . . . . .at St. Louis	**SEPTEMBER**
19-21 . . .San Francisco		19-21 . . . .Philadelphia	1 . . . . at Colorado
22-25 . . . . .Arizona	**JUNE**	22-25 . . . . St. Louis	3-5. . . . . .Miami
26-28 . at Los Angeles (NL)	1-2. . . . . .Milwaukee	26-28 . . at New York (NL)	6-8. . . . . St. Louis
30 . . . . .at Texas	4-6. . . . . Atlanta	29-31 . . . . .at Cincinnati	9-12 . . . . at San Francisco
	7-9. . . . . . at Milwaukee		13-15 . . . .at Chicago (NL)
MAY	10-13 . . . . . at Atlanta	**AUGUST**	17-19 . . . . Seattle
1 . . . . .at Texas	14-16 . . . . at Miami	2-4. . . . . . .New York (NL)	20-22 . . . . at Milwaukee
3-5. . . . . Oakland	18-19 . . . . Detroit	5-7. . . . . .Milwaukee	24-26 . . . . . Chicago (NL)
	21-23 . . . . . . San Diego	9-11 . . . . . . .at St. Louis	27-29 . . . . Cincinnati

GENERAL INFORMATION
Stadium (year opened):
PNC Park (2001).
Team Colors: Black and gold.

Home Dugout: Third Base.
Playing Surface: Grass.

BASEBALL OPERATIONS

Executive VP/General Manager: Neal Huntington. **VP, Assistant General Manager:** Kyle Stark. **Assistant GM:** Kevan Graves. **Special Assistants to GM:** Ron Hopkins, Sean McNally, Matt Ruebel, Jax Robertson, Greg Smith, Doug Strange. **Special Assistants to Baseball Operations:** Jeff Banister, Jamey Carroll (Defensive Coordinator), David Eckstein, Scott Elarton, Grady Little, Kevin Young (Offensive Coordinator). **Senior Advisor, Baseball Operations:** Nick Leyva. **Director, Personnel:** Dr. Chris Johnson. **Senior Director, Baseball Informatics:** Dan Fox. **Director, Baseball Operations:** Will Lawton. **Baseball Operations Assistant:** Trey Rose. **Assistant Director, Baseball Informatics:** Andrew Gibson. **Senior Quantitative Analyst:** Joe Douglas. **Quantitative Analyst:** Justin Newman. **Data Architect:** Matt Reiersgaard. **Senior Developer, Baseball Informatics:** Brian Hulick. **Director, Cultural Initiatives:** Hector Morales. **Special Assistant to GM/Cultural Initiatives:** Mike Gonzalez. **Video Coordinator:** Kevin Roach. **Major League Advance Coordinator, Baseball Informatics:** Aaron Razum. **Major League Assistant:** Tim McKeithan.

Neal Huntington

MAJOR LEAGUE STAFF

Manager: Clint Hurdle. **Coaches: Bench**—Tom Prince, **Coach**—Dave Jauss, **Pitching**—Ray Searage, **Assistant Pitching**—Justin Meccage, **Hitting**—Rick Eckstein, **Assistant Hitting**—Jacob Cruz, **First Base**—Kimera Bartee, **Third Base**—Joey Cora, **Bullpen**—Euclides Rojas. **Bullpen Catchers:** Herberto Andrade, Jordan Comadena.

MEDICAL/TRAINING

Medical Director: Dr. Patrick DeMeo. **Team Physicians:** Dr. Darren Frank, Dr. Dennis Phillips, Dr. Michael Scarpone, Dr. Robert Schilken, Dr. Edward Snell. **Director of Sports Medicine:** Todd Tomczyk. **Head Major League Athletic Trainer:** Brian Housand. **Assistant Major League Athletic Trainer:** Ben Potenziano. **Major League Strength/Conditioning Coach:** Jim Malone. **Physical Therapist:** Kevin "Otis" Fitzgerald. **Physical Therapist:** Seth Steinhauer. **Sports Science Coordinator:** Brendon Huttmann.

PLAYER DEVELOPMENT

Senior Director, Minor League Operations: Larry Broadway. **Assistant Director, Minor League Operations:** Brian Selman. **Coordinator, Minor League Operations:** TJ Large. **Senior Field Coordinator:** Brad Fischer. **Field Coordinator:** Bobby Scales. **Coordinator of Instruction:** Dave Turgeon. **Senior Pitching Coordinator:** Scott Mitchell. **Assistant Pitching Coordinator:** Tom Filer. **Rehab Pitching Coach:** Matt Ford. **Roving Infield Coordinator:** Gary Green. **Assistant Hitting Coordinator & Minor League Manager:** Drew Saylor. **Minor League Video Coordinator:** Ryan Gaynor. **Minor League Equipment Manager:** Pat Hagerty. **Medical Services Coordinator:** Carl Randolph. **Senior Coordinator, Rehab/Athlete Development:** AJ Patrick. **Strength & Conditioning Coordinator:** Joe Hughes. **Director, Mental Conditioning:** Bernie Holliday. **Mental Conditioning Coordinator:** Tyson Holt. **EAP/Coordinator, Personal/Professional Development:** Jon Hammermeister. **Nutritionist:** Allison Mauer. **Senior Advisor, Latin American Operations:** Luis Silverio. **Senior Advisor, Player Development:** Woody Huyke, Mike Lum. **Latin American Field Coordinator:** Mendy Lopez. **Latin American Pitching Coordinator:** Amaury Telemaco. **Senior Advisor, DSL:** Cecilio Beltre. **Education Coordinator:** Mayu Fielding.

FARM SYSTEM

Class	Club (League)	Manager	Hitting Coach	Pitching Coach
Triple-A	Indianapolis (IL)	Brian Esposito	Ryan Long	Brian Hickerson
Double-A	Altoona (EL)	Michael Ryan	Jon Nunnally	Joel Hanrahan
High A	Bradenton (FSL)	Wyatt Toregas	Butch Wynegar	Drew Benes
Low A	Greensboro (SAL)	Miguel Perez	Chris Peterson	Stan Kyles
Short-season	West Virginia (NYP)	Drew Saylor	Jonathan Tucker	Tom Filer
Rookie	Bristol (APP)	Kieran Mattison	Jonathan Preito	Eric Marshall
Rookie	Pirates (GCL)	Gera Alvarez	Kory DeHaan	Fernando Nieve
Rookie	Pirates 1 (DSL)	Stephen Morales	Luis Borges	Randor Bierd
Rookie	Pirates 2 (DSL)	Shawn Bowman	Julio Bruno	Yorman Bazzardo

SCOUTING

Fax: (412) 325-4414. **Senior Director, Amateur Scouting:** Joe DelliCarri. **Assistant Director, Amateur Scouting:** Mike Mangan. **Coordinator, Amateur Scouting:** Matt Skirving. **National Supervisors:** Jack Bowen (Bethel Park, PA), Jimmy Lester (Columbus, GA). **Regional Supervisors:** Jesse Flores (Sacramento, CA), Trevor Haley (Temperance, MI), Sean Heffernan (Florence, SC). **Area Supervisors:** Rick Allen (Moorpark, CA), Matt Bimeal (Olathe, KS), Adam Bourassa (Cincinnati, OH), Eddie Charles (Auburn, NY), Phil Huttmann, (McKinney, TX), Jerry Jordan (Kingsport, TN), Wayne Mathis (Cuero, TX), Darren Mazeroski (Panama City Beach, FL), Cam Murphy (Seattle, WA), Nick Presto (Palm Beach Gardens, FL), Dan Radcliff (Palmyra, VA), Mike Sansoe (Fairfield, CA), Matt Taylor (Atlanta, GA), Brian Tracy (Yorba Linda, CA), Derrick Van Dusen (Phoenix, AZ), Anthony Wycklendt (Oak Creek, WI). **Director, Pro Scouting:** Steve Williams. **Major League Scouts:** Mike Basso, Ricky Bennett, Jim Dedrick, Bob Minor. **Pro Scouts:** Carlos Berroa, Rodney Henderson, Andrew Lorraine, Alvin Rittman, Everett Russell, Gary Varsho. **Scouting Assistants:** John Birkbeck, Joe Hutlzen. **Director, International Scouting:** Junior Vizcaino. **Assistant Director, International Scouting:** Max Kwan. **Coordinator of International Operations:** Matt Benedict. **International Supervisors:** Emilio Carrasquel (Venezuela); Raul Lopez (Mexico); Tony Harris (International/Australia); Fu-Chun Chiang (Far East); Tom Gillespie (Europe/Africa); Orlando Covo (Central & South America/Colombia). **International Scouts:** Esteban Alvarez, Emmanuel Gomez, Daury Nin, Victor Santana, Cristino Valdez (Dominican Republic); Victor Alvarez, Pedro Avila, Omar Gonzalez, Jesus Morelli, Jessie Nava, Saul Torres (Venezuela); Roberto Saucedo (Mexico); Marcos Guimaraes (Brasil); Eugene Helder (Aruba); Jose Mosquera, Robinson Ortega, Cristobal Santoya (Columbia); Mark Van Zanten (Curacao); Jose Pineda (Panama); Oleg Boyko, Christian Dresel (Europe).

ST. LOUIS CARDINALS

Office Address: 700 Clark Street, St. Louis MO 63102.
Telephone: (314) 345-9600. **Fax:** (314) 345-9523. **Website:** www.cardinals.com.

OWNERSHIP

Operated By: St. Louis Cardinals, LLC. **Chairman/Chief Executive Officer:** William DeWitt, Jr. **President:** Bill DeWitt III. **Senior Administrative Assistant to Chairman:** Grace Kell. **Senior Administrative Assistant to President:** Julie Laningham. **Sr. VP & General Counsel:** Mike Whittle. **Associate Counsel:** Nick Garzia. **VP, Business Development:** Dan Good.

BUSINESS OPERATIONS

FINANCE

Fax: (314) 345-9520.
Senior VP/Chief Financial Officer: Brad Wood. **Director, Risk Management:** Rex Carter. **Director, Human Resources:** Ann Seeney. **VP, Event Services/Merchandising:** Vicki Bryant.

MARKETING/SALES/COMMUNITY RELATIONS

Fax: (314) 345-9529.
Senior VP, Sales & Marketing: Dan Farrell. **Administrative Assistant, VP, Sales & Marketing:** Gail Ruhling. **VP, Corporate Sales, Marketing & Stadium Entertainment:** Thane Van Breusegen. **Director, Scoreboard, Productions & Fan Entertainment, Senior Account Executive:** Tony Simokaitis. **Director, Publications:** Steve Zesch. **VP, Community Relations & Executive Director, Cardinals Care:** Michael Hall. **Administrative Assistant:** Bonnie Parres.

Bill DeWitt III

COMMUNICATIONS

Fax: (314) 345-9530.
Director, Communications: Brian Bartow. **Director, Multimedia Communications:** Jill Falk. **Manager, Baseball Communications:** Michael Whitty. **Administrator, Baseball Information & Media Services:** Chris Tunno. **Spanish Interpreter:** Carlos Villoria. **PA Announcer:** John Ulett. **Official Scorers:** Gary Muller, Jeff Durbin, Mike Smith.

STADIUM OPERATIONS

Fax: (314) 345-9535.
VP, Stadium Operations: Matt Gifford. **VP, Facility Planning & Engineering:** Joe Abernathy. **Administrative Assistant:** Hope Baker. **Director, Security:** Philip Melcher. **Director Facility, Security & Stadium Operations:** Hosei Maruyama. **Head Groundskeeper:** Bill Findley.

TICKETING

Fax: (314) 345-9522.
VP, Ticket Sales/Service: Joe Strohm. **Director, Ticket Sales & Marketing:** Martin Coco. **Director, Ticket Sales & Retention:** Rob Fasoldt. **Director, Ticket Operations:** Kerry Emerson.

2019 SCHEDULE

Standard Game Times: Mon.-Sat., 7:15 pm; Sun., 1:15 pm.

MARCH
28-31 . . . . . at Milwaukee

APRIL
1-3 . . . . at Pittsburgh
4-7 . . . . San Diego
8-11 . . . Los Angeles (NL)
13-14 . . . . . at Cincinnati
15-17 . . . . . at Milwaukee
19-21 . . . . . New York (NL)
22-24 . . . . Milwaukee
26-28 . . . . . . Cincinnati
29-30 . . . . at Washington

MAY
1-2 . . . . . at Washington
3-5 . . . . . at Chicago (NL)
6-8 . . . . Philadelphia

9-12 . . . . Pittsburgh
14-16 . . . . . . at Atlanta
17-19 . . . . at Texas
21-22 . . . . . Kansas City
24-26 . . . . Atlanta
28-30 . . . . at Philadelphia
31 . . . . Chicago (NL)

JUNE
1-2 . . . . . . Chicago (NL)
4-6 . . . . Cincinnati
7-9 . . . . . at Chicago (NL)
10-12 . . . . at Miami
13-16 . . . at New York (NL)
17-20 . . . . Miami
21-23 . . . Los Angeles (AL)
25-26 . . . . Oakland

28-30 . . . . . at San Diego

JULY
2-4 . . . . at Seattle
5-7 . . . . . at San Francisco
12-14 . . . . Arizona
15-17 . . . . . . Pittsburgh
18-21 . . . . . at Cincinnati
22-25 . . . . at Pittsburgh
26-28 . . . . Houston
30-31 . . . . . Chicago (NL)

AUGUST
1 . . . . Chicago (NL)
3-4 . . . . at Oakland
5-7 . . . at Los Angeles (NL)
9-11 . . . . Pittsburgh
13-14 . . . . at Kansas City

15-18 . . . . . at Cincinnati
19-21 . . . . . . Milwaukee
22-25 . . . . Colorado
26-28 . . . . at Milwaukee
30-31 . . . . . . Cincinnati

SEPTEMBER
1 . . . . Cincinnati
2-5 . . . . . . San Francisco
6-8 . . . . . . at Pittsburgh
10-12 . . . at Colorado
13-15 . . . . . . Milwaukee
16-18 . . . . . Washington
19-22 . . . at Chicago (NL)
23-25 . . . . . . at Arizona
27-29 . . . . . Chicago (NL)

GENERAL INFORMATION

Stadium (year opened): Busch Stadium (2006).
Team Colors: Red and white.
Home Dugout: First Base.
Playing Surface: Grass.

TRAVEL/CLUBHOUSE
Fax: (314) 345-9523.
Traveling Secretary: Ernie Moore. **Equipment Manager:** Mark Walsh. **Visiting Clubhouse Manager:** Rip Rowan.
Video Coordinator: Chad Blair.

BASEBALL OPERATIONS

John Mozeliak

President of Baseball Operations: John Mozeliak. **Vice President & General Manager:** Michael Girsch. **Senior Executive Assistant to the President of Baseball Operations:** Linda Brauer. **Assistant GM:** Moises Rodriguez. **Assistant GM & Director of Scouting:** Randy Flores. **Senior Special Assistant to GM:** Bob Gebhard. **Special Assistant to GM:** Ryan Franklin. **Special Assistant to GM, Player Procurement:** Matt Slater. **Director, Baseball Administration:** John Vuch. **Director, Baseball Development:** Dane Sorensen. **Director, Baseball Analytics & Systems:** Jeremy Cohen. **Director, Major League Administration:** Judy Carpenter-Barada. **Manager, Player Communications:** Melody Yount. **Manager, Baseball Systems:** Patrick Casanta. **Senior Developer:** Brian Seyfert. **Baseball Operations Analyst, Player Development & Performance:** Emily Wiebe. **Baseball Development Analysts:** Kevin Seats, Javier Duren, Julia Prusaczyk. **Baseball Analyst:** Garrett Greenwood.

MAJOR LEAGUE STAFF
Telephone: (314) 345-9600.
Manager: Mike Shildt. **Coaches: Bench**—Oliver Marmol. **Pitching**—Mike Maddux. **Hitting**—Jeff Albert. **Assistant Hitting Coach**—Mark Budaska. **First Base**—Richard "Stubby" Clapp. **Third Base**—Ron "Pop" Warner. **Bullpen**—Bryan Eversgerd. **Assistant Coach:** Willie McGee. **Pitching Specialist:** Chris Carpenter. **Bullpen Catchers**—Jamie Pogue, Kleininger Teran.

MEDICAL/TRAINING
Head Orthopedist Surgeon: Dr. George Paletta. **Coordinator of Medical Services & Team Physician:** Brian Mahaffey. **Director of Medical Operations:** Adam Olsen. **Director of Performance:** Robert Butler. **Assistant Athletic Trainers:** Jeremy Clipperton, Chris Conroy. **Assistant Director, Performance:** Thomas Knox. **Performance Specialist & Physical Therapist:** Jason Shutt. **Strength & Conditioning Coach:** Lance Thomason.

PLAYER DEVELOPMENT
Director, Player Development: Gary LaRocque. **Administrator Minor League Operations:** Tony Ferreira. **Minor League Equipment Manager:** Dave Vondarhaar. **Field Coordinator:** Mark DeJohn. **Assistant Field Coordinator:** Chris Swauger. **Coordinators:** Jose Leger (Latin America Field & Academy Development), Tim Leveque (senior pitching), George Greer (offensive strategist), Randy Niemann (pitching), Jose Oquendo (roving), Johnny Rodriguez (infield), Tony Cruz (catching), Ryan Ludwick (hitting), Jason Isringhausen (pitching), Barry Weinberg (medical advisor), Keith Joynt (medical coordinator, player development), Matt Leonard (rehab coordinator), Aaron Rhodes (strength & conditioning), DC MacLea (performance speacialist), Victor Kuri (assistant rehab coordinator).

FARM SYSTEM

Class	Club (League)	Manager	Hitting Coach	Pitching Coach
Triple-A	Memphis (PCL)	Ben Johnson	Jobel Jimenez	Dernier Orozco
Double-A	Springfield (TL)	Joe Kruzel	Brandon Allen	Darwin Marrero
High A	Palm Beach (FSL)	Dann Bilardello	Tyger Pederson	Will Ohman
Low A	Peoria (MWL)	Erick Almonte	Russ Chambliss	Cale Johnson
Short-season	State College (NYP)	Jose Leon	Cody Gabella	Adrian Martin
Rookie	Johnson City (APP)	Roberto Espinoza	Brian Burgamy	Rick Harig
Rookie	Cardinals (GCL)	Joshua Lopez	Joe Hawkins	Giovanni Carrara
Rookie	Cardinals 1 (DSL)	John Matos	Nabo Martinez	Renee Cortez
Rookie	Cardinals 2 (DSL)	Fray Peniche	Ismael Castro	Billy Villanueva

SCOUTING
Fax: (314) 345-9519.
Assistant General Manager & Director of Scouting: Randy Flores. **Manager, Pro Scouting:** Jared Odom. **Manager, Scouting Analytics:** Matt Bayer. **Amateur Scouting Coordinator/Analyst:** Tyler Hadzinsky. **Special Assistant to Amateur Scouting:** Mike Roberts. **Special Advisor to the Scouting Director:** Jamal Strong. **Professional Scouts:** Chris Bourjos (Scottsdale, AZ), Brian Hopkins (Holly Springs, NC), Jeff Ishii (Chino, CA), Aaron Klinic (Baltimore, MD), Deric McKamey (Cincinnati, OH), Ricky Meinhold (Springfield, MO), Craig Richmond (Tampa, FL) Joe Rigoli (Parsippany, NJ), Kerry Robinson (Ballwin, MO). **National Crosscheckers:** Aaron Looper (Shawnee, OK), Sean Moran (Doylestown, PA). **Regional Crosscheckers:** Dominic "Ty" Boyles (Dallas, TX), Aaron Krawiec (Gilbert, AZ), Zach Mortimer (Pilesgrove, NJ), Kevin Saucier (Pensacola, FL). **Area Scouts:** Clint Brown (Tuscaloosa, AL), Jason Bryans (Tecumseh, ON), TC Calhoun (Abingdon, VA), Mike Dibiase (Tampa, FL), Jim Foster (St. Louis, MO), Mike Garciaparra (Manhattan Beach, CA), Dirk Kinney (Lenexa, KS), Tom Lipari (Aubrey, TX), Jim Negrych (Phoenixville, PA), Charles Peterson (Columbia, SC), Stacey Pettis (Brentwood, CA), Chris Rodriguez (Vancouver, WA), Mauricio Rubio (Tempe, AZ), Nathan Sopena (Cary, IL), Eli Tupuola (San Diego, CA). **Video Scout:** Patrick Elkins (Olathe, KS). **Part-Time Scouts:** Jim Foster (St. Louis, MO), Karl Sakuda (Honolulu, HI), Juan Ramos (Carolina, PR). **Director, International Operations & Administration:** Luis Morales. **Coordinator, International Operations:** Joseph Quezada. **Senior International Crosschecker:** Joe Almaraz. **International Scouts:** Filberto Fernandez, Raymi Dicent, Braly Guzman, Angel Ovalles, Alix Martinez (Dominican Republic); Johan Acevedo, Adel Granadillo, Jesus Perez , Estuar Ruiz (Venezuela); Ramon Garcia (Mexico); Carlos Balcazar (Colombia); Damaso Espino (Panama); Nahim Attaf (Curacao).

SAN DIEGO PADRES

Office Address: Petco Park, 100 Park Blvd, San Diego, CA 92101.
Mailing Address: PO Box 122000, San Diego, CA 92112. **Telephone:** (619) 795-5000.
E-mail address: comments@padres.com. **Website:** www.padres.com. **Twitter:** @padres.
Facebook: www.facebook.com/padres. **Instagram:** www.instagram.com/padres

OWNERSHIP

Operated By: Padres LP. **Executive Chairman:** Ron Fowler. **Managing Partner:** Peter Seidler. **Special Advisor to the Executive Chariman:** Bill Johnston.

BUSINESS OPERATIONS

President, Business Operations: Erik Greupner. **Senior VP, Chief Financial Officer:** Ronda Sedillo. **Vice President, Information Technology:** Ray Chan. **Sr. Director, Human Resources:** Sara Greenspan. **Director, Accounting:** Chris James.

Ron Fowler

LEGAL

Senior Vice President/General Counsel: Caroline Perry. **Associate General Counsel/ Baseball Operations Compliance Officer:** Stephanie Wilka.

COMMUNITY RELATIONS/MILITARY AFFAIRS

Telephone: (619) 795-5265. **Fax:** (619) 795-5266. **Senior VP, Community/Military Affairs:** Tom Seidler. **Military Affairs Advisor:** J.J. Quinn. **Director, Public Affairs:** Diana Puetz.

ENTERTAINMENT/MARKETING/COMMUNICATIONS/CREATIVE SERVICES

Sr. VP/Chief Marketing Officer: Wayne Partello. **Director, Communications:** Craig Hughner. **Director, Content:** Nicky Patriarca. **Sr. Director, Entertainment/Broadcasting/Archives:** Erik Meyer. **VP, Marketing:** Katie Jackson. **Director, Creative Services:** Brendan Nieto.

BALLPARK OPERATIONS/HOSPITALITY

VP, Ballpark Operations/GM, Petco Park: Mark Guglielmo. **VP/Chief Hospitality Officer:** Scott Marshall. **Senior Director, Security/Transportation:** Len Davey. **Senior Director, Event Operations:** Ken Kawachi. **Director, Field Operations:** Matt Balough. **Director, Guest Experience:** Erin Sheehan. **Official Scorers:** Jack Murray, Bill Zavestoski.

TICKETING

Telephone: (619) 795-5500. **Fax:** (619) 795-5034. **Senior VP, Corporate Partnerships:** Sergio Del Prado. **Senior Director, Ticket Sales:** Curt Waugh. **Director, Group Tickets/Hospitality:** Matt Clark. **Director, Membership Services:** Sindi Edelstein. **Director, Partnership Services:** Eddie Quinn. **Director, Ticket Operations:** Jim Kiersnowski. **Director, Petco Parks Events:** Kristie Ewing, Allie Asuncion.

TRAVEL/CLUBHOUSE

Director, Player & Staff Services: T.J. Lasita. **Manager, Equipment & Clubhouse:** Spencer Dallin. **Assistant Equipment Manager/Umpire Room Attendant:** Tony Petricca. **Visiting Clubhouse Manager:** TJ Laidlaw.

2019 SCHEDULE

Standard Game Times: Mon.-Fri., 7:10 pm; Sat., 5:40 pm; Sun,. 1:40 pm.

MARCH
28-31 . . . . . San Francisco

APRIL
1-3 . . . . Arizona
4-7 . . . . at St. Louis
8-10 . . . . at San Francisco
11-14 . . . . at Arizona
15-16 . . . . Colorado
18-21 . . . . Cincinnati
23-24 . . . . Seattle
26-28 . . . . at Washington
29-30 . . . . at Atlanta

MAY
1-2 . . . . at Atlanta
3-5 . . . . Los Angeles (NL)

6-8 . . . . . . New York (NL)
10-12 . . . . . . at Colorado
14-15 . at Los Angeles (NL)
16-19 . . . . . . Pittsburgh
20-22 . . . . Arizona
24-26 . . . . . . at Toronto
27-29 . . . at New York (AL)
31 . . . . Miami

JUNE
1-2 . . . . Miami
3-5 . . . . Philadelphia
6-9 . . . . Washington
11-12 . . . at San Francisco
13-16 . . . . . . at Colorado
17-19 . . . . . . Milwaukee
21-23 . . . . at Pittsburgh

25-26 . . . . . . at Baltimore
28-30 . . . . St. Louis

JULY
1-3 . . . . . . San Francisco
4-7 . . at Los Angeles (NL)
12-14 . . . . Atlanta
16-18 . . . . at Miami
19-21 . . .at Chicago (NL)
23-25 . . . at New York (NL)
26-28 . . . . . San Francisco
29-30 . . . . Baltimore

AUGUST
1-4 . . . at Los Angeles (NL)
6-7 . . . . .at Seattle
8-11 . . . . Colorado

12-14 . . . . Tampa Bay
16-18 . . . . at Philadelphia
19-21 . . . . . .at Cincinnati
23-25 . . . . Boston
26-28 . . . Los Angeles (NL)
29-31 . . . at San Francisco

SEPTEMBER
1 . . . . . . at San Francisco
2-4 . . . . at Arizona
6-8 . . . . Colorado
9-12 . . . . . Chicago (NL)
13-15 . . . . . at Colorado
16-19 . . . . at Milwaukee
20-22 . . . . Arizona
24-26 . . . Los Angeles (NL)
27-29 . . . . at Arizona

GENERAL INFORMATION

Stadium (year opened):
Petco Park (2004).
Team Colors: Padres Blue and White

Home Dugout: First Base.
Playing Surface: Grass.

BASEBALL OPERATIONS

A.J. Preller

Telephone: (619) 795-5077. **Fax:** (619) 795-5361.

Executive VP/General Manager: A.J. Preller. **VP/Assistant GM:** Fred Uhlman Jr. **Senior Advisor/Director, Player Personnel:** Logan White. **Assistant GM:** Josh Stein. **Special Assistant to the GM:** James Keller. **Director, Baseball Operations:** Nick Ennis. **Director, Baseball Information Systems:** Matt Klotsche. **Director, Player Staff and Services:** TJ Lastia. **Director, Player Health and Performance:** Don Tricker.. **Special Assistant, Scouting:** David Post. **Director, Baseball Systems:** Wells Oliver. **Developer, Baseball Systems:** Garret Doe. **Director, Baseball Research & Development:** Adam Esquer. **Analyst, Baseball Research and Development:** Nathan Landau. **Manager, Baseball Administration:** Michaelene Courtis. **Senior Analyst:** Dave Cameron. **Assistant Director, Baseball Operations:** David Longley. **Coordinatior, Baseball Operations:** Brett Becker. **Coordinator, Video Scouting/Baseball Operations:** Max Kraust.

MAJOR LEAGUE STAFF

Manager: Andy Green. **Bench Coach:** Rod Barajas. **Pitching Coach:** Darren Balsley. **Hitting Coach:** Johnny Washington. **Assistant Hitting/Infielders Coach:** Damion Easley. **First Base:** Skip Schumaker. **Third Base:** Glenn Hoffman. **Bullpen:** Doug Bochtler.

MEDICAL/TRAINING

Club Physician: UC San Diego Health—Dr. Catherine Robertson, Dr. Kenneth Taylor. **Head Athletic Trainer:** Mark Rogow. **Assistant Athletic Trainers:** Michael Salazar, Kevin Pillifant. **Head Strength & Conditioning Coach:** John Philbin. **Assistant Strength & Conditioning Coach:** Scott Cline. **Physical Therapist:** Scott Hacker. **Massage Therapist:** Atsushi Nakasone.

PLAYER DEVELOPMENT

Telephone: (619) 795-5343. **Fax:** (619) 795-5036.

Senior Director, Player Development: Sam Geaney. **Director, Player Development:** Ben Sestanovich. **Special Assistants, Player Development:** Moises Alou, Steve Finley. **Director, Professional Development:** Jason Amoroso. **Instructor, Player Development:** Dave Bingham. **International Player Development/Infield Instructor:** Vicente Cafaro. **Director, International Operations:** Cesar Rizik. **Administrator, International Operations:** Franklyn Peguero. **Manager, Minor Leagues/Peoria Operations:** Todd Stephenson. **Manager, Minor League Equipment & Clubhouse:** Zach Nelson. **Coordinatiors/Roving Instructors:** Ryley Westman (instruction), Steve Lyons (pitching development), Eric Junge (pitching), Gorman Heimueller (pitching), Kevin Hooper (infield), Oscar Bernard (hitting), Ben Fritz (Arizona/rehab), Ben Fraser (minor leagye ATC), JoJo Tarantino (minor league medical administration), Dan Byrne (strength/conditioning).

FARM SYSTEM

Class	Farm Club (League)	Manager	Hitting Coach	Pitching Coach
Triple-A	El Paso (PCL)	Edwin Rodriguez	Morgan Burkhart	Bronswell Patrick
Double-A	Amarillo (TL)	Philip Wellman	Raul Padron	Jimmy Jones
High A	Lake Elsinore (CAL)	Tony Tarasco	Doug Banks	Pete Zamora
Low A	Fort Wayne (MWL)	Anthony Contreras	Jonathan Mathews	Burt Hooton
Short-season	Tri-City (NWL)	Mike McCoy	Pat O'Sullivan	Leo Rosales
Rookie	Padres 1 (AZL)	Vinny Lopez	Jed Morris	Giancarlo Alvarado
Rookie	Padres 2 (AZL)	Aaron Levin	Raul Gonzalez	John Halama
Rookie	Padres (DSL)	Miguel Del Castillo	Yunir Garcia	N. Cruz/J. Quezada

SCOUTING

Director, Amateur Scouting: Mark Conner. **Director, Professional Scouting:** Pete DeYoung. **Director, International Scouting/Field Coordinator:** Chris Kemp. **Director, Pacific Rim Operations:** Acey Kohrogi. **Assistant Scouting Director:** Kurt Kemp. **National Crosschecker:** Chip Lawrence. **Coordinator, Amateur Scouting:** Sam Ray. **Coordinator, Amateur Scouting/Baseball Operations:** Ethan Dixon. **Manager, Professional Scouting:** Preston Mattingly. **Special Assistant, Professional Scouting:** Spencer Graham (Gresham, OR). **Professional Scouting Crosscheckers:** Mike Juhl (Charlotte, NC), Chuck LaMar (Victoria, TX), Dominic Viola (Holly Springs, NC). **Professional Scouts:** Keith Boeck (Phoenix, AZ), Kimball Crossley (Providence, RI) Tim Holt (Allen, TX), Mark Merila (Minneapolis, MN), Dominic Scavone (Palm Harbor, FL), Duane Shaffer (Goodyear, AZ), Matt Simonetti (Manalapan, NJ), Tyler Tufts (Macedonia, OH), Mike Venafro (Fort Myers, FL), Cory Wade (Zionsville, IN). **Amateur Scouting Supervisors:** Matt Haas, Yancy Ayres, Josh Emmerick, Chris Kelly, Andrew Salvo. **Amateur Scouts:** Stephen Baker (Pensacola, FL), Justin Baughman (Portland, OR), Nick Brannon (Huntersville, NC), Brian Cruz (Pembroke Pines, FL), Carlos Fisher (Los Angeles, CA), Kevin Ham (Katy, TX), Troy Hoerner (Greenville, WI), Jake Koenig (Hartford, CT), Nick Long (Lake Forest, CA), Matt Maloney (Granville, OH), John Martin (Tampa, FL), Steve Moritz (Kennesaw, GA), James Parker (Phoenix, AZ), Tim Reynolds (Livermore, CA), Willie Ronda (Las Lomas Rio Piedras, PR), Daniel Sader (Overland Park, KS), Matt Schaffner (Dallas, TX), Tyler Stubblefield (Canton, GA), Murray Zuk (Souris, Manitoba). **International Scouting Supervisor:** Trevor Schumm. **Coordinator, Latin American Scouting:** Felix Feliz. **Supervisor, Venezuela:** Yfrain Linares. **International Crosschecker/Mexico Supervisor:** Bill McLaughlin. **Supervisor, Dominican Republic:** Alvin Duran. **International Scouts:** Antonio Alejos (Venezuela), Andres Cabadias (Colombia), Milton Croes (Aruba), Emenejildo Diaz (Dominican Republic), Jhonathan Feliz (Dominican Republic), Po-Husan Keng (Taiwan), Martin Jose (Dominican Republic), Victor Magdaleno (Venezuela), Manuel Marin (Venezuela), Richard Montenegro (Panama), Hoon Namgung (Korea/Taiwan), Luis Prieto (Venezuela), Ysrael Rojas (Dominican Republic), Takashi Saito (Japan), Jose Salado (Dominican Republic), Damian Shanahan (Australia).

SAN FRANCISCO GIANTS

Office Address: Oracle Park, 24 Willie Mays Plaza, San Francisco, CA 94107.
Telephone: (415) 972-2000. **Fax:** (415) 947-2800. **Website:** sfgiants.com, sfgigantes.com.

OWNERSHIP
Operated By: San Francisco Baseball Associates L.P.

BUSINESS OPERATIONS
President/Chief Executive Officer: Laurence M. Baer. **Executive VP:** Brian R. Sabean.
Special Assistants: Will Clark, Willie Mays. **Special Advisor:** Barry Bonds

FINANCE/LEGAL/INFORMATION TECHNOLOGY
Executive VP/General Counsel: Jack F. Bair. **VP/General Counsel:** Amy Tovar. **Senior VP/Chief Financial Officer:** Lisa Pantages. **Senior VP/CIO/Chairman, San Jose Giants:** Bill Schlough. **VP, Information Technology:** Ken Logan. **VP, Finance:** Matt Causey.

Laurence M. Baer

ADMINISTRATION
Executive VP, Administration: Alfonso Felder. **Senior VP, Operations/Facilities:** Jorge Costa. **VP, Ballpark Operations:** Gene Telucci. **VP, Guest Services:** Rick Mears. **Senior VP/Chief People Officer:** Leilani Gayles. **President, Giants Enterprises:** Stephen Revetria. **Senior VP, Event Strategy & Services:** Sara Grauf.

COMMUNICATIONS
Telephone: (415) 972-2445. **Fax:** (415) 947-2800.
Executive VP, Communications/Senior Advisor to the CEO: Staci Slaughter. **VP, Public Affairs/Community Relations:** Shana Daum. **Executive Director, Giants Community Fund:** Sue Petersen. **Senior Director, Broadcast Communications & Media Operations:** Maria Jacinto. **Senior Director, Media Relations:** Matt Chisholm. **Senior Manager, Hispanic Communications & Marketing:** Erwin Higueros. **Media Relations Manager:** Megan Brown. **Baseball Information Manager:** Mike Passanisi.

BUSINESS OPERATIONS
Executive VP, Business Operations: Mario Alioto. **Senior VP, Partnerships/Business Development:** Jason Pearl. **VP, Partnership Sales & Business Development:** Brenden Mallette. **VP, Retail Operations:** Dave Martinez. **VP, Marketing/Advertising:** Danny Dann. **VP, SFG Productions:** Paul Hodges. **VP, Brand Development/Digital Media:** Bryan Srabian. **VP, Creative Services/Visual Identity:** Nancy Donati. **PA Announcer:** Renel Brooks-Moon.

TICKETING
Telephone: (415) 972-2000. **Fax:** (415) 972-2500.
Senior VP, Ticket Sales/Services: Russ Stanley. **VP, Ticket Sales/Premium Seating:** Jeff Tucker. **VP, Ticket Operations & Services:** Steve Fanelli. **VP, Strategic Revenue Services:** Jerry Drobny. **VP, Business Analytics:** Rocky Koplik.

2019 SCHEDULE
Standard Game Times: Mon.-Sat., 7:15 pm; Sun., 1:05 pm.

MARCH	10-12 . . . . . . Cincinnati	27-30 . . . . Arizona	15-18 . . . . . . at Arizona
28-31 . . . . . at San Diego	14-15 . . . . Toronto	**JULY**	20-22 . . . . at Chicago (NL)
	17-19 . . . . . . at Arizona	1-3 . . . . . . at San Diego	24-25 . . . . at Oakland
APRIL	20-23 . . . . Atlanta	5-7 . . . . St. Louis	26-27 . . . . Arizona
1-3 . . . at Los Angeles (NL)	24-26 . . . . Arizona	12-14 . . . . at Milwaukee	29-31 . . . . San Diego
5-7 . . . . Tampa Bay	28-30 . . . . . . at Miami	15-17 . . . . . at Colorado	
8-10 . . . . San Diego	31 . . . . at Baltimore	18-21 . . . . . New York (NL)	**SEPTEMBER**
11-14 . . . . Colorado		22-24 . . . . Chicago (NL)	1 . . . . San Diego
16-18 . . . at Washington	**JUNE**	26-28 . . . . at San Diego	2-5 . . . . at St. Louis
19-21 . . . . at Pittsburgh	1-2 . . . . . . at Baltimore	30-31 . . . at Philadelphia	6-8 . . at Los Angeles (NL)
23-24 . . . . . . at Toronto	4-6 . . . . at New York (NL)		9-12 . . . . Pittsburgh
26-28 . . . . New York (AL)	7-9 . . . . Los Angeles (NL)	**AUGUST**	13-15 . . . . Miami
29-30 . . . Los Angeles (NL)	11-12 . . . . San Diego	1 . . . . . . at Philadelphia	17-19 . . . . . . at Boston
	14-16 . . . . . . Milwaukee	2-4 . . . . . . at Colorado	20-22 . . . . . at Atlanta
MAY	17-20 . at Los Angeles (NL)	5-7 . . . . Washington	24-26 . . . . Colorado
1 . . . . . Los Angeles (NL)	21-23 . . . . . . at Arizona	8-11 . . . . . . Philadelphia	27-29 . . . Los Angeles (NL)
3-6 . . . . at Cincinnati	24-26 . . . . . . Colorado	13-14 . . . . Oakland	
7-9 . . . . . . at Colorado			

GENERAL INFORMATION
Stadium (year opened): Oracle Park (2000).   **Playing Surface:** Grass.
Team Colors: Black, orange and cream.
Home Dugout: Third Base.

BASEBALL OPERATIONS

Telephone: (415) 972-1922. **Fax:** (415) 947-2929.
President of Baseball Ops.: Farhan Zaidi. **Senior Advisor to President of Baseball Ops:** JP Ricciardi, Dick Tidrow, John Barr. **VP/Assistant GM:** Jeremy Shelley. **VP, Baseball Ops.:** Yeshayah Goldfarb. **Special Assistant, Scouting:** Craig Weissmann. **Special Assist. to Baseball Ops:** Felipe Alou, Dave Righetti. **Executive Assist. to Baseball Ops/Admin.:** Karen Sweeney. **Director of Baseball Personnel Admin:** Clara Ho. **Director of Baseball Analytics:** Paul Bien. **Senior Advisor to Baseball Ops:** Tony Siegle. **Coord. of Org Travel:** Mike Scardino.

Farhan Zaidi

MAJOR LEAGUE STAFF

Manager: Bruce Bochy. **Coaches: Bench**—Hensley Meulens. **Pitching**—Curt Young. **Hitting**—Alonzo Powell/Rick Schu. **First Base**—Jose Alguacil, **Third Base**—Ron Wotus. **Bullpen**—Matt Herges. **Coach/Video Replay Analyst:** Shawon Dunston. **Bullpen Catcher:** Taira Uematsu, Brant Whiting. **Manager, Baseball Video Systems:** Yo Miyamoto. **Coordinator, Baseball Video Systems:** Patrick Yount.

MEDICAL/TRAINING

Team Physicians: Dr. Anthony Saglimbeni, Dr. Ken Akizuki, Dr. Robert Murray, Dr. Chris Chung, Dr. Tim McAdams. **Senior Dir. of Athletic Training:** Dave Groeschner. **Head Athletic Trainer:** Anthony Reyes. **Asst. Athletic Trainer:** Eric Ortega. **Physical Therapist:** Tony Reale. **Strength & Conditioning Coach:** Brad Lawson. **Asst. Strength & Conditioning Coach/Sports Science Coordinator:** Saul Martinez. **Massage Therapist:** Haro Ogawa. **Coordinator, Medical Admin. :** Chrissy Yuen. **Director of Mental Skill:** Derin McMains. **Director, EAP & Org. Health:** Mike Mombrea.

PLAYER DEVELOPMENT

Director, Player Development: Kyle Haines. **Asst. Dir, Player Development (Hitting):** Alan Zinter. **Asst. Dir, Player Development (Administration):** Eric Flemming. **Asst. Dir, Player Development (Medical):** Geoff Head. **Field Coordinator:** Antoan Richardson. **Coordinator, Minor League Pitching:** Mark Allen. **Coordinator, Minor League Hitting:** David Hansen. **Coordinator of Pitching Analysis:** Matt Daniels. **Assistant Pitching Coordinator:** Ethan Katz. **Sr. Analyst, Player Development:** Michael Gries. **Development Coach:** Dan O'Brien. **Coordinator, Fundamentals:** Tom Trebelhorn. **Outfield and Baserunning Coordinator:** Vince Coleman. **Manager, Arizona Baseball Ops.:** Gabe Alvarez. **Coordinator, Education/Cultural Development:** Laura Nunez. **Special Assistant, Player Development:** Joe Amalfitano, Gene Clines. **Director, Arizona Field Operations:** Josh Warstler.

FARM SYSTEM

Class	Farm Club (League)	Manager	Hitting Coach	Pitching Coach
Triple-A	Sacramento (PCL)	Dave Brundage	Damon Minor	Steve Kline
Double-A	Richmond (EL)	Willie Harris	Francisco Morales	Glenn Dishman
High A	San Jose (CAL)	Billy Hayes	Thomas Neal	Matt Yourkin
Low A	Augusta (SAL)	Carlos Valderrama	Jake Fox	Clayton Rapada
Short-season	Salem-Keizer (NWL)	Mark Hallberg	Doug Clark	Dwight Bernard
Rookie	Giants 1 (AZL)	Michael Johnson	Travis Ishikawa	Mike Rodriguez
Rookie	Giants 2 (AZL)	Alvaro Espinoza	Casey Chenoweth	Mike Couchee
Rookie	Giants (DSL)	Jose Montilla	Juan Parra	M. Aguasvivas/O. Matos

SCOUTING

Telephone: (415) 972-2360. **Fax:** (415) 947-2929.
Director of Pro Scouting: Zack Minasian. **Director of Amateur Scouting:** Michael Holmes. **Asst. Dir, Pro & Amateur Scouting:** Adam Nieting. **Asst. Baseball Ops.:** Mike Navolio. **Pro Scouts:** Steve Balboni (Watchung, NJ), Keith Champion (Ballwin, MO), Joe Bochy (Plant City, FL), Ellis Burks (Moreland Hills, OH), Steve Decker (Keizer, OR), Lee Elder (Biloxi, MS), Paul Gale (Phoenix, AZ), Brian Johnson (Detroit, MI), Michael Kendall (Rancho Palos Verde, CA), Joe Lefebvre (Chichester, NH), Bob Mariano (Fountain Hills, AZ), Matt Nerland (Escalon, CA), Tim Rock (Orlando, FL), Andy Skeels (Prescott, AZ), Glenn Tufts (Bridgewater, MA), Paul Turco Jr (Chicago, IL), Shane Turner (Sinking Spring, PA), Randy Winn (Alamo, CA), Darren Wittcke (Sherwood, OR). **Part Time:** Tom Zimmer (Seminole, FL) **Senior Advisors, Amateur Scouting:** Ed Creech (Moultrie, GA). **PT– Senior Advisor:** Doug Mapson (Chandler, AZ). **National Crosschecker:** John Castleberry (High Point, NC). **National Pitching Coordinator:** Daniel Murray (Prairie Village, KS). **Special Assignment Scout:** Bert Bradley (Mattoon, IL). **Supervisors: Northeast**—Arnold Brathwaite (Linthicum Heights, MD). **Midwest**—Andrew Jefferson (St.Louis, MO). **Southeast**—Mike Metcalf (Sarasota, FL). **West**— Matt Woodward (Camas, WA). **Area Scouts:** Ray Callari (Cote Saint Luc, Quebec), Kevin Christman (Noblesville, IN), Todd Coryell (Louisville, KY), John DiCarlo (Glenwood, NJ), Mark O'Sullivan (Haverhill, MA), Jose Alou (Boynton Beach, FL), Jim Gabella (Deltona, FL), Tim Osborne (Woodstock, GA), Junior Roman (Puerto Rico), Jeff Wood (Birmingham, AL), DJ Jauss (Chicago, IL), James Mouton (Missouri City, TX), Jared Schlehuber (Tulsa, OK), Todd Thomas (Dallas, TX), Brad Cameron (Los Alamitos, CA), Larry Casian (Salem, OR), Chuck Fick (Newbury Park, CA), Chuck Hensley Jr. (Mesa, AZ), Keith Snider (Stockton, CA). **Part-Time Scout:** Jorge Posada Sr. (Rio Piedras, PR). **International Scouting, Director of Operations:** Joe Salermo. **Manager, International Operations:** Jose Bonilla. **International Crosschecker:** Charlie Sullivan. **Latin America Crosschecker:** Junior Roman. **Director, Dominican Republic Operations:** Pablo Peguero. **Scouting Supervisor, Venezuela:** Ciro Villalobos. **Assistant Director, DR Operations/Latin America Crosschecker:** Felix Peguero. **Dominican Republic Crosschecker:** Jesus Stephens. **International Scouts (Domincan Republic):** Abner Abreu, Jonathan Bautista, Gabriel Elias, Luis Polonia Jr.. **International Scouts (Venezuela):** Jonathan Arraiz, Edgar Fernandez, Juan Marquez, Oscar Montero, Neriel Morillo, Robert Moron, Ciro Villalobos Jr. **International Scouts:** Jim Patterson (Austrailia), Daniel Mavarez (Colombia), Quincy Martina (Curacao/Bonaire/Aruba), Jeff Kusumoto (Japan), Luis Pena (Mexico), Ernesto Cantu (Mexico), Sandy Moreno (Nicaragua), Rogelio Castillo (Panama), Evan Hsueh (Pacific Rim). **International Baseball Operations Administrator:** Joan Cuevas.

SEATTLE MARINERS

Office Address: 1250 First Ave. South, Seattle, WA 98134.
Mailing Address: PO Box 4100, Seattle, WA 98194.
Telephone: (206) 346-4000. **Fax:** (206) 346-4400. **Website:** www.mariners.com.

OWNERSHIP

Board of Directors: John Stanton (Chairman), John Ellis, Buck Ferguson, Chris Larson, Howard Lincoln, Jeff Raikes, Frank Shrontz.
President/CEO: Kevin Mather. **Senior VP & Special Advisor to the Chairman and CEO:** Randy Adamack.

BUSINESS OPERATIONS

John Stanton

FINANCE

Executive Vice President and CFO: Tim Kornegay. **VP, Finance:** Greg Massey. **Director, Internal Audit Operations:** Connie McKay. **VP, Human Resources:** Lisa Winsby.

LEGAL & GOVERNMENTAL AFFAIRS/ COMMUNITY RELATIONS

Executive Vice President and General Counsel: Fred Rivera. **Deputy General Counsel:** Melissa Robertson. **VP, Corporate Business & Community Relations:** Joe Chard. **Senior Director, Community Relations:** Gina Hasson.

SALES

Senior VP, Sales: Frances Traisman. **Senior Director, Corporate Business:** Ingrid Russell-Narcisse. **Senior Director, Ticket Sales:** Cory Carbary. **Director, Group Business Development:** Bob Hellinger.

MARKETING/COMMUNICATIONS

Telephone: (206) 346-4000. **Fax:** (206) 346-4400.
Senior VP, Marketing/Communications: Kevin Martinez. **VP, Communications:** Tim Hevly. **Senior Director, Public Information:** Rebecca Hale. **Senior Manager, Baseball Information:** Kelly Munro. **Coordinator, Baseball Information:** Ryan Hueter. **Senior Director, Mariners Productions:** Ben Mertens. **Senior Director, Marketing:** Gregg Greene. **Director, Marketing:** Mandy Lincoln. **Director, Graphic Design:** Carl Morton.

TICKETING

Telephone: (206) 346-4001. **Fax:** (206) 346-4100.
Senior Director, Ticketing & Parking Operations: Malcolm Rogel. **Director, Ticket Services:** Jennifer Sweigert.

STADIUM OPERATIONS

Senior VP, Ballpark Events & Operations: Trevor Gooby. **Senior Director, Engineering/Maintenance:** Ryan van Maarth. **Senior Director, Event Sales:** Alisia Anderson. **Director, Ballpark Event Operations:** Michael Hilburn. **VP, Information Services:** Dave Curry. **Director, Information Systems:** Oliver Roy. **Director, Database/Applications:** Justin Stolmeier.

2019 SCHEDULE

Standard Game Times: Mon.-Sat., 7:10 pm; Sun., 1:10 pm.

MARCH		
20-21 . . . . . . .at Oakland	
28-31 . . . . Boston	

APRIL
1-2. . . . . Los Angeles (AL)
4-7. . . . . .at Chicago (AL)
8-11 . . . . .at Kansas City
12-14 . . . . Houston
15-17 . . . . Cleveland
18-21 . at Los Angeles (AL)
23-24 . . . . . at San Diego
25-28 . . . . Texas
30 . . . . Chicago (NL)

MAY
1 . . . . Chicago (NL)
3-5. . . . . . . .at Cleveland

6-9. . . . . at New York (AL)
10-12 . . . . .at Boston
13-14 . . . . Oakland
16-19 . . . . . . Minnesota
20-22 . . . . .at Texas
24-26 . . . . . .at Oakland
27-29 . . . . Texas
30-31 . . . Los Angeles (AL)

JUNE
1-2. . . . . Los Angeles (AL)
3-6. . . . . Houston
7-9. . at Los Angeles (AL)
11-13 . . . . . at Minnesota
14-16 . . . . . . .at Oakland
17-19 . . . . . Kansas City
20-23 . . . . Baltimore

25-27 . . . . . at Milwaukee
28-30 . . . . . . .at Houston

JULY
2-4. . . . . St. Louis
5-7. . . . . Oakland
12-14 . at Los Angeles (AL)
16-17 . . . . . . .at Oakland
19-21 . . . Los Angeles (AL)
22-24 . . . . Texas
25-28 . . . . Detroit
30-31 . . . . .at Texas

AUGUST
2-4. . . . . .at Houston
6-7. . . . . San Diego
9-11 . . . . . . .Tampa Bay
13-15 . . . . . . .at Detroit

16-18 . . . . at Toronto
19-21 . . . . at Tampa Bay
23-25 . . . . .Toronto
26-28 . . . . .New York (AL)
29-31 . . . . .at Texas

SEPTEMBER
1 . . . . .at Texas
2-3. . . . . .at Chicago (NL)
5-8. . . . . . . .at Houston
10-12 . . . . Cincinnati
13-15 . . . . . Chicago (AL)
17-19 . . . at Pittsburgh
20-22 . . . . . .at Baltimore
24-25 . . . . Houston
26-29 . . . . Oakland

GENERAL INFORMATION

Stadium (year opened): T-Mobile Park (1999). **Home Dugout:** First Base.
Team Colors: Northwest green, silver and navy blue. **Playing Surface:** Grass.

Senior Director, Procurement: Norma Cantu. Head Groundskeeper: Bob Christofferson. Assistant Head Groundskeepers: Tim Wilson, Leo Liebert. PA Announcer: Tom Hutyler. Official Scorer: Eric Radovich.

MERCHANDISING
Sr. Director, Operations: Julie McGillivray. Director, Merchandising: Renee Steyh. Director, Stores: Mary Beeman.

TRAVEL/CLUBHOUSE
Director, Major League Operations: Jack Mosimann. Clubhouse Manager: Ryan Stiles. Visiting Clubhouse Manager: Jeff Bopp. Video Coordinator: Jimmy Hartley. Assistant Video Coordinator: Craig Manning.

BASEBALL OPERATIONS

Jerry Dipoto

Executive VP/General Manager: Jerry Dipoto.
Assistant GM: Justin Hollander. Special Assistants to the GM: Joe Bohringer, Roger Hansen, Tom McNamara. Director, Major League Operations: Jack Mosimann. Manager, Baseball Operations: Tim Stanton. Coordinator, Baseball Operations: David Hesslink. Coodinator, Advance Scouting: Frankie Piliere. Assistant, Advance Scouting: Skylar Shibayama. Director, Analytics: Jesse Smith. Manager, Analytics: Joel Firman. Analysts: John Choiniere, Ben Aronow, Forrest Diamond. Assistant, High Performance: Anthony Ortiz.

MAJOR LEAGUE STAFF
Manager: Scott Servais. Bench—Manny Acta. Pitching—Paul Davis. Hitting—Tim Laker. First Base—Perry Hill. Third Base—Chris Prieto. Bullpen—Jim Brower. Bullpen Catcher — Fleming Baez. Field Coordinator—Jared Sandberg. Director, Pitching & Strategies: Brian Delunas. Director, Hitting Development and Strategies: Dustin Lind.

MEDICAL/TRAINING
Medical Director: Dr. Ed Khalfayan. Team Doctor: Dr. Tim Johnson. Head Athletic Trainer: Rob Nodine. Athletic Trainers: Matt Toth, Yoshi Nakazawa. Physical Therapist: Ryan Bitzel. Head Performance/Strength & Conditioning Coach: James Clifford. Assistant Strength & Conditioning Coach: Derek Cantieni.

PLAYER DEVELOPMENT
Telephone: (206) 346-4316. Fax: (206) 346-4300.
Director, Player Development: Andy McKay. Coordinator, Player Development: Mat Snider. Administrator, Player Development: Jan Plein. Special Assistant, Pitching Coach: Pete Harnisch. Special Assistants, Player Development: Alvin Davis, Dan Wilson. Peak Performance Coaches: David Franco, Adam Bernero, Jimmy VanOstrand. Rehab Coach: Moises Hernandez. Athlete Monitoring: Dan Adams. Pitching Strategists: Trent Blank, Forrest Hermann. Hitting Strategist: Jarret DeHart. Field Coordinator: Carson Vitale. Hitting Coordinator: Hugh Quattlebaum. Pitching Coordinator: Max Weiner. Assistant Hitting/Catching Coordinator: Tony Arnerich. Latin American Development Coodinator: Cesar Nicolas. Performance Specialist Coordinator: Rob Fumagalli. Asst. Coordinator, Performance Specialists: Aaron Reis.

FARM SYSTEM

Class	Club (League)	Manager	Hitting Coach	Pitching Coach
Triple-A	Tacoma (PCL)	Daren Brown	Roy Howell	Lance Painter
Double-A	Arkansas (TL)	Mitch Canham	Kyle Wilson	Pete Woodworth
High A	Modesto (CAL)	Denny Hocking	Jose Umbria	Rob Marcello
Low A	West Virginia (SAL)	Dave Berg	Eric Farris	Alon Leichman
Short-season	Everett (NWL)	Jose Moreno	Joe Thurston	Ari Ronick
Rookie	Peoria (AZL)	Zac Livingston	Connor Dawson	Yoel Monzon
Rookie	Mariners (DSL)	Austin Knight	David Flores	Jose Amancio

SCOUTING
VP, Scouting: Tom Allison. Director, Amateur Scouting: Scott Hunter. Player Personnel Managers: West: Emanuel Sifuentes. East: Brendan Domaracki. Central: Jason Karegeannes. Scouting Coordinator: Andrew Herrera. Asst. Amateur Scouting Coordinator: Ty Bowman (Phoenix, AZ). Special Assistants to Scouting: Mark Lummus (Godley, TX), Bill Masse (Manchester, CT), Howard McCullough (Greenville, NC), Woody Woodward (Palm Coast, FL). Pro Scouts: John Hester (Scottsdale, AZ), Preston Higbe (Phoenix, AZ), Greg Hunter (Seattle, WA), Bobby Korecky (Estero, FL), John McMichen (Cincinnati, OH), Chris Pelekoudas (Mesa, AZ), Chris Rosenbaum (Arlington, VA), Tyler Warmoth (Orlando, FL). Independent League Scout: Ross Vecchio (Canonsburg, PA) Territorial Crosscheckers: West: Taylor Cameron (Long Beach, CA), Northeast: Devitt Moore (Bryn Mawr, PA), Southeast: Jesse Kapellusch (Cooper City, FL). Area Scouts: Jordan Bley (Dallas, TX), Ben Collman (German Valley, IL), Dan Holcomb (Birmingham, AL), Ryan Holmes (Moorpark, CA), Tyler Holub (Durham, NC), Chris Hom (Benicia, CA), Amanda Hopkins (Phoenix, AZ), Robert Keller (Mobile, AL), Jackson Laumann (Florence, KY), Les McTavish (Lethbridge, Alberta), Derek Miller (Sugar Land, TX), Rob Mummau (Palm Harbor, FL), Patrick O'Grady (Conshohocken, PA), Gary Patchett (Wildomar, CA), David Pepe (Caldwell, NJ), Alex Ross (Kirkland, WA), Dan Rovetto (Davie, FL), Rafael Santo Domingo (San Juan, PR), John Wiedenbauer (Cumming, GA). Director, International Amateurs: Frankie Thon (Doral, FL). International Crosschecker: Kevin Fox (Roseville, CA), Supervisor, Dominican Republic: Eddy Toledo (Santo Domingo, DR). Coordinator, Special Projects: Ted Heid (Peoria, AZ). Latin America Supervisor: David Brito (Valencia, Venezuela). International Scouts: Tim Ballard (Australia), Felipe Burin (Brazil), Alfredo Celestin (Dominican Republic), Emilio De Los Santos (Dominican Republic), Luis Fuenmayor (Venezuela), Sam Kao (Taiwan), Tristan Loetzsch (Australia), Luis Martinez (Venezuela), Diego Mina (Colombia), Manabu Noto (Japan), Rigoberto Rangel (Panama), Ismael Rosado (Dominican Republic), Francisco Rosario (Dominican Republic), Illich Salazar (Venezuela), Karel Williams (Aruba), Audo Vicente (Dominican Republic).

TAMPA BAY RAYS

Office Address: Tropicana Field, One Tropicana Drive, St. Petersburg, FL 33705.
Telephone: (727) 825-3137. **Fax:** (727) 825-3111.

OWNERSHIP
Principal Owner: Stuart Sternberg

BUSINESS OPERATIONS

Presidents: Brian Auld, Matt Silverman.
Chief Development Officer: Melanie Lenz. **Senior Vice President, Administration/General Counsel:** John Higgins. **Senior Vice President, Baseball Operations/General Manager:** Erik Neander. **Senior Vice President, Baseball Operations:** Chaim Bloom. **VP, Public Affairs:** Rafaela A. Amador. **VP, Baseball Operations:** James Click. **VP/Chief Financial Officer:** Rob Gagliardi. **VP, Communications:** Dave Haller. **VP, Operations/Facilities:** Rick Nafe. **VP, Information Technology:** Juan Ramirez. **VP, Corporate Partnerships:** Brian Richeson. **VP, Ticket Sales and Service:** Jeff Tanzer. **VP, Human Resources and Organizational Engagement:** Jennifer Lyn Tran. **VP, Strategy and Development:** Bill Walsh. **VP, Marketing and Creative Services:** Eric Weisberg. **VP, Employee and Community Development:** Bill Wiener, Jr.

Stuart Sternberg

FINANCE
Senior Director, Controller: Patrick Smith. **Senior Director, Business Operations & Analytics:** Barry Newell. **Director, Financial Planning and Analysis:** Jason Gray.

MARKETING/COMMUNITY RELATIONS
Director, Creative: Warren Hypes. **Director, Marketing & Creative Services:** Emily Miller. **Executive Director, Rays Baseball Foundation:** Stephen Thomas.

COMMUNICATIONS/BROADCASTING
Senior Director, Broadcasting: Larry McCabe.

TICKET SALES
Phone: (888) FAN-RAYS. **Director, Ticket Sales:** Dan Newhart. **Director, Ticket Services and Technology:** Matt Fitzpatrick. **Director, Season Ticket Services:** Josh Muirhead. **Director, Ticket Operations:** Robert Bennett. **Assistant Director, Ticket Operations:** Ken Mallory

STADIUM OPERATIONS
Senior Director, Game Operations and Security: Jim Previtera. **Senior Director, Guest Relations:** Cass Halpin. **Director, Stadium Operations:** Chris Raineri. **Head Groundskeeper:** Dan Moeller. **Travel/Clubhouse:** Chris Westmoreland. **Manager, Home Clubhouse:** Ryan Denlinger. **Manager, Visitor Clubhouse:** Guy Gallagher. **Video Coordinator:** Chris Fernandez

2019 SCHEDULE

Standard Game Times: 7:10 p.m.; Sun. 1:10.

MARCH
28-31 . . . . Houston

APRIL
1-3 . . . . Colorado
5-7 . . . . . at San Francisco
8-10 . . . . . at Chicago (AL)
12-14 . . . . at Toronto
16-18 . . . . Baltimore
19-21 . . . . Boston
22-24 . . . . . Kansas City
26-28 . . . . at Boston
29-30 . . . . at Kansas City

MAY
1-2 . . . . . . at Kansas City
3-5 . . . . at Baltimore
6-8 . . . . Arizona

10-12 . . . . . New York (AL)
14-15 . . . . at Miami
17-19 . . at New York (AL)
21-22 . . . Los Angeles (NL)
23-26 . . . . . at Cleveland
27-29 . . . . Toronto
30-31 . . . . Minnesota

JUNE
1-2 . . . . Minnesota
4-6 . . . . at Detroit
7-9 . . . . at Boston
10-12 . . . . Oakland
13-16 . . . Los Angeles (AL)
17-19 . . at New York (AL)
20-23 . . . . . . at Oakland
25-27 . . . . at Minnesota
28-30 . . . . Texas

JULY
1-3 . . . . Baltimore
4-7 . . . . . . New York (AL)
12-14 . . . . . at Baltimore
15-18 . . at New York (AL)
19-21 . . . . Chicago (AL)
22-24 . . . . Boston
26-28 . . . . . . at Toronto
30-31 . . . . . . at Boston

AUGUST
1 . . . . at Boston
3-4 . . . . Miami
5-7 . . . . Toronto
9-11 . . . . at Seattle
12-14 . . . . at San Diego
16-18 . . . . Detroit

19-21 . . . . Seattle
22-25 . . . . . at Baltimore
27-29 . . . . . . at Houston
30-31 . . . . . . Cleveland

SEPTEMBER
1 . . . . Cleveland
2-4 . . . . Baltimore
5-8 . . . . Toronto
10-12 . . . . at Texas
13-15 . at Los Angeles (AL)
17-18 . at Los Angeles (NL)
20-23 . . . . Boston
24-25 . . . . New York (AL)
27-29 . . . . . at Toronto

GENERAL INFORMATION

Stadium (year opened): Tropicana Field (1998). **Playing Surface:** AstroTurf
Team Colors: Dark blue, light blue, yellow. Game Day Grass 3D-60 H.
Home Dugout: First Base.

BASEBALL OPERATIONS

Senior VP Baseball Operations/GM: Erik Neander. **Senior VP, Baseball Operations:** Chaim Bloom. **VP, Baseball Operations:** James Click. **Coordinator, Baseball Administration:** Samantha Bireley. **Coordinator, Major League Operations:** Jeremy Sowers. **Special Assistant to the GM:** Bobby Heck. **Special Assistant, Baseball Operations:** Tom Foley. **Director, Baseball Development:** Peter Bendix. **Coordinator, Baseball Development:** Simon Rosenbaum. **Assistant, Baseball Development:** Brad Ballew. **Director, Staff Development and Recruiting:** Chanda Lawdermilk **Director, Development Strategy:** Sandy Sternberg. **Director, Team Travel and Logistics:** Chris Westmoreland. **Assistant Director, Hitting Development:** Cole Figueroa. **Director, Baseball Performance Science:** Joe Myers **Coordinator, Baseball Performance Science:** Ryan Pennell. **Lead Sports Dietician:** Ryan Harmon. **Biomechanist:** Mike McNally. **Analyst, Baseball Performance Science:** Winston Doom. **Director, Baseball Systems:** Brian Plexico. **Programmer, Baseball Systems:** Daniel Nolan. **Analytics Developer, Baseball Systems:** Michael Vanger. **Developers, Baseball Systems:** Brandon Cordell, Ryan Kelley, Nick Siefken. **Senior Data Scientist:** Will Cousins. **Data Engineer, Baseball Systems:** Clayton Elger. **Data Technician, R&D:** Michael Topol. **Analysts, R&D:** Anirudh Kilambi, Michael McClellan, David Marshall, Taylor Smith.

SKIP MILOS

Erik Neander

MAJOR LEAGUE STAFF

Manager: Kevin Cash. **Coaches: Bench**—Matt Quatraro, **Pitching**—Kyle Snyder, **Hitting**—Chad Mottola, **First Base**—Ozzie Timmons, **Third Base**—Rodney Linares, **Bullpen**—Stan Boroski, **Field Coordinator**—Paul Hoover.

MEDICAL/TRAINING

Medical Director: Dr. James Andrews. **Orthopedic Team Physician:** Dr. Koco Eaton. **Team Chiropractor:** Christopher Williams. **Massage Therapist:** Ray Allen. **ML Medical Coordinator:** Paul Harker. **Head Athletic Trainer:** Joe Benge. **First Assistant Athletic Trainer:** Mark Vinson. **Assistant Athletic Trainer:** Mike Sandoval. **Strength/Conditioning Coach:** Trung Cao. **Strength/Conditioning Assistant:** Joe Greany. **Mental Skills:** Justin Su'a.

PLAYER DEVELOPMENT

Telephone: (727) 825-3267. **Fax:** (727) 825-3493.

Director, Minor League Operations: Mitch Lukevics. **Assistant Director, Minor League Operations:** Jeff McLerran. **Assistant, International/Minor League Operations:** George Pappas. **Administrator, International/Minor League Operations:** Giovanna Rodriguez. **Assistant, Minor League Operations:** Wilson Made. **Minor League Equipment Manager:** Tim McKechney. **Assistant Minor League Equipment Manager:** Shane Rosetti. **Florida Education Coordinator:** Lenore Sutton. **Field Coordinators:** Craig Albernaz, Michael Johns. **Minor League Coordinators:** Tomas Francisco (catching), Skeeter Barnes (outfield/baserunning), Hector Torres (infield), Dewey Robinson (pitching), Jorge Moncada (pitching), Steve Livesey (hitting), Steve Henderson (hitting) Aaron Scott (medical), Joel Smith (rehabilitation), Chris Tomashoff (Latin American medical), Jairo De La Rosa (Latin American cultural), Patrick Trainor (strength/conditioning), Lance Green (mental skills), James Schwabach (mental skills).

FARM SYSTEM

Class	Club (League)	Manager	Hitting Coach	Pitching Coach
Triple-A	Durham (IL)	Brady Williams	Dan DeMent	Rick Knapp
Double-A	Montgomery (SL)	Morgan Ensberg	J. Nelson/G. Redus	R.C. Lichtenstein
High A	Charlotte (FSL)	Jeff Smith	J. Szekely	Steve Watson
Low A	Bowling Green (MWL)	Reinaldo Ruiz	M. Castillo/J. Owens	Brian Reith
Short-season	Hudson Valley (NYP)	Blake Butera	A. Freire/S. Smedley	Jose Gonzalez
Rookie	Princeton (APP)	Danny Sheaffer	W. Rincones/G. Melendez	Jim Paduch
Rookie Rays	(GCL)	Rafael Valenzuela	B.North/J. Morrison	M. DeMerritt/ A.Bastardo
Rookie Rays 1	(DSL)	Julio Zorrilla	Omar Luna	L. Urena/Y. Almonte
Rookie Rays 2	(DSL)	Esteban Gonzalez	Alejandro Segovia	L. Romero/J. Sanchez

SCOUTING

Director, Pro Scouting: Kevin Ibach. **Assistant Director, Pro Scouting:** Ryan Bristow. **Assistant, Pro Scouting:** Tyler Chamberlain-Simon. **Director, Amateur Scouting:** Rob Metzler. **Assistant Director, Amateur Scouting:** Hamilton Marx. **Senior Advisor, Scouting/Baseball Operations:** R.J. Harrison. **Assistant, Amateur Scouting:** Jeff Johnson. **Administrator, Scouting:** Sydney Malone. **Special Assignment Scout:** Fred Repke. **Professional/International Crosschecker:** Mike Brown. **Professional Scouting Crosschecker:** Jason Cole. **Pro Scouts:** Michael Brown, Ken Califano, Max Cohen, JD Elliby, Jose Gomez, Jason Grey, Nate Howard, Brian Keegan, Ken Kravec, Mike Langill, Dave Myers, Jaylon Pimentel, Jeff Stewart, Tyler Stohr. **National Crosschecker:** Chuck Ricci. **Midwest Regional Supervisor:** Jeff Cornell. **Northeastern Regional Supervisor:** Brian Hickman. **Southeastern Regional Supervisor:** Kevin Elfering. **Western Regional Supervisor:** Jake Wilson. **Pitching Crosschecker:** Ryan Henderson. **Scout Supervisors:** Matt Alison, Steve Ames, James Bonnici, Zach Clark, Tom Couston, Rickey Drexler, Brett Foley, Jonathan Hall, David Hamlett, Joe Hastings, Milt Hill, Alan Hull, Jaime Jones, Paul Kirsch, Pat Murphy, Victor Rodriguez, Greg Whitworth, Lou Wieben. **Part-Time Area Scouts:** Jose Hernandez, Dave Jorn, Gil Martinez, Casey Onaga, Jack Sharp, Donald Turley. **Director, International Scouting:** Carlos Rodriguez. **Assistant Director, International Operations:** Patrick Walters. **International Crosschecker:** Steve Miller. **International Crosschecker:** Brad Budzinski. **Director, South American Operations:** Ronnie Blanco. **Consultant, International Operations:** John Gilmore. **Scouting Supervisor, Colombia:** Angel Contreras. **Scouting Supervisor, Mexico:** Eddie Diaz. **Scouting Supervisor, Dominican Republic:** Danny Santana. **International Scout:** Marlon Roche. **International Scouts:** Abraham Despradel, Remmy Hernandez, Victor Torres (Dominican Republic), William Bergolla, Juan Francisco Castillo, Federico Hernandez, Carlos Leon, Edward Rojas (Venezuela), Tiago Campos, Keith Hsu (Taiwan), Chairon Isenia (Curacao), Joe Park (Korea), Tateki Uchibori (Japan), Gustavo Zapata (Panama).

TEXAS RANGERS

Office Address: 1000 Ballpark Way, Arlington, TX 76011. **Mailing Address:** P.O. Box 90111, Arlington, TX 76011. **Telephone:** (817) 273-5222. **Fax:** (817) 273-5110. **Website:** www.texasrangers.com. **Twitter:** @Rangers.

OWNERSHIP

Co-Chairman/Managing Partner: Ray C. Davis. **Co-Chairman:** Bob R. Simpson. **Chief Operating Officer:** Neil Leibman.

BUSINESS OPERATIONS

Executive VP, Business Operations: Rob Matwick. **Executive VP, Chief Marketing & Revenue Officer:** Joe Januszewski. **Executive VP/CFO:** Kellie Fischer. **Executive VP/ General Counsel:** Katie Pothier. **Executive VP, Communications:** John Blake. **Executive VP, Entertainment/Productions:** Chuck Morgan. **VP/Controller:** Starr Gulledge.

HUMAN RESOURCES/LEGAL/INFORMATION TECHNOLOGY

Sr. VP, Human Resources/Risk Management: Terry Turner. **Corporate Counsel:** Ilana Miller. **Director, Human Resources:** Mercedes Riley. **VP, Info Technology:** Mike Bullock. **Asst. VP, Customer Service:** Donnie Pordash. **Asst. VP, Business Operations:** Richard Price.

PROJECT DEVELOPMENT

Senior VP, Project Development: Jack Hill. **Project Accountant:** Kelley Walker.

Ray Davis

COMMUNICATIONS/COMMUNITY RELATIONS

VP, Broadcasting/Communications: Angie Swint. **Asst. VP, Player/Alumni Relations:** Taunee Taylor. **Sr. Director, Media Relations:** Rich Rice. **Manager, Photography:** Kelly Gavin. **Manager, Media Relations:** Brian SanFilippo. **Manager, Communications:** Madison Pelletier. **Manager, Baseball Information:** Matt Mallian. **Coordinator, Communications:** Kate Munson. **Asst. Director, Player Relations:** Monique Corralez. **Coordinator, Player Relations:** Stephanie Gentile. **VP, Community Outreach/Executive Director, Foundation:** Karin Morris. **Director, Youth Baseball and Youth Academy Programs:** Juan Leonel Garciga. **Manager, Development:** Justin Henry. **Manager, Foundation & Community Outreach:** Reynaldo Casas.

FACILITIES/RETAIL/EVENTS

Sr. VP, Operations & Events: Sean Decker. **VP, Ballpark Operations & Guest Services:** Mike Healy. **VP, Security & Parking:** Blake Miller. **Sr. Director, Parking & Security:** Mike Smith. **Sr. Director, Maintenance:** Mike Call. **Sr. Director, Facility Operations:** Duane Arber. **Director, Major League Grounds:** Dennis Klein. **Director, Complex Grounds:** Steve Ballard. **Director, Retail:** George Dunn. **Director, Tours & Experiences:** Lindsey Hopper. **Director, Sales:** Jared Schrom. **Director, Event Operations:** Pedro Soto, Jr.

TICKET AND SPONSORSHIP SALES

Sr. VP, Ticket Sales & Service: Paige Farragut. **Sr. VP, Partnerships & Client Services:** Jim Cochrane. **Director, Season Tickets:** Dan Hessling. **Director, Inside Sales:** Nick Richardson. **Director, Group Sales:** Jamie Roberts.

2019 SCHEDULE

Standard Game Times: 7:05 p.m.; Sun. 2:05.

MARCH			
28-31 . . . . . Chicago (NL)	7-8 . . . . at Pittsburgh	25-27 . . . . .at Detroit	12-14 . . . . at Toronto
	9-12 . . . . .at Houston	28-30 . . . . . at Tampa Bay	15-18 . . . . Minnesota
APRIL	14-16 . . . . .at Kansas City		19-21 . . . Los Angeles (AL)
1-3 . . . . Houston	17-19 . . . . St. Louis	**JULY**	22-25 . . . .at Chicago (AL)
4-7 . . . at Los Angeles (AL)	20-22 . . . . Seattle	1-4 . . . . . Los Angeles (AL)	27-28 . at Los Angeles (AL)
9-10 . . . . at Arizona	24-26 . at Los Angeles (AL)	5-7 . . . . . . at Minnesota	29-31 . . . . Seattle
12-14 . . . . Oakland	27-29 . . . . .at Seattle	11-14 . . . . Houston	
15-17 . . . Los Angeles (AL)	30-31 . . . . . Kansas City	16-17 . . . . Arizona	**SEPTEMBER**
19-21 . . . . Houston		19-21 . . . . . .at Houston	1 . . . . Seattle
22-24 . . . . . .at Oakland	**JUNE**	22-24 . . . . .at Seattle	2-4 . . . . at New York (AL)
25-28 . . . . . . .at Seattle	1-2 . . . . Kansas City	25-28 . . . . . . .at Oakland	5-8 . . . . . . .at Baltimore
30 . . . . Pittsburgh	4-6 . . . . Baltimore	30-31 . . . . Seattle	10-12 . . . . . .Tampa Bay
	7-9 . . . . Oakland		13-15 . . . . Oakland
MAY	10-13 . . . . . . .at Boston	**AUGUST**	17-18 . . . . . .at Houston
1 . . . . Pittsburgh	14-16 . . . . .at Cincinnati	2-4 . . . . Detroit	20-22 . . . . . .at Oakland
3-5 . . . . .Toronto	17-20 . . . . . . Cleveland	5-7 . . . . . . .at Cleveland	24-26 . . . . Boston
	21-23 . . . . . Chicago (AL)	9-11 . . . . . at Milwaukee	27-29 . . . .New York (AL)

GENERAL INFORMATION

Stadium (year opened): Globe Life Park in Arlington (1994). **Team Colors:** Royal blue and red.

Home Dugout: First Base. **Playing Surface:** Grass.

Director, Suites & Premium Services: Delia Wilms. **Director Ticket Services:** Mike Lentz. **Director, Business Analytics:** Katie Morgan. **Director, Partnerships:** Guy Tomcheck. **Director, Client Services:** Rose Swenson.

MARKETING/GAME PRESENTATION

VP, Marketing: Travis Dillon. **Director, Advertising/Marketing:** Sarah Opgenorth. **Senior Director, Game Entertainment/Productions:** Chris DeRuyscher. **Manager, Social Media:** Kyle Smith.

BASEBALL OPERATIONS

Jon Daniels

Telephone: (817) 273-5222. **Fax:** (817) 273-5285.

President, Baseball Operations/General Manager: Jon Daniels. **Executive Assistant to President, Baseball Operations/GM:** Joda Parent. **Assistant General Managers:** Josh Boyd, Mike Daly, Shiraz Rehman. **Special Assistants to the GM:** Colby Lewis, Brandon McCarthy, Darren Oliver, Ivan Rodriguez, Michael Young. **Senior Director, Baseball Systems:** Todd Slavinsky. **Director, Pitching Research/Development:** Todd Walther. **Director, Baseball Analytics:** Ryan Murray. **Assistant Director, Baseball Operations:** Ben Baroody. **Senior Developers, Baseball Systems:** Bradley Ankrom, Kim Eskew. **Jr. Analyst, Baseball Analytics:** Vinesh Kanthan. **Developer, Baseball Systems:** Alexander Booth. **Analysts, Baseball Operations:** Bobby Bandelow, Andrew Koo, R.J. Walsh.

MAJOR LEAGUE STAFF

Manager: Chris Woodward.

Coaches: Bench—Don Wakamatsu. **Pitching**—Julio Rangel. **Hitting**—Luis Ortiz. **First Base**—Hector Ortiz. **Third Base**—Tony Beasley. **Bullpen**—Oscar Marin. **Assistant Hitting Coach**—Callix Crabbe. **ML Player Development Field Coordinator:** Jayce Tingler.

MEDICAL/TRAINING

Senior Director, Medical Operations/Sports Science: Jamie Reed. **Team Physician:** Dr. Keith Meister. **Head Trainer:** Matt Lucero. **Assistant Trainer:** Jacob Newburn. **Physical Therapist:** Regan Wong. **Director, Strength/Conditioning:** Jose Vazquez. **Team Nutritionist:** Stephanie Fernandes.

PLAYER DEVELOPMENT

Telephone: (817) 436-5999. **Fax:** (817) 273-5285.

Director, Player Development: Matt Blood. **Director, Minor League Operations:** Paul Kruger. **Assistant, Player Development:** Casey Fox. **Field Coordinator:** Corey Ragsdale. **Pitching Coordinator:** Danny Clark. **Coordinators:** Josue Perez (hitting), Dwayne Murphy (assistant hitting/outfield), Kenny Holmberg (infield), Jono Armold (roving pitching), Jeff Andrews (special assignment coach-pitching), Keith Comstock (rehab pitching), Napoleon Pichardo (strength/conditioning), Jack Blake (Peak Performance, A-Ball), Jason Roberts (minor league medical administration), Sean Fields (Arizona medical), Chris Olson (international medical). **Coordinator, Arizona Operations:** Stosh Hoover. **Minor League Equipment Manager:** Chris Ackerman.

FARM SYSTEM

Class	Club (League)	Manager	Hitting Coach	Pitching Coach
Triple-A	Nashville (PCL)	Jason Wood	Howard Johnson	Brian Shouse
Double-A	Frisco (TL)	Joe Mikulik	Jason Hart	Greg Hibbard
High A	Down East (CL)	Corey Ragsdale	Chase Lambin	Steve Mintz
Low A	Hickory (SAL)	Matt Hagen	Jared Goedert	Jose Jaimes
Short-season	Spokane (NWL)	Kenny Hook	Salomon Manriquez	Henderson Lugo
Rookie	Rangers (AZL)	Carlos Cardoza	C. Comer/E. Dorton/G. Rodriguez	B. Conger/S.Cashman
Rookie	Rangers (DSL)	S. Adriana/C.Maldonado	J. Moore/L.Sumoza	J. Delgado/P. Blanco/R.Valencia

SCOUTING

Director, Pro Scouting: Ross Fenstermaker. **Assistant, Pro Scouting:** Mike Parnell. **Special Assistants:** Mike Anderson (Austin, TX), Scot Engler (Montgomery, IL), Scott Littlefield (Long Beach, CA), Greg Smith (Gettysburg, PA). **Pro Scouts:** Russ Ardolina (Rockville, MD), Jay Eddings (Tulsa, OK), Mike Grouse (Lubbock,TX), Jonathan George (Pittsburgh, PA), Donzell McDonald (Chandler, AZ), Elliott Blair (Argyle, TX), Vinny Rottino (Milwaukee, WI). **Senior Director, Amateur Scouting:** Kip Fagg. **Assistant Director, Amateur Scouting:** Adam Lewkowicz. **National Crosscheckers:** Jake Krug (Flower Mound, TX), Bobby Crook (Fort Worth, TX). **West Coast Crosschecker:** Casey Harvie (Lake Stevens, WA). **Midwest Crosschecker:** Demond Smith (Carrollton, TX). **Eastern Crosschecker:** Ryan Coe (Acworth, GA). **Southeast Crosschecker:** Brian Williams (Cincinnati, OH). **Area Scouts:** Josh Simpson (Chandler, AZ), Brett Campbell (Orlando, FL), Chris Collias (Royal Oak, MI), Steve Flores (Temecula, CA), Brian Matthews (Mount Joy, PA), Todd Guggiana (Long Beach, CA), Jay Heafner (Charlotte, NC), Levi Lacey (Mesa, AZ), Gary McGraw (Gaston, OR), Michael Medici (Danville, IN), Brian Morrison (Birmingham, AL), Patrick Perry (St. George, UT), Takeshi Sakurayama (Manchester, CT), Dustin Smith (Olathe, KS), Cliff Terracuso (Jupiter, FL), Derrick Tucker (Kennesaw, GA). **Part-Time Scout:** Rick Schroeder (Phoenix, AZ). **Director, International Scouting:** Rafic Saab. **Assistant Director, International Scouting:** Hamilton Wise. **Asst. International Scouting:** Jonny Clum. **Supervisor, Dominican Republic:** Willy Espinal. **Supervisor, Venezuela:** Jhonny Gomez. **Dominican Program Coordinator:** Danilo Troncoso. **Latin America Crosschecker:** Chu Halabi. **International Scouts:** Jose Fernandez (Special Projects, International Scouting). JC Alvarez (Dominican Republic), Carlos Gonzalez (Venezuela), Jose Gabriel Rodriguez (Venezuela), Juan Salazar (Venezuela), Carlos Plaza (Venezuela), Carlos Barrios (Venezuela), Rafael Cedeno (Panama), Eduardo Thomas (Panama), Hamilton Sarabia (Colombia), Efrain Lara (Mexico). **Video Scout, Dominican Republic:** Michael Acevedo. **Assistant, International Operations:** Jose Vargas. **DR Complex Administrator:** Marlenis Alejo. **Director, Pacific Rim Operations:** Joe Furukawa (Japan). **Manager, Pacific Rim:** Hajime Watabe (Japan). **International Scout:** Daniel Chang (Taiwan).

TORONTO BLUE JAYS

Office/Mailing Address: 1 Blue Jays Way, Suite 3200, Toronto, Ontario M5V 1J1.
Telephone: (416) 341-1000. **Fax:** (416) 341-1245. **Website:** www.bluejays.com.

OWNERSHIP

Operated by: Toronto Blue Jays Baseball Club. **Principal Owner:** Rogers Communications Inc. **Chairman, Toronto Blue Jays:** Edward Rogers. **Vice Chairman, Rogers Communications Inc.:** Phil Lind. **President and CEO, Rogers Communication:** Joe Natale. **President, Media Business Unit:** Rick Brace. **Chief Financial Officer, Rogers Communication:** Tony Staffieri.

BUSINESS OPERATIONS

President and CEO: Mark A. Shapiro. **President Emeritus:** Paul Beeston. **Executive Vice President, Baseball Operations/General Manager:** Ross Atkins. **Executive Vice President, Business Operations:** Andrew Miller. **Executive Assistant to the President/CEO:** Gail Ricci.

Mark Shapiro

FINANCE/ADMINISTRATION

Director, Finance: Janet Chant. **Director, Blue Jays Payroll:** Brenda Dimmer. **Senior Manager, Blue Jays US Payroll & Benefits:** Sharon Dykstra. **Senior Manager, Finance:** Josh Hoffman. **Manager, Financial Business:** Leslie Galant-Gardiner. **Manager, Finance:** Derek Nicholson. **Manager, Treasury & Vault Operations:** Garrett Mercer. **Senior Payroll Analyst:** Samantha Randolph. **Senior Financial Analyst:** Jan Andrejuk. **Financial Analyst:** Dylan Hewko. **Financial Analyst:** Troy Mercuri. **Financial Analyst:** Melissa Paterson. **Senior Payroll Administrator:** Marichu Estrella. **Payroll Analyst:** Joyce Chan.

MARKETING/COMMUNITY RELATIONS

Vice President, Marketing & Events: Marnie Starkman. **Director, Marketing:** Kristy Boone. **Director, Creative Services & Marketing Management:** Sherry Oosterhuis. **Acting Director, Marketing:** Michelle Seniuk. **Senior Manager, Game Entertainment & Producer:** Stefanie Wright. **Senior Manager, Events:** Laura Attwell. **Manager, Player Relations:** Shannon Curley. **Manager, Events Production:** Carol Balfour. **Program Manager, Amateur Baseball:** T.J. Burton. **Program Manager, MyBlueJays:** Maureen Kinghorn. **Department Manager, Marketing & Events:** Maria Cresswell. **Manager, Game Entertainment:** Laura Spratt.

BASEBALL MEDIA

Director, Baseball Media: Richard Griffin. **Manager, Business Communications:** Jessica Beard. **Manager, Baseball Media:** Ryan Brown. **Manager, Social Media:** Simone Gervais. **Social Content Specialist:** Graeme Campbell. **Social Community Manager:** Alykhan Ravjiani. **Coordinator, Business Communications:** Madeleine Davidson. **Coordinator, Baseball Media:** Adam Felton. **Associate, Baseball Media:** Rodney Hiemstra.

TRAVEL/CLUBHOUSE

Director, Team Travel/Clubhouse Operations: Mike Shaw. **Senior Manger, Visiting Clubhouse:** Kevin Malloy. **Clubhouse Manager:** Scott Blinn. **Clubhouse Manager, Equipment:** Mustafa Hassan.

2019 SCHEDULE

Standard Game Times: 7:07 p.m.; Sat/Sun: 1:07

MARCH
28-31 . . . . Detroit

APRIL
1-3 . . . . Baltimore
4-7 . . . . . . .at Cleveland
9-11 . . . . .at Boston
12-14 . . . . . . .Tampa Bay
15-18 . . . . . at Minnesota
19-21 . . . . . .at Oakland
23-24 . . . .San Francisco
26-28 . . . . Oakland
30 . . . at Los Angeles (AL)

MAY
1-2 . . . at Los Angeles (AL)
3-5 . . . . .at Texas
6-8 . . . . Minnesota

10-12 . . . . . Chicago (AL)
14-15 . . . at San Francisco
16-19 . . . .at Chicago (AL)
20-23 . . . . Boston
24-26 . . . . . . San Diego
27-29 . . . at Tampa Bay
31 . . . . at Colorado

JUNE
1-2 . . . . at Colorado
4-6 . . . . . .New York (AL)
7-9 . . . . .Arizona
11-13 . . . . . .at Baltimore
14-16 . . . . . .at Houston
17-20 . . . Los Angeles (AL)
21-23 . . . . . . .at Boston
24-26 . . . at New York (AL)

28-30 . . . . . Kansas City

JULY
1 . . . . Kansas City
2-4 . . . . Boston
5-7 . . . . Baltimore
12-14 . . . at New York (AL)
15-18 . . . . . . .at Boston
19-21 . . . . . . .at Detroit
22-24 . . . . . Cleveland
26-28 . . . . . .Tampa Bay
29-31 . . . .at Kansas City

AUGUST
1-4 . . . . .at Baltimore
5-7 . . . . . . at Tampa Bay
8-11 . . . . . .New York (AL)
12-14 . . . . Texas

16-18 . . . . Seattle
20-22 . at Los Angeles (NL)
23-25 . . . . .at Seattle
27-28 . . . . Atlanta
30-31 . . . . Houston

SEPTEMBER
1 . . . . Houston
2-3 . . . . at Atlanta
5-8 . . . . . . at Tampa Bay
10-12 . . . . Boston
13-15 . . . .New York (AL)
17-19 . . . .at Baltimore
20-22 . . . at New York (AL)
23-25 . . . . . . Baltimore
27-29 . . . . . .Tampa Bay

GENERAL INFORMATION

Stadium (year opened): Rogers Centre (1989). **Team Colors:** Blue and white.

Home Dugout: Third Base. **Playing Surface:** AstroTurf 3D Xtreme.

BASEBALL OPERATIONS

Vice President, Baseball Operations & Assistant General Manager: Tony Lacava. **Vice President, Baseball Operations:** Ben Cherington. **Assistant General Manager:** Andrew Tinnish. **Assistant General Manager:** Joe Sheehan. **Director, Baseball Operations:** Michael Murov. **Director, Team Travel & Clubhouse Operations:** Michael Shaw. **Senior Manager, Visiting Clubhouse:** Kevin Malloy. **Senior Manager, Baseball Administration:** Heather Connolly. **Clubhouse Manager, Operations:** Scott Blinn. **Clubhouse Manager, Equipment:** Mustafa Hassan. **Manager, Baseball Analytics:** Sanjay Choudhury. **Manager, Baseball Research:** Jeremy Reesor. **Assistant, Baseball Research:** Adam Yudelman. **Assistant, Baseball Research:** Graydon Carruthers. **Assistant, Advance Scouting:** John Babocsi. **Fellow:** Ginger Poulson. **Data Architect:** Peter Saunders. **Baseball Systems Developer:** Spencer Estey. **Bullpen Catcher:** Alex Andreopoulos. **Interpreter:** Josue Peley. **Major League Video Coordinator:** Eric Slotter. **Executive Assistant to the General Manager:** Anna Coppola.

Ross Atkins

MAJOR LEAGUE STAFF

Manager: Charlie Montoyo. **Coaches: Bench**—Dave Hudgens, **Pitching**—Pete Walker, **Hitting**—Guillermo Martinez, **First Base**—Mark Budzinski, **Third Base**—Luis Rivera, **Bullpen**—Matt Buschmann, **Major League Field Coordinator**—Shelley Duncan. **Major League Coach** — John Schneider. **Bullpen Catcher:** Alex Andreopoulos.

HIGH PERFORMANCE/MEDICAL STAFF

Director, High Performance: Angus Mugford. **Assistant Director, High Performance:** Clive Brewer. **Assistant Director, Operations:** Dehra Harris. **Major League Head Athletic Trainer:** Nikki Huffman. **Major League Assistant Athletic Trainer:** Jose Ministral. **Major League Assistant Athletic Trainer:** Voon Chong. **Major League Assistant Physical Therapist:** Scott Peters. **Head of Strength & Conditioning:** Donovan Santas. **Major League Assistant Strength & Conditioning Coach:** Scott Weberg. **Medical Coordinator:** Pat Chasse. **Assistant Medical Coordinator:** Drew MacDonald. **Assistant Medical Coordinator:** Garrett Valls. **GCL ATC & Latin American Coordinator:** Jon Woodworth. **ATC & Transaction Coordinator:** Jeff Stevenson.

PLAYER DEVELOPMENT

Telephone: (727) 734-8007. **Fax:** (727) 734-8162.

Director, Player Development: Gil Kim. **Director, Minor League Operations:** Charlie Wilson. **Coordinator, Latin America Operation:** Blake Bentley. **Coordinator, Minor League Operations:** Michael Nielsen. **Coordinator, Player Development:** Joe Sclafani. **Assistant, Player Development:** Megan Evans. **Administrative Assistant:** Kim Marsh. **Field Coordinator:** Eric Wedge. **Coordinator, Practice Design/Skill Development:** Casey Candaele. **Pitching Coordinator:** Jeff Ware. **Senior Pitching Advisor:** Rick Langford. **Rehab Pitching Coordinator:** Darold Knowles. **Hitting Coordinator:** Hunter Mense. **Catching Coordinator:** Ken Huckaby. **Infield Coordinator:** Danny Solano. **Special Assistant to Player Development:** Tim Raines. **Outfield Coordinator:** Antoan Richardson. **Latin American Field Coordinator:** John Tamargo. **Latin America Player Advisor:** Omar Malave. **Video Coordinator:** Ryan Monsevalles. **Performance and Development Analyst:** Evan Short. **Equipment Coordinator:** Billy Wardlow.

FARM SYSTEM

Class	Club (League)	Manager	Hitting Coach	Pitching Coach	Position Coach
Triple-A	Buffalo (IL)	Bobby Meacham	Corey Hart	Doug Mathis	Devon White
Double-A	New Hampshire (EL)	Mike Mordecai	Donnie Murphy	Vince Horsman	Andy Fermin
High A	Dunedin (FSL)	Cesar Martin	Matt Young	Jim Czajkowski	J. McGuiggan
Low A	Lansing (MWL)	Dallas McPherson	Logan Bone	Antonio Caceres	Dave Pano
Short-season	Vancouver (NWL)	Casey Candaele	Aaron Mathews	Demetre Kokoris	Danny Canellas
Rookie	Bluefield (APP)	Luis Hurtado	Paul Elliott	Rafael Lazo	Chris Schaeffer
Rookie	Blue Jays (GCL)	Dennis Holmberg	Michel Abreu	Mark Worrell	George Carroll
Rookie	Blue Jays (DSL)	Jose Mayorga	Petr Stribrcky	Yoel Hernandez	Jose Mateo

SCOUTING

Director, Pro Scouting: Ryan Mittleman. **Manager, Baseball Operations & Pro Scouting:** David Haynes. **Special Assignment Scout:** Russ Bove. **Special Assignment Scout:** Dean Decillis. **Major League Scouts:** Sal Butera, Jon Lalonde, Jim Skaalen. **Professional Scouts:** Matt Anderson, Kevin Briand, Blake Bentley, David May Jr, Jeremy Gordon, Marc Lippman, Mitch Leeds, Tim Rooney. **Player Personnel Coordinators:** Carson Cistulli, Nick Manno, Brent Urcheck.

Director, Amateur Scouting: Steve Sanders. **Manager, Amateur & International Scouting:** Harry Einbinder. **Coordinator, Amateur Scouting:** Kory Lafreniere. **National Supervisor:** Blake Crosby. **Regional Crosscheckers:** CJ Ebarb, Tim Rooney, Paul Tinnell, Jamie Lehman. **Area Scouts:** Joey Aversa, Coulson Barbiche Jr., Jason Beverlin., Matt Bishoff, Dallas Black, Darold Brown, Ryan Fox, Pete Holmes, Randy Kramer, Jim Lentine, Nate Murrie, Don Norris, Matt O'Brien, Wes Penick, Bud Smith, Mike Tidick, Brandon Bishoff, Gerald Turner. **Amateur Scouting Video Coordinators:** Chris Curtis, Kyle Fleming. **Canadian Scouting:** Jay Lapp, Adam Arnold, Jasmin Roy.

Director, Latin American Operations: Sandy Rosario. **Assistant, International Scouting:** Julio Ramirez. **Dominican Scouting Supervisor:** Lorenzo Perez. **Mexican Scouting Supervisor:** Aaron Acosta. **Venezuelan Scouting Supervisor:** Jose Contreras. **International Scouting —Caracas, VZ:** Franklin Briceno. **Santo Domingo, DR:** Alexis de la Cruz, Luciano del Rosario, Fausto Espinosa, Eric Ramirez. **Cartagena, COL:** Enrique Falcon. **Mao, DR:** Jhoan Gomez. **Barquisimeto, VZ:** Miguel Leal. **San Pedro de Macoris, DR:** Luis Natera. **Aragua, VZ:** Francisco Plasencia. **Managua, NIC:** Daniel Sotelo. **Colon, PAN:** Alex Zapata.

WASHINGTON NATIONALS

Office Address: 1500 South Capitol Street SE, Washington, DC 20003.
Telephone: (202) 640-7000. **Fax:** (202) 547-0025.
Website: www.nationals.com.

OWNERSHIP

Managing Principal Owner: Mark D. Lerner. **Founding Principal Owner:** Theodore N. Lerner.
Principal Owners: Annette M. Lerner, Marla Lerner Tanenbaum, Debra Lerner Cohen, Robert K. Tanenbaum, Edward L. Cohen, Judy Lenkin Lerner.

BUSINESS OPERATIONS

Chief Operating Officer, Lerner Sports: Alan H. Gottlieb. **Chief Financial Officer:** Lori Creasy. **Senior Vice President:** Elise Holman.

BALLPARK ENTERPRISES

Executive Director, Ballpark Enterprises: Emily Dunham. **Senior Manager, Event Sales:** Kathryn Fincher.

LEGAL

Senior Vice President & General Counsel, Baseball & Business Operations: Damon Jones. **Deputy General Counsel:** Betsy Philpott.

Mark Lerner

HUMAN RESOURCES

Vice President, Human Resources: Alexa Herndon. **Senior Director, Human Resources:** Kelvin Scott. **Director, Benefits:** Stephanie Giroux.

COMMUNICATIONS

Vice President, Communications: Jennifer Giglio. **Executive Director, Communications:** Elizabeth Alexander. **Director, Communications:** Kyle Brostowitz. **Manager, Communications:** Melissa Strozza. **Manager, Communications:** Christopher Browne. **Coordinator, Communications:** Alec Scercy.

COMMUNITY RELATIONS

Vice President, Community Engagement: Gregory McCarthy. **Executive Director, Player & Community Relations:** Shawn Bertani. **Senior Manager, Community Relations:** Collin Lever. **Senior Manager, Community Relations:** Nicole Murray.

BROADCASTING/GAME PRESENTATION

Senior Vice President, Broadcasting & Game Presentation: Jacqueline Coleman. **Vice President, Production & Broadcasting:** David Lundin. **Director, Game Production:** Mike Masino

TICKETING/SALES

Vice President, Ticket Sales & Service: Ryan Bringger. **Senior Director, Ticket Sales:** Joseph Dellwo. **Vice President, Ticket Operations & Sales Optimization:** Andrew Bragman. **Director, Ticket Operations:** Tyler Hubbard.

2019 SCHEDULE

Standard Game Times: Mon.-Sat., 7:05 pm; Sun., 1:35 pm.

MARCH		
28-31 . . . . .New York (NL)		

APRIL
2-3. . . . . .Philadelphia
4-7. . . . . at New York (NL)
8-10 . . . . . at Philadelphia
12-14 . . . . Pittsburgh
16-18 . . . . . San Francisco
19-21 . . . . at Miami
22-24 . . . . . . at Colorado
26-28 . . . . San Diego
29-30 . . . . St. Louis

MAY
1-2. . . . . St. Louis
3-5. . . . . . at Philadelphia

6-8. . . . . . . at Milwaukee
9-12 . . at Los Angeles (NL)
14-16 . . . . .New York (NL)
17-19 . . . . . Chicago (NL)
20-23 . . . at New York (NL)
24-27 . . . . .Miami
28-29 . . . . at Atlanta
31 . . . . .at Cincinnati

JUNE
1-2. . . . . . . .at Cincinnati
4-5. . . . . . . Chicago (AL)
6-9. . . . . . at San Diego
10-11 . . . .at Chicago (AL)
13-16 . . . . Arizona
17-20 . . . . . .Philadelphia
21-23 . . . . Atlanta

25-27 . . . . at Miami
28-30 . . . . .at Detroit

JULY
2-4. . . . . .Miami
5-7. . . . . . . Kansas City
12-14 . . . . at Philadelphia
16-17 . . . . . .at Baltimore
18-21 . . . . . . at Atlanta
22-25 . . . . .Colorado
26-28 . . . Los Angeles (NL)
29-31 . . . . Atlanta

AUGUST
2-4. . . . . at Arizona
5-7. . . . . at San Francisco
9-11 . . . . at New York (NL)

12-14 . . . . Cincinnati
16-18 . . . . . . .Milwaukee
19-22 . . . . at Pittsburgh
23-25 . . .at Chicago (NL)
27-28 . . . . . . Baltimore
30-31 . . . . .Miami

SEPTEMBER
1 . . . . .Miami
2-4. . . . . . .New York (NL)
5-8. . . . . at Atlanta
10-12 . . . at Minnesota
13-15 . . . . Atlanta
16-18 . . . . . .at St. Louis
20-22 . . . . at Miami
23-26 . . . . .Philadelphia
27-29 . . . . Cleveland

GENERAL INFORMATION

Stadium (year opened):
Nationals Park (2008).
Team Colors: Red, white and blue.

Home Dugout: First Base.
Playing Surface: Grass.

BUSINESS STRATEGY & ANALYTICS

Senior VP, Consumer Revenue: Mike Shane. **Executive Director, Strategy:** Mike Carney.

BALLPARK OPERATIONS

Senior Vice President, Ballpark Operations: Frank Gambino. **Vice President, Ballpark Ops:** Jonathan Stahl.

BASEBALL OPERATIONS

Mike Rizzo

President of Baseball Operations and General Manager: Mike Rizzo. **Assistant General Manager & Vice President, Player Personnel:** Doug Harris. **Assistant General Manager & Vice President, Scouting Operations:** Kris Kline. **Assistant General Manager & Vice President, Finance:** Ted Towne.

MAJOR LEAGUE OPERATIONS

Vice President, Clubhouse Operations & Team Travel: Rob McDonald. **Senior Advisor to the General Manager:** Jack McKeon, Phillip Rizzo. **Special Assistant, Major League Administration:** Harolyn Cardozo. **Assistant, Major League Administration:** Jordan Missal. **Director, Baseball Operations:** Michael DeBartolo. **Analyst, Baseball Operations:** James Badas. **Coordinator, Baseball Operations:** John Wulf. **Baseball Operations Video Coordinator:** James Goodwin. **Clubhouse & Equipment Manager:** Mike Wallace. **Visiting Clubhouse Manager:** Matt Rosenthal. **Equipment Manager:** Dan Wallin. **Clubhouse Assistants:** Mike Gordon, Andrew Melnick, Gregory Melnick.

MAJOR LEAGUE STAFF

Manager: Dave Martinez. **Coaches: Bench**—Chip Hale. **Pitching**—Derek Lilliquist. **Hitting**—Kevin Long. **First Base**—Tim Bogar. **Third Base**—Bob Henley. **Bullpen**—Henry Blanco. **Assistant Hitting Coach:** Joe Dillon.

MEDICAL/TRAINING

Executive Director, Medical Services: Harvey Sharman. **Lead Team Physician:** Dr. Robin West. **Chairman, Medical Services Advisory Board:** Dr. Keith Pyne. **Director, Mental Conditioning:** Mark Campbell. **Director, Athletic Training:** Paul Lessard. **Head Athletic Trainer:** Dale Gilbert. **Athletic Trainer:** Greg Barajas. **Team Physician and Internist:** Dr. Dennis Cullen. **Team Physician, Minor League and Florida Operations:** Dr. Bruce Thomas. **Strength & Conditioning Coach:** Matt Eiden. **Assistant Major League Strength Coach:** Brett Henry. **Corrective Exercise Specialist:** Patrick Panico. **Team Chiropractor:** Dr. Hirad Bagy. **Director of Visual Performance:** Dr. Keith Smithson, .O.D. **Team Dentist:** Dr. Hugo Bonilla, DDS MS. **EAP Coordinator:** Frank Jans. **Physical Therapist:** Seth Blee. **Nutritionist:** Sue Saunders.

PLAYER DEVELOPMENT

Vice President, Senior Advisor to the General Manager: Bob Boone. **Director, Player Development:** Mark Scialabba. **Director, Minor League Operations:** Ryan Thomas. **Senior Advisor, Player Development:** Spin Williams. **Manager, Minor League Operations:** JJ Estevez. **Florida Operations Manager:** Dianne Wiebe. **Co-Field Coordinators:** Jeff Garber, Tommy Shields. **Pitching Coordinator:** Paul Menhart. **Hitting Coordinator:** Troy Gingrich. **Outfield/Baserunning Coordinator:** Gary Thurman. **Catching Coordinator:** Michael Barrett. **Information/Roving Coordinator:** Billy Gardner Jr., Mark Grater. **Medical and Rehab Coordinator:** Jon Kotredes. **Assistant Minor League Medical Coordinator:** Jeff Allred. **Rehab Pitching Coordinator:** Mark Grater. **Strength and Conditioning Coordinator:** Tony Rogowski. **Minor League Equipment Coordinator:** Calvin Minasian.

FARM SYSTEM

Class	Club	Manager	Hitting Coach	Pitching Coach
Triple-A	Fresno (PCL)	Randy Knorr	Brian Daubach	Brad Holman
Double-A	Harrisburg (EL)	Matt LeCroy	Brian Rupp	Michael Tejera
High A	Potomac (CL)	Tripp Keister	Luis Ordaz	Sam Narron
Low A	Hagerstown (SAL)	Patrick Anderson	Amaury Garcia	Mack Jenkins
Short-season	Auburn (NYP)	Rocket Wheeler	Mark Harris	Franklin Bravo
Rookie	Nationals (GCL)	Mario Lisson	Jorge Mejia	Larry Pardo
Rookie	Nationals (DSL)	Sandy Martinez	Freddy Guzman	Pablo Frias

SCOUTING

Director, Player Procurement: Kasey McKeon. **Director, Scouting Operations:** Eddie Longosz. **Assistant Director, Amateur Scouting:** Mark Baca. **Director, Pitching Evaluation & Special Asst. to the President of Baseball Ops & GM:** Jeff Zona. **Special Assistants to the President of Baseball Operations & GM:** Steve Arnieri, Chuck Cottier, Mike Cubbage, Mike Daughtry, Dan Jennings, Ron Rizzi, Jay Robertson, Bob Schaefer, Pete Vukovich, De Jon Watson, Terry Wetzel. **Manager, Advance Scouting:** Jonathan Tosches. **Coordinator, Advance Scouting:** Greg Ferguson. **Major League Advance Scout:** Jim Cuthbert. **Major League Professional Scout:** Colin Sabean. **West/Midwest Crosschecker:** Fred Costello, **East/Midwest Crosschecker:** Jimmy Gonzales. **Area Supervisors:** Justin Bloxom (IA, IN, IL, MN, WI, MO), Bryan Byrne (N. CA, NV), Brian Cleary (KY, OH, TN, MI), Ben Gallo (S. CA, HI), Jerad Head (KS, ND, NE, SD, AR, OK), Brandon Larson (S. TX, S. LA), Steve Leavitt (C. CA, S. CA), John Malzone (CT, MA, ME, NH, NJ, NY, RI, VT), Alan Marr (C. FL, N. FL), Alex Morales (Puerto Rico, S. FL), Bobby Myrick (D.C., MD, VA, DE, WV, NC, PA), Scott Ramsay (AK, ID, MT, OR, WA, WY, Canada), Eric Robinson (AL, GA, SC, Independent League Coordinator), Mitch Sokol (AZ, CO, El Paso, Las Vegas, NM, UT), Tyler Wilt (N. TX, N. LA, MS). **Vice President, International Operations:** Johnny DiPuglia. **Director, Dominican Republic Academy & Scout, Puerto Rico:** Alex Rodriguez. **Coordinator, Venezuela:** German Robles. **Assistant, International Scouting:** Taisuke Sato. **Crosscheckers:** Fausto Severino, Modesto Ulloa. **Colombia:** Eduardo Cabrera. **Curacao and Aruba:** David Leer. **Dominican Republic Supervisor:** Pablo Arias. **Dominican Republic:** Virgilio De Leon, Carlos Ulloa, Riki Vasquez. **Panama:** Miguel Ruiz. **Venezuela:** Salvador Donadelli, Juan Indriago, Ronald Morillo, Juan Munoz, Oscar Alvarado.

MEDIA INFORMATION

LOCAL MEDIA INFORMATION

AMERICAN LEAGUE

BALTIMORE ORIOLES
Radio Announcers: Joe Angel, Ben McDonald, Brian Roberts. **Flagship Station:** WJZ-FM 105.7 The Fan.
TV Announcers: Mike Bordick, Tom Davis, Rick Dempsey, Jim Hunter, Jim Palmer, Gary Thorne. **Flagship Station:** Mid-Atlantic Sports Network (MASN).

BOSTON RED SOX
Radio Announcers: Joe Castiglione. **Flagship Station:** WEEI (93.7 FM/850 AM).
TV Announcers: Dave O'Brien, Jerry Remy. **Flagship Station:** New England Sports Network (regional cable).

CHICAGO WHITE SOX
Radio Announcers: Ed Farmer, Darrin Jackson, Chris Rongey (pre/post). **Flagship Station:** WLS-AM 890.
TV Announcers: Steve Stone, Jason Benetti. **Flagship Stations:** WGN TV-9, WPWR-TV, Comcast SportsNet Chicago (regional cable).

CLEVELAND INDIANS
Radio Announcers: Tom Hamilton, Jim Rosenhaus. **Flagship Station:** WTAM 1100-AM.
TV Announcers: Rick Manning, Matt Underwood, Andre Knott, Jensen Lewis, Al Pawlowski (Pre/post). **Flagship Station:** SportsTime Ohio.

DETROIT TIGERS
Radio Announcers: Dan Dickerson, Jim Price. **Flagship Station:** WXYT 97.1 FM and AM 1270.
TV Announcers: Mario Impemba, Rod Allen, Craig Monroe, John Keating. **Flagship Station:** FOX Sports Detroit (regional cable).

HOUSTON ASTROS
Radio Announcers: Steve Sparks, Robert Ford. **Spanish:** Alex Trevino, Francisco Romero. **Flagship Stations:** KBME 790-AM, KLAT 1010-AM (Spanish).
TV Announcers: Todd Kalas, Geoff Blum. **Flagship Station:** ROOT Sports Houston.

KANSAS CITY ROYALS
Radio Announcers: Denny Matthews, Steve Physioc, Steve Stewart. **Kansas City Affiliate:** KCSP 610-AM.
TV Announcers: Ryan Lefebvre, Rex Hudler, Joel Goldberg, Jeff Montgomery (pre-game). **Flagship Station:** FOX Sports Kansas City.

LOS ANGELES ANGELS
Radio Announcers: Terry Smith, Mark Langston. **Flagship Station:** AM 830, 1330 KWKW (Spanish).
TV Announcers: Victor Rojas, Mark Gubicza. **Spanish TV Announcers:** Jose Tolentino, Jose Mota. **Flagship TV Station:** Fox Sports West (regional cable).

MINNESOTA TWINS
Radio Announcers: Cory Provus, Dan Gladden. **Radio Network Studio Host:** Kris Atteberry. **Radio Engineer:** Kyle Hammer. **Spanish Radio Play-by-Play:** Alfonso Fernandez. **Spanish Radio Analyst:** Tony Oliva. **Flagship Station:** 1500 ESPN. **TV Announcers:** Bert Blyleven, Dick Bremer, Roy Smalley, Jack Morris, Torii Hunter. **Flagship Station:** Fox Sports North.

NEW YORK YANKEES
Radio Announcers: John Sterling, Suzyn Waldman. **Flagship Station:** WFAN 660-AM, WADO 1280-AM. **Spanish Radio Announcers:** Francisco Rivera, Rickie Ricardo.
TV Announcers: David Cone, Jack Curry, John Flaherty, Michael Kay, Bob Lorenz, Meredith Marakovits, Paul O'Neill, Ken Singleton. **Flagship Station:** YES Network (Yankees Entertainment & Sports).

OAKLAND ATHLETICS
Radio Announcers: Vince Cotroneo, Ken Korach. **Flagship Station:** KGMZ 95.7 The Game, FM.
TV Announcers: Ray Fosse, Glen Kuiper, Dallas Braden. **Flagship Stations:** Comcast SportsNet California.

SEATTLE MARINERS
Radio Announcers: Rick Rizzs, Aaron Goldsmith. **Flagship Station:** 710 ESPN Seattle (KIRO-AM 710).
TV Announcers: Mike Blowers, Dave Sims. **Flagship Station:** ROOT Sports Northwest.

TAMPA BAY RAYS
Radio Announcers: Andy Freed, Dave Wills. **Flagship Station:** WDAE 620 AM/95.3 FM Tampa/St. Petersburg **TV Announcers:** Brian Anderson, Dewayne Staats. **Flagship Station:** FOX Sports Sun.

TEXAS RANGERS
Radio Announcers: Eric Nadel, Matt Hicks, Jared Sandler. **Spanish:** Eleno Ornelas, Jose Guzman. **Flagship Station:** 105.3 The FAN FM, KFLC 1270 AM (Spanish).
TV Announcers: Dave Raymond, Tom Grieve, C.J. Nitkowski, Emily Jones. **Flagship Station:** FOX Sports Southwest (regional cable).

TORONTO BLUE JAYS
Radio Announcers: Ben Wagner, Mike Wilner. **Flagship Station:** SportsNet Radio Fan 590-AM.
TV Announcers: Buck Martinez, Pat Tabler, Dan Shulman. **Flagship Station:** Rogers Sportsnet.

NATIONAL LEAGUE

ARIZONA DIAMONDBACKS
Radio Announcers: Greg Schulte, Tom Candiotti, Mike Ferrin, Rodrigo Lopez (Spanish), Arturo Ochoa, Oscar Soria (Spanish), Richard Saenz (Spanish). **Flagship Stations:** Arizona Sports 98.7 FM.
TV Announcers: Steve Berthiaume, Bob Brenly. **Flagship Stations:** FOX Sports Arizona (regional cable).

ATLANTA BRAVES
Radio Announcers: Jim Powell, Don Sutton. **Flagship Stations:** WCNN-AM 680, The Fan (93.7 FM), WYAY-FM (106.7).
TV Announcers: Chip Caray, Joe Simpson, Tom Glavine. **Flagship Stations:** FOX Sports South/Southeast (regional cable).

CHICAGO CUBS
Radio Announcers: Pat Hughes, Ron Coomer. **Flagship Station:** 670 The Score.
TV Announcers: Len Kasper, Jim Deshaies. **Flagship Stations:** CSN Chicago (regional cable), ABC7 Chicago, WGN-TV (OTAs).

CINCINNATI REDS
Radio/TV Announcers: Marty Brennaman, Thom Brennaman, Jeff Brantley, Jim Day, Doug Flynn. **Flagship Station:** WLW 700-AM.

COLORADO ROCKIES
Radio Announcers: Jack Corrigan, Jerry Schemmel. **Flagship Station:** KOA 850-AM & 94.1 FM.
TV Announcers: Drew Goodman, Jeff Huson, Ryan Spilborghs.

LOS ANGELES DODGERS
Radio Announcers: Rick Monday, Charley Steiner. **Spanish:** Jaime Jarrín, Jorge Jarrin. **Flagship Stations:** AM570 Fox Sports LA, KTNQ 1020-AM (Spanish).
TV Announcers: Ned Colletti, Joe Davis, Orel Hershiser, Nomar Garciaparra, Alanna Rizzo, John Hartung, Jerry Hairston, Jr. **Spanish:** Pepe Yniguez, Fernando Valenzuela, Manny Mota. **Flagship Stations:** SportsNet LA (regional cable).

MIAMI MARLINS
Radio Announcers: Dave Van Horne, Glenn Geffner. **Flagship Stations:** WINZ 940-AM, WAQI 710-AM (Spanish).
TV Announcers: Paul Severino, Todd Hollandsworth.
Spanish Radio Announcers: Felo Ramirez, Yiky Quintana. **Flagship Stations:** FSN Florida (regional cable).

MILWAUKEE BREWERS
Radio Announcers: Bob Uecker, Jeff Levering, Lane Grindle. **Flagship Station:** WTMJ 620-AM.
TV Announcers: Brian Anderson, Bill Schroeder, Matt Lepay. **Flagship Station:** Fox Sports Wisconsin.

NEW YORK METS
Radio Announcers: Howie Rose, Josh Lewin and Wayne Randazzo. **Flagship Station:** WOR 710-AM.
TV Announcers: Gary Cohen, Keith Hernandez, Ron Darling, Steve Gelbs, Todd Zeile. **Flagship Stations:** Sports Net New York (regional cable), PIX11-TV.

PHILADELPHIA PHILLIES
Radio Announcers: Scott Franzke, Larry Andersen, Jim Jackson. **Flagship Station:** SportsRadio 94WIP (94.1 FM).
TV Announcers: Tom McCarthy, Ben Davis, Kevin Frandsen, John Kruk, Gregg Murphy, Mike Schmidt. **Flagship Stations:** CSNPhilly, NBC 10.

PITTSBURGH PIRATES
Radio Announcers: Joe Block, Steve Blass, Greg Brown, Bob Walk, John Wehner. **Flagship Station:** Sports Radio 93.7 FM The Fan.
TV Announcers: Joe Block, Steve Blass, Greg Brown, Bob Walk, John Wehner. **Flagship Station:** ROOT SPORTS (regional cable).

ST. LOUIS CARDINALS
Radio Announcers: Mike Shannon, John Rooney, Ricky Horton. **Flagship Station:** KMOX 1120 AM.
TV Announcers: Jim Edmonds, Ricky Horton, Al Hrabosky, Tim McCarver, Dan McLaughlin, Mike Claiborne. **Flagship Station:** Fox Sports Midwest.

SAN DIEGO PADRES
Radio Announcers: Ted Leitner and Jesse Agler. **Flagship Stations:** Entercom FM 949.
TV Announcers: Don Orsillo, Mark Grant, Tony Gwynn Jr. **Flagship Station:** Fox Sports San Diego. **Spanish Announcers:** Eduardo Ortega, Carlos Hernandez on XEMO-860-AM.

SAN FRANCISCO GIANTS
Radio Announcers: Mike Krukow, Duane Kuiper, Jon Miller, Dave Flemming.
Spanish: Tito Fuentes, Edwin Higueros. **Flagship Station:** KNBR 680-AM (English); ESPN Deportes-860AM (Spanish).
TV Announcers: CSN Bay Area—Mike Krukow, Duane Kuiper; **KNTV-NBC 11**—Jon Miller, Mike Krukow. **Flagship Stations:** KNTV-NBC 11, CSN Bay Area (regional cable).

WASHINGTON NATIONALS
Radio Announcers: Charlie Slowes, Dave Jageler. **Flagship Station:** WJFK 106.7 FM.
TV Announcers: Bob Carpenter, FP Santangelo, Dan Kolko. **Flagship Station:** Mid-Atlantic Sports Network (MASN).

NATIONAL MEDIA INFORMATION

BASEBALL STATISTICS

ELIAS SPORTS BUREAU INC. NATIONAL MEDIA BASEBALL STATISTICS
Official Major League Statistician Mailing Address: 500 Fifth Ave., Suite 2140, New York, NY 10110.
Telephone: (212) 869-1530. **Fax:** (212) 354-0980. **Website:** www.esb.com.
President: Seymour Siwoff.
Executive Vice President: Steve Hirdt. **Vice President:** Chris Thorn, Peter Hirdt.

MLB ADVANCED MEDIA
Official Minor League Statistician Mailing Address: 75 Ninth Ave., New York, NY 10011.
Telephone: (212) 485-3444. **Fax:** (212) 485-3456. **Website:** MiLB.com.
Director, Stats: Chris Lentine. **Senior Manager, Stats:** Shawn Geraghty.
Senior Stats Supervisors: Jason Rigatti, Ian Schwartz. **Stats Supervisors:** Lawrence Fischer, Jake Fox, Dominic French, Kelvin Lee.

MILB.COM OFFICIAL WEBSITE OF MINOR LEAGUE BASEBALL
Mailing Address: 75 Ninth Ave, New York, NY 10011.
Telephone: (212) 485-3444. **Fax:** (212) 485-3456. **Website:** MiLB.com.
Director, Minor League Club Initiatives: Nathan Blackmon. **Sr. Producer, MiLB.com:** Dan Marinis.

STATS LLC
Mailing Address: 203 N. LaSalle St. Chicago, IL, 60601.
Telephone: (847) 583-2100. **Fax:** (847) 470-9140. **Website:** www.stats.com.
Email: sales@stats.com. **Twitter:** @STATSBiznews; @STATS_MLB. **CEO:** Ken Fuchs. **Chief Operating Officer:** Robert Schur. **EVP, Global Sales & Marketing:** Greg Kirkorsky. **SVP, Products:** Jim Corelis. **VP, Marketing:** Kirsten Porter. **Associate Vice President, Data Operations:** Allan Spear. **Manager, Baseball Operations:** Jeff Chernow

GENERAL INFORMATION

SCOUTING

PROFESSIONAL BASEBALL SCOUTS FOUNDATION
Mailing Address: 3914 Corte Cancion, Thousand Oaks, CA 91360.
Telephone: (818) 224-3906 / **Fax** (805) 378-7126. **Email:** cindy.pbsf@yahoo.com. **Website:** www.pbsfonline.com
Chairman: Dennis J. Gilbert. **Executive Director:** Cindy Picerni. **Board of Directors:** Billy Eppler, Bill "Chief" Gayton, Pat Gillick, Derrick Hall, Roland Hemond, Gary Hughes, Jeff Idelson, Dan Jennings, JJ Lally, Tommy Lasorda, Frank Marcos, Roberta Mazur, Danny Montgomery, Bob Nightengale, Pat O'Conner, Damon Oppenheimer, Jared Porter, Tracy Ringolsby, John Scotti, Brian Stephenson, Dale Sutherland, Dave Yoakum.

SCOUT OF THE YEAR FOUNDATION
Mailing Address: P.O. Box 211585, West Palm Beach, FL 33421.
Telephone: (561) 798-5897, (561) 818-4329. **E-mail Address:** bertmazur@aol.com.
President: Roberta Mazur. **Vice President:** Tracy Ringolsby. **Treasurer:** Ron Mazur II. **Board of Advisers:** Pat Gillick, Roland Hemond, Gary Hughes, Tommy Lasorda. **Scout of the Year Program Advisory Board:** Grady Fuson, Roland Hemond, Gary Hughes, Dan Jennings, Linda Pereira, Gene Watson.

MUSEUMS

NATIONAL BASEBALL HALL OF FAME AND MUSEUM
Address: 25 Main St., Cooperstown, NY 13326.
Telephone: (888) 425-5633, (607) 547-7200. **Fax:** (607) 547-2044. **E-mail Address:** info@baseballhall.org. **Website:** www.baseballhall.org.
Year Founded: 1939.
Chairman: Jane Forbes Clark. **Vice Chairman:** Joe Morgan. **President:** Jeff Idelson.
Museum Hours: Open daily, year-round, closed only Thanksgiving, Christmas and New Year's Day. 9 a.m.-5 p.m. Summer hours, 9 a.m.-9 p.m. (Memorial Day weekend through the day before Labor Day.)
2019 Hall of Fame Induction Weekend: July 19-22, Cooperstown, N.Y.

NEGRO LEAGUES BASEBALL MUSEUM
Mailing Address: 1616 E. 18th St., Kansas City, MO 64108.
Telephone: (816) 221-1920. **Fax:** (816) 221-8424.
E-mail Address: bkendrick@nlbm.com. **Website:** www.nlbm.com.
Year Founded: 1990.
President: Bob Kendrick.
Museum Hours: Tues.-Sat. 9 a.m.-6 p.m.; Sun. noon-6 p.m.

RESEARCH

SOCIETY FOR AMERICAN BASEBALL RESEARCH

Mailing Address: Cronkite School at ASU, 555 N Central Ave., #416 , Phoenix, AZ 85004.
Website: www.sabr.org.
Year Founded: 1971.
President: Vince Gennaro. **Vice President:** Leslie Heaphy. **Secretary:** Todd Lebowitz. **Treasurer:** F.X. Flinn. **Directors:** Bill Nowlin, Mark Armour, Chris Dial, Emily Hawks. **CEO:** Scott Bush. **Director of Editorial Content:** Jacob Pomrenke.

ALUMNI ASSOCIATIONS

MAJOR LEAGUE BASEBALL PLAYERS ALUMNI ASSOCIATION

Mailing Address: 1631 Mesa Ave., Copper Building, Suite D, Colorado Springs, CO 80906.
Telephone: (719) 477-1870. **Fax:** (719) 477-1875.
E-mail Address: postoffice@mlbpaa.com. **Website:** www.baseballalumni.com.
Facebook: facebook.com/majorleaguebaseballplayersalumniassociation. **Twitter:** @MLBPAA.
Chief Executive Officer: Dan Foster (dan@mlbpaa.com). **Chief Operating Officer:** Geoffrey Hixson (geoff@mlbpaa.com). **Vice President, Operations:** Mike Groll (mikeg@mlbpaa.com). **Director, Communications:** Nikki Warner (nikki@mlbpaa.com). **Director, Membership:** Kate Hutchinson (Kate@mlbpaa.com). **Director, Memorabilia:** Greg Thomas (greg@mlbpaa.com). **Database Administrator:** Chris Burkeen (cburkeen@mlbpaa.com).

BASEBALL ASSISTANCE TEAM (B.A.T.)

Mailing Address: 245 Park Ave., 31st Floor, New York, NY 10167.
Telephone: (212) 931-7822, **Fax:** (212) 949-5433.
Website: www.baseballassistanceteam.com.

MINISTRY

BASEBALL CHAPEL

Mailing Address: P.O. Box 10102, Largo FL 33773.
Telephone: (610) 999-3600.
E-mail Address: office@baseballchapel.org. **Website:** www.baseballchapel.org.
Year Founded: 1973.
President: Vince Nauss. **Hispanic Ministry:** Cali Magallanes, Gio Llerena. **Ministry Operations:** Rob Crose, Steve Sisco. **Board of Directors:** Don Christensen, Greg Groh, Dave Howard, Vince Nauss, Walt Wiley.

CATHOLIC ATHLETES FOR CHRIST

Mailing Address: 3703 Cameron Mills Road, Alexandria, VA 22305.
Telephone: (703) 239-3070.
E-mail Address: info@catholicathletesforchrist.org. **Website:** www.catholicathletesforchrist.org.
Year Founded: 2006.
President: Ray McKenna. **MLB Ministry Coordinator:** Kevin O'Malley. **MLB Athlete Advisory Board Members:** Mike Sweeney (Chairman), Jeff Suppan (Vice Chairman), Sal Bando, Tom Carroll, David Eckstein, Tyler Flowers, Terry Kennedy, Jack McKeon, Darrell Miller, Mike Piazza, Vinny Rottino, Craig Stammen.

TRADE/EMPLOYMENT

BASEBALL WINTER MEETINGS

Mailing Address: P.O. Box A, St. Petersburg, FL 33731.
Telephone: (727) 822-6937. **Fax:** (727) 821-5819.
E-Mail Address: BaseballWinterMeetings@milb.com. **Website:** www.baseballwintermeetings.com.
2019 Convention: Dec. 9-12, San Diego

BASEBALL TRADE SHOW

Mailing Address: P.O. Box A, St. Petersburg, FL 33731-1950.
Telephone: (866) 926-6452. **Fax:** (727) 683-9865.
E-Mail Address: TradeShow@MiLB.com. **Website:** www.BaseballTradeShow.com.
Contact: Noreen Brantner, Sr. Asst. Director, Exhibition Services & Sponsorships.
2019 Convention: Dec. 9-12, San Diego

PROFESSIONAL BASEBALL EMPLOYMENT OPPORTUNITIES

Mailing Address: P.O. Box A, St. Petersburg, FL 33731-1950.
Telephone: 866-WE-R-PBEO. **Fax:** 727-821-5819.
Email: info@PBEO.com. **Website:** www.PBEO.com.
Contact: Paige Hegedus, Manager, Special Events/Affiliate Programming.

REVIVING BASEBALL IN INNER CITIES

Mailing Address: 245 Park Avenue 30th Fl, New York, NY 10167
Telephone: (212) 931-7800. **Fax:** (212) 949-5695
Year Founded: 1989
Senior Vice President, Youth Programs: Tony Reagins (Tony.Reagins@mlb.com). **Vice President, Youth Programs:** David James (David.James@mlb.com). **E-mail:** rbi@mlb.com. **Website:** www.mlb.com/rbi

MLB YOUTH ACADEMIES

CINCINNATI REDS YOUTH ACADEMY
Director: Jerome Wright
Asst. Director: Jeremy Hamilton
Mailing Address: 2026 E. Seymour Avenue. Cincinnati , OH 45327
Phone Number: 513-765-5000

COMPTON YOUTH ACADEMY
Vice President: Darrell Miller
Mailing Address: 901 East Artesia Blvd. Compton, CA

HOUSTON ASTROS YOUTH ACADEMY
Director: Daryl Wade
Mailing Address: 2801 South Victory Drive. Houston, TX 77088.
Email: uya@astros.com

KANSAS CITY ROYALS URBAN YOUTH ACADEMY
Director: Darwin Pennye
Email: Darwin.Pennye@royals.com

NEW ORLEANS YOUTH ACADEMY
Director: Eddie Anthony Davis III
Mailing Address: 6403 Press Drive. New Orleans, LA 70126
Phone Number: 504-282-0443

PHILADELPHIA YOUTH ACADEMY
Director: Jon Joaquin
Phone Number: 215-218-5634
Director: Rob Holiday
Phone Number: 215-218-5204

PUERTO RICO BASEBALL ACADEMY AND HIGH SCHOOL
Director: Luis Cintron
Phone Number: 787-712-0700
Lucy Batista: Headmaster
Phone Number: 787-531-1768

TEXAS RANGERS YOUTH ACADEMY
Director: Karin Morris
Mailing Address: 3500 Goldman Street. Dallas, TX 75212
Phone Number: 817-273-5297

WASHINGTON NATIONALS YOUTH ACADEMY
Executive Director: Tal Alter
Mailing Address: 3675 Ely Place SE. Washington, DC 20019
Phone Number: 202-827-8960

SPRING TRAINING

CACTUS LEAGUE

ARIZONA DIAMONDBACKS

MAJOR LEAGUE

Complex Address: Salt River Fields at Talking Stick, 7555 North Pima Road, Scottsdale, AZ 85256. **Telephone:** (480) 270-5000. **Seating Capacity:** 11,000 (7,000 fixed seats, 4,000 lawn seats). **Location:** From Loop-101, use exit 44 (Indian Bend Road) and proceed west for approximately one-half mile; turn right at Pima Road to travel north and proceed one-quarter mile; three entrances to Salt River Fields will be available on the right-hand side.

MINOR LEAGUE

Complex Address: Same as major league club.

CHICAGO CUBS

MAJOR LEAGUE

Complex Address: Sloan Park, 2330 West Rio Salado Parkway, Mesa, AZ 85201. **Telephone:** (480) 668-0500. **Seating Capacity:** 15,000. **Location:** on the land of the former Riverview Golf Course, bordered by the 101 and 202 interchange in Mesa.

MINOR LEAGUE

Complex Address: 2510 W. Rio Salado Parkway, Mesa, AZ 85201. **Telephone:** (480) 668-0500

CHICAGO WHITE SOX

MAJOR LEAGUE

Complex Address: Camelback Ranch-Glendale, 10710 West Camelback Road, Phoenix, AZ 85037. **Telephone:** (623) 302-5000. **Seating Capacity:** 13,000. **Hotel Address:** Residence Inn Phoenix Glendale Sports and Entertainment District, 7350 N Zanjero Blvd, Glendale, AZ 85305, **Telephone:** (623) 772-8900. **Hotel Address:** Renaissance Glendale Hotel & Spa, 9495 W Coyotes Blvd, Glendale, AZ 85305. **Telephone:** 629-937-3700.

MINOR LEAGUE

Complex/Hotel Address: Same as major league club.

CINCINNATI REDS

MAJOR LEAGUE

Complex Address: Cincinnati Reds Player Development Complex, 3125 S Wood Blvd, Goodyear, AZ 85338. **Telephone:** (623) 932-6590. **Ballpark Address:** Goodyear Ballpark, 1933 S Ballpark Way, Goodyear, AZ 85338. **Telephone:** (623) 882-3120. **Hotel Address:** Marriott Residence Inn, 7350 N Zanjero Blvd, Glendale, AZ 85305. **Telephone:** (623) 772-8900. **Fax:** (623) 772-8905.

MINOR LEAGUE

Complex/Hotel Address: Same as major league club.

CLEVELAND INDIANS

MAJOR LEAGUE

Complex Address: Cleveland Indians Player Development Complex 2601 S Wood Blvd, Goodyear, AZ 85338; Goodyear Ballpark 1933 S Ballpark Way, Goodyear, AZ 85338. **Telephone:** (623) 882-3120. **Location: From Downtown Phoenix/East Valley:** West on I-10 to

Exit 127, Bullard Avenue and proceed south (left off exit), Bullard Avenue turns into West Lower Buckeye Road. Turn left onto Wood Blvd. **Hotel Address:** (Media) Hampton Inn and Suites, 2000 N Litchfield Rd, Goodyear, AZ 85395. **Telephone:** (623) 536-1313. **Hotel Address:** Holiday Inn Express, 1313 N Litchfield Rd, Goodyear, AZ 85395. **Telephone:** (623) 535-1313. **Hotel Address:** TownePlace Suites, 13971 West Celebrate Life Way, Goodyear, AZ 85338. **Telephone:** (623) 535-5009. **Hotel Address:** Residence Inn by Marriott, 2020 N Litchfield Rd, Goodyear, AZ 85395. **Telephone:** (623) 866-1313.

MINOR LEAGUE

Complex Address: Same as major league club.

COLORADO ROCKIES

MAJOR LEAGUE

Complex Address: Salt River Fields at Talking Stick, 7555 North Pima Rd, Scottsdale, AZ 85258. **Telephone:** (480) 270-5800. **Seating Capacity:** 11,000 (7,000 fixed seats, 4,000 lawn seats). **Location:** From Loop-101, use exit 44 (Indian Bend Road Talking Stick Way) and proceed west for approximately one-half mile; turn right at Pima Road to travel north and proceed one-quarter mile; three entrances to Salt River Fields will be available on the right-hand side. **Visiting Team Hotel:** The Scottsdale Plaza Resort, 7200 North Scottsdale Road, Scottsdale, AZ 85253. **Telephone:** (480) 948-5000. **Fax:** (480) 951-5100.

MINOR LEAGUE

Complex/Hotel Address: Same as major league club.

KANSAS CITY ROYALS

MAJOR LEAGUE

Complex Address: Surprise Stadium, 15850 North Bullard Ave, Surprise, AZ 85374. **Telephone:** (623) 222-2000. **Seating Capacity:** 10,700. **Location:** I-10 West to Route 101 North, 101 North to Bell Road, left on Bell for five miles, stadium on left. **Hotel Address:** Wigwam Resort, 300 East Wigwam Blvd, Litchfield Park, Arizona 85340. **Telephone:** (623) 935-3811.

MINOR LEAGUE

Complex Address: Same as major league club. **Hotel Address:** Comfort Hotel and Suites, 13337 W Grand Ave, Surprise, AZ 85374. **Telephone:** (623) 583-3500.

LOS ANGELES ANGELS

MAJOR LEAGUE

Complex Address: Tempe Diablo Stadium, 2200 West Alameda Drive, Tempe, AZ 85282. **Telephone:** (480) 858-7500. **Fax:** (480) 438-7583. **Seating Capacity:** 9,558. **Location:** I-10 to exit 153B (48th Street), south one mile on 48th Street to Alameda Drive, left on Alameda.

MINOR LEAGUE

Complex Address: Tempe Diablo Minor League Complex, 2225 W Westcourt Way, Tempe, AZ 85282. **Telephone:** (480) 858-7558.

LOS ANGELES DODGERS

MAJOR LEAGUE

Complex Address: Camelback Ranch, 10710 West Camelback Rd, Phoenix, AZ 85037. **Seating Capacity:** 13,000, plus standing room. **Location:** I-10 or I-17 to Loop 101 West or North, Take Exit 5, Camelback Road West to ballpark. **Telephone:** (623) 302-5000. **Hotel:** Unavailable.

MINOR LEAGUE

Complex/Hotel Address: Same as major league club.

MILWAUKEE BREWERS

MAJOR LEAGUE

Complex Address: Maryvale Baseball Park, 3600 N 51st Ave, Phoenix, AZ 85031. **Telephone:** (623) 245-5555. **Seating Capacity:** 9,000. **Location:** I-10 to 51st Ave, north on 51st Ave. **Hotel Address:** Unavailable.

MINOR LEAGUE

Complex Address: Maryvale Baseball Complex, 3805 N 53rd Ave, Phoenix, AZ 85031. **Telephone:** (623) 245-5600. **Hotel Address:** Unavailable.

OAKLAND ATHLETICS

MAJOR LEAGUE

Complex Address: Hohokam Stadium, 1235 North Center Street, Mesa, AZ 85201. **Telephone:** 480-907-5489. **Seating Capacity:** 10,000.

MINOR LEAGUE

Complex Address: Fitch Park, 160 East 6th Place, Mesa, AZ 85201. **Telephone:** 480-387-5800. **Hotel Address:** Unavailable.

SAN DIEGO PADRES

MAJOR LEAGUE

Complex Address: Peoria Sports Complex, 8131 West Paradise Lane, Peoria, AZ 85382. **Telephone:** (619) 795-5720. **Fax:** (623) 486-7154. **Seating Capacity:** 12,000. **Location:** I-17 to Bell Road exit, west on Bell to 83rd Ave. **Hotel Address:** La Quinta Inn & Suites (623) 487-1900, 16321 N 83rd Avenue, Peoria, AZ 85382.

MINOR LEAGUE

Complex/Hotel: Country Inn and Suites (623) 879-9000, 20221 N 29th Avenue, Phoenix, AZ 85027.

SAN FRANCISCO GIANTS

MAJOR LEAGUE

Complex Address: Scottsdale Stadium, 7408 East Osborn Rd, Scottsdale, AZ 85251. **Telephone:** (480) 990-7972. **Fax:** (480) 990-2643. **Seating Capacity:** 11,500. **Location:** Scottsdale Road to Osborne Road, east on Osborne for a 1/2 mile. **Hotel Address:** Hilton Garden Inn Scottsdale Old Town, 7324 East Indian School Rd, Scottsdale, AZ 85251. **Telephone:** (480) 481-0400.

MINOR LEAGUE

Complex Address: Giants Minor League Complex 8045 E Camelback Road, Scottsdale, AZ 85251. **Telephone:** (480) 990-0052. **Fax:** (480) 990-2349.

SEATTLE MARINERS

MAJOR LEAGUE

Complex Address: Seattle Mariners, 15707 North 83rd Street, Peoria, AZ 85382. **Telephone:** (623) 776-4800. **Fax:** (623) 776-4829. **Seating Capacity:** 12,339. **Location:** I-17 to Bell Road exit, east on Bell to 83rd Ave, south on 83rd Ave. **Hotel Address:** La Quinta Inn & Suites, 16321 N 83rd Ave, Peoria, AZ 85382. **Telephone:** (623) 487-1900.

MINOR LEAGUE

Complex Address: Peoria Sports Complex (1993), 15707 N 83rd Ave, Peoria, AZ 85382. **Telephone:** (623) 776-4800. **Fax:** (623) 776-4828. **Hotel Address:** Hampton Inn, 8408 W Paradise Lane, Peoria, AZ 85382. **Telephone:** (623) 486-9918.

TEXAS RANGERS

MAJOR LEAGUE

Complex Address: Surprise Stadium, 15754 North Bullard Ave, Surprise, AZ 85374. **Telephone:** (623) 266-8100. **Seating Capacity:** 10,714. **Location:** I-10 West to Route 101 North, 101 North to Bell Road, left at Bell for seven miles, stadium on left. **Hotel Address:** Residence Inn Surprise, 16418 N Bullard Ave, Surprise, AZ 85374. **Telephone:** (623) 249-6333.

MINOR LEAGUE

Complex Address: Same as major league club. **Hotel Address:** Holiday Inn Express and Suites Surprise, 16549 North Bullard Ave, Surprise AZ 85374. **Telephone:** (800) 939-4249.

GRAPEFRUIT LEAGUE

ATLANTA BRAVES

MAJOR LEAGUE
Stadium Address: Champion Stadium at ESPN Wide World of Sports Complex, 700 S Victory Way, Kissimmee, FL 34747. **Telephone:** (407) 939-1500. **Seating Capacity:** 9,500. **Location:** I-4 to exit 25B (Highway 192 West), follow signs to Magic Kingdom/Wide World of Sports Complex, right on Victory Way. **Hotel Address:** World Center Marriott, World Center Drive, Orlando, FL 32821. **Telephone:** (407) 239-4200.

MINOR LEAGUE
Complex Address: Same as major league club. **Telephone:** (407) 939-2232. **Fax:** (407) 939-2225. **Hotel Address:** Marriot Village at Lake Buena Vista, 8623 Vineland Ave, Orlando, FL 32821. **Telephone:** (407) 938-9001.

BALTIMORE ORIOLES

MAJOR LEAGUE
Complex Address: Ed Smith Stadium, 2700 12th Street, Sarasota, FL 34237. **Telephone:** (941) 893-6300. **Fax:** (941) 893-6377. **Seating Capacity:** 7,500. **Location:** I-75 to exit 210, West on Fruitville Road, right on Tuttle Avenue.

MINOR LEAGUE
Complex Address: Buck O'Neil Baseball Complex at Twin Lakes Park, 6700 Clark Rd, Sarasota, FL 34241. **Telephone:** (941) 923-1996.

BOSTON RED SOX

MAJOR LEAGUE
Complex Address: JetBlue Park at Fenway South, 11500 Fenway South Drive, Fort Myers, FL 33913. **Telephone:** (239) 334-4700. **Directions: From the North:** Take I-75 South to Exit 131 (Daniels Parkway); Make a left off the exit and go east for approximately two miles; JetBlue Park will be on your left. **From the South:** Take I-75 North to Exit 131 (Daniels Parkway); Make a right off exit and go east for approximately two miles; JetBlue Park will be on your left.

MINOR LEAGUE
Complex/Hotel Address: Fenway South, 11500 Fenway South Drive, Fort Myers, FL 33913.

DETROIT TIGERS

MAJOR LEAGUE
Complex Address: Joker Marchant Stadium, 2301 Lakeland Hills Blvd, Lakeland, FL 33805. **Telephone:** (863) 686-8075. **Seating Capacity:** 9,568. **Location:** I-4 to exit 33 (Lakeland Hills Boulevard).

MINOR LEAGUE
Complex Address: Tigertown, 2125 N Lake Ave, Lakeland, FL 33805. **Telephone:** (863) 686-8075.

HOUSTON ASTROS

MAJOR LEAGUE
Complex Address: The Ballpark of the Palm Beaches, 5444 Haverhill Road, West Palm Beach, FL 33407. **Telephone:** (844) 676-2017. **Seating Capacity:** 7,838. **Location:** Exit Florida's Turnpike onto Okeechobee Blvd.

Proceed east to Haverhill Road turning left onto Haverhill Road. On game days, all vehicles may park in one of two grass parking areas. Proceed toward the stadium for disabled parking or drop-off. The North entrance on Haverhill Road will be right-out only. **Hotel Address:** Unavailable.

MINOR LEAGUE
Complex Information: Same as major league club. **Hotel Address:** Unavailable.

MIAMI MARLINS

MAJOR LEAGUE
Complex Address: Roger Dean Stadium, 4751 Main Street, Jupiter, FL 33458. **Telephone:** (561) 775-1818. **Telephone:** (561) 799-1346. **Seating Capacity:** 7,000. **Location:** I-95 to exit 83, east on Donald Ross Road for one mile to Central Blvd, left at light, follow Central Boulevard to circle and take Main Street to Roger Dean Stadium. **Hotel Address:** Palm Beach Gardens Marriott, 4000 RCA Boulevard, Palm Beach Gardens, FL 33410. **Telephone:** (561) 622-8888. **Fax:** (561) 622-0052.

MINOR LEAGUE
Complex/Hotel Address: Same as major league club.

MINNESOTA TWINS

MAJOR LEAGUE
Complex Address: Centurylink Sports Complex/Hammond Stadium, 14100 Six Mile Cypress Parkway, Fort Myers, FL 33912. **Telephone:** (239) 533-7610. **Seating Capacity:** 8,100. **Location:** Exit 21 off I-75, west on Daniels Parkway, left on Six Mile Cypress Parkway. **Hotel Address:** Four Points by Sheraton, 13600 Treeline Avenue South, Ft. Myers, FL 33913. **Telephone:** (800) 338-9467.

MINOR LEAGUE
Complex/Hotel Address: Same as major league club.

NEW YORK METS

MAJOR LEAGUE
Complex Address: Tradition Field, 525 NW Peacock Blvd, Port St. Lucie, FL 34986. **Telephone:** (772) 871-2100. **Seating Capacity:** 7,000. **Location:** Exit 121C (St Lucie West Blvd) off I-95, east 1/4 mile, left onto NW Peacock. **Hotel Address:** Hilton Hotel, 8542 Commerce Centre Drive, Port St. Lucie, FL 34986. **Telephone:** (772) 871-6850.

MINOR LEAGUE
Complex Address: Same as major league club. **Hotel Address:** Main Stay Suites, 8501 Champions Way, Port St. Lucie, FL 34986. **Telephone:** (772) 460-8882.

NEW YORK YANKEES

MAJOR LEAGUE
Complex Address: George M. Steinbrenner Field, One Steinbrenner Drive, Tampa, FL 33614. **Telephone:** (813) 875-7753. **Hotel:** Unavailable.

MINOR LEAGUE
Complex Address: Yankees Player Development/Scouting Complex, 3102 N Himes Ave, Tampa, FL 33607. **Telephone:** (813) 875-7569. **Hotel:** Unavailable.

PHILADELPHIA PHILLIES

MAJOR LEAGUE

Complex Address: Spectrum Field, 601 N Old Coachman Road, Clearwater, FL 33765. **Telephone:** (727) 467-4457. **Fax:** (727) 712-4498. **Seating Capacity:** 8,500. **Location:** Route 60 West, right on Old Coachman Road, ballpark on right after Drew Street. **Hotel Address:** Holiday Inn Express, 2580 Gulf to Bay Blvd, Clearwater, FL 33765. **Telephone:** (727) 797-6300. **Hotel Address:** La Quinta Inn, 21338 US 19 North, Clearwater, FL 33765. **Telephone:** (727) 799-1565.

MINOR LEAGUE

Complex Address: Carpenter Complex, 651 N Old Coachman Rd, Clearwater, FL 33765. **Telephone:** (727) 799-0503. **Fax:** (727) 726-1793. **Hotel Addresses:** Hampton Inn, 21030 US Highway 19 North, Clearwater, FL 34625. **Telephone:** (727) 797-8173. **Hotel Address:** Econolodge, 21252 US Hwy 19, Clearwater, FL 34625. **Telephone:** (727) 799-1569.

PITTSBURGH PIRATES

MAJOR LEAGUE

Stadium Address: 17th Ave West and Ninth Street West, Bradenton, FL 34205. **Seating Capacity:** 8,500. **Location:** US 41 to 17th Ave, west to 9th Street. **Telephone:** (941) 747-3031. **Fax:** (941) 747-9549.

MINOR LEAGUE

Complex: Pirate City, 1701 27th St E, Bradenton, FL 34208.

ST. LOUIS CARDINALS

MAJOR LEAGUE

Complex Address: Roger Dean Stadium, 4751 Main Street, Jupiter, FL 33458. **Telephone:** (561) 775-1818. **Fax:** (561) 799-1380. **Seating Capacity:** 7,000. **Location:** I-95 to exit 58, east on Donald Ross Road for 1/4 mile. **Hotel Address:** Embassy Suites, 4350 PGA Blvd, Palm Beach Gardens, FL 33410. **Telephone:** (561) 622-1000.

MINOR LEAGUE

Complex: Same as major league club. **Hotel:** Double Tree Palm Beach Gardens. **Telephone:** (561) 622-2260.

TAMPA BAY RAYS

MAJOR LEAGUE

Stadium Address: Charlotte Sports Park, 2300 El Jobean Road, Port Charlotte, FL 33948. **Telephone:** (941) 206-4487. **Seating Capacity:** 6,823 (5,028 fixed seats). **Location:** I-75 to US-17 to US-41, turn left onto El Jobean Rd. **Hotel Address:** None.

MINOR LEAGUE

Complex: Same as major league club.

TORONTO BLUE JAYS

MAJOR LEAGUE

Stadium Address: Florida Auto Exchange Stadium, 373 Douglas Ave, Dunedin, FL 34698. **Telephone:** (727) 733-9302. **Seating Capacity:** 5,509. **Location:** US 19 North to Sunset Point; west on Sunset Point to Douglas Avenue; north on Douglas to Stadium; ballpark is on the southeast corner of Douglas and Beltrees.

MINOR LEAGUE

Complex Address: Bobby Mattick Training Center at Englebert Complex, 1700 Solon Ave, Dunedin, FL 34698. **Telephone:** (727) 734-8007. **Hotel Address:** Clarion Inn & Suites, 20967 US Highway 19 North Clearwater, FL 33765. **Telephone:** (727) 799-1181.

WASHINGTON NATIONALS

MAJOR LEAGUE

Stadium Address: The Ballpark of the Palm Beaches, 5444 N. Haverhill Road, West Palm Beach, FL 33407. **Telephone:** (844) 676-2017.

MINOR LEAGUE

Complex: Same as major league club.

MINOR
LEAGUES

MINOR LEAGUE BASEBALL

MINOR LEAGUE BASEBALL

THE NATIONAL ASSOCIATION OF PROFESSIONAL BASEBALL LEAGUES

Street Address: 9550 16th St. North, St. Petersburg, FL 33716.
Mailing Address: PO Box A, St. Petersburg, FL 33731-1950.
Telephone: (727) 822-6937. **Fax:** (727) 821-5819.
Fax/Marketing: (727) 894-4227. **Fax/Licensing:** (727) 825-3785.
President & CEO: Pat O'Conner. **Vice President:** Stan Brand. **Chief Marketing & Commercial Officer:** David Wright. **Chief Financial Officer:** Sean Brown. **Senior VP, Legal Affairs & General Counsel:** D. Scott Poley. **Senior VP, Digital Strategy & Business Development:** Katie Davison. **Senior VP, Baseball & Business Operations:** Tim Brunswick. **VP, Marketing Strategy & Research:** Kurt Hunzeker. **VP, Business Development & Media:** Gerald Jones. **Head of Licensing & Consumer Products:** Brian Earle. **Sr. Executive Advisor to the President:** Dan O'Brien Jr. **Assistant to the President:** Bill Smith. **Sr. Dir., Communications:** Jeff Lantz. **Dir., Information Technology:** Rob Colamarino. **Dir., Special Events:** Stefanie Loncarich. **Dir., Diversity & Inclusion:** Vince Pierson. **Dir., Partnership Marketing:** Heather Raburn. **Dir., Human Resources:** Tara Thornton. **Deputy General Counsel:** Robert Fountain. **Special Counsel:** George Yund. **Controller:** James Dispanet. **Asst. Dir., Licensing:** Carrie Adams. **Asst. Dir., Baseball & Business Operations:** Andy Shultz. Asst. **Dir., Community Engagement:** Courtney Nehls. **Asst. Dir., Corporate Communications:** Mary Marandi. **Marketing Strategy & Research:** Cory Bernstine. **Asst. Dir., Special Events & Affiliate Programming:** Mark Labban. **Asst. Dir., Sr. Mgr., Brand Development:** Ryan Foose. **Senior Mgr., Digital Marketing & Communications:** Mallory Roberts. **Assoc. Counsel:** Shannon Finucane. **Contract Mgr./Legal Asst.:** Jeannette Machicote. **Mgr., Event Partners & Trade Show Services:** Eileen Sahin-Murphy. **Mgr., Business Development & Media:** Curtis Walker. **Mgr., Baseball Ops./Exec. Asst. To President:** Mary Wooters. **Mgr., Partnership Marketing:** William Kent Jr. **Mgr., Partnership Marketing:** Scott Ester. **Manager, Special Events & Affiliate Programming:** Paige Hegedus. **Manager, Business and Data Processes:** Belicia Montgomery. **Senior Digital Project Manager:** Laurie Nygren. **Production Designer:** Vincent Pettofrezzo. **Sr. Accountant:** Michelle Heystek. **Coord., Social Media Marketing:** Brad Friedman. **Coord., Enterprise Marketing:** Meghan Madson. **Coord., Trademarks & Intellectual Properties:** Melissa Giesler-Hassell. **Coordinator, Events & Partnerships:** Jessica Nori. **Coordinator, Ecommerce:** Tajma Brown. **Office Coordinator:** Anthony Franceschini.

Pat O'Conner

AFFILIATED MEMBERS/COUNCIL OF LEAGUE PRESIDENTS

Triple-A

League	President	Telephone	Fax Number
International	Randy Mobley	(614) 791-9300	(614) 791-9009
Mexican	Javier Salinas	01152-55571007	01152-53952454
Pacific Coast	Branch Rickey	(512) 310-2900	(512) 310-8300

Double-A

League	President	Telephone	Fax Number
Eastern	Joe McEacharn	(207) 761-2700	(207) 761-7064
Southern	Lori Webb	(770) 321-0400	(770) 321-0037
Texas	Tim Purpura	(682) 316-4100	(682) 316-4100

High Class A

League	President	Telephone	Fax Number
California	Charlie Blaney	(805) 985-8585	(805) 985-8580
Carolina	Geoff Lassiter	(336) 691-9030	(336) 464-2737
Florida State	Ken Carson	(727) 224-8244	(386) 252-7495

Low Class A

League	President	Telephone	Fax Number
Midwest	Dick Nussbaum	(574) 231-3000	(574) 231-3000
South Atlantic	Eric Krupa	(727) 538-4270	(727) 499-6853

Short-Season

League	President	Telephone	Fax Number
New York-Penn	Ben Hayes	(727) 289-7112	(727) 683-9691
Northwest	Mike Ellis	(406) 541-9301	(406) 543-9463

Rookie Advanced

League	President	Telephone	Fax Number
Appalachian	Dan Moushon	(919) 656-5357	Unavailable
Pioneer	Jim McCurdy	(509) 456-7615	(509) 456-0136

Rookie

League	President	Telephone	Fax Number
Arizona	Bob Richmond	(208) 429-1511	(208) 429-1525
Dominican Summer	Orlando Diaz	(809) 532-3619	(809) 532-3619
Gulf Coast	Operated by MiLB	(727) 456-1734	(727) 821-5819

NATIONAL ASSOCIATION BOARD OF TRUSTEES

TRIPLE-A
At-large: Ken Young (Norfolk). **International League:** Ken Schnacke, Chairman (Columbus). **Pacific Coast League:** Sam Bernabe (Iowa). **Mexican League:** Gerardo Benavides Pape (Monclova).

DOUBLE-A
Eastern League: Joe Finley (Trenton). **Southern League:** Stan Logan, Secretary (Birmingham). **Texas League:** Matt Gifford (Springfield).

CLASS A
California League: Tom Volpe (Stockton). **Carolina League:** Chuck Greenberg (Myrtle Beach). **Florida State League:** Ron Myers (Lakeland). **Midwest League:** Tom Dickson (Lansing). **South Atlantic League:** Chip Moore (Rome).

SHORT-SEASON
New York-Penn League: Marv Goldklang, Vice Chairman (Hudson Valley). **Northwest League:** Bobby Brett (Spokane).

ROOKIE
Appalachian League: Mitch Lukevics (Princeton). **Pioneer Baseball League:** Dave Elmore, (Idaho Falls). **Gulf Coast League:** Reid Ryan (Astros).

PROFESSIONAL BASEBALL UMPIRE CORP.

President & CEO: Pat O'Conner.
Secretary/Sr. VP, Legal Affairs & General Counsel: D. Scott Poley.
Senior VP, Baseball/Business Operations: Tim Brunswick. **Director, MiLB Umpire Development:** Dusty Dellinger.
Mgr., Umpire Technology: Tom Honec. **Mgr., Umpire Development:** Jess Schneider. **Chief of Instruction:** Mike Felt.
Field Evaluators/Instructors: Jorge Bauza, Tyler Funneman, Jay Pierce, Brian Sinclair, Darren Spagnardi. **Medical Coordinator:** Mark Stubblefield.

GENERAL INFORMATION

Medical Coordinator: Mark Stubblefield.
VP, Baseball/Business Operations: Tim Brunswick. **Director, MiLB Umpire Development:** Dusty Dellinger. **Chief of Instruction:** Mike Felt. **Field Evaluators/Instructors:** Jorge Bauza, Tyler Funneman, Mark Lollo, Larry Reveal, Brian Sinclair, Darren Spagnardi. **Video Technician:** Tom Honec. **Medical Coordinator:** Mark Stubblefield. **Special Assistant:** Lillian Patterson.

			Regular Season		All-Star Games	
	Teams	Games	Opening Day	Closing Day	Date	Host
International	14	140	April 4	Sept. 2	* July 10	Columbus
Pacific Coast	16	140	April 4	Sept. 2	* July 10	Columbus
Eastern	12	140	April 4	Sept. 2	July 10	Richmond
Southern	10	140	April 4	Sept. 2	June 18	Biloxi
Texas	8	140	April 4	Sept. 2	June 25	Tulsa
California	8	140	April 4	Sept. 2	June 18	Inland Empire
Carolina	10	140	April 4	Sept. 2	June 18	Frederick
Florida State	12	140	April 4	Sept. 1	June 15	Jupiter/PB
Midwest	16	140	April 4	Sept. 2	June 18	South Bend
South Atlantic	14	140	April 4	Sept. 2	June 18	West Virginia
New York-Penn	14	76	June 14	Sept. 2	Aug. 21	Staten Island
Northwest	8	76	June 14	Sept. 2	^ Aug. 6	Boise
Appalachian	10	68	June 18	Aug. 28	None	
Pioneer	8	76	June 14	Sept. 5	^ Aug. 6	Boise
Arizona	15	56	June 17	Aug. 26	None	
Gulf Coast	18	56	June 17	Aug. 24	None	

*Triple-A All-Star Game. ^Northwest League vs. Pioneer Baseball League.

DINGERBATS.COM
SWING DINGER
BIG LEAGUE WOOD. BIG LEAGUE HOMERS.
SHOP BATS
WORLD CLASS WOOD
made in the USA
KS-10
PROFESSIONAL MAPLE
MODEL KS-10 34/31

INTERNATIONAL LEAGUE

Randy Mobley

Address: 55 South High St., Suite 202, Dublin, Ohio 43017.
Telephone: (614) 791-9300. **Fax:** (614) 791-9009.
E-Mail Address: office@ilbaseball.com.
Website: www.ilbaseball.com.
Years League Active: 1884.
President/Treasurer: Randy Mobley.

Vice President: Ken Young. **League Administrator:** Chris Sprague. **Corporate Secretary:** Max Schumacher.

Directors: Don Beaver (Charlotte); Jeff Wilpon (Syracuse); Joe Finley (Lehigh Valley); Mike Birling (Durham); Erik Ibsen (Toledo); North Johnson (Gwinnett); Stuart Katzoff (Louisville); Bob Rich Jr. (Buffalo); Joe Gregory (Norfolk); Josh Olerud (Scranton/Wilkes-Barre); Ken Schnacke (Columbus); Bruce Schumacher (Indianapolis); Naomi Silver (Rochester); Mike Tamburro (Pawtucket). **Office Manager:** Gretchen Addison.

Division Structure: North—Buffalo, Lehigh Valley, Pawtucket, Rochester, Scranton/Wilkes-Barre, Syracuse. **West**—Columbus, Indianapolis, Louisville, Toledo. **South**—Charlotte, Durham, Gwinnett, Norfolk.

Regular Season: 140 games. **2018 Opening Date:** April 4. **Closing Date:** Sept 2.

All-Star Game: July 11 at Columbus (IL vs Pacific Coast League).

Playoff Format: South winner meets West winner in best of five series; wild card (non-division winner with best winning percentage) meets North winner in best of five series. Winners meet in best-of-five series for Governors' Cup championship.

Triple-A Championship Game: Sept. 18 at Columbus (IL vs Pacific Coast League).

Roster Limit: 25. **Player Eligibility:** No restrictions.

Official Baseball: Rawlings ROM-INT.

Umpires: Ryan Additon (Davie, FL); Erich Bacchus (Germantown, MD); Adam Beck (Winter Springs, FL); John Bacon (Sherrodsville, OH); Sean Barber (Lakeland, FL); Jeff Carnahan (Crystal River, FL); Scott Costello (Barrie, Canada); Travis Godec (Roanoke, VA); Rich Grassa (Limehurst, NY); Christopher Graham (Newmarket, Canada); Nic Lentz (Holland, MI); Shane Livensparger (Jacksonville Beach, FL); Brennan Miller (Woodbridge, VA); Daniel Merzel (Hopkinton, MA); Brian Peterson (Wilmington, DE); Charlie Ramos (Grand Rapids, MI); Jeremie Rehak (Monroesville, PA); Jeremy Riggs (Suffolk, VA); Richard Riley (Alexandria, VA); Skyler Shown (Owensboro, KY); Alex Tosi (Lake Villa, IL); Jansen Visconti (Latrobe, PA); Chad Whitson (Dublin, OH); Ryan Wills (Williamsburg, VA); Mike Wiseman (White Lake, MI).

STADIUM INFORMATION

Club	Stadium	Opened	LF	CF	RF	Capacity	2018 Att.
Buffalo	Sahlen Field	1988	325	404	325	18,025	527,988
Charlotte	BB&T Ballpark	2015	325	400	315	10,002	619,639
Columbus	Huntington Park	2009	325	400	318	10,100	587,067
Durham	Durham Bulls Athletic Park	1995	305	400	327	10,000	536,304
Gwinnett	Coolray Field	2009	335	400	335	10,427	195,955
Indianapolis	Victory Field	1996	320	402	320	14,500	619,122
Lehigh Valley	Coca-Cola Park	2008	336	400	325	10,000	561,745
Louisville	Louisville Slugger Field	2000	325	400	340	13,131	466,026
Norfolk	Harbor Park	1993	333	400	318	12,067	341,369
Pawtucket	McCoy Stadium	1946	325	400	325	10,031	394,811
Rochester	Frontier Field	1997	335	402	325	10,840	437,974
Scranton/WB	PNC Field	2013	330	408	330	10,000	386,819
Syracuse	NBT Bank Stadium	1997	330	400	330	11,671	277,332
Toledo	Fifth Third Field	2002	320	408	315	10,300	507,965

BUFFALO BISONS

Address: Sahlen Field, One James D. Griffin Plaza, Buffalo, NY 14203.
Telephone: (716) 846-2000. **Fax:** (716) 852-6530.
E-Mail Address: info@bisons.com. **Website:** www.bisons.com.
Affiliation (first year): Toronto Blue Jays (2013). **Years in League:** 1886-90, 1912-70, 1998-

OWNERSHIP/MANAGEMENT

Operated By: Rich Products Corp.

Principal Owner/President: Robert Rich Jr. **President, Rich Entertainment Group:** Melinda Rich. **Vice President/ Chief Operating Officer, Rich Entertainment Group:** Joseph Segarra. **President, Rich Baseball Operations:** Jon Dandes. **VP/General Manager:** Mike Buczkowski. **VP/Secretary:** William Gisel. **Corporate Counsel:** Jill Bond, William Grieshober. **VP/Operations & Finance:** Kevin Parkinson. **VP/Food Service Operations:** Robert Free. **Assistant**

MINOR LEAGUES

General Manager: Anthony Sprague. **Director, Stadium Operations:** Tom Sciarrino. **Senior Accountants:** Chas Fiscella. **Accountants:** Amy Delaney, Tori Dwyer. **Director, Ticket Operations:** Mike Poreda. **Director, Marketing & Public Relations:** Brad Bisbing. **Graphic Design:** Michele Lange. **Director, Corporate Sales:** Jim Harrington. **Director, Sales:** Geoff Lundquist. **Entertainment/Promotions Manager:** Mike Simoncelli. **Sales Coordinators:** Rachel Osucha. **Account Executives:** Mark Gordon, Nick Iacona, Kim Milleville, Burt Mirti, Shaun O'Lay. **Manager, Merchandise:** Theresa Cerabone. **Social Media & Sponsorship Coordinator:** Bethany Sickler. **Manager, Office Services:** Margaret Russo. **Executive Assistant:** Tina Lesher. **Community Relations:** Gail Hodges. **General Manager, Food Service Operations:** Sean Regan. **Food Service Operations Supervisor:** Curt Anderson. **Head Groundskeeper:** Danny Keene. **Chief Engineer:** Pat Chella. **Home Clubhouse/Baseball Operations Coordinator:** Scott Lesher. **Visiting Clubhouse Manager:** Steve Morris.

FIELD STAFF
Manager: Bobby Meacham. **Hitting Coach:** Corey Hart. **Pitching Coach:** Doug Mathis. **Coach:** Devon White. **Athletic Trainer:** Bob Tarpey. **Strength/Conditioning Coach:** Brian Pike.

GAME INFORMATION
Radio Announcers: Pat Malacaro, Duke McGuire. **No. of Games Broadcast:** 140. **Flagship Station:** ESPN 1520. **PA Announcer:** Jerry Reo, Tom Burns. **Official Scorers:** Kevin Lester, Jon Dare.
Stadium Name: Sahlen Field. **Location:** From north, take I-190 to Elm Street exit, left onto Swan Street; From east, take I-190 West to exit 51 (Route 33) to end, exit at Oak Street, right onto Swan Street; From west, take I-190 East, exit 53 to I-90 North, exit at Elm Street, left onto Swan Street. **Standard Game Times:** 7:05 pm, Sun 1:05. **Ticket Price Range:** $9-17. **Visiting Club Hotel:** Adams Mark, 120 Church St, Buffalo, NY 14202. **Telephone:** (716) 845-5100.

CHARLOTTE KNIGHTS

Address: BB&T Ballpark, 324 S. Mint St., Charlotte, NC 28202.
Telephone: (704) 274-8300. **Fax:** 704-274-8330.
E-Mail Address: knights@charlotteknights.com. **Website:** www.charlotteknights.com.
Affiliation (first year): Chicago White Sox (1999). **Years in League:** 1993-

OWNERSHIP/MANAGEMENT
Operated by: Knights Baseball, LLC.
Principal Owners: Don Beaver, Bill Allen.
Chief Operating Officer: Dan Rajkowski. **General Manager:** Rob Egan. **Director, Special Projects:** Julie Clark. **VP, Marketing:** Mark Smith. **VP, Sales:** Chuck Arnold. **VP, Communications:** Tommy Viola. **VP, Ticket Sales:** Matt Millward. **VP, Entertainment:** David Ruckman. **VP, Stadium Operations:** Tom Gorter. **Finance/HR Manager:** Matt Tate. **Director, Broadcasting/Team Travel:** Matt Swierad. **Director, Community Relations:** Cassidy MacQuarrie. **Director, Video Production:** Chase Christiansen. **Director, Stadium Operations:** Nick Braun. **Director, Season Membership Sales:** Brett Butler. **Director, Group Sales:** Yogi Brewington. **Director, Ticket Operations:** Jonathan English. **Business Development Executives:** Mark Dacko, Dallas Godfrey. **Client Services Manager:** Natalee Jarrett. **Creative Director:** Bill Walker. **Promotions Manager:** Courtney Wright. **Entertainment Coordinator:** Nick Farmer. **Ticket Sales Account Executives:** Otto Loor, Michael Rapp. **Inside Sales Manager:** David Woodard. **Ticket Sales Service Representative:** Amanda Bullard. **Premium Services Manager:** Nicole Dietrich. **Community Relations Manager:** Megan Smithers. **Manager, Hispanic/Latino Marketing:** Rafael Bastidas. **Head Groundskeeper:** Matt Parrott. **Operations Coordinator:** Colby Barlowe. **Director, Special Events:** Kerry Krull. **Special Events Coordinator:** Briana Iorio.

FIELD STAFF
Manager: Mark Grudzielanek. **Pitching Coach:** Steve McCatty. **Hitting Coach:** Frank Menechino. **Coach:** Guillermo Quiroz. **Trainer:** Josh Fallin. **Conditioning:** Shawn Powell.

GAME INFORMATION
Radio Announcers: Matt Swierad, Mike Pacheco. **No. of Games Broadcast:** 140. **Flagship Station:** 730 The Game ESPN Charlotte. **PA Announcer:** Ken Conrad. **Official Scorers:** Jerry Bowers, Dave Friedman, Jack Frost, Richard Walker. **Stadium Name:** BB&T Ballpark. **Location:** Exit 10 off Interstate 77. **Ticket Price Range:** $9-$22. **Visiting Club Hotel:** Doubletree by Hilton Charlotte, 895 W. Trade St., Charlotte, NC 28202.

COLUMBUS CLIPPERS

Address: 330 Huntington Park Lane, Columbus, OH 43215.
Telephone: (614) 462-5250. **Fax:** (614) 462-3271. **Tickets:** (614) 462-2757.=
E-Mail Address: info@clippersbaseball.com. **Website:** www.clippersbaseball.com.
Affiliation (first year): Cleveland Indians (2009). **Years in League:** 1955-70, 1977-

OWNERSHIP/MANAGEMENT
General Manager: Ken Schnacke. **Director, Merchandising:** Krista Oberlander. **Director, Marketing/Sales:** Mark Galuska. **Director, Communications/Media:** Joe Santry.
Assistant Director, Sales, Special Events/Birthday Parties: Travis Allard. **Director, Game Operations/Creative Services:** Yoshi Ando. **Director, Ballpark Operations:** Steve Dalin. **Assistant Director, Ticket Sales:** Kevin Daniels. **Ballpark Superintendent:** Gary Delozier. **Support Services:** Marvin Dill. **Assistant Director, Marketing:** Michael

Eckstein. **Assistant Director, Ticket Sales:** Jacob Fleming. **Home Clubhouse Manager:** Tanner Graham. **Assistant Director, Group Sales:** Cedric Hatton. **Director, Corporate Sales:** Jason Hillyer. **Executive Assistant to the President/ GM:** Ashley Held. **Director, Promotions/In-Game Entertainment:** Steve Kuilder. **Assistant Director, Ticket Operations:** Eddie Langhenry. **Assistant Director, Broadcasting:** Scott Leo. **Maintenance Supervisor:** Curt Marcum. **Director, Sponsorship Relations:** Joyce Martin. **Director, Multimedia/Telecast:** Larry Mitchell. **Assistant Office Manager:** Beth Morris. **Assistant Director, Marketing/School Programs/Kids Club:** Emily Poynter. **Director, Finance/ Administration:** Ashley Ramirez. **Assistant Director, Ballpark Operations:** Tom Rinto. **Visiting Clubhouse Manager:** Colin Shaub. **Director, Event Planning:** Micki Shier. **Assistant Director, Media Relations/Statistics:** Anthony Slosser. **Assistant Director, Event Planning/Catering/Suites:** Amanda Smithey. **Assistant GM:** Mark Warren. **Assistant Director, Multimedia/Telecast:** Pat Welch. **Assistant Director, Business Operations:** Shelby White. **Assistant Director, Merchandising:** Schuyler Wright. **Director, Ticket Operations:** Scott Ziegler. **Head Groundskeeper:** Wes Ganobcik. **Director, Multimedia:** Ryan Mitchell. **Director, Social Media/Website:** Matt Leininger. **GM, Levy Food/ Beverage:** Jeff Roberts.

FIELD STAFF

Field Manager: Tony Mansolino. **Pitching Coach:** Rigo Beltran. **Hitting Coach:** Andy Tracy. **Bench Coach:** Kyle Hudson. **Trainer:** Jeremy Heller. **Strength/Conditioning Coach:** Scott Nealon.

GAME INFORMATION

Radio Announcers: Ryan Mitchell, Scott Leo. **No of Games Broadcast:** 140. **Flagship Station:** WMNI 920 AM/easy 95.1 FM. **PA Announcer:** Matt Leininger. **Official Scorer:** Jim Habermehl, Ty Debevoise and Paul Pennell.

Stadium Name: Huntington Park. **Location: From North:** South on I-71 to I-670 west, exit at Neil Avenue, turn left at intersection onto Neil Avenue. **From south:** North on I-71, exit at Front Street (#100A); turn left at intersection onto Front Street, turn left onto Nationwide Blvd. **From East:** West on I-70, exit at Fourth Street, continue on Fulton Street to Front Street, turn right onto Front Street, turn left onto Nationwide Blvd. **From West:** East on I-70, exit at Fourth Street, continue on Fulton Street to Front Street, turn right onto Front Street, turn left onto Nationwide Blvd. **Ticket Price Range:** $4-20. **Visiting Club Hotel:** Crowne Plaza, 33 East Nationwide Blvd, Columbus, OH 43215. **Telephone:** (877) 348-2424. **Visiting Club Hotel:** Drury Hotels Columbus Convention Center, 88 East Nationwide Blvd, Columbus, OH 43215. **Telephone:** (614) 221-7008. **Visiting Club Hotel:** Hyatt Regency Downtown, 350 North High Street, Columbus, OH 43215. **Telephone:** (614) 463-1234. **Visiting Club Hotel:** Red Roof Inn, 111 East Nationwide Blvd., Columbus Ohio 43215. **Telephone:** 614-224-6539.

DURHAM BULLS

Office Address: 409 Blackwell St., Durham, NC 27701. **Mailing Address:** PO Box 507, Durham, NC 27702
Telephone: (919) **687-6500 Fax:** (919) 687-6560
Website: durhambulls.com. **Twitter:** @DurhamBulls
Affiliation (first year): Tampa Bay Rays (1998). **Years in League:** 1998-

OWNERSHIP/MANAGEMENT

Operated by: Capitol Broadcasting Company, Inc.
President/CEO: Jimmy Goodmon. **Vice President:** Mike Birling. **Assistant General Manager, Sales:** Chip Allen. **Assistant General Manager, Operations:** Scott Strickland. **Business Manager:** Rhonda Carlile. **Accounting Supervisor:** Theresa Stocking. **Staff Accountant:** Alicia McMillen. **Receptionist:** Caitlynn Walker. **Director of Corporate Partnerships:** Nick Bavin. **Sponsorship Services Manager:** Ashley Crabtree. **Sponsorship Account Executive:** Andrew Ferrier, Edward Richards. **Head Groundskeeper:** Cameron Brendle. **Operations Manager:** Cortlund Beneke. **Head Groundskeeper, Durham Athletic Park:** Joe Stumpo. **Director, Special Events:** LaTosha Smith. **Director of Marketing/Communications:** Matt Sutor. **Promotions Director:** Faith Inman. **Radio/TV Broadcaster:** Patrick Kinas. **Mascot/Community Relations Coordinator:** Nico Tennant. **Production Designer:** Amy Zirkle. **Video Manager: Patrick Norwood Media Relations Coordinator:** Alex McKeon. **Director of Merchandising/Team Travel:** Bryan Wilson. **Merchandising Assistant:** Ashley Adams. **Director of Ticketing:** Peter Wallace. **Director of Ticket Sales:** Brian Simorka. **Box Office Manager:** Daniel Nobles. **Senior Corporate Account Executive:** Chris Jones. **Corporate Account Executive:** Izzy Piedmonte, Brad Cook. **Senior Account Executive, Group Sales:** Cassie Fowler. **Group Sales Account Executive:** Max Gagnon, Marcus Carlson. **Ticket Sales Representative:** Will McPherson, Danlee Wallace, Caitlin Wallen. **Director of Food and Beverage:** Dave Levey. **Executive Chef:** Curtis Wong. **Assistant Food and Beverage Director:** Todd Feneley. **Hospitality & Catering Manager:** Matt Messner. **Concessions Manager:** Andrew Houston. **Chef:** John Horn.

FIELD STAFF

Manager: Brady Williams. **Pitching Coach:** Rick Knapp. **Coach:** Dan DeMent, Quinton McCracken. **Athletic Trainer:** Scott Thurston. **Strength & Conditioning Coach:** Bryan King.

GAME INFORMATION

Broadcasters: Patrick Kinas, Scott Pose. **No. of Games Broadcast:** 140. **Flagship Station:** 96.5 FM and 99.3 FM. **PA Announcer:** Tony Riggsbee. **Official Scorer:** Brent Belvin. **Stadium Name:** Durham Bulls Athletic Park. **Location:** From Raleigh, I-40 West to Highway 147 North, exit 12B to Willard, two blocks on Willard to stadium; From I-85, Gregson Street exit to downtown, left on Chapel Hill Street, right on Mangum Street. **Standard Game Times:** 7:05 pm, Sat. 6:35 pm, Sun. 5:05 pm. **Ticket Price Range:** $7-14.
Visiting Club Hotel: Millennium Durham. 2800 Campus Walk Ave. Durham, NC 27705. **Telephone:** (919) 383-8575.

GWINNETT STRIPERS

Office Address: 2500 Buford Drive, Lawrenceville, GA 30043.
Mailing Address: P.O. Box 490310, Lawrenceville, GA 30049.
Telephone: (678) 277-0300. **Fax:** (678) 277-0338.
E-Mail Address: stripersinfo@braves.com. **Website:** www.gostripers.com.
Affiliation (first year): Atlanta Braves (1966). **Years in League:** 1884, 1915-17, 1954-64, 1966-

OWNERSHIP/MANAGEMENT

Vice President & General Manager: Adam English. **Assistant GM:** Erin O'Donnell. **Office Manager:** Tyra Williams. **Corporate Partnerships Account Representative:** Gabe Rendon. **Partnership Services Coordinator:** Hannah Craig. **Ticket Sales Manager:** Jerry Pennington. **Account Executives:** Ryan Logan, Zach Mandelblatt, Dylan Powers, Katie Soraghan. **Ticket Operations Coordinator:** Elizabeth Brooks. **Media Relations Manager:** Dave Lezotte. **Social Media Coordinator:** Anastasia Meenach. **Community Relations Coordinator:** Kelly Watrous. **Creative Services Coordinator:** Nick Gosen. **Director, Stadium Operations:** Ryan Stoltenberg. **Stadium Operations Coordinator:** Rick Fultz. **Facilities Engineer:** Gary Hoopaugh. **Sports Turf Manager:** McClain Murphy. **Sports Turf Assistant:** Glen Blackwell. **Team Store Merchandise Coordinator:** Leah Benton. **Clubhouse Manager:** Nick Dixon.

FIELD STAFF

Manager: Damon Berryhill. **Pitching Coach:** Mike Maroth. **Hitting Coach:** Bobby Magallanes. **Coach:** Einar Diaz. **Trainer:** Nick Jensen.

GAME INFORMATION

Radio Announcer: Tony Schiavone.
No. of Games Broadcast: 140. **Flagship Station:** 97.7 FM.
PA Announcer: Kevin Kraus. **Official Scorers:** Guy Curtright, Jack Woodard, Phil Engel, Stan Awtrey, Paul Melendez. **Stadium Name:** Coolray Field.
Location: I-85 (at Exit 115, State Road 20 West) and I-985 (at Exit 4); follow signs to park. **Ticket Price Range:** $8-45.
Visiting Club Hotels: Courtyard by Marriott Buford/Mall of Georgia, 1405 Mall of Georgia Boulevard, Buford, GA 30519. **Telephone:** (678) 745-3380. Fairfield Inn & Suites Atlanta Buford/Mall of Georgia, 1355 Mall of Georgia Boulevard, Buford, GA 30519. **Telephone:** (678) 714-0248.

INDIANAPOLIS INDIANS

Address: 501 W. Maryland Street, Indianapolis, IN 46225.
Telephone: (317) 269-3542. **Fax:** (317) 269-3541.
E-Mail Address: Indians@IndyIndians.com. **Website:** www.indyindians.com.
Affiliation (first year): Pittsburgh Pirates (2005). **Years in League:** 1963, 1998-

OWNERSHIP/MANAGEMENT

Operated By: Indians Inc.
Chairman of the Board/Chief Executive Officer: Bruce Schumacher. **President & General Manager:** Randy Lewandowski. **Senior Vice President, Community Affairs:** Cal Burleson. **Chairman Emeritus:** Max Schumacher. **Assistant General Manager, Corporate Sales/Marketing:** Joel Zawacki. **Assistant General Manager, Tickets/ Operations:** Matt Guay. **Director, Communications:** Charlie Henry. **Baseball Communications Manager:** Cheyne Reiter. **Community Relations Manager:** Emily Hitchcock. **Community Relations Coordinator:** Zach McDonald. **Social Media Coordinator:** Casey McGaw. **Voice of the Indians:** Howard Kellman. **Broadcaster:** Andrew Kappes. **Director, Corporate Sales:** Christina Toler. **Corporate Sales Account Executives:** Erica Otey, Jeremy Smith. **Partnership Activation Manager:** Kylie Kinder. **Partnership Activation Coordinator:** Sydney Glover. **Director, Marketing/ Promotions:** Kim Stoebick. **Game Presentation/Promotions Manager:** Hayden Barnack. **Digital Marketing Manager:** Shayla Smith. **Telecast/Production Coordinator:** Alex Leachman. **Graphic Designers:** Jessica Davis, Matthew Lipke. **Director, Merchandise:** Mark Schumacher. **Merchandise Manager:** Patrick Westrick. **Director, Field Operations:** Joey Stevenson. **Field Operations Manager:** Adam Basinger. **Senior Director, Business Operations:** Brad Morris. **Business Operations Coordinator:** Sarah Haynes. **Senior Director, Facilities:** Tim Hughes. **Senior Facilities Manager:** Allan Danehy. **Facilities Maintenance Tech:** Kyle Winters. **Stadium Operations Manager:** Eddie Acheson. **Stadium Operations Coordinator:** Joshua Ball. **Operations Support:** Ricky Floyd, Ki Hubbard, Sandra Reaves. **Home Clubhouse Manager/Operations Support:** Bobby Martin. **Visiting Clubhouse Manager:** Jeremy Martin. **Director of Tickets, Sales/Services:** Chad Bohm. **Director, Tickets, Premium Services/Events:** Kerry Vick. **Senior Ticket Services Manager/Internship Coordinator:** Bryan Spisak. **Inside Ticket Sales Manager:** Garrett Rosh. **Senior Ticket Sales Account Executives:** Ryan Barrett, Jonathan Howard. **Ticket Sales Account Executives:** Ty Eaton, David Diehl, Courtney Fowler. **Guest Relations Coordinator:** Cara Carrion. **Premium Services/Events Coordinator:** Kaylin Pellegrini. **Inside Sales Representatives:** Brandon Brinsey, Myles Busby, Ian Cooper, Nic Lash. **ARAMARK General Manager:** Chris Scherrer. **Concession Manager:** Jamie Nicholson.

FIELD STAFF

Manager: Brian Esposito. **Hitting Coach:** Ryan Long. **Pitching Coach:** Bryan Hickerson. **Athletic Trainer:** Dru Scott. **Strength & Conditioning Coach:** Alan Burr.

GAME INFORMATION
  Radio Announcers: Howard Kellman, Andrew Kappes. **Flagship Station:** Fox Sports 97.5 FM/1260 AM.
  PA Announcer: David Pygman. **Official Scorers:** Ed Holdaway, Bill McAfee, Kim Rogers, Kit Stetzel, Jeff Williams.
  Stadium Name: Victory Field. **Location:** I-70 to West Street exit, north on West Street to ballpark; I-65 to Martin Luther King and West Street exit, south on West Street to ballpark. **Standard Game Times:** 7:05 pm; 1:35 (Wed/Sun.); 7:15 (Fri.). **Ticket Price Range:** $11-17. **Visiting Club Hotel:** Holiday Inn Indy Downtown, 515 S. West Street, Indianapolis, IN 46225. **Telephone:** (317) 631-9000.

LEHIGH VALLEY IRONPIGS

  Address: 1050 IronPigs Way, Allentown, PA 18109.
  Telephone: (610) 841-7447. **Fax:** (610) 841-1509.
  E-Mail Address: info@ironpigsbaseball.com. **Website:** www.ironpigsbaseball.com.
  Affiliation (first year): Philadelphia Phillies (2008). **Years in League:** 2008-

OWNERSHIP/MANAGEMENT
  Ownership: LV Baseball LP.
  President & General Manager: Kurt Landes. **Vice President, Marketing & Entertainment:** Lindsey Knupp. **Vice President, Ticket Sales:** Brian DeAngelis. **Media Relations & Broadcasting:** Mike Ventola. **Director, Digital Media & Communications:** Chris Dunham Jr. **Director, Multimedia Design & Entertainment:** Rob Sternberg. **Manager, Multimedia Design & Entertainment:** Matt Cech. **Executive Director, IronPigs Charities:** Diane Donaher. **Manager, Community Relations:** Maddison Kendrick. **Senior Director, Food & Beverage:** Alex Rivera. **Director, Concessions:** Brock Hartranft. **Director, Special Events:** Allison Valentine. **Manager, Catering &Hospitality:** Jared Takacs. **Executive Chef:** Mike Hermes. **Director, Corporate Partnerships:** Tom Bendetti. **Managers, Marketing Services:** Dean Hirschberg, Maria Valentyn. **Administrative Assistant:** Pat Golden. **Director, Field Operations:** Ryan Hills. **Senior Director, Stadium Operations:** Jason Kiesel. **Managers, Stadium Operations:** Mike Moneta, Chris Kiefer. **Director, Finance:** Denise Ahner. **Director, Administration:** Michelle Perl. **Managers, Corporate Partnerships:** Pete Kandianis, Nick Wilder. **Manager, Promotions & Entertainment:** Zach Betkowski. **Director, Guest Experience:** Brad Ludwig. **Director, Group Sales:** Ryan Hines. **Senior Manager, Group Sales:** Billy Misiti. **Managers, Group Sales:** Matthew Duddy, Josh Mullin, Mike Pascarella, Daniel Sterenberg. **Director, Memberships:** Erik Hoffman. **Senior Manager, Ticket Operations:** Brittany Balonis. **Manager, Ticket Operations & Analytics:** Collin DeJong. **Manager, Premium Sales:** Adam Puskar. **Managers, Memberships:** Nick DiChristofaro, Cody Hallman. **Director, Merchandise:** Mike Luciano.

FIELD STAFF
  Manager: Gary Jones. **Hitting Coach:** Darryl Robinson. **Pitching Coach:** Steve Schrenk. **Assistant Coach:** Greg Legg. **Trainer:** Mickey Kozack. **Strength/Conditioning:** Mike Lidge.

GAME INFORMATION
  Radio Announcers: TBD. **No. of Games Broadcast:** 140. **Flagship Radio Station:** ESPN 1160/1240/1320 AM. **Television Station:** TV2. **Television Announcers:** Mike Zambelli, Steve Degler, Doug Heater. **No. of Games Televised:** 70 (all home games). **PA Announcer:** Jim Walck. **Official Scorers:** Mike Falk, Jack Logic, David Sheriff, Dick Shute. **Stadium Name:** Coca-Cola Park. **Location:** Take US 22 to exit for Airport Road South, head south, make right on American Parkway, left into stadium. **Standard Game Times:** 7:05 pm, Sat. 6:35, Sun. 1:35.

LOUISVILLE BATS

  Address: 401 E Main St, Louisville, KY 40202.
  Telephone: (502) 212-2287. **Fax:** (502) 515-2255.
  E-Mail Address: info@batsbaseball.com. **Website:** www.batsbaseball.com.
  Affiliation (first year): Cincinnati Reds (2000). **Years in League:** 1998-

OWNERSHIP/MANAGEMENT
  Chairman: Stuart and Jerry Katzoff (MC Sports).
  Board of Directors: Dan Ulmer Jr., Edward Glasscock, Gary Ulmer, Kenny Huber, Steve Trager, Michael Brown. **President/CEO:** Gary Ulmer. **Senior Vice President:** Greg Galiette. **Vice President, Stadium Operations/Technology:** Scott Shoemaker. **Controller:** Michele Anderson. **Accounting Assistant:** Becky Reeves. **Director, Media/Public Relations:** Alex Mayer. **Director, Broadcasting:** Nick Curran. **Director, Baseball Operations:** Josh Hargreaves. **Director, Online Media/Design:** Tony Brown. **Graphic Designer:** Rachel Suding. **Director of Ticket Sales:** Bryan McBride. **Director, Business Operations:** Kyle Reh. **Director, Corporate Suites:** Malcolm Jollie. **Assistant Director, Ticket Operations:** Andrew Siers. **Corporate Marketing Manager:** Michael Harmon. **Corporate Marketing Manager:** Kristen Stonicher. **Corporate Marketing Manager:** David Barry. **Corporate Marketing Manager:** Peyton Rhea. **Director of Entertainment:** Casey Rusnak. **Manager, Corporate Partnerships:** Shelby Harding. **Manager, Team Store/Merchandise:** Kat Steponovich. **Manager, Corporate Partnerships:** Chip Sobel. **Manager/Coordinator, Stadium Operations:** Nathan Renfrow. **Head Clubhouse Manager:** Derrick Jewell. **Visiting Clubhouse Manager:** Tyler Smith. **Head Groundskeeper:** Tom Nielsen. **Assistant Groundskeeper:** Bobby Estienne. **Club Physicians:** Walter Badenhausen, M.D.; John A. Lach, Jr., M.D. **Club Dentist:** Pat Carroll, D.M.D. **Chaplains:** Bob Bailey, Jose Castillo.

FIELD STAFF

Manager: Jody Davis. **Pitching Coach:** Jeff Fassero. **Hitting Coach:** Leon Durham. **Bench Coach:** Dick Schofield. **Trainer:** Steve Gober. **Strength/Conditioning Coach:** Matt Hall.

GAME INFORMATION

Radio Announcers: Nick Curran. **No. of Games Broadcast:** 140. **Flagship Station:** WKRD 790-AM. **PA Announcer:** Charles Gazaway. **Official Scorer:** Nick Evans, Neil Rohrer. **Organist:** Bob Ramsey. **Stadium Name:** Louisville Slugger Field. **Location:** I-64 and I-71 to I-65 South/North to Brook Street exit, right on Market Street, left on Jackson Street; stadium on Main Street between Jackson and Preston. **Ticket Price Range:** $8-18. **Visiting Club Hotel:** Omni Hotel, 400 South 2nd Street, Louisville, KY 40202. **Telephone:** (502) 313-6664.

NORFOLK TIDES

Address: 150 Park Ave, Norfolk, VA 23510.
Telephone: (757) 622-2222. **Fax:** (757) 624-9090.
E-Mail Address: receptionist@norfolktides.com. **Website:** www.norfolktides.com.
Affiliation (first year): Baltimore Orioles (2007). **Years in League:** 1969-

OWNERSHIP/MANAGEMENT

Operated By: Tides Baseball Club Inc.
President: Ken Young. **General Manager:** Joe Gregory.
Director, Media Relations: Ian Locke. **Director, Community Relations:** John Rogerson. **Director, Ticket Operations:** Sze Fong. **Director, Group Sales:** John Muszkewycz. **Director, Premium Services:** Stephanie Hierstein. **Director, Stadium Operations:** Mike Zeman. **Business Manager:** Dawn Coutts. **Director, Business Development/ Gameday Experience:** Mike Watkins. **Corporate Sponsorships/Promotions:** Jonathan Mensink. **Manager, Merchandising:** AnnMarie Piddisi Ambler. **Assistant Director, Stadium Operations:** Mike Cardwell. **Administrative Assistant:** Lisa Blocker. **Head Groundskeeper:** Kenny Magner. **Assistant Groundskeeper:** Justin Hall. **Visiting Clubhouse Manager:** Jack Brenner. **Media Relations Assistant:** Dan Laverde. **Community Relations Assistant:** Laurel Zarcilla. **Group Sales Representatives:** Tee Austin, Symone McCollum.

FIELD STAFF

Manager: Gary Kendall. **Hitting Coach:** Butch Davis. **Pitching Coach:** Mike Griffin. **Athletic Trainer:** Chris Poole. **Strength/Conditioning Coach:** Trevor Howell.

GAME INFORMATION

Radio Announcers: Pete Michaud, Jeff McCarragher. **No. of Games Broadcast:** 140. **Flagship Station:** ESPN 94.1 FM. **PA Announcer:** Jack Ankerson. **Official Scorers:** Mike Holtzclaw, Jim Hodges. **Stadium Name:** Harbor Park. **Location:** Exit 9, 11A or 11B off I-264, adjacent to the Elizabeth River in downtown Norfolk. **Standard Game Times:** 6:35 pm during weekdays in April & May, 7:05 pm, Sun 1:05 pm (first half of season); 4:05 pm (second half of season). **Ticket Price Range:** $10-15. **Visiting Club Hotel:** Sheraton Waterside, 777 Waterside Dr, Norfolk, VA 23510. **Telephone:** (757) 622-6664.

PAWTUCKET RED SOX

Office Address: One Ben Mondor Way, Pawtucket, RI 02860.
Mailing Address: PO Box 2365, Pawtucket, RI 02861.
Telephone: (401) 724-7300. **Fax:** (401) 724-2140.
E-Mail Address: info@pawsox.com. **Website:** www.pawsox.com.
Affiliation (first year): Boston Red Sox (1973). **Years in League:** 1973-

OWNERSHIP/MANAGEMENT

Principal Owner and Chairman: Larry Lucchino.
Vice Chairman: Mike Tamburro. **President:** Dr. Charles Steinberg. **Executive Vice President/General Manager:** Dan Rea III. **Treasurer:** Jeff White. **Executive Vice President/General Counsel:** Kim Miner. **Senior Vice President/ Communications:** Bill Wanless. **Senior Vice President/Sales & Marketing:** Rob Crain. **Vice President/Facilities Management:** Dave Johnson. **Vice President/Partnerships:** Michael Gwynn. **Special Assistant to the Chairman:** Bart Harvey. **Special Assistant to the President:** Jackie Dempsey. **Senior Director of Ticket Sales:** Matt Harper. **Senior Director of Fan Services:** Rick Medeiros. **Director of Marketing & Merchandising:** Brooke Cooper. **Director of McCoy Events:** Grace Eng. **Director of Partnerships:** Jack Verducci. **Director of Baseball Operations & Community Relations:** Joe Bradlee. **Director of Hospitality & Client Services:** Julie Hershkowitz. **Director of Accounting & Data Analytics:** Matt Levin. **Director of Ticket Operations:** Sam Saccoia-Beggs. **Director of Concessions:** Jenn Boisclair. **Office Manager:** Carol Krushnowski. **Manager of Client Services:** Bernadette Provost. **Premium Hospitality Coordinator:** Hannah Butler. **Corporate Partnerships Sales:** Mike Lyons. **Corporate Event Managers:** Anthony Cahill & Jim Cain. **Group Event Manager:** Ben Proctor. **Community Sales Manager:** Alli Katterheinrich. **Creative Services Specialist:** Joe Jacobs. **Staff Accountant:** Dan Fontaine. **Field Superintendent:** Matt McKinnon. **Clubhouse Manager:** Josh Liebenow. **Radio Broadcasters:** Josh Maurer, Will Flemming.

FIELD STAFF

Field Manager: Billy McMillon. **Hitting Coach:** Rich Gedman. **Pitching Coach:** Kevin Walker. **Coach:** Bruce Crabbe.

Trainer: David Herrera. **Strength & Conditioning Coach:** Chris Messina.

GAME INFORMATION
Radio Announcers: Josh Maurer, Will Flemming. **No. of Games Broadcast:** 140. **Flagship Station:** WHJJ 920-AM. **PA Announcers:** Ben DeCastro, Scott Fraser. **Official Scorer:** Bruce Guindon.
Stadium Name: McCoy Stadium. **Location:** From north, 95 South to exit 2A in Massachusetts (Newport Ave); follow Newport Ave for 2 miles, right on Columbus Ave, follow one mile, stadium on right; From south, 95 North to exit 28 (School Street); right at bottom of exit ramp, through two sets of lights, left onto Pond Street, right on Columbus Ave, stadium entrance on left; From west (Worcester); 295 North to 95 South and follow directions from north; From east (Fall River); 195 West to 95 North and follow directions from south. **Standard Game Times:** 7 pm, Sat. 6, Sun 1. **Ticket Price Range:** $5-11. **Visiting Club Hotel:** Hampton Inn Pawtucket, 2 George St, Pawtucket, RI 02860. **Telephone:** (401) 723-6700.

ROCHESTER RED WINGS

Address: One Morrie Silver Way, Rochester, NY 14608.
Telephone: (585) 454-1001. **Fax:** (585) 454-1056.
E-Mail: info@redwingsbaseball.com. **Website:** RedWingsBaseball.com.
Affiliation (first year): Minnesota Twins (2003). **Years in League:** 1885-89, 1891-92, 1895-present

OWNERSHIP/MANAGEMENT
Operated by: Rochester Community Baseball, Inc.
President/CEO/COO: Naomi Silver.
Chairman: Gary Larder. **General Manager:** Dan Mason. **Assistant GM:** Will Rumbold. **Controller:** Michelle Schiefer. **Director, Human Resources:** Paula LoVerde. **Ticket Office Mgr. & Business Coordinator:** Dave Welker. **Manager, Operations:** Marcia DeHond. **Director, Communications:** Nate Rowan. **Director, Corporate Development:** Nick Sciarratta. **Manager, Social Media & Promotions:** Tim Doohan. **Director, Group Sales:** Bob Craig. **Group Sales & Tickets Reps:** Kevin Lute & Mike Ewing. **Senior Director, Sales:** Matt Cipro. **Director, Ticket Operations:** Rob Dermody. **Assistant Director, Ticket Operations:** Eric Friedman. **Director, Game Day Operations:** Travis Sick. **Director, Video Production:** Matt Miller. **Director, Merchandising:** Casey Sanders. **Merchandising Assistant:** Kathy Bills. **Head Groundskeeper:** Gene P Buonomo. **Assistant Groundskeeper:** Geno Buonomo. **Office Mgr. & Community Relations Coordinator:** Gini Darden. **GM, Food/Beverage:** Jeff Dodge. **Business Manager, Food/Beverage:** Dave Bills. **Manager, Concessions:** Jeff DeSantis. **Director, Catering:** Courtney Trawitz. **Sales Manager, Catering:** Steve Gonzalez. **Executive Chef:** Ryan Donalty. **Manager, Warehouse:** Tyler Klobusicky.

FIELD STAFF
Manager: Joel Skinner. **Hitting Coach:** Javier Valentin. **Pitching Coach:** Stu Cliburn. **Trainer:** Chris Johnson. **Strength Coach:** Jacob Dean. **Bullpen Coach:** Mike McCarthy.

GAME INFORMATION
Radio Announcer: Josh Whetzel. **No. of Games Broadcast:** 140. **Flagship Stations:** WHTK 1280-AM.
PA Announcers: Kevin Spears, Rocky Perrotta. **Official Scorers:** Warren Kozireski, Brendan Harrington, Craig Bodensteiner. **Stadium Name:** Frontier Field. **Location:** I-490 East to exit 12 (Brown/Broad Street) and follow signs; I-490 West to exit 14 (Plymouth Ave) and follow signs. **Standard Game Times:** 7:05 pm, Sun 1:35. **Ticket Price Range:** $9-14. **Visiting Club Hotel:** Holiday Inn Rochester Downtown, 70 State St, Rochester, NY 14608. **Telephone:** (585) 546-3450.

SCRANTON/WILKES-BARRE
RAILRIDERS

Address: 235 Montage Mountain Rd., Moosic, PA 18507.
Telephone: (570) 969-2255. **Fax:** (570) 963-6564.
E-Mail Address: info@swbrailriders.com.
Website: www.swbrailriders.com.
Affiliation (first year): New York Yankees (2007). **Years in League:** 1989-

OWNERSHIP/MANAGEMENT
Team President/General Manager: Josh Olerud. **Chief Financial Officer/Financial Controller:** Scott A'Hara. **VP, Assistant General Manager:** Katie Beekman. **VP, Ticket Sales:** Andrew Yarnall. **Sr. Box Office Manager:** Heather Holston. **Sr. Director, Corporate Services & Design:** Kristina Knight. **Director, Marketing & Media/ Broadcasting:** Adam Marco. **Director, Community Relations:** Jordan Maydole. **Director, Video Production:** Victor Sweet. **Chief Sales Officer:** Sal Lombardo. **Corporate Sales Executive:** Jordan Perrine. **Corporate Sales Executive:** Jamie Monahan. **Sr. Corporate Services Manager:** Noelle Richard. **Corporate Service Managers:** Allie Bowen. **Director, Season Ticket Sales & Service:** Kelly Cusick. **Account Executive, Client Retention:** Joe Yudichak. **Account Executives, Premium Sales:** Nick Bolka, Tim Duggan, Ricky Goykin, Amanda Hutchison, Joe Tucciarone. **Group Sales Manager:** Mike Harvey.

MINOR LEAGUES

Director, Youth Baseball & Sports Sales: Robby Judge. **Media Relations Manager/Broadcaster:** Adam Giardino. **Business Operations Manager:** Amy Miller. **Special Events/ Social Media Manager:** Kat Sokirka. **Administrative Assistant:** Melissa Pitz. **Manager, Director, Field Operations:** Steve Horne. **Assistant Groundskeeper:** Chris Stephens. **Director, Ballpark Operations:** Joe Villano.

FIELD STAFF

Manager: Jay Bell. **Hitting Coach:** Phil Plantier. **Pitching Coach:** Tommy Phelps. **Bullpen Coach:** Doug Davis. **Athletic Trainer:** Darren London. **Strength & Conditioning Coach:** Brad Hyde. **Clubhouse Manager:** Mike Macciocco.

GAME INFORMATION

Radio Announcers: Adam Marco, Adam Giardino. **No. of Games Broadcast:** 140. **Flagship Stations:** 1340 WYCK-AM, 1400 WICK-AM, 1440 WCDL-AM. **Television Announcer:** Adam Marco. **No. of Games Broadcast:** TBA. **Flagship Station:** TBA. **PA Announcers:** Dean Corwin, Rob Nolan. **Official Scorers:** Dean Corwin, Dick Devans, Mark Ligi &Armand Rosamilia. **Stadium Name:** PNC Field. **Location:** Exit 182 off Interstate 81; stadium is on Montage Mountain Road. **Standard Game Times:** 6:35 pm (April/May) 7:05 pm (June-August); Sun. 1:05 pm. **Ticket Price Range:** $10-$16. **Visiting Club Hotel:** Hilton Scranton & Conference Center. **Telephone:** (570) 343-3000.

SYRACUSE METS

Address: One Tex Simone Drive, Syracuse NY, 13208
Telephone: 315-474-7833. **Fax:** 315-474-2658.
E-Mail Address: baseball@syracusemets.com **website:** syracusemets.com
Affiliation (First year): New York Mets (2019). **Years in league:** 1885-1889, 1891-92, 1894-1901, 1918, 1920-1927, 1934-1955, 1961-present

OWNERSHIP/MANAGEMENT

Operated by: NY Mets.
General Manager: Jason Smorol. **Assistant GM:** Clint Cure. **Sales/Marketing:** Kathleen McCormick. **Director, Finance:** Frank Santoro. **Director, Group Sales:** Arnold Malloy. **Director, Broadcasting/Public Relations:** Eric Gallanty. **Director, Ticket Sales:** Will Commisso. **Director, Multimedia Production:** Anthony Cianchetta. **Manager, Corporate Sales:** Julie Cardinali. **Manager, Luxury Suites/Guest Relations:** Bill Ryan. **Director, Community Relations/Social Media:** Kyle Fussner/Danny Tripodi. **Head Groundskeeper:** John Stewart.

FIELD STAFF

TBA

GAME INFORMATION

Radio Announcers: Eric Gallanty, Mike Tricarico. **No. of Games Broadcast:** 142. **Flagship Station:** The Score 1260 AM. **PA Announcers:** Nick Aversa. **Official Scorer:** Dom Leo. **Stadium Name:** NBT Bank Stadium. **Location:** New York State Thruway to exit 36 (I-81 South); to 7th North Street exit, left on 7th North, right on Hiawatha Boulevard. **Standard Game Times:** 7:05 pm, Sun. 1:05 pm. **Ticket Price Range:** $6-14. **Visiting Club Hotel:** Embassy Suites @ Destiny USA.

TOLEDO MUD HENS

Address: 406 Washington St., Toledo, OH 43604.
Telephone: (419) 725-4367. **Fax:** (419) 725-4368.
E-Mail Address: mudhens@mudhens.com. **Website:** www.mudhens.com.
Affiliation (first year): Detroit Tigers (1987). **Years in League:** 1889, 1965-

OWNERSHIP/MANAGEMENT

Operated By: Toledo Mud Hens Baseball Club, Inc.
Chairman of the Board: Michael Miller. **Vice President:** David Huey. **Secretary/Treasurer:** Charles Bracken. **President/CEO:** Joseph Napoli. **GM/Executive Vice President:** Erik Ibsen. **President, Chief Marketing Officer:** Kim McBroom. **CFO:** Brian Leverenz. **Accounting:** Sheri Kelly, Shelly Solis. **Assistant Controller:** Tom Mitchell. **Director, Strategic Planning and Projects:** Michael Keedy. **Director, Communications/Media:** Andi Roman. **Director, Ticket Sales/Services:** Thomas Townley. **Director of Operations, Food & Beverage:** Chris Shannon. **Manager, Picnics:** Matt Anzalone. **Manager, Banquets:** Tiffany Muszynski. **Catering Coordinator:** Ann Marie Biesiada. **Gameday Operations Manager:** Greg Setola. **Director Corporate Partnerships:** Ed Sintic. **Corporate Sales Consultant:** Rob Rice. **Game Plan Consultants:** Logan Ankney Phil Bargardi, PJ Carr, John Dotson, Becky Fitts, Adam Haman, Stephen Salens. **Group Sales Manager:** Kyle Moll. **Group Consultant:** Rita Natter, Brian Wilson. **Manager, Ticket Service Team:** Troy Hammersmith. **Ticket Services Team:** Haley Dennis, Samantha Hoot, Tori Larsick. **Manager, Box Office Sales:** Jennifer Hill. **Assistant Manager Box Office Sales:** Jessica MacFarlane. **Manager, Digital Communications:** Nathan Steinmetz. **Special Events Coordinator:** Emily Croll. **Game Day Coordinator:** Tyler Clark, CJ O'Leary. **Director, Broadcast Services:** Greg Tye. **Creative Director:** Dan Royer. **Graphic Design Assistants:** Will Melon, Troy Hester, Director, **Merchandise & Licensing:** Craig Katz. **Manager, Swamp Shop:** Adam Stone. **Office Manager:** Carol Hamilton. **Executive Assistants:** Beth Loy, Brenda Murphy, Pam Miranda. **Turf Manager:** Jake Tyler. **Clubhouse Manager:** Joe Sarkisian. **Team Historian:** John Husman.

FIELD STAFF

Manager: Doug Mientkiewicz. **Hitting:** Mike Hessman. **Pitching Coach:** Juan Nieves. **Third Base Coach:** Basilio Cabrera. **Trainer:** Chris McDonald. Strength and Conditioning, Jeff Mathers.

GAME INFORMATION

Radio Announcer: Jim Weber. **No. of Games Broadcast:** 140. **Flagship Station:** WCWA 1230-AM. **TV Announcers:** Jim Weber, Matt Melzak. **No. of Games Broadcast:** 70 (all home games). **TV Flagship:** Buckeye Cable Sports Network (BCSN). **PA Announcer:** Mason. **Official Scorers:** Jeff Businger, Ron Kleinfelter, John Malkoski Jr., John Malkoski Sr., Lee Schuh, Jason Parkins. **Stadium Name:** Fifth Third Field. **Location:** From Ohio Turnpike 80/90, exit 54 (4A) to I-75 North, follow I-75 North to exit 201-B, left onto Erie Street, right onto Washington Street; From Detroit, I-75 South to exit 202-A, right onto Washington Street; From Dayton, I-75 North to exit 201-B, left onto Erie Street, right on Washington Street; From Ann Arbor, Route 23 South to I-475 East, I-475 east to I-75 South, I-75 South to exit 202-A, right onto Washington Street. **Ticket Price Range:** $12. **Visiting Club Hotel:** Park Inn, 101 North Summit, Toledo, OH 43604. **Telephone:** (419) 241-3000.

PACIFIC COAST LEAGUE

PACIFIC COAST LEAGUE

Address: One Chisholm Trail, Suite 4200, Round Rock, Texas 78681.
Telephone: (512) 310-2900. **Fax:** (512) 310-8300.
E-Mail Address: office@pclbaseball.com.
Website: www.pclbaseball.com.
President: Branch B. Rickey.

Vice President: Don Logan (Las Vegas).

Directors: John Traub (Albuquerque), Josh Hunt (El Paso), Michael Baker (Fresno), Sam Bernabe (Iowa), Don Logan (Las Vegas), Peter B. Freund (Memphis), Frank Ward (Nashville), Lou Schwechheimer (New Orleans), Gary Green (Omaha), Larry Freedman (Oklahoma City), Eric Edelstein (Reno), Chris Almendarez (Round Rock), Jeff Savage (Sacramento), Marc Amicone (Salt Lake), Dave Elmore (San Antonio), Aaron Artman (Tacoma).

Director, Business: Melanie Fiore. **Vice President, Baseball Operations:** Dwight Hall.
Public Relations & Operations Manager: Matt Grilli.

Branch Rickey

Division Structure: American Conference—Northern: Iowa, Memphis, Nashville, Omaha; **Southern:** Oklahoma City, New Orleans, Round Rock, San Antonio. **Pacific Conference— Northern:** Fresno, Reno, Sacramento, Tacoma. **Southern:** Albuquerque, El Paso, Las Vegas, Salt Lake.

Regular Season: 140 games. **2019 Opening Date:** April 4. **Closing Date:** Sept 2.

All-Star Game: July 10 at El Paso (PCL vs International League).

Playoff Format: Pacific Conference/Northern winner meets Southern winner, and American Conference/Northern winner meets Southern winner in best-of-five semifinal series. Winners meet in best-of-five series for league championship.

Triple-A Championship Game: Sept 17 at Memphis (PCL vs International League).

Roster Limit: 25. **Player Eligibility Rule:** No restrictions; **Brand of Baseball:** Rawlings ROM.

Umpires: Sean Allen (Fresno, CA), David Arrieta (Maracaibo, Zulia, Venezuela), Ryan Blakney (Phoenix, AZ), Nestor Ceja (Arleta, CA), Paul Clemons (Oxford, KS), Ramon De Jesus (Santo Domingo, Dominican Republic), Derek Eaton (Elk Grove, CA), Bryan Fields (Phoenix, AZ), Reid Gibbs (Glendale, AZ), Clayton Hamm (Spicewood, TX), Javerro January (Southaven, MS), John Libka (Port Huron, MI), Nick Mahrley (Phoenix, AZ), Ben May (Milwaukee, WI), Kyle McCrady (Longview, WA), Lee Meyers (Madera, CA), Malachi Moore (Compton, CA), Edwin Moscoso (Santiago, Chile), Cody Oakes (Oelwein, IA), Roberto Ortiz (Kissimmee, FL), Sean Ryan (Waunakee, WI), Chris Segal (Fairfax, VA), Jason Starkovich (San Tan Valley, AZ), Nate Tomlinson (Ogdensburg, WI), Junior Valentine (Maryville, TN), Clint Vondrak (Reno, NV), Lewis Williams III (Lodi, CA), Tom Woodring (Las Vegas, NV), Alex Ziegler (Metairie, LA).

STADIUM INFORMATION

Club	Stadium	Opened	LF	CF	RF	Capacity	2018 Att.
Albuquerque	Isotopes Park	2003	340	400	340	13,500	556,330
Colorado Springs	Security Service Field	1998	350	410	350	8,500	262,657
El Paso	Southwest University Park	2014	322	406	322	8,018	539,520
Fresno	Chukchansi Park	2002	324	400	335	12,500	405,403
Iowa	Principal Park	1992	335	400	335	11,000	463,399
Las Vegas	Cashman Field	1983	328	433	328	11,500	332,224
Memphis	AutoZone Park	2000	319	400	322	10,000	340,476
Nashville	First Tennessee Park	2015	330	405	310	10,000	603,135
New Orleans	Shrine on Airline	1997	325	400	325	10,000	252,614
Oklahoma City	Chickasaw Bricktown Ballpark	1998	325	400	325	9,000	463,195
Omaha	Werner Park	2011	310	402	315	9,023	345,830
Reno	Aces Ballpark	2009	339	410	340	9,100	351,298
Round Rock	Dell Diamond	2000	330	405	325	8,722	616,636
Sacramento	Raley Field	2000	330	403	325	14,014	538,785
Salt Lake	Smith's Ballpark	1994	345	420	315	14,511	477,528
Tacoma	Cheney Stadium	1960	325	425	325	6,500	372,780

ALBUQUERQUE ISOTOPES

Address: 1601 Avenida Cesar Chavez SE, Albuquerque, NM 87106
Telephone: (505) 924-2255. **Fax:** (505) 242-8899.
E-Mail Address: info@abqisotopes.com. **Website:** www.abqisotopes.com.
Affiliation (first year): Colorado Rockies (2015). **Years in League:** 1972-2000, 2003-

OWNERSHIP/MANAGEMENT

President: Ken Young. **Vice President/Secretary/Treasurer:** Emmett Hammond. **VP/GM:** John Traub. **VP, Corporate Development:** Nick LoBue. **Assistant GM, Business Operations:** Chrissy Baines. **Assistant GM, Sales/ Marketing:** Adam Beggs. **Director, Public Relations:** Kevin Collins. **Director, Retail Operations:** Kara Hayes. **Director, Stadium Operations:** Bobby Atencio. **Director, Accounting/Human Resources:** Cynthia DiFrancesco. **Box Office/ Administration Manager:** Mark Otero. **Community Relations Manager:** Michelle Montoya. **Marketing/Promotions**

Manager: Dylan Storm. **Game Production Manager:** Kris Shepard. **Suite Relations Manager:** Lorraine Chavez. **Travel Coordinator/Home Clubhouse Manager:** Ryan Maxwell. **Season Tickets/Group Sales Manager:** Jason Buchta. **Ticket Sales Executives:** Alex Clark, Terry Clark, Aaron Robinson, CJ Scroger, Malcolm Smith. **Graphic Designer:** Alvin Garcia. **Public Relations Assistant:** Andrew Cockrum. **Front Office Assistant:** Margaret Harris. **Retail Operations Assistant:** Michael Malgieri. **Stadium Operations Assistant:** Tony Troyer. **Head Groundskeeper:** Clint Belau. **Assistant Groundskeeper:** Ryan Coleman. **GM, Spectra Food & Hospitality:** Nick Korth. **Premium Services Manager:** Jennifer Schurman. **Head Chef:** Ryan Curry. **Spectra Office Manager:** Angela Goniea.

FIELD STAFF

Manager: Glenallen Hill. **Hitting Coach:** Tim Doherty. **Pitching Coach:** Brandon Emanuel. **Athletic Trainer:** Heath Townsend. **Physical Performance Coach:** Marcus Lefton

GAME INFORMATION

Radio Announcer: Josh Suchon. **No. of Games Broadcast:** 140. **Flagship Station:** KNML 95.9-FM & 610-AM. **PA Announcer:** Francina Walker. **Official Scorers:** Gary Herron, Brent Carey, John Miller, Frank Mercogliano. **Stadium Name:** Isotopes Park. **Location:** From 1-25, exit east on Avenida Cesar Chavez SE to University Boulevard; From I-40, exit south on UniversityBoulevard SE to Avenida Cesar Chavez. **Standard Game Times:** 6:35 pm / 7:05 pm. **Sun** 1:35/6:05 pm. **Ticket Price Range:** $8-$27. **Visiting Club Hotel:** Sheraton Albuquerque Airport Hotel, 2910 Yale Blvd SE, Albuquerque, NM 87106. **Telephone:** (505) 843-7000.

EL PASO CHIHUAHUAS

Address: 1 Ballpark Plaza, El Paso, TX 79901.
Telephone: (915) 533-2273. **Fax:** (915) 242-2031.
E-Mail Address: info@epchihuahuas.com. **Website:** www.epchihuahuas.com.
Affiliation (first year): San Diego Padres (2014). **Years in League:** 2014-

OWNERSHIP/MANAGEMENT

Owner/Chairman of the Board: Paul Foster. **Owner/CEO/Vice Chairman:** Josh Hunt. **Owners:** Alejandra de la Vega Foster, Woody Hunt. **President:** Alan Ledford. **Senior Vice President/General Manager:** Brad Taylor. **Director, Finance & Administration:** Pamela De La O. **Accounting Manager:** Heather Hagerty. **Accounting Assistant:** Pamela Nieto. **Administrative Services Coordinator:** Nicole Ortega. **Director, Corporate Partnerships & Suites:** Judge Scott. **Corporate Partnerships Service Coordinator:** Adrian Arvizo. **Corporate Partnerships Activation Specialist:** Alex O'Connor. **Account Executive, Corporate Partnerships:** Ryan Knox. **Director, Ticket Sales & Service:** Nick Seckerson. **Manager, Season Seat Sales:** Primo Martinez. **Hospitality & Military Sales:** Monica Castillo. **Manager, Ticket Operations & Analytics Manager:** Ross Rotwein. **Manager, Group Sales:** Brittany Morgan. **Group Sales Ticket Services Supervisor:** Killian Valleiu. **Account Executives, Ticket Sales:** Corey Cerrone, Brittany Kaaihue, Alex Lakinske, Jay Morris, Austin Weber. **Account Executives, Group Sales:** Matt Heiligenberg, Lauren Marquis, Janine Quiroz. **Ticket Operations Assistant:** Ruben Armendariz. **Ticket Sales Assistant:** Eduardo Cabrera. **Director, Marketing & Communications:** Angela Olivas. **Manager, Video & Digital Production:** Juan Gutierrez. **Manager, Broadcast & Media Relations:** Tim Hagerty. **Manager, Promotions & Community Relations:** Andy Imfeld. **Mascot & Entertainment Supervisor:** Grant Gorham. **Production & Social Media Coordinator:** Gage Freeman. **Community Relations & Promotions Coordinator:** Kate Lewis. **Creative Services Coordinator:** Ilene Serna. **Director, Guest Services & Baseball Operations:** Lizette Espinosa. **Director, Ballpark Operations:** Douglas Galeano. **Manager Grounds, Head Groundskeeper:** Travis Howard. **Assistant Groundskeeper:** Tony Tafoya. **Assistant Coordinator, Groundskeeping:** Andrew Faust. **Baseball Operations Assistant & Facilities Supervisor:** Michael Raymundo. **Guest Services & Operations Supervisor:** Evan Ruiz. **Baseball Operations & Guest Services Specialist:** Latoya Wright. **Manager, Retail & Merchandise Operations:** Denise Richardson.

FIELD STAFF

Manager: Edwin Rodriguez. **Hitting Coach:** Morgan Burkhart. **Pitching Coach:** Bronswell Patrick. **Coach:** Lance Burkhart. **Trainers:** Dan Turner, Dan Leja.

GAME INFORMATION

Radio Announcer: Tim Hagerty. **No. of Games Broadcast:** 140. **Flagship Station:** ESPN 600 AM El Paso. **PA Announcer:** Larry Berg. **Official Scorer:** Bernie Ricono. **Stadium Name:** Southwest University Park. **Standard Game Times:** 7:05, Sun 1:05. **Ticket Price Range:** $5-10.50. **Visiting Club Hotel:** Hilton Garden Inn.

FRESNO GRIZZLIES

Address: 1800 Tulare St, Fresno, CA 93721.
Telephone: (559) 320-4487. **Fax:** (559) 264-0795.
E-Mail Address: info@fresnogrizzlies.com. **Website:** www.FresnoGrizzlies.com.
Affiliation (first year): Washington Nationals (2019). **Years in League:** 1998-

OWNERSHIP/MANAGEMENT

Operated By: Fresno Sports & Events
Managing Partner: Michael Baker. **Chief Financial Officer:** Michael Moran.
President: Derek Franks. **Vice President, Ticket Sales:** Andrew Milios. **Vice President, Partnership Marketing:**

Andrew Melrose. **Director, Marketing Creative:** Sam Hansen. **Director, Marketing Communication:** Jamie Dierking. **Director, Operations:** Shaun O'Brien. **Director, Stadium Maintenance:** Harvey Kawasaki. **Stadium Maintenance Manager:** Ira Calvin. **Director, Corporate Partnerships:** Jason Hannold. **Ticket Sales Manager:** Cody Holden. **Assistant Ticket Sales Manager:** Eric Moreno. **Ticket Sales Assistant:** Angie Cazares. **Group Sales Manager:** Kyle Selna. **Inside Sales Manager:** Brandon Aurecchione. **Group Account Executive:** Zach Gilman. **Group Account Executive:** Caleb Kephart. **Group Account Executive:** Owen Blake. **Entertainment Manager:** Ray Ortiz. **Media Relations Manager:** Paul Braverman. **Graphic Designer:** Dorian Castro. **Merchandise Manager:** Lalonnie Calderon. **Assistant Merchandise Manager:** Chris Calderon. **Ballpark Development Manager:** Jon Stockton. **Controller:** Allison Ferrell. **Entertainment/Mascot Manager:** Troy Simeon. **Community Engagement Coordinator:** Madeline Hamada. **Partnership Activation Manager:** Belinda Gonzalez-Diaz. **Partnership Activation Coordinator:** Jazzmine Young. **Business Manager:** Yanet Richardson. **Head Groundskeeper:** David Jacinto. **Assistant Head Groundskeeper:** David Jacinto, Jr. **Home Clubhouse Manager:** Louie Raya. **Visiting Clubhouse Manager:** Jeff Little. **Administrative Assistant:** Norma Mata. **Director, Pro Sports Catering:** Kendyl Brown. **Assistant Director, Pro Sports Catering:** Alex Lilley.

FIELD STAFF

Manager: Randy Knorr. **Hitting Coach:** Brian Daubach. **Pitching Coach:** Brad Holman. **Trainer:** Eric Montague. **Strength & Conditioning:** Mike Warren.

GAME INFORMATION

Radio Announcer: Doug Greenwald. **No. of Games Broadcast:** 140. **Flagship Radio Station:** 99.7 FM KKDJ. **Stadium Name:** Chukchansi Park. **Location:** 1800 Tulare St, Fresno, CA 93721. **Directions:** From 99 North, take Fresno Street exit, left on Fresno Street, left on Inyo or Tulare to stadium. From 99 South, take Fresno Street exit, left on Fresno Street, right on Broadway to H Street. From 41 North, take Van Ness exit toward Fresno, left on Van Ness, left on Inyo or Tulare, stadium is straight ahead. From 41 South, take Tulare exit, stadium is located at Tulare and H Streets, or take Van Ness exit, right on Van Ness, left on Inyo or Tulare, stadium is straight ahead.
Ticket Price Range: $10-19. **Visiting Club Hotel:** Doubletree Downtown Fresno, 2233 Ventura St. Fresno, CA 93721. **Telephone:** (559)-268-1000.

IOWA CUBS

Address: One Line Drive, Des Moines IA 50309.
Telephone: (515) 243-6111. **Fax:** (515) 243-5152.
Website: www.iowacubs.com.
Affiliation (first year): Chicago Cubs (1981). **Years in League:** 1969-

OWNERSHIP/MANAGEMENT

Operated By: Raccoon Baseball Inc.
Chairman/Principal Owner: Michael Gartner. **Executive Vice President:** Michael Giudicessi. **President/General Manager:** Sam Bernabe. **Vice Chairman/Shareholder:** Mike C. Gartner. **Shareholder:** Dr. Doug Dorner. **VP/Assistant GM:** Randy Wehofer. **VP/CFO:** Sue Tollefson. **Director, Media Relations:** Shelby Cravens. **Director, Video and Multimedia Arts:** Justin Walters. **Director, Ticket Operations:** Clayton Grandquist. **Director, Broadcasting:** Alex Cohen. **Director, Group Outings:** Jason Gellis. **VP/Director, Luxury Suites:** Brent Conkel. **VP/Stadium Operations:** Jeff Tilley. **VP/Catering and Event Sales:** Brandie Willson. **Manager, Stadium Operations:** Nic Peters, Andrew Quillin, Dustin Halderson. **Account Executive:** John Rodgers, Nick Long. **Group Sales:** Beth Kneeskern. **VP/Head Groundskeeper:** Chris Schlosser. **Assistant Groundskeeper:** Chase Manning. **Director, Merchandise:** Lisa Hufford. **Manager, Merchandise:** Jody Shough. **Accounting:** Lori Auten, Jill Vento. **Chief Technology Officer:** Ryan Clutter. **Manager, Social and Digital Media:** Matt Evers. **Manager, Game Day Events:** Danae Ziggafoos. **Manager, Events and Catering:** Alivia Sprenger. **Broadcaster:** Deene Ehlis. **Landscape Coordinator:** Shari Kramer.

FIELD STAFF

Manager: Marty Pevey. **Hitting Coaches:** Desi Wilson, Keoni DeRenne. **Pitching Coach:** Rod Nichols. **Athletic Trainers:** Ed Halbur, Mike McNulty. **Strength/Conditioning:** Ryan Clausen.

GAME INFORMATION

Radio Announcers: Alex Cohen, Deene Ehlis. **No. of Games Broadcast:** 140. **Flagship Station:** AM 940 KPSZ. **PA Announcers:** Aaron Johnson, Mark Pierce, Corey Coon, Rick Stageman, Joe Hammen. **Official Scorers:** Doug Howard, Michael Pecina, James Hilchen, Steve Mohr. **Stadium Name:** Principal Park. **Location:** I-80 or I-35 to I-235, to Third Street exit, south on Third Street, left on Line Drive. **Standard Game Times:** 12:08/7:08 pm, Sun. 1:08. **Ticket Price Range:** $5-16. **Visiting Hotel:** Hampton Inn and Suites Downtown, 120 SW Water Street, Des Moines IA 50309. **Telephone:** (515) 244-1650.

LAS VEGAS AVIATORS

Address: 1650 S. Pavilion Center Drive, Las Vegas, NV 89135.
Telephone: (702) 943-7200. **Fax:** (702) 943-7214.
E-Mail Address: info@aviatorslv.com. **Website:** www.aviatorslv.com.
Affiliation (first year): Oakland Athletics (2019). **Years in League:** 1983 - present (36 years)

OWNERSHIP/MANAGEMEN

Operated By: Summerlin Las Vegas Baseball Club LLC.
President/COO: Don Logan. **General Manager/Vice President, Sales/Marketing:**
Chuck Johnson. **Vice President, Ticket Sales:** Erik Eisenberg. **VP of Community Relations
& Special Events:** Melissa Harkavy. **Vice President/Stadium Operations:** Jay Cline. **Director/Engineering &
Stadium Operations:** Raymond Brown. **VP/Ballpark Support:** Nick Fitzenreider. **Director, Ticket Operations:**
Siobhan Steiermann. **Director, Ticket Sales:** TJ Thedinga. **Director, Sponsorships:** James Jensen. **VP/Accounting:**
Scott Montes. **Staff Accountant:** Brad Winslow. **Accounting/Human Resources Clerk:** Esther Lomeli. **Director,
Broadcasting:** Russ Langer. **Director, Digital Media & Marketing:** Ashley Paxton. **Director, Business Development:**
Larry Brown. **Media Relations Director:** Jim Gemma. **Administrative Assistants:** Jan Dillard, Michelle Taggart. **Senior
Account Executive, Ticket Sales:** Bryan Frey. **Account Executives, Ticket Sales:** Nathan Erbach, Ariel Greenberg, David
Moses, Kyle Nakama, Corey Silva. **Director, Retail Operations:** Jason Weber. **Ballpark Support Manager:** Chip Vespe.
Director/Team Operations: Steve Dwyer. **Director/Game Entertainment:** Gary Arlitz. **Box Office Manager:** Brad
Hudecek. **Team Store Manager:** Edward Dorville.

FIELD STAFF

Manager: Fran Riordan. **Hitting Coach:** Eric Martins. **Pitching Coach:** Rick Rodriguez. **Coach:** Craig Conklin. **Athletic
Trainer:** Brad LaRosa. **Strength/Conditioning Coach:** Henry Torres.

GAME INFORMATION

Radio Announcer: Russ Langer. **No. of Games Broadcast:** 140. **Flagship Station:** NBC Sports AM 920 'The Game'.
PA Announcer: Dick Calvert. **Official Scorer:** Peter Legner. **Stadium Name:** Las Vegas Ballpark. **Location:** I 215
North Beltway to Sahara Avenue (exit east), left on Pavilion Center Drive; 1 215 South Beltway to Charleston Blvd. (exit
east), right on Pavilion Center Drive. **Standard Game Time:** 7:05 pm. **Ticket Price Range:** $12-35.
Visiting Club Hotel: Red Rock Casino Resort & Spa, 11011 W. Charleston Blvd. Las Vegas, NV 89135. **Telephone:**
(702) 797-7777.

MEMPHIS REDBIRDS

Office Address: 198 Union, Memphis, TN 38103.
Stadium Address: 198 Union Ave, Memphis, TN 38103.
Telephone: (901) 721-6000. **Fax:** (901) 328-1102. **Website:** www.memphisredbirds.
com. **Affiliation (first year):** St. Louis Cardinals (1998). **Years in League:** 1998-

OWNERSHIP/MANAGEMENT

Ownership: Peter B. Freund.
President/General Manager: Craig Unger. **Vice President, Marketing and Sales:** Andy Steavens. **Vice President,
Stadium and Baseball Operations:** Mike Voutsinas. **Director, Media and Public Relations:** Michael Schroeder.
Director, Ticket Sales: Kyle Krebs. **Director, Field Operations:** Brian Bowe. **Manager, Ticket Operations:** Gian
D'Amico. **Manager, Corporate Sales:** Tyler Gilles. **Manager, Marketing:** Nikki Paine. **Manager, Guest Services and
Baseball Operations:** Marissa Zvolanek. **Accounting Manager:** Cindy Neal. **Office Manager:** Jackie Likens. **Facilities
Manager:** Spencer Shields.

FIELD STAFF

Manager: TBA. **Hitting Coach:** TBA. **Pitching Coach:** Dernier Orozco. **Trainer:** Matt Corvo.

GAME INFORMATION

Radio Announcer: Steve Selby. **No. of Games Broadcast:** 140. **Flagship Station:** online. **PA Announcer:** TBA.
Official Scorers: J.J. Guinozzo, Eric Opperman. **Stadium Name:** AutoZone Park. **Location:** North on I-240, exit at Union
Avenue West, one and half miles to park. **Standard Game Times:** 7:05, Sat. 6:35, Sun 2:05. **Ticket Price Range:** $9-24.
Visiting Club Hotel: TBA.

NASHVILLE SOUNDS

Address: 19 Junior Gilliam Way, Nashville, TN 37219.
Telephone: (615) 690-HITS. **Fax:** (615) 256-5684.
E-Mail address: info@nashvillesounds.com. **Website:** www.nashvillesounds.com.
Affiliation (first year): Oakland Athletics (2015). **Years in League:** 1998-

OWNERSHIP/MANAGEMENT

Operated By: MFP Baseball. **Owners:** Frank Ward, Masahiro Honzawa.

GM/Chief Operating Officer: Adam Nuse. **VP, Operations:** Doug Scopel. **VP, Fan Relations:** Amy Schoch. **VP, Sales:** Bryan Mayhood. **Director, Finance:** Barb Walker. **Director, Sales:** Taylor Fisher. **Director, Corporate Partnerships:** Danielle Gaw. **Director, Media Relations:** Chad Seely. **Director, Marketing:** Alex Wassel. **Director, Entertainment:** Mary Hegley. **Director, Retail:** Katie Ward. **Director, Advertising:** Ryan Madar. **Director, Broadcasting:** Jeff Hem. **Director, Stadium Operations:** Jeremy Wells. **Director, Video and Digital Production:** Erik Sharpnack. **Manager, Business Development:** Sierra Seigel. **Business Development, Corporate Partnerships:** Jon Brownfield. **Merchandise Manager:** Wade Becker. **Community Relations Manager:** Destiny Whitmore. **Ticket Operations Manager:** CJ Berthelsen. **Stadium Operations Manager:** Austin Brunk, Caleb Yorks. **Account Executive, Ticket Sales:** Mandy Valentine, Mahalie Shorrock, Anton Calvin. **Ticket Operations Coordinator:** Irving Alvarez. **Ticket Sales Representatives:** Jon Bellis, Randi Bivens, Zach Booth, Nate Card, Hayley Greenwell, Matt Walker. **Promotions and Activation Coordinator:** Shannyn Wong. **Partnership Activation Coordinator:** Allie Doheny. **Mascot Coordinator:** Buddy Yelton. **Production Event Coordinator:** Stephen Hart. **Creative Assistant:** RV Oliver. **Graphic Designer:** Joe Masterson. **Fan Services Seasonal Associate:** Travis Williams. **Social Media Seasonal Associate:** Abby Holman. **Head Groundskeeper:** Thomas Trotter. **Assistant Groundskeepers:** Shay Adams, Bryce Huebner. **Clubhouse & Equipment Manager:** Matt Gallant. **Team Photographer:** Casey Gower.

FIELD STAFF

Manager: Jason Wood. **Hitting Coach:** Howard Johnson. **Pitching Coach:** Brian Shouse. **Bench Coach:** Geno Petralli. **Bullpen Coach:** Eric Gagne. **Athletic Trainer:** Carlos Olivas. **Strength/Conditioning Coach:** Al Sandoval.

GAME INFORMATION

Radio Announcer: Jeff Hem. **No. of Games Broadcast:** 140. **Flagship Station:** ALT 97.5 FM
PA Announcer: Eric Berner. **Official Scorers:** Eric Jones, Cody Bush, Eric Moyer.
Stadium Name: First Tennessee Park. **Location:** I-65 to exit 85 (Rosa L Parks Blvd) and head south; Turn left on Jefferson St, then turn right onto 5th Ave North, then turn left on Jackson St. **Standard Game Times:** 7:05, Sat 6:35, 7:05 pm, Sun 2:05 (April-June 19), 6:35 (June 26-August 14). **Ticket Price Range:** $9-35. **Visiting Club Hotel:** Millennium Maxwell House, 2025 Rosa L Parks Blvd, Nashville, TN, 37228.

NEW ORLEANS BABY CAKES

Address: 6000 Airline Dr, Metairie, LA 70003.
Telephone: (504) 734-5155. **Fax:** (504) 734-5118.
E-Mail Address: TBA. **Website:** www.cakesbaseball.com.
Affiliation (first year): Miami Marlins (2009). **Years in League:** 1998-

OWNERSHIP/MANAGEMENT

Principal Owner/President: Lou Schwechheimer. **Chief Operating Officer:** Matt White Senior. **Vice President/General Manager:** Augusto "Cookie" Rojas. **General Counsel:** Walter Leger. **Assistant General Manager, Fan Experience:** Bob Moullette. **Director, Broadcasting/Team Travel:** Tim Grubbs. **Director, Public Relations:** Dave Sachs. **Director, Stadium Operations:** Craig Schaffer. **Director, Clubhouse:** Brett Herbert. **Group Sales Manager:** Trevor Johnson. **Group Sales:** Jonathan Boraski. **Corporate Sales Executives:** Kyle Guillie, Kristin Rojas. **Game Operations Manager:** Alex Knudsen. **Box Office Manager:** Joseph Kuchler. **Marketing Coordinator:** Nicole Foto. **Merchandise Coordinator:** Margaret Schleismann. **Head Groundskeeper:** Scott Blanchette. **Administrative Assistant:** Susan Radkovich.

FIELD STAFF

Manager: Keith Johnson. **Hitting Coach:** Justin Mashore. **Pitching Coach:** Jeremy Powell. **Defensive Coach:** Chris Briones. **Athletic Trainer:** Greg Harrel. **Strength & Conditioning:** Robert Reichert.

GAME INFORMATION

Radio Announcers: Tim Grubbs, Ron Swoboda. **No. of Games Broadcast:** 140. **Flagship Station:** 1280 AM.
PA Announcer: TBA. **Official Scorer:** TBA. **Stadium Name:** Shrine on Airline. **Location:** I-10 West toward Baton Rouge, exit at Clearview Pkwy (exit 226) and continues south, right on Airline Drive (US 61 North) for 1 mile, stadium on left; From airport, take Airline Drive (US 61) east for 4 miles, stadium on right. **Standard Game Times:** 7 pm, Sat. 6, Sun. 1. **Ticket Price Range:** $5-13. **Visiting Club Hotel:** Crowne Plaza New Orleans Airport, 2829 Williams Blvd, Kenner, LA 70062. **Telephone:** (504) 467-5611.

OKLAHOMA CITY DODGERS

Address: 2 S Mickey Mantle Dr., Oklahoma City, OK 73104.
Telephone: (405) 218-1000. **Fax:** (405) 218-1001.
E-Mail Address: info@okcdodgers.com. **Website:** www.okcdodgers.com.
Affiliation (first year): Los Angeles Dodgers (2015). **Years in League:** 1963-1968, 1998-

OWNERSHIP/MANAGEMENT

Operated By: MB OKC LLC. **Principal Owner:** Mandalay Baseball.
President/General Manager: Michael Byrnes. **Senior Vice President:** Jenna Byrnes. **Vice President, Ticket**

Sales: Kyle Daugherty. **Vice President, Corporate Partnerships:** Scott Sterling. **Senior Director, Operations:** Mitch Stubenhofer. **Director, Finance/Accounting:** Jon Shaw. **Director, Business Intelligence:** Kyle Logan. **Director, Ticket Operations:** Russell Durrant. **Director, Partner Services:** Ben Beecken. **Director, Facility Operations:** Harlan Budde. **Director, Communications/Broadcasting:** Alex Freedman. **Director, Marketing:** Travis Piercefield. **Director, Food Service Operations:** Al Splisbury. **Executive Director, OKC Dodgers Baseball Foundation:** Jill vanEgmond. **Communications Coordinator:** Lisa Johnson. **Baseball Operations Coordinator:** Billy Maloney. **Game Presentation Manager:** A.J. Navarro. **Office Manager:** Travis Hunter. **Head Groundskeeper:** Monte McCoy. **Clubhouse Manager:** T.J. Leonard.

FIELD STAFF

Manager: Travis Barbary. **Hitting Coach:** Scott Coolbaugh. **Pitching Coach:** Bill Simas. **Coach:** Jeremy Rodriguez. **Athletic Trainer:** Jason Kirkman. **Strength/Conditioning Coach:** Tyler Norton.

GAME INFORMATION

Radio Announcer: Alex Freedman. **No. of Games Broadcast:** 144. **Station:** KGHM-AM 1340 (www.1340thegame. com).

PA Announcer: Jared Gallagher. **Official Scorers:** Jim Byers, Mark Heusman, Rich Tortorelli.

Stadium Name: Chickasaw Bricktown Ballpark. **Location:** Bricktown area in downtown Oklahoma City, near interchange of I-235 and I-40, off I-235 take Sheridan exit to Bricktown; off I-40 take Shields exit, north to Bricktown. **Standard Game Times:** 7:05 pm, Sun 2:05 (April-May), 6:05 (June-Aug). **Ticket Price Range:** $9-28.

Visiting Club Hotel: Courtyard Oklahoma City Downtown, 2 West Reno Ave., Oklahoma City, OK 73102. **Telephone:** (405) 232-2290.

OMAHA STORM CHASERS

Address: Werner Park, 12356 Ballpark Way, Papillion, NE 68046.
Administrative Office Phone: (402) 734-2550. **Ticket Office Phone:** (402) 738-5100. **Fax:** (402) 734-7166. **E-mail Address:** info@omahastorm-chasers.com. **Website:** www.omahastormchasers.com. **Affiliation (first year):** Kansas City Royals (1969). **Years in League:** 1998-

OWNERSHIP/MANAGEMENT

Operated By: Alliance Baseball Managing Partners. **Owners:** Gary Green, Larry Botel, Brian Callaghan, Eric Foss, Stephen Alepa, Peter Huff, Evan Friend.

CEO: Gary Green. **President/General Manager:** Martie Cordaro. **Assistant GM:** Laurie Schlender. **Assistant GM, Operations:** Andrea Bedore. **Assistant GM, Sales:** Sean Olson. **Human Resources Manager:** Laura Warnock. **Director, Broadcasting:** Mark Nasser. **Director, Business Development:** Dave Endress. **Head Groundskeeper:** Scott Rowedder. **Manager of Marketing/Communications:** Josh Tague. **Facilities Manager:** Louie Page. **Marketing/Promotions Manager:** Andrew Asbury. **Promotions/Game Operations Manager:** Nick Sandberg. **Community Relations Manager:** Becki Frishman. **Senior Corporate Account Manager:** Jason Kinney. **Client Services Manager:** Cory Livingston. **Media Operations Manager:** Andrew Green. **Creative Services Manager:** Lauren Kirk. **Video/Multimedia Coordinator:** Scott Popp. **Ticket Operations Manager:** Anna Del Castillo. **Group Sales Manager:** Zach Ziler. **Group Ticket Sales Executive:** Harrison Zornes. **Accounting Manager:** Luke Aggeler. **Retail Manager:** Mitch Cunningham. **Broadcast Assistant:** Donny Baarns. **Sales Assistant:** Sara Howard. **Ticket Operations Assistant:** Michael McCoy. **Senior Ballpark Operations Assistant:** Kory Foster. **Ballpark Operations Assistant:** Jordan King. **Grounds Manager:** Tom Walter. **Front Office Assistant:** Donna Kostal and Michelle VanBemmelen.

FIELD STAFF

Manager: Brian Poldberg. **Hitting Coach:** Brian Buchanan. **Pitching Coach:** Andy Hawkins. **Athletic Trainer:** James Stone. **Strength Coach:** Phil Falco.

GAME INFORMATION

Radio Announcers: Mark Nasser, Donny Baarns. **No. of Games Broadcast:** 140. **Flagship Station:** KZOT-AM 1180. **PA Announcer:** Chris Chapman & Craig Evans. **Official Scorers:** Frank Adkisson, Ryan White, and Gary Sharp. **Stadium Name:** Werner Park. **Location:** Highway 370, just east of I-80 (exit 439). **Standard Game Times:** 6:35 pm (April-May), 7:05 (June-Sept), Fri./Sat. 7:05, Sun. 2:05. **Visiting Club Hotel:** Courtyard Omaha La Vista, 12560 Westport Parkway, La Vista, NE 68128. **Telephone:** (402) 339-4900. **Fax:** (402) 339-4901.

RENO ACES

Address: 250 Evans Ave, Reno, NV 89501.
Telephone: (775) 334-4700. **Fax:** (775) 334-4701.
Website: www.renoaces.com.
Affiliation (first year): Arizona Diamondbacks (2009). **Years in League:** 2009-

OWNERSHIP/MANAGEMENT

President: Eric Edelstein.

General Manager: Emily Jaenson. **Chief Operations Officer:** Chris Holland. **Chief Revenue Officer:** Samantha Hicks. **Chief Financial Officer:** Stacey Bowman. **VP of Corporate Partnership:** Doug Raftery. **VP of Business**

MINOR LEAGUES

Development: Brian Moss. **Director of Ticket Operations:** Sarah Bliss. **Director of Broadcasting:** Ryan Radtke. **Director of Field Operations:** Joe Hill. **Senior Accountant:** Jamie Smith. **Communications Manager:** Jackson Gaskins. **Marketing Manager:** Vince Ruffino. **Senior Marketing Implementation Manager:** Candice Vialpando. **Group Sales Manager:** Alex Strathearn. **Entertainment Manager:** Jon Reisdorf. **Merchandise Manager:** Joey Santos. **Ticket Operations Manager:** Liz Bell. **Fan Experience Manager:** Marisa Ochoa. **Facilities Manager:** Miguel Paredes. **Creative Manager:** McKenna Bush. **Manager: Corporate Partnerships:** Max Margulies. **Outside Sales Manager:** Denis O'Grady. **Community Relations Manager:** Jared Cooper. **Special Events Manager:** Sean Smock. **Visiting Clubhouse Manager:** Bubba Hearn. **Retail Sales Coordinator:** Corinne Guerra. **Corporate Partnerships Services Coordinator:** Courtney Baker. **Corporate Partnerships Coordinator:** Max Simpson. **Account Executive - Corporate Partnerships:** Stevie McElheny. **Entertainment Coordinator:** Joey Thyne. **Member Services Coordinator, Aces:** Chloe Marquardt. **Sales & Analytics Coordinator:** Shane Kocick. **Stadium Superintendent:** Ben Sanchez. **Ticket Operations Supervisor:** John Ashley. **Account Executive, Group Sales:** Miles Hendrick. **Account Executive:** Reed Gibson. **Outside Sales Executive:** Thomas Beckley. **Account Executive:** Katherine Davison. **Sales Academy Reps:** Dominic Breshears, JJ Baldivia. **Sales Academy Rep:** Ryan Gordon. **Sales Academy Rep:** Shawnee McFadden.

FIELD STAFF

Manager: Chris Cron. **Hitting Coach:** Jason Camilli. **Pitching Coach:** Jeff Bajenaru. **Coach:** Greg Gross. **Athletic Trainer:** Paul Porter. **Strength & Conditioning Coach:** Steven Candelaria.

GAME INFORMATION

Radio Announcer: Ryan Radtke. **No. of Games Broadcast:** 142. **Flagship Station:** Fox Sports 630 AM. **PA Announcers:** Cory Smith, Chris Payne. **Official Scorers:** Derek Neff, Nick Saccomanno, Katie Rihn, Gregg Zive. **Stadium Name:** Greater Nevada Field. **Location: From north, south and east:** I-80 West, Exit 14 (Wells Ave.), left on Wells, right at Kuenzli St., field on right; From West, I-80 East to Exit 13 (Virginia St.), right on Virginia, left on Second, field on left. **Standard Game Times:** 7:05 p.m., 6:35 p.m., 1:05 p.m. **Ticket Price Range:** $8-35.

ROUND ROCK EXPRESS

Address: 3400 East Palm Valley Blvd, Round Rock, TX 78665.
Telephone: (512) 255-2255. **Fax:** (512) 255-1558.
E-Mail Address: info@rrexpress.com. **Website:** www.roundrockexpress.com.
Affiliation (first year): Houston Astros (2019). **Year in League:** 2005-

OWNERSHIP/MANAGEMENT

Operated By: Ryan Sanders Baseball, LP. **Principal Owners:** Nolan Ryan, Don Sanders. **Owners:** Reese Ryan, Reid Ryan, Brad Sanders, Bret Sanders, Eddie Maloney.
CEO, Ryan Sanders Baseball: Reese Ryan. **Chief Operating Officer, Ryan Sanders Baseball:** JJ Gottsch. **Executive Assistant, Ryan Sanders Baseball:** Debbie Bowman. **Administrative Assistant, Ryan Sanders Baseball:** Jacqueline Bowman. **President:** Chris Almendarez. **General Manager:** Tim Jackson. **Advisor to President/General Manager:** Dave Fendrick. **Senior Vice President, Marketing:** Laura Fragoso. **Vice President, Corporate Sales:** Henry Green. **Vice President, Ticket Sales:** Gary Franke. **Vice President, Administration/Accounting:** Debbie Coughlin. **Senior Director, United Heritage Center:** Scott Allen. **Senior Director, Ticket Operations:** Ross Scott. **Director, Broadcasting:** Mike Capps. **Director, Ballpark Entertainment:** Steve Richards. **Director, Community Relations and Special Events:** Elisa Fogle. **Director, Retail Operations:** Joe Belger. **Director, Stadium Maintenance:** Aurelio Martinez. **Director, Stadium Operations:** Gene Kropff. **Director, IT:** Sam Isham. **Director, Express Select:** Chris Godwin. **Manager, PR/Communications:** Andrew Felts. **Manager, Client Services:** Zach Pustka. **Manager, Stadium Operations:** Justin Botkins. **Coordinator, Creative Marketing:** Julia Price. **Coordinator, Grassroots Marketing:** Casey Wright. **Coordinator, Amateur Baseball:** Chase Almendarez. **Digital Content Specialist:** Taylor Shipp. **Coordinator, Season Memberships and Suite Services:** Aschley Eschenburg. **Senior Account Executives:** Alyssa Coggins, Oscar Rodriguez. **Account Executives:** Lucas Allison, Chaniel Nelson. **Guest Experience Specialist:** Jake Foust. **Head Groundskeeper:** Nick Rozdilski. **Clubhouse Manager:** Kenny Bufton. **Maintenance Staff:** Ofelia Gonzalez. **Electrician/HVAC Maintenance Staff:** Leslie Hitt. **Office Manager:** Wendy Abrahamsen. **Accounting Assistant:** Sandy Tucker.

FIELD STAFF

Manager: Mickey Storey. **Hitting Coach:** Ben Rosenthal. **Pitching Coach:** Drew French. **Coach:** TBA. **Trainer:** TBA. **Strength Coach:** TBA.

GAME INFORMATION

Radio Announcers: Mike Capps. **No. of Games Broadcast:** 140. **Flagship Station:** AM 1300 The Zone. **PA Announcer:** Glen Norman. **Official Scorer:** Tommy Tate. **Stadium Name:** Dell Diamond. **Location:** US Highway 79, 3.5 miles east of Interstate 35 (exit 253) or 1.5 miles west of Texas Tollway 130. **Standard Game Times:** 7:05 pm, 6:05, 1:05. **Ticket Price Range:** $7-$30. **Visiting Club Hotel:** Hilton Garden Inn, 2310 North IH-35, Round Rock, TX 78681. **Telephone:** (512) 341-8200.

SACRAMENTO RIVER CATS

Address: 400 Ballpark Drive, West Sacramento, CA 95691
Telephone: (916) 376-4700. **Fax:** (916) 376-4710.

E-Mail Address: reception@rivercats.com. **Website:** www.rivercats.com
Affiliation (first year): San Francisco Giants (2015). **Years in League:** 1903, 1909-11, 1918-60, 1974-76, 2000-

OWNERSHIP/MANAGEMENT

Majority Owner/CEO: Susan Savage. **President:** Jeff Savage.
General Manager: Chip Maxson. **Manager, Human Resources:** Isabella Guedes. **Coordinator, Human Resources:** Stacey Lee. **Vice President, Finance:** Maddie Strika. **Accounting Coordinator:** Darcy Kooman. **Executive Assistant:** Shari Koepplin. **Receptionist:** Vanessa Villanueva. **Vice President, Partner Services:** Greg Coletti. **Director, Business Development:** Kasey Carlock. **Manager, Partnership Services:** Kim Bare. **Manager, Key Accounts:** Ellese Iliff. **Director, Marketing:** Emily Williams. **Manager, Communications/Baseball Operations:** Daniel Emmons. **Radio Broadcaster:** Johnny Doskow. **Multimedia Designer:** Mike Villarreal. **Coordinator, Creative Services:** Aaron Davis. **Coordinator, Marketing:** Melissa Adams. **Coordinator, Digital Marketing:** Sasha Margulies. **Mascot Coordinator:** Stephen Webster. **Promotions Coordinator:** Amber Wyatt. **Assistant, Graphic Design:** Nina Berghausen. **Director, Ticket Sales & Membership Services:** Joey Van Cleave. **Director, Ticket Operations:** Joe Carlucci
Manager, Corporate Sales: John Watts. **Senior Account Executive, Corporate Sales:** Jack Barbour. **Senior Account Executive, Corporate Sales:** Troy Loparco. **Account Executives, Corporate Sales:** Kelsie Monroe, Aaron Gray, Sean Piper. **Manager, Group Sales:** Jeff Goldsmith. **Account Executive, Group Events:** Daniel Mason. **Manager, Inside Sales:** Alexis Stevens. **Representatives, Inside Sales:** Lydia Brown, Jake Thompson, Jonathan Arrow, Mohammed Halabi. **Account Executives, Inside Sales:** Collyn Carter, J'son Bennett, Kaz Gibney. **Account Executives, Group Sales:** Peyton Burnham, Austin Kromminga, Justin Wiley, Tyler Kadison, Michael Rodgers. **Senior Membership Experience Specialist:** Kyle Strom. **Membership Experience Specialists:** Christine Visitacion, Kayla Vidal. **Manager, Merchandise:** Rose Holland. **Manager, Merchandise Marketing & Online Sales:** Erin Kilby. **Coordinator, Website/Research:** Brent Savage. **Director, Stadium Operations:** Brett Myers. **Director, Events/Entertainment:** Brittney Nizuk. **Coordinator, Events/Entertainment:** Aubrey Schmidt. **Assistant, Events & Entertainment:** Simonne Sacco. **Director, Field Operations:** Chris Shastid. **Facility Supervisor:** Anthony Hernandez. **Manager, Security:** Rich Bentley. **Facility Operations:** Mike Correa. **Coordinator, Field Opertations:** Marcello Clamar. **Landscaper:** Rafael Quiroz. **Vice President, Ballpark Experience:** Corey Brandt. **Executive Chef:** Tim Benham. **Manager, Concessions:** Sean Gerkensmeyer. **Manager, Suites & Premium Hospitality:** Alexander Ross. **Coordinator, Office Recruiter:** Courtney Cino.

FIELD STAFF

Manager: Dave Brundage. **Hitting Coach:** Damon Minor. **Pitching Coach:** Steve Kline. **Fundamentals Coach:** Jolbert Cabrera. **Athletic Trainer:** David Getsoff. **Athletic Trainer:** Hiro Sato. **Strength & Conditioning Coach:** Andy King.

GAME INFORMATION

Radio Broadcaster: Johnny Doskow. **No. of Games Broadcast:** 140. **PA Announcer:** TBD. **Official Scorers:** Mark Honbo, Doug Kelly, Brian Berger.
Stadium Name: Raley Field. **Location:** I-5 to Business-80 West, exit at Jefferson Boulevard. **Standard Game Time:** 7:05 pm. **Ticket Price Range:** $10-$70. **Visiting Club Hotel:** Holiday Inn Capitol Plaza.

SALT LAKE BEES

Address: 77 W 1300 South, Salt Lake City, UT 84115.
Telephone: (801) 325-2337. **Fax:** (801) 485-6818.
E-Mail Address: info@slbees.com. **Website:** www.slbees.com.
Affiliation (first year): Los Angeles Angels (2001). **Years in League:** 1915-25, 1958-65, 1970-84, 1994-.

OWNERSHIP/MANAGEMENT

Operated by: Larry H. Miller Baseball Inc.
Principal Owner: Gail Miller. **President, Miller Sports & Entertainment:** Steve Starks. **President, Vivint Smart Home Arena:** Jim Olson. **Chief Revenue Officer:** Don Stirling. **Chief Customer Officer:** Craig Sanders. **Chief Financial Officer:** John Larson. **President/General Manager:** Marc Amicone. **Assistant GM:** Bryan Kinneberg. **Senior VP, Corporate Partnerships:** Ted Roberts. **Senior VP, Communications:** Frank Zang. **General Counsel:** Sam Harkness. **VP of Corporate Partnerships:** John Kimball. **Director, Broadcasting:** Steve Klauke. **Director, Ticket Sales:** Brad Jacoway. **Director, Corporate Partnerships:** Kim Brown. **Director, Marketing:** Brady Brown. **Director, Ticket Operations:** Derrek DeGraaff. **Communications Manager:** Kraig Williams. **Game Operations and Marketing Manager:** Nikki Sim. **Youth Programs Coordinator:** Nate Martinez. **Home Clubhouse Manager:** Cole Filosa. **Visiting Clubhouse Manager:** Sam Robbins. **Head Groundskeeper:** Brian Soukup. **Asst. Head Groundskeeper:** Paul Sheffield.

FIELD STAFF

Manager: Lou Marson. **Hitting Coach:** Brian Betancourth. **Pitching Coach:** Pat Rice. **Trainer:** Brian Reinker.

GAME INFORMATION

Radio Announcer: Steve Klauke. **No. of Games Broadcast:** 140. **Flagship Station:** 1280 AM. **PA Announcer:** Jeff Reeves. **Official Scorers:** Jeff Cluff, Brooke Frederickson. **Stadium Name:** Smith's Ballpark. **Location:** I-15 North/South to 1300 South exit, east to ballpark at West Temple. **Standard Game Times:** 6:35 (April-May), 7:05 (June-Sept). **Ticket Price Range:** $10-24.

SAN ANTONIO MISSIONS

Address: 5757 Highway 90 West, San Antonio, TX 78227.
Telephone: (210) 675-7275. **Fax:** (210) 670-0001.
E-Mail Address: sainfo@samissions.com. **Website:** www.samissions.com.
Affiliation (first year): Milwaukee Brewers (2019). **Years in League:** 2019-

OWNERSHIP/MANAGEMENT

Operated by: Elmore Sports Group. **Principal Owner:** David Elmore.
President: Burl Yarbrough. **General Manager:** Dave Gasaway. **Assistant GMs:** Mickey Holt, Jeff Long, Bill Gerlt.
Director, Baseball Operations: Rich Weimert. **GM, Diamond Concessions:** Joe Demma. **Controller:** Eric Olivarez.
Director, Broadcasting: Mike Saeger. **Office Manager:** Delia Rodriguez. **Director, Operations:** John Hernandez.
Director, Public Relations: Mark Meyers. **Field Superintendent:** Travis Joslin. **Director, Ticketing:** Michael Ford.

FIELD STAFF

Manager: Rick Sweet. **Hitting Coach:** Al LeBoeuf. **Pitching Coach:** Fred Dabney. **Coach:** Ned Yost IV. **Trainer:** Aaron Hoback. **Strength Coach:** Andrew Emmick

GAME INFORMATION

Radio Announcer: Mike Saeger. **No. of Games Broadcast:** 140. **Flagship Station:** 860-AM.
PA Announcer: Roland Ruiz. **Official Scorer:** David Humphrey.
Stadium Name: Nelson Wolff Stadium. **Location:** From I-10, I-35 or I-37, take US Hwy 90 West to Callaghan Road exit. **Standard Game Times:** 7:05 pm, Sun 2:05pm/6:05pm.
Visiting Club Hotel: Holiday Inn Northwest/Sea World. **Telephone:** (210) 520-2508.

TACOMA RAINIERS

Address: 2502 South Tyler St, Tacoma, WA 98405.
Telephone: (253) 752-7707. **Fax:** (253) 752-7135.
Website: www.tacomarainiers.com
Affiliation (first year): Seattle Mariners (1995). **Years in League:** 1960-Present

OWNERSHIP/MANAGEMENT

Owners: The Baseball Club of Tacoma.
President: Aaron Artman. **CFO:** Brian Coombe. **Vice President, Sales:** Shane Santman. **Director, Administration/ Asst. to the President:** Patti Stacy. **Senior Director, Ticket Sales:** Tim O'Hollaren. **Director, Business Development:** Ben Nelson. **Director, Ticket Operations:** TBD. **Director, Baseball Operations and Merchandise:** Ashley Schutt. **Director, Stadium Operations:** Nick Cherniske. **Director, Group Sales and Event Marketing:** Caitlin Calnan. **Creative Director:** Casey Catherwood. **Vice President, Marketing:** Megan Mead. **Graphic Designer:** Delaney Saul. **Director, Media Relations and Content Creation:** AJ Garcia. **Manager, Stadium Operation:** Isaiah Dowdell. **Director Partner Services:** Yvette Yzaguirre. **Manager, Partner Services:** Sarah Lopes. **Manager, Ticket Operations:** TBD. **Manager, Group Sales:** Chris Aubertin. **Manager, Box Office:** Necia Borba. **Manager, Corporate Sales:** Devon Barker, Kevin Drugge, Kyle Milton, Danny Muno, Matthew Hummel. **Coordinator, Group Events:** Michael Landrum, Hayley Hacker. **Coordinator, Technical:** Anthony Phinney. **Head Groundskeeper:** Michael Huie. **Financial Analyst:** Jack Kelly. **Coordinator, Front Desk/Reception:** Allie Brown. **Premium Experience:** Hannah Hall. **Manager, Team Store:** Kyle McGilvray. **Home Clubhouse Manager:** Shane Hickenbottom.

FIELD STAFF

Manager: Daren Brown. **Hitting Coach:** Roy Howell. **Pitching Coach:** Lance Painter. **Trainers:** Tom Newberg and Josh DiLoreto. **Performance Specialist:** Derek Mendoza.

GAME INFORMATION

Radio Broadcaster: Mike Curto. **No. of Games Broadcast:** 140/140. **Flagship Station:** KHHO 850-AM. **PA Announcer:** Randy McNair. **Official Scorers:** Kevin Kalal, Gary Brooks, Michael Jessee, Jon Gilbert. **Stadium Name:** Cheney Stadium. **Location:** From I-5, take exit 132 (Highway 16 West) for 1.2 miles to 19th Street East exit, merge right onto 19th Street, right onto Clay Huntington Way and follow into parking lot of ballpark. **Standard Game Times:** 7:05, Sun. 1:35. (Monday – Wednesday games start at 6:05pm in April – June). **Ticket Price Range:** $7.50-$25.50. **Visiting Club Hotel:** Hotel Murano, 1320 Broadway Plaza, Tacoma, WA 98402. **Telephone:** (253) 238-8000.

EASTERN LEAGUE

Address: 27 Gorham Rd, Suite 221, Scarborough, ME 04074.
Telephone: (207) 289-6206. **Fax:** (207) 219-8958.
E-Mail Address: elpb@easternleague.com.
Website: www.easternleague.com.
Years League Active: 1923-
President/Treasurer: Joe McEacharn.

Vice President/Secretary: Charlie Eshbach. **VP:** Chuck Domino. **Director of Operations:** Bill Rosario. **Directors:** Fernando Aguirre (Erie), Ken Babby (Akron), Art Solomon (New Hampshire), Mark Butler (Harrisburg), Lou DiBella (Richmond), Geoff Iacuessa (Portland), Joe Finley (Trenton), John Hughes (Binghamton), Bob Lozinak (Altoona), Brian Shallcross (Bowie), Josh Solomon (Hartford), Craig Stein (Reading).

Division Structure: Eastern—Binghamton, Hartford, New Hampshire, Portland, Reading, Trenton. **Western**—Akron, Altoona, Bowie, Erie, Harrisburg, Richmond.

Regular Season: 140 games. **2019 Opening Date:** April 4. **Closing Date:** Sept 2.
All-Star Game: July 10 at Richmond.
Playoff Format: The first half winner and second half winner from each division meet in best-of-five series. Winners meet in best-of-five series for league championship.
Roster Limit: 25. **Player Eligibility Rule:** No restrictions.
Brand of Baseball: Rawlings.
Umpires: Joseph Gonzalez (El Monte, CA), Thomas Hanahan (Mentor, OH), Aaron Higgins (Elk Grove, CA), John Mang (Youngstown, OH), Christopher Marco (Waterdown, Ontario), David Martinez (Bayonne, NJ), Takahito Matsuda (Seiyo, Japan), Jacob Metz (Edmonds, WA), Michael Rains (Plano, TX), Thomas Roche (Hamden, CT), Greg Roemer (Richfield, OH), Randy Rosenberg (Arlington, VA), Michael Savakinas (Fairborn, OH), Chris Scott (Davidsonville, MD), Sean Shafer-Markle (Grand Rapids, MI), Patrick Sharshel (Highlands Ranch, CO), Derek Thomas (Cape Coral, FL), Thomas West (Scarborough, Australia).

Joe McEacharn

STADIUM INFORMATION

Club	Stadium	Opened	Dimensions LF	CF	RF	Capacity	2018 Att.
Akron	Canal Park	1997	331	400	337	7,630	344,754
Altoona	Peoples Natural Gas Field	1999	325	405	325	7,210	297,118
Binghamton	NYSEG Stadium	1992	330	400	330	6,012	220,279
Bowie	Prince George's Stadium	1994	309	405	309	10,000	230,347
Erie	UPMC Park	1995	317	400	328	6,000	205,055
Harrisburg	Metro Bank Park	1987	325	400	325	6,300	259,243
Hartford	Dunkin' Donuts Park	2018	325	400	325	6,146	408,942
New Hampshire	Northeast Delta Dental Stadium	2005	326	400	306	6,500	319,099
Portland	Hadlock Field	1994	315	400	330	7,368	346,341
Reading	FirstEnergy Stadium	1951	330	400	330	9,000	388,510
Richmond	The Diamond	1985	330	402	330	9,560	396,686
Trenton	Arm & Hammer Park	1994	330	407	330	6,150	351,297

AKRON RUBBERDUCKS

Address: 300 S Main St, Akron, OH 44308.
Telephone: (330) 253-5151. **Fax:** (330) 253-3300.
E-Mail Address: information@akronrubberducks.com.
Website: www.akronrubberducks.com.
Affiliation (first year): Cleveland Indians (1989). **Years in League:** 1989-

OWNERSHIP/MANAGEMENT

Operated By: Fast Forward Sports Group / Akron Baseball, LLC. **Principal Owner/CEO:** Ken Babby.
President: Jim Pfander. **CFO:** Shawn Carlson. **General Manager/COO:** Jim Pfander. **Assistant GM/Vice President, Operations:** Scott Riley. **Vice President, Sales:** Dave Burke. **Controller:** Leslie Wenzlawsh. **Assistant, Finance:** Bryson Lenderman. **Coordinator, Promotions:** Kyle Hixenbaugh. **Director, Public/Media Relations:** Adam Liberman. **Lead Broadcaster:** Marco LaNave. **Director, Merchandise:** Jeff Campano. **Coordinator, Creative Services:** Gabe Wasylko. **Director, Stadium Operations:** Adam Horner. **Head Groundskeeper:** Chris Walsh. **Assistant Groundskeeper:** James Petrella. **Assistant Director, Ballpark Operations:** James Parsons. **Director, Food/Beverage:** Brian Manning. **Assistant Director, Food/Beverage:** Bob Demyan. **Director, Premium Experience:** Sam Dankoff. **Executive Chef:** James Phillips. **Office Manager:** Missy Dies. **Coordinator, Community Relations:** Sonia Bravo-Murillo. **Manager, Season Ticket Sales & Service:** Mitch Cromes. **Manager, Group Sales & Service:** Roy Jacobs. **Ticket Sales Executives:** Dom DeMarco, Thyran Nowden, Rik Segal, Ian Wilkinson, Trevor McGuire. **Manager, Corporate Partnerships:** Anthony Chadwick. **Coordinator, Corporate Partnerships:** Brian Lobban. **Art Director:** Scott Watkins. **Director, Player Facilities:** Shad Gross.

FIELD STAFF
Manager: Rouglas Odor. **Hitting Coach:** Justin Toole. **Pitching Coach:** Tony Arnold. **Bench Coach:** Juan De la Cruz. **Trainer:** Bobby Ruiz.

GAME INFORMATION
Radio Announcers: Marco LaNave, Jim Clark. **No. of Games Broadcast:** 140. **Flagship Station:** Fox Sports Radio 1350-AM. **PA Announcer:** DJ Nivens. **Official Scorer:** Chuck Murr.

Stadium Name: Canal Park. **Location:** From I-76 East or I-77 South, exit onto Route 59 East, exit at Exchange/ Cedar, right onto Cedar, left at Main Street; From I-76 West or I-77 North, exit at Main Street/Downtown, follow exit onto Broadway Street, left onto Exchange Street, right at Main Street. **Standard Game Time:** 6:35 (April-May); 7:05 pm (June-Sept), Sun 2:05. **Ticket Price Range:** $5-11. **Visiting Club Hotel:** Fairfield Inn & Suites by Marriott Akron Fairlawn. **Telephone:** (330) 665-0641.

ALTOONA CURVE

Address: Peoples Natural Gas Field, 1000 Park Avenue, Altoona, PA 16602
Telephone: (814) 943-5400. **Fax:** (814) 942-9132
E-Mail Address: frontoffice@altoonacurve.com. **Website:** www.altoonacurve.com
Affiliation (first year): Pittsburgh Pirates (1999). **Years in League:** 1999-

OWNERSHIP/MANAGEMENT
Operated By: Lozinak Professional Baseball.

Managing Members: Bob and Joan Lozinak. **COO:** David Lozinak. **CFO:** Mike Lozinak. **General Manager:** Derek Martin. **Senior Advisor:** Sal Baglieri. **Assistant General Manager:** Nathan Bowen. **Director of Finance:** Mary Lamb. **Assistant Director of Finance:** Aaron McGuire. **Administrative Assistant:** Donna Harpster. **Director of Communications & Broadcasting:** Garett Mansfield. **Communications & Broadcasting Assistant:** Michael Marcantonini. **Director of Ticketing:** Jess Knott. **Box Office Manager:** Joel Fox. **Senior Ticket Account Manager:** Ed Moffett. **Ticket Sales Manager:** Briana Hornung. **Ticket Sales Manager:** Bryan Sowers. **Ticket Sales Manager:** Jeremy Snyder. **Director of Business Development & Sponsorship:** Corey Homan. **Manager of Partnership Services:** Jade Giantini. **Director of Community Relations:** Emily Rosencrants. **Director of Ballpark Operations:** Doug Mattern. **Head Groundskeeper:** Chris Mason. **Director of Concessions:** Glenn McComas. **Assistant Director of Concessions:** Michelle Anna. **Director of Entertainment and Branding:** Isaiah Arpino. **Director of Creative Services:** David Gallagher. **Director of Marketing, Promotions & Special Events:** Mike Kessling. **Social Media Manager:** Annie Choiniere. **Director of Merchandise:** Michelle Gravert.

FIELD STAFF
Manager: Michael Ryan. **Hitting Coach:** Jon Nunnally. **Pitching Coach:** Joel Hanrahan. **Coach:** Salvador Paniagua. **Trainer:** Justin Ahrens. **Strength/Conditioning:** Joe Schlesinger.

GAME INFORMATION
Radio Announcers: Garett Mansfield and Michael Marcantonini. **No. of Games Broadcast:** 140. **Flagship Station:** 1240 AM, WRTA. **PA Announcer:** Rich DeLeo. **Official Scorers:** Ted Beam, Dick Wagner. **Stadium Name:** Peoples Natural Gas Field. **Location:** Located just off the Frankstown Road Exit off I-99. **Standard Game Times:** 7 p.m., 6:30 p.m. (Weekdays, June-August), 6 p.m. (April-May); Sat. 6 p.m.; Sun 1 p.m., 6 p.m. **Ticket Price Range:** $8-15. **Visiting Club Hotel:** Altoona Grand Hotel.

BINGHAMTON RUMBLE PONIES

Office Address: 211 Henry St., Binghamton, NY 13901.
Mailing Address: PO Box 598, Binghamton, NY 13902.
Telephone: (607) 722-3866. **Fax:** (607) 723-7779.
E-Mail Address: info@bingrp.com. **Website:** www.bingrp.com.
Affiliation (first year): New York Mets (1992). **Years in League:** 1923-37, 1940-63, 1966-68, 1992-

OWNERSHIP/MANAGEMENT
President: John Hughes. **Managing Director:** John Bayne. **Director of Business Operations:** Amy Mercadante. **Director of Broadcasting & Media Relations:** Tim Heiman. **Director of Community Relations:** Eddie Saunders. **Director of Video Production:** Ryan Nicholson. **Director of Marketing & Promotions:** Catie Graf. **Box Office Manager:** Bob Way. **Director of Stadium Operations:** Richard Tylicki. **Sales Manager:** Steve Poploski. **Director of Merchandise & Retail Sales:** Jessica Swartz. **Senior Account Executive:** Tony Rogers. **Scholastic Programs Coordinator:** Lou Ferraro.

FIELD STAFF
Manager: Kevin Boles. **Hitting Coach:** TBA. **Pitching Coach:** TBA. **Bench Coach:** TBA.

GAME INFORMATION
Radio Announcer: Tim Heiman. **No. of Games Broadcast:** 140. **Flagship Station:** WNBF 1290-AM. **PA Announcer:** Frank Perney. **Official Scorer:** Matt Ferraro. **Stadium Name:** NYSEG Stadium. **Location:** I-81 to exit 4S (Binghamton), Route 11 exit to Henry Street. **Standard Game Times:** 6:35, 7:05 (Fri-Sat), 1:05 (Day Games). **Ticket Price Range:** $7 - $14. **Visiting Club Hotel:** Holiday Inn Downtown.

BOWIE BAYSOX

Address: Prince George's Stadium, 4101 NE Crain Hwy, Bowie, MD 20716.
Telephone: (301) 805-6000. **Fax:** (301) 464-4911.
E-Mail Address: info@baysox.com. **Website:** www.baysox.com.
Affiliation (first year): Baltimore Orioles (1993). **Years in League:** 1993-

OWNERSHIP/MANAGEMENT

Owned By: Maryland Baseball Holding LLC.
President: Ken Young. **General Manager:** Brian Shallcross. **Assistant GM:** Phil Wrye. **Director, Ticket Operations:** Charlene Fewer. **Director, Sponsorships:** Matt McLaughlin. **Assistant Director, Ticket Operations:** Sean Banks. **Promotions Manager:** Chris Rogers. **Communications Manager:** Robby Veronesi. **Sponsorship Account Manager/ Director of Broadcasting:** Adam Pohl. **Group Events Managers:** Mauricio Simms, Scott Rupp. **Box Office Manager:** Landon Ferrell. **Director, Video Production:** Mitchell Block. **Facility Manager & Head Groundskeeper:** Richard Douglas. **Stadium Operations Manager:** Jessica Briggs. **Groundskeeper Assistant:** Colin Tyzinski Director. **Gameday Personnel:** Darlene Mingioli. **Clubhouse Manager:** TBA. **Bookkeeper:** Carol Terwilliger.

FIELD STAFF

Manager: Buck Britton. **Hitting Coach:** Keith Bodie. **Pitching Coach:** Kennie Steenstra.

GAME INFORMATION

Radio Announcer: Adam Pohl. **No. of Games Broadcast:** 140. **Flagship Station:** www.1430wnav.com.
PA Announcer: Adrienne Roberson. **Official Scorers:** Ted Black, Dan Gretz, Jason Lee. **Stadium Name:** Prince George's Stadium. **Location:** 1/4 mile south of US 50/Route 301 Interchange in Bowie. **Standard Game Times:** Mon-Thu, Sat. 6:35 pm, Fri 7:05 pm, Sun 1:35 pm. **Ticket Price Range:** $7-17. **Visiting Club Hotel:** Crowne Plaza Annapolis, 173 Jennifer Rd, Annapolis, MD 21401. **Telephone:** (410) 266-3131.

ERIE SEAWOLVES

Address: 110 E 10th St, Erie, PA 16501.
Telephone: (814) 456-1300. **Fax:** (814) 456-7520.
E-Mail Address: seawolves@seawolves.com. **Website:** www.seawolves.com.
Affiliation (first year): Detroit Tigers (2001). **Years in League:** 1999-

OWNERSHIP/MANAGEMENT

Principal Owners: At Bat Group, LLC.
CEO: Fernando Aguirre. **President:** Greg Coleman. **Assistant GM, Communications:** Greg Gania. **Assistant GM, Sales:** Mark Pirrello. **Director, Accounting/Finance:** Amy McArdle. **Director, Operations:** Christopher McDonald. **Director, Entertainment:** TBD. **Director, Ticket Sales:** Dan Jones. **Account Executive:** Joe Peer. **Community Engagement Manager:** TBD. **Director, Merchandise:** Christy Buchar. **Director, Food/Beverage:** Jeff Burgess. **Ticket Operations Manager:** Tom Barnes. **Executive Chef:** Ed Coleman.

FIELD STAFF

Manager: Mike Rabelo. **Hitting Coach:** Brian Harper. **Pitching Coach:** Mark Johnson. **Coach:** Santiago Garrido. **Trainer:** T.J. Obergefell. **Strength/Conditioning Coach:** Matt Rosenhammer.

GAME INFORMATION

Radio Announcer: Greg Gania. **No. of Games Broadcast:** 140. **Flagship Station:** Fox Sports Radio WFNN 1330-AM.
PA Announcer: Bob Shreve. **Official Scorer:** Les Caldwell. **Stadium Name:** UPMC Park. **Location:** US 79 North to East 12th Street exit, left on State Street, right on 10th Street. **Standard Game Times:** 6:05 p.m. (April-May), 7:05 p.m. (June-Aug), Sun 1:35 p.m. **Ticket Price Range:** $10-16. **Visiting Club Hotel:** Baymont Inn & Suites, 8170 Perry Hwy., Erie, PA 16509. **Telephone:** (814) 866-8808.

HARRISBURG SENATORS

Office Address: FNB Field, City Island, Harrisburg, PA 17101.
Mailing Address: PO Box 15757, Harrisburg, PA 17105. **Telephone:** (717) 231-4444. **Fax:** (717) 231-4445.
E-Mail address: information@senatorsbaseball.com. **Website:** www.senatorsbaseball.com.
Affiliation (first year): Washington Nationals (2005). **Years in League:** 1924-35, 1987-

OWNERSHIP/MANAGEMENT

Principal Owner: Mark Butler. **President:** Kevin Kulp.
General Manager: Randy Whitaker. **Assistant General Manager/Ticket Sales Manager:** Jon Boles. **Accounting Manager:** Donna Demczak. **Senior Corporate Sales Executive:** Todd Matthews. **Director, Group Sales:** Jessica Moyer. **Account Executives:** Sage Berry, Erin Carr and Tyler Liles. **Group Sales Account Executives:** Jeff Bell and Kyle Kondracki. **Sales Service Coordinator:** Josh Bleyer. **Group Sales Interns:** Trent Sneidman and Sam West. **Box Office Manager:** Matt McGrady. **Box Office Intern:** TBD. **Director, Merchandise:** Ann Marie Naumes. **Director of Stadium**

MINOR LEAGUES

Operations: Tim Foreman. **Head Groundskeeper:** Brandon Forsburg. **Stadium Operations and Groundskeeping intern:** TBD. **Director of Media Relations & Broadcaster:** Terry Byrom. **Broadcasting and Media Assistant:** Seth Smit. **Director, Marketing:** Ashley Grotte. **Community Relations Coordinator:** JK McKay. **Marketing/Community Relations Intern:** Chelsie Bingham. **Director of Game Entertainment:** Scott Ciaccia. **Game Entertainment Coordinator:** Sami Lesniak.

FIELD STAFF

Manager: Matt LeCroy. **Coach:** Brian Rupp. **Pitching Coach:** Michael Tejera. **Trainer:** T.D. Swinford. **Strength Coach:** R.J. Guyer.

GAME INFORMATION

Radio Announcers: Terry Byrom & Seth Smith. **No. of Games Broadcast:** Home-70 Road-70 CBSSports Radio Harrisburg. **PA Announcer:** TBD. **Official Scorers:** Andy Linker and Mick Reinhard. **Stadium Name:** FNB Field. **Location:** I-83, exit 23 (Second Street) to Market Street, bridge to City Island. **Ticket Price Range:** $9-35. **Visiting Club Hotel:** Holiday Inn Harrisburg East, 815 S. Eisenhower Blvd, Middletown, Pa. 17057. **Telephone:** (717) 939-1600. **Visiting Team Workout Facility:** TBD.

HARTFORD YARD GOATS

Address: Dunkin' Donuts Park, 1214 Main Street, Hartford CT 06103
Telephone: (860) 246-4628. **Fax:** (860) 247-4628
E-Mail Address: info@yardgoatsbaseball.com. **Website:** www.YardGoatsBaseball.com
Affiliation (first year): Colorado Rockies (2015). **Years in League:** 2015-

OWNERSHIP/MANAGEMENT

President: Tim Restall. **General Manager:** Mike Abramson.
Assistant General Manager, Sales: Josh Montinieri. **Assistant General Manager, Operations:** Dean Zappalorti. **Director, Broadcasting & Media Relations:** Jeff Dooley. **Executive Director of Business Development:** Steve Given. **Human Resources Manager:** Thulani LeGrier. **Director of Event Services:** Conor Geary. **Events Marketing Manager:** Jacqueline Crockwell. **Hospitality and External Business Coordinator:** Jessica Gorman. **Director of Game Day Operations:** John Netkovick. **Stadium Operations Manager:** Ryan Mariotti. **Stadium Operations Coordinator:** Andrew Girard. **Operations Assistant:** Jimmy Bruno. **Director, Community Partnerships:** Tiffany Young. **Fundraising and Community Engagement Manager:** Tom Baxter. **Controller:** Jim Bonfiglio. **Client & Team Relations Manager:** Amanda Goldsmith. **Promotions & Marketing Manager:** Danielle Chylinski. **Creative Services Coordinator:** Karishma Pinto. **Game Production Manager:** Mike Delgado. **Merchandise Manager:** AJ Massaro. **Box Office Manager:** Sage Vigliarolo. **Ticket Operations Assistant:** Rick Hoffman. **Ticket Sales Manager:** Steve Mekkelsen. **Ticket Sales Account Executive:** Matt DiBona. **Ticket Sales Account Executive:** Shawn Perry. **Ticket Sales Account Executive:** Kyle Abad. **Ticket Sales Account Executive:** Kylah Hudson. **Ticket Sales Account Executive:** Jacob Michney. **Ticket Sales Account Executive:** Jordan Carrion. **Sports Turf Manager:** Kyle Calhoon. **Administrative Assistant:** Brisely Tifa.
Professional Sports Catering — Director of Operations: Scott Gustafson. **Assistant Director of Operations:** Jenny Nelson. **Concessions Manager:** Andrew Labov. **Executive Chef:** Joe Bartlett. **Business Manager:** Denise Picard.

FIELD STAFF

Manager: Warren Schaeffer. **Hitting Coach:** Lee Stevens. **Pitching Coach:** Steve Merriman. **Trainer:** Hoshito Mizutani. Phil Bailey Physical Performance Coach.

GAME INFORMATION

Radio Announcers: Jeff Dooley, Dan Lovallo. **No. of Games Broadcast:** 140. **Flagship Station:** News Radio 1410*FM 100.9 Spanish Danny Rodriguez, Derik Rodriguez. **PA Announcer:** Jared Doyon. **Official Scorer:** Jim Keener. **Stadium Name:** Dunkin' Donuts Park. **Directions: From the West:** Take 84 East to Exit 50 (Main Street). Take Exit 50 toward Main St. Use the left lane to merge onto Chapel St S. Turn left onto Trumbull St. Use the middle lane to turn left onto Main St. **From the East:** Take 84 West to Exit 50 (US-44 W/Morgan Street). Follow I-91 S/Main St. Take a slight right onto Main St. **From the North:** Take 91 South to Exit 32A - 32B (Trumbull St). Turn left onto Market St. Turn right onto Morgan St. Take a slight right onto Main St. **From the South:** Take 91 North to Exit 32A - 32B (Market St). Use the left lane to take Exit 32A-32B for Trumbull St. Use the middle lane to turn left onto Market St. Turn right onto Morgan St. Take a slight right onto Main St. **Ticket Price Range:** $6-22. **Visiting Club Hotel:** Holiday Inn Express, 2553 Berlin Turnpike, Newington, CT 06111. (860) 372-4000.

NEW HAMPSHIRE
FISHER CATS

Address: 1 Line Dr, Manchester, NH 03101.
Telephone: (603) 641-2005. **Fax:** (603) 641-2055.
E-Mail Address: info@nhfishercats.com. **Website:** www.nhfishercats.com.

Affiliation (first year): Toronto Blue Jays (2004). **Years in League:** 2004-

OWNERSHIP/MANAGEMENT

Operated By: DSF Sports. **Owner:** Art Solomon.
President: Mike Ramshaw. **General Manager:** Jim Flavin. **Senior VP, Sales:** Jeff Tagliaferro. **VP, Stadium Operations:** Tim Hough. **VP, Business Development:** Erik Lesniak. **Executive Director, Ticket Sales:** Shane Stout. **Director, Hospitality and Special Events:** Stephanie Fournier. **Director of Promotions & Entertainment:** Tyler Zickel. **Senior Account Executive:** John Evans. **Corporate Controller:** Jennifer Egan. **Client Relations Manager:** Christina Carrillo. **Corporate Sales Manager:** Tom Devarenne. **Box Office Manager:** Tara Leeth. **Marketing and Promotions Manager:** Sarah Lenau. **Broadcasting and Media Relations Manager:** Tyler Murray. **Production Manager:** Evan O'Brien. **Facility Operations Manager:** D.J. Peer. **Merchandise Manager:** Samantha Stawarz. **Turf Manager:** Greg Nigrello. **Corporate Sales and Promotions Coordinator:** Andrew Marais. **Ticket Sales Account Executives:** Colin Cyr, Andrew Larson, Garth Vincent, Chris Conery. **Professional Sports Catering, Director, Food & Beverage:** Jesse DaSilva.

FIELD STAFF

Manager: Mike Mordecai. **Hitting Coach:** Donnie Murphy. **Pitching Coach:** Vince Horsman. **Athletic Trainer:** Caleb Daniel. **Strength/Conditioning:** Ryan Maedel. **Dietitian:** Lauren Poole.

GAME INFORMATION

Radio Announcers: Tyler Murray, Bob Lipman, Tyler Zickel, Charlie Sherman.
No. of Games Broadcast: 140. **Flagship Station:** WGIR 610-AM. **PA Announcer:** Ben Altsher. **Official Scorers:** Chick Smith, Lenny Parker. **Stadium Name:** Northeast Delta Dental Stadium. **Location:** From I-93 North, take I-293 North to exit 5 (Granite Street), right on Granite Street, right on South Commercial Street, right on Line Drive. **Ticket Price Range:** $12. **Visiting Club Hotel:** Country Inn & Suites, 250 South River Rd., Bedford, N.H. 03110. **Telephone:** (603) 666-4600.

PORTLAND SEA DOGS

Office Address: 271 Park Ave, Portland, ME 04102. **Mailing Address:** PO Box 636, Portland, ME 04104.
Telephone: (207) 874-9300. **Fax:** (207) 780-0317.
E-Mail address: seadogs@seadogs.com. **Website:** www.seadogs.com.
Affiliation (first year): Boston Red Sox (2003). **Years in League:** 1994-

OWNERSHIP/MANAGEMENT

Operated By: Portland, Maine Baseball, Inc.
Chairman: Bill Burke. **Treasurer:** Sally McNamara. **President/General Manager:** Geoff Iacuessa. **Senior VP:** John Kameisha. **VP/ Financial Affairs & Game Operations:** Jim Heffley. **VP/ Communications & Fan Experience:** Chris Cameron. **Assistant General Manager/Sales:** Dennis Meehan. **Director, Corporate Sales:** Justin Phillips. **Account Manager-Sales:** John Muzzy. **Ticket Office Manager:** Bryan Pahigian. **Assistant Ticket Office Manager:** Allison Casiles. **Director, Creative Services:** Ted Seavey. **Mascot Coordinator:** Tim Jorn. **Director, Media Relations & Broadcasting:** Mike Antonellis. **Director, Food Services:** Mike Scorza. **Assistant Director, Food Services:** Greg Moyes. **Ticket Office Coordinator:** Alan Barker, Samantha Fletcher. **Senior Advisor:** Charlie Eshbach. **Clubhouse Managers:** Mike Coziahr, Mike McHugh. **Head Groundskeeper:** Jason Cooke. **Assistant Groundskeeper:** Andy Cashman.

FIELD STAFF

Manager: Joe Oliver. **Hitting Coach:** Lee May Jr. **Pitching Coach:** Paul Abbott. **Athletic Trainer:** Scott Gallon. **Strength & Conditioning Coach:** Ben Chadwick.

GAME INFORMATION

Radio Announcer: Mike Antonellis. **No. of Games Broadcast:** 140. **Flagship Station:** WPEI 95.9 FM. **PA Announcer:** Paul Coughlin. **Official Scorer:** Thom Hinton. **Stadium Name:** Hadlock Field. **Location:** From South, I-295 to exit 5, merge onto Congress Street, left at St John Street, merge right onto Park Ave; From North, I-295 to exit 6A, right onto Park Ave. **Ticket Price Range:** $6-11.
Visiting Club Hotel: Fireside Inn & Suites, 81 Riverside St., Portland, ME 04103. **Telephone:** (207) 774-5601.

READING FIGHTIN PHILS

Office Address: Route 61 South/1900 Centre Ave, Reading, PA 19605. **Mailing Address:** PO Box 15050, Reading, PA 19612.
Telephone: (610) 370-2255. **Fax:** (610) 373-5868.
E-Mail Address: info@fightins.com. **Website:** www.fightins.com.
Affiliation (first year): Philadelphia Phillies (1967). **Years in League:** 1933-35, 1952-61, 1963-65, 1967-

OWNERSHIP/MANAGEMENT

Operated By: E&J Baseball Club, Inc. **Principal Owner:** Reading Baseball LP. **Managing Partner:** Craig Stein.
General Manager: Scott Hunsicker.
Assistant General Manager: Matt Hoffmaster. **Exec. Director, Sales:** Joe Bialek. **Exec. Director, Baseball**

Operations & Merchandise: Kevin Sklenarik. **Exec. Director, Tickets:** Mike Becker. **Exec. Director, Community & Fan Development:** Mike Robinson. **Exec. Director, Business Development:** Anthony Pignetti. **Controller:** Kris Haver. **Head Groundskeeper:** Dan Douglas. **Chief Director, Promotions:** Todd Hunsicker. **Director, Marketing & Exec. Director, Baseballtown Charities:** Tonya Petrunak. **Video Director:** Andy Kauffman. **Director, Food & Beverage:** Travis Hart. **Office Manager:** Deneen Giesen. **Director, Groups:** Jon Nally. **Director, Public Relations/Media Relations & Radio Broadcaster:** TBA. **Director, Client Fulfillment/Clubhouse Operations:** Andrew Nelson. **Director, Graphic Arts/ Merchandise:** Ryan Springborn. **Asst. Director, Groups:** Brian Wells. **Asst. Director, Food & Beverage:** Nick Crosby. **Group Outings Manager:** Nick Mayer. **Extra Events Manager:** Nicole Fetchko. **Stadium Operations Manager:** Heath Skimski. **Diversity Outreach Coordinator:** Roberto Sanchez.

FIELD STAFF

Manager: Shawn Williams. **Hitting Coach:** Kevin Riggs. **Pitching Coach:** Aaron Fultz. **Assistant Coach:** Nelson Prada.

GAME INFORMATION

Radio Announcer: Gregg Caserta. **No. of Games Broadcast:** 140. **Flagship Station:** 610 ESPN. **Official Scorers:** Kyle Matschke, Brian Kopetsky, Josh Leiboff, Dick Shute. **Stadium Name:** FirstEnergy Stadium. **Location:** From east, take Pennsylvania Turnpike West to Morgantown exit, to 176 North, to 422 West, to Route 12 East, to Route 61 South exit; From west, take 422 East to Route 12 East, to Route 61 South exit; From north, take 222 South to Route 12 exit, to Route 61 South exit; From south, take 222 North to 422 West, to Route 12 East exit at Route 61 South. **Standard Game Times:** 7:05 pm, 6:35 (April-May), Sun. 2:05. **Ticket Price Range:** $5-11.

Visiting Club Hotel: Crowne Plaza Reading Hotel 1741 Papermill Road, Wyomissing, PA 19610. **Telephone:** (610) 376-3811.

RICHMOND FLYING SQUIRRELS

Address: 3001 N Boulevard, Richmond, VA 23230.
Telephone: (804) 359-3866. **Fax:** (804) 359-1373.
E-Mail Address: info@squirrelsbaseball.com. **Website:** www.squirrelsbaseball.com.
Affiliation: San Francisco Giants (2010). **Years in League:** 2010-

OWNERSHIP/MANAGEMENT

Operated By: Navigators Baseball LP. **President/Managing Partner:** Lou DiBella.
CEO: Chuck Domino. **Vice President/COO:** Todd "Parney" Parnell.
General Manager: Ben Rothrock. **Controller:** Faith Casey-Harriss. Assistant Controller, Debbie Srock. **Executive Director, Corporate Sales:** Ben Terry. **Executive Director, Business Development:** Marty Steele. **Corporate Sales Executives:** Lydia Novalis, Clint Goulden, Drew Norris. **Executive Director, Marketing & Promotions:** Anthony Oppermann. **Director of Communications & Broadcasting:** Trey Wilson. **Communications & Broadcasting Assistant:** Jake Eisenberg. **Community Relations Manager:** Cassidy Koch. **Manager of Funn:** Matt Wease. **Special Events Manager:** Hannah DeFrank. **Social Media & Promo Manager:** Caroline Phipps. **Creative Services & Production Manager:** Nick Elder. **Executive Director, Group Sales:** Camp Peery. **Assistant Director, Group Sales:** Garrett Erwin. **Group Sales Executives:** Donovan Havens, Hayden Nachtigal. **Director of Ticketing:** Eric Harrell. **Ticket Sales Manager:** Shelby Moody. **Suites Coordinator:** Sam Mireles. **Director of Food & Beverage:** Josh Barban. **Food & Beverage Operations Manager:** Tom Pritzl. **Executive Director, Field & Ballpark Operations:** Steve Ruckman. **Director of Stadium Operations:** Evan Smith. **Grounds Assistant:** Kyle Nichols. **Retail & Merchandise Manager:** Jackson Hairfield.

FIELD STAFF

Manager: Willie Harris. **Hitting Coach:** Francisco Morales. **Pitching Coach:** Glenn Dishman. **Fundamentals Coach:** Lipso Nava. **Bullpen Coach:** Eliezer Zambrano. **Athletic Trainer:** Garrett Havig. **Strength Coach:** Jonathan Medici.

GAME INFORMATION

Radio Announcers: Trey Wilson, Jake Eisenberg. **No. of Games Broadcast:** 140. **Flagship Station:** Fox Sports Richmond WRNL. **PA Announcer:** Anthony Opperman. **Official Scorer:** Scott Day. **Stadium Name:** The Diamond. **Location:** Right off I-64 at the Boulevard exit. **Standard Game Times:** 6:35 pm, Fri., 7:05, Sat. 6:05, Sun. 1:05. **Ticket Price Range:** $8-12. **Visiting Club Hotel:** Fairfield Inn & Suites by Marriott Richmond Short Pump/1-64. **Telephone:** (804) 545-4200.

TRENTON THUNDER

Address: One Thunder Road, Trenton, NJ 08611.
Telephone: (609) 394-3300. **Fax:** (609) 394-9666.
E-Mail address: fun@trentonthunder.com. **Website:** www.trentonthunder.com.
Affiliation (first year): New York Yankees (2003). **Years in League:** 1994-Present

OWNERSHIP/MANAGEMENT

Operated By: Garden State Baseball, LLP.
General Manager/COO: Jeff Hurley. **Senior VP, Corporate Sales/Partnerships:** Eric Lipsman. **VP Ticket Sales:** John

Fierko. **VP, Marketing/Sponsorship:** Lydia Rios. **Director, Merchandising:** Joe Pappalardo. **Director, Food/Beverage:** Kelly Kromer. **Director, Creative Services:** Dee Lugo. **Director, Ticket Sales:** Jon Bodnar. **Head Groundskeeper:** Jason Smith. **Controller:** Trevor Hain. **Director, Broadcasting and Media Relations:** Jon Mozes. **Director, Baseball & Stadium Operations:** Bryan Rock. **Manager, Web & Creative Services:** Dylan DeSimine. **Video Production Coordinator:** Ben Wolverton. **Manager, Box Office:** Sean O'Brien. **Group Sales and Special Events Representative:** Casey Borish. **Manager, Corporate Sales:** Juli Donlen. **Stadium Operations Manager:** Shane Eldridge. **Senior Group Sales Account Executive:** Brian Davis. **Group Sales Account Executives:** Seth English, Matt Lutz. **Ticket Sales Account Executive:** Bernadette Marco, Tyler Gleason, Tommy Kay, Teddy Smallwood. **Database Manager:** Jackie Mott. **Chef:** Corey Anderson. **Office Manager:** Morgan Schroll. **Broadcast and Media Relations Assistant:** Spenser Smith

FIELD STAFF

Manager: Patrick Osborn. **Hitting Coach:** Ty Hawkins. **Pitching Coach:** Tim Norton. **Defensive Coach:** Raul Dominguez. **Bullpen Coach:** Jason Phillips. **Trainer:** Jimmy Downam. **Strength/Conditioning Coach:** Anthony Velazquez.

GAME INFORMATION

Radio Announcers: Jon Mozes, Spenser Smith. **No. of Games Broadcast:** 140. **Flagship Station:** 920 AM The Jersey – Fox Sports Radio. **PA Announcer:** Kevin Scholla, Kevin Casey, Ryan Shute. **Official Scorers:** Jay Dunn, Greg Zak, Greg Zak Sr. **Stadium Name:** ARM & HAMMER Park. **Location:** From I-95, take Route 1 North to Route 29 South, stadium entrance just before tunnel; From NJ Turnpike, take Exit 7A and follow I-195 West, Road will become Route 29, Follow through tunnel and ballpark is on left. **Standard Game Times:** Monday-Friday: 10: 30, 11:00, 12:00, 7:00. Sat. 5:00, 7:00. Sun 1:00, 5:00. **Ticket Price Range:** $11-13.

SOUTHERN LEAGUE

Telephone: (770) 321-0400. **Fax:** (770) 321-0037.
E-Mail Address: office@southernleague.com.
Website: www.southernleague.com.
Years League Active: 1964-
President: Lori Webb.

Lori Webb

Vice President: Doug Kirchhofer. **Directors:** Hunter Reed (Biloxi), Jonathan Nelson (Birmingham), Jason Freier (Chattanooga), Reese Smith (Jackson), Ken Babby (Jacksonville), Chip Moore (Mississippi), Ralph Nelson (Mobile), Todd Parnell (Montgomery), Jonathan Griffith (Pensacola), Doug Kirchhofer (Tennessee).

Director, Media Relations: Michael Guzman

Division Structure: North—Birmingham, Chattanooga, Jackson, Montgomery, Tennessee. **South**—Biloxi, Jacksonville, Mississippi, Mobile, Pensacola.

Regular Season: 140 games (split schedule). **2019 Opening Date:** April 4. **Closing Date:** Sept. 2. **All-Star Game:** June 18 in Biloxi, MS.

Playoff Format: First-half division winners meet second-half division winners in best-of-five series. Winners meet in best of five series for league championship.

Roster Limit: 25. **Player Eligibility Rule:** No restrictions.
Brand of Baseball: Rawlings.
Umpires: Unavailable.

STADIUM INFORMATION

| Club | Stadium | Opened | Dimensions | | | Capacity | 2018 Att. |
			LF	CF	RF		
Biloxi	MGM Park	2015	335	400	335	6,000	160,364
Birmingham	Regions Field	2013	320	400	325	8,500	391,061
Chattanooga	AT&T Field	2000	325	400	330	6,362	214,811
Jackson	The Ballpark at Jackson	1998	310	395	320	6,000	110,798
Jacksonville	Baseball Grounds of Jacksonville	2003	321	420	317	11,000	317,335
Mississippi	Trustmark Park	2005	335	402	332	7,416	151,352
Mobile	Hank Aaron Stadium	1997	325	400	310	6,000	69,504
Montgomery	Riverwalk Stadium	2004	314	380	332	7,000	238,538
Pensacola	Blue Wahoos Stadium	2012	325	400	335	6,000	300,002
Tennessee	Smokies Stadium	2000	330	400	330	6,000	308,069

BILOXI SHUCKERS

Address: 105 Caillavet Street, Biloxi, MS 39530
Telephone: (228) 233-3465.
E-Mail Address: info@biloxishuckers.com. **Website:** www.biloxishuckers.com.
Affiliation (first year): Milwaukee Brewers (1999). **Years in League:** 1985-2015.

OWNERSHIP/MANAGEMENT

Operated By: Biloxi Baseball LLC.
President: Ken Young. **General Manager:** Hunter Reed. **Assistant General Manager:** Trevor Matifes. **Media Relations Manager and Broadcaster:** Garrett Greene. **Director of Sales:** Ricky Cunningham. **Director of Ticket Operations:** Allan Lusk. **Ticket Sales Executives:** Kory DuMond, Layton Markwood, Stephanie Chapman. **Community Relations Manager:** Kelsey Thompson. **Promotions Manager:** Jourdan Natale. **Marketing Manager:** Dani Polen. **Retail Manager:** Megan Ondrey. **Head Groundkeeper:** Quince Landry. **Human Resources & Accounting Manager:** Lisa Turner. **Box Office Coordinator:** Racheal Prosise. **Stadium Operations Manager:** Kennedy Helms. **Team Ambassador:** Barry Lyons.

FIELD STAFF

Manager: Mike Guerrero. **Bench Coach:** Chuckie Caufield. **Hitting Coach:** Danny Santin. **Pitching Coach:** Bob Milacki. **Athletic Trainer:** Jeff Bodenhamer. **Strength/Conditioning Coach:** Nate Dine.

GAME INFORMATION

PA Announcer: Kyle Curley. **Official Scorer:** Scotty Berkowitz.
Stadium Name: MGM Park. **Location:** I-10 to I-110 South toward beach, take Ocean Springs exit onto US 90 (Beach Blvd), travel east one block, turn left on Caillavet Street, stadium is on left. **Ticket Price Range:** $7-$24. **Visiting Club Hotel:** Double Tree by Hilton Biloxi on Beach Blvd.

BIRMINGHAM BARONS

Office Address: 1401 1st Ave South, Birmingham, AL, 35233. **Mailing Address:**
PO Box 877, Birmingham, AL, 35201.
  Telephone: (205) 988-3200. **Fax:** (205) 988-9698.
  E-Mail Address: barons@barons.com. **Website:** www.barons.com.
  Affiliation (first year): Chicago White Sox (1986). **Years in League:** 1964-65, 1967-75, 1981-

OWNERSHIP/MANAGEMENT

  Principal Owners: Don Logan, Jeff Logan, Stan Logan.
  President/General Manager: Jonathan Nelson. **Vice President of Sales:** John Cook. **HR & Payroll Manager:**
Ty Reed. **Corporate Sales Manager:** Don Leo. **Director of Group Sales:** Cory Ausderau. **Group Sales/ Educational
Outreach Coordinator:** Tyler Gore. **Group Sales Manager:** Sam Allen. **Group Sales Associates:** Jordan Smith &
Morgan Long. **Sponsorship Sales Coordinator:** Cole Buck. **Corporate Sales Manager:** Richard Coats. **Vice President
of Finance:** Randy Prince. **Director, Broadcasting:** Curt Bloom. **Marketing & Promotions Manager:** Samantha
Beck. **Creative Services Manager:** Courtney LeSueur. **Ticket Sales Manager:** Caleb Young. **Box Office Manager:**
John McCracken. **Director of Events:** Jennifer McGee. **Director of Hospitality Sales:** Jessica O'Rear. **Premium Sales
Manager:** Abby Southerland. **Director, Stadium Operations:** Mike Craven. **Director, Customer Service:** George
Chavous. **Head Groundskeeper:** Zach Van Voorhees. **Director of Retail Sales:** Gabe Harris. **General Manager of Food
& Beverage:** David Madison. **Concessions Manager:** Andy Jackson. **Director of Catering:** Sarah Spires. **Executive
Chef:** Nick Tittle. **Sous Chef:** Vic Arnold.

FIELD STAFF

  Manager: Omar Vizquel. **Hitting Coach:** Wes Helms. **Bench Coach:** Charlie Poe. **Pitching Coach:** Richard Dotson.
Head Athletic Trainer: Cory Barton. **Strength and Conditioning Coach:** Tim Rodmaker.

GAME INFORMATION

  Radio Announcer: Curt Bloom. **No of Games Broadcast:** 140. **Flagship Station:** JOX 94.5-WJOX-FM
  PA Announcers: Derek Scudder, Andy Parish. **Official Scorers:** AA Moore, David Tompkins.
  Stadium Name: Regions Field. **Location:** I-65 (exit 259B) in Birmingham. **Standard Game Times:** 7:05 pm, Sat. 6:30,
Sun 4:00. **Ticket Price Range:** $8-15.
  Visiting Club Hotel: Sheraton Birmingham Hotel, 2101 Richard Arrington Junior Boulevard North, Birmingham, AL
35203. **Telephone:** (205) 324-5000.

CHATTANOOGA LOOKOUTS

Office Address: 201 Power Alley, Chattanooga, TN 37402.
Mailing Address: PO Box 11002, Chattanooga, TN 37401.
Telephone: (423) 267-2208. **Fax:** (423) 267-4258.
E-Mail Address: lookouts@lookouts.com. **Website:** www.lookouts.com.
Affiliation (first year): Cincinnati Reds (2019). **Years in League:** 1964-65, 1976-

OWNERSHIP/MANAGEMENT

  Operated By: Chattanooga Lookouts, LLC
  Principal Owner: Hardball Capital. **Managing Partner:** Jason Freier.
  President: Rich Mozingo. **Public/Media Relations Manager:** Dan Kopf. **Head Groundskeeper:** Mike Showe.
Marketing & Promotions Manager: Alex Tainsh. **Director of Broadcasting:** Larry Ward. **Director, Operations/
Concessions Manager:** Anthony Polito. **Vice President:** Andrew Zito. **Ticket Partnership Manager:** Jennifer Crum.
Corporate Partnership Manager: Coralee Bryan. **Ticket Partnership Manager:** Bret Cranston. **Ticket Partnership
Manager:** Jarrah Vella-Wright. **Ticket Operations Manager:** Aaron Glachman. **Ticket Operations Manager:** Graham
Hartman.

FIELD STAFF

  Manager: Pat Kelly. **Hitting Coach:** Daryle Ward. **Pitching Coach:** Danny Darwin. **Coach:** Darren Bragg. **Strength &
Conditioning Coach:** Joseph Miranda. **Trainer:** Tyler Moos

GAME INFORMATION

  Radio Announcers: Larry Ward. **No. of Games Broadcast:** 140. **Flagship Station:** 98.1 The LAKE.
  PA Announcer: Ron Hall. **Official Scorers:** Andy Paul, David Jenkins.
  Stadium Name: AT&T Field. **Location:** From I-24, take US 27 North to exit 1C (4th Street), first left onto Chestnut
Street, left onto Third Street. **Ticket Price Range:** $5-10. **Visiting Club Hotel:** Holiday Inn, 2232 Center Street,
Chattanooga, TN 37421. **Telephone:** (423) 485-1185.

JACKSON GENERALS

  Address: 4 Fun Place, Jackson, TN 38305.
  Telephone: (731) 988-5299. **Fax:** (731) 988-5246.

E-Mail Address: sarge@jacksongeneralsbaseball.com.
Website: www.jacksongeneralsbaseball.com
Affiliation (first year): Arizona Diamondbacks (2017). **Years in League:** 1998-

OWNERSHIP/MANAGEMENT

Operated by: Jackson Baseball Club LLC.
Chairman: David Freeman. **Owner:** Reese Smith III. **President & General Manager:** Jason Compton. **Vice President, Finance:** Charles Ferrell. **Assistant General Manager:** Marcus Sabata. **Sales Manager:** Tory Goodman. **Turf Manager:** Jacob Barber. **Manager, Media Relations/Broadcasting:** Tyler Springs. **Manager, Tickets & Merchandise:** Ian Ueltschi. **Manager, Stadium Operations & Security:** Matt Malone. **Manager, Catering/Concessions:** Jeremy Wyatt. **Manager of Promotions/Production:** Robbie Perry. **Sales Exec:** Daniel Jones. **Sales Exec:** Milt Canovan. **Sales Exec:** Marcus Sabata. **Sales Exec:** Mark Cunningham.

FIELD STAFF

Manager: Blake Lalli. **Hitting Coach:** Rick Short. **Pitching Coach:** Doug Drabek. **Coach:** Jorge Cortes. **Strength/Conditioning Coach:** Mike Locasto. **Trainer:** Joe Rosauer.

GAME INFORMATION

Radio Announcer: Tyler Springs. **No. of Games Broadcast:** 70 (Home). **PA Announcer:** Mike Coburn. **Official Scorer:** Mike Henson. **Stadium Name:** The Ballpark at Jackson. **Location:** From I-40, take exit 85 South on FE Wright Drive, left onto Ridgecrest Road. **Standard Game Times:** 6:05, Sun. 2:05 or 6:05. **Ticket Price Range:** $8-12. **Visiting Club Hotel:** Doubletree by Hilton Jackson, 1770 Hwy 45 Bypass, Jackson, TN 38305. **Telephone:** (731) 664-6900.

JACKSONVILLE JUMBO SHRIMP

Office Address: 301 A. Philip Randolph Blvd, Jacksonville, FL 32202.
Telephone: (904) 358-2846. **Fax:** (904) 358-2845.
E-Mail Address: info@jaxshrimp.com. **Website:** www.jaxshrimp.com.
Affiliation (first year): Miami Marlins (2009). **Years In League:** 1970-

OWNERSHIP/MANAGEMENT

Operated by: Jacksonville Baseball LLC
Owner & Chief Executive Officer: Ken Babby. **Executive Assistant to Ken Babby:** Jill Popov.
President, Fast Forward Sports Group: Jim Pfander. **Chief Financial Officer:** Shawn Carlson. **General Manager:** Harold Craw. **Assistant General Manager:** Noel Blaha. **Vice President, Sales and Marketing:** Linda McNabb. **Director, Stadium Operations:** Weill Casey. **Director, Field Operations:** Christian Galen. **Director, Food & Beverage:** Ernest Hopkins. **Director, Ticket Operations:** Corey Marnik. **Director, Corporate Partnerships:** Gary Nevolis. **Director, Community Relations:** Andrea Williams. **Director, Broadcasting:** Roger Hoover. **Senior Business Development & Military Affairs:** Theresa Viets. **Creative Services Manager:** Brian DeLettre. **Merchandise Manager:** Brennan Earley. **Box Office Manager:** Peter Ercey. **Food/Beverage Manager:** Chris Harper. **Media/Public Relations Manager:** Scott Kornberg. **Accounting Manager:** Teresa Lively-Hall. **Partner Services Manager:** Ashley McCallen. **Food & Beverage Manager:** Nevious Love. **Promotions & Special Events Manager:** David Ratz. **Account Executives:** James Abbatinozzi, Alex Bell, John Bennett Costello, Robert Dorfman, Justin Lemminn, Tom Snyder, Julian Staiano. **Office Manager:** Christine Collins. **Accounting Assistant:** Jacob Yurdakul.

FIELD STAFF

Manager: Kevin Randel. **Pitching Coach:** Bruce Walton. **Hitting Coach:** Sean Berry. **Defensive Coach:** Jose Ceballos. **Athletic Trainer:** TBA. **Strength/Conditioning Coach:** Brady Fitzgerald. **Video Assistant:** TBA.

GAME INFORMATION

Radio Announcers: Roger Hoover & Scott Kornberg. **No. of Games Broadcast:** 140. **Flagship Station:** 102.3 FM.
PA Announcer: TBA. **Official Scorer:** Jason Eliopulos.
Stadium Name: Bragan Field at The Baseball Grounds of Jacksonville.
Location: I-95 South to Martin Luther King Parkway exit, follow Gator Bowl Blvd around Everbank Field; I-95 North to Exit 347 (Emerson Street), go right to Hart Bridge Expressway, take Sports Complex exit, left at light to stop sign, take left and follow around Everbank Field; From Mathews Bridge, take A Philip Randolph exit, right on A Philip Randolph, straight to stadium. **Standard Game Times:** 7:05 pm, Sat. 6:35 pm, Sun. 3:05 pm. **Ticket Price Range:** $5-$18.
Visiting Club Hotel: Hyatt Regency Jacksonville Riverfront, 225 Coastline Drive, Jacksonville, FL 32202. **Telephone:** (904) 360-8665.

MISSISSIPPI BRAVES

Office Address: Trustmark Park, 1 Braves Way, Pearl, MS 39208.
Mailing Address: PO Box 97389, Pearl, MS 39288.
Telephone: (601) 932-8788. **Fax:** (601) 936-3567.
E-Mail Address: mississippibraves@braves.com. **Web site:** www.mississippibraves.com.
Affiliation (first year): Atlanta Braves (2005). **Years in League:** 2005-

OWNERSHIP/MANAGEMENT

Operated By: Atlanta National League Baseball Club Inc.
Vice President & General Manager: Pete Laven. **Assistant General Manager/Director of Sales:** Tim Mueller.
Office Manager: Christy Shaw. **Ticket Manager:** Jeff Olson. **Account Executive:** Darius Green. **Account Executive:** Daylin Britt. **Account Executive:** Jacob Lord. **Director of Field & Facility Operations:** Matt Taylor. **Stadium Operations Manager:** Zach Evans. **Assistant Stadium Operations Manager:** Tony Duong. **Director of Communications, Media & Broadcasting:** Chris Harris. **Promotions & Entertainment Manager:** Dan Oleskowicz. **Graphic Design Manager:** Garrett Steiger. **Merchandise Manager:** Sarah Banta. **Food & Beverage Director:** Felicia Thompson.

FIELD STAFF

Manager: Chris Maloney. **Hitting Coach:** Carlos Mendez. **Pitching Coach:** Dennis Lewallyn. **Coach:** Alfredo Amézaga. **Trainer:** TJ Saunders.

GAME INFORMATION

Radio Announcer: Chris Harris. **No. of Games Broadcast:** 140. **Flagship Station:** WYAB 103.9 FM.
PA Announcer: Derrel Palmer. **Official Scorer:** Mark Beason.
Stadium Name: Trustmark Park. **Location:** I-20 to exit 48/Pearl (Pearson Road). **Ticket Price Range:** $6-$25.
Visiting Club Hotel: Hilton Garden Inn Jackson Flowood, 118 Laurel Park Cove, Flowood, MS 39232. **Telephone:** (601) 487-0800.

MOBILE BAYBEARS

Address: Hank Aaron Stadium, 755 Bolling Brothers Blvd., Mobile, AL 36606.
Telephone: (251) 479-2327. **Fax:** (251) 476-1147.
E-Mail Address: Info@mobilebaybears.com. **Web site:** www.MobileBayBears.com.
Affiliation (first year): Los Angeles Angels (2017). **Years in League:** 1966, 1970, 1997-current

OWNERSHIP/MANAGEMENT

Operated by: BallCorps Management. **Principal Owner:** Ralph Nelson.
Vice President: Jenny Askins. **General Manager:** Ken Clary. **Assistant General Manager:** Ari Rosenbaum. **Sales Manager:** JR Wittner. **Director of Stadium Operations:** Stephen Warren. **Director of Food & Beverage:** Gary Johnson. **Senior Account Executive:** Brice Ballentine. **Head Groundskeeper:** Kevin Grimes.

FIELD STAFF

Manager: David Newhan. **Hitting Coach:** Matt Spring. **Pitching Coach:** Jairo Cuevas.

GAME INFORMATION

Radio Announcer: Steve Goldberg. **No. of Games Broadcast:** 140. **Website:** www.BayBearsRadio.com. MiLB.tv.
PA Announcer: David Haney. **Official Scorer:** Greg Sufana. **Stadium Name:** Hank Aaron Stadium. **Location:** I-65 to exit 1 (Government Blvd East), right at Satchel Paige Drive, right at Bolling Bros Blvd. **Standard Game Times:** 6:35pm (Weekday), 7:05 (Fri-Sat) 7:05 (Sun), 2:05 (April-May), **Sunday:** 5:05 pm (June-Sept). **Ticket Price Range:** $6-16. **Visiting Club Hotel:** Riverview Plaza, 64 S Water St, Mobile, AL 36602. **Telephone:** (251) 438-4000.

MONTGOMERY BISCUITS

Address: 200 Coosa St., Montgomery, AL 36104.
Telephone: (334) 323-2255. **Fax:** (334) 323-2225.
E-Mail address: info@biscuitsbaseball.com. **Web site:** www.biscuitsbaseball.com.
Affiliation (first year): Tampa Bay Rays (2004). **Years in League:** 1965-1980, 2004-

OWNERSHIP/MANAGEMENT

Operated By: Biscuits Baseball LLC. **Managing Owner:** Lou DiBella
President: Todd "Parney" Parnell. **Chief Operating Officer:** Brendon Porter. **General Manager:** Michael Murphy.
Executive Consultant: Greg Rauch. **Corporate & Military Partnerships:** Jay Jones. **Corporate Partnerships Executive:** Matt Mulvanny. **Director of Group Sales:** Chris Walker. **Group Sales Manager:** Matt Baranofsky.
Community Engagement: Katie Parker. **Box Office Manager, Season Ticket Coordinator:** Justin Ross. **Marketing & Multimedia:** Jared McCarthy. **Broadcaster, Media Relations:** Chris Adams-Wall. **Retail Manager:** Ashley Williams.
Director, Food & Beverage: Risa Juliano. **Special Events/Catering Manager:** Sabrina Tew. **Executive Chef:** Mark Johnson. **Special Events/Catering Coordinator:** Kellsie Winkler. **Director, Stadium Operations:** Steve Blackwell.
Stadium Operations Assistant: Thomas Constant. **Head Groundskeeper:** Alex English. **Business Manager:** Tracy Mims. **Financial Specialist:** Joan Burden. **Executive Administrator:** Jeannie Burke.

FIELD STAFF

Manager: Morgan Ensberg. **Pitching Coach:** RC Lichtenstein. **Coach:** Gary Redus. **Coach:** Jamie Nelson. **Athletic Trainer:** Kris Russell. **Conditioning Coach:** Carlos Gonzalez

GAME INFORMATION

Radio Announcer: Chris Adams-Wall. **No of Games Broadcast:** 140. **Flagship Station:** WMSP 740-AM. **PA Announcer:** Rick Hendrick. **Official Scorer:** Brian Wilson. **Stadium Name:** Montgomery Riverwalk Stadium.

Location: I-65 to exit 172, east on Herron Street, left on Coosa Street. **Ticket Price Range:** $9-13. **Visiting Club Hotel:** Candlewood Suites, 9151 Boyd-Cooper Pkwy, Montgomery, AL 36117. **Telephone:** (334) 277-0677.

PENSACOLA BLUE WAHOOS

Address: 351 West Cedar St., Pensacola, FL 32502.
Telephone: (850) 934-8444. **Fax:** (850) 791-6256.
E-Mail Address: info@bluewahoos.com. **Website:** www.bluewahoos.com
Affiliation (first year): Minnesota Twins (2019). **Years in League:** 2012-

OWNERSHIP/MANAGEMENT
Operated by: Northwest Florida Professional Baseball LLC. **Principal Owners:** Quint Studer, Rishy Studer. **Minority Owner:** Bubba Watson, Derrick Brooks.
President: Jonathan Griffith. **Vice President of Operations:** Donna Kirby. **Vice President of Sales:** Alex Sides. **Receptionist:** Dawn Williams. **Operations Coordinator:** Mike Crenshaw. **Director, Sports Turf Management:** Dustin Hannah. **Director, Human Relations:** Candice Miller. **Media Relations Manager:** Daniel Venn. **Senior Writer:** Bill Vilona. **Broadcaster:** Chris Garagiola. **Creative Services Manager:** Adam Waldron. **Creative Services Assistant Manager:** Derek Diamond. **Director, Merchandise:** Anna Striano. **Box Office Manager:** Dakota Lee. **Box Office Assistant Manager:** Danny Do. **Sales Executives:** Bailie Tate, Wesley Donald, Steven Unser, Gracey McDonald. **CFO:** Amber McClure. **Assistant CFO:** Sally Jewell, Pam Handlin.

FIELD STAFF
Manager: Ramon Borrego. **Hitting Coach:** Steve Singleton. **Pitching Coaches:** Cibney Bello, Justin Willard. **Athletic Trainer:** Davey LaCroix. **Strength & Conditioning Coach:** Travis Koon.

GAME INFORMATION
Radio Announcer: Chris Garagiola. **No. of Games Broadcast:** 140. **Flagship Station:** The Ticket 97.1 FM.
PA Announcer: Josh Gay, Kevin Peterson, Chris James. **Official Scorer:** Craig Cooper.
Stadium Name: Blue Wahoos Stadium. **Standard Game Times:** 6:35 pm, Sat. 6:05, Sun. 1:05, 5:05 pm. **Ticket Price Range:** $7-$19.
Visiting Club Hotels: Hilton Garden Inn, Hampton Inn, Homewood Suites.

TENNESSEE SMOKIES

Address: 3540 Line Drive, Kodak, TN 37764.
Telephone: (865) 286-2300. **Fax:** (865) 523-9913.
E-Mail Address: info@smokiesbaseball.com. **Website:** www.smokiesbaseball.com.
Affiliation (first year): Chicago Cubs (2007-). **Years in League:** 1964-67, 1972-

OWNERSHIP/MANAGEMENT
Owners: Randy and Jenny Boyd.
CEO: Doug Kirchhofer. **President/COO:** Chris Allen. **Vice President:** Jeremy Boler. **General Manager:** Tim Volk. **Assistant General Manager, Stadium Operations:** Bryan Webster. **Operations Assistant:** Caleb Miles. **Special Events Manager:** Jason Moody. **Director of Broadcasting:** Mick Gillispie. **Head Groundskeeper:** Eric Taylor. **Administrative Assistant:** Tolena Trout. **Director of Corporate Partnerships:** Thomas Kappel. **Corporate Sales Executive:** Corey Smart. **Partnership Activation Manager:** Baylor Love. **Partnership Activation Manager:** Morgan Harlan. **Business Manager:** Suzanne French. **Admin/Finance Assistant:** Michelle Conway. **Director of Food and Beverage:** Chris Franklin. **Hospitality Manager:** Morgan Messick. **Merchandise Manager:** Ashley Binder. **Marketing and Community Relations Manager:** Connor Pearce. **Director of Video Production:** Aris Theofanopoulos. **Creative Services Manager:** Jonathan Bentley. **Group Sales and Ticketing Manager:** Andrew O'Gara. **Senior Account Executive:** Matt Graves. **Account Executive/Ticket Operations:** Brett Adams. **Account Executive:** Courtney Yarbrough. **Account Executive:** Evan Courtney.

FIELD STAFF
Manager: Mark Johnson. **Hitting Coach:** Chad Allen. **Pitching Coach:** Terry Clark. **Coach:** Ben Carhart. **Strength Coach:** Jason Morriss. **Athletic Trainer:** Toby Williams.

GAME INFORMATION
Radio Announcer: Mick Gillispie. **No. of Games Broadcast:** 140. **Flagship Station:** WNML 99.1-FM/990-AM.
PA Announcer: George Yardley. **Official Scorer:** Wade Mitchell. **Stadium Name:** Smokies Stadium. **Location:** I-40 to exit 407, Highway 66 North. **Standard Game Times:** 7:00 pm, Sat. 7:00 pm, Sun. 2/5:30. **Ticket Price Range:** $10-$14.
Visiting Club Hotel: Hampton Inn & Suites Sevierville, 105 Stadium Drive, Kodak, TN 37764. **Telephone:** (865) 465-0590.

TEXAS LEAGUE

Mailing Address: 505 Main St., Suite 250, Fort Worth, TX 76102
Telephone: (682) 316-4100. **Fax:** (682) 316-4100.
E-Mail Address: office@texasleague.com
Website: www.texasleague.com.
Years League Active: 1888-1890, 1892, 1895-1899, 1902-1942, 1946-
President/Treasurer: Tim Purpura.

Tim Purpura

Vice President: Justin Cole **Corporate Secretary:** Monty Hoppel, **Assistant to the President:** Tyler King **Directors:** Jon Dandes (Northwest Arkansas), Ken Schrom (Corpus Christi), Matt Gifford (Springfield), Dale Hubbard (Tulsa), Chuck Greenberg (Frisco), Miles Prentice (Midland), Russ Meeks (Arkansas), Burl Yarbrough (San Antonio).

Division Structure: North—Arkansas, Northwest Arkansas, Springfield, Tulsa. South—Corpus Christi, Frisco, Midland, San Antonio.

Regular Season: 140 games (split-schedule). **2019 Opening Date:** April 4. **Closing Date:** Sept 2.

All-Star Game: June 25 at Tulsa

Playoff Format: First-half division winners play second-half division winners in best-of-five series. Winners meet in best-of-five series for league championship.

Roster Limit: 25. **Player Eligibility Rule:** No restrictions.

Brand of Baseball: Rawlings.

Umpires: Unavailable.

Club	Stadium	Opened	LF	CF	RF	Capacity	2018 Att.
Amarillo	Hodgetown	2019	—	—	—	7,000	N/A
Arkansas	Dickey-Stephens Park	2007	332	413	330	5,842	296,847
Corpus Christi	Whataburger Field	2005	325	400	315	5,362	340,607
Frisco	Dr Pepper Ballpark	2003	335	409	335	10,216	468,259
Midland	Security Bank Ballpark	2002	330	410	322	4,669	263,024
NW Arkansas	Arvest Ballpark	2008	325	400	325	6,500	304,526
Springfield	John Q. Hammons Field	2003	315	400	330	6,750	326,362
Tulsa	ONEOK Field	2010	330	400	307	7,833	350,396

(Header spans: **Dimensions** over LF, CF, RF)

AMARILLO SOD POODLES

Ballpark Address: 715 S. Buchanan Street, Amarillo, TX 79101
Temporary Office Address: 821 South Johnson Street, Amarillo, TX 79101
Temporary Mailing Address: P.O. Box 9880, Amarillo, TX 79105
Main Phone: (806) 803-7762
Stadium Name: Hodgetown. **Estimated Capacity:** 7,000
Affiliation (first year): San Diego Padres (2019). **Years in League:** 2019-

OWNERSHIP/MANAGEMENT

Owners: Elmore Sports Group.

President & General Manager: Tony Ensor. **Director of Finance:** Ben Knowles. **Executive Assistant:** Shannon Cook. **Director of Public Relations and Baseball Operations:** Shane Philipps. **Director of Broadcasting:** Sam Levitt. **Video Production Manager:** Joe Corbisiero. **Director of Marketing:** Tess Bloom. **Director of Partnerships:** Nick Hall. **Corporate Partnerships Manager:** Matt Hamilton. **Promotions and Community Relations Manager:** Sierra Todd. **Director of Merchandise:** Katarina Burns. **Director of Ticket Sales and Service:** Jeff Turner. **Director of Group Sales:** Dustin True. **Ticket Operations Manager:** Nick Yardley. **Account Executive:** Jacob Helmus. **Account Executive:** Matt Sutherland. **Account Executive:** Ryan Williams. **Director of Stadium Operations:** Wayne Loeblein. **Head Groundskeeper:** Jordan Barr. Director of Food and Beverage (Diamond Concessions): Mike Lindal.

FIELD STAFF

Manager: Phillip Wellman. **Hitting Coach:** Raul Padron. **Pitching Coach:** Jimmy Jones. **Fielding Coach:** Freddy Flores.

GAME INFORMATION

Radio Announcer: Sam Levitt. **No. of Games Broadcast:** 140.. **Flagship Station:** N/A.

PA Announcer: N/A. **Official Scorer:** N/A. **Stadium Name:** Hodgetown. **Standard Game Times:** 11:05 a.m., 12:05 p.m., 1:05 p.m., 6:05 p.m., 7:05 p.m. CT. **Ticket Price Range:** $6-18. **Visiting Club Hotel:** N/A. **Telephone:** 806-803-7762.

ARKANSAS TRAVELERS

Office Address: Dickey-Stephens Park, 400 West Broadway, North Little Rock, AR 72114.
Mailing Address: PO Box 3177, Little Rock, AR 72203.
Telephone: (501) 664-1555. **Fax:** (501) 664-1834.
E-Mail address: travs@travs.com. **Website:** www.travs.com.
Affiliation (third year): Seattle Mariners (2017). **Years in League:** 1966-

OWNERSHIP/MANAGEMENT

Ownership: Arkansas Travelers Baseball Club, Inc.
President: Russ Meeks.
General Manager: Paul Allen. **Assistant GM, Merchandise:** Rusty Meeks. **Broadcaster:** Steven Davis. **Controller:** Brad Eagle. **Director, Finance:** Patti Clark. **Director, In-Game Entertainment:** Tommy Adam. **Park Superintendent:** Greg Johnston. **Assistant Park Superintendent:** Reggie Temple. **Director, Stadium Operations:** Andrew Heideman. **Director, Tickets:** Chris Fleischmann **Director, Marketing/Media Relations:** Lance Restum. **Corporate Event Planners:** John Sjobeck, Sophie Ozier, Montag Genser.

FIELD STAFF

Manager: Mitch Canham. **Hitting Coach:** Kyle Wilson. **Pitching Coach:** Pete Woodworth. **Performance Coach:** Michael Apodaca. **Trainer:** B.J. Downie.

GAME INFORMATION

Radio Announcer: Steven Davis. **No. of Games Broadcast:** 140. **Flagship Station:** KARN 920 AM.
PA Announcer: Russ McKinney. **Official Scorer:** Tim Cooper. **Stadium Name:** Dickey-Stephens Park. **Location:** I-30 to Broadway exit, proceed west to ballpark, located at Broadway Avenue and the Broadway Bridge. **Standard Game Time:** 7:10 pm. **Ticket Price Range:** $3-13. **Visiting Club Hotel:** Crowne Plaza, 201 S. Shackleford Rd, Little Rock, AR 72211. **Telephone:** (501) 223-3000.

CORPUS CHRISTI HOOKS

Address: 734 East Port Ave, Corpus Christi, TX 78401.
Telephone: (361) 561-4665. **Fax:** (361) 561-4666.
E-Mail Address: info@cchooks.com. **Website:** www.cchooks.com.
Affiliation (first year): Houston Astros (2005). **Years in League:** 1958-59, 2005-

OWNERSHIP/MANAGEMENT

Owned/Operated By: Houston Astros.
President: Ken Schrom. **General Manager:** Wes Weigle.
Senior Director, Finance: Kim Harris. **Senior Director, Stadium Operations:** Jeremy Sturgeon. **Director, Media Relations/Broadcasting:** Michael Coffin. **Director, Marketing:** JD Davis. **Director, Business Development:** Maggie Freeborn. **Director, Premium/Membership Sales:** Zach Kaddatz. **Field Superintendent:** Andrew Batts. **Marketing Manager:** Carly Boatwright. **Account Executive:** Amanda Boman. **Ticket Operations Manager:** Ray Cervenka. **Accounting Manager:** Jessica Fearn. **Customer Service Manager:** Brett Howsley. **Special Events/Operations Coordinator:** Jorden Klaevemann. **Community Outreach Coordinator:** Courtney Merritt. **Account Executive:** Sean Phelan. **Video Production Manager:** Neil Rosan. **Stadium Operations:** Michael Shedd. **Business Development Manager:** Diana Sleep. **Retail Manager:** Rudy Soliz.

FIELD STAFF

Manager: Omar Lopez. **Hitting Coach:** Tim LaMonte. **Pitching Coach:** Graham Johnson.

GAME INFORMATION

Radio Announcers: Michael Coffin, Gene Kasprzyk. **No. of Games Broadcast:** 140. **Flagship Station:** KKTX-AM 1360.
PA Announcer: TBA. **Stadium Name:** Whataburger Field. **Location:** I-37 to end of interstate, left at Chaparral, left at Hirsh Ave. **Ticket Price Range:** $6-20.
Visiting Club Hotel: Holiday Inn Corpus Christi Downtown Marina, 707 North Shoreline Blvd, Corpus Christi, Texas, 78401. **Telephone:** (361) 882-1700.

FRISCO ROUGHRIDERS

Address: 7300 RoughRiders Trail, Frisco, TX 75034.
Telephone: (972) 334-1900. **Fax:** (972) 731-5355.
E-Mail Address: info@ridersbaseball.com. **Website:** www.ridersbaseball.com.
Affiliation (first year): Texas Rangers (2003). **Years in League:** 2003-

OWNERSHIP/MANAGEMENT

Operated by: Frisco RoughRiders LP

Chairman/CEO/General Partner: Chuck Greenberg. **President & General Manager:** Andy Milovich. **Chief Operating Officer:** Scott Burchett. **Chief Sales Officer:** John Alper. **Chief Financial Officer:** Bernie Miller. **Director of Business Intelligence & Strategy:** Ankit Agrawal. **Assistant VP, Partner & Event Services:** Kathryne Buckley. **Director, Partner Services:** David Kosydar. **Partner Services Coordinators:** Jenny Katlein, Alexis Summers. **Director, Human Resources:** Kenya Allen. **Customer Service Agents:** Claudia Kipp, Vicki Sohn. **VP, Ticket Sales & Services:** Ross Lanford. **Senior Director, Ticket Sales & Services:** David Dwyer. **Premium Corporate Sales Manager:** Tyler Ellis. **Premium Group Sales Manager:** Monica Man. **Sr. Corporate Sales Executive:** Tom Baker. **Corporate Sales Executives:** Andrew Dance, Annie Millay, Jamaal Wilkins, Crystal Vasquez, Ryan Biddlecombe, Garrett Evans, Kasey Klopfenstein, Gustavo Rodriguez. **Group Sales Executives:** Mikaya Carlisle, Nate Doederlein, Cameron Pipes, Trevor Rolofson, Sydney Ryan, Alex Sandborn, Jenna Swafford, Ryan McFarland, Matthew Petrov. **Ticket Sales Coordinators:** Sydney Peterson, Skylor Rodriguez, Rachel Bilke, Amanda Standley. **Director, Ticket Operations:** Stephen Christ. **Ticket Operations Coordinator:** Katie Castillon. **Director, Marketing:** Jennifer Johnson. **Media/Marketing Coordinator:** Krystin King. **Graphic Design Coordinator:** Duncan Stanley. **Manager, Game Entertainment:** Jordan Gracey. **VP, Community Development:** Breon Dennis, Jr. **Community Intern:** Julie Gaona. **Broadcaster:** Ryan Rouillard. **VP, Ballpark Operations:** Tim Arseneau. **Operations Coordinator:** Ryan Wojdula. **Operations Assistant:** Eric Smith. Senior Director, **Sports Turf & Grounds Manager:** David Bicknell. **Clubhouse Manager:** Mitch Brasher. **Maintenance Director:** Alfonso Bailon. **Merchandise Manager:** Courtney Ward.

FIELD STAFF
Manager: Joe Mikulik. **Hitting Coach:** Jason Hart. **Pitching Coach:** Greg Hibbard. **Bench Coach:** Brad Flanders. **Athletic Trainer:** Alex Rodriguez. **Strength & Conditioning Coach:** Wade Lamont.

GAME INFORMATION
Broadcaster: Ryan Rouillard. **No. of Games Broadcast:** 140. **Flagship Station:** www.RidersBaseball.com. **PA Announcer:** Sean Heath. **Official Scorer:** Larry Bump. **Stadium Name:** Dr Pepper Ballpark. **Location:** Intersection of Dallas North Tollway & State Highway 121. **Standard Game Times:** 7:05 PM, Sunday 4:05 PM (April-May), 6:05 PM (June-August). **Visiting Club Hotel:** Comfort Suites at Frisco Square, 9700 Dallas Parkway, Frisco, TX 75033. **Visiting Club Hotel Phone:** (972) 668-9700. **Visiting Club Hotel Fax:** (972) 668-9701.

MIDLAND ROCKHOUNDS

Address: Security Bank Ballpark, 5514 Champions Drive, Midland, TX 79706.
Telephone: (432) 520-2255. **Fax:** (432) 520-8326.
Website: www.midlandrockhounds.org.
Affiliation (first year): Oakland Athletics (1999). **Years in League:** 1972-

OWNERSHIP/MANAGEMENT
Operated By: Midland Sports, Inc. **Principal Owners:** Miles Prentice, Bob Richmond.
President: Miles Prentice. **Executive Vice President:** Bob Richmond. **General Manager:** Monty Hoppel.
Assistant GM: Jeff VonHolle. **Assistant GM, Marketing/Tickets:** Jamie Richardson. **Assistant GM, Operations:** Ray Fieldhouse. **Director, Broadcasting/Publications:** Bob Hards. **Director, Business Operations:** Eloisa Galvan. **Director, Sales:** Matthew Barnett. **Director, Ticketing/Office Manager:** Jordan Loya. **Director, Client Services/Sports Complex Marketing:** Shelly Haenggi. **Director, Community Relations:** Rachael DiLeonardo. **Media Relations Coordinator:** Nathan Hymel. **Director, Marketing:** Matt Bari. **Director, Facilities:** Joe Peters. **Director, Operations:** Cannon Schrank. **Head Groundskeeper:** Eric Peckham. **Game Entertainment/Video Board Coordinator:** Russ Pinkerton. **Sales Executive:** Mike Castillo. **Assistant Concessions Manager:** Al Melville. **Home Clubhouse Manager:** Vernon Koslow. **Visiting Clubhouse Manager:** Seth Miller.

FIELD STAFF
Manager: Scott Steinmann. **Hitting Coach:** Tommy Everidge. **Pitching Coach:** Steve Connelly. **Coach:** Bobby Crosby. **Trainer:** Justin Whitehouse. **Strength/Conditioning:** Omar Aguilar.

GAME INFORMATION
Radio Announcer: Bob Hards. **No. of Games Broadcast:** 140. **Flagship Station:** KCRS 550 AM. **PA Announcer:** Wes Coles. **Official Scorer:** Mac Gipson. **Stadium Name:** Security Bank Ballpark. **Location:** From I-20, exit Loop 250 North to Highway 191 intersection. **Standard Game Times: Sunday:** 2:00 pm, Monday-Wednesday: 6:30 pm, Thursday-Saturday: 7:00 pm. **Ticket Price Range:** $8-16. **Visiting Club Hotel:** Springhill Suites by Marriott, 5716 Deauville Blvd, Midland, TX 79706. **Telephone:** (432) 695-6870.

NORTHWEST ARKANSAS
NATURALS

Address: 3000 Gene George Blvd, Springdale, AR 72762.
Telephone: (479) 927-4900. **Fax:** (479) 756-8088.
E-Mail Address: tickets@nwanaturals.com. **Website:** www.nwanaturals.com.
Affiliation (first year): Kansas City Royals (1995). **Years in League:** 2008-Present

OWNERSHIP/MANAGEMENT

Principal Owner: Rich Products Corp.
Chairman: Robert Rich Jr. **President, Rich Entertainment:** Melinda Rich. **President, Rich Baseball:** Jon Dandes.
Vice President/General Manager: Justin Cole. **Sales Manager:** Mark Zaiger. **Business Manager:** Morgan Helmer.
Marketing/PR Manager: Dustin Dethlefs. **Ballpark Operations Director:** Jeff Windle. **Ballpark Operations Assistant:**
Corey Lewis. **Head Groundskeeper:** Brock White. **Business Department Assistant:** Sarah Giesen. **Ticket Office
Manager:** Sam Ahern. **Broadcaster/Baseball Operations Coordinator:** Benjamin Kelly. **Promotions Coordinator:**
Roxanne Grundmeier. **Production Coordinator:** Adam Annaratone. Sr. **Account Executive:** Brad Ziegler. **Account
Executives:** Matt Fanning, Trey Garner, Josh Hill. **Clubhouse Manager:** Danny Helmer.

FIELD STAFF

Manager: Darryl Kennedy. **Hitting Coach:** Abraham Nunez. **Pitching Coach:** Doug Henry. **Athletic Trainer:** Justin
Kemp. **Strength & Conditioning Coach:** Will Gilmore.

GAME INFORMATION

Radio Announcer: Benjamin Kelly. **No. of Games Broadcast:** 140. **Flagship:** KQSM 92.1-FM. **PA Announcer:**
Bill Rogers, Jon Williams. **Official Scorers:** Kyle Stiles, Walter Woodie & Paul Boyd. **Stadium Name:** Arvest Ballpark.
Location: I-49 to US 412 West (Sunset Ave), Left on Gene George Blvd. **Ticket Price Range:** $8.75-14.75. **Standard
Game Times:** 7:05 pm (Monday-Friday), 6:05 pm (Saturday), 2:05 pm (Sunday). **Visiting Club Hotel:** Holiday Inn
Springdale, 1500 S 48th St, Springdale, AR 72762. **Telephone:** (479) 751-8300.

SPRINGFIELD CARDINALS

Address: 955 East Trafficway, Springfield, MO 65802.
Telephone: (417) 863-0395. **Fax:** (417) 832-3004.
E-Mail Address: springfield@cardinals.com. **Website:** springfieldcardinals.com.
Affiliation (first year): St. Louis Cardinals (2005). **Years in League:** 2005-

OWNERSHIP/MANAGEMENT

Operated By: St. Louis Cardinals.
Vice President/General Manager: Dan Reiter. **VP, Baseball/Business Operations:** Scott Smulczenski. **Director,
Market Development:** Brad Beattie. **Director, Ticket Operations:** Angela Deke. **Manager, Public Relations/
Broadcaster:** Andrew Buchbinder. **Public Relations Coordinator:** Matt Turer. **Marketing/Event Coordinator:** Regina
Norris. **Manager, Production:** Kent Shelton. **Graphic Designer:** T.J. Patton. **Manager, Premium Sales/Marketing:**
Zack Pemberton. **Manager, Ticket Sales:** Eric Tomb. **Memberships Coordinator:** Ross Fuller. **Director, Stadium
Operations:** Aaron Lowrey. **Head Groundskeeper:** Brock Phipps. **Assistant Head Groundskeeper:** Derek Edwards.

FIELD STAFF

Manager: Joe Kruzel. **Hitting Coach:** Brandon Allen. **Pitching Coach:** Darwin Marrero. **Trainer:** Dan Martin.

GAME INFORMATION

Radio Announcer: Andrew Buchbinder. **No. of Games Broadcast:** 140. **Flagship Station:** JOCK 98.7 FM.
PA Announcer: Eric Tomb. **Official Scorers:** Mark Stillwell, Tim Tourville.
Stadium Name: Hammons Field. **Location:** Highway 65 to Chestnut Expressway exit, west to National, south
on National, west on Trafficway. **Standard Game Time:** 7:10 pm. **Ticket Price Range:** $7-28. **Visiting Club Hotel:**
University Plaza Hotel, 333 John Q Hammons Parkway, Springfield, MO 65806. **Telephone:** (417) 864-7333.

TULSA DRILLERS

Address: 201 N. Elgin Ave, Tulsa, OK 74120.
Telephone: (918) 744-5998. **Fax:** (918) 747-3267.
E-Mail Address: mail@tulsadrillers.com. **Website:** www.tulsadrillers.com.
Affiliation (first year): Los Angeles Dodgers (2015). **Years in League:** 1933-42, 1946-65, 1977-present

OWNERSHIP/MANAGEMENT

Operated By: Tulsa Baseball Inc.
Co-Chairman: Dale Hubbard. **Co-Chairman:** Jeff Hubbard. **President/GM:** Mike Melega.
Executive VP/Assistant GM: Jason George. **Vice President, Operations:** Mark Hilliard. **Vice President, Media &
Public Relations:** Brian Carroll. **Vice President, Sales & Analytics:** Eric Newendorp. **Vice President, Marketing:** Justin
Gorski. **Vice President, Director of Food Service:** Robert Founds. **Director of Merchandise:** Tom Jones. **Director,
Ticket Sales:** Joanna Hubbard. **Corporate Sales Executive:** Robin Flores. **Account Executives:** Phil Sidoti, Cameron
Gordon, Katy Pace. **Graphic Design & Social Media Manager:** Evan Brown. **Community Relations Manager:** Taylor
Levacy. **Ticket Operations Assistants:** Katie Revlett, Jack Long. **Ticket Sales Assistants:** Nick Hill, Justin Perkins,
Corey Wilson, Jake Plotnik. **Promotions Assistant:** Alex Kossakoski. **Media & Public Relations Assistant:** Mark Verace.
Graphic Design & Social Media Assistant: Reo Radford. **Video Production Manager:** Alan Davidson. **Bookkeeper:**
Jenna Savill. **Assistant Bookkeeper:** Amy Eden. **Executive Assistant:** Lynda Davis. **Receptionist & Administrative
Assistant:** Jordan Saia. **Head Groundskeeper:** Gary Shepherd. **Facilities Manager:** Stevelan Hamilton. **Stadium
Operations Manager:** Marshall Schellhardt. **Mascot Coordinator:** Taylor Foote. **Executive Chef:** Aloha Manahan.
Radio Broadcaster: Dennis Higgins. **Team Photographer:** Rich Crimi.

FIELD STAFF

Manager: Scott Hennessey. **Hitting Coach:** Adam Melhuse. **Pitching Coach:** Dave Borkowski. **Coach:** Petie Montero. **Strength Coach:** Shaun Alexander. **Trainer:** Kalie Swain.

GAME INFORMATION

Radio Announcer: Dennis Higgins. **No. of Games Broadcast:** 140. **Flagship Station:** KTBZ 1430-AM. **PA Announcer:** Kirk McAnany. **Official Scorers:** Bruce Howard, Duane DaPron, Larry Lewis, Barry Lewis. **Stadium Name:** ONEOK Field. **Location:** I-244 to Cincinnati/Detroit Exit (6A), north on Detroit Ave, right onto John Hope Franklin Blvd, right on Elgin Ave. **Standard Game Times:** 7:05 pm, Sun. 1:05 (April-June), 7:05 (July-Aug). Mon. 11:05 am (May-June). **Visiting Club Hotel:** Marriott Tulsa Hotel Southern Hills, 1902 E 71st Street, Tulsa, OK 74136. **Telephone:** (918) 493-7000.

CALIFORNIA LEAGUE

Address: 3600 South Harbor Blvd, Suite 122, Oxnard, CA 93035.
Telephone: (805) 985-8585. **Fax:** (805) 985-8580.
Website: www.californialeague.com.
E-Mail: info@californialeague.com.
Years League Active: 1941-1942, 1946-
President: Charlie Blaney.

Vice President: Tom Volpe. **Directors:** Bobby Brett (Rancho Cucamonga), Jake Kerr (Lancaster), Dave Elmore (Inland Empire), Gary Jacobs (Lake Elsinore), Mike Savit (Modesto), Tom Seidler (Visalia), Tom Volpe (Stockton), Dan Orum (San Jose).

Director, Operations: Matt Blaney. **Historian:** Chris Lampe.

Legal Counsel: Jonathan Light. **CPA:** Mike Owen.

Division Structure: North—Modesto, San Jose, Stockton, Visalia. **South**—Inland Empire, Lake Elsinore, Lancaster, Rancho Cucamonga.

Regular Season: 140 games (split schedule).

2018 Opening Date: April 4. **Closing Date:** Sept 2.

Playoff Format: Four teams make the playoffs. First-half winners in each division play second-half winners (or wild card if the same team wins both halves) in best-of-five semifinals. Winners meet in best-of-five series for league championship.

All-Star Game: June 18 at Inland Empire.

Roster Limit: 25 active (35 under control). **Player Eligibility:** No more than two players and one player/coach on active list may have more than six years experience.

Brand of Baseball: Rawlings. **Umpires:** TBD.

Charlie Blaney

STADIUM INFORMATION

Club	Stadium	Opened	LF	CF	RF	Capacity	2018 Att.
Inland Empire	San Manuel Stadium	1996	330	410	330	5,000	193,992
Lake Elsinore	The Diamond	1994	330	400	310	7,866	214,955
Lancaster	The Hangar	1996	350	410	350	4,500	155,573
Modesto	John Thurman Field	1952	312	400	319	4,000	145,028
Rancho Cucamo.	LoanMart Field	1993	335	400	335	6,615	171,767
San Jose	Municipal Stadium	1942	320	390	320	5,208	147,668
Stockton	Banner Island Ballpark	2005	300	399	326	5,200	187,966
Visalia	Recreation Ballpark	1946	320	405	320	2,468	124,208

Dimensions (LF, CF, RF)

INLAND EMPIRE 66ERS

Address: 280 South E St., San Bernardino, CA 92401.
Telephone: (909) 888-9922. **Fax:** (909) 888-5251. **Website:** www.66ers.com.
Affiliation (first year): Los Angeles Angels (2011). **Years in League:** 1941, 1987-

OWNERSHIP/MANAGEMENT

Operated by: Inland Empire 66ers Baseball Club of San Bernardino. **Principal Owners:** David Elmore, Donna Tuttle.
President: David Elmore. **Chairman:** Donna Tuttle. **General Manager:** Joe Hudson. **Director, Sales /Assistant GM:** Alex Groh. **Director, Corporate Sales & Marketing/Assistant GM:** Steve Pelle. **Director, Broadcasting:** Steve Wendt. **Director, Group Sales:** Hollee Haines. **Director, Ticket Operations/Sales:** Sean Peterson. **Manager, Community Groups:** Stephanie O'Quinn. **Manager, Creative Services:** Dusty Ferguson. **Group Account Executive:** Jarrett Stark. **Manager, Promotions:** Vincent Zielen. **Coordinator, Corporate Sales:** Anna Forslin. **Coordinator, Ticket Operations:** George Bateman. **Administrative Assistant:** Marlena Garcia. **Manager, Facility:** Richard Morales. **Head Groundskeeper:** Dominick Guerrero. **Accountant:** Sarah Arechiga. **Director, Food & Beverage (Diamond Creations):** Ryan Liptrot. **Operations Manager, Food & Beverage (Diamond Creations):** Mike Liotta.

FIELD STAFF

Manager: Ryan Barba. **Hitting Coach:** Derek Florko. **Pitching Coach:** Michael Wuertz.

GAME INFORMATION

Radio Announcer: Steve Wendt. **Flagship Station:** 66ers Radio on TuneIn. **PA Announcer:** Renaldo Gonzales.
Official Scorer: Bill Maury-Holmes. **Stadium Name:** San Manuel Stadium. **Location:** From south, I-215 to 2nd Street exit, east on 2nd, right on G Street; from north, I-215 to 3rd Street exit, left on Rialto, right on G Street. **Standard Game Times:** Mon.-Fri. 7:05 pm; Sat. 6:05 pm; Sun. 2:05 pm (1st Half) 5:35 pm (2nd Half). **Ticket Price Range:** $9-$18. **Visiting Club Hotel:** TBA. **Telephone:** TBA.

LAKE ELSINORE STORM

Address: 500 Diamond Drive, Lake Elsinore, CA 92530
Telephone: (951) 245-4487. **Fax:** (951) 245-0305.
E-Mail Address: info@stormbaseball.com. **Website:** www.stormbaseball.com.
Affiliation (first year): San Diego Padres (2001). **Years in League:** 1994-

OWNERSHIP/MANAGEMENT

Owners: Gary Jacobs, Len Simon.
General Manager/Director of Sales: Raj Narayanan. **Assistant GM (Marketing/Digital Media)/Senior Designer:** Mark Beskid. **Chief Financial Officer:** Christine Kavic. **Director of Broadcasting:** Sean McCall. **VP of Business Development:** Paul Stiritz. **Director of Merchandising:** Arlene Spahn. **Director of Ticketing:** Eric Colunga. **Ticket Operations Coordinator/Box Office Manager:** Lucas Wedgewood. **Senior Group Sales Executives:** Eric Theiss, Kasey Rawitzer. **Media Manager:** Matt Rodriguez. **Corporate Partnerships Sales Executive/Clubhouse Manager:** Terrance Tucker. **Stadium Operations Manager:** Daniel Limon. **Head Groundskeeper:** Joe Jimenez. **Assistant Groundskeeper:** Brandon Castaneda. **Executive Chef:** Johnny McCloskey. **Director of Diamond Club Events:** Margie McCloskey. **Sous Chef:** Jason Natale.

FIELD STAFF

Manager: Tony Tarasco. **Hitting Coach:** Doug Banks. **Pitching Coach:** Pete Zamora. **Fielding Coach:** Felipe Blanco. **Strength Coach:** Jay Young. **Trainer:** Ricky Huerta.

GAME INFORMATION

Radio Announcer: Sean McCall. **No. of Games Broadcast:** 140. **Flagship Station:** Radio 94.5. **PA Announcer:** Unavailable. **Official Scorer:** Lloyd Nixon. **Stadium Name:** The Diamond. **Location:** From I-15, exit at Diamond Drive, west one mile to stadium. **Standard Game Times:** Mon.-Thurs. 6 p.m. Fri-Sat. 7 p.m. Sunday (first half): 1 p.m. (second half) 5 p.m. **Ticket Price Range:** $13-16. **Visiting Club Hotel:** Lake Elsinore Hotel and Casino, 20930 Malaga St, Lake Elsinore, CA 92530. **Telephone:** (951) 674-3101.

LANCASTER JETHAWKS

Address: 45116 Valley Central Way, Lancaster, CA 93536.
Telephone: (661) 726-5400. **Fax:** (661) 726-5406.
Email Address: info@jethawks.com. **Website:** www.jethawks.com.
Affiliation (first year): Colorado Rockies (2017). **Years in League:** 1996-

OWNERSHIP/MANAGEMENT

Operated By: JetHawks Baseball, LP. **Principal Owner/Managing General Partner:** Jake Kerr. **Partner:** Jeff Mooney. **President:** Andy Dunn. **Executive Vice President/General Manager:** Tom Backemeyer. **Assistant General Manager:** Dylan Baker. **Assistant General Manager:** Katie Woods Director, **Facility/Baseball Operations:** John Laferney. **Director, Broadcasting & Media Relations:** Jason Schwartz. **Box Office/Merchandise Manager:** Taylor Dunn. **Community Relations/Marketing Manager:** Julianna Clyne. **Ticket Sales Account Executive:** Jamie Martin. **Ticket Sales Account Executive:** Nicklaus DiPaola. **Ticket Sales Account Executive:** Adan Rodriguez. **Special Advisor:** Mark Bozigian.

FIELD STAFF

Developmental Supervisor: Frank Gonzales. **Manager:** Scott Little. **Hitting Coach:** Tom Sutaris. **Pitching Coach:** Dave Burba. **Athletic Trainer:** Josh Guterman.

GAME INFORMATION

Radio Announcer: Jason Schwartz. **No. of Games Broadcast:** 140. **Flagship Station:** www.jethawks.com. **PA Announcer:** TBD. **Official Scorer:** David Guenther. **Stadium Name:** The Hangar. **Location:** Highway 14 in Lancaster to Avenue I exit, west one block to stadium. **Standard Game Times:** 6:35 pm, Sun. 2:05pm (April-June), 5:05pm (July-Sept). **Ticket Price Range:** $10-17. **Visiting Club Hotel:** Comfort Inn, 1825 W Avenue J-12, Lancaster CA 93534. **Telephone:** (661) 723-2001.

MODESTO NUTS

Office Address: 601 Neece Dr, Modesto, CA 95351. **Mailing Address:** PO Box 883, Modesto, CA 95353. **Telephone:** (209) 572-4487. **Fax:** (209) 572-4490
E-Mail Address: fun@modestonuts.com. **Website:** www.modestonuts.com.
Affiliation (first year): Seattle Mariners (2017). **Years in League:** 1946-64, 1966-

OWNERSHIP/MANAGEMENT

Operated by: HWS Group IV. **Majority Owners:** Seattle Mariners.
General Manager: Zach Brockman. **Director of Marketing & Promotions:** Veronica Hernandez. **Head Groundskeeper:** TBA. **Account Executive:** TBA. **Community Relations Manager:** Deanna Gill. **Director of Ticket**

Sales: Gary Olson. **Account Executive:** Steven Webster. **In-Game Entertainment Manager:** Madison Brophy. **Director, Broadcasting:** Keaton Gillogly. **Office Manager:** Kate Mendoza. **Food and Beverage Manager:** Kyle Gogo. **Director of Stadium Operations:** Christian Lomeli.

FIELD STAFF

Manager: Denny Hocking. **Pitching Coach:** Rob Marcello. **Hitting Coach:** Jose Umbria. **Trainer:** Taylor Bennett.

GAME INFORMATION

Radio Announcer: Keaton Gillogly. **PA Announcer:** Unavailable. **Official Scorer:** Unavailable. **Stadium Name:** John Thurman Field. **Location:** Highway 99 in southwest Modesto to Tuolumne Boulevard exit, west on Tuolumne for one block to Neece Drive, left for 1/4 mile to stadium. **Standard Game Times:** 7:05 pm, Sun. 2:05pm/6:05 pm. **Ticket Price Range:** $8-14. **Visiting Club Hotel:** Unavailable.

RANCHO CUCAMONGA
QUAKES

Office Address: 8408 Rochester Ave., Rancho Cucamonga, CA 91730.
Mailing Address: P.O. Box 4139, Rancho Cucamonga, CA 91729.
Telephone: (909) 481-5000. **Fax:** (909) 481-5005. **E-Mail Address:** info@rcquakes.com.
Website: www.rcquakes.com. **Affiliation (first year):** Los Angeles Dodgers (2011). **Years in League:** 1993-

OWNERSHIP/MANAGEMENT

Operated By: Bobby Brett. **Principal Owner:** Bobby Brett.
President: Brent Miles. **Vice President/General Manager:** Grant Riddle. **Vice President/Tickets:** Monica Ortega. **Vice President/Groups:** Linda Rathfon. **Vice President/Sponsorships:** Chris Pope. **Sponsorship Account Executive:** David Fields. **Sponsorship Account Executive:** Trevor Morehead. **Promotions Assistant:** Chloe Melanson. **Director, Fan Engagement:** Bobbi Salcido. **Director, Group Sales:** Kyle Burleson. **Director, Season Tickets/Operations:** Eric Jensen. **Group Sales Coordinator:** Emily Lokovic, Michael Lopez, Sarah Mansour. **Director, Accounting:** Amara McCellan. **Director, Public Relations/Voice of the Quakes:** Mike Lindskog. **Office Manager:** Shelley Scebbi. **Director, Food/Beverage:** Michael Garcia.

FIELD STAFF

Manager: Mark Kertenian. **Hitting Coach:** Dustin Kelly. **Pitching Coach:** Connor McGuiness. **Assistant Coach:** Elian Herrera.

GAME INFORMATION

Radio Announcer: Mike Lindskog. **No. of Games Broadcast:** 140. **Flagship Station:** NewsTalk AM 1290 PA. **Announcer:** Chris Albaugh. **Official Scorer:** Steve Wishek/Curt Christiansen. **Stadium Name:** LoanMart Field. **Location:** I-10 to I-15 North, exit at Foothill Boulevard, left on Foothill, left on Rochester to Stadium. **Standard Game Times:** 7:05 pm; Sun. 2:05 pm. **Visiting Club Hotel:** Best Western Heritage Inn, 8179 Spruce Ave, Rancho Cucamonga, CA 91730. **Telephone:** (909) 466-1111.

SAN JOSE GIANTS

Office Address: 588 E Alma Ave, San Jose, CA 95112.
Mailing Address: PO Box 21727, San Jose, CA 95151.
Telephone: (408) 297-1435. **Fax:** (408) 297-1453.
E-Mail Address: info@sjgiants.com. **Website:** www.sjgiants.com.
Affiliation (first year): San Francisco Giants (1988). **Years in League:** 1942, 1947-58, 1962-76, 1979-

OWNERSHIP/MANAGEMENT

Operated by: Progress Sports Management. **Principal Owners:** San Francisco Giants, Heidi Stamas, Richard Beahrs. **President/CEO:** Daniel Orum. **Chief Operating Officer/General Manager:** Mark Wilson. **Senior VP, Ballpark Operations:** Lance Motch. **VP, Sales:** Jeff Di Giorgio. **VP, Marketing:** Jeff Black. **VP, Game Day Operations and Human Resources:** Tara Tallman. **Director, Player Personnel:** Linda Pereira. **Director, Broadcasting:** Joe Ritzo. **Director, Group Sales:** Justin Frederickson. **Manager, Accounting/ Payroll:** Joshua Chang. **Manager, Marketing:** DJ Bettinger. **Manager, Retail/Merchandise:** Sierra Hanley. **Manager, Food and Beverage:** Ramiro Mijares. **Coordinator, Ticket Operations:** Ryan Anthony. **Coordinator, Social Media/Community Relations:** Nicole Hernandez. **Head Groundskeeper:** Danny Alverson.

FIELD STAFF

Manager: Bill Hayes. **Hitting Coach:** Thomas Neal. **Pitching Coach:** Matt Yourkin. **Fundamentals Coach:** Gary Davenport. **Athletic Trainer:** Ryo Watanabe. **Strength & Conditioning Coach:** TBD. **Bullpen Coach:** Ydwin Villegas.

GAME INFORMATION

Radio Announcers: Joe Ritzo, Justin Allegri. **No. of Games Broadcast:** 140.
Flagship: sjgiants.com. **Television Announcers:** Joe Ritzo, 70 home games on MiLB.TV. **PA Announcer:** Russ Call.
Official Scorer: Mike Hohler. **Stadium Name:** Municipal Stadium. **Location:** South on I-280: Take 10th/11th Street Exit,

turn right on 10th Street, turn left on Alma Ave. North on **I-280:** Take the 10th/11th Street Exit, Turn left on 10th Street, turn left on Alma Ave. **Standard Game Times:** 7 p.m., 6:30 p.m, Sat. 5 p.m., Sun 1 p.m. (5 p.m. after June 30). **Ticket Price Range:** $8-24.

STOCKTON PORTS

Address: 404 W Fremont St, Stockton, CA 95203. **Telephone:** (209) 644-1900.
Fax: (209) 644-1931. **E-Mail Address:** info@stocktonports.com.
Website: www.stocktonports.com.
Affiliation (first year): Oakland Athletics (2005). **Years in League:** 1941, 1946-72, 1978-

OWNERSHIP/MANAGEMENT

Operated By: 7th Inning Stretch LLC. **Chairman/CEO:** Tom Volpe.
President: Pat Filippone. **General Manager:** Taylor McCarthy. **Assistant General Manager:** Justice Hoyt. **Director, Partnerships/Marketing:** Peter Fiorentino. **Community Relations Manager:** Allie Bakalar. **Group Sales Manager:** Riley Robar. **Account Executive/Stadium Operations Manager:** Seth Unger. **Box Office Manager:** Christine Bowling. **Marketing Manager:** Katie Schulz. **Account Executives:** Chris Griesche, Tony Capretto. **Front Office Manager:** Christa Leri. **Finance Manager:** Sydney Snodgrass.

FIELD STAFF

Manager: Webster Garrison. **Hitting Coach:** Brian McArn. **Pitching Coach:** Chris Smith. **Athletic Trainer:** Shane Zdebiak. **Strength & Conditioning Coach:** Matt Mosiman.

GAME INFORMATION

Radio Announcer: Zack Bayrouty. **No of Games Broadcast:** 140. **Flagship Station:** TuneIn App. **TV:** Comcast Hometown Network, Channel 104, regional telecast. **PA Announcer:** Mike Conway. **Official Scorer:** Paul Muyskens. **Stadium Name:** Banner Island Ballpark. **Location:** From I-5/99, take Crosstown Freeway (Highway 4) exit El Dorado Street, north on El Dorado to Fremont Street, left on Fremont. **Standard Game Times:** 7:05 pm. **Ticket Price Range:** $7-$20. **Visiting Club Hotel:** Quality Inn Lathrop, 16855 Harlan Rd, Lathrop, CA 95330. **Telephone:** 209-598-1524.

VISALIA RAWHIDE

Address: 300 N Giddings St, Visalia, CA 93291.
Telephone: (559) 732-4433. **Fax:** (559) 739-7732.
E-Mail Address: info@rawhidebaseball.com. **Website:** www.rawhidebaseball.com.
Affiliation (first year): Arizona Diamondbacks (2007). **Years in League:** 1946-62, 1968-75, 1977-

OWNERSHIP/MANAGEMENT

President: Tom Seidler. **General Manager:** Jennifer Reynolds. **Assistant General Manager:** Jill Webb and Charlie Saponara. **Director of Baseball Operations:** Julian Rifkind. **Director of Groups and Ticketing:** Markus Hagglund. **Director of Broadcasting & Media Relations:** Jill Gearin. **Head Groundskeeper:** James Templeton. **Manager of Ballpark Operations:** Brady Hochhalter. **Community Partnership Manager:** Joe Ross. **Merchandise Manger:** Jake Davis. **Events and Promotions Manager:** Caitlin Carter.

FIELD STAFF

Manager: Shawn Roof. **Hitting Coach:** Travis Denker. **Pitching Coach:** Shane Loux. **Coach:** Nick Evans. **Trainer:** Michael Powell.

GAME INFORMATION

Radio Announcers: Jill Gearin. **No. of Games Broadcast:** 70. **Flagship Station:** Unavailable.
PA Announcer: Brian Anthony. **Official Scorer:** Harry Kargenian and Mark "Scooter" Cossentine. **Stadium Name:** Rawhide Ballpark. **Location:** From Highway 99, take 198 East to Mooney Boulevard exit, left at second signal on Giddings; four blocks to ballpark. **Standard Game Times:** 7 pm, Sun. 1pm (first half), 6 pm (second half). **Ticket Price Range:** $7-30. **Visiting Club Hotel:** Quality Inn, 1010 E Prosperity Ave, Tulare, CA 93274.

CAROLINA LEAGUE

Address: 3206 Buena Vista Road, Winston-Salem, NC 27106
Telephone: (336) 691-9030. **Fax:** (336) 464-2737.
E-Mail Address: office@carolinaleague.com.
Website: www.carolinaleague.com.
Years League Active: 1945-
President/Treasurer: Geoff Lassiter.
Vice President: Billy Prim (Winston-Salem). **Executive VP:** Tim Zue (Salem). **Corporate Secretary:** Ken Young (Frederick). **Directors:** DG Elmore (Lynchburg), Chuck Greenberg (Myrtle Beach), Dave Ziedelis (Frederick), Tyler Barnes (Carolina), Dave Heller (Wilmington), Billy Prum (Winston-Salem), Art Silber (Potomac), David Lane (Fayetteville), Joe Januszeswki (Down East). **Media Director:** Brian Boesch. **Division Structure: North**—Frederick, Lynchburg, Potomac, Salem, Wilmington. **South**—Buies Creek, Carolina, Down East, Myrtle Beach, Winston-Salem. **Regular Season:** 140 games (split schedule).

Geoff Lassiter

2019 Opening Date: April 4. **Closing Date:** Sept 2.
All-Star Game: South Division vs. North Division at Frederick, June 18.
Playoff Format: First-half division winners play second-half division winners in best-of- three series. If a team wins both halves it plays division opponent with next-best second- half record. Division series winners meet in best-of-five series for Mills Cup. **Roster Limit:** 25 active. **Player Eligibility Rule:** No age limit. No more than two players and one player/coach on active list may have six or more years of prior minor league service. **Brand of Baseball:** Rawlings.
Umpires: Unavailable.

STADIUM INFORMATION

Club	Stadium	Opened	Dimensions LF	CF	RF	Capacity	2018 Att.
Buies Creek	Jim Perry Stadium*	2012	337	395	328	2,000	24,068
Carolina	Five County Stadium	1991	330	400	309	6,500	181,122
Down East	Grainger Stadium	1949	335	390	335	4,100	116,835
Frederick	Harry Grove Stadium	1990	325	400	325	5,400	275,001
Lynchburg	City Stadium	1939	325	390	325	4,000	112,228
Myrtle Beach	TicketReturn.com Field	1999	308	400	328	5,200	219,589
Potomac	Pfitzner Stadium	1984	315	400	315	6,000	237,244
Salem	Salem Memorial Stadium	1995	325	401	325	6,415	192,621
Wilmington	Frawley Stadium	1993	325	400	325	6,532	249,746
Winston-Salem	BB&T Ballpark	2010	315	399	323	5,500	292,774

CAROLINA MUDCATS

Office Address: 1501 NC Hwy 39, Zebulon, NC 27597.
Mailing Address: PO Drawer 1218, Zebulon, NC 27597. **Telephone:** (919) 269-2287.
Fax: (919) 269-4910. **E-Mail Address:** muddy@carolinamudcats.com.
Website: www.carolinamudcats.com.
Affiliation: Milwaukee Brewers (2018-). **Years in League:** 2012-

OWNERSHIP/MANAGEMENT

Ownership: Milwaukee Brewers Baseball Club, L.P. **Operated by:** Milwaukee Brewers Baseball Club, L.P.
Vice President/General Manager: Joe Kremer. **Assistant General Manager, Operations:** Eric Gardner. **Assistant GM, Sales:** David Lawrence. **Business Manager:** Joshua Perry. **Manager, Ticket Package Sales:** Taylor Gustafson.
Coordinator, Box Office: Ryan Rainey. **Director, Group Sales:** Mike Link. **Associate, Group Sales:** Aaron Freeman, Cameron Dennis, Jack Noble. **Director, Promotions and Fan Experience:** Patrick Ennis. **Director of Marketing & Community Relations:** Samantha Barry. **Coordinator, Community Relations:** Cassie Tomasello. **Manager, Multimedia:** Evan Moesta. **Coordinator, Social Media/Marketing/Graphics:** Aaron Bayles. **Manager, Merchandise:** Amy Peterson. **Coordinator, Stadium Operations:** Michael Lincoln. **Director, Food and Beverage:** Dwayne Lucas. **Coordinator, Food and Beverage:** Josh Clark. **Director, Broadcasting and Media Relations:** Greg Young. **Manager, Grounds:** John Packer.

FIELD STAFF

Manager: Joe Ayrault. **Pitching Coach:** Cameron Castro. **Hitting Coach:** Bobby Bell. **Coach:** Fidel Pena. **Athletic Trainer:** Matt Deal. **Strength & Conditioning Coach:** Jonah Mergen.

GAME INFORMATION

Radio Announcer: Greg Young. **No. of Games Broadcast:** 140. **Flagship Station:** The Big Dawg 98.5 FM, WDWG. **PA Announcer:** Hayes Permar. **Official Scorer:** Bill Woodward. **Stadium Name:** Five County Stadium.
Location: From Raleigh, US 64 East to 264 East, exit at Highway 39 in Zebulon. **Standard Game Times:** 7:00, Sat. 5:00, Sun. 2:00. **Ticket Price Range:** $10-12. **Visiting Club Hotel:** Holiday Inn Raleigh.

DOWN EAST WOOD DUCKS

Address: 400 East Grainger Avenue, Kinston, NC 28502
Telephone: (252) 686-5165
E-Mail Address: jbullock@woodducksbaseball.com. **Website:** woodducksbaseball.com
Affiliation (first year): Texas Rangers (2017). **Years in League:** 2017-

OWNERSHIP/MANAGEMENT

Operated By: Texas Rangers, LLC.
President: Neil Leibman. **General Manager:** Wade Howell. **Assistant GM of Operations:** Janell Bullock. **Head Groundskeeper:** Stephen Watson. **Assistant GM Of Sales:** Jon Clemmons. **Creative Services Director:** Matthew Edwards. **Director of Marketing:** Alexa Kay. **Director of Broadcasting:** Matt Present. **Group Sales:** Charlie Casey. **Group Sales:** Chris Jacob.

FIELD STAFF

Manager: Corey Ragsdale. **Hitting Coach:** Chase Lambin. **Pitching Coach:** Steve Mintz. **Coach:** Turtle Thomas. **Trainer:** Luke Teeters. **Strength & Conditioning Coach:** Adam Noel.

GAME INFORMATION

Radio Announcer: Matt Present. **PA Announcer:** Bryan Hanks. **Stadium Name:** Grainger Stadium.
Standard Game Times: 7:00 (weekdays), 6:00 (Saturdays), 1:00 (Sundays). **Ticket Price Range:** $7-11.
Visiting Club Hotel: Mother Earth Motor Lodge, 501 N Herritage St., Kinston, NC 28501.

FAYETTEVILLE WOODPECKERS

Address: 225 Ray Avenue. Fayetteville, NC 28301.
Telephone: 910-339-1989.
E-Mail Address: Woodpeckers@astros.com. **Website:** fayettevillewoodpeckers.com
Affiliation (first year): Houston Astros (2019). **Years in League:** 2019-

OWNERSHIP/MANAGEMENT

Principal Owner: Houston Astros.
President: Mark Zarthar. **General Manager:** David Lane. **Vice President, Sales and Marketing:** Austin Schwartz. **Director, Finance:** Jennifer Carpenter. **Manager, Marketing and Communications:** Ben Hughes. **Manager, Retail:** Brittany Tschida. **Account Executive, Sponsorships:** Chaz Dawson. **Account Executive, Ticketing:** Elizabeth Adams. **Manager, Ballpark Entertainment:** Pete Subsara. **Manager, Corporate Partnerships:** Sarah Suggs. **Manager, Stadium Operations:** Chris Cominse. **Manager, Baseball Operations:** Mike Montesino. **Manager, Ticket Operations:** Gabriel Evans. **Manager, Events:** Rachel Smith.

FIELD STAFF

Manager: Nate Shaver. **Hitting Coach:** Jason Kanzler. **Pitching Coach:** Thomas Whitsett.

GAME INFORMATION

Radio Announcer: N/A. **No. of Games Broadcast:** 140. **Flagship Station:** N/A.
PA Announcer: N/A. **Official Scorer:** N/A.
Stadium Name: N/A. **Standard Game Times:** N/A.
Visiting Club Hotel: N/A. **Telephone:** N/A.

FREDERICK KEYS

Address: 21 Stadium Dr., Frederick, MD 21703.
Telephone: (301) 662-0013. **Fax:** (301) 662-0018.
E-Mail Address: info@frederickkeys.com. **Website:** www.frederickkeys.com.
Affiliation (first year): Baltimore Orioles (1989). **Years in League:** 1989-

OWNERSHIP/MANAGEMENT

Ownership: Maryland Baseball Holding LLC.
President: Ken Young. **General Manager:** Dave Ziedelis. **Director, Assistant General Manager Sales:** Andrew Klein. **Director of Marketing:** Erin Lawson. **Director Broadcasting/ Public Relations:** Geoff Arnold. **Promotions and Creative Services Manager:** Kevin Hernandez. **Director of Stadium Operations:** Kari Collins. **Ticket Operations Manager:** Jackson Bushong-Taylor. **Sponsorship Sales Account Managers:** Casey O'Brien, George Cluster. **Group Sales Manager:** Ellery Price. **Group Sales Account Managers:** Marcus Jenkins, Ben Underwood, Kirby Sauble. **Broadcasting/PR/CR Assistant:** Jack Keffer. **Marketing Assistant:** Sarah Kleinhans. **Head Groundskeeper:** Mike Dunn. **Clubhouse Manager:** Jared Weiss. **Director of Finance & Human Resources:** Tami Hetrick. **General Manager, Spectra:** Alan Cranfill.

FIELD STAFF

Manager: Ryan Minor. **Hitting Coach:** Bobby Rose. **Pitching Coach:** Justin Lord.

GAME INFORMATION

Radio Announcers: Geoff Arnold, Jack Keffer. **PA Announcer:** Andy Redmond. **Official Scorers:** Jason Lee, Luke Stillson, Dave Musil, Geoff Goyne, Bob Roberson, Dennis Hetrick. **Stadium Name:** Harry Grove Stadium. **Location:** From I-70, take exit 54 (Market Street), left at light; From I-270, take exit 32 (I-70Baltimore/Hagerstown toward Baltimore (I-70), to exit 54 at Market Street. **Ticket Price Range:** $9-15. **Visiting Club Hotel:** Comfort Inn Frederick, 7300 Executive Way, Frederick, MD 21704. **Telephone:** (301) 668-7272.

LYNCHBURG HILLCATS

Address: Lynchburg City Stadium, 3180 Fort Ave, Lynchburg, VA 24501. **Telephone:** (434) 528-1144. **Fax:** (434) 846-0768.
E-Mail Address: info@lynchburg-hillcats.com. **Website:** www.Lynchburg-hillcats.com.
Affiliation (first year): Cleveland Indians (2015). **Years in League:** 1966-

OWNERSHIP/MANAGEMENT

Operated By: Elmore Sports Group.
President/General Manager: Chris Jones. **Assistant General Manager:** Matt Klein. **Assistant General Manager of Tickets:** Peter Billups. **Director of Sales:** Max Rettig. **Account Executive:** Hanna Tyree. **Head Groundskeeper:** Joe Knight. **Director of Concessions:** Matt Ramstead. **Director of Broadcasting and Communications:** Max Gun. **Broadcast and Media Relations Assistant:** Anders Jorstad. **Creative Services Coordinator:** Emily Messina. **Public Relations Assistant:** Riley Bedford. **Social Media and Marketing Coordinator:** Morgan Tabor. **Emcee and Director of Entertainment:** Jeff Raymond. **Community Outreach and Promotions:** Kathryn Doherty. **Operations/Clubhouse Manager:** Ryan Henson. **Director, Finance/Accounting:** Crystal Williamson. **Accounting Assistant:** Austin Amos. **Head Groundskeeper:** Joe Knight.

FIELD STAFF

Manager: Jim Pankovits. **Hitting Coach:** Johnny Narron. **Pitching Coach:** Joe Torres. **Bench Coach:** Mike Mergenthaler. **Strength & Conditioning Coach:** Eric Ortego. **Athletic Trainer:** Jake Legan.

GAME INFORMATION

Radio Announcer: Max Gun. **No. of Games Broadcast:** 140. **PA Announcer:** TBA. **Official Scorers:** TBA. **Stadium Name:** Calvin Falwell Field at Lynchburg City Stadium. **Location:** US 29 Business South to Lynchburg City Stadium (exit 6); US 29 Business North to Lynchburg City Stadium (exit 4). **Ticket Price Range:** $6-12. **Visiting Club Hotel:** La Quinta Inn & Suites, 3320 Candlers Mountain Rd., Lynchburg, VA 24502. **Telephone:** (434) 847-8655.

MYRTLE BEACH PELICANS

Mailing Address: 1251 21st Avenue N. Myrtle Beach, SC 29577.
Telephone: (843) 918-6000. **Fax:** (843) 918-6001.
E-Mail Address: info@myrtlebeachpelicans.com.
Website: www.myrtlebeachpelicans.com.
Affiliation (first year): Chicago Cubs (2015). **Years in League:** 1999-

OWNERSHIP/MANAGEMENT

Owners, Greenberg Sports Group: Chuck Greenberg.
President, Greenberg Sports Group: Andy Milovich. **General Manager:** Ryan Moore. **Sr. Director, Finance:** Anne Moore. **Assistant GM, Operations:** Mike Snow. **Assistant GM, Marketing:** Kristin Call. **Administrative Assistant:** Beth Freitas. **Director, Business Development:** Ryan Waters. **Director, Sales:** Ryan Cannella. **Box Office Manager:** Shannon Barbee. **Sports & Tourism Sales Manager:** Todd Chapman. **Corporate Sales Representative:** Robert Buchanan. **Merchandise Manager/Pro Shop:** Dan Bailey. **Director, Food & Beverage:** Brad Leininger. **Sports Turf Manager:** JC Blackhurst. **Director, Fan Engagement:** Hunter Horenstein. **Director, Video Productions:** Kyle Guertin. **Media Relations:** Zach Bigley.

FIELD STAFF

Manager: Jimmy Gonzalez. **Pitching Coach:** Brian Lawrencew. **Hitting Coach:** Ricardo Medina. **Athletic Trainer:** Logan Severson.

GAME INFORMATION

PA Announcer: Jerrod Schmidt-Dubose. **Official Scorer:** B.J. Scott. **Stadium Name:** Ticketreturn.com Field at Pelicans Ballpark. **Location:** US Highway 17 Bypass to 21st Ave. North, half mile to stadium. **Standard Game Times:** 7:05 p.m. **Ticket Pirce Range:** $9-$15. **Visiting Club Hotel:** Courtyard Marriott Barefoot Landing, 1000 Commons Blvd., Myrtle Beach, S.C., 29572. **Telephone:** (843) 916-0600.

POTOMAC NATIONALS

Office Address: 7 County Complex Ct, Woodbridge, VA 22192.
Mailing Address: PO Box 2148, Woodbridge, VA 22195.
Telephone: (703) 590-2311. **Fax:** (703) 590-5716.
E-Mail Address: info@potomacnationals.com.
Website:www.potomacnationals.com.
Affiliation (first year): Washington Nationals (2005). **Years in League:** 1978-

OWNERSHIP/MANAGEMENT

Operated By: Potomac Baseball LLC. **Principal Owner:** Art Silber.
President: Lani Silber Weiss. **General Manager, Sales:** Bryan Holland. **General Manager, Operations:** Aaron Johnson. **Director of Season Ticket & Group Tickets:** Alec Manriquez. **Director, Broadcasting, Media, & Local Corporate Partnerships:** Mike Weisman. **Stadium Operations & Merchandising Manager, Corporate Sales Executive:** Will Darmstead. **Ticket Operations Manager:** Matt LeBlanc. **Corporate Partnership Fulfillment, Community Relations/Promotions Manager:** Brice Walker. **Director of Graphic Design, Video Production, & Social Media:** Alexis Deegan. **Business Operations Manager:** Theresa Coffey.

FIELD STAFF

Manager: Tripp Keister. **Hitting Coach:** Luis Ordaz. **Pitching Coach:** Sam Narron. **Athletic Trainer:** Don Neidig. **Strength & Conditioning Coach:** Shane Hill.

GAME INFORMATION

Radio Announcer: Mike Weisman. **No. of Games Broadcast:** 140. **Flagship:** www.potomacnationals.com. **PA Announcer:** Jeremy Whitham. **Official Scorer:** Ben Trittipoe, Dave McAndrew, Tony Black. **Stadium Name:** G. Richard Pfitzner Stadium. **Location:** From I-95, take exit, 158B and continue on Prince William Parkway for five miles, right into County Complex Court. **Standard Game Times:** 7:05 pm, Sat. 6:35, Sun. 1:05. **Ticket Price Range:** $10-16. **Visiting Club Hotel:** Country Inn and Suites, Prince William Parkway, Woodbridge, VA 22192. **Telephone:** (703) 492-6868.

SALEM RED SOX

Office Address: 1004 Texas St., Salem, VA 24153.
Mailing Address: PO Box 842, Salem, VA 24153. **Telephone:** (540) 389-3333.
Fax: (540) 389-9710. **E-Mail Address:** info@salemsox.com.
Website: www.salemsox.com. **Affiliation (first year):** Boston Red Sox (2009).
Years in League: 1968-

OWNERSHIP/MANAGEMENT

Operated By: Carolina Baseball LLC/Fenway Sports Group.
Managing Director: Tim Zue. **President/General Manager:** Ryan Shelton. **VP/Assistant GM:** Allen Lawrence. **VP of Operations:** Tim Anderson. **Director, Corporate Sponsorships:** Steven Elovich. **Marketing/Promotions Manager:** Suzie Cool. **Facilities Manager/Head Groundskeeper:** Joey Elmore. **Manager of Group Sales & Community Programs:** Charlie Umland. **Ticket Operations/Retention Manager:** Dave Malerk. **Food/Beverage Manager:** Patrick Pelletier. **Premium Sales Account Executive:** Grant Harmon. **New Business Account Executive:** Bobby Howland. **Senior Premium Sales Account Executive:** Alex Michel. **Bookkeeper:** Barry Stephens. **Video Production Manager:** Cameron Moist. **Clubhouse Manager:** Tom Wagner.

FIELD STAFF

Manager: Corey Wimberly. **Hitting Coach:** Lance Zawadski. **Pitching Coach:** Lance Carter. **Trainer:** Nick Kuchwara.

GAME INFORMATION

Radio Announcer: Dominic Cotroneo. **No. of Games Broadcast:** 140. **Flagship Station:** ESPN Radio 1240 AM. **PA Announcer:** Emile Brown. **Official Scorer:** Billy Wells. **Stadium Name:** Haley Toyota Field at Salem Memorial Ballpark. **Location:** I-81 to exit 141 (Route 419), follow signs to Salem Civic Center Complex. **Standard Game Times:** 7:05 pm, Sat./Sun. 6:**05**/4:05. **Ticket Price Range:** $7-14. **Visiting Club Hotel:** Comfort Suites Ridgewood Farms, 2898 Keagy Rd., Salem, VA 24153. **Telephone:** (540) 375-4800.

WILMINGTON BLUE ROCKS

Address: 801 Shipyard Drive, Wilmington, DE 19801.
Telephone: (302) 888-2015. **Fax:** (302) 888-2032.
E-Mail Address: info@bluerocks.com. **Website:** www.bluerocks.com.
Affiliation (first year): Kansas City Royals (2007). **Years in League:** 1993-

OWNERSHIP/MANAGEMENT

Operated by: Wilmington Blue Rocks LP. **Honorary President:** Matt Minker. **Club President:** Clark Minker.
Owners: Main Street Baseball. Managing Partner/League Director & **CEO, Main Street Baseball:** Dave Heller.

General Manager: Andrew Layman. **Director of Broadcasting & Video:** Cory Nidoh. **Director of Media Relations:** Matt Janus. **Director, Merchandise:** Jim Beck. **Director, Community Affairs:** Kevin Linton. **Director of Web and Creative Services:** Mike Diodati. **Director of Business Development:** Robert Ford. **Client Services Manager:** Liz Welch. **Director of Ticket Operations:** Joe McCarthy. **Director of Marketing:** Jason Estes. **Ticket Sales Manager:** Shea Macagnone. **Group Sales Executives:** Ryan Blaire, Mike Rice and Antoine Ray.

FIELD STAFF

Manager: Scott Thorman. **Hitting Coach:** Larry Sutton. **Pitching Coach:** Steve Luebber. **Athletic Trainer:** Saburo Hagihara.

GAME INFORMATION

Radio Announcer: Cory Nidoh. **No. of Games Broadcast:** 140. **Flagship Station:** 89.7 WGLS-FM. **PA Announcer:** Kevin Linton. **Official Scorer:** Dick Shute. **Stadium Name:** Judy Johnson Field at Daniel Frawley Stadium. **Location:** I-95 North to Maryland Ave (exit 6), right on Maryland Ave, and through traffic light onto Martin Luther King Blvd, right at traffic light on Justison St, follow to Shipyard Dr; I-95 South to Maryland Ave (exit 6), left at fourth light on Martin Luther King Blvd, right at fourth light on Justison St, follow to Shipyard Dr.

Standard Game Times: 6:35 pm, (Mon-Thur) 7:05 (Fri) 6:05 (Sat) Sun. 1:35 p.m. **Ticket Price Range:** $6-$15. **Visiting Club Hotel:** Quality Inn & Suites Skyways 147 North Dupont Highway New Castle, DE 19720 (302) 328-6666.

WINSTON-SALEM DASH

Office Address: 926 Brookstown Ave, Winston-Salem, NC 27101.
Stadium Address: 951 Ballpark Way, Winston-Salem, NC 27101.
Telephone: (336) 714-2287. **Fax:** (336) 714-2288. **E-Mail Address:** info@wsdash.com. **Website:** www.wsdash.com.
Affiliation (first year): Chicago White Sox (1997). **Years in League:** 1945-

OWNERSHIP/MANAGEMENT

Operated by: W-S Dash. **Principal Owner:** Billy Prim.
President: CJ Johnson. **VP, Chief Financial Officer:** Kurt Gehsmann. **VP, Baseball Operations:** Ryan Manuel.
VP, Corporate Partnerships: Corey Bugno. **Director, Entertainment/Community Relations:** Jessica Aveyard.
Director of Ticket Sales: Paul Stephens. **Director of Corporate Partnership Sales:** Jenny Fulton. **Broadcast and Media Relations Manager:** Joe Weil. **Head Groundskeeper:** Paul Johnson. **Accounting Manager:** Amanda Elbert.
Corporate Partnerships Manager: Zach Alderman. **Corporate Partnerships Representative:** Ayla Acosta. **Corporate Partnerships Assistant:** Adam Natzke. **Group Sales Representatives:** Benjamin Kendrew, LaToya Wilson. **Business Development Representatives:** Autumn Sharp, Drew Fisch and Will Wyatt. **Sales Coordinator:** Rosanna Stewart. **Box Office Manager:** Owen Wilson. **Ticket Sales & Service Representative:** Jordan McGinnis. **Box Office Manager:** Owen Wilson.

FIELD STAFF

Manager: Justin Jirschele. **Hitting Coach:** Jamie Dismuke. **Pitching Coach:** Matt Zaleski. **Trainer:** Hyeon Kim.
Strength Coach: George Timke.

GAME INFORMATION

Radio Announcer: Joe Weil. **No. of Games Broadcast:** 140. **Flagship Station:** The Triad Sports Hub - 101.5 FM & 600 AM (Thursdays) or wsdash.com (all games). **PA Announcer:** Jeffrey Griffin. **Official Scorer:** TBD. **Stadium Name:** BB&T Ballpark. **Location:** I-40 Business to Peters Creek Parkway exit (exit 5A). **Standard Game Times:** M-F 7 p.m., Sat. 6 p.m., Sun. 2 p.m. **Visiting Club Hotel:** Unavailable.

FLORIDA STATE LEAGUE

Office Address: 3000 Gulf To Bay, Suite 219 Clearwater, FL 33759.
Mailing Address: 3000 Gulf To Bay, Suite 219 Clearwater, FL 33759.
Telephone: (727) 724-6146.
E-Mail Address: office@floridastateleague.com.
Website: www.floridastateleague.com.
Years League Active: 1919-1927, 1936-1941, 1946- .
Chairman/President/Treasurer: Ken Carson.
Executive Vice President: John Timberlake. **VPs: North**—Ron Myers. **South**—Mike Bauer.
Corporate Secretary: Steve Smith.
Directors: Mike Bauer (Jupiter/Palm Beach), Shelby Nelson (Dunedin), Jordan Kobritz (Charlotte), Jeff Podobnik (Bradenton), Andrew Kaufmann (Fort Myers), Reese Smith, III (Daytona), Ron Myers (Lakeland), Erik Anderson (Osceola), Vance Smith (Tampa), Traer Van Allen (St. Lucie), John Timberlake (Clearwater). **League Executive Assistant:** Laura LeCras.

Ken Carson

Division Structure: North— Clearwater, Daytona, Dunedin, Lakeland, Osceola, Tampa.
South—Bradenton, Charlotte, Fort Myers, Jupiter, Palm Beach, St. Lucie.
Regular Season: 140 games (split schedule). **2018 Opening Date:** April 4. **Closing Date:** September 1. **All-Star Game:** June 15 at Jupiter.
Playoff Format: First-half division winners meet second-half winners in best of three series. Winners meet in best of five series for league championship. **Roster Limit:** 25. **Player Eligibility Rule:** No age limit. No more than two players and one player-coach on active list may have six or more years of prior minor league service.
Brand of Baseball: Rawlings.
Umpires: Brandon Blome, Acosta Mercedes, Jonathan Biarreta Castillo, Jonathon Benken, Donald Carlyon, Zachary Dobson, Garry Kelley, Jude Koury, Lucas Krupa, Robert Nunez, Kelvin Velez Caminero, Dillon Wilson

STADIUM INFORMATION

Club	Stadium	Opened	Dimensions LF	CF	RF	Capacity	2018 Att.
Bradenton	McKechnie Field	1923	335	400	335	8,654	66,769
Charlotte	Charlotte Sports Park	2009	343	413	343	5,028	76,705
Clearwater	Spectrum Field	2004	330	400	330	8,500	150,843
Daytona	Jackie Robinson Ballpark	1930	317	400	325	4,200	95,274
Dunedin	Florida Auto Exchange Stadium	1977	335	400	327	5,509	24,750
Florida	Heritage Park	1994	340	404	340	8,100	27,118
Fort Myers	Hammond Stadium	1991	330	405	330	7,900	95,553
Jupiter	Roger Dean Chevrolet Stadium	1998	330	400	325	6,871	42,881
Lakeland	Publix Field at Joker Marchant Stadium	1966	340	420	340	7,961	42,235
Palm Beach	Roger Dean Chevrolet Stadium	1998	330	400	325	6,871	48,020
St. Lucie	First Data Field	1988	338	410	338	7,000	80,830
Tampa	Steinbrenner Field	1996	318	408	314	10,270	58,816

BRADENTON MARAUDERS

Address: 1701 27th Street East, Bradenton, FL 34208.
Telephone: (941) 747-3031. **Fax:** (941) 747-9442.
E-Mail Address: MaraudersInfo@pirates.com. **Website:** www.BradentonMarauders.com.
Affiliation (first year): Pittsburgh Pirates (2010). **Years in League:** 1919-20, 1923-24, 1926, 2010-.

OWNERSHIP/MANAGEMENT

Operated By: Pittsburgh Associates of Florida
Senior Director, Florida Operations: Jeff Podobnik. **General Manager, Director of Sales:** Rachelle Madrigal. **Manager, Florida Operations:** Ray Morris. **Manager, Concessions:** Chuck Knapp. **Assistant General Manager, Sales:** Craig Warzecha. **Coordinator, Sponsorship/Tickets:** Zach Henkel. **Coordinator, Sales:** Nolan Bialek. **Coordinator, Sales:** Taylor Fraise; **Coordinator, Marketing/ Community Relations:** Mary Lanzino. **Coordinator, Stadium Operations:** Nick Long. **Manager, Communications & In-Game Entertainment:** Nate March. **Head Groundskeeper:** Victor Madrigal.

FIELD STAFF

Manager: Wyatt Toregas. **Hitting Coach:** Butch Wynegar. **Pitching Coach:** Drew Benes. **Athletic Trainer:** Matt DenBleyker.

GAME INFORMATION

PA Announcer: Jeff Phillips. **Official Scorer:** Dave Taylor. **Stadium Name:** LECOM Park. **Location:** I-75 to exit 220 (220B from I-75N) to SR 64 West/Manatee Ave, Left onto 9th St West, LECOM PARK on the left. **Standard Game Times:**

6:30 pm, Sun. 1:00 pm (1st half), 5 pm (second half). **Ticket Price Range:** $6-12. **Visiting Club Hotel:** Holiday Inn Express West, 4450 47th St W, Bradenton, FL 34210. **Telephone:** (941) 795-4633.

CHARLOTTE STONE CRABS

Address: 2300 El Jobean Road, Building A, Port Charlotte, FL 33948.
Telephone: (941) 206-4487. **Fax:** (941) 206-3599.
E-Mail Address: info@stonecrabsbaseball.com. **Website:** www.stonecrabsbaseball.com.
Affiliation (first year): Tampa Bay Rays (2009). **Years in League:** 2009-

OWNERSHIP/MANAGEMENT

Operated By: CBI-Rays.
General Manager: Jared Forma. **Assistant GM:** Jeff Cook. **Finance Director:** Lori Engleman. **Director of Group Sales:** Hallie Rubins. **Director of Fan Engagement:** Ashley Stephenson. **Director of Food & Beverage:** Brittany Jones. **Stadium Operations Manager:** Andrew Crawford. **Broadcasting & Media Relations Manager:** John Vittas. **Video Production Manager:** Chance Fernandez. **Box Office Manager:** Jennifer Lundrigan.

FIELD STAFF

Manager: Jeff Smith. **Pitching Coach:** Steve "Doc" Watson. **Coach:** Joe Szekely. **Coach:** Ivan Ochoa.

GAME INFORMATION

PA Announcer: Josh Grant. **Official Scorer:** Steve Posilovich. **Scoreboard Stats:** R.J. Fraser. **Gameday Stringer:** Jack Melton. **Stadium Name:** Charlotte Sports Park. **Location:** I-75 to Exit 179, turn left onto Toledo Blade Blvd then right on El Jobean Rd. **Ticket Price Range:** $8-10. **Visiting Club Hotel:** Sleep Inn, 806 Kings Hwy., Port Charlotte, FL 33980. **Phone:** 941-613-6300.

CLEARWATER THRESHERS

Address: 601 N Old Coachman Road, Clearwater, FL 33765.
Telephone: (727) 712-4300. **Fax:** (727) 712-4498.
Website: www.threshersbaseball.com.
Affiliation (first year): Philadelphia Phillies (1985). **Years in League:** 1985-

OWNERSHIP/MANAGEMENT

Operated by: Philadelphia Phillies.
Director of Florida Operations: John Timberlake. **General Manager of Clearwater Threshers:** Jason Adams. **Senior Manager of Corporate Partnerships:** Dan McDonough. **Manager of Business Operations:** Dianne Gonzalez. **General Manager, Spectrum Field:** Doug Kemp. **Assistant GM, Clearwater Threshers:** Dan Madden. **Ballpark Operations Manager:** Jay Warren. **Community Engagement/Media Manager:** Robert Stretch. **Food and Beverage Manager:** Justin Gunsaulus. **Assistant Food and Beverage Manager:** Justin Stone. **Office Manager:** DeDe Angelillis. **Senior Sales Associate:** Bobby Mitchell. **Corporate Sales Associate:** Cory Sipe. **Merchandise Manager:** Robin Warner. **Clubhouse Manager:** Mark Meschede. **Bar Manager:** Damian Heinz. **Manager, Ticket Operations:** Pat Prevelige. **Assistant Manager, Ticket Operations:** Kyle Webb. **Facility and Operations Coordinator:** Sean McCarthy. **Manager, Promotions and Game Entertainment:** Dominic Repper. **Suites Coordinator:** Wendy Smith. **Merchandise Assistant:** Shan Isett. **Group Sales Assistant:** Victoria Phipps. **Operations Assistant:** Will Priest. **Threshers Broadcaster:** Kirsten Karbach.

FIELD STAFF

Manager: Marty Malloy. **Hitting Coach:** Tyler Henson. **Pitching Coach:** Brad Bergesen.

GAME INFORMATION

PA Announcer: Don Guckian. **Official Scorer:** Larry Wiederecht. **Stadium Name:** Spectrum Field. **Location:** US 19 North and Drew Street in Clearwater. **Standard Game Times:** Mon.-Thu. 7 pm, Fri.-Sat. 6:30 pm, Sun. 1 p.m., most Wednesdays are day games. **Ticket Price Range:** $6-10. **Visiting Club Hotel:** La Quinta Inn, 21338 US Highway 19 N, Clearwater, FL 33765. **Telephone:** (727) 799-1565.

DAYTONA TORTUGAS

Address: 110 E Orange Ave, Daytona Beach, FL 32114. **Telephone:** (386) 257-3172. **Fax:** (386) 523-9490. **E-Mail Address:** info@daytonatortugas.com. **Website:** www.daytonatortugas.com. **Affiliation (first year):** Cincinnati Reds (2015 **Years in League:** 1920-24,1928, 1936-41, 1946-73, 1977-87, 1993-

OWNERSHIP/MANAGEMENT

Operated By: Tortugas Baseball Club LLC. **Principal Owner/President:** Reese Smith III.
President: Ryan Keur. **General Manager:** Jim Jaworski. **Manager, Broadcasting/Media/Communications:** Justin Rocke. **Director, Ticket Operations:** Paul Krenzer. **Manager, Food/Beverage:** Alex Swartz. **Manager, Community**

Relations: Trevor Fay. **Director, Corporate Partnerships:** Austin Scher. **Stadium Ops/Events Manager:** Thomas Vickers. **Marketing Coordinator:** Harolin Alvarez. **Manager, Partnership Fulfillment:** Amy Cecil. **Account Executive:** Max Furbee. **Director, Ticket Sales:** Melissa Balbach. **Business Development Manager:** Anderson Rathbun. **Controller:** David Manning.

FIELD STAFF
   Manager: Ricky Gutierrez. **Hitting Coach:** Alex Pelaez. **Pitching Coach:** Tom Brown. **Bench Coach:** Lenny Harris. **Athletic Trainer:** Ryan Ross. **Strength & Conditioning Coach:** Trey Strickland.

GAME INFORMATION
   Radio Announcer: Justin Rocke. **No. of Games Broadcast:** 140. **Flagship Station:** AM-1230 WSBB. **PA Announcer:** Tim Lecras. **Official Scorer:** Don Roberts. **Stadium Name:** Jackie Robinson Ballpark. **Location:** I-95 to International Speedway Blvd Exit, east to Beach Street, south to Magnolia Ave east to ballpark; A1A North/South to Orange Ave west to ballpark. **Standard Game Time:** 7:05 p.m. **Ticket Price Range:** $7-13.00. **Visiting Club Hotel:** Holiday Inn Resort Daytona Beach Oceanfront, 1615 S. Atlantic Ave Daytona Beach, FL 32118. **Telephone:** (386) 255-0921.

DUNEDIN BLUE JAYS

   Address: 373 Douglas Ave Dunedin, FL 34698.
   Telephone: (727) 733-9302. **Fax:** (727) 734-7661.
   E-Mail Address: dunedin@bluejays.com. **Website:** dunedinbluejays.com.
   Affiliation (first year): Toronto Blue Jays (1987). **Years in League:** 1978-79, 1987-

OWNERSHIP/MANAGEMENT
   Director Florida Operations: Shelby Nelson. **General Manager:** Mike Liberatore. **Accounting Manager:** Gayle Gentry. **Manager, Retail Sales and Community Relations:** Kathi Beckman. **Manager, Ticket Operations and Box office:** Jackie Purcell. **Administrative Assistant/Receptionist:** Dea Jones. **Manager, Security and Stadium Operations:** Zac Phelps. **Head Superintendent:** Patrick Skunda.

FIELD STAFF
   Manager: Cesar Martin. **Hitting Coach:** Matt Young. **Pitching Coach:** Jim Czajkowski. **Analyst/Coach:** Jake McGuiggan. **Strength & Conditioning Coach:** Kyle Edlhuber. **Athletic Trainer:** Michael Rendon.

GAME INFORMATION
   PA Announcer: Bill Christie. **Official Scorer:** Steven Boychuk. **Stadium Name:** Jack Russell Stadium. **Location:** From I-275, north on Highway 19, exit on Drew Street for 2.8 miles, right on North Highland Avenue, left onto Palmetto Road; stadium is on the left. **Standard Game Times:** 6:30 pm, Sun. 1:00 pm. **Ticket Price Range:** $5. **Visiting Club Hotel:** La Quinta, 21338 US Highway 19 North, Clearwater, FL. **Telephone:** (727) 799-1565.

FLORIDA FIRE FROGS

   Address: 631 Heritage Park Way Kissimmee, FL 34741
   Telephone: (321) 697-3156 . **E-Mail Address:** info@floridafirefrogs.com.
   Website: www.floridafirefrogs.com.
   Affiliation (first year): Atlanta Braves (2017). **Years in League:** 2017-

OWNERSHIP/MANAGEMENT
   Operated By: Manatees Baseball Club LLC.
   Chairman: CEO: President/GM: Erik Anderson. **Assistant General Manager:** Adam Whitlow. **Clubhouse Manager:** TBA. **Head Groundskeeper:** Wayne Thompson.

FIELD STAFF
   Manager: Barrett Kleinknecht. **Pitching Coach:** Dan Meyer. **Hitting Coach:** Doug DeVore.

GAME INFORMATION
   PA Announcer: Alfredo Muente. **Official Scorer:** Unavailable.
   Radio Broadcaster: Thaddeus Krzus. **Radio Station:** TuneIn. **Stadium Name:** Osceola County Stadium. **Location:** Take either I-4 or the Florida Turnpike to US 192. Follow US 192 (Irlo Bronson Memorial Highway) to Bill Beck Boulevard. Turn onto Bill Beck Boulevard, then take a left onto Heritage Park Way. To get to US 192 from I-4, take Exit 64. From the Turnpike, take either Exit 242 (northbound) or Exit 244 (southbound).

FORT MYERS MIRACLE

   Address: 14400 Six Mile Cypress Pkwy, Fort Myers, FL 33912.
   Telephone: (239) 768-4210. **Fax:** (239) 768-4211.
   E-Mail Address: miracle@miraclebaseball.com.
   Website: www.miraclebaseball.com. **Affiliation (first year):** Minnesota Twins (1993).
   Years in League: 1926, 1978-87, 1991-

OWNERSHIP/MANAGEMENT

Operated By: Kaufy Baseball, LLC. **Owner:** Andrew Kaufmann. **Partner:** Jason Hochberg
President/General Manager: Chris Peters. **Assistant General Manager, Operations:** Judd Loveland. **Assistant General Manager, Sales:** Paul Kleinhans-Schulz. **Senior Director, Business Operations:** Suzanne Reaves. **Sales Manager:** Andy Wood. **Broadcast & Media Relations Manager:** Marshall Kelner. **Promotions Manager & Corporate Sales Executive:** Daniel Straney. **Community Relations Manager & Account Executive:** Karlee Montgomery. **Social Media & Creative Services Manager:** Alexis Farinacci. **Account Executive:** Micah Beutell. **Account Executive:** Kyle Hamer. **Food & Beverage Director:** Loren Merrigan. **Catering Manager:** Sarah Keelen. **Merchandise Manager:** Lynn Izzo. **Ballpark and Concessions Operations:** Nate Whiteaker.

FIELD STAFF

Manager: Toby Gardenhire. **Hitting Coach:** Matt Borgschulte. **Pitching Coach:** Luis Ramirez. **Coach:** Frank Jagorda. **Trainer:** Ben Myers. **Strength & Conditioning Coach:** Chuck Bradway.

GAME INFORMATION

Radio Announcer: Marshall Kelner. **No. of Games Broadcast:** 140. **Internet Broadcast:** www.miraclebaseball.com. **PA Announcer:** Allen Woodard. **Official Scorer:** Scott Pedersen. **Stadium Name:** William H. Hammond Stadium at the CenturyLink Sports Complex. **Location:** Exit 131 off I-75, west on Daniels Parkway, left on Six Mile Cypress Parkway. **Standard Game Times:** Mon-Fri 6:30 or 7:00 pm, Sat. 6:00; Sun. 1:00. **Ticket Price Range:** $7.50-$13. **Visiting Club Hotel:** Four Points by Sheraton, 13600 Treeline Ave S, Fort Myers, FL 33913.

JUPITER HAMMERHEADS

Address: 4751 Main Street, Jupiter, FL 33458.
Telephone: (561) 775-1818. **Fax:** (561) 691-6886.
E-Mail Address: jupiterhammerheads@rogerdeanchevroletstadium.com.
Website: www.jupiterhammerheads.com.
Affiliation (first year): Miami Marlins (2002). **Years in League:** 1998-

OWNERSHIP/MANAGEMENT

Owned By: Miami Marlins, Jupiter Stadium, LTD.
General Manager, Jupiter Stadium, LTD: Mike Bauer. **General Manager:** Jamie Toole. **Executive Assistant:** Lynn Besaw. **Media Relations Coordinator:** Andrew Miller **Media Relations Assistant:** Abby Piper. **Director of Accounting:** Pam Satory. **Director of Corporate Partnerships:** Jamie Toole. **Director of Ticketing:** Andrew Seymour. **Marketing & Promotions Manager:** Sarah Campbell. **Building Manager:** Walter Herrera. **Event Services Manager:** Dan Knapinski. **Director, Grounds & Facilities:** Jordan Treadway. **Assistant Director, Grounds & Facilities:** Mitchell Moenster. **Merchandise Manager:** Taryn Taylor. **Ticket Office Manager:** Louis Reyes.

FIELD STAFF

Manager: Todd Pratt. **Pitching Coach:** Reid Cornelius. **Hitting Coach:** Kevin Witt. **Strength & Conditioning Coach:** Gregory Bourn. **Athletic Trainer:** Eric Reigelsberger. **Defensive Coach:** Danny Black.

GAME INFORMATION

PA Announcers: John Frost, Jay Zeager. **Official Scorer:** Brennan McDonald. **Stadium Name:** Roger Dean Chevrolet Stadium. **Location:** I-95 to exit 83, east on Donald Ross Road for 1/4 mile, left on Parkside Dr. **Standard Game Times:** 6:30 pm, Sat. 5:30 pm, Sun. 1:00 pm. **Ticket Price Range:** $7- $10. **Visiting Club Hotel:** Fairfield Inn by Marriott, 6748 Indiantown Road, Jupiter, FL 33458. **Telephone:** (561) 748-5252.

LAKELAND FLYING TIGERS

Address: 2301 Lakeland Hills Blvd., Lakeland, FL 33805.
Telephone: (863) 686-8075. **Fax:** (863) 687-4127.
Website: www.lakelandflyingtigers.com.
Affiliation (first year): Detroit Tigers (1967). **Years in League:** 1919-26, 1953-55, 1960, 1962-64, 1967-.

OWNERSHIP/MANAGEMENT

Owned By: Detroit Tigers, Inc.
Principal and CEO of Illitch Holdings, Inc. and Detroit Tigers: Christoper Illitch. **Director, Florida Operations:** Ron Myers. **General Manager:** Zach Burek. **Manager, Administration/Operations Manager:** Shannon Follett. **Ticket Manager:** Ryan Eason. **Assistant General Manager:** Dan Lauer. **Administration/ Operations Assistant:** Alison Streicher.

FIELD STAFF

Manager: Andrew Graham. **Hitting Coach:** Tim Garland. **Pitching Coach:** Jorge Cordova. **Coach:** Francisco Contreras. **Trainer:** Jason Schwartzman. **Strength & Conditioning Coach:** Dax Fiore. **Video Coordinator:** TBD. **Clubhouse Manager:** Pete Mancuso.

GAME INFORMATION

PA Announcer: Unavailable. **Official Scorer:** Joe Falatek. **Stadium Name:** Publix Field at Joker Marchant Stadium. **Location:** Exit 33 on I-4 to 33 South (Lakeland Hills Blvd.), 1.5 miles on left. **Standard Game Times:** Mon.-Fri. 6:30,

Sat. 6:00, Sun. 1:00. **Ticket Price Range:** $5-10. **Visiting Club Hotel:** Ecco Suites Lakeland, 4360 Lakeland Park Drive, Lakeland, FL 33809. **Telephone:** (863) 904-2050 .

PALM BEACH CARDINALS

Address: 4751 Main Street, Jupiter, FL 33458.
Telephone: (561) 775-1818. **Fax:** (561) 691-6886.
E-Mail Address: PalmBeachCardinals@rogerdeanchevroletstadium.com.
Affiliation (first year): St. Louis Cardinals (2003). **Years in League:** 2003-

OWNERSHIP/MANAGEMENT

Owned By: St. Louis Cardinals, Jupiter Stadium, LTD.
General Manager, Jupiter Stadium, LTD: Mike Bauer. **General Manager:** Jamie Toole. **Executive Assistant:** Lynn Besaw. **Media Relations Coordinator:** Andrew Miller. **Media Relations Assistant:** Abby Piper. **Director of Accounting:** Pam Satory. **Director of Corporate Partnerships:** Jamie Toole. **Director of Ticketing:** Andrew Seymour. **Marketing & Promotions Manager:** Sarah Campbell. **Building Manager:** Walter Herrera. **Event Services Manager:** Dan Knapinski. **Director, Grounds & Facilities:** Jordan Treadway. **Assistant Director, Grounds & Facilities:** Mitchell Moenster. **Merchandise Manager:** Taryn Taylor. **Ticket Office Manager:** Louis Reyes.

FIELD STAFF

Manager: Dann Bilardello. **Pitching Coach:** Will Ohman. **Hitting Coach:** Tyger Pederson. **Strength & Conditioning Coach:** Ross Hasegawa. **Certified Athletic Trainer:** Chris Whitman.

GAME INFORMATION

PA Announcers: John Frost, **Jay Zeager, Official Scorer:** Brennan McDonald. **Stadium Name:** Roger Dean Chevrolet Stadium. **Location:** I-95 to exit 83, east on Donald Ross Road for 1/4 mile, left on Parkside Dr. **Standard Game Times:** 6:30 pm, Sat. 5:30pm, Sun. 1:00pm. **Ticket Price Range:** $7- $10. **Visiting Club Hotel:** Fairfield Inn by Marriott, 6748 Indiantown Road, Jupiter, FL 33458. **Telephone:** (561) 748-5252.

ST. LUCIE METS

Address: 525 NW Peacock Blvd., Port St Lucie, FL 34986.
Telephone: (772) 871-2100. **Fax:** (772) 878-9802.
Website: www.stluciemets.com.
Affiliation (first year): New York Mets (1988). **Years in League:** 1988-

OWNERSHIP/MANAGEMENT

Operated by: Sterling Mets LP.
Chairman/CEO: Fred Wilpon. **President:** Saul Katz. **COO:** Jeff Wilpon. **Executive Director, Minor League Facilities:** Paul Taglieri. **General Manager:** Traer Van Allen. **Executive Assistant:** Mary O'Brien. **Coordinator, Group Sales:** Josh Sexton. **Staff Accountant:** Shannon Murray. **Accounting Clerk:** Christina Rivera. **Director, Sales/Corporate Partnerships:** Lauren DeAcetis. **Director, Ticketing/Merchandise:** Kyle Gleockler. **Manager, Media/Broadcast Relations:** Adam MacDonald. **Director, Group Sales/Community Relations:** Kasey Blair. **Coordinator, Social Media and Graphic Design:** Marissa Kappus. **Maintenance:** Jerry Lanigan.

FIELD STAFF

Manager: Chad Kreuter. **Hitting Coach:** TBD. **Pitching Coach:** TBD. **Trainer:** Hiroto Kawamura. **Strength & Conditioning Coach:** Tanner Miracle.

GAME INFORMATION

PA Announcer: Evan Nine. **Official Scorer:** Bill Whitehead. **Stadium Name:** First Data Field. **Location:** Exit 121 (St Lucie West Blvd) off I-95, east 1/2 mile, left on NW Peacock Blvd. **Standard Game Times:** 6:30 pm, Sun 1pm. **Ticket Price Range:** $6 - $10. **Visiting Club Hotel:** Holiday Inn Express, 1601 NW Courtyard Circle, Port St Lucie, FL 34986. **Telephone:** (772) 879-6565.

TAMPA TARPONS

Address: One Steinbrenner Drive, Tampa, FL 33614.
Telephone: (813) 875-7753. **Fax:** (813) 673-3186
E-Mail Address: vsmith@yankees.com. **Website:** tarponsbaseball.com
Affiliation (first year): New York Yankees (1994).
Years in League: 1919-27, 1957-1988, 1994-

OWNERSHIP/MANAGEMENT

Operated by: Florida Bomber Baseball LLC. **VP Business Operations:** Vance Smith. **General Manager:** Matt Gess
Assistant GM: Jeremy Ventura. **Premium Ticket Services:** Jennifer Magliocchetti. **Ticket Operations & Promotions:**
Allison Stortz. **Digital Media Coordinator:** Maddie Erhardt. **Operations Coordinator:** Kate Harvey, **Director,**
Grounds: Ritchie Anderson. **Stadium Supervisor:** Ron Kaufman. **Head Groundskeeper:** Jeff Eckert.

FIELD STAFF

Manager: Aaron Holbert. **Hitting Coach:** Joe Migliaccio. **Pitching Coach:** Jose Rosado. **Catching Coach:** Michel
Hernandez. **Defensive Coach:** Kevin Mahoney. **Athletic Trainer:** Michael Becker. **Strength & Conditioning Coach:**
Jacob Dunning. **Video Coordinator:** Dylan Elber. **Clubhouse/Equipment Manager:** Kenneth "JR" Bassett.

GAME INFORMATION

Radio: www.tarponsbaseball.com. **PA Announcer:** Unavailable. **Official Scorer:** Unavailable.
Stadium Name: George M Steinbrenner Field. **Location:** I-275 to Dale Mabry Hwy, North on Dale Mabry Hwy
(Facility is at corner of West Martin Luther King Blvd/Dale Mabry Hwy). **Standard Game Times:** Mon - Sat. 6:30pm,
Sun 1pm. **Ticket Price Range:** $5-8. **Visiting Club Hotel:** Double Tree by Hilton Tampa Airport - Westshore.

MIDWEST LEAGUE

Address: 210 S. Michigan St., South Bend, Ind. 46601.
Telephone: (574) 234-3000. **Fax:** (574) 234-4220.
E-Mail Address: mwl@midwestleague.com, dickn@sni-law.com.
Website: www.midwestleague.com.
Years League Active: 1947-
President/Legal Counsel/Secretary: Richard A. Nussbaum, II.

Richard Nussbaum

Vice President: Lew Chamberlin. **Directors:** Andrew Berlin (South Bend). Jack Blackstock (Bowling Green). Kim Parker (Burlington). Lew Chamberlin (West Michigan). Dennis Conerton (Beloit). Paul Davis (Clinton). Tom Dickson (Lansing). Jason Freier (Fort Wayne). David Heller (Quad Cities). Doug Nelson (Cedar Rapids). Greg Rosenbaum (Dayton). Peter Carfagna (Lake County). Scott Litle (Great Lakes). Jason Mott (Peoria). Dr. Bob Froehlich (Kane County). Rob Zerjav (Wisconsin). **Director Emeritus:** Dave Walker. **League Administrator:** Holly Voss.
Division Structure: East—Bowling Green, Dayton, Fort Wayne, Lake County, Lansing, South Bend, Great Lakes, West Michigan. **West—**Beloit, Burlington, Cedar Rapids, Clinton, Kane County, Peoria, Quad Cities, Wisconsin.

Regular Season: 140 games (split schedule). **Opening Date:** April 4. **Closing Date:** Sept 2. **All-Star Game:** June 18 at South Bend, Indiana. **Playoff Format:** Eight teams qualify. First-half and second-half division winners and wild- card teams meet in best of three quarterfinal series. Winners meet in best of three series for division championships. Division champions meet in best-of-five series for league championship. **Roster Limit:** 25 active. **Player Eligibility Rule:** No age limit. No more than two players and one player-coach on active list may have more than five years experience. **Brand of Baseball:** Rawlings ROM-MID. **Umpires:** Unavailable.

STADIUM INFORMATION

Club	Stadium	Opened	Dimensions LF	CF	RF	Capacity	2018 Att.
Beloit	Pohlman Field	1982	325	380	325	3,500	64,574
Bowling Green	Bowling Green Ballpark	2009	318	400	326	4,559	178,329
Burlington	Community Field	1947	338	403	318	3,200	53,259
Cedar Rapids	Veterans Memorial Stadium	2002	315	400	325	5,300	160,165
Clinton	Ashford University Field	1937	335	401	325	5,000	121,678
Dayton	Fifth Third Field	2000	338	402	338	6,830	550,725
Fort Wayne	Parkview Field	2009	336	400	318	8,100	376,422
Great Lakes	Dow Diamond	2007	332	400	325	5,200	187,220
Kane County	Northwestern Medicine Field	1991	335	400	335	10,973	350,028
Lake County	Classic Park	2003	320	400	320	6,157	202,124
Lansing	Cooley Law School Stadium	1996	305	412	305	11,000	313,592
Peoria	Dozer Park	2002	310	400	310	7,000	208,275
Quad Cities	Modern Woodmen Park	1931	343	400	318	7,140	215,061
South Bend	Four Winds Fields	1987	336	405	336	5,000	343,763
West Michigan	Fifth Third Ballpark	1994	317	402	327	9,281	386,609
Wisconsin	Neuroscience Group Field	1995	325	400	325	5,170	225,897

BELOIT SNAPPERS

Office Address: 2301 Skyline Drive, Beloit, WI 53511.
Mailing Address: P.O. Box 855, Beloit, WI 53512.
Telephone: (608) 362-2272. **Fax:** (608) 362-0418.
E-Mail: snappy@snappersbaseball.com. **Website:** www.snappersbaseball.com.
Affiliation (first year): Oakland Athletics (2013). **Years in League:** 1982-

OWNERSHIP/MANAGEMENT
Operated by: Beloit Professional Baseball Association, Inc. **President:** Dennis Conerton.
General Manager: Jeff Gray. **Marketing and Media Manager:** Ben Vigliarolo. **Tickets and Group Sales Manager:** Tommy Himebaugh. **Corporate Partnerships Manager:** Tom Finn. **Head Groundskeeper:** Alan Jones.

FIELD STAFF
Manager: Lloyd Turner. **Hitting Coach:** Juan Dilone. **Pitching Coach:** Don Schulze. **Assistant Coach:** Anthony Phillips. **Athletic Trainer:** Brian Thorson. **Strength & Conditioning Coach:** Scott Smith.

GAME INFORMATION
Radio Announcer: Unavailable. **No. of Games Broadcast:** Unavailable. **Flagship Station:** Unavailable. **PA Announcer:** Unavailable. **Official Scorer:** Unavailable. **Stadium Name:** Pohlman Field. **Location:** I-90 to exit 185-A, right at Cranston Road for 1 1/2 miles; I-43 to Wisconsin 81 to Cranston Road, right at Cranston for 1 1/2 miles. **Standard Game Times:** 6:30 pm, Sat. 4 pm (April), Sun 2 pm. **Ticket Price Range:** $7.50-$12.00. **Visiting Club Hotel:** Rodeway Inn, 2956 Milwaukee Rd, Beloit, WI 53511. **Telephone:** (608) 364-4000.

BOWLING GREEN HOT RODS

Address: Bowling Green Ballpark, 300 8th Avenue, Bowling Green, KY 42101.
Telephone: (270) 901-2121. **Fax:** (270) 901-2165.
E-Mail Address: fun@bghotrods.com. **Website:** www.bghotrods.com.
Affiliation (first year): Tampa Bay Rays (2009). **Years in League:** 2010-

OWNERSHIP/MANAGEMENT
Operated By: BG SKY, LLC.
President/Managing Partner: Jack Blackstock. **General Manager/COO:** Eric C. Leach. **Assistant General Manager:** Matt Ingram. **Director, Sales:** Kyle Wolz. **Director, Stadium Operations:** Wallace Brown. **Assistant Director, Stadium Operations:** Brock Wilson. **Head Groundskeeper:** Tradd Jones. **Manager, Promotions and Community Relations:** Laura Feese. **Creative Services Manager, Video:** Todd Warren. **Creative Services Manager, Graphics:** Emma Reece. **Group Sales Manager:** Daniel Kline. **Account Executive/Retail Store Manager:** Nathan Baer. **Manager, Box Office:** Jon Barhorst. **Manager, Broadcast/Media Relations:** Shawn Murnin. **Account Executive:** George Collins. **Corporate Sales Executive:** Barry Vincent.

FIELD STAFF
Manager: Reinaldo Ruiz. **Pitching Coach:** Brian Reith. **Assistant Coach:** Manny Castillo, Jeremy Owens. **Athletic Trainer:** Brian Newman. **Strength & Conditioning Coach:** James McCallie.

GAME INFORMATION
Radio Announcer: Shawn Murnin. **No. of Games Broadcast:** 140. **Flagship Station:** WBGN 94.1 FM. **PA Announcer:** Unavailable. **Official Scorer:** Unavailable. **Stadium Name:** Bowling Green Ballpark. **Location:** From I-65, take Exit 26 (KY-234/Cemetery Road) into Bowling Green for 3 miles, left onto College Street for .2 miles, right onto 8th Avenue. **Standard Game Times:** Mon.-Sat., 6:35 pm, Sun., 4:05 pm. **Ticket Price Range:** $8-24. **Visiting Club Hotel:** Clarion Inn. **Telephone:** (270) 282-7130.

BURLINGTON BEES

Office Address: 2712 Mount Pleasant St., Burlington, IA 52601.
Mailing Address: PO Box 824, Burlington, IA 52601.
Telephone: (319) 754-5705. **Fax:** (319) 754-5882.
E-Mail Address: staff@gobees.com. **Website:** www.gobees.com.
Affiliation (first year): Los Angeles Angels (2013). **Years in League:** 1962-

OWNERSHIP/MANAGEMENT
Operated By: Burlington Baseball Association Inc.
President: Scott Zaiser. **General Manager:** Kim Parker. **Director of Ticketing & Front Office Administrator:** Jill Mason. **Sales/Stadium Operations Executive:** Tad Lowary. **Director Media Relations:** Ted Gutman. **Groundskeeper:** Lance Weber. **Clubhouse Manager:** Corbin Schindler.

FIELD STAFF
Manager: Jack Howell. **Hitting Coach:** Will Bradley. **Pitching Coach:** Unavailable.

GAME INFORMATION
Radio Announcer: RJ Larson. **No. of Games Broadcast:** 67 home games. **PA Announcer:** Marty Mogk. **Official Scorer:** Ted Gutman. **Stadium Name:** Community Field. **Location:** From US 34, take US 61 North to Mt. Pleasant St, east 1/8 mile. **Standard Game Times:** Mon.-Sat., 6:30 pm, Sat., 5:00 pm (April-May) Sun., 2 pm. **Ticket Price Range:** $5-10. **Visiting Club Hotel:** Pzazz Best Western FunCity, 3001 Winegard Dr., Burlington, IA 52601. **Telephone:** (319) 753-2223.

CEDAR RAPIDS KERNELS

Office Address: 950 Rockford Road SW, Cedar Rapids, IA 52404.
Mailing Address: PO Box 2001, Cedar Rapids, IA 52406.
Telephone: (319) 363-3887. **Fax:** (319) 363-5631.
E-Mail: kernels@kernels.com. **Website:** www.kernels.com.
Affiliation (first year): Minnesota Twins (2013). **Years in League:** 1962-

OWNERSHIP/MANAGEMENT
President: Greg Seyfer. **Chief Executive Officer:** Doug Nelson. **General Manager:** Scott Wilson. **Manager, IT/Communications:** Andrew Pantini. **Sports Turf Manager:** Jesse Roeder. **Sr. Director, Ticket/Group Sales:** Andrea Brommelkamp. **Accounting Manager:** Tracy Barr. **Director, Broadcasting:** Morgan Hawk. **Manager, Community Relations:** Aron Brecht. **Sr. Director, Corporate Sales/Marketing:** Jessica Fergesen. **Coordinator, History:** Marcia Moran. **Manager, Ticket Office:** Peter Keleher. **Manager, Stadium Operations:** Brad Mochal. **Clubhouse Manager:** Taylor Hoth. **Office Manager/Donations Coordinator:** Sherry Downey.

FIELD STAFF

Manager: Brian Dinkelman. **Hitting Coach:** Ryan Smith. **Pitching Coach:** Virgil Vazquez. **Infield Coach:** Luis Rodriguez. **Athletic Trainer:** Tyler Blair. **Strength & Conditioning Coach:** Kyle Kelly.

GAME INFORMATION

Radio Announcer: Morgan Hawk, Chris Kleinhans-Schulz. **No. of Games Broadcast:** 140. **Flagship Station:** KMRY 1450-AM/93.1-FM. **PA Announcer:** Unavailable. **Official Scorers:** Steve Meyer, Shane Severson. **Stadium Name:** Perfect Game Field at Veterans Memorial Stadium. **Location:** From I-380 North, take the Wilson Ave exit, turn left on Wilson Ave, after the railroad tracks, turn right on Rockford Road, proceed .8 miles, stadium is on left; From I-380 South, exit at First Avenue, proceed to Eighth Avenue (first stop sign) and turn left, stadium entrance is on right. **Standard Game Times:** Mon.-Sat., 6:35 pm, Sun. 2:05 pm. **Ticket Price Range:** $8-12 in advance, $9-13 day of game. **Visiting Club Hotel:** Comfort Inn & Suites, 2025 Werner Ave NE, Cedar Rapids, IA 52402. **Telephone:** (319) 378-8888.

CLINTON LUMBERKINGS

Office Address: 537 Ball Park Drive, Clinton, IA 52732.
Mailing Address: PO Box 1295, Clinton, IA 52733.
Telephone: (563) 242-0727. **Fax:** (563) 242-1433.
E-Mail Address: lumberkings@lumberkings.com. **Website:** www.lumberkings.com.

OWNERSHIP/MANAGEMENT

Operated By: Clinton Baseball Club Inc.
President: Paul Davis. **General Manager:** Ted Tornow. **Director, Broadcasting/Media Relations:** Erik Oas. **Director, Operations:** Tyler Oehmen. **Accountant:** Ryan Marcum. **Assistant Director, Operations:** Morty Kriner. **Director, Facility Compliance:** Tom Whaley. **Office Procurement Manager:** Les Moore. **Clubhouse Manager:** Unavaiable. **Community Service Representative:** Tammy Johnson. **Assistant Groundskeeper:** Matt Dunbar. **Special Events Coordinator:** Tom Krogman.

FIELD STAFF

Manager: Mike Jacobs. **Hitting Coach:** Frank Moore. **Pitching Coach:** Mark DiFelice. **Athletic Trainer:** Melissa Hampton. **Strength & Conditioning Coach:** Amanda Sartoris.

GAME INFORMATION

Radio Announcer: Erik Oas. **No. of Games Broadcast:** 140. **Flagship Station:** WCCI 100.3 FM. **PA Announcer:** Brad Seward. **Official Scorer:** Alex Miller. **Stadium Name:** LumberKings Stadium. **Location:** Highway 67 North to Sixth Ave. North, right on Sixth, cross railroad tracks, stadium on right. **Standard Game Times:** 6:30 pm, Sun. 2:00. **Ticket Price Range:** $5-8. **Visiting Club Hotel:** AmericInn & Suites, 1301 17th Street, Fulton, Ill. 61252. **Telephone:** (815) 589-3333.

DAYTON DRAGONS

Office Address: Fifth Third Field, 220 N. Patterson Blvd., Dayton,OH 45402.
Mailing Address: PO Box 2107, Dayton, OH 45401.
Telephone: (937) 228-2287. **Fax:** (937) 228-2284.
E-Mail Address: dragons@daytondragons.com. **Website:** www.daytondragons.com.
Affiliation (first year): Cincinnati Reds (2000). **Years in League:** 2000-

OWNERSHIP/MANAGEMENT

Operated By: Palisades Arcadia Baseball LLC.
President & General Manager: Robert Murphy. **Executive Vice President:** Eric Deutsch. **Office Manager/Executive Assistant to the President:** Leslie Stuck. **VP, Assistant General Manager:** Brandy Guinaugh. **VP, Accounting/Finance:** Mark Schlein. **VP, Corporate Partnerships:** Brad Eaton, Trafton Eutsler. **Director, Media Relations & Broadcasting:** Tom Nichols. **Senior Director, Operations:** John Wallace. **Director, Facility Operations:** Jason Fleenor. **Senior Director, Entertainment:** Kaitlin Rohrer. **Director, Entertainment:** Katrina Gibbs. **Director, Creative Services:** James Westerheide. **Director, Ticket Operations:** Stefanie Mitchell. **Director, Ticket Sales:** Andrew Hayes. **Senior Group Sales Manager:** Carl Hertzberg. **Senior Manager of Corporate Partnerships:** Greg Lees. **Senior Business Development Manager:** Sam Schneider. **Senior Inside Sales Manager:** Mandy Roselli. **Group Sales Managers:** Matt Dombrowski, Grant Hall, Dosh Hyde, Seth Mackesy, Andrew Majzan, Ben Shockley. **Business Development Managers:** Sam Bowers, Randy Stites. **Corporate Partnerships Managers:** Christine Burns, Megan Norkunas, Brandon Rexin, Alex Wilker. **Corporate Partnership Assistants:** Brittany Snyder, Tyler Hess. **Ticket Operations Manager:** Jordyn Lewis. **Graphic Designer:** Ali Beach. **Multimedia Designer:** Connor Boyle. **Sports Turf Manager:** Tanner Turner. **Operations Manager:** Tyler Dunton. **Manager of Retail Operations:** Kyle Dunlap. **Operations Assistants:** Chandler Dawson, Shane Hale. **Media Relations Assistant:** Josh Hess. **Entertainment Assistant:** Jamie Penwell. **Clubhouse Manager:** Austin Coleman. **Staff Accountant:** Dawn Reed. **Administrative Secretary:** Barbara Van Schaik.

FIELD STAFF

Manager: Luis Bolivar. **Hitting Coach:** Mike Devereaux. **Pitching Coach:** Seth Etherton. **Bench Coach:** Kevin Mahar.

GAME INFORMATION

Radio Announcers: Tom Nichols and Josh Hess. **No. of Games Broadcast:** 140. **Flagship Station:** WONE 980 AM.

Television Announcer: Tom Nichols and Jack Pohl. No. of Games Broadcast: Home-25. Flagship Station: WBDT Channel 26. PA Announcer: Ben Oburn. Official Scorers: Matt Lindsay, Mike Lucas, Matt Zircher. Stadium Name: Fifth Third Field. Location: I-75 South to downtown Dayton, left at First Street; I-75 North, right at First Street exit. Ticket Price Range: $9-$19. Visiting Club Hotel: Courtyard by Marriott, 100 Prestige Place, Miamisburg, OH 45342. Telephone: 937-433-3131. Fax: 937-433-0285.

FORT WAYNE TINCAPS

Address: 1301 Ewing St., Fort Wayne, IN 46802.
Telephone: (260) 482-6400. Fax: (260) 471-4678.
E-Mail Address: info@tincaps.com. Website: www.tincaps.com.
Affiliation (first year): San Diego Padres (1999). Years in League: 1993-

OWNERSHIP/MANAGEMENT

Operated By: Hardball Capital. Owner: Jason Freier. President: Mike Nutter. Vice President, Corporate Partnerships: David Lorenz. VP, Finance: Brian Schackow. VP, Marketing & Promotions: Michael Limmer. Creative Director: Tony DesPlaines. Director of Video Production: Melissa Darby. Assistant Video Production Manager: Tim Bajema. Broadcasting/Media Relations Manager: John Nolan. Community Engagement Manager: Morgan Olson. Digital Content Manager: Cory Stace. Group Sales Director: Jared Parcell. Group Sales Assistant Director: Brent Harring. Senior Ticket Account Manager: Austin Allen. Ticket Account Manager: Dalton McGill. Ticket Account Manager: Jenn Sylvester. Ticket Account Manager: Tyler Lantz. Ticketing Director: Paige Watson. Reading Program Director/Assistant Director of Ticketing: Kade Zvokel. Corporate Partnerships Manager: Devon Merder. Special Events Coordinator: Holly Raney. Banquet Event Manager: Alexis Strabala. Food/Beverage Director: Bill Lehn. Executive Chef/Culinary Director: Pisarn Amornarthakij. VIP Services Manager: Dominick Catanzarite. Food/Beverage Operations Manager: Nathan Seaman. Commissary Manager: Eric Sauer. Head Groundskeeper: Keith Winter. Assistant Groundskeeper: Ryan Lehrman. Facilities Director: Tim Burkhart. Accounting Manager/ Facilities Manager: Erik Lose. Groundskeeping/Ballpark Operations Assistant: Jake Sperry. Ballpark Cleaning Crew Supervisor: Jeff Johnson. Merchandise Manager: Jen Klinker. Human Resources/Office Manager: Cathy Tinney.

FIELD STAFF

Manager: Anthony Contreras. Hitting Coach: Jonathan Matthews. Pitching Coach: Burt Hooton. Fielding Coach: Jhonny Carvajal. Athletic Trainer: Allyse Kramer. Strength & Conditioning Coach: Sam Hoffman.

GAME INFORMATION

Radio Announcers: John Nolan, Evan Stockton, Mike Maahs. No. of Radio Games Broadcast: 140. Flagship Station: WKJG 1380-AM/100.9-FM. TV Announcers: John Nolan, Dave Doster, Javi DeJesus, Brett Rump, Tracy Coffman. No. of TV Games Broadcast: Home–70. Flagship Station: Comcast Network 81. PA Announcer: Jared Parcell. Official Scorers: Rich Tavierne, Bill Scott, Dan Watson Dave Coulter. Stadium Name: Parkview Field. Location: 1301 Ewing St., Fort Wayne, IN, 46802. Ticket Price Range: $6-$15. Visiting Club Hotel: Quality Inn, 1734 West Washington Center Rd., Fort Wayne, IN, 46818. Telephone: (260-489-5554).

GREAT LAKES LOONS

Address: 825 East Main St., Midland, MI 48640.
Telephone: (989) 837-2255. Fax: (989) 837-8780.
E-Mail Address: info@loons.com. Website: www.loons.com.
Affiliation (first year): Los Angeles Dodgers (2007). Years in League: 2007-

OWNERSHIP/MANAGEMENT

Stadium Ownership: Michigan Baseball Foundation.
Founder: William Stavropoulos. Director, ESPN 100.9-FM Sales: Jay Arons. Business Manager, Concessions: Andrew Booms. Vice President, CFO: Jana Chotivkova. Assistant GM, Marketing & Communication: Matt DeVries. Director, Production: Trent Elliott. Manager, Retail: Kimberley Emerick. Coordinator, ESPN 100.9-FM Content & Play-by-Play Broadcaster: Blake Froling. Manager, Group Venue Sales: Tony Garant. General Manager, Dow Diamond Events: Dave Gomola. Manager, ESPN 100.9-FM Business: Robin Gover. Administrative Support Assistant: Melissa Kehoe. Director, Partnership Activation: Tyler Kring. Corporate Account Executive: Drew Moomey. Vice President, CRO: Chris Mundhenk. Executive Chef: Andrea Noonan. Director, ESPN 100.9-FM Production & Operations: Jerry O'Donnell. Coordinator, Group Ticket Sales: Riley Paulus. Manager, Group Ticket Sales: Sam PeLong. Assistant GM, Ticket Sales: Thom Pepe. Director, Business Applications & Analytics: Eric Ramseyer. Head Groundskeeper: Kelly Rensel. Coordinator, Group Ticket Sales: Rickey Rissman. Manager, Creative Services: Alex Seder. Manager, Accounting: Holly Snow. Director, Accounting: Jamie Start. Assistant GM, Facility Operations: Dan Straley. Manager, Catering: Ryan Teeple. Manager, ESPN 100.9-FM Programming & Play-by-Play Broadcaster: Brad Tunney. Executive Assistant & MBF Grants: Carol VanWert. Corporate Account Executive: Joe Volk. Vice President, Baseball Operations & Gameday Experience: Tiffany Wardynski.

FIELD STAFF

Manager: John Shoemaker. Hitting Coach: Jair Fernandez. Pitching Coach: Bobby Cuellar. Bench Coach: Seth Conner.

GAME INFORMATION

Play-by-Play Broadcaster: Brad Tunney & Blake Froling. **No. of Games Broadcast:** 140. **Flagship Station:** WLUN, ESPN 100.9-FM (ESPN1009.com). **PA Announcer:** Jerry O'Donnell. **Official Scorers:** Steve Robb. **Stadium Name:** Dow Diamond. **Location:** I-75 to US-10 W, Take the M-20/US-10 Business exit on the left toward downtown Midland, Merge onto US-10 W/MI-20 W (also known as Indian Street), Turn left onto State Street, the entrance to the stadium is at the intersection of Ellsworth and State Streets. **Standard Game Times:** Mon.-Sat., 6:05 pm (April), 7:05 pm (May-Sept), Sun. 2:05 pm. **Ticket Price Range:** $6-9. **Visiting Club Hotel:** Holiday Inn, 810 Cinema Drive, Midland, MI 48642. **Telephone:** (989) 794-8500.

KANE COUNTY COUGARS

Address: 34W002 Cherry Lane, Geneva, IL 60134. **Telephone:** (630) 232-8811.
Fax: (630) 232-8815. **Website:** www.kccougars.com.
Affiliation (first year): Arizona Diamondbacks (2015). **Years in League:** 1991-

OWNERSHIP/MANAGEMENT

Operated By: Cougars Baseball Partnership/American Sports Enterprises, Inc. **Chairman/Chief Executive Officer/President:** Dr. Bob Froehlich. **Owners:** Dr. Bob Froehlich, Cheryl Froehlich. **Board of Directors:** Dr. Bob Froehlich, Cheryl Froehlich, Stephanie Froehlich, Chris Neidhart, Marianne Neidhart. **Vice President/General Manager:** Curtis Haug. **Senior Director, Finance/Administration:** Douglas Czurylo. **Finance/Accounting Manager:** Lance Buhmann. **Accounting:** Sally Sullivan. **Senior Director, Ticketing:** R. Michael Patterson. **Senior Ticket Sales Representative:** Alex Miller. **Sales Representatives:** Dave Grochowski, Kelton Zimmerman. **Director, Ticket Services/Community Relations:** Amy Mason. **Assistant Director of Ticket Operations:** Paul Quillia. **Ticket Operations Representative:** Jeff Weaver. **Director, Security:** Dan Klinkhamer. **Promotions Director:** Caela McBride. **Communications Coordinator:** Jacquie Boatman. **Design/Graphics:** Emmet Broderick. **Media Placement Coordinator:** Bill Baker. **Office Manager:** Sherri Johnson. **Video Director:** Andy Cozzi. **Director, Food/Beverage:** Benito Suero. **Business Manager:** Robin Hull. **Executive Chef:** Ron Kludac. **Senior Director, Stadium Operations:** Mike Klafehn. **Director, Maintenance:** Jeff Snyder. **Head Groundskeeper:** Sean Ehlert.

FIELD STAFF

Manager: Vince Harrison. **Hitting Coach:** Micah Franklin. **Pitching Coach:** Mike Parrott. **Bench Coach:** Carlos Mesa. **Athletic Trainer:** Kelly Boyce. **Strength & Conditioning Coach:** Tim Queck. **Clubhouse Manager:** Scott Anderson.

GAME INFORMATION

Radio Announcer: Joe Brand. **No. of Games Broadcast:** 140. **Flagship Station:** WBIG 1280-AM. **Official Scorer:** Bill Baker. **Stadium Name:** Northwestern Medicine Field. **Location:** From east or west, I-88 Ronald Reagan Memorial Tollway) to Farnsworth Ave. North exit, north five miles to Cherry Lane, left into stadium; from northwest, I-90 (Jane Addams Memorial Tollway) to Randall Rd. South exit, south to Fabayan Parkway, east to Kirk Rd., north to Cherry Lane, left into stadium complex. **Standard Game Times:** Mon.-Sat., 6:30 pm, Sun., 1 pm. **Ticket Price Range:** $9-15. **Visiting Club Hotel:** Pheasant Run Resort, 4051 E Main St, St. Charles, IL 60174. **Telephone:** (630) 584-6300.

LAKE COUNTY CAPTAINS

Address: Classic Park, 35300 Vine St., Eastlake, OH 44095-3142.
Telephone: (440) 975-8085. **Fax:** (440) 975-8958.
E-Mail Address: nstein@captainsbaseball.com.
Website: www.captainsbaseball.com.
Affiliation (first year): Cleveland Indians (2003). **Years in League:** 2010-

OWNERSHIP/MANAGEMENT

Operated By: Cascia LLC. **Owners:** Peter and Rita Carfagna, Ray and Katie Murphy.
Chairman/Secretary/Treasurer: Peter Carfagna. **Vice Chairman:** Rita Carfagna. **Vice President:** Ray Murphy. **General Manager:** Neil Stein. **Assistant General Manager:** Jen Yorko. **Manager of Promotions, Graphics Coordinator:** Rachel Wallbrown. **Sr. Director, Food and Beverage:** John Klein. **Director, Ticket Operations & Special Events:** Justin Cartor. **Director, Finance:** Nicole Owens. **Director of Production & Corporate Partnership Development:** Tim O'Brien. **Director, Stadium Operations:** Matthew Boes. **Manager, Turf Operations:** Charlie Erlenbach. **Asst. Manager, Food and Beverage:** Helen Scholar. **Sr. Director Corporate Sales & Media Relations:** Craig Deas. **Director, Ticket Sales:** Kate Roth. **Ticket Sales Account Executive:** Olivia Vocke. **Ticket Sales Account Executive:** Kevin Clements. **Manager, Community Relations & Game Presentation:** Devin Levan-Galang. **Office Assistant:** Jim Carfagna. **Radio Broadcaster:** Andrew Luftglass.

FIELD STAFF

Field Manager: Luke Carlin. **Hitting Coach:** Jason Esposito. **Pitching Coach:** Owen Dew. **Bench Coach:** Jordan Smith. **Athletic Trainer:** Unavailable. **Strength & Conditioning Coach:** Travis Roberson.

GAME INFORMATION

Radio Announcer: Craig Deas and Andrew Luftglass. **No. of Games Broadcast:** 140. **Flagship Station:** allsportsc-leveland.net. **PA Announcer:** Jasen Sokol. **Official Scorers:** Mike Mohner, Chuck Murr. **Stadium Name:** Classic Park. **Location:** From Ohio State Route 2 East, exit at Ohio 91, go left and the stadium is 1/4 mile north on your right; From

Ohio State Route 90 East, exit at Route 91, go right and the stadium in approximately five miles north on your right. **Standard Game Times:** Mon.-Sat., 6:30 pm (April-May), Mon.-Sat., 7:00 pm (May-Sept), Sun. 1:30 pm. **Visiting Club Hotel:** Red Roof Inn 4166 State Route 306, Willoughby, Ohio 44094. **Telephone:**(440)-946-9872.

LANSING LUGNUTS

Address: 505 E. Michigan Ave., Lansing, MI 48912.
Telephone: (517) 485-4500. **Fax:** (517) 485-4518.
E-Mail Address: info@lansinglugnuts.com. **Website:** www.lansinglugnuts.com.
Affiliation (first year): Toronto Blue Jays (2005). **Years in League:** 1996-

OWNERSHIP/MANAGEMENT
Operated By: Take Me Out to the Ballgame LLC. **Principal Owners:** Tom Dickson, Sherrie Myers.
President: Nick Grueser. **General Manager:** Tyler Parsons. **Executive Administrator:** Angela Sees. **Director of Finance:** Brianna Pfeil. **Director of Sales:** Ross Combs. **Group Sales Manager, Senior Manager of Sales and Ticket Services:** Eric Pionk. **Season Ticket Specialist:** Greg Kruger. **Director of Retail:** Matt Hicks. **Director of Stadium Operations:** Dennis Busse. **Senior VP of Operations Food & Beverage:** Patrick Day. **Food/Beverage Director:** John Thompson. **Assistant F&B Manager & Non-Profit Coordinator:** Paul Ciucci. **Director of Special Events & Meetings Manager:** Malinda Barr. **Special Events Coordinator:** Monica Edwards. **Production Manager:** Ryan LeFevre. **Manager of Fan Engagement:** Stephanie Smigiel. **Corporate Partnerships Manager:** Ashley Loudan. **Head Grounds Manager:** Zach Severns.

FIELD STAFF
Manager: Dallas McPherson. **Hitting Coach:** Logan Bone. **Pitching Coach:** Antonio Caceres. **Position Player Coach:** Dave Pano. **Athletic Trainer:** Hiroki Yoshimoto. **Strength & Conditioning Coach:** Aaron Spano.

GAME INFORMATION
Radio Announcer: Jesse Goldberg-Strassler. **No. of Games Broadcast:** 140. **Flagship Station:** WQTX 92.1-FM. **PA Announcer:** Unavailable. **Official Scorer:** Timothy Zeko. **Stadium Name:** Cooley Law School Stadium. **Location:** I-96 East/West to US 496, exit at Larch Street, north of Larch, stadium on left. **Ticket Price Range:** $8-$36. **Visiting Club Hotel:** Radisson Hotel.

PEORIA CHIEFS

Address: 730 SW Jefferson, Peoria, IL 61605.
Telephone: (309) 680-4000. **Fax:** (309) 680-4080.
E-Mail Address: feedback@chiefsnet.com. **Website:** www.peoriachiefs.com.
Affiliation (first year): St. Louis Cardinals (2013). **Years in League:** 1983-

OWNERSHIP/MANAGEMENT
Operated By: Peoria Chiefs Community Baseball Club LLC.
General Manager: Jason Mott. **Manager, Box Office:** Ryan Sivori. **Director, Media/Baseball Ops/Community Engagement:** Nathan Baliva. **Director, Creative Services:** Allison Rhoades. **Director, Stadium Operations:** Patrick Walker. **Manager, Marketing & Game Presentation:** Stephen Brown. **Director, Ticket Sales:** Kate Voss. **Manager, Corporate Sales:** Kevin Kurowski. **Manager, Inside Sales:** John Phelps. **Account Executive:** Kyle Belback. **Inside Sales Representative:** Will Lyznicki, Connor Meehan, Terry Ward, Zach Kozoduj. **Head Groundskeeper:** Mike Reno.

FIELD STAFF
Manager: Erick Almonte. **Hitting Coach:** Russell Chambliss. **Pitching Coach:** Cale Johnson.
Athletic Trainer: Chris Walsh. **Strength & Conditioning Coach:** Kyle Richter.

GAME INFORMATION
Radio Announcer: Nathan Baliva. **No. of Games Broadcast:** 140. **Flagship Station:** www.peoriachiefs.com, Tune-In Radio. **PA Announcer:** Lee Hall, Rodney Knuppel, Dustin Fitzpatrick. **Official Scorers:** Bryan Moore, Brad Kupiec, Nathan Baliva. **Stadium Name:** Dozer Park. **Location:** From South/East, I-74 to exit 93 (Jefferson St), continue one mile, stadium is one block on left; From North/West, I-74 to Glen Oak Exit, turn right on Glendale, which turns into Kumpf Blvd, turn right on Jefferson, stadium on left. **Standard Game Times:** Mon.-Sat., 7 pm, Sun., 6:30 pm (April-May, after Aug. 26), Sat., 6:30 pm, Sun. 2 p.m. **Ticket Price Range:** $7-14. **Visiting Club Hotel:** Quality Inn & Suites, 4112 Brandywine Dr, Peoria, IL, 61614. **Telephone:** (309) 685-2556.

QUAD CITIES RIVER BANDITS

Address: 209 S. Gaines St., Davenport, IA 52802.
Telephone: (563) 324-3000. **Fax:** (563) 324-3109.
E-Mail Address: bandit@riverbandits.com. **Website:** www.riverbandits.com.
Affiliation (first year): Houston Astros (2013). **Years in League:** 1960-

OWNERSHIP/MANAGEMENT

Operated by: Main Street Iowa LLC, Dave Heller, Roby Smith. **General Manager:** Jacqueline Holm. **VP, Sales:** Shawn Brown. **VP, Ticketing:** Mike Candela. **Assistant GM, Special Events:** Amy Richey. **Director, Special Events:** Deanna Foster, **Director, Amusements:** Bill Duncan. **Manager, Baseball Finance:** Steve Hawk. **Director, Community Relations:** Kaylee Golden. **Manager, Promotions:** Allie Bettenhausen. **Director, Media Relations:** Jason Kempf. **Manager, Stadium Operations:** Seth Reeve. **Manager, Creative Services and Production:** Evan Wiseman. **Director, Merchandise:** Darren Pitra. **Manager, First Impressions:** Rae Mittan. **Manager, Box Office:** Julia McNeil. **Head Groundskeeper:** Andrew Marking. **Director, Food/Beverage:** Jonny Williams. **Account Executive, Group Sales:** Amanda Adee. **Account Executive, Group Sales:** Aaron Wilson. **Account Executive, Group Sales:** John Barrett.

FIELD STAFF

Manager: Ray Hernandez. **Hitting Coach:** Rafael Pena. **Pitching Coach:** Erick Abreu.

GAME INFORMATION

Radio Announcer: Jason Kempf. **No. of Games Broadcast:** 140. **Flagship Station:** 1170-AM KBOB. **PA Announcer:** Unavailable. **Official Scorer:** Unavailable. **Stadium Name:** Modern Woodmen Park. **Location:** From I-74, take Grant Street exit left, west onto River Drive, left on South Gaines Street; from I-80, take Brady Street exit south, right on River Drive, left on S. Gaines Street. **Standard Game Times:** Mon.-Sat., 6:35 pm; Sun. 1:15 pm (April and Sept.), Sun. 5:15 pm (May-August). **Ticket Price Range:** $5-13. **Visiting Club Hotel:** Radisson Quad City Plaza Hotel,111 E. 2nd St, Davenport, IA 52801. **Telephone:** (563) 322-2200.

SOUTH BEND CUBS

Office Address: 501 W. South St., South Bend, IN 46601.
Mailing Address: PO Box 4218, South Bend, IN 46634.
Telephone: (574) 235-9988. **Fax:** (574) 235-9950.
E-Mail Address: cubs@southbendcubs.com. **Website:** www.southbendcubs.com
Affiliation (first year): Chicago Cubs (2015). **Years in League:** 1988-

OWNERSHIP/MANAGEMENT

Owner: Andrew Berlin.
President: Joe Hart. **Vice President/General Manager, Business Development:** Nick Brown. **Assistant GM, Tickets:** Andy Beuster. **Director, Ticket Operations and Customer Service:** Devon Hastings. **Senior Account Executive:** Mitch McKamey. **Account Executives:** Logan Lee, Brey Tyson. **Ticket Operations Assistant:** Collin Gray. **Director, Finance/Human Resources:** Cheryl Carlson. **Director, Food/Beverage:** Nick Barkley. **Catering/Business Manager:** Kelly Kalsch. **Executive Chief:** Josh Farmer. **Concession Manager:** Kyle Hoffmann. **Director, Media/Promotions:** Chris Hagstrom-Jones. **Production Assistant:** Kyle Arnett. **Promotions Assistant & Office Manager:** Sydney Ezell. **Merchandise Manager:** Mary-Lou Pallo. **Assistant GM, Operations:** Peter Argueta. **Stadium Operations Assistant:** Brandon Dunnam. **Head Groundskeeper:** T.J. Wohlever. **Groundskeeper:** Jeremy Harper.

FIELD STAFF

Manager: Buddy Bailey. **Hitting Coach:** Paul McAnulty. **Pitching Coach:** Jamie Vermilyea. **Bench Coach:** Pedro Gonzalez. **Athletic Trainer:** James Edwards. **Strength & Conditioning Coach:** Dallas Lopez.

GAME INFORMATION

Radio Announcers: Darin Pritchett, Brenden King. **Flagship Station:** 96.1 FM WSBT. **PA Announcer:** Gregg Sims, Jon Thompson. **Official Scorer:** Peter Yarbro. **Stadium Name:** Four Winds Field. **Location:** I-80/90 toll road to exit 77, take US 31/33 south to South Bend to downtown (Main Street), to Western Ave., right on Western, left on Taylor. **Standard Game Times:** Mon.-Thu., Sat., 7:05 pm, Fri. 7:35 pm, Sun. 2:05 pm. **Ticket Price Range:** Advance $11-13, Day of Game $12-14. **Visiting Club Hotel:** Aloft South Bend. **Hotel Telephone:** (574) 288-8000.

WEST MICHIGAN WHITECAPS

Office Address: 4500 West River Dr., Comstock Park, MI 49321. **Mailing Address:** PO Box 428, Comstock Park, MI 49321. **Telephone:** (616) 784-4131. **Fax:** (616) 784-4911. **E-Mail Address:** playball@whitecapsbaseball.com. **Website:** www.whitecapsbaseball.com. **Affiliation (first year):** Detroit Tigers (1997). **Years in League:** 1994-

OWNERSHIP/MANAGEMENT

Operated By: Whitecaps Professional Baseball Corp. **Principal Owners:** Denny Baxter, Lew Chamberlin. **President:** Steve McCarthy. **Vice President:** Jim Jarecki. **Vice President, Sales:** TBD. **Facility Events Manager:** Mike Klint. **Operations Manager:** TBD. **Director, Food/Beverage:** Matt Timon. **Community Relations Coordinator:** Jessica Muzevuca. **Director, Marketing/Media:** Mickey Graham. **Promotions Manager:** Matt Hoffman. **Creative and Digitial Design Manager:** Elaine Cunningham. **Box Office Manager:** Shaun Pynnonen. **Groundskeeper:** Mitch Hooten. **Facility Maintenance Manager:** Jason Ross. **Director, Ticket Sales:** Chad Sayen.

FIELD STAFF

Manager: Lance Parrish. **Hitting Coach:** John Vander Wal. **Pitching Coach:** Willie Blair. **Bench Coach:** Ed Dennis. **Athletic Trainer:** Chris Vick.

GAME INFORMATION

Radio Announcers: Dan Hasty. **No. of Games Broadcast:** 140. **Flagship Station:** WBBL 107.3-FM. **PA Announcers:** Mike Newell, Bob Wells. **Official Scorers:** Mike Dean, Don Thomas. **Stadium Name:** Fifth Third Ballpark. **Location:** US 131 North from Grand Rapids to exit 91 (West River Drive). **Ticket Price Range:** $8-18. **Visiting Club Hotel:** Crowne Plaza 5700 28th Street SE Grand Rapids, MI 49546. **Telephone:** (616) 957-1770.

WISCONSIN TIMBER RATTLERS

Office Address: 2400 N. Casaloma Dr., Appleton, WI 54913.
Mailing Address: PO Box 7464, Appleton, WI 54912.
Telephone: (920) 733-4152. **Fax:** (920) 733-8032.
E-Mail Address: info@timberrattlers.com. **Website:** www.timberrattlers.com.
Affiliation (first year): Milwaukee Brewers (2009). **Years in League:** 1962-

OWNERSHIP/MANAGEMENT

Operated By: Appleton Baseball Club, Inc.
Chairman: Jim Britt. **President/General Manager:** Rob Zerjav. **Vice President/Assistant GM:** Aaron Hahn. **Director, Marketing/ Assistant GM:** Hilary Bauer. **Director, Food/Beverage:** Ryan Grossman. **Director, Stadium Operations/ Security:** Ron Kaiser. **Director, Community Relations:** Dayna Baitinger. **Director, Corporate Partnerships:** Ryan Cunniff. **Director of Grounds:** Kyle Slaton. **Director, Tickets:** Sam Connell. **Director, Merchandise:** Jay Gruszonski. **Director, Media Relations:** Chris Mehring. **Group Sales:** Kyle Fargen, Jared Jirschele. **Corporate Marketing Manager:** Seth Merrill. **Manager, Ticket Operations & Season Sales:** Lance Kays. **Controller:** Eric Dresang. **Director, Catering & Events:** Terry Lagarde. **Wedding Sales & Events Manager:** Kim McGownd. **Executive Chef:** Charles Behrmann. **Executive Sous Chef:** Chris Gosz. **Assistant, Food/Beverage Director:** Chris Prentice. **Stadium Operations Manager:** Justin Peterson. **Creative Director:** Ann Lindeman. **Entertainment Coordinator:** Jacob Jirschele. **Graphic Designer:** Nick Guenther. **Accounting/Human Resources Manager:** TBA. **Production Manager:** Jerred Drake. **Clubhouse Manager:** Mason Kubly. **Office Manager:** Mary Robinson.

FIELD STAFF

Manager: Matt Erickson. **Hitting Coach:** Dave Joppie. **Pitching Coach:** Jim Henderson. **Athletic Trainer:** Jeff Paxson.

GAME INFORMATION

Radio Announcer: Chris Mehring. **No. of Games Broadcast:** 140. **Flagship Station:** WNAM 1280-AM. **Television Announcer:** Chris Mehring (Radio Simulcast). **Television Affiliates:** WACY-TV. **No. of Games Broadcast:** Unavailable. **PA Announcer:** Joey D. **Official Scorer:** Jay Grusznski. **Stadium Name:** Neuroscience Group Field at Fox Cities Stadium. **Location:** Highway 41 to Highway 15 (00) exit, west to Casaloma Drive, left to stadium. **Standard Game Times:** Mon.- Fri., 6:35 pm (April-May), 7:05 pm (June-Sept.), Sat., 6:35 pm, Sun., 1:05 pm. **Ticket Price Range:** $9-31. **Visiting Club Hotel:** Country Inn & Suites; 355 N Fox River Dr, Appleton, WI 54913. **Telephone:** (920) 830-3240.

SOUTH ATLANTIC LEAGUE

EST. 1903
SOUTH ATLANTIC LEAGUE
"THE LEAGUE OF CHOICE"

Address: 2451 McMullen Booth Rd., Ste. 245, Clearwater, FL, 33759.
Telephone: (727) 538-4270. **Fax:** (727) 499-6853.
E-Mail Address: office@saloffice.com.
Website: www.southatlanticleague.com.
Years League Active: 1904-1964, 1979-
President/Secretary/Treasurer: Eric Krupa.
First Vice President: Chip Moore (Rome). **Second Vice President:** Craig Brown (Greenville).
Directors: Brian DeWine (Asheville), Jeff Eiseman (Augusta), Marvin Goldklang (Charleston),
Jason Freier (Columbia), Tom Volpe (Delmarva), Cooper Brantley (Greensboro), Craig Brown
(Greenville), Bruce Quinn (Hagerstown), Neil Leibman (Hickory), Andrew Sandler (Kannapolis),
Art Matin (Lakewood), Andy Shea (Lexington), Chip Moore (Rome), Tim Wilcox (West Virginia).
Division Structure: North—Delmarva, Greensboro, Hagerstown, Hickory, Kannapolis,
Lakewood, West Virginia. **South**—Asheville, Augusta, Charleston, Columbia, Greenville,

Eric Krupa

Lexington, Rome. **Regular Season:** 140 games (split schedule). **2019 Opening Date:** April 4.
Closing Date: September 2. **All-Star Game:** June 18 at West Virginia. **Playoff Format:** First-
half and second-half division winners meet in best-of-three series. Winners meet in best of five series for league champion-
ship. **Roster Limit:** 25 active. **Player Eligibility Rule:** No age limit. No more than two players and one player-coach
on active list may have more than five years of experience. **Brand of Baseball:** Rawlings. **Umpires:** Matthew Baldwin
(Annapolis, MD), Colin Baron (Wilmington, NC), Sean Cassidy (Arlington, VA), Nolan Early (Kennewick, WA), Benjamin
Fernandez (Cape Coral, FL), Thomas Fornarola (Webster, NY), Joshua Gilreath (Buford, GA), James Jean (Lake Park, FL),
Evin Johnson (Chesterfield, VA), Tanner Moore (Omaha, NE), Jen Pawol (Fort Myers, FL), Drew Saluga (Boardman, OH),
Christopher Silvestri (Chesterfield, VA), Justin Whiddon (Savannah, GA).

STADIUM INFORMATION

Club	Stadium	Opened	Dimensions LF	CF	RF	Capacity	2018 Att.
Asheville	McCormick Field	1992	326	373	297	4,000	170,389
Augusta	SRP Park	2018	330	395	318	4,782	255,155
Charleston	Joseph P. Riley, Jr. Ballpark	1997	306	386	336	5,800	305,040
Columbia	Segra Park	2016	319	400	330	7,501	251,586
Delmarva	Arthur W. Perdue Stadium	1996	309	402	309	5,200	201,329
Greensboro	First National Bank Field	2005	322	400	320	7,599	322,156
Greenville	Fluor Field at the West End	2006	310	400	302	5,000	313,507
Hagerstown	Municipal Stadium	1931	335	400	330	4,600	64,957
Hickory	L.P. Frans Stadium	1993	330	401	330	5,062	125,394
Kannapolis	Intimidators Stadium	1995	330	400	310	4,700	64,688
Lakewood	FirstEnergy Park	2001	325	400	325	6,588	293,413
Lexington	Whitaker Bank Ballpark	2001	320	401	318	6,033	281,134
Rome	State Mutual Stadium	2003	335	400	330	5,100	146,276
West Virginia	Appalachian Power Park	2005	330	400	320	4,300	112,273

ASHEVILLE TOURISTS

Address: McCormick Field, 30 Buchanan Place, Asheville, NC 28801.
Telephone: (828) 258-0428. **E-Mail Address:** info@theashevilletourists.com.
Website: www.theashevilletourists.com.
Affiliation (first year): Colorado Rockies (1994). **Years in League:** 1976-

OWNERSHIP/MANAGEMENT
Operated By: DeWine Seeds Silver Dollar Baseball, LLC. **President:** Brian DeWine. **General Manager:** Larry Hawkins.
Senior Sales Executive: Chris Smith. **Creative Marketing Manager:** Sam Fischer. **Director of Broadcasting/Media
Relations:** Doug Maurer. **Director of Ticket Operations:** Hannah Martin. **Executive Assistant:** Avery Page. **Group
Sales Associates:** Michael Grimes, Matthew Wisniewski, Robert Mantey, Samantha Cook. **Outside Sales Associate:** Bob
Jones. **Stadium Operations Director:** Eliot Williams. **Director of Food & Beverage:** Tyler Holt. **Head Groundskeeper:**
Matt Dierdorff. **Merchandise Manager:** Kali DeWine. **Publications:** Bill Ballew.

FIELD STAFF
Manager: Robinson Cancel. **Hitting Coach:** Norberto "Paco" Martin. **Pitching Coach:** Mark Brewer.
Development Supervisor: Randy Ingle. **Athletic Trainer:** Kelsey Branstetter.

GAME INFORMATION
Radio Announcer: Doug Maurer. **No. of Games Broadcast:** 140. **Flagship Station:** Asheville Tourists Online Radio
Network. **PA Announcer:** Tim Lolley. **Official Scorer:** Steven Grady. **Stadium Name:** McCormick Field. **Location:** I-240
to Charlotte Street South exit, south one mile on Charlotte, left on McCormick Place. **Ticket Price Range:** $6.50-13.50.
Visiting Club Hotel: Unavailable. **Telephone:** Unavailable.

AUGUSTA GREENJACKETS

Office Address: 187 Railroad Ave. North Augusta, SC 29841.
Mailing Address: 187 Railroad Ave. North Augusta, SC 29841.
Telephone: (803) 349-9467. **Fax:** (803) 349-9434.
E-Mail Address: info@greenjacketsbaseball.com. **Website:** www.greenjacketsbaseball.com.
Affiliation (first year): San Francisco Giants (2005). **Years in League:** 1988-

OWNERSHIP/MANAGEMENT

Ownership Group: AGON Sports & Entertainment. **Owner:** Chris Schoen.
President: Jeff Eiseman. **Vice President:** Tom Denlinger. **General Manager:** Brandon Greene. **Manager, Ticket Sales:** Matt Szczupakowski. **Accounting:** Debbie Brown. **Stadium Operations Director:** Billy Nowak. **Marketing & Community Relations Manager:** Shannon Mitchell. **Manager, Corporate Partnerships:** Greg Dietz. **Assistant Ticket Sales Manager:** Troy Pakusch. **Manager, Group Sales:** Yari Natal. **Group Sales Account Executive:** James Mullins. **Ticket Operations Manager:** Tyler Henderson. **Retail Sales Manager:** Chelsea Galbraith. **Food & Beverage Director:** Joshua Shea. **Food & Beverage Supervisor:** David Hutto. **Groundskeeper:** Darrell Lemmer.

FIELD STAFF

Manager: Carlos Valderrama. **Hitting Coach:** Jake Fox. **Pitching Coach:** Clay Rapada. **Fundamentals Coach:** Willie Romero.

GAME INFORMATION

PA Announcer: Unavailable. **Stadium Name:** SRP Park. **Standard Game Times:** Mon.-Fri., 7:05 pm, Sat., 6:05 pm, Sun., 2:05 pm through All Star Break, Sun., 5:05 pm after All Star Break. **Ticket Price Range:** $9-$28. **Visiting Club Hotel:** Comfort Suites, 2911 Riverwest Dr, Augusta, GA. **Telephone:** (706) 434-2540.

CHARLESTON RIVERDOGS

Office Address: 360 Fishburne St, Charleston, SC 29403.
Mailing Address: PO Box 20849, Charleston, SC 29403.
Telephone: (843) 723-7241. **Fax:** (843) 723-2641.
E-Mail Address: admin@riverdogs.com. **Website:** www.riverdogs.com.
Affiliation (first year): New York Yankees (2005). **Years in League:** 1973-78, 1980-

OWNERSHIP/MANAGEMENT

Operated by: The Goldklang Group/South Carolina Baseball Club LP.
Chairman: Marv Goldklang. **President:** Jeff Goldklang. **Club President/General Manager:** Dave Echols. **President Emeritus:** Mike Veeck. **Director, Fun:** Bill Murray. **Co-Owners:** Peter Freund, Gene Budig, Al Phillips. **VP, Corporate Sales:** Andy Lange. **Assistant GM:** Ben Abzug. **Director of Client Services:** Melissa Azevedo. **Director, Promotions:** Nate Kurant. **Director, Broadcasting/Media Relations:** Matt Dean. **Director, Food/Beverage:** Jesse White. **Director, Community Relations:** Walter Nolan-Cohn. **Director, Ticket Sales:** Garret Randle. **Director, Operations:** Josh Otterline. **Director, Special Events:** Lisa Dingman. **Director, Video Production:** Jeremy Schrank. **Business Manager:** Dale Stickney. **Box Office Manager:** Morgan Powell. **Marketing & Creative Services Manager:** Courtney Lewis. **Special Events Manager:** Kayli Varner. **Riley Park Club Events Manager:** Bailey Linderman. **Food/Beverage Manager:** Kristina Wilkins. **Hospitality Manager:** Sara Carpenter. **Operations Manager:** Jordan Wiley. **Sales Representative:** Daniel Armas, Claudia Davis, Mike Ryan, Serg Saradjian, Jake Terrell. **Office Manager:** Cynthia Linhart. **Head Groundskeeper:** Kevin Coyne. **Clubhouse Manager:** Matt Seletsky.

FIELD STAFF

Manager: Julio Mosquera. **Hitting Coach:** Greg Colbrunn. **Pitching Coach:** Gabe Luckert. **Defensive Coaches:** Travis Chapman, Francisco Leandro. **Athletic Trainer:** Michael Sole. **Strength & Conditioning Coach:** Danny Russo.

GAME INFORMATION

Radio Announcer: Matt Dean. **No. of Games Broadcast:** 140. **Flagship Station:** WTMA 1250-AM. **PA Announcer:** Ken Carrington. **Official Scorer:** Mike Hoffman. **Stadium Name:** Joseph P. Riley, Jr. **Location:** 360 Fishburne St, Charleston, SC 29403, From US 17, take Lockwood Dr. North, right on Fishburne St. **Standard Game Times:** Mon.-Fri., 7:05pm, Sat. 6:05 pm, Sun. 5:05 pm. **Ticket Price Range:** $8-20. **Visiting Club Hotel:** Aloft Charleston Airport.

COLUMBIA FIREFLIES

Office Address: 1640 Freed Street, Columbia, SC 29201.
Mailing Address: 1640 Freed Street, Columbia, SC 29201.
Telephone: (803) 726-4487. **Fax:** (803) 726-3126.
E-Mail Address: info@columbiafireflies.com. **Website:** www.columbiafireflies.com.
Affiliation (first year): New York Mets (2016). **Years in League:** 2016-

OWNERSHIP/MANAGEMENT

Operated By: Columbia Fireflies Baseball, LLC.
President: John Katz. **Executive Vice President:** Brad Shank. **Senior Vice President/Food & Beverage:** Scott Burton. **Vice President, Marketing & Public Relations:** Abby Naas. **Director of Corporate Partnerships:** Blake Buchanan. **Director, Accounting & Baseball Operations:** Jonathan Mercier. **Office Manager:** Katie Maroney. **Director, Ticketing:** Joe Shepard. **Director, Group Sales:** Juan Encarnacion. **Assistant Director, Ticketing/Reading Program Manager:** Kyle Williamson. **Senior Corporate Account Manager:** Jeff Berger, Scott Rhodes. **Ticket Account Manager:** Nick Spano, Kenny Anderson, Ashley Studebaker. **Graphics Manager:** Marcus Walker. **New Media Engagement & Promotions Manager:** Kyle Spinner. **Video Production Manager:** Jared Law. **Community Engagement Manager:** McKenzie Brown. **Promotions/Client Services Manager:** Ashlie DeCarlo. **Merchandise Manager:** Alex Watson. **Executive Chef:** Bobby Hunter. **Catering Manager:** Terry Stevenson. **Food & Beverage Manager:** Michael Bolt. **Luxury Suite & Club Level Manager:** Lexie Brensinger. **Director of Stadium Operations:** Anthony Altamura. **Stadium Operations Manager:** Matt Lundquist. **Head Groundskeeper:** Drew Tice.

FIELD STAFF

Manager: Pedro Lopez. **Hitting Coach:** Luis Rivera. **Pitching Coach:** Royce Ring. **Bench Coach:** Gilbert Gomez. **Assistant Coach:** Derek Swartout-Mosher. **Athletic Trainer:** Daichi Arima. **Strength & Conditioning Coach:** Sam Nickelsen.

GAME INFORMATION

Radio Announcer: Unavailable. **No. of Games Broadcast:** 140. **Flagship Station:** Unavailable. **PA Announcer:** Bryan Vacchio. **Official Scorer:** Unavailable. **Stadium Name:** Segra Park. **Location:** 1640 Freed Street, Columbia, SC 29201. **Standard Game Times:** Mon.-Sat., 7:05pm, Sun. 2:05 pm, 5:05pm. **Ticket Price Range:** $5-$10. **Visiting Club Hotel:** Hyatt Place Columbia/Harbison, 1130 Kinley Road, Irmo, SC 29063.

DELMARVA SHOREBIRDS

Office Address: 6400 Hobbs Rd, Salisbury, MD 21804.
Mailing Address: PO Box 1557, Salisbury, MD 21802.
Telephone: (410) 219-3112. **Fax:** (410) 219-9164.
E-Mail Address: info@theshorebirds.com. **Website:** www.theshorebirds.com.
Affiliation: Baltimore Orioles (1997). **Years in League:** 1996-

OWNERSHIP/MANAGEMENT

Operated By: 7th Inning Stretch, LP. **Owner:** Tom Volpe. **President:** Pat Filippone. **General Manager:** Chris Bitters. **Assistant GM:** Jimmy Sweet. **Assistant GM of Marketing:** Eric Sichau. **Director, Business Development:** Andrew Bryda. **Director, Tickets:** Brandon Harms. **Director, Ticket Operations:** Benjamin Posner. **Ticket Sales Account Executive:** Kevin Odell. **Ticket Sales Account Executive:** Joseph DeLucia. **Ticket Sales Account Executive:** Chip Woytowitz. **Community Relations Manager:** Kathy Damato. **Director, Stadium Operations:** Unavailable. **Head Groundskeeper:** Tim Young. **Director, Broadcasting:** Will DeBoer. **Communication Services Coordinator:** Bobby Coon. **Accounting Manager:** Matt Figard. **Merchandise & Office Manager:** Audrey Vane.

FIELD STAFF

Manager: Kyle Moore. **Hitting Coach:** Unavailable. **Pitching Coach:** Justin Ramsey.

GAME INFORMATION

Radio Announcer: Will DeBoer. **No. of Games Broadcast:** 140. **Flagship Station:** Fox Sports 960 WTGM. **PA Announcer:** Tyler Horton. **Stadium Name:** Arthur W. Perdue Stadium. **Location:** From US 50 East, right on Hobbs Rd; From US 50 West, left on Hobbs Road. **Standard Game Time:** 7:05 pm. **Ticket Price Range:** $8-13. **Visiting Club Hotel:** Sleep Inn, 406 Punkin Court, Salisbury, MD 21804. **Telephone:** (410) 572-5516.

GREENSBORO GRASSHOPPERS

Address: 408 Bellemeade St, Greensboro, NC 27401.
Telephone: (336) 268-2255. **Fax:** (336) 273-7350.
E-Mail Address: info@gsohoppers.com. **Website:** www.gsohoppers.com.
Affiliation (first year): Pittsburgh Pirates (2019) **Years in League:** 1979-

OWNERSHIP/MANAGEMENT

Operated By: Greensboro Baseball LLC. **Principal Owners:** Cooper Brantley, Wes Elingburg, Len White.
President/General Manager: Donald Moore. **Vice President, Baseball Operations:** Katie Dannemiller. **Assistant General Manager:** Tim Vangel. **Chief Financial Officer:** Brad Falkiewicz. **Director of Sales:** Todd Olson. **Director, Ticket/Box Office Operations:** Andy Webb. **Director, Production/Partnership Services:** Josh Feldman. **Director, Creative Services:** Amanda Williams. **Coordinator, Promotions/Community Relations:** Mary DeFriest. **Manager, Video Production:** Jak Kerley. **Director, Merchandise:** Corey Brothers. **Sales Associates:** Erich Dietz, Stephen Johnson. **Director, Stadium Operations:** Chris Naiberk. **Assistant Groundskeeper:** Anthony Alejo.

FIELD STAFF

Manager: Miguel Perez. **Hitting Coach:** Chris Petersen. **Pitching Coach:** Stan Kyles. **Bench Coach:** Unavailable.
Athletic Trainer: Jorge Islas. **Strength & Conditioning Coach:** Jim Seratt.

GAME INFORMATION

Radio Announcer: Andy Durham. **No. of Games Broadcast:** 140. **Flagship Station:** WPET 950-AM. **PA Announcer:** Unavailable. **Official Scorer:** Wesley Gullet. **Stadium Name:** First National Bank Field. **Location:** From I-85, take Highway 220 South (exit 36) to Coliseum Blvd, continue on Edgeworth Street, ballpark at corner of Edgeworth and Bellemeade Streets. **Standard Game Times:** Mon.-Sat., 7 pm, Sun., 2 pm (April, May, June), Sun., 4 pm (July, Aug., Sept.) **Ticket Price Range:** $7-11. **Visiting Club Hotel:** Days Inn — 6102 Landmark Center Boulevard, Greensboro, NC 27407. **Telephone:** (336) 553-2763.

GREENVILLE DRIVE

Address: 935 South Main St, Suite 202, Greenville, SC 29601
Telephone: (864) 240-4500. **E-Mail Address:** info@greenvilledrive.com.
Website: www.greenvilledrive.com.
Affiliation (first year): Boston Red Sox (2005). **Years in League:** 2005-

OWNERSHIP/MANAGEMENT

Operated By: Greenville Drive, LLC. **Owner/President:** Craig Brown. **General Manager:** Eric Jarinko.
VP, Sales: Thomas Berryhill. **VP, Marketing:** Jeff Brown. **VP, Operations/Grounds:** Greg Burgess. **VP, Finance:** Jordan Smith. **Director, Sponsorships & Community Engagement:** Katie Batista. **Director, Inside Sales:** Ned Kennedy. **Director, Food & Beverage:** Mike Agostino. **Director, Game Entertainment:** Alex Guest. **Director, Operations:** Timmy Hinds. **Director, Ticket Operations:** Patrick Innes. **Director, West End Events:** Beth Rusch. **Media Relations Manager:** Cameron White. **Design Services Managers:** Lance Fowler, Davis Simpson. **Sponsor Services & Activations Manager:** Matthew Tezza. **Sponsorship & Community Events Manager:** Melissa Welch. **Special Events Coordinator:** Kristin Kipper. **Senior Account Executives:** Micah Gold, Molly Mains. **Account Executives:** Houghton Flanagan, Jayson Osteen. **Inside Sales Representatives:** Tyler Melson, Toby Sandblom. **Assistant Director, Food and Beverage:** Rebekah Miller. **Food and Beverage Manager:** Tyler Kenney. **Premium Services Manager:** Elise Parish. **Clubhouse Manager:** Bob Wagner. **Assistant Groundskeeper:** Zack Pagans. **Accounting Manager:** Adam Baird. **Business & Team Operations Manager:** Amanda Medlin. **Office Manager:** Allison Roedell.

FIELD STAFF

Manager: Iggy Suarez. **Hitting Coach:** Nelson Paulino. **Pitching Coach:** Bob Kipper.

GAME INFORMATION

Radio Announcer: Ed Jenson. **No. of Games Broadcast:** Home-70. **Flagship Station:** www.greenvilledrive.com. **PA Announcer:** Chuck Hussion. **Official Scorers:** Jordan Caskey, Scott Keeler, Chandler Simpson. **Stadium Name:** Fluor Field at the West End. **Location:** From south, I-85N to exit 42 toward downtown Greenville, turn left onto Augusta Road, stadium is two miles on the left; From north, I-85S to I-385 toward Greenville, turn left onto Church St., turn right onto University Ridge. **Standard Game Times:** Mon.-Sat., 7:05 pm, Sun., 3:05 pm. **Ticket Price Range:** $7-12. **Visiting Club Hotel:** Wingate by Wyndham, Greenville Airport, 33 Beacon Drive, Greenville, SC 29615. **Telephone:** (864) 288-1200.

HAGERSTOWN SUNS

HAGERSTOWN SUNS

Address: 274 E Memorial Blvd, Hagerstown, MD 21740.
Telephone: (301) 791-6266. **Fax:** (301) 791-6066.
E-Mail Address: info@hagerstownsuns.com. **Website:** www.hagerstownsuns.com.
Affiliation (first year): Washington Nationals (2007). **Years in League:** 1993-

OWNERSHIP/MANAGEMENT
Principal Owner/Operated by: Hagerstown Baseball LLC.
President: Bruce Quinn. **General Manager:** Travis Painter. **Assistant GM/Head Groudnskeeper:** Brian Saddler. **Director, Media Relations:** John Kocsis Jr. **F&B Operations:** Center Plate. **Manager, Promotions/Game Day Production:** Tom Burtman. **Manager, Box Office/Ticket Operations:** Unavailable. **Sales Executive:** Cory Chatfield, Ross Jones. **Assistant Head Groundskeeper:** Mark Rabideau.

FIELD STAFF
Manager: Patrick Anderson. **Hitting Coach:** Amaury Garcia. **Pitching Coach:** Mack Jenkins. **Trainer:** Darren Yoos.

GAME INFORMATION
Radio Announcer: John Kocsis Jr. **No. of Games Broadcast:** Home-70. **Flagship Station:** Unavailable. **PA Announcer:** Johnny Castle. **Official Scorer:** Will Kauffman. **Stadium Name:** Municipal Stadium. **Location:** Exit 32B (US 40 West) on I-70 West, left at Eastern Boulevard; Exit 6A (US 40 East) on I-81, right at Eastern Boulevard. **Standard Game Times:** Mon.-Fri., 7:05 pm (April 6:05 pm), Sat., 6:05 pm (April 4:05 pm), Sun. 2:05 pm. **Ticket Price Range:** $10-13.

HICKORY CRAWDADS

Office Address: 2500 Clement Blvd. NW, Hickory, NC 28601.
Mailing Address: PO Box 1268, Hickory, NC 28603.
Telephone: (828) 322-3000. **E-Mail Address:** crawdad@hickorycrawdads.com.
Website: www.hickorycrawdads.com.
Affiliation (first year): Texas Rangers (2009). **Years in League:** 1952, 1960, 1993-

OWNERSHIP/MANAGEMENT
Operated by: Hickory Baseball Inc. **Principal Owners:** Texas Rangers.
President: Neil Leibman. **General Manager:** Mark Seaman. **Assistant GM:** Douglas Locascio. **Business Manager:** Donna White. **Director of Promotions and Community Relations:** Chris Dillon. **Director of Creative Services and Media Relations:** Ashley Salinas. **Operations Manager:** Skip Moser. **Head Groundskeeper:** Andrew Tallent. **Group Sales Executives:** Daniel Barkley, John Ryan. **General Manager of Food and Beverage:** Shawn Sullivan.

FIELD STAFF
Manager: Matt Hagen. **Hitting Coach:** Jared Goedert. **Pitching Coach:** Jose Jaimes. **Bench Coach:** Josh Johnson. **Athletic Trainer:** Bronson Santillan.

GAME INFORMATION
PA Announcers: Jason Savage, Rob Eastwood. **Official Scorers:** Mark Parker. **Stadium Name:** LP Frans Stadium. **Location:** I-40 to exit 123 (Lenoir North), 321 North to Clement Blvd, left for 1/2 mile. **Standard Game Times:** First half—Mon.-Wed. & Sat., 6:30 pm, Thur. & Fri., 7 pm, Sun., 3 pm; Second half—Mon.-Sat., 7 pm, Sun., 5 pm. **Visiting Club Hotel:** Crowne Plaza, 1385 Lenior-Rhyne Boulevard SE, Hickory, NC 28602. **Telephone:** (828) 323-1000.

KANNAPOLIS INTIMIDATORS

Office Address: 2888 Moose Road, Kannapolis, NC 28083.
Mailing Address: PO Box 64, Kannapolis, NC 28082.
Telephone: (704) 932-3267. **Fax:** (704) 938-7040.
E-Mail Address: info@intimidatorsbaseball.com.
Website: www.intimidatorsbaseball.com.
Affiliation (first year): Chicago White Sox (2001). **Years in League:** 1995-

OWNERSHIP/MANAGEMENT
Operated by: Temerity Baseball Club, LLC.
Assistant GM: Vince Marcucci. **Finance Manager:** Paige Tamaro. **Group Sales Executive:** Kyle Teegardin. **Group Sales Executive:** Rachel Kilinski. **Director of Marketing & Community Relations:** Blair Jewell. **Broadcasting & Baseball Ops Executive:** Trevor Wilt. **Graphics & Digital Media Coordinator:** Caitlyn Gardner. **Director of Ballpark and Ticket Operations:** Mike Wolf. **Head Groundskeeper:** Billy Ball. **Assistant Groundskeeper:** Brian Mroz.

FIELD STAFF
Manager: Ryan Newman. **Hitting Coach:** Cole Armstong. **Pitching Coach:** Jose Bautista. **Athletic Trainer:** Joe Geck. **Strength & Conditioning Coach:** Goldy Simmons.

GAME INFORMATION

Radio Announcer: Trevor Wilt. **No. of Games Broadcast:** 70. **Flagship Station:** www.intimidatorsbaseball.com. **PA Announcer:** Bill Jones. **Official Scorer:** Brent Stastny. **Stadium Name:** Intimidators Stadium. **Location:** Exit 63 on I-85, west on Lane Street to Stadium Drive. **Standard Game Times:** Mon.-Sat., 7:00 pm, Sun., 3:00 pm (April-June), 5:00 pm (July-Sept.). **Ticket Price Range:** $6-$10. **Visiting Club Hotel:** Uptown Suites, 7850 Commons Park Cir NW, Concord, NC 28027.

LAKEWOOD BLUECLAWS

Address: 2 Stadium Way, Lakewood, NJ 08701.
Telephone: (732) 901-7000. **Fax:** (732) 901-3967.
E-Mail Address: info@blueclaws.com. **Website:** www.blueclaws.com
Affiliation (first year): Philadelphia Phillies (2001). **Years in League:** 2001-

OWNERSHIP/MANAGEMENT

Managing Partner/Shore Town Baseball: Art Matin. **President/General Manager:** Joe Ricciutti. **Assistant General Manager:** Kevin Fenstermacher. **Sr. VP, Ticket Sales:** Bob McLane. **VP, Ticket Sales:** Jim McNamara. **VP, Commnity Relations:** Jim DeAngelis. **VP, Finance:** Don Rodgers. **Sr. Director, Sponsorship:** Rob Vota. **Director of Communications:** Greg Giombarrese. **Director of Production:** Kirsten Boye. **Director, Marketing & Promotions:** Jamie Stone. **Director, Food & Beverage:** Brian Genis. **Director, Partnership Services:** Zack Nicol. **Director, Merchandise:** Ben Cecil. **Director, Season Tickets:** Rob McGillick. **Corporate Sales Manager:** Anthony Arena, Mike Kasel. **Senior Sales Executive:** Craig Ebinger. **Ticket Sales Manager:** Juwan Jackson, Michael Troy. **Ticket Memberships Manager:** Joel Podos, Elias Riginos. **Group Sales Executive:** Brian O'Shaughnessy, Dave McKurth. **Ticket Operations Manager:** Garrett Herr. **Food & Beverage Manager:** Kathryn Raso. **Events & Operations Manager:** Steve Woloshin, Kevin McNellis. **Accounting Manager:** Annette Clark. **Ticket Operations Coordinator:** Tyler Odle. **Partnership Services Coordinator:** Arielle Roth. **Heads Groundskeeper:** Mike Morvay. **Front Office Manager:** JoAnne Bell.

FIELD STAFF

Manager: Unavailable. **Hitting Coach:** Christian Marrero. **Pitching Coach:** Matt Hockenberry.

GAME INFORMATION

Radio Announcers: Greg Giombarrese. **No. of Games Broadcast:** 140. **Flagship Station:** WOBM 1160-AM. **PA Announcers:** Kevin Clark. **Official Scorers:** Joe Bellina. **Stadium Name:** FirstEnergy Park. **Location:** Route 70 to New Hampshire Avenue, North on New Hampshire for 2.5 miles to ballpark. **Standard Game Times:** Mon.-Sat., 6:35 pm (April-May), 7:05 pm (June-Sept.), Sun., 1:05 pm. **Ticket Price Range:** $7-15. **Visiting Team Hotel:** Days Hotel, Toms River, 290 NJ-37, Toms River, NJ 08753. **Telephone:** 732-244-4000.

LEXINGTON LEGENDS

Address: 207 Legends Lane, Lexington, KY 40505.
Telephone: (859) 252-4487. **Fax:** (859) 252-0747.
E-Mail Address: webmaster@lexingtonlegends.com.
Website: www.lexingtonlegends.com.
Affiliation (first year): Kansas City Royals (2013). **Years in League:** 2001-

OWNERSHIP/MANAGEMENT

Operated By: STANDS LLC. **Principal:** Susan Martinelli.
President/CEO: Andy Shea. **Executive Vice President:** Gary Durbin. **Vice President, Operations:** Shannon Kidd. **Vice President, Business Development:** Sarah Bosso. **Director, Stadium Operations/Manager, Human Resources:** Shannon Kidd. **Accounting and Business Operations Manager:** Leslie Taylor. **Special Projects Manager:** Anne Mapson. **Director, Corporate Sales:** Jesse Scaglion. **Director of Ticket Sales:** Mike Allison. **Ticket Sales Manager:** Kyle Hargrove. **Marketing Specialist:** Jillian Waitkus. **Director, Broadcasting/Media Relations:** Emma Tiedemann. **Director of Group Sales:** Mike Allison. **Senior Account Executive:** Ron Borkowski. **Head Groundskeeper:** Johnny Youngblood. **Facility Specialist:** Steve Moore.

FIELD STAFF

Manager: Brooks Conrad. **Hitting Coach:** Jesus Azuaje. **Pitching Coach:** Mitch Stetter. **Bench Coach:** Glenn Hubbard. **Athletic Trainer:** Saburo Hagihara.

GAME INFORMATION

Radio Announcer: Emma Tiedemann. **No. of Games Broadcast:** 140. **Flagship Station:** WLXG 1300-AM. **PA Announcer:** Unavailable. **Official Scorer:** Joseph Hardiman. **Stadium Name:** Whitaker Bank Ballpark. **Location:** From I-64/75, take exit 113, right onto North Broadway toward downtown Lexington for 1.2 miles, past New Circle Road (Highway 4), right into stadium, located adjacent to Northland Shopping Center. **Standard Game Times:** Mon., Tues., Thurs., Fri., 7:05 pm, Wed., 12:35 pm, Sat., 6:35 pm. Sun., 2:05 pm. **Ticket Price Range:** $5-$25. **Visiting Club Hotel:** Clarion Hotel Conference Center South, 5532 Athens-Boonesboro Rd, Lexington, KY 40509. **Phone:** (859) 263-5241.

ROME BRAVES

Office Address: State Mutual Stadium, 755 Braves Blvd, Rome, GA 30161.
Mailing Address: PO Box 1915, Rome, GA 30162-1915.
Telephone: (706) 378-5100. **Fax:** (706) 368-6525.
E-Mail Address: rome.braves@braves.com. **Website:** www.romebraves.com.
Affiliation (first year): Atlanta Braves (2003). **Years in League:** 2003-

OWNERSHIP MANAGEMENT
Operated By: Atlanta National League Baseball Club Inc. **VP and General Manager:** Jim Bishop. **Assistant General Manager:** Jim Jones. **Director, Stadium Operations:** Morgan McPherson. **Ticket Manager:** Jalaam Robinson. **Director of Group Sales:** Jeff Fletcher. **Community Relations and Special Events:** Lori George. **Director, Business Operations:** Miranda Black. **Digital Manager:** Drew Gibby. **Account Representative:** Katie Aspin. **Account Representative:** Matt Pinson. **Director, Head Groundskeeper:** Joseph Brooks. **Retail Manager:** Starla Roden. **Warehouse Operations Manager:** Tyler Stinson. **Food and Beverage Director:** Jonathan Jackson. **Culinary Director:** Owen Reppert.

FIELD STAFF
Manager: Matt Tuiasosopo. **Hitting Coach:** Bobby Moore. **Pitching Coach:** Kanekoa Texeira.
Athletic Trainer: Eric Hrycko.

GAME INFORMATION
Radio Announcer: Kevin Karel. **No. of Games Broadcast:** 140. **Flagship Station:** 99.5 FM The Jock, RomeBraves.com (home games). **PA Announcer:** Jeff McDermott. **Official Scorers:** Jim O'Hara, Lyndon Huckaby. **Stadium Name:** State Mutual Stadium. **Location:** I-75 North to exit 190 (Rome/Canton), left off exit and follow Highway 411/Highway 20 to Rome, right at intersection on Highway 411 and Highway 1 (Veterans Memorial Highway), stadium is at intersection of Veterans Memorial Highway and Riverside Parkway. **Ticket Price Range:** $5-12. (purchased in advance). **Visiting Club Hotel:** Days Inn, 840 Turner McCall Blvd, Rome, GA 30161. **Telephone:** (706) 295-0400.

WEST VIRGINIA POWER

Address: 601 Morris St, Suite 201, Charleston, WV 25301.
Telephone: (304) 344-2287. **Fax:** (304) 344-0083.
E-Mail Address: info@wvpower.com. **Website:** www.wvpower.com.
Affiliation (first year): Seattle Mariners (2019). **Years in League:** 1987-

OWNERSHIP MANAGEMENT
Operated By: West Virginia Baseball, LLC.
Managing Partner: Tim Wilcox. **General Manager:** Jeremy Taylor. **Community Outreach and Merchandise Manager:** Hannah Frenchick. **Accountant:** Darren Holstein. **Broadcast & Media Relations Manager:** David Kahn. **Head Groundskeeper:** Paul Kuhna. **Box Office Manager:** Zach Kurdin. **Director of Ticket Sales:** George Levandoski. **Stadium Operations Manager:** Jesus Paez. **Director of Food & Beverage:** Aaron Simmons. **Assistant, Food & Beverage:** Nathan Richard. **Game Entertainment/Production Manager:** Dean Thomas. **Suites & Community Outreach Coordinator:** Lindsey Webb.

FIELD STAFF
Manager: Dave Berg. **Hitting Coach:** Eric Farris. **Pitching Coach:** Alon Leichman.

GAME INFORMATION
Radio Announcer: David Kahn. **No. of Games Broadcast:** 140. **Flagship Stations:** The Jock-WJYP-1300 AM & WMON-1340 AM. **PA Announcer:** Unavailable. **Official Scorer:** Unavailable. **Stadium Name:** Appalachian Power Park. **Location:** I-77 South to Capitol Street exit, left on Lee Street, left on Brooks Street. **Standard Game Times:** Mon.-Fri., 7:05 pm, Sat., 6:05 pm, Sun., 2:05 pm. **Ticket Price Range:** $6-11. **Visiting Club Hotel:** Holiday Inn Civic Center, 100 Civic Center Drive, Charleston, WV 25301. **Telephone:** (304) 345-0600.

NEW YORK-PENN LEAGUE

Address: 204 37th Ave. N., #366, St. Petersburg, Florida 33704.
Telephone: (727) 289-7111. **Fax:** (727) 683-9691.
Website: www.newyork-pennleague.com.
Years League Active: 1939-
President: Ben J. Hayes, J.D.

President Emeritus: Robert Julian. **Treasurer:** Jon Dandes (West Virginia). **Corporate Secretary:** Doug Estes (Williamsport).

League Administrator: Laurie Hayes. **League Media Associate:** Tricia Burrows.

Directors: Matt Slatus (Aberdeen), Jeff Dygert (Auburn), None (Batavia), Steve Cohen (Brooklyn), E. Miles Prentice (Connecticut), Marvin Goldklang (Hudson Valley), Dave Heller (Lowell), Michael Savit (Mahoning Valley), Chuck Greenberg (State College), Glenn Reicin (Staten Island), Bill Gladstone (Tri-City), Kyle Bostwick (Vermont), Jon Dandes (West Virginia), Peter Freund (Williamsport).

Ben Hayes

Division Structure: McNamara—Aberdeen, Brooklyn, Hudson Valley, Staten Island. **Pinckney**—Auburn, Batavia, Mahoning Valley, State College, West Virginia, Williamsport. **Stedler**—Lowell, Connecticut, Tri-City, Vermont. **Regular Season:** 76 games. **2019 Opening Date:** June 14. **Closing Date:** Sept 2.

All-Star Game: Aug. 21, Staten Island.

Playoff Format: Division winners and wild-card team meet in best of three series. Winners meet in best of three series for league championship. **Roster Limit:** 35 active and eligible to play in any given game. **Player Eligibility Rule:** No more than four players 23 or older; no more than three players on active list may have four or more years of prior service. **Brand of Baseball:** Rawlings. **Umpires:** Unavailable.

STADIUM INFORMATION

Club	Stadium	Opened	Dimensions			Capacity	2018 Att.
			LF	CF	RF		
Aberdeen	Ripken Stadium	2002	310	400	310	6,000	121,907
Auburn	Falcon Park	1995	330	400	330	2,800	43,343
Batavia	Dwyer Stadium	1996	325	400	325	2,600	29,005
Brooklyn	KeySpan Park	2001	315	412	325	7,500	202,495
Connecticut	Dodd Stadium	1995	309	401	309	6,270	75,810
Hudson Valley	Dutchess Stadium	1994	325	400	325	4,494	148,156
Lowell	Edward LeLacheur Park	1998	337	400	301	4,842	118,319
Mahoning Valley	Eastwood Field	1999	335	405	335	6,000	97,204
State College	Medlar Field at Lubrano Park	2006	325	399	320	5,412	119,986
Staten Island	Richmond County Bank Ballpark	2001	325	400	325	6,500	72,894
Tri-City	Joseph L. Bruno Stadium	2002	325	400	325	5,000	140,036
Vermont	Centennial Field	1922	323	405	330	4,000	83,956
West Virginia	WVU Baseball Park	2015	325	400	325	3,500	69,430
Williamsport	Bowman Field	1923	345	405	350	4,200	68,475

ABERDEEN IRONBIRDS

Address: 873 Long Drive, Aberdeen, MD 21001
Telephone: (410) 297-9292. **Fax:** (210) 297-6653
E-Mail Address: Info@ironbirdsbaseball.com. **Website:** ironbirdsbaseball.com
Affiliation (first year): Baltimore Orioles (2002). **Years in league:** 2002-

OWNERSHIP/MANAGEMENT

Operated By: Ripken Professional Baseball LLC. **Principal Owner:** Cal Ripken Jr. **Co-Owner/Executive Vice President:** Bill Ripken. **General Manager:** Matt Slatus. **Director, Ticketing:** Adam Barbato. **Director, Creative Services:** Kevin Jimenez. **Assistant General Manager, Operations:** Jack Graham. **Sr. Director, Business Development:** Vince Bulik. **Partnership Activation Coordinator:** Zoe Derrickson. **Director, Human Resources:** Lavorette Preston. **Director, Retail Merchandise:** Don Eney. **Sports Turf Superintendent:** Todd Bradley. **Manager, Facilities:** Larry Gluch. **Facilities Assistant:** David Dawson. **Sr. Box Office Coordinator:** Nat Giblin. **Manager, Accounting:** Elly Ripken. **Director, Finance & Administration:** Wayne Leonard. **Business Marketing Specialist:** Tyler Weigandt. **Group Event Specialist:** Ryan Ebert, Megan Ward. **Membership Services & Retention:** Justin Gentilcore. **Marketing & Social Media Coordinator:** Matthew Stratton. **Coordinator, Community Relations & Retail:** Amelia Adams.

FIELD STAFF

Manager: Kevin Bradshaw. **Hitting Coach:** TBD. **Pitching Coach:** Robbie Aviles.

GAME INFORMATION

Radio Announcer: Michael Lehr. **No. of Games Broadcast:** TBD. **Flagship Station:** WAMD 970 AM. **PA Announcer:**

Unavailable. **Official Scorer:** Joe Stetka. **Stadium Name:** Leidos Field at Ripken Stadium. **Location:** I-95 to exit 85 (route 22), west on 22, right onto long drive. **Ticket Price Range:** $5-$39. **Visiting Club Hotel:** Comfort Inn-Aberdeen, Marriott Courtyard-Aberdeen, Residence Inn-Aberdeen.

AUBURN DOUBLEDAYS

Address: 130 N Division St, Auburn, NY 13021. **Telephone:** (315) 255-2489.
E-Mail Address: info@auburndoubledays.com. **Website:** www.auburndoubledays.com.
Affiliation (first year): Washington Nationals (2011). **Years in League:** 1958-80, 1982-

OWNERSHIP/MANAGEMENT

Owned by: City of Auburn. **Operated by:** Auburn Community Baseball, LLC. **President:** Jeff Dygert.
General Manager: Adam Winslow. **Assistant General Managers:** Shane Truman, Robert Scarbrough.

FIELD STAFF

Manager: Ralph "Rocket" Wheeler. **Hitting Coach:** Mark Harris. **Pitching Coach:** Franklin Bravo.

GAME INFORMATION

Radio Announcer: Jack McMullens, JD Raucci. **No. of Games Broadcast:** 38. **Flagship Station:** WAUB. **PA Announcer:** Mike DeForrest. **Official Scorer:** Terry Clifford. **Stadium Name:** Leo Pinckney Field at Falcon Park. **Location:** I-90 to exit 40, right on Route 34 South for 8 miles to York Street, right on York, left on North Division Street. **Standard Game Times:** Unavailable. **Ticket Price Range:** $6-11. **Visiting Club Hotel:** Unavailable.

BATAVIA MUCKDOGS

Address: Dwyer Stadium, 299 Bank St, Batavia, NY 14020.
Telephone: 585-483-3647. **E-Mail Address:** bkelly@muckdogs.com.
Website: www.muckdogs.com.
Affiliation (first year): Miami Marlins (2013). **Years in League:** 1939-53, 1957-59, 1961-

OWNERSHIP/MANAGEMENT

Operated By: Batavia Muckdogs, Inc. **General Manager:** Brendan Kelly. **Sales and Marketing Coordinator:** Kerri Schmidt. **Director of Grounds:** Cooper Thomson.

FIELD STAFF

Manager: Jorge Hernandez. **Hitting Coach:** Unavailable. **Pitching Coach:** Chad Rhoades. **Defensive Coach:** Nathan Mikolas. **Athletic Trainer:** Jordan Wheat. **Strength & Conditioning Coach:** Justin Weiss. **Video Assistant:** Unavailable.

GAME INFORMATION

Radio Announcer: Unavailable. **No. of Games Broadcast:** Home-38. **Flagship Station:** WBTA 1490- AM/100.1 FM. **PA Announcer:** Paul Spiotta. **Official Scorer:** Paul Spiotta. **Stadium Name:** Dwyer Stadium. **Location:** I-90 to exit 48, left on Route 98 South, left on Richmond Avenue, left on Bank Street. **Standard Game Times:** Mon.-Sat., 7:05 pm, Sun., 5:05 pm. **Ticket Price Range:** $7-9 (in advance), $8-$10 (day of). **Visiting Club Hotel:** Red Roof Inn.

BROOKLYN CYCLONES

Address: 1904 Surf Ave, Brooklyn, NY 11224.
Telephone: (718) 372-5596. **Fax:** (718) 449-6368.
E-Mail Address: info@brooklyncyclones.com. **Website:** www.brooklyncyclones.com.
Affiliation (first year): New York Mets (2001) **Years in League:** 2001-

OWNERSHIP/MANAGEMENT

Chairman, CEO: Fred Wilpon. **President:** Saul Katz. **COO:** Jeff Wilpon. **Vice President:** Steve Cohen. **General Manager:** Kevin Mahoney. **Assistant GM:** Gary Perone. **Director, Communications:** Billy Harner. **Director, Ticketing:** Greg Conway. **Operations Manager:** Vladimir Lipsman. **Marketing Manager:** Alyssa Morel. **Director, Community Relations:** Christina Moore. **Community Outreach/Promotions:** King Henry. **Account Executives:** Tommy Cardona, Nicole LaMonica, Rafael Guerreo, Joe Ferrucci, Jeremy Allen, Anthony Genna, Ricky Viola. **Staff Accountant:** Tatiana Isdith. **Administrative Assistant, Community Relations:** Sharon Lundy.

FIELD STAFF

Manager: Edgardo Alfonzo. **Hitting Coach:** Delwyn Young. **Pitching Coach:** Josue Matos.

GAME INFORMATION

Radio Announcer: Keith Raad. **No. of Games Broadcast:** 76. **Flagship Station:** Web Streaming Only. **PA Announcer:** Mark Frotto. **Official Scorer:** Howard Kaplan, Patrick McCormack. **Stadium Name:** MCU Park. **Location:** Belt Parkway to Cropsey Ave South, continue on Cropsey until it becomes West 17th St, continue to Surf Ave, stadium on south side of Surf Ave; By subway, west/south to Stillwell Ave./Coney Island station. **Ticket Price Range:** $10-17. **Visiting Club Hotel:** Unavailable.

CONNECTICUT TIGERS

Address: 14 Stott Avenue, Norwich, CT 06360.
Telephone: (860) 887-7962. **Fax:** (860) 886-5996.
E-Mail Address: info@cttigers.com. **Website:** www.cttigers.com.
Affiliation (first year): Detroit Tigers (1999). **Years in League:** 2010-

OWNERSHIP/MANAGEMENT

Operated By: Oneonta Athletic Corp. **President:** Miles Prentice. **Senior Vice President:** CJ Knudsen. **General Manager:** Dave Schermerhorn. **Director, Concessions/Merchandise:** Heather Bartlett. **Director, Ticket Operations:** Josh Postler. **Director, Community & Fan Development:** Ed McMahon. **Business Development Manager:** Lee Walter, Jr. **Head Groundskeeper:** Ryan Lefler.

FIELD STAFF

Manager: Brayan Pena. **Hitting Coach:** Bill Springman. **Pitching Coach:** Carlos Bohorquez. **Athletic Trainer:** Shane McFarland.

GAME INFORMATION

PA Announcer: Ed Weyant. **Official Scorer:** Chris Cote. **Stadium Name:** Dodd Stadium. **Location:** Exit 14 (old exit 82) off I-395. **Standard Game Times:** Mon.-Fri., 7:05 pm, Sat., 6:05 pm, Sun., 4:05 pm. **Ticket Price Range:** $10-20. **Visiting Club Hotel:** Holiday Inn Norwich.

HUDSON VALLEY RENEGADES

Office Address: Dutchess Stadium, 1500 Route 9D, Wappingers Falls, NY 12590.
Mailing Address: PO Box 661, Fishkill, NY 12524.
Telephone: (845) 838-0094. **Fax:** (845) 838-0014.
E-Mail Address: info@hvrenegades.com. **Website:** www.hvrenegades.com.
Affiliation (first year): Tampa Bay Rays (1996). **Years in League:** 1994-

OWNERSHIP/MANAGEMENT

Operated by: Keystone Professional Baseball Club Inc. **Principal Owner:** Marv Goldklang.
President/General Manager: Steve Gliner. **Vice President:** Rick Zolzer. **Vice President of Community Partnerships:** Kristen Huss. **Assistant GM/Director of Ticket Sales:** Bryan Viggiano. **Director, Baseball Operations:** Joe Ausanio. **Director, Business Operations:** Vicky DeFreese. **Director, Food & Beverage/Merchandise:** Teri Bettencourt. **Manager, New Business Development:** Dave Neff. **Head Groundskeeper:** Tim Merante. **Box Office Manager:** Nick Leitner. **Ticket Sales Executives:** Jeremiah DeLine, Kyler DeMale. **Promotions Manager:** Marc Coppola.

FIELD STAFF

Manager: Blake Butera. **Hitting Coach:** Alejandro Freire. **Pitching Coach:** Jose Gonzalez. **Bench Coach:** Sean Smedley. **Athletic Trainer:** Tsutomu Kamiya. **Strength & Conditioning Coach:** Dan Rousseau. **Clubhouse Manager:** John Horaz.

GAME INFORMATION

Radio Announcer: Josh Carey. **No. of Games Broadcast:** Home—38 at hvrenegades.com. **PA Announcer:** Rick Zolzer. **Official Scorer:** Mike Ferraro. **Stadium Name:** Dutchess Stadium. **Location:** I-84 to exit 11 (Route 9D North), north one mile to stadium. **Standard Game Times:** Mon.-Fri., 7:05 pm, Sat, 6:05 pm, Sun., 4:35 pm. **Visiting Club Hotel:** Magnuson Hotel, 20 Schuyler Blvd and Route 9, Fishkill, NY 12524. **Telephone:** (845) 896-4995.

LOWELL SPINNERS

Address: 450 Aiken St, Lowell, MA 01854.
Telephone: (978) 459-2255. **Fax:** (978) 459-1674.
E-Mail Address: info@lowellspinners.com. **Website:** www.lowellspinners.com.
Affiliation (first year): Boston Red Sox (1996). **Years in League:** 1996-

OWNERSHIP/MANAGEMENT

Operated by: Main Street Baseball. **Owner:** Dave Heller.
President/General Manager: Shawn Smith. **Vice President:** Brian Lindsay. **VP, Finance:** Priscilla Harbour. **Box Office Manager:** TJ Konstant. **Creative Services Representative:** Erin Reynolds. **Grounds Manager:** Kyle Wood. **Director of Grounds Management:** Jack Schmidgall. **Director of Merchandise:** Shawn Bergeron. **Coordinator of Marketing Partnerships:** Frank Pimentel. **Coordinator of Operations:** Kristin Kinchla.

FIELD STAFF

Manager: Luke Montz. **Hitting Coach:** Nate Spears. **Pitching Coach:** Nick Green. **Athletic Trainer:** Taylor Boucher.

GAME INFORMATION

Radio Announcer: John Leahy. **No. of Games Broadcast:** 76. **Flagship Station:** WCAP 980-AM. **PA Announcer:**

Unavailable. **Official Scorer:** David Rourke. **Stadium Name:** Edward A LeLacheur Park. **Location:** From Route 495 and 3, take exit 35C (Lowell Connector), follow connector to exit 5B (Thorndike Street) onto Dutton Street, left onto Father Morrissette Boulevard, right on Aiken Street. **Standard Game Times:** 7:05 pm. **Ticket Price Range:** $7-10 (advance); $9-12 (day of game). **Visiting Club Hotel:** Radisson of Chelmsford, 10 Independence Dr, Chelmsford, MA 01879. **Telephone:** (978) 356-080.

MAHONING VALLEY
SCRAPPERS

Address: 111 Eastwood Mall Blvd, Niles, OH 44446.
Telephone: (330) 505-0000. **Fax:** (303) 505-9696.
E-Mail Address: info@mvscrappers.com. **Website:** www.mvscrappers.com.
Affiliation (first year): Cleveland Indians (1999). **Years in League:** 1999-

OWNERSHIP/MANAGEMENT
Operated By: HWS Baseball Group. **Managing General Partner:** Michael Savit. **Vice President, HWS Baseball/ General Manager:** Jordan Taylor. **Assistant GM, Marketing:** Heather Sahli. **Assistant GM, Sales:** Matt Thompson. **Director of Tickets & Game Operations:** Kate Walsh. **Director of Ticket Sales:** Kaylin Rose. **Manager, Box Office:** Clayton Sibilla. **Assistant GM, Operations:** Brad Hooser. **Head Groundskeeper:** Kyle Nagy. **Manager, Accounting & Human Resources:** Roxanne Polichetti. **Manager, Production:** Drew Masirovits.

FIELD STAFF
Manager: Dennis Malave. **Hitting Coach:** Grant Fink. **Pitching Coach:** Jason Blanton. **Bench Coach:** Omir Santos. **Athletic Trainer:** Patrick Reynolds. **Strength & Conditioning Coach:** Juan Acevedo.

GAME INFORMATION
Radio Announcer: Tim Pozsgai. **No. of Games Broadcast:** 76. **Flagship Station:** TBD. **PA Announcer:** Robb Schmidt. **Official Scorer:** Craig Antush. **Stadium Name:** Eastwood Field. **Location:** I-80 to 11 North to 82 West to 46 South; stadium located behind Eastwood Mall. **Ticket Price Range:** $8-12. **Visiting Club Hotel:** Days Inn & Suites, 1615 Liberty St, Girard, OH 44429. **Telephone:** (330) 759-9820.

STATE COLLEGE SPIKES

Address: 112 Medlar Field at Lubrano Park, University Park, PA 16802.
Telephone: (814) 272-1711. **Fax:** (814) 272-1718.
Website: www.statecollegespikes.com.
Affiliation (first year): St. Louis Cardinals (2013). **Years in League:** 2006-

OWNERSHIP/MANAGEMENT
Operated By: Spikes Baseball LP. **Chairman/Managing Partner:** Chuck Greenberg.
General Manager: Scott Walker. **Assistant GM, Operations:** Dan Petrazzolo. **Director of Ticket Sales:** David Woodard. **Senior Sales Executive:** Taylor Young. **Ticket Account Executive:** Fiona Frassinelli. **Director, Promotions/ In-Game Entertainment:** Ben Love. **Manager of Communications:** Joe Putnam. **Senior Sports Turf Manager:** Matt Neri. **Accounting Manager:** Beth Hamilton. **Box Office/Business Ops Specialist:** Robert DeLusa. **Off the Rack Outfitters Team Store Manager:** Julie Henry.

FIELD STAFF
Manager: Jose Leon. **Hitting Coach:** Cody Gabella. **Pitching Coach:** Adrian Martin. **Athletic Trainer:** Joey Olsiewicz. **Strength & Conditioning Coach:** Don Trapp.

GAME INFORMATION
PA Announcer: Jeff Brown. **Official Scorers:** Dave Baker, John Dixon. **Stadium Name:** Medlar Field at Lubrano Park. **Location:** From west, US 322 to Mount Nittany Expressway, I-80 to exit 158 (old exit 23/Milesburg), follow Route 150 South to Route 26 South; From east, I-80 to exit 161 (old exit 24/Bellefonte) to Route 26 South or US 220/I-99 South. **Standard Game Times:** Mon.-Sat., 7:05 pm, Sun., 6:05 pm. **Ticket Price Range:** $8-18. **Visiting Club Hotel:** Ramada Conference & Golf Hotel, 1450 Atherton St, State College, PA 16801. **Telephone:** (814) 238-3001.

STATEN ISLAND YANKEES

Stadium Address: 75 Richmond Terrace, Staten Island, NY 10301.
Telephone: (718) 720-9265. **Fax:** (718) 273-5763. **Website:** www.siyanks.com.
Affiliation (first year): New York Yankees (1999). **Years in League:** 1999-Present.

OWNERSHIP/MANAGEMENT
Principal Owners: Nostalgic Partners. **President/Operating Partner:** Will Smith. **General Manager:** Jane Rogers.

Vice President of Business Development: Adam Lorber. **CFO:** Jason Nazzaro. **Vice President of Operations:** T.J. Jahn. **Director of Corporate Partnerships:** Steve Devcich. **Finance Associate, Corporate Sales:** Mike Gerbasi. **Group Sales Manager:** David Percarpio. **Group Sales Executives:** Jesse Lopresti, David Budash, Megan Bloyd, Mitchell Lister. **Production & Marketing Manager:** Michael Galayda. **Head Groundskeeper:** Unavailable. **Stadium Operations Manager:** Anthony Silvia.

FIELD STAFF

Manager: David Adams. **Hitting Coach:** Ken Joyce. **Pitching Coach:** Travis Phelps. **Defensive Coach:** Tyson Blaser.

GAME INFORMATION

Radio Announcer: Unavailable. **No. of Games Broadcast:** Unavailable. **Flagship Station:** Unavailable. **PA Announcer:** Unavailable. **Official Scorer:** Unavailable. **Stadium Name:** Richmond County Bank Ballpark at St George. **Location:** 75 Richmond Terrace, Staten Island, NY 10301 (located next to Staten Island Ferry and Staten Island Railway-St. George) **Standard Game Times:** Mon.-Sat., 7 p.m., Sun., 1 p.m. **Visiting Club Hotel:** Unavailable.

TRI-CITY VALLEYCATS

Office Address: Joseph L Bruno Stadium, 80 Vandenburg Ave, Troy, NY 12180.
Mailing Address: PO Box 694, Troy, NY 12181.
Telephone: (518) 629-2287. **Fax:** (518) 629-2299.
E-Mail Address: info@tcvalleycats.com. **Website:** www.tcvalleycats.com.
Affiliation (first year): Houston Astros (2002). **Years in League:** 1999-

OWNERSHIP/MANAGEMENT

Operated By: Tri-City ValleyCats Inc. **Principal Owners:** Martin Barr, John Burton, William Gladstone, Rick Murphy, Alfred Roberts, Stephen Siegel. **President:** William Gladstone. **Executive Vice President/Chief Operating Officer:** Rick Murphy. **General Manager:** Matt Callahan. **Assistant GM:** Michelle Skinner. **Media Relations Manager:** Chris Chenes. **Ticket Office and Operations Manager:** Jessica Guido. **Food & Beverage Manager:** Missy Henry. **Community & Promotions Coordinator:** Elyse Zima. **Account Executive:** Matt Sammarco. **Sales & Operations Associate:** Jordan Mitchell. **Client Services Associate:** Lizzy Tripoli.

FIELD STAFF

Manager: Ozney Guillen. **Hitting Coach:** Sean Godfrey. **Pitching Coach:** John Kovalik.

GAME INFORMATION

Radio Announcer: Unavailable. **No. of Games Broadcast:** 38. **Flagship Station:** MiLB.com. **PA Announcer:** Anthony Pettograsso. **Official Scorer:** Jim Pertierra. **Stadium Name:** Joseph Bruno Stadium. **Location:** From north, I-87 to exit 7 (Route 7), go east 1 1/2 miles to I-787 South, to Route 378 East, go over bridge to Route 4, right to Route 4 South, one mile to Hudson Valley Community College campus on left; From south, I-87 to exit 23 (I-787), I-787 north six miles to exit for Route 378 east, over bridge to Route 4, right to Route 4 South, one mile to campus on left; From east, Massachusetts Turnpike to exit B-1 (I-90), nine miles to Exit 8 (Defreestville), left off ramp to Route 4 North, five miles to campus on right; From west, I-90 to exit 24 (I-90 East), I-90 East for six miles to I-787 North (Troy), 2.2 miles to exit for Route 378 East, over bridge to Route 4, right to Route 4 south for one mile to campus on left. **Standard Game Times:** 7pm, Sun. 5 pm. **Ticket Price Range:** $5.50-$12.50. **Visiting Club Hotel:** The Desmond Hotel Albany, 660 Albany-Shaker Road, Albany, NY 12211. **Telephone:** (518) 869-8100.

VERMONT LAKE MONSTERS

Address: 1 King Street Ferry Dock, Burlington, VT 05401.
Telephone: (802) 655-4200. **Fax:** (802) 655-5660.
E-Mail Address: info@vermontlakemonsters.com.
Website: www.vermontlakemosters.com.
Affiliation (first year): Oakland Athletics (2011). **Years in League:** 1994-

OWNERSHIP/MANAGEMENT

Operated by: Vermont Expos Inc.
Principal Owner/President: Ray Pecor Jr. **Vice President:** Kyle Bostwick. **General Manager:** Joe Doud. **Assistant General Manager:** Adam Matth. **Executive Director, Sales & Marketing:** Nate Cloutier. **Marketing and In-Game Promotions Manager:** Jeff Kent. **Box Office and Team Operations Manager:** Hannah Carlin. **Staff Accountant:** Heather Regnaud. **Director, Media Relations:** Paul Stanfield. **Clubhouse Operations:** Jack Zagursky. **Head Groundskeeper:** John Thibeault.

FIELD STAFF

Manager: Aaron Nieckula. **Hitting Coach:** Kevin Kouzmanoff. **Pitching Coach:** Carlos Chavez. **Bench Coach:** Rick Magnante.

GAME INFORMATION

Radio Announcers: George Commo. **No. of Games Broadcast:** Home-38 (Internet Only). **PA Announcer:** Rich Haskell, Jamey McGowan. **Official Scorer:** Bruce Bosley. **Stadium Name:** Centennial Field. **Location:** I-89 to exit 14W, right on East Avenue for one mile, right at Colchester Avenue. **Standard Game Times:** Mon.-Fri., 7:05 pm, Sat., 6:05 pm, Sun., 5:05 pm.

Ticket Price Range: $5-8. Visiting Club Hotel: Doubletree By Hilton (formerly Sheraton). Telephone: (802) 865-6600.

WEST VIRGINIA BLACK BEARS

Office Address: 2040 Jedd Gyorko Drive, Granville, WV 26534
Mailing Address: PO Box 4680 Morgantown, WV 26504.
Telephone: (304) 293-7910. Website: www.westvirginiablackbears.com
Affiliation (first year): Pittsburgh Pirates (2015). Years in League: 2015-

OWNERSHIP/MANAGEMENT

Operated By: Rich Baseball Operations. President: Robert Rich Jr. Chief Operating Officer: Jonathan Dandes. General Manager: Matthew Drayer. Assistant GM: Jackie Riggleman. Sponsorship & Promotions Manager: Travis O'Neal. Stadium Manager: Craig McIntosh. Groundskeeper: Logan Elliott.

FIELD STAFF

Manager: Drew Saylor. Hitting Coach: John Tucker. Pitching Coach: Tom Filer.

GAME INFORMATION

PA Announcer: Bill Nevlin. Official Scorer: Unavailable. Stadium Name: Monongalia County Ballpark. Standard Game Times: Mon.-Fri., 6:35 pm, Sat., 7:05 pm, Sun., TBA. Visiting Club Hotel: Fairfield Inn & Suites by Marroitt.

WILLIAMSPORT CROSSCUTTERS

Office Address: BB&T Ballpark at Historic Bowman Field, 1700 W Fourth St, Williamsport, PA 17701. Mailing Address: PO Box 3173, Williamsport, PA 17701.
Telephone: (570) 326-3389. Fax: (570) 326-3494.
E-Mail Address: mail@crosscutters.com. Website: www.crosscutters.com.
Affiliation (first year): Philadelphia Phillies (2007). Years in League: 1968-72, 1994-

OWNERSHIP/MANAGEMENT

Operated By: Cutting Edge Baseball, LLC. Principal Owner: Peter Freund.
Vice President/General Manager: Doug Estes. Vice-President, Marketing/Public Relations: Gabe Sinicropi. Director, Food/Beverage: Bill Gehron. Director, Ticket Operations/Community Relations: Sarah Budd. Director, Client Services: Nate Schneider.

FIELD STAFF

Manager: Pat Borders. Hitting Coach: Joel McKeithan. Pitching Coach: Hector Berrios. Bench Coach: Greg Brodzinski.

GAME INFORMATION

Radio Announcers: Todd Bartley, Ian Catherine. No. of Games Broadcast: 76. Flagship Station: WLYC 1050-AM & 104.1 FM (FoxSports Williamsport). Stadium Name: BB&T Ballpark at Historic Bowman Field. Location: 1700 W. Fourth St., Williamsport, PA. From the North: Follow Route 15 South. Take the Fourth Street exit. Turn left onto Fourth Street. Ballpark will be on your left. From the South: Follow Route 15 North. Cross the Susquehanna River via the Market Street Bridge and follow into Downtown Williamsport. At the second traffic light, turn left onto Fourth Street. Follow approx. 3 miles. Ballpark will be on your right. Ballpark will be your right. Ticket Price Range: $8-$15. Visiting Club Hotel: Best Western, 1840 E Third St, Williamsport, PA 17701. Telephone: (570) 326-1981.

NORTHWEST LEAGUE

Address: 140 N Higgins Ave., No. 211, Missoula, MT, 59802.
Telephone: (406) 541-9301.
E-Mail Address: mellisnwl@aol.com.
Website: www.northwestleague.com.
Years League Active: 1954-
President/Treasurer: Mike Ellis.
Vice President: Andy Dunn (Vancouver). **Corporate Secretary:** Jerry Walker (Salem-Keizer).
Directors: Dave Elmore (Eugene), Bobby Brett (Spokane), Tom Volpe (Everett), Jake Kerr (Vancouver), Mike McMurray (Hillsboro), Brent Miles (Tri-City), Jerry Walker (Salem-Keizer), Jeff Eiseman (Boise). **Administrative Assistant:** Judy Ellis.
Division Structure: South—Boise, Hillsboro, Eugene, Salem-Keizer. **North**—Everett, Spokane, Tri-City, Vancouver. **Regular Season:** 76 games (split schedule).
2019 Opening Date: June 14. **Closing Date:** Sept. 2. **All-Star Game:** Aug. 6 at Boise (Northwest League vs. Pioneer Baseball League). **Playoff Format:** First-half division winners meet second-half division winners in best-of-three series. Winners meet in best-of-five series for league championship. **Roster Limit:** 35 active, 35 under control. **Player Eligibility Rule:** No more than three players on active list may have four or more years of prior service. **Brand of Baseball:** Rawlings. **Umpires:** Unavailable.

Mike Ellis

STADIUM INFORMATION

| Club | Stadium | Opened | Dimensions | | | Capacity | 2018 Att. |
			LF	CF	RF		
Boise	Memorial Stadium	1989	335	400	335	3,426	126,192
Eugene	PK Park	2010	335	400	325	4,000	125,967
Everett	Everett Memorial Stadium	1984	324	380	330	3,682	111,599
Hillsboro	Hillsboro Ballpark	2013	325	400	325	4,500	130,286
Salem-Keizer	Volcanoes Stadium	1997	325	400	325	4,100	72,094
Spokane	Avista Stadium	1958	335	398	335	7,162	198,423
Tri-City	Dust Devils Stadium	1995	335	400	335	3,700	86,283
Vancouver	Nat Bailey Stadium	1951	335	395	335	6,500	239,086

BOISE HAWKS

Address: 5600 N. Glenwood St. Boise, ID 83714.
Telephone: (208) 322-5000. **Fax:** (208) 322-6846.
Website: www.boisehawks.com.
Affiliation (first year): Colorado Rockies (2015).
Years in League: 1975-76, 1978, 1987-

OWNERSHIP/MANAGEMENT

Operated by: Boise Professional Baseball LLC. **President:** Jeff Eiseman. **Vice President, Operations:** Missy Martin. **General Manager:** Bob Flannery. **Assistant General Manager:** Mike Van Hise. **Director, Stadium Ops/Food & Beverage:** Jake Lusk. **Manager, Accounting/Office:** Judy Peterson. **Corporate Sales Manager:** Matt Osbon. **Ticket Sales Manager:** Jon Jensen. **Account Executive, Group Sales:** Colton Hampson. **Account Executive:** Mikayla Leroue, Jamie Wolph, Hailey Gavett, Jacob Cluff. **Box Office Manager:** Reilly Raube. **Stadium Operations Manager:** Carl Koster. **Food and Beverage Coordinator:** Adam Pinckard. **Media Relations/Marketing Manager:** Carly McCullough. **Marketing Coordinator:** Melissa Mione. **Graphics/Video Production Coordinator:** Megan Corcoran. **Media Relations & Play-by-Play Broadcaster:** Unavailable. **Head Groundskeeper:** John Gides.

FIELD STAFF

Manager: Steve Soliz. **Hitting Coach:** Cesar Galvez. **Pitching Coach:** Ryan Kibler. **Athletic Trainer:** Mickey Clarizio. **Development Supervisor:** Fred Ocasio.

GAME INFORMATION

Radio Announcer: Unavailable. **No. of Games Broadcast:** 76. **Flagship Station:** 101.5 KOOL-FM. **PA Announcer:** Jeremy Peterson. **Official Scorer:** Curtis Haines. **Stadium Name:** Memorial Stadium. **Location:** I-84 to Cole Rd., north to Western Idaho Fairgrounds at 5600 North Glenwood St. **Standard Game Time:** 7:15 pm. **Ticket Price Range:** $8-35. **Visiting Club Hotel:** Wyndham Garden Hotel, 3300 South Vista Ave. Boise, ID.

EUGENE EMERALDS

Office Address: 2760 Martin Luther King Jr. Blvd, Eugene, OR 97401.
Mailing Address: PO Box 10911, Eugene, OR 97440.
Telephone: (541) 342-5367. **Fax:** (541) 342-6089.
E-Mail Address: info@emeraldsbaseball.com. **Website:** www.emeraldsbaseball.com.
Affiliation (first year): Chicago Cubs (2015). **Years in League:** 1955-68, 1974-

OWNERSHIP/MANAGEMENT

Operated By: Elmore Sports Group Ltd. **Principal Owner:** David Elmore.
General Manager: Allan Benavides. **Assistant GM:** Matt Dompe. **Director, Food/Beverage:** Turner Elmore.
Director, Tickets: David Roth. **Event Manager:** Chris Bowers. **Event Manager:** Patrick Zajac. **Graphic Designer:**
Danny Cowley. **Director, Community Affairs:** Anne Culhane. **Ticket Sales:** Andrew Brown, Cam LaFerle, Kindra Bates.
Merchandise and Social Media: Shelby Holteen. **Sponsorship Sales:** Brian Vucovich. **Home Radio:** Matt Dompe.
Away Radio: Patrick Zajac.

FIELD STAFF

Manager: Steve Lerud. **Hitting Coach:** Ty Wright. **Pitching Coach:** Armando Gabino. **Assistant Coach:** Carlos Rojas.
Athletic Trainer: Sean Folan.

GAME INFORMATION

Radio Announcer: Matt Dompe. **No. of Games Broadcast:** 76. **Flagship Station:** 95.3-FM The Score. **PA
Announcer:** Ted Welker. **Official Scorer:** George McPherson. **Stadium Name:** PK Park. **Standard Game Time:** Mon.-
Sat., 7:05 p.m., Sun., 5:05pm. **Ticket Price Range:** $8-$15. **Visiting Club Hotel:** Holiday Inn Express, Eugene Springfield.

EVERETT AQUASOX

Mailing Address: 3802 Broadway, Everett, WA 98201.
Telephone: (425) 258-3673. **Fax:** (425) 258-3675.
E-Mail Address: info@aquasox.com. **Website:** www.aquasox.com.
Affiliation (first year): Seattle Mariners (1995). **Years in League:** 1984-

OWNERSHIP/MANAGEMENT

Operated by: 7th Inning Stretch, LLC.
Directors: Tom Volpe, Pat Filippone. **General Manager:** Danny Tetzlaff. **Assistant GM:** Rick Maddox. **Director,
Corporate Partnerships/Broadcasting:** Pat Dillon. **Director, Tickets:** Dan Ferguson. **Corporate Partnership and
Team Operations Manager:** Alex Clausius. **Director of Community Relations & Merchandise:** Ashlea LaPlant.
Director of Marketing & Digital Media: Jason Grohoske. **Account Executives:** Scott Brownlee, Conner Grant.

FIELD STAFF

Manager: Jose Moreno. **Hitting Coach:** Joe Thurston. **Pitching Coach:** Ari Ronick.

GAME INFORMATION

Radio Announcer: Pat Dillon. **No. of Games Broadcast:** 76. **Flagship Station:** KRKO 1380-AM, 95.3-FM. **PA
Announcer:** Tom Lafferty. **Official Scorer:** Patrick Lafferty. **Stadium Name:** Everett Memorial Stadium. **Location:** I-5,
exit 192. **Standard Game Times:** Mon.-Sat., 7:05 pm, Sun., 4:05 pm. **Ticket Price Range:** $8-18. **Visiting Club Hotel:**
Best Western Cascadia Inn, 2800 Pacific Ave, Everett, WA 98201. **Telephone:** (425) 258-4141.

HILLSBORO HOPS

Address: 4460 NE Century Blvd., Hillsboro, OR, 97124. **Telephone:** (503) 640-0887.
E-Mail Address: info@hillsborohops.com. **Website:** www.hillsborohops.com.
Affiliation (first year): Arizona Diamondbacks (2001). **Years in League:** 2013-

OWNERSHIP/MANAGEMENT

Operated by: Short Season LLC. **Managing Partners:** Mike McMurray, Josh Weinman, Myron Levin.
Chairman and CEO: Mike McMurray. **President and General Manager:** K.L. Wombacher. **Chief Financial
Officer:** Laura McMurray. **Director, Ballpark Operations:** Ryan Kees. **Vice President, Tickets:** Jason Gavigan. **Senior
Director, Merchandise:** Lauren Wombacher. **Manager, Marketing and Communications:** Casey Sawyer. **Director,
Broadcasting:** Rich Burk.

FIELD STAFF

Manager: Javier Colina. **Hitting Coach:** Franklin Stubbs. **Pitching Coach:** Barry Enright. **Coach:** Hatuey Mendoza.
Coach: Ben Petrick.

GAME INFORMATION

PA Announcer: Unavailable. **Official Scorer:** Blair Cash. **Stadium Name:** Ron Tonkin Field. **Location:** 4460 NE
Century Blvd., Hillsboro, OR. 97124. **Standard Game Times:** Mon.-Sat., 7:05 pm, Sun., 4:05 pm. **Ticket Price Range:**
$7-$20. **Visiting Club Hotel:** Extended Stay America—Portland/Hillsboro, Hillsboro, OR. **Telephone:** (503) 221-0140.

SALEM-KEIZER VOLCANOES

Office Address: 6700 Field of Dreams Way, Keizer, OR 97303.
Mailing Address: PO Box 20936, Keizer, OR 97307.
Telephone: (503) 390-2225. **Fax:** (503) 390-2227.
E-Mail Address: Volcanoes@volcanoesbaseball.com. **Website:** www.volcanoesbaseball.com.
Affiliation (first year): San Francisco Giants (1997). **Years in League:** 1997-

OWNERSHIP/MANAGEMENT
Operated By: Sports Enterprises Inc. **Principal Owners:** Jerry Walker, Lisa Walker. **President/General Manager:** Jerry Walker. **Vice President:** Lisa Walker. **President, Business Operations:** Mitche Graf. **President, Stadium Operations:** Rick Nelson. **Senior Account Executive, Game Day Operations:** Jerry Howard. **Sales Manager, Group Sales:** Eric Fisk. **Director of Ticketing:** Vicky Swearingin. **Director, Business Development:** Justin Lacche. **Director of Concessions:** Mickey Walker.

FIELD STAFF
Manager: Mark Hallber. **Hitting Coach:** Doug Clark. **Pitching Coach:** Dwight Bernard. **Fundamentals Coach:** Nestor Rojas. **Athletic Trainer:** Charlene Wichman. **Strength & Conditioning Coach:** Joe Palazzolo.

GAME INFORMATION
Radio Announcer: Unavailable. **No. of Games Broadcast:** 76. **Flagship Station:** Unavailable. **PA Announcer:** Unavailable. **Official Scorer:** Scott Sepich. **Stadium Name:** Volcanoes Stadium. **Location:** I-5 to exit 260 (Chemawa Road), west one block to Stadium Way NE, north six blocks to stadium. **Standard Game Times:** Mon.-Sat., 6:35 pm, Sun., 5:05 p.m. **Ticket Price Range:** $7-22. **Visiting Club Hotel:** Comfort Suites, 630 Hawthorne Ave SE, Salem, OR 97301. **Telephone:** (503) 585-9705.

SPOKANE INDIANS

Office Address: Avista Stadium, 602 N Havana, Spokane, WA 99202.
Mailing Address: PO Box 4758, Spokane, WA 99220.
Telephone: (509) 535-2922. **Fax:** (509) 534-5368.
E-Mail Address: mail@spokaneindians.com. **Website:** www.spokaneindians.com.
Affiliation (first year): Texas Rangers (2003). **Years in League:** 1972, 1983-Present-

OWNERSHIP/MANAGEMENT
Operated By: Longball Inc. **Principal Owner:** Bobby Brett. **Co-Owner/Senior Advisor:** Andrew Billig.
Vice President/General Manager: Chris Duff. **Senior Vice President:** Otto Klein. **VP, Development:** Josh Roys.
VP, Business Operations: Lesley DeHart. **Assistant General Manager:** Sean Bozigian. **Assistant GM, Sponsorships:** Kyle Day. **Assistant GM, Tickets:** Nick Gaebe. **Director of Promotions & Events:** Darby Moore. **Partner Services & Sustainable Operations Manager:** Kat O'Melinn. **Business Operations Manager:** MacKenzie White. **Director of Public Relations:** John Collett. **Communications Consultant:** Bud Bareither. **Senior Account Executive:** Jake Browne. **Account Executives:** Wyatt Shelley, Jordan Vela. **Director of Group Sales:** Sean Dorsey. **Group Sales Coordinators:** Gina Giesseman, Kaitlyn Tisch. **Personal Account Managers:** Forest Salgado, James Lange. **Chief Financial Officer:** Greg Sloan. **Controller:** Tim Gittel. **Director of Facilities & Grounds:** Tony Lee. **Assistant Director, Stadium Operations:** Larry Blumer.

FIELD STAFF
Manager: Kenny Hook. **Pitching Coach:** Salomon Manriquez. **Hitting Coach:** Henderson Lugo. **Strength & Conditioning Coach:** Ed Yong.

GAME INFORMATION
Radio Announcer: Mike Boyle. **No. of Games Broadcast:** 76. **Flagship Station:** 1510 AM/103.5 FM. **PA Announcer:** Unavailable. **Official Scorer:** Todd Gilkey. **Stadium Name:** Avista Stadium. **Location:** From west, I-90 to exit 283B (Thor/Freya), east on Third Avenue, left onto Havana; From east, I-90 to Broadway exit, right onto Broadway, left onto Havana. **Standard Game Time:** Mon.-Sat., 6:30 pm, Sun., 3:30 pm. **Ticket Price Range:** $5-13. **Visiting Club Hotel:** Mirabeau Park Hotel & Convention Center, 1100 N. Sullivan Rd, Spokane, WA 99037. **Telephone:** (509) 924-9000.

TRI-CITY DUST DEVILS

Address: 6200 Burden Blvd, Pasco, WA 99301.
Telephone: (509) 544-8789. **Fax:** (509) 547-9570.
E-Mail Address: info@dustdevilsbaseball.com.
Website: www.dustdevilsbaseball.com.
Affiliation (first year): San Diego Padres (2015).
Years in League: 1955-1974, 1983-1986, 2001-

OWNERSHIP/MANAGEMENT

Operated by: Northwest Baseball Ventures. **Principal Owners:** George Brett, Yoshi Okamoto, Brent Miles. **President:** Brent Miles. **Vice President/General Manager:** Derrel Ebert. **Assistant General Manager, Business Operations:** Trevor Shively. **Assistant General Manager, Sponsorships:** Ann Shively. **Sponsorships Account Executive:** Michael Allen. **Sponsorships Account Executive:** Kimberly Bullis. **Director of Ticket Sales:** Riley Shintaffer. **Group Sales Manager:** Marcus Manderbach. **Account Executive:** Alex Cornwell. **Account Executive:** Preston Eder. **Head Groundskeeper:** Michael Angel.

FIELD STAFF

Manager: Mike McCoy. **Hitting Coach:** Pat O'Sullivan. **Pitching Coach:** Leo Rosales. **Fielding Coach:** Oscar Salazar.

GAME INFORMATION

Radio Announcer: Chris King. **No. of Games Broadcast:** 76. **Flagship Station:** 870-AM KFLD. **PA Announcer:** Patrick Harvey. **Official Scorers:** Tony Wise, Scott Tylinski. **Stadium Name:** Gesa Stadium. **Location:** I-182 to exit 9 (Road 68), north to Burden Blvd, right to stadium. **Standard Game Time:** 7:15 pm. **Ticket Price Range:** $8-12. **Visiting Club Hotel:** Hampton Inn & Suites Pasco/Tri-Cities, 6826 Burden Blvd., Pasco, WA 99301. **Telephone:** (509) 792-1660.

VANCOUVER CANADIANS

Address: Scotiabank Field at Nat Bailey Stadium, 4601 Ontario St, Vancouver, B.C. V5V 3H4. **Telephone:** (604) 872-5232. **Fax:** (604) 872-1714. **E-Mail Address:** staff@canadiansbaseball.com. **Website:** www.canadiansbaseball.com. **Affiliation (first year):** Toronto Blue Jays (2011). **Years in League:** 2000-

OWNERSHIP/MANAGEMENT

Operated by: Vancouver Canadians Professional Baseball LLP. **Managing General Partner:** Jake Kerr. **Co-Owner:** Jeff Mooney. **President:** Andy Dunn. **General Manager:** Allan Bailey. **Financial Controller:** Brenda Chmiliar. **VP, Sales/Marketing:** Graham Wall. **Director, Communications:** Rob Fai. **Director, Sales/Game Day Operations:** Michael Richardson. **Director, Sales & Marketing:** Lindsay Scharf. **Director, Group Sales & Social Media:** Stephani Ellis. **Manager, Community Relations:** Lori Stankiewicz. **Manager, Ticket Operations:** Reilly Simmonds. **Coordinator, Sales:** Chelsea Jenner. **Coordinator, Sales & Game Day Operations:** Jordan Skavinsky. **Head Groundskeeper:** Ross Baron. **Manager, Ballpark Operations/Home Clubhouse Attendant:** John Stewart. **Manager, Concessions:** Iain Graham (Aramark).

FIELD STAFF

Manager: Casey Candaele. **Hitting Coach:** Aaron Mathews. **Pitching Coach:** Demetre Kokoris.

GAME INFORMATION

Radio/TV Announcer: Rob Fai (13th season), Ricky Romero (1st season). **No. of Games Broadcast:** 76. **Flagship Station:** Sportsnet650 AM. **PA Announcer:** Niall O'Donohoe. **Official Scorer:** Mike Hanafin. **Stadium Name:** Scotiabank Field at Nat Bailey Stadium. **Location:** From downtown, take Cambie Street Bridge, left on East 29th Ave., left on Ontario St. to stadium; From south, take Highway 99 to Oak Street, right on 41st Ave, left on Cambie St. right on East 29th Ave., left on Ontario St to stadium. **Standard Game Times:** Mon.-Sat., 7:05 pm, Sun., 1:05 pm. **Ticket Price Range:** $16-27. **Visiting Club Hotel:** Sandman Hotel Vancouver Airport, 3233 St. Edwards Dr., Richmond, B.C., V6X 1N4. **Telephone:** (604) 303-8888.

APPALACHIAN LEAGUE

Mailing Address: 1340 Environ Way, Chapel Hill, NC 27517
Telephone: 919-913-4590. **E-Mail Address:** dan@appyleague.com
Website: www.appyleague.com.
Years League Active: 1921-25, 1937-55, 1957-
President/Treasurer: Dan Moushon.
Corporate Secretary: David Cross (Danville).**League Publicist:** Betsy Haugh (Pulaski).
President Emeritus: Lee Landers.
Directors: Charlie Wilson (Toronto), Larry Broadway (Pittsburgh), Alec Zumwalt (Kansas City), Dom Chiti (Atlanta), Jeremy Zoll (Minnesota), Eric Lee (Cincinnati), Gary LaRocque (St. Louis), Jared Banner (New York Mets), Mitch Lukevics Tampa Bay), Eric Schmitt (New York Yankees).
Executive Committee: Mike Mains (Elizabethton), Brian Paupeck (Kingsport), Betsy Haugh (Pulaski), Gary La Rocque (St. Louis), Charlie Wilson (Toronto), Larry Broadway (Pittsburgh).
Board of Trustees Representative: Mitch Lukevics (Tampa Bay).
Baseball Chapel Representative: Mikie Morrison (Burlington).
Division Structure: East—Bluefield, Burlington, Danville, Princeton, Pulaski. **West**—Bristol, Elizabethton, Greeneville, Johnson City, Kingsport.
Regular Season: 68 games. **2019 Opening Date:** June 18. **Closing Date:** August 28.
All-Star Game: None. **Playoff Format:** First-and second-place teams in each division play each other in best-of-three series. Winners meet in best-of-three series for league championship. **Roster Limit:** 35 active, 35 under control.
Player Eligibility Rule: No more than three players on the active roster may have three or more years of prior minor league service. **Brand of Baseball:** Rawlings. **Umpires:** Unavailable.

Dan Moushon

STADIUM INFORMATION

| Club | Stadium | Opened | Dimensions | | | Capacity | 2018 Att. |
			LF	CF	RF		
Bluefield	Bowen Field	1939	335	400	335	2,046	20,018
Bristol	DeVault Memorial Stadium	1969	325	400	310	2,000	21,941
Burlington	Burlington Athletic Stadium	1960	335	410	335	3,216	36,541
Danville	Dan Daniel Memorial Park	1993	330	400	330	2,755	34,766
Elizabethton	Joe O'Brien Field	1974	335	414	326	1,500	15,329
Greeneville	Pioneer Park	2004	331	400	331	2,672	48,021
Johnson City	TVA Credit Union Ballpark	1956	320	410	320	2,897	68,881
Kingsport	Hunter Wright Stadium	1995	330	410	330	2,418	28,928
Princeton	Hunnicutt Field	1988	330	396	330	2,000	23,549
Pulaski	Calfee Park	1935	335	405	310	2,912	91,226

BLUEFIELD BLUE JAYS

Office Address: Stadium Drive, Bluefield, WV 24701. **Mailing Address:** PO Box 356, Bluefield, WV 24701. **Telephone:** (304) 324-1326. **Fax:** (304) 324-1318.
E-Mail Address: babybirds1@comcast.net. **Website:** www.bluefieldjays.com.
Affiliation (first year): Toronto Blue Jays (2011). **Years in League:** 1946-55, 1957-

OWNERSHIP/MANAGEMENT
Director: Charlie Wilson (Toronto Blue Jays). **President:** George McGonagle. **Vice President:** David Kersey. **Counsel:** Brian Cochran. **General Manager:** Patrick (Rocky) Malamisura.

FIELD STAFF
Manager: Luis Hurtado. **Hitting Coach:** Paul Elliott. **Pitching Coach:** Rafael Lazo. **Position Player Coach:** Chris Schaeffer. **Athletic Trainer:** Brandon Hammerstrom. **Strength & Conditioning Coach:** Casey Callison.

GAME INFORMATION
PA Announcer: Unavailable. **Official Scorer:** Unavailable. **Stadium Name:** Bowen Field. **Location:** I-77 to Bluefield exit 1, Route 290 to Route 460 West, fourth light right onto Leatherwood Lane, left at first light, past Hometown Shell station and turn right, stadium quarter-mile on left. **Ticket Price Range:** $6. **Visiting Club Hotel:** Quality Inn Bluefield, 3350 Big Laurel Highway/460 West, Bluefield, WV 24701. **Telephone:** (304) 325-6170.

BRISTOL PIRATES

Office Address: 1501 Euclid Ave, Bristol, VA 24201.
Mailing Address: PO Box 1434, Bristol, VA 24203.
Telephone: (276) 206-9946. **Fax:** (423)-968-2636.
E-Mail Address: gm@bristolbaseball.com. **Website:** www.bristolpiratesbaseball.com.
Twitter: @BriBucs. **Facebook:** www.facebook.com/bristolpiratesbaseball.
Affiliation (first year): Pittsburgh Pirates (2014). **Years in League:** 1921-25, 1940-55, 1969-

OWNERSHIP/MANAGEMENT

Owned by: Pittsburgh Pirates. **Director:** Larry Broadway (Pittsburgh Pirates). **Operated by:** Bristol Baseball Inc.
President/General Manager: Mahlon Luttrell. **Vice President:** Craig Adams, Mark Young. **Treasurer:** Delma Luttrell.
Secretary: Connie Kinkead.

FIELD STAFF

Manager: Kieran Mattison. **Hitting Coach:** Jonathan Prieto. **Pitching Coach:** Eric Minshall. **Athletic Trainer:** Matt
McNamee. **Strength & Conditioning Coach:** Unavailable.

GAME INFORMATION

Radio: milb.com. **PA Announcer:** Unavailable. **Official Scorer:** Connie Kinkead. **Stadium Name:** DeVault Memorial
Stadium. **Location:** I-81 to exit 3 onto Commonwealth Ave, right on Euclid Ave for half-mile. **Standard Game Times:**
Mon.-Sat., 7 pm, Sun., 6 pm. **Ticket Price Range:** $4-$8. **Visiting Club Hotel:** Holiday Inn, 3005 Linden Drive Bristol, VA
24202. **Telephone:** (276) 466-4100.

BURLINGTON ROYALS

Office Address: 1450 Graham St, Burlington, NC 27217.
Mailing Address: PO Box 1143, Burlington, NC 27216. **Telephone:** (336) 222-0223.
E-Mail Address: info@burlingtonroyals.com. **Website:** www.burlingtonroyals.com
Affiliation (first year): Kansas City Royals (2007). **Years in League:** 1986-

OWNERSHIP/MANAGEMENT

Operated by: Burlington Baseball Club Inc. **Director:** Alec Zumwalt (Kansas City).
President: Miles Wolff. **General Manager:** Mikie Morrison. **Assistant GM:** Lauren Wagaman.
Director of Operations: Brett Burke

FIELD STAFF

Manager: Chris Widger. **Hitting Coach:** Andy LaRoche. **Pitching Coach:** Carlos Martinez.

GAME INFORMATION

Radio Announcer: Unavailable. **No. of Games Broadcast:** Home-34, Away-4. **Flagship:** www.burlingtonroyals.
com. **PA Announcer:** Unavailable. **Official Scorer:** Unavailable. **Stadium Name:** Burlington Athletic Stadium. **Location:**
I-40/85 to exit 145, north on Route 100 (Maple Avenue) for 1.5 miles, right on Mebane Street for 1.5 miles, right on
Beaumont, left on Graham. **Standard Game Time:** 6:30 pm. **Ticket Price Range:** $6-10. **Visiting Club Hotel:** Best
Western Plus Burlington.

DANVILLE BRAVES

Office Address: Dan Daniel Memorial Park, 302 River Park Dr, Danville, VA 24540.
Mailing Address: PO Box 378, Danville, VA 24543.
Telephone: (434) 797-3792. **Fax:** (434) 797-3799.
E-Mail Address: danvillebraves@braves.com. **Website:** www.dbraves.com.
Affiliation (first year): Atlanta Braves (1993). **Years in League:** 1993-

OWNERSHIP/MANAGEMENT

Operated by: Atlanta National League Baseball Club LLC.
Director: Dom Chiti (Atlanta Braves). **VP/General Manager:** David Cross. **Assistant GM:** Brandon Bennett.
Sales & Marketing Manager: Stephen Brunson. **Head Groundskeeper:** Ryan Brown.

FIELD STAFF

Manager: Anthony Nuñez. **Hitting Coach:** Danny Santiesteban. **Pitching Coach:** Jason Stanford. **Bench Coach:**
Connor Narron. **Athletic Trainer:** Koji Kanemura. **Strength & Conditioning Coach:** Unavailable.

GAME INFORMATION

Radio Announcer: Nick Pierce. **No. of Games Broadcast:** Home-34. **Flagship Station:** www.dbraves.com.
PA Announcer: Jay Stephens. **Official Scorer:** Mark Bowman. **Stadium Name:** American Legion Field Post 325 Field at
Dan Daniel Memorial Park. **Location:** US 29 Bypass to River Park Drive/Dan Daniel Memorial Park exit; follow signs to
park. **Standard Game Times:** Mon.-Sat., 6:30 pm, Sun., 4 pm. **Ticket Price Range:** $5-10. **Visiting Club Hotel:** Comfort
Inn & Suites, 100 Tower Drive, Danville, VA 24540.

ELIZABETHTON TWINS

Office Address: 300 West Mill St., Elizabethton, TN 37643.
Stadium Address: 208 N. Holly Lane, Elizabethton, TN 37643.
Mailing Address: 300 West Mill St., Elizabethton, TN 37643.
Telephone: (423) 547-6441. **Fax:** (423) 547-6442.
Affiliation (first year): Minnesota Twins (1974). **Years in League:** 1937-42, 1945-51, 1974-

OWNERSHIP/MANAGEMENT
Operated by: Unavailable. **Director:** Jeremy Zoll. **President:** Harold Mains. **General Manager:** Mike Mains.

FIELD STAFF
Manager: Ray Smith. **Hitting Coach:** Jeff Reed. **Pitching Coach:** Richard Salazar. **Athletic Trainer:** Matt Kalies.
Strength & Conditioning Coach: Connor Derrickson.

GAME INFORMATION
Radio Announcer: Mike Gallagher. **No. of Games Broadcast:** 34–Home, 6–Away. **Flagship Station:** WBEJ 1240-AM.
PA Announcer: Tom Banks. **Official Scorer:** Gene Renfro. **Stadium Name:** Joe O'Brien Field. **Location:** I-81 to Highway
I-26, exit at Highway 321/67, left on Holly Lane. **Standard Game Times:** 7 pm. **Ticket Price Range:** $3-7. **Visiting Club
Hotel:** Holiday Inn, 101 W Springbrook Dr, Johnson City, TN 37601. **Telephone:** (423) 282-4611.

GREENEVILLE REDS

Office Address: 135 Shiloh Road, Greeneville, TN 37745
Mailing Address: 135 Shiloh Road, Greeneville, TN 37745
Telephone: (423) 609-7400. **E-Mail Address:** contact@greenevillereds.com.
Website: www.greenevillereds.com.

OWNERSHIP/MANAGEMENT
Owned by: Boyd Sports, LLC. **Director:** Shawn Pender (Cincinnati Reds) **General Manager:** Kristen Atwell.

FIELD STAFF
Manager: Gookie Dawkins. **Hitting Coach:** Luis Terrero. **Pitching Coach/Assistant to the Pitching Coordinator:**
Derrin Ebert. **Bench Coach:** Reggie Williams. **Athletic Trainer:** Josh Hobson. **Strength & Conditioning Coach:** Alex
Puskarich.

GAME INFORMATION
Radio Announcer: Unavailable. **Flagship Station:** greenevillereds.com. **PA Announcer:** Unavailable. **Official
Scorer:** Johnny Painter. **Stadium Name:** Pioneer Park. **Location:** On the campus of University, 135 Shiloh Rd
Greeneville, TN 37745. **Standard Game Time:** Mon-Fri., 7 pm, Sat., 7 pm, Sun., 5 pm (times could change due to new
6:30 p.m. proposal). **Ticket Price Range:** $5 group discount, $7 reserved, $8 premium. **Visiting Club Hotel:** Quality Inn,
3160 E Andrew Johnson Hwy, Greeneville, TN 37745. **Telephone:** (423) 638-7511.

JOHNSON CITY CARDINALS

Office Address: 510 Bert St., Johnson City, TN 37601.
Mailing Address: PO Box 179, Johnson City, TN 37605.
Telephone: (423) 461-4866. **E-Mail Address:** contact@jccardinals.com.
Website: www.jccardinals.com. **Affiliation (first year):** St. Louis Cardinals (1975).
Years in League: 1911-13, 1921-24, 1937-55, 1957-61, 1964-

OWNERSHIP/MANAGEMENT
Owned by: St. Louis Cardinals. **Operated by:** Boyd Sports, LLC. **President:** Chris Allen.
Director: Gary Larocque. **General Manager:** Zac Clark. **Assistant General Manager:** Kat Deal.

FIELD STAFF
Manager: Roberto Espinoza. **Hitting Coach:** Brian Burgamy. **Pitching Coach:** Rick Harig.

GAME INFORMATION
PA Announcer: Unavailable. **Official Scorer:** Unavailable. **Stadium Name:** TVA Credit Union Ballpark. **Location:** I-26
to exit 23, left on East Main, through light onto Legion Street. **Standard Game Time:** 7 pm. **Ticket Price Range:** $6-$9.
Visiting Club Hotel: Holiday Inn, 101 W Springbrook Dr, Johnson City, TN 37601. **Telephone:** (423) 282-4611.

KINGSPORT METS

Address: 800 Granby Rd, Kingsport, TN 37660.
Telephone: (423) 224-2626. **Fax:** (423) 224-2625.
E-Mail Address: info@kmets.com. **Website:** www.kmets.com
Affiliation (first year): New York Mets (1980).
Years in League: 1921-25, 1938-52,1957, 1960-63, 1969-82, 1984-

OWNERSHIP/MANAGEMENT
Owner/Operated By: New York Mets. **Director:** Jared Banner. **General Manager:** Brian Paupeck. **Staff:** Josh Lawson. **Clubhouse Manager:** Carlos Martell.

FIELD STAFF
Manager: Rich Donnelly. **Hitting Coach:** Rafael Fernandez. **Pitching Coach:** Jerome Williams.

GAME INFORMATION
PA Announcer: Mike Ezekiel. **Official Scorer:** Zeke Newton. **Stadium Name:** Hunter Wright Stadium. **Location:** I-26, Exit 1 (Stone Drive), left on West Stone Drive (US 11W), right on Granby Road. **Standard Game Times:** Mon-Sat., 6:30 pm, Sun., 4 pm; **Doubleheaders—Mon-Sun.,** 4 pm. **Ticket Price Range:** $5-$8. **Visiting Club Hotel:** Quality Inn, 3004 Bays Mountain Plaza, Kingsport, TN 37664. **Telephone:** (423) 230-0534.

PRINCETON RAYS

Office Address: 345 Old Bluefield Rd, Princeton, WV 24739.
Mailing Address: PO Box 5646, Princeton, WV 24740. **Telephone:** (304) 487-2000.
Fax: (304) 487-8762. **E-Mail Address:** princetonrays@frontier.com. **Website:** www.princetonrays.net.
Affiliation (first year): Tampa Bay Rays (1997). **Years in League:** 1988-

OWNERSHIP/MANAGEMENT
Operated By: Princeton Baseball Association Inc. **Director:** Mitch Lukevics. **President:** Dewey Russell. **General Manager:** Danny Shingleton. **Director, Stadium Operations:** Dewey Russell, Adam Sarver. **Chaplain:** Craig Stout.

FIELD STAFF
Manager: Danny Sheaffer. **Pitching Coach:** Jim Paduch. **Coach:** Wuarnner Rincones. **Coach:** German Melendez. **Athletic Trainer:** Ruben Santiago.

GAME INFORMATION
Radio Announcer: Kyle Cooper. **No. of Games Broadcast:** 34–Away. **Flagship Station:** WAEY-103.3FM. **PA Announcer:** Tommy Lester. **Official Scorer:** Unavailable. **Stadium Name:** Hunnicutt Field. **Location:** Exit 9 off I-77, US 460 West to downtown exit, left on Stafford Drive; stadium located behind Mercer County Technical Education Center. **Standard Game Times:** Mon.-Sat., 6:30 pm, Sun., 5 pm. **Ticket Price Range:** $5-8. **Visiting Club Hotel:** Days Inn, I-77 and Ambrose Lane, Princeton, WV 24740. **Telephone:** (304) 425-8100.

PULASKI YANKEES

Office Address: 529 Pierce Avenue, Pulaski, VA 24301.
Mailing Address: PO Box 852, Pulaski, VA 24301. **Telephone:** (540) 980-1070.
Email Address: info@pulaskiyankees.net. **Affiliation (first season):** New York Yankees (2015).
Years in League: 1942-1951, 1952-55, 1957-58, 1969-77, 1982-92, 1997-2002, 2003-2006, 2008-2014, 2015-

OWNERSHIP/MANAGEMENT
Operated By: Calfee Park Baseball Inc. **Park Owners:** David Hagan, Larry Shelor. **General Manager:** Betsy Haugh. **Assistant General Manager:** James Cahilellis.

FIELD STAFF
Manager: Luis Dorante. **Hitting Coach:** Scott Seabol. **Pitching Coach:** Gerardo Casadiego. **Defensive Coach:** Teuris Olivares. **Athletic Trainer:** Manny Ozoa. **Strength & Conditioning Coach:** Larry Adegoke.

GAME INFORMATION
PA Announcer: Unavailable. **Official Scorer:** Unavailable. **Stadium Name:** Historic Calfee Park. **Location:** Interstate 81 to Exit 89-B (Route 11), north to Pulaski, right on Pierce Avenue. **Ticket Price Range:** $5-11. **Visiting Club Hotel:** Quality Inn, Dublin, Va.

PIONEER BASEBALL LEAGUE

Office Address: 812 W. 30th Avenue, Spokane, WA 99203.
Mailing Address: PO Box 2564, Spokane, WA 99220.
Telephone: (509) 456-7615. **Fax:** (509) 456-0136.
E-Mail Address: fanmail@pioneerleague.com.
Website: www.pioneerleague.com.
Years League Active: 1939-42, 1946-
President: Jim McCurdy.

Jim McCurdy

Directors: Dave Baggott (Ogden), Peter C. Davis (Missoula), DG Elmore (Colorado Springs), Kevin Greene (Idaho Falls), Michael Baker (Grand Junction), Jeff Katofsky (Orem), Vinny Purpura (Great Falls), Dave Heller (Billings). **League Administrator:** Teryl MacDonald.

Executive Director: Mary Ann McCurdy.

Division Structure: North—Billings, Great Falls, Idaho Falls, Missoula. **South**—Colorado Springs, Grand Junction, Ogden, Orem.

Regular Season: 76 games (split schedule). **2018 Opening Date:** June 14. **Closing Date:** Sept. 7. **All-Star Game:** Aug. 6 at Boise (Pioneer Baseball League vs. Northwest League).

Playoff Format: First-half division winners meet second-half division winners in best-of-three series. Winners meet in best-of-three series for league championship. **Roster Limit:** 35 active, 35 dressed for each game. **Player Eligibility Rule:** No player on active list may have three or more years of prior minor league service. **Brand of Baseball:** Rawlings. **Umpires:** Unavailable.

STADIUM INFORMATION

Club	Stadium	Opened	Dimensions LF	CF	RF	Capacity	2018 Att.
Billings	Dehler Park	2008	329	410	350	3,071	93,466
Grand Junction	Sam Suplizio Field	1949	302	400	333	7,014	84,416
Great Falls	Centene Stadium at Legion Park	1956	335	414	335	3,800	47,625
Idaho Falls	Melaleuca Field	1976	340	400	350	3,400	101,448
Missoula	Ogren Park at Allegiance Field	2004	309	398	287	3,500	65,919
Ogden	Lindquist Field	1997	335	396	334	5,000	129,285
Orem	Home of the Owlz	2005	305	408	312	4,500	51,092
Rocky Mountain	Security Service Field	1988	350	410	350	8,500	N/A

BILLINGS MUSTANGS

Office Address: Dehler Park, 2611 9th Avenue North, Billings, MT 59101.
Mailing Address: PO Box 1553, Billings, MT 59103-1553.
Telephone: (406) 252-1241. **Fax:** (406) 252-2968.
E-Mail Address: mustangs@billingsmustangs.com. **Website:** billingsmustangs.com.
Affiliation (first year): Cincinnati Reds (1974). **Years in League:** 1948-63, 1969-

OWNERSHIP/MANAGEMENT

Operated By: Mustangs Baseball LLC.
President/CEO: Dave Heller. **General Manager:** Gary Roller. **Director, Corporate Sales/Partnerships:** Chris Marshall. **Director, Stadium Operations:** Matt Schoonover. **Director, Broadcasting/Media Relations:** Dustin Daniel. **Director, Food and Beverage Services:** Curt Prchal. **Director, Field Operations:** Jeff Limburg.

FIELD STAFF

Manager: Ray Martinez. **Hitting Coach:** Darryl Brinkley. **Pitching Coach:** Chris Booker. **Bench Coach:** Bryan LaHair. **Athletic Trainer:** Brandon Blascak. **Strength & Conditioning Coach:** Blaine Taylor.

GAME INFORMATION

Radio Broadcaster: Dustin Daniel. **No. of Games Broadcast:** 76. **Flagship Station:** ESPN 910-AM KBLG. **PA Announcer:** Sarah Spangle. **Official Scorer:** Evan O'Kelly. **Stadium Name:** Dehler Park. **Location:** I-90 to Exit 450, north on 27th Street North to 9th Avenue North. **Standard Game Times:** Mon.–Sat., 6:35 pm, Sun., 1:05 pm. **Ticket Price Range:** $5-$11.

GRAND JUNCTION ROCKIES

Address: 1315 North Ave., Grand Junction, CO, 81501
Telephone: (970) 255-7625. **Fax:** (970) 241-2374
Email: mritter@gjrockies.com. **Website:** www.gjrockies.com
Affiliation (first year): Colorado Rockies (2001). **Years in League:** 2001–

OWNERSHIP/MANAGEMENT
Principal Owners/Operated by: GJR, LLC. **President:** Joe Kubly. **Assistant GM:** Mick Ritter. **Operations Manager:** Matt Allen. **Marketing Manager:** Jarah Wright.

FIELD STAFF
Manager: Jake Opitz. **Hitting Coach:** Zach Osborne. **Pitching Coach:** Blaine Beatty. **Supervisor:** Andy Gonzalez.

GAME INFORMATION
Radio Announcer: Kyle Kercheval . **No. of Games Broadcast:** 76. **Flagship Station:** MiLB.TV, gjrockies.com. **Television Announcer:** Kyle Kercheval. **No. of Games Televised:** Unavailable. **Flagship:** KGJT—My Network, Dish Network. **Produced by:** Colorado Mesa University. **PA Announcer:** Tim Ray. **Official Scorers:** Unavailable. **Stadium Name:** Suplizio Field. **Location:** 1315 North Ave. Grand Junction, CO 81501. **Standard Game Times:** 6:40 pm. **Ticket Price Range:** $7-$11.

GREAT FALLS VOYAGERS

Address: 1015 25th St N, Great Falls, MT 59401.
Telephone: (406) 452-5311. **Fax:** (406) 454-0811.
E-Mail Address: voyagers@gfvoyagers.com. **Website:** www.gfvoyagers.com.
Affiliation (first year): Chicago White Sox (2003). **Years in League:** 1948-1963, 1969-

OWNERSHIP/MANAGEMENT
Operated By: Great Falls Baseball Club.
President: Vinney Purpura. **General Manager:** Scott Reasoner. **Assistant General Manager:** Scott Lettre.
Community Relations Director: Bailey Johnson. **Marketing and Groups Manager:** Deaven Palm.

FIELD STAFF
Manager: Tim Esmay. **Hitting Coach:** Cameron Seitzer. **Pitching Coach:** John Ely.

GAME INFORMATION
Radio Announcer: Shawn Tiemann. **No. of Games Broadcast:** 76. **Flagship Station:** KXGF-1400 AM. **PA Announcer:** Chris Evans. **Official Scorer:** Mike Lewis. **Stadium Name:** Centene Stadium. **Location:** From I-15 to exit 281 (10th Ave S), left on 26th, left on Eighth Ave North, right on 25th, ballpark on right, past railroad tracks. **Ticket Price Range:** $5-10. **Visiting Club Hotel:** Days Inn, 101 14th Ave NW, Great Falls, MT 59404. **Telephone:** (406) 727-6565.

IDAHO FALLS CHUKARS

Office Address: 900 Jim Garchow Way, Idaho Falls, ID 83402.
Mailing Address: PO 2183, Idaho, ID 83403.
Telephone: (208) 522-8363. **Fax:** (208) 522-9858.
E-Mail Address: chukars@ifchukars.com. **Website:** www.ifchukars.com.
Affiliation (first year): Kansas City Royals (2004). **Years in League:** 1940-42, 1946-

OWNERSHIP/MANAGEMENT
Operated By: The Elmore Sports Group. **Principal Owner:** David Elmore.
President/General Manager: Kevin Greene. **Vice President:** Paul Henderson. **Assistant GM:** Josh Michalsen.
Director, Operations: Aaron Madero. **Clubhouse Manager:** Patrick Greene. **Head Groundskeeper:** Brenden Seaver.

FIELD STAFF
Manager: Omar Ramirez. **Hitting Coach:** Damon Hollins. **Pitching Coach:** Clayton Mortensen.

GAME INFORMATION
Radio Announcer: John Balginy. **No. of Games Broadcast:** 76. **Flagship Station:** ESPN 980-AM & 94.5 and 105.1FM.
PA Announcer: Javier Hernandez. **Official Scorer:** John Balginy. **Stadium Name:** Melaleuca Field. **Location:** I-15 to
West Broadway exit, left onto Memorial Drive, right on Mound Avenue, 1/4 mile to the stadium. **Standard Game
Times:** Mon.-Sat., 7:15 pm, Sun., 4:00 pm. **Ticket Price Range:** $8-12. **Visiting Club Hotel:** Fairbridge Inn & Suites, 850
Lindsay Blvd, Idaho Falls, ID 83402. **Telephone:** (208) 522-6260.

MISSOULA OSPREY

Address: 140 N Higgins, Suite 201, Missoula, MT 59802. **Telephone:** (406) 543-3300.
E-Mail Address: info@missoulaosprey.com. **Website:** www.missoulaosprey.com.
Affiliation (first year): Arizona Diamondbacks (1999). **Years in League:** 1956-60, 1999-

OWNERSHIP/MANAGEMENT
Operated By: Big Sky Baseball LLC. **Co-Chairs:** Peter & Susan Crampton Davis.
Vice President: Matt Ellis. **Director/Sales:** Tono Lippy. **Office Manager/Bookkeeper:** Nola Hunter. **Director/
Community Engagement & Retail:** Kim Klages Johns. **Director of Operations/Sales Executive:** Taylor Rush.
Ticket Sales & Box Office Specialist: Robert Rink.

FIELD STAFF
Manager: Juan Francia. **Hitting Coach:** KC Judge. **Pitching Coach:** Manny Garcia. **Bench Coach:** Mike Benjamin.
Athletic Trainer: Daniel Fifer. **Strength & Conditioning Coach:** Nathan Friedman.

GAME INFORMATION
Radio Announcer: Unavailable. **No. of Games Broadcast:** 76. **Flagship Station:** ESPN 102.9 FM. **PA Announcer:**
RJ Hentz. **Official Scorer:** Unavailable. **Stadium Name:** Ogren Park Allegiance Field. **Location:** Take Orange Street to
Cregg Lane, west on Cregg Lane, stadium west of McCormick Park past railroad trestle. **Standard Game Times:** Mon.-
Sat., 7:05 pm, Sun., 5:05 pm. **Ticket Price Range:** $8-14. **Visiting Club Hotel:** Comfort Inn-University, 1021 E. Broadway,
Missoula, MT 59802. **Telephone:** (406) 549-7600.

OGDEN RAPTORS

Address: 2330 Lincoln Ave, Ogden, UT 84401. **Telephone:** (801) 393-2400. **Fax:** (801)
393-2473.
E-Mail Address: homerun@ogden-raptors.com. **Website:** www.ogden-raptors.com.
Affiliation (first year): Los Angeles Dodgers (2003). **Years in League:** 1939-42,
1946-55, 1966-74, 1994-

OWNERSHIP/MANAGEMENT
Operated By: Ogden Professional Baseball, Inc. **Principal Owners:** Dave Baggott, John Lindquist.
President/General Manager: Dave Baggott. **Director, Media Relations/Broadcaster:** Andrew Haynes. **Director,
Food Services:** Stacy Oliver. **Director, Security:** Scott McGregor. **Director, Social Media:** Kevin Johnson. **Director,
Ticket Operations:** Trevor Wilson. **Director, Information Technology:** Chris Greene. **Public Relations:** Pete Diamond.
Groundskeeper: Kenny Kopinski. **Assistant Groundskeeper:** Bob Richardson.

FIELD STAFF
Manager: Jeremy Rodriguez. **Hitting Coach:** Dustin Kelly. **Pitching Coach:** Dean Stiles. **Clubhouse Manager:** Dave
"MacGyver" Ackerman.

GAME INFORMATION
Radio Announcer: Andrew Haynes. **No. of Games Broadcast:** 76. **Flagship Station:** ogden-raptors.com. **PA
Announcer:** Pete Diamond. **Official Scorer:** Dennis Kunimura. **Stadium Name:** Lindquist Field. **Location:** I-15 North to

21th Street exit, east to Lincoln Avenue, south three blocks to park. **Standard Game Times:** Mon.-Sat., 7 pm, Sun., 4pm. **Ticket Price Range:** $4-10. **Visiting Club Hotel:** Unavailable.

OREM OWLZ

Address: 970 W. University Parkway, Orem, UT 84058. **Telephone:**(801) 377-2255.
E-Mail Address: matt@oremowlz.com. **Website:** www.oremowlz.com.
Affiliation (first year): Los Angeles Angels (2001). **Years in League:**2001-

OWNERSHIP/MANAGEMENT
Operated By: Bery Bery Gud To Me LLC. **Principal Owner:** Jeff Katofsky.
General Manager: Rick Berry. **Assistant GM:** Julie Hatch. **Director, Sales & Marketing:** Connor Cude. **Director, Public Relations:** Cory Snyder.

FIELD STAFF
Manager: Jack Santora. **Hitting Coach:** Ryan Sebra. **Pitching Coach:** J. Watson/B. Garman

GAME INFORMATION
Radio Announcer: Michael Broskowski. **No. of Games Broadcast:** 76. **Flagship Station:** Unavailable. **PA Announcer:** Doug Warr. **Official Scorer:** Unavailable. **Stadium Name:** Home of the Owlz. **Location:** Exit 269 (University Parkway) off I-15 at Utah Valley University campus. **Ticket Price Range:**$6-11. **Visiting Club Hotel:** La Quinta Inn & Suites Orem University Parkway, 521 W Universtiy Prky, Orem, UT 84058. **Telephone:** (801) 226-0440.

ROCKY MOUNTAIN VIBES

Address: 4385 Tutt Blvd., Colorado Springs, CO 80922.
Telephone: (719) 597-1449. **Fax:** (719) 597-2491.
E-Mail address: info@vibesbaseball.com. **Website:** www.vibesbaseball.com.
Affiliation (first year): Milwaukee Brewers (2015). **Years in League:** 2019-

OWNERSHIP/MANAGEMENT
Operated By: Rocky Mountain Vibes. **Principal Owner:** Dave Elmore. **President/General Manager:** Chris Phillips. **Assistant GM:** Keith Hodges. **Director, Public & Media Relations:** Travis Arnold. **Sr. Director, Ticketing/Merchandise:** Patrick Trainor. **Director, Accounting:** Ed Duffett. Director, **Production & Promotions:** Abby Kappel. **Director, Marketing:** Kyle Fritzke. **VP, Field Operations:** Steve DeLeon. **Manager, Community Relations:** Crystal Mazey. **Manager, Group Sales/Military Liaison:** Jonathan Basil. **Manager, Group Sales:** Josh Preli. **Event Manager:** Brien Smith. **GM, Diamond Creations:** Don Giuliano. **Executive Chef:** Chris Evans. **Clubhouse Manager:** Christian Andreas.

FIELD STAFF
Manager: Nestor Corredor. **Hitting Coach:** Liu Rodriguez. **Pitching Coach:** Rolando Valles.

GAME INFORMATION
No. of Games Broadcast: 76. **Flagship Station:** Xtra Sports 1300. **PA Announcer:** Don Arcuri. **Official Scorers:** Marty Grantz, Rich Wastler. **Stadium Name:** Security Service Field. **Location:** I-25 South to Woodmen Road exit, east on Woodmen to Powers Blvd., right on Powers to Barnes Road. **Standard Game Times:** Mon.-Fri., 6:40 pm, Sat., 6:00 pm, Sun., 1:30 pm. **Ticket Price Range:** $5-15.

ARIZONA LEAGUE

Office Address: 620 W Franklin St., Boise, ID 83702. **Mailing Address:** PO Box 1645, Boise, ID 83701.
Telephone: (208) 429-1511. **Fax:** (208) 429-1525. **E-Mail Address:** bobrichmond@qwestoffice.net
Years League Active: 1988- **President/Treasurer:** Bob Richmond. **Vice President:** Mike Bell (D-backs).
Corporate Secretary: Zak Basch. **Administrative Assistant:** Rob Richmond.

Divisional Alignment: East—Athletics Green, Athletics Gold, Cubs 1, Cubs 2, Giants Orange, Giants Black, Angels
and Diamondbacks. **Central**—Brewers Gold, Dodgers 2, Indians Blue, Padres 2, White Sox, and Reds. **West**—Brewers
Blue, Dodgers 1, Indians Red, Padres 1, Mariners, Royals, and Rangers. **Regular Season:** 56 games (split schedule).
2018 Opening Date: June 18. **Closing Date:** Aug. 25. **Playoff Format:** Six teams qualify. The three division champions
from each half qualify for the single-elimination playoffs. If the same team wins a division in both halves, the team with
the second-best overall record from the other division teams would qualify as the second team from that division. The
two clubs with the best overall records receive first-round byes. Quarterfinal winners advance to a one-game playoff
against one of the clubs that received a bye. Semifinal winners meet in a best-of-three series for the league championship. **All-Star Game:** None. **Roster Limit:** 35 active. **Player Eligibility Rule:** No player may have three or more years of
prior minor league service.

Clubs	Playing Site	Manager	Hitting Coach	Pitching Coach
Angels	Angels Complex, Tempe	David Stapleton	T. Jeske/D. Ortega	T. Anderson/TBD
Athletics Green	Fitch Park, Mesa	Eddie Menchaca	Francisco Santana	Gabriel Ozuna
Athletics Gold	Fitch Park, Mesa	Hiram Bocachica	Ruben Escalera	Bryan Coney
Brewers Blue	Maryvale Baseball Complex, Phoenix	Rafael Neda	Brenton Del Chiaro	Hiram Burgos
Brewers Gold	Maryvale Baseball Complex, Phoenix	Liu Rodriguez	Bobby Spain	Steve Cline
Cubs 1	Cubs Park, Mesa	Carmelo Martinez	Michael Carter	Anderson Tavarez
Cubs 2	Cubs Park, Mesa	Lance Rymel	Claudio Almonte	Manny Olivera
D-backs	Salt River Fields at Talking Stick	Wellington Cepeda	Jose Amado	Rich Sauveur
Dodgers	Camelback Ranch, Phoenix	Jair Fernandez	Jarek Cunningham	Stephanos Stroop
Giants 1	Giants Complex, Scottsdale	Michael Johnson	Travis Ishikawa	Mike Rodriguez
Giants 2	Giants Complex, Scottsdale	Alvaro Espinoza	Casey Chenoweth	Mike Couchee
Indians 1	Goodyear Ballpark	Larry Day	Jordan Becker	Joel Mangrum
Indians 2	Goodyear Ballpark	Jerry Owens	Junior Betances	Mike Steele
Mariners	Peoria Sports Complex	Zac Livingston	Connor Dawson	Yoel Monzon
Padres 1	Peoria Sports Complex	Vinny Lopez	Jed Morris	Giancarlo Alvarado
Padres 2	Peoria Sports Complex	Aaron Levin	Raul Gonzalez	John Halama
Rangers	Surprise Recreation Campus	Carlos Cardoza	C. Comer/E. Dorton/G. Rodrigues	B. Conger/S. Cashman
Reds	Goodyear Ballpark	Jose Nieves	Todd Takayoshi	Elmer Dessens
Royals	Surprise Recreation Campus	Tony Pena Jr.	R. Castro/W. Aikens	M. Davis/J. Pimentel
White Sox	Camelback Ranch, Phoenix	Evan Magallanes	Gary Ward	Felipe Lira

GULF COAST LEAGUE

Operated By: Minor League Baseball.
Office Address: 9550 16th Street North, St Petersburg, FL 33716.
Telephone: 727-456-1734. **Fax:** 727-456-1745. **Website:** www.milb.com. **Email Address:** gcl@milb.com.
Senior Vice President, Baseball & Business Operations: Tim Brunswick. **Assistant Director, Baseball & Business Operations:** Andy Shultz. **2019 Opening Date:** June 24. **Closing Date:** August 31. **Regular Season:** 56 Games (East, South)/52 Games (North). **Divisional Alignment: East**—Astros, Cardinals, Marlins, Mets, Nationals. **North**—Blue Jays, Phillies East, Phillies West, Tigers East, Tigers West, Yankees East, Yankees West. **South**—Braves, Orioles, Pirates, Rays, Red Sox, Twins. **Playoff Format:** The division winner with the best winning percentage plays the wild card (the non-division winner with best winning percentage) and the other two division winners meet in a one game semifinal. The winners meet in a best-of-three series for the Gulf Coast League championship. **All-Star Game:** None. **Roster Limit:** 35 active and in uniform and eligible to play in any given game. At least 10 must be pitchers as of July 1. **Player Eligibility Rule:** No player may have three or more years of prior minor league service. **Brand of Baseball:** Rawlings. **Statistician:** Major League Baseball Advanced Media.

Clubs	Playing Site	Manager	Hitting Coach	Pitching Coach
Astros	The Ballpark of the Palm Beaches	Wladimir Sutil	Rene Rojas	Jose Rada
Blue Jays	Bobby Mattick Training Center,	Dennis Holmberg	Abreu, Carroll	Mark Worrell
Braves	Braves Complex,	Nestor Perez	Albert, Garvey, Narron	Elvin Nina
Cardinals	Cardinals Complex	Joshua Lopez	Joe Hawkins	Giovanni Carrara
Marlins	Roger Dean Stadium Complex	Robert Rodriguez	Jesus Merchan	Jason Erickson
Mets	Mets Complex	David Davillilo	Joel Fuentes	Ariel Prieto
Nationals	The Ballpark of the Palm Beaches	Mario Lisson	Jorge Mejia	Larry Pardo
Orioles	Ed Smith Stadium Complex	Alan Mills	Milt May, Carols Tosca	Wilson Alvarez
Phillies E.	Carpenter Complex, Clearwater	Roly deArmas	Rafael De Lima,	Hector Mercado
Phillies W.	Carpenter Complex, Clearwater	Milver Reyes	Charlie Hayes	Heintz, Wernes, Billings
Pirates	Pirate City, Bradenton	Jera Alvarez	Petersen, Gustavo	Fernando Nieve
Rays	Charlotte Sports Park	Rafael Valenzuela	North, Morrison	Bastardo, DeMerritt
Red Sox	Jet Blue Park, Fort Myers	Tom Kotchman	Zamora, Berroa, Jiang	Bonilla, Such
Tigers East	Tigertown, Lakeland	Luis Lopez	Rafael Gil	Jose Parra
Tigers West	Tigertown, Lakeland	Gary Cathcart	John Murrian	Mike Alvarez
Twins	Lee County Sports Complex,	Robbie Robinson	Rasmussen, Abney	Bove, Hernandez
Yankees E.	Himes Complex, Tampa	Dan Fiorito	Pacheco,Coa	Gabriel Tatis
Yankees W.	Himes Complex, Tampa	Nick Ortiz	Hirst, Diaz, Rabago	Pope, Nieve

TEAM SCHEDULES

TRIPLE-A

INTERNATIONAL LEAGUE

BUFFALO BISONS

APRIL
4-7 . . . . Scranton/WB
8-10 . . . . .Pawtucket
11-14 . . . at Scranton/WB
15-17 . . . . . at Pawtucket
19-20 . . . . . Scranton/WB
22-25 . . . . . at Syracuse
26-28 . . . at Lehigh Valley
29-30 . . . . . . .Pawtucket

MAY
1-2 . . . . .Pawtucket
3-5 . . . . . Lehigh Valley
7-9 . . . . . . at Gwinnett
10-12 . . . . . at Norfolk
14-16 . . . . . . Gwinnett
17-19 . . . . . Louisville
21-23 . . . . at Rochester
24-27 . . . at Lehigh Valley
28-30 . . . . . . .Syracuse
31 . . . . . . at Rochester

JUNE
1-2 . . . . . at Rochester
3-6 . . . . . . Scranton/WB
7-9 . . . . . Lehigh Valley
11-13 . . . . at Indianapolis
14-16 . . . . at Louisville
18-20 . . . . . .Indianapolis

CHARLOTTE KNIGHTS

APRIL
4-7 . . . . Durham
8-10 . . . . .Norfolk
11-14 . . . at Indianapolis
15-18 . . . . . at Gwinnett
19-21 . . . . . at Norfolk
23-25 . . . . Toledo
26-28 . . . . .Indianapolis
29-30 . . . . . . Gwinnett

MAY
1 . . . . Gwinnett
2-5 . . . . . . at Norfolk
7-9 . . . . . at Columbus
10-12 . . . . at Louisville
14-16 . . . . . Rochester
17-19 . . . . Lehigh Valley
21-23 . . . . at Gwinnett
24-27 . . . . . . Durham
28-30 . . . at Indianapolis
31 . . . . .at Toledo

JUNE
1-2 . . . . .at Toledo
3-5 . . . . Gwinnett
6-9 . . . . Louisville
11-13 . . . . . at Syracuse
14-16 . . . . at Rochester
18-20 . . . . . . Syracuse

COLUMBUS CLIPPERS

APRIL
4-7 . . . . .Indianapolis
8-10 . . . . . . Louisville
11-14 . . . . . . .at Durham

21-23 . . . . .Norfolk
24-25 . . . . . at Pawtucket
26-27 . . . at Scranton/WB
28-30 . . . . Syracuse

JULY
1-3 . . . . . . Lehigh Valley
4-7 . . . . . . at Syracuse
11-14 . . . . at Pawtucket
15-18 . . . . . . Charlotte
19-21 . . . . . . Columbus
23-25 . . . . . at Charlotte
26-28 . . . . . .at Durham
29-30 . . . . . . Rochester
31 . . . . . at Lehigh Valley

AUGUST
1 . . . . . at Lehigh Valley
2-4 . . . . Syracuse
6-8 . . . . .at Toledo
9-11 . . . . . at Columbus
13-15 . . . . Toledo
16-18 . . . . Durham
19-22 . . . . . at Rochester
23-25 . . . . . .Pawtucket
26-29 . . . . . . Rochester
30-31 . . . at Scranton/WB

SEPTEMBER
1-2 . . . . . at Scranton/WB

APRIL
21-23 . . . . . . Louisville
24-25 . . . . . .at Durham
26-27 . . . . . . Gwinnett
28-30 . . . . . at Norfolk

JULY
1-3 . . . . .at Durham
4-7 . . . . .Norfolk
11-14 . . . . . . Gwinnett
15-18 . . . . . at Buffalo
19-21 . . . at Pawtucket
23-25 . . . . .Buffalo
26-28 . . . . . .Pawtucket
29-30 . . . . at Norfolk
31 . . . . Durham

AUGUST
1 . . . . Durham
2-4 . . . . . . at Gwinnett
6-8 . . . . . at Scranton/WB
9-11 . . . at Lehigh Valley
13-15 . . . Scranton/WB
16-18 . . . . . . .Columbus
19-22 . . . . . .at Durham
23-25 . . . . . . .Norfolk
26-29 . . . . . . Durham
30-31 . . . . . at Norfolk

SEPTEMBER
1-2 . . . . at Norfolk

APRIL
15-18 . . . . . .at Louisville
19-21 . . . . .at Toledo
23-25 . . . . . . .Norfolk
26-28 . . . . Durham

29-30 . . . . .at Indianapolis

MAY
1 . . . . . . at Indianapolis
2-5 . . . . .at Toledo
7-9 . . . . Charlotte
10-12 . . . . . . Syracuse
14-16 . . . . at Pawtucket
17-19 . . . . at Syracuse
21-23 . . . . Toledo
24-27 . . . . .Indianapolis
28-30 . . . . . at Norfolk
31 . . . . at Durham

JUNE
1-2 . . . . . . .at Durham
3-5 . . . . Toledo
6-9 . . . . .Norfolk
11-13 . . . . at Rochester
14-16 . . . at Lehigh Valley
18-20 . . . . . Rochester
21-23 . . . . Lehigh Valley
24-25 . . . . Toledo
26-27 . . . .at Indianapolis
28-30 . . . . .at Louisville

DURHAM BULLS

APRIL
4-7 . . . . .at Charlotte
8-9 . . . . at Gwinnett
11-14 . . . . . . Columbus
15-18 . . . . . at Norfolk
19-21 . . . . . . Gwinnett
23-25 . . . . .at Louisville
26-28 . . . . at Columbus
29-30 . . . . .Norfolk

MAY
1 . . . . .Norfolk
2-6 . . . . Gwinnett
7-9 . . . . at Lehigh Valley
10-12 . . . . at Rochester
14-16 . . . . Lehigh Valley
17-19 . . . . . Rochester
21-23 . . . . at Norfolk
24-27 . . . . at Charlotte
28-30 . . . . . Louisville
31 . . . . Columbus

JUNE
1-2 . . . . Columbus
3-5 . . . . .Norfolk
6-9 . . . . . . at Gwinnett
11-13 . . . . Toledo
14-16 . . . . Scranton/WB
18-20 . . . . at Pawtucket
21-23 . . . at Scranton/WB

24-25 . . . . Charlotte
26-27 . . . . .Norfolk
28-30 . . . . . . .at Toledo

JULY
1-3 . . . . Charlotte
4-7 . . . . at Gwinnett
11-14 . . . . .Norfolk
15-18 . . . . . . .at Toledo
19-21 . . . at Indianapolis
23-25 . . . . . .Pawtucket
26-28 . . . . .Buffalo
29-30 . . . . . at Gwinnett
31 . . . . at Charlotte

AUGUST
1 . . . . at Charlotte
2-4 . . . . at Norfolk
6-8 . . . . Syracuse
9-11 . . . . . .Indianapolis
13-15 . . . . at Syracuse
16-18 . . . . . at Buffalo
19-22 . . . . . . Charlotte
23-25 . . . . . . Gwinnett
26-29 . . . . at Charlotte
30-31 . . . . . . Gwinnett

SEPTEMBER
1-2 . . . . Gwinnett

GWINNETT STRIPERS

APRIL
4-7 . . . . .Norfolk
8-9 . . . . Durham
11-14 . . . . .at Louisville
15-18 . . . . . . Charlotte
19-21 . . . . . .at Durham
23-25 . . . . .Indianapolis
26-28 . . . . . . Toledo
29-30 . . . . .at Charlotte

MAY
1 . . . . at Charlotte
2-6 . . . . .at Durham

7-9 . . . . .Buffalo
10-12 . . . . . . .Pawtucket
14-16 . . . . . at Buffalo
17-19 . . . . at Pawtucket
21-23 . . . . . . Charlotte
24-27 . . . . . . .Norfolk
28-30 . . . . . . .at Toledo
31 . . . . . .at Indianapolis

JUNE
1-2 . . . . . at Indianapolis
3-5 . . . . .at Charlotte
6-9 . . . . Durham

11-13 . . . . at Lehigh Valley
14-16 . . . . . . at Syracuse
18-20 . . . . Louisville
21-23 . . . . Syracuse
24-25 . . . . . . at Norfolk
26-27 . . . . . at Charlotte
28-30 . . . . .Indianapolis

JULY
1-3 . . . . at Norfolk
4-7 . . . . Durham
11-14 . . . . . at Charlotte
15-18 . . . . . Lehigh Valley
19-21 . . . . . . Rochester
23-25 . . . . . at Louisville
26-28 . . . . . at Columbus
29-30 . . . . Durham
31 . . . . .Norfolk

AUGUST
1 . . . . .Norfolk
2-4 . . . . Charlotte
6-8 . . . . . at Rochester
9-11 . . . at Scranton/WB
13-15 . . . . . . Columbus
16-18 . . . . Scranton/WB
19-22 . . . . . at Norfolk
23-25 . . . . .at Durham
26-29 . . . . . . .Norfolk
30-31 . . . . . .at Durham

SEPTEMBER
1-2 . . . . .at Durham

INDIANAPOLIS INDIANS

APRIL
4-7 . . . . . . at Columbus
9-10 . . . . .at Toledo
11-14 . . . . . . Charlotte
15-18 . . . . Toledo
19-21 . . . . . . Louisville
23-25 . . . . . at Gwinnett
26-28 . . . . at Charlotte
29-30 . . . . . . Columbus

MAY
1 . . . . Columbus
2-5 . . . . Louisville
7-9 . . . at Scranton/WB
10-12 . . at Lehigh Valley
14-16 . . . . Scranton/WB
17-19 . . . . . .Norfolk
21-23 . . . .at Louisville
24-27 . . . . at Columbus
28-30 . . . . . Charlotte
31 . . . . Gwinnett

JUNE
1-2 . . . . Gwinnett
3-5 . . . . . . at Louisville
6-9 . . . . . . .at Toledo
11-13 . . . . Buffalo
14-16 . . . . . . Pawtucket
18-20 . . . . . at Buffalo
21-23 . . . . . at Pawtucket
24-25 . . . . . . Louisville
26-27 . . . . . . Columbus
28-30 . . . at Gwinnett

JULY
1-3 . . . . . at Louisville
4-7 . . . . Toledo
11-14 . . . . . at Columbus
15-18 . . . . . . Syracuse
19-21 . . . . . . Durham
23-25 . . . . at Syracuse
26-28 . . . . at Rochester
29-30 . . . . . Columbus
31 . . . . .at Toledo

AUGUST
1 . . . . .at Toledo
2-4 . . . . Columbus
6-8 . . . . . at Norfolk
9-11 . . . . . .at Durham
13-15 . . . . . Rochester
16-18 . . . Lehigh Valley
19-22 . . . . . .at Toledo
23-24 . . . . . . Louisville
25 . . . . . at Louisville
26-29 . . . . . Toledo
30-31 . . . . . Columbus

SEPTEMBER
1-2 . . . . . at Louisville

LEHIGH VALLEY IRONPIGS

APRIL
4-7 . . . . Rochester
8-10 . . . . . Scranton/WB
11-14 . . . . . at Rochester
15-17 . . . at Scranton/WB
18-20 . . . . . . Rochester
22-25 . . . . at Pawtucket
26-28 . . . . . . Buffalo
29-30 . . . . . . Syracuse

MAY
1-2 . . . . Syracuse
3-5 . . . . . . at Buffalo
7-9 . . . . Durham
10-12 . . . .Indianapolis
14-16 . . . .at Durham
17-19 . . .at Charlotte
21-23 . . . . . . Syracuse
24-27 . . . . . . Buffalo
28-30 . . . . at Pawtucket
31 . . . . . at Scranton/WB

JUNE
1-2 . . . . at Scranton/WB
3-4 . . . . . at Pawtucket
5-6 . . . . . at Pawtucket
7-9 . . . . at Buffalo
11-13 . . . . . . Gwinnett
14-16 . . . . . . Columbus
18-20 . . . . . .at Toledo
21-23 . . . . at Columbus
24-25 . . . . at Syracuse
26-27 . . . . . Rochester
28-30 . . . . Scranton/WB

JULY
1-3 . . . . at Buffalo
4-7 . . . . .Pawtucket
11-14 . . . . at Rochester
15-18 . . . .at Gwinnett
19-21 . . . . at Norfolk
23-25 . . . . . . Toledo
26-28 . . . . . .Norfolk
29-30 . . . . .Pawtucket
31 . . . . Buffalo

AUGUST
1 . . . . Buffalo
2-4 . . . . at Scranton/WB
6-8 . . . . Louisville
9-11 . . . . . . Charlotte
13-15 . . . . at Louisville

16-18 . . . . . at Indianapolis
19-22 . . . . . . Syracuse
23-25 . . . . Scranton/WB
26-29 . . . . at Syracuse

LOUISVILLE BATS

APRIL
4-7 . . . . .at Toledo
8-10 . . . . at Columbus
11-14 . . . . . Gwinnett
15-18 . . . . . Columbus
19-21 . . . at Indianapolis
23-25 . . . . . Durham
26-28 . . . . . .Norfolk
29-30 . . . .at Toledo

MAY
1 . . . . .at Toledo
2-5 . . . . . at Indianapolis
7-9 . . . . Syracuse
10-12 . . . . . Charlotte
14-16 . . . . at Syracuse
17-19 . . . . . at Buffalo
21-23 . . . .Indianapolis
24-27 . . . . . . Toledo
28-30 . . . .at Durham
31 . . . . . at Norfolk

JUNE
1-2 . . . . at Norfolk
3-5 . . . . . . .Indianapolis
6-9 . . . . . at Charlotte
11-13 . . . . .Pawtucket
14-16 . . . . . Buffalo
18-20 . . . . at Gwinnett
21-23 . . . . at Charlotte
24-25 . . . . at Indianapolis
26-27 . . . . . Toledo
28-30 . . . . Columbus

JULY
1-3 . . . . . . .Indianapolis
4-7 . . . . . at Columbus
11-14 . . . . . Toledo
15-18 . . . . at Pawtucket
19-21 . . . at Scranton/WB
23-25 . . . . . Gwinnett
26-28 . . . . Scranton/WB
29-30 . . . .at Toledo
31 . . . . . at Columbus

AUGUST
1 . . . . at Columbus
2-4 . . . . Toledo
6-8 . . . . . at Lehigh Valley
9-11 . . . . at Rochester
13-15 . . . . Lehigh Valley
16-18 . . . . . Rochester
19-22 . . . at Columbus
23-24 . . . at Indianapolis
25 . . . . . .Indianapolis
26-29 . . . . . Columbus
30-31 . . . . .at Toledo

SEPTEMBER
1-2 . . . . . .Indianapolis

NORFOLK TIDES

APRIL
4-7 . . . . . . at Gwinnett
8-10 . . . . at Charlotte
11-14 . . . . . . Toledo
15-18 . . . . . Durham
19-21 . . . . . Charlotte
23-25 . . . at Columbus
26-28 . . . at Louisville
29-30 . . . . .at Durham

MAY
1 . . . . .at Durham
2-5 . . . . . Charlotte
7-9 . . . . . . .Pawtucket
10-12 . . . . . Buffalo
14-16 . . . .at Toledo
17-19 . . . at Indianapolis
21-23 . . . . . Durham
24-27 . . . at Gwinnett
28-30 . . . . . Columbus
31 . . . . . . Louisville

JUNE
1-2 . . . . . Louisville
3-5 . . . . .at Durham
6-9 . . . . at Columbus
11-13 . . . . Scranton/WB
14-16 . . . . . Toledo
18-20 . . . at Scranton/WB
21-23 . . . . . at Buffalo
24-25 . . . . . Gwinnett
26-27 . . . .at Durham
28-30 . . . . Charlotte

JULY
1-3 . . . . Gwinnett
4-7 . . . . .at Charlotte
11-14 . . . . .at Durham
15-18 . . . Rochester
19-21 . . . . . Lehigh Valley
23-25 . . . . at Rochester
26-28 . . . at Lehigh Valley
29-30 . . . . . Charlotte
31 . . . . . .at Gwinnett

AUGUST
1 . . . . at Gwinnett
2-4 . . . . Durham
6-8 . . . . . .Indianapolis
9-11 . . . . . . Syracuse
13-15 . . . at Pawtucket
16-18 . . . . at Syracuse
19-22 . . . . . Gwinnett
23-25 . . . .at Charlotte
26-29 . . . .at Gwinnett
30-31 . . . . Charlotte

SEPTEMBER
1-2 . . . . . Charlotte

PAWTUCKET RED SOX

APRIL
4-7 . . . . . at Syracuse
8-10 . . . . . at Buffalo
11-14 . . . . .Syracuse
15-17 . . . . . . Buffalo
19-21 . . . . at Syracuse
22-25 . . . Lehigh Valley
26-28 . . . at Rochester
29-30 . . . . at Buffalo

MAY
- 1-2 . . . . at Buffalo
- 3-5 . . . . Rochester
- 7-9 . . . . at Norfolk
- 10-12 . . . . at Gwinnett
- 14-16 . . . . Columbus
- 17-19 . . . . Gwinnett
- 21-23 . . . . at Scranton/WB
- 24-27 . . . . at Rochester
- 28-30 . . . . Lehigh Valley
- 31 . . . . Syracuse

JUNE
- 1-2 . . . . Syracuse
- 3-4 . . . . Lehigh Valley
- 5-6 . . . . at Lehigh Valley
- 7-9 . . . . Rochester
- 11-13 . . . . at Louisville
- 14-16 . . . . at Indianapolis
- 18-20 . . . . Durham
- 21-23 . . . . Indianapolis
- 24-25 . . . . Buffalo
- 26-27 . . . . at Syracuse
- 28-30 . . . . at Rochester

JULY
- 1-3 . . . . Scranton/WB
- 4-7 . . . . at Lehigh Valley
- 11-14 . . . . Buffalo
- 15-18 . . . . Louisville
- 19-21 . . . . Charlotte
- 23-25 . . . . at Durham
- 26-28 . . . . at Charlotte
- 29-30 . . . . at Lehigh Valley
- 31 . . . . at Syracuse

AUGUST
- 1 . . . . at Syracuse
- 2-4 . . . . Rochester
- 6-8 . . . . at Columbus
- 9-11 . . . . at Toledo
- 13-15 . . . . Norfolk
- 16-18 . . . . Toledo
- 19-22 . . . . at Scranton/WB
- 23-25 . . . . at Buffalo
- 26-29 . . . . Scranton/WB
- 30-31 . . . . Lehigh Valley

SEPTEMBER
- 1-2 . . . . Lehigh Valley

(continued, top right)
- 4-7 . . . . Rochester
- 11-14 . . . . at Syracuse
- 15-18 . . . . Columbus
- 19-21 . . . . Louisville
- 23-25 . . . . at Columbus
- 26-28 . . . . at Louisville
- 29-30 . . . . Syracuse
- 31 . . . . at Rochester

AUGUST
- 1 . . . . at Rochester
- 2-4 . . . . Lehigh Valley

(continued, far right)
- 6-8 . . . . Charlotte
- 9-11 . . . . Gwinnett
- 13-15 . . . . at Charlotte
- 16-18 . . . . at Gwinnett
- 19-22 . . . . Pawtucket
- 23-25 . . . . at Lehigh Valley
- 26-29 . . . . at Pawtucket
- 30-31 . . . . Buffalo

SEPTEMBER
- 1-2 . . . . Buffalo

ROCHESTER RED WINGS

APRIL
- 4-7 . . . . at Lehigh Valley
- 8-10 . . . . at Syracuse
- 11-14 . . . . Lehigh Valley
- 15-17 . . . . Syracuse
- 18-20 . . . . at Lehigh Valley
- 22-25 . . . . Scranton/WB
- 26-28 . . . . Pawtucket
- 29-30 . . . . at Scranton/WB

MAY
- 1-2 . . . . at Scranton/WB
- 3-5 . . . . at Pawtucket
- 7-9 . . . . Toledo
- 10-12 . . . . Durham
- 14-16 . . . . at Charlotte
- 17-19 . . . . at Durham
- 21-23 . . . . Buffalo
- 24-27 . . . . Pawtucket
- 28-30 . . . . at Scranton/WB
- 31 . . . . Buffalo

JUNE
- 1-2 . . . . Buffalo
- 3-6 . . . . at Syracuse
- 7-9 . . . . at Pawtucket
- 11-13 . . . . Columbus
- 14-16 . . . . Charlotte
- 18-20 . . . . at Columbus

- 21-23 . . . . at Toledo
- 24-25 . . . . Scranton/WB
- 26-27 . . . . at Lehigh Valley
- 28-30 . . . . Pawtucket

JULY
- 1-3 . . . . Syracuse
- 4-7 . . . . at Scranton/WB
- 11-14 . . . . Lehigh Valley
- 15-18 . . . . at Norfolk
- 19-21 . . . . at Gwinnett
- 23-25 . . . . Norfolk
- 26-28 . . . . Indianapolis
- 29-30 . . . . at Buffalo
- 31 . . . . Scranton/WB

AUGUST
- 1 . . . . Scranton/WB
- 2-4 . . . . at Pawtucket
- 6-8 . . . . Gwinnett
- 9-11 . . . . Louisville
- 13-15 . . . . at Indianapolis
- 16-18 . . . . at Louisville
- 19-22 . . . . Buffalo
- 23-25 . . . . at Syracuse
- 26-29 . . . . at Buffalo
- 30-31 . . . . Syracuse

SEPTEMBER
- 1-2 . . . . Syracuse

SCRANTON/WILKES-BARRE RAILRIDERS

APRIL
- 4-7 . . . . at Buffalo
- 8-10 . . . . at Lehigh Valley
- 11-14 . . . . Buffalo
- 15-17 . . . . Lehigh Valley
- 19-20 . . . . at Buffalo
- 22-25 . . . . at Rochester
- 26-28 . . . . Syracuse
- 29-30 . . . . Rochester

MAY
- 1-2 . . . . Rochester
- 3-5 . . . . at Syracuse
- 7-9 . . . . Indianapolis
- 10-12 . . . . Toledo
- 14-16 . . . . at Indianapolis
- 17-19 . . . . at Toledo
- 21-23 . . . . Pawtucket

- 24-27 . . . . at Syracuse
- 28-30 . . . . Rochester
- 31 . . . . Lehigh Valley

JUNE
- 1-2 . . . . Lehigh Valley
- 3-6 . . . . at Buffalo
- 7-9 . . . . Syracuse
- 11-13 . . . . at Norfolk
- 14-16 . . . . at Durham
- 18-20 . . . . Norfolk
- 21-23 . . . . Durham
- 24-25 . . . . at Rochester
- 26-27 . . . . Buffalo
- 28-30 . . . . at Lehigh Valley

JULY
- 1-3 . . . . at Pawtucket

SYRACUSE METS

APRIL
- 4-7 . . . . Pawtucket
- 8-10 . . . . Rochester
- 11-14 . . . . at Pawtucket
- 15-17 . . . . at Rochester
- 19-21 . . . . Pawtucket
- 22-25 . . . . Buffalo
- 26-28 . . . . at Scranton/WB
- 29-30 . . . . at Lehigh Valley

MAY
- 1-2 . . . . at Lehigh Valley
- 3-5 . . . . Scranton/WB
- 7-9 . . . . at Louisville
- 10-12 . . . . at Columbus
- 14-16 . . . . Louisville
- 17-19 . . . . Columbus
- 21-23 . . . . at Lehigh Valley
- 24-27 . . . . Scranton/WB
- 28-30 . . . . at Buffalo
- 31 . . . . at Pawtucket

JUNE
- 1-2 . . . . at Pawtucket
- 3-6 . . . . Rochester
- 7-9 . . . . at Scranton/WB
- 11-13 . . . . Charlotte
- 14-16 . . . . Gwinnett
- 18-20 . . . . at Charlotte

- 21-23 . . . . at Gwinnett
- 24-25 . . . . Lehigh Valley
- 26-27 . . . . Pawtucket
- 28-30 . . . . at Buffalo

JULY
- 1-3 . . . . at Rochester
- 4-7 . . . . Buffalo
- 11-14 . . . . Scranton/WB
- 15-18 . . . . at Indianapolis
- 19-21 . . . . at Toledo
- 23-25 . . . . Indianapolis
- 26-28 . . . . Toledo
- 29-30 . . . . at Scranton/WB
- 31 . . . . Pawtucket

AUGUST
- 1 . . . . Pawtucket
- 2-4 . . . . at Buffalo
- 6-8 . . . . at Durham
- 9-11 . . . . at Norfolk
- 13-15 . . . . Durham
- 16-18 . . . . Norfolk
- 19-22 . . . . at Lehigh Valley
- 23-25 . . . . Rochester
- 26-29 . . . . Lehigh Valley
- 30-31 . . . . at Rochester

SEPTEMBER
- 1-2 . . . . at Rochester

TOLEDO MUD HENS

APRIL
- 4-7 . . . . Louisville
- 9-10 . . . . Indianapolis
- 11-14 . . . . at Norfolk
- 15-18 . . . . at Indianapolis
- 19-21 . . . . Columbus
- 23-25 . . . . at Charlotte
- 26-28 . . . . at Gwinnett
- 29-30 . . . . Louisville

MAY
- 1 . . . . Louisville
- 2-5 . . . . Columbus
- 7-9 . . . . at Rochester
- 10-12 . . . . at Scranton/WB
- 14-16 . . . . Norfolk
- 17-19 . . . . Scranton/WB
- 21-23 . . . . at Columbus
- 24-27 . . . . at Louisville
- 28-30 . . . . Gwinnett
- 31 . . . . Charlotte

JUNE
- 1-2 . . . . Charlotte
- 3-5 . . . . at Columbus
- 6-9 . . . . Indianapolis
- 11-13 . . . . at Durham
- 14-16 . . . . at Norfolk
- 18-20 . . . . Lehigh Valley
- 21-23 . . . . Rochester

- 24-25 . . . . at Columbus
- 26-27 . . . . at Louisville
- 28-30 . . . . Durham

JULY
- 1-3 . . . . Columbus
- 4-7 . . . . at Indianapolis
- 11-14 . . . . at Louisville
- 15-18 . . . . Durham
- 19-21 . . . . Syracuse
- 23-25 . . . . at Lehigh Valley
- 26-28 . . . . at Syracuse
- 29-30 . . . . Louisville
- 31 . . . . Indianapolis

AUGUST
- 1 . . . . Indianapolis
- 2-4 . . . . at Louisville
- 6-8 . . . . Buffalo
- 9-11 . . . . Pawtucket
- 13-15 . . . . at Buffalo
- 16-18 . . . . at Pawtucket
- 19-22 . . . . Indianapolis
- 23-25 . . . . at Columbus
- 26-29 . . . . at Indianapolis
- 30-31 . . . . Louisville

SEPTEMBER
- 1-2 . . . . Columbus

PACIFIC COAST LEAGUE

ALBUQUERQUE ISOTOPES

APRIL	
4-8	Salt Lake
9-11	at Reno
12-15	at Tacoma
16-18	Reno
19-22	Tacoma
24-28	at Salt Lake
29-30	Sacramento

MAY	
1-2	Sacramento
3-6	at Tacoma
7-10	at El Paso
11-14	at Fresno
16-20	El Paso
21-24	at Las Vegas
25-28	Sacramento
29-31	Reno

JUNE	
1-2	Reno
4-6	at Omaha
7-10	at Iowa
12-14	Oklahoma City
15-18	New Orleans
20-24	at Reno

25-28	Tacoma
29-30	at Sacramento

JULY	
1-3	at Sacramento
4-7	Las Vegas
11-14	at El Paso
15-18	Fresno
19-21	El Paso
23-25	at Salt Lake
26-28	Salt Lake
30-31	at Memphis

AUGUST	
1	at Memphis
2-5	at Nashville
7-9	San Antonio
10-13	Round Rock
15-18	at Las Vegas
19-21	at Sacramento
22-25	Fresno
26-29	Las Vegas
30-31	at Fresno

SEPTEMBER	
1-2	at Fresno

EL PASO CHIHUAHUAS

APRIL	
4-8	Las Vegas
9-11	at Tacoma
12-15	at Reno
16-18	Tacoma
19-22	Reno
24-28	at Las Vegas
29-30	at Fresno

MAY	
1-2	at Fresno
3-6	Salt Lake
7-10	Albuquerque
11-14	at Sacramento
16-20	at Albuquerque
21-24	Reno
25-28	at Fresno
29-31	Tacoma

JUNE	
1-2	Tacoma
4-6	at Iowa
7-10	at Omaha
12-14	New Orleans
15-18	Oklahoma City
20-24	at Tacoma

25-28	Sacramento
29-30	Fresno

JULY	
1-3	Fresno
4-7	at Salt Lake
11-14	Albuquerque
15-18	at Reno
19-21	at Albuquerque
23-25	at Las Vegas
26-28	Las Vegas
30-31	at Nashville

AUGUST	
1	at Nashville
2-5	at Memphis
7-9	Round Rock
10-13	San Antonio
15-18	at Salt Lake
19-21	Fresno
22-25	Sacramento
26-29	Salt Lake
30-31	at Sacramento

SEPTEMBER	
1-2	at Sacramento

FRESNO GRIZZLIES

APRIL	
4-8	Reno
9-11	at Salt Lake
12-15	at Las Vegas
16-18	Salt Lake
19-22	Las Vegas
24-28	at Reno
29-30	El Paso

MAY	
1-2	El Paso
3-6	at Las Vegas
7-10	at Sacramento
11-14	Albuquerque
16-20	Sacramento

21-24	at Tacoma
25-28	El Paso
29-31	Salt Lake

JUNE	
1-2	Salt Lake
4-6	at New Orleans
7-10	at Oklahoma City
12-14	Iowa
15-18	Omaha
20-24	at Salt Lake
25-28	Las Vegas
29-30	at El Paso

JULY	
1-3	at El Paso
4-6	Tacoma
11-14	at Sacramento
15-18	at Albuquerque
19-21	at Reno
23-25	Sacramento
26-28	Reno
30-31	at Round Rock

AUGUST	
1	at Round Rock

IOWA CUBS

APRIL	
4-8	at Nashville
9-11	New Orleans
12-15	Oklahoma City
17-18	at New Orleans
19-22	at Oklahoma City
24-28	Nashville
29-30	San Antonio

MAY	
1-2	San Antonio
3-6	at Omaha
7-10	at Memphis
11-14	Omaha
16-20	New Orleans
21-24	at Omaha
25-29	at New Orleans
30-31	at Round Rock

JUNE	
1-2	at Round Rock
4-6	El Paso
7-10	Albuquerque
12-14	at Fresno
15-18	at Sacramento
20-24	Round Rock

25-28	Omaha
29-30	at San Antonio

JULY	
1-3	at San Antonio
4-7	Memphis
11-14	at Round Rock
15-18	Oklahoma City
19-21	at Nashville
23-25	at San Antonio
26-28	Round Rock
30-31	at Reno

AUGUST	
1	at Reno
2-5	at Tacoma
7-9	Las Vegas
10-13	Salt Lake
15-18	at Memphis
19-22	San Antonio
23-25	Nashville
26-29	at Oklahoma City
30-31	Memphis

SEPTEMBER	
1-2	Memphis

LAS VEGAS AVIATORS

APRIL	
4-8	at El Paso
9-11	Sacramento
12-15	Fresno
16-18	at Sacramento
19-22	at Fresno
24-28	El Paso
29-30	at Reno

MAY	
1-2	at Reno
3-6	Fresno
7-10	Salt Lake
11-14	Tacoma
16-20	at Salt Lake
21-24	Albuquerque
25-28	at Reno
29-31	at Sacramento

JUNE	
1-2	at Sacramento
4-6	Round Rock
7-10	San Antonio
12-14	at Nashville
15-18	at Memphis
20-24	Sacramento

25-28	at Fresno
29-30	Reno

JULY	
1-3	Reno
4-7	at Albuquerque
11-14	Salt Lake
15-18	at Tacoma
19-21	at Salt Lake
23-25	El Paso
26-28	at El Paso
30-31	New Orleans

AUGUST	
1	New Orleans
2-5	Oklahoma City
7-9	at Iowa
10-13	at Omaha
15-18	Albuquerque
19-21	Reno
22-25	at Tacoma
26-29	at Albuquerque
30-31	Tacoma

SEPTEMBER	
1-2	Tacoma

MEMPHIS REDBIRDS

APRIL	
4-8	Omaha
9-11	at San Antonio
12-15	at Round Rock

16-18	San Antonio
19-22	Round Rock
24-28	at Omaha
29-30	at New Orleans

MAY
1-2 . . at New Orleans
3-6 . . . at Nashville
7-10 . . . . Iowa
11-14 . . . . . . .Nashville
16-20 . . . . at San Antonio
21-24 . . . . at Nashville
25-29 . . . . San Antonio
30-31 . . . . Oklahoma City

JUNE
1-2 . . . . . Oklahoma City
4-6 . . . . at Tacoma
7-10 . . . . .at Reno
12-14 . . . . Salt Lake
15-18 . . . . . . Las Vegas
20-24 . . . at Oklahoma City
25-28 . . . . . . .Nashville
29-30 . . . . . New Orleans

JULY
1-3 . . . . . . New Orleans

NASHVILLE SOUNDS

APRIL
4-8 . . . . Iowa
9-11 . . . . . at Round Rock
12-15 . . . . at San Antonio
16-18 . . . . . .Round Rock
19-22 . . . . . San Antonio
24-28 . . . . at Iowa
29-30 . . . . .Omaha

MAY
1-2 . . . . .Omaha
3-6 . . . . Memphis
7-10 . . . . at Oklahoma City
11-14 . . . . .at Memphis
16-20 . . . . at Round Rock
21-24 . . . . . . Memphis
25-29 . . . . . .Round Rock
30-31 . . . . . New Orleans

JUNE
1-2 . . . . New Orleans
4-6 . . . . .at Reno
7-10 . . . . at Tacoma
12-14 . . . . Las Vegas
15-18 . . . . .Salt Lake
20-24 . . .at New Orleans

NEW ORLEANS BABY CAKES

APRIL
4-8 . . . . .Round Rock
9-11 . . . . .at Iowa
12-15 . . . . . . at Omaha
17-18 . . . . Iowa
19-22 . . . . .Omaha
24-28 . . . . at Round Rock
29-30 . . . . Memphis

MAY
1-2 . . . . Memphis
3-6 . . . . . .Oklahoma City
7-10 . . . . .at San Antonio
11-14 . . . . . San Antonio
16-20 . . . . at Iowa
21-24 . . . . Oklahoma City
25-29 . . . . Iowa
30-31 . . . . . . at Nashville

JUNE
1-2 . . . . at Nashville
4-6 . . . . Fresno
7-10 . . . . .Sacramento
12-14 . . . . at El Paso
15-18 . . . . at Albuquerque
20-24 . . . . .Nashville

4-7 . . . . at Iowa
11-14 . . . . .Oklahoma City
15-18 . . . . at Round Rock
19-21 . . . . at Omaha
23-25 . . . . . New Orleans
26-28 . . . at Oklahoma City
30-31 . . . . . Albuquerque

AUGUST
1 . . . . Albuquerque
2-5 . . . . El Paso
7-9 . . . . at Sacramento
10-13 . . . . . . .at Fresno
15-18 . . . . Iowa
19-22 . . . . . .Round Rock
23-25 . . . . .Omaha
26-29 . . . .at New Orleans
30-31 . . . . .at Iowa

SEPTEMBER
1-2 . . . . at Iowa

25-28 . . . . . .at Memphis
29-30 . . . . Oklahoma City

JULY
1-3 . . . . Oklahoma City
4-7 . . . . at Omaha
11-14 . . . . . New Orleans
15-18 . . . at San Antonio
19-21 . . . . Iowa
23-25 . . . . . Oklahoma City
26-28 . . . .at New Orleans
30-31 . . . . El Paso

AUGUST
1 . . . . El Paso
2-5 . . . . Albuquerque
7-9 . . . . .at Fresno
10-13 . . . . at Sacramento
15-18 . . . . .Omaha
19-22 . . at Oklahoma City
23-25 . . . . .at Iowa
26-29 . . . . . at Omaha
30-31 . . . . . San Antonio

SEPTEMBER
1-2 . . . . San Antonio

OKLAHOMA CITY DODGERS

APRIL
4-8 . . . . San Antonio
9-11 . . . . at Omaha
12-15 . . . . .at Iowa
16-18 . . . . .Omaha
19-22 . . . . Iowa
24-28 . . . . at San Antonio
29-30 . . . . . .Round Rock

MAY
1-2 . . . . .Round Rock
3-6 . . . . . .at New Orleans
7-10 . . . . .Nashville
11-14 . . . . at Round Rock
16-20 . . . . .Omaha
21-24 . . . .at New Orleans
25-29 . . . . . . at Omaha
30-31 . . . . . at Memphis

JUNE
1-2 . . . . at Memphis
4-6 . . . . .Sacramento
7-10 . . . . Fresno
12-14 . . . . at Albuquerque
15-18 . . . . . . at El Paso
20-24 . . . . Memphis

OMAHA STORM CHASERS

APRIL
4-8 . . . . .at Memphis
9-11 . . . . . Oklahoma City
12-15 . . . . . New Orleans
16-18 . . . at Oklahoma City
19-22 . . . .at New Orleans
24-28 . . . . Memphis
29-30 . . . . . . at Nashville

MAY
1-2 . . . . . . at Nashville
3-6 . . . . Iowa
7-10 . . . . . . .Round Rock
11-14 . . . . .at Iowa
16-20 . . . at Oklahoma City
21-24 . . . . Iowa
25-29 . . . .Oklahoma City
30-31 . . . . at San Antonio

JUNE
1-2 . . . . . at San Antonio
4-6 . . . . Albuquerque
7-10 . . . . El Paso
12-14 . . . . at Sacramento
15-18 . . . . . . .at Fresno
20-24 . . . . . . San Antonio

RENO ACES

APRIL
4-8 . . . . .at Fresno
9-11 . . . . . . Albuquerque
12-15 . . . . El Paso
16-18 . . . . at Albuquerque
19-22 . . . . . . at El Paso
24-28 . . . . Fresno
29-30 . . . . . . Las Vegas

MAY
1-2 . . . . Las Vegas
3-6 . . . . . . at Sacramento
7-10 . . . . at Tacoma
11-14 . . . . .Salt Lake
16-20 . . . . .Tacoma
21-24 . . . . . . at El Paso
25-28 . . . . Las Vegas

25-28 . . . . . New Orleans
29-30 . . . . . . at Nashville

JULY
1-3 . . . . at Nashville
4-7 . . . . .Round Rock
11-14 . . . . . .at Memphis
15-18 . . . . .at Iowa
19-21 . . . . . San Antonio
23-25 . . . . . at Nashville
26-28 . . . . Memphis
30-31 . . . . at Salt Lake

AUGUST
1 . . . . at Salt Lake
2-5 . . . . . . .at Las Vegas
7-9 . . . . .Tacoma
10-13 . . . . Reno
15-18 . . . . at Round Rock
19-22 . . . . .Nashville
23-25 . . . .at San Antonio
26-29 . . . . Iowa
30-31 . . . . . New Orleans

SEPTEMBER
1-2 . . . . New Orleans

25-28 . . . . .at Iowa
29-30 . . . . . at Round Rock

JULY
1-3 . . . . at Round Rock
4-7 . . . . .Nashville
11-14 . . . . at San Antonio
15-18 . . . . . New Orleans
19-21 . . . . Memphis
23-25 . . . . at Round Rock
26-28 . . . . . . San Antonio
30-31 . . . . at Tacoma

AUGUST
1 . . . . at Tacoma
2-5 . . . . .at Reno
7-9 . . . . .Salt Lake
10-13 . . . . Las Vegas
15-18 . . . . . . at Nashville
19-22 . . . .at New Orleans
23-25 . . . . . .at Memphis
26-29 . . . . .Nashville
30-31 . . . . . . .Round Rock

SEPTEMBER
1-2 . . . . .Round Rock

29-31 . . . . at Albuquerque

JUNE
1-2 . . . . . at Albuquerque
4-6 . . . . .Nashville
7-10 . . . . Memphis
12-14 . . . . at Round Rock
15-18 . . . . at San Antonio
20-24 . . . . . Albuquerque
25-28 . . . . at Salt Lake
29-30 . . . . .at Las Vegas

JULY
1-3 . . . . .at Las Vegas
4-7 . . . . .Sacramento
11-14 . . . . . . at Tacoma
15-18 . . . . El Paso

19-21 . . . . Fresno
23-25 . . . . .Tacoma
26-28 . . . . . . .at Fresno
30-31 . . . . Iowa

AUGUST
1 . . . . Iowa
2-5 . . . . Omaha
7-9 . . . .at New Orleans

ROUND ROCK EXPRESS

APRIL
4-8 . . . . . .at New Orleans
9-11 . . . . .Nashville
12-15 . . . . Memphis
16-18 . . . . at Nashville
19-22 . . . . . .at Memphis
24-28 . . . . . New Orleans
29-30 . . . at Oklahoma City

MAY
1-2 . . . . at Oklahoma City
3-6 . . . . .at San Antonio
7-10 . . . . . . at Omaha
11-14 . . . .Oklahoma City
16-20 . . . . . .Nashville
21-24 . . . . . San Antonio
25-29 . . . . at Nashville
30-31 . . . . Iowa

JUNE
1-2 . . . . Iowa
4-6 . . . . .at Las Vegas
7-10 . . . . at Salt Lake
12-14 . . . . Reno
15-18 . . . . .Tacoma
20-24 . . . . . . .at Iowa

SACRAMENTO RIVER CATS

APRIL
4-8 . . . . .Tacoma
9-11 . . . . . .at Las Vegas
12-15 . . . . at Salt Lake
16-18 . . . . . Las Vegas
19-22 . . . . .Salt Lake
24-28 . . . . at Tacoma
29-30 . . . at Albuquerque

MAY
1-2 . . . . . at Albuquerque
3-6 . . . . Reno
7-10 . . . . Fresno
11-14 . . . . El Paso
16-20 . . . . . . .at Fresno
21-24 . . . . .Salt Lake
25-28 . . . at Albuquerque
29-31 . . . . . Las Vegas

JUNE
1-2 . . . . . Las Vegas
4-6 . . . . at Oklahoma City
7-10 . . . .at New Orleans
12-14 . . . . . .Omaha
15-18 . . . . . . Iowa
20-24 . . . . . .at Las Vegas

SALT LAKE BEES

APRIL
4-8 . . . . . at Albuquerque
9-11 . . . . Fresno
12-15 . . . . .Sacramento
16-18 . . . . . . .at Fresno
19-22 . . . at Sacramento
24-28 . . . . Albuquerque

10-13 . . . at Oklahoma City
15-18 . . . . . .Sacramento
19-21 . . . .at Las Vegas
22-25 . . . . . Salt Lake
26-29 . . . at Sacramento
30-31 . . . . at Salt Lake

SEPTEMBER
1-2 . . . . . . at Salt Lake

25-28 . . . . at San Antonio
29-30 . . . . . . .Omaha

JULY
1-3 . . . . .Omaha
4-7 . . . . at Oklahoma City
11-14 . . . . Iowa
15-18 . . . . . . Memphis
19-21 . . .at New Orleans
23-25 . . . . .Omaha
26-28 . . . . .at Iowa
30-31 . . . . Fresno

AUGUST
1 . . . . Fresno
2-5 . . . . .Sacramento
7-9 . . . . at El Paso
10-13 . . . . at Albuquerque
15-18 . . . . Oklahoma City
19-22 . . . .at Memphis
23-25 . . . . New Orleans
26-29 . . . . San Antonio
30-31 . . . . . at Omaha

SEPTEMBER
1-2 . . . . at Omaha

25-28 . . . . . . at El Paso
29-30 . . . . .Albuquerque

JULY
1-3 . . . . . . .Albuquerque
4-7 . . . . .at Reno
11-14 . . . . Fresno
15-18 . . . . at Salt Lake
19-21 . . . . . . at Tacoma
23-25 . . . . . . .at Fresno
26-28 . . . . .Tacoma
30-31 . . . . at San Antonio

AUGUST
1 . . . . at San Antonio
2-5 . . . . . at Round Rock
7-9 . . . . Memphis
10-13 . . . . . . .Nashville
15-18 . . . . .at Reno
19-21 . . . . . Albuquerque
22-25 . . . . . at El Paso
26-29 . . . . Reno
30-31 . . . . . . El Paso

SEPTEMBER
1-2 . . . . El Paso

29-30 . . . . .Tacoma

MAY
1-2 . . . . .Tacoma
3-6 . . . . at El Paso
7-10 . . . . .at Las Vegas
11-14 . . . . .at Reno

16-20 . . . . . . Las Vegas
21-24 . . . at Sacramento
25-28 . . . . .Tacoma
29-31 . . . . . . .at Fresno

JUNE
1-2 . . . . .at Fresno
4-6 . . . . San Antonio
7-10 . . . . .Round Rock
12-14 . . . . at Memphis
15-18 . . . at Nashville
20-24 . . . . Fresno
25-28 . . . . Reno
29-30 . . . . . . .at Tacoma

JULY
1-3 . . . . .at Tacoma
4-7 . . . . El Paso
11-14 . . . .at Las Vegas

SAN ANTONIO MISSIONS

APRIL
4-8 . . . . . at Oklahoma City
9-11 . . . . Memphis
12-15 . . . . . .Nashville
16-18 . . . . . at Memphis
19-22 . . . . at Nashville
24-28 . . . .Oklahoma City
29-30 . . . . . . .at Iowa

MAY
1-2 . . . . .at Iowa
3-6 . . . . . . .Round Rock
7-10 . . . . . New Orleans
11-14 . . .at New Orleans
16-20 . . . . . . Memphis
21-24 . . . . at Round Rock
25-29 . . . . .at Memphis
30-31 . . . . . . .Omaha

JUNE
1-2 . . . . .Omaha
4-6 . . . . . . at Salt Lake
7-10 . . . . .at Las Vegas
12-14 . . . . . . .Tacoma
15-18 . . . . Reno
20-24 . . . . . at Omaha

TACOMA RAINIERS

APRIL
4-8 . . . . . . at Sacramento
9-11 . . . . El Paso
12-15 . . . . Albuquerque
16-18 . . . . . at El Paso
19-22 . . . at Albuquerque
24-28 . . . . .Sacramento
29-30 . . . . . at Salt Lake

MAY
1-2 . . . . . at Salt Lake
3-6 . . . . . Albuquerque
7-10 . . . . Reno
11-14 . . . . .at Las Vegas
16-20 . . . . . . .at Reno
21-24 . . . . Fresno
25-28 . . . . at Salt Lake
29-31 . . . . . . at El Paso

JUNE
1-2 . . . . . . at El Paso
4-6 . . . . Memphis
7-10 . . . . . . .Nashville
12-14 . . . .at San Antonio
15-18 . . . . at Round Rock
20-24 . . . . El Paso
25-28 . . . at Albuquerque

15-18 . . . . . .Sacramento
19-21 . . . . . Las Vegas
23-25 . . . . . Albuquerque
26-28 . . . . at Albuquerque
30-31 . . . . Oklahoma City

AUGUST
1 . . . . . . .Oklahoma City
2-5 . . . . . New Orleans
7-9 . . . . at Omaha
10-13 . . . . . .at Iowa
15-18 . . . . El Paso
19-21 . . . . . at Tacoma
22-25 . . . . . . at Reno
26-29 . . . . . at El Paso
30-31 . . . . Reno

SEPTEMBER
1-2 . . . . Reno

25-28 . . . . . .Round Rock
29-30 . . . . Iowa

JULY
1-3 . . . . Iowa
4-7 . . . . . .at New Orleans
11-14 . . . . .Omaha
15-18 . . . . . . .Nashville
19-21 . . . at Oklahoma City
23-25 . . . . Iowa
26-28 . . . . . at Omaha
30-31 . . . . .Sacramento

AUGUST
1 . . . . .Sacramento
2-5 . . . . Fresno
7-9 . . . . . at Albuquerque
10-13 . . . . . . at El Paso
15-18 . . . . . New Orleans
19-22 . . . . .at Iowa
23-25 . . . . Oklahoma City
26-29 . . . . at Round Rock
30-31 . . . . . at Nashville

SEPTEMBER
1-2 . . . . at Nashville

29-30 . . . . .Salt Lake

JULY
1-3 . . . . .Salt Lake
4-6 . . . . .at Fresno
11-14 . . . . Reno
15-18 . . . . . Las Vegas
19-21 . . . . .Sacramento
23-25 . . . . .at Reno
26-28 . . . . at Sacramento
30-31 . . . . .Omaha

AUGUST
1 . . . . .Omaha
2-5 . . . . Iowa
7-9 . . . . at Oklahoma City
10-13 . . . .at New Orleans
15-18 . . . . Fresno
19-21 . . . . . .Salt Lake
22-25 . . . . . Las Vegas
26-29 . . . . . . .at Fresno
30-31 . . . . .at Las Vegas

SEPTEMBER
1-2 . . . . .at Las Vegas

DOUBLE-A

EASTERN LEAGUE

AKRON RUBBERDUCKS

APRIL
4-7 . . . . Altoona
8-10 . . . . Trenton
11-14 . . . . at Altoona
15-17 . . . . at Trenton
18-20 . . . . .Bowie
22-24 . . . . . . Binghamton
25-28 . . . . at Bowie
29-30 . . . . at Binghamton

MAY
1 . . . . . .at Binghamton
2-5 . . . . Reading
7-9 . . . . at Erie
10-12 . . . . . .at Reading
13-15 . . . . .Bowie
16-19 . . . . at Richmond
21-23 . . . . . .Harrisburg
24-27 . . . . . . .Richmond
28-30 . . . . . at Bowie
31 . . . . at Erie

JUNE
1-2 . . . . at Erie
4-6 . . . . Reading
7-9 . . . . .at Altoona
11-13 . . . . . . Hartford
14-16 . . . . . . Portland

18-20 . . . . . .at Reading
21-23 . . . . Erie
24-26 . . . . at Harrisburg
27-30 . . . . . . .at Bowie

JULY
1-3 . . . . Altoona
4-7 . . . .at Binghamton
11-14 . . . . .Bowie
15-17 . . . . at Erie
18-21 . . . . . Binghamton
22-24 . . . . . . at Trenton
25-28 . . . . . at Hartford
30-31 . . . New Hampshire

AUGUST
1 . . . . . . New Hampshire
2-4 . . . . . . Binghamton
6-8 . . . at New Hampshire
9-11 . . . . . . at Portland
13-15 . . . . Trenton
16-18 . . . . . . at Erie
19-21 . . . . . .Harrisburg
22-25 . . . . . . .Richmond
26-29 . . . .at Altoona
30-31 . . . . Erie

SEPTEMBER
1-2 . . . . Erie

ALTOONA CURVE

APRIL
4-7 . . . . at Akron
8-10 . . . . at Erie
11-14 . . . . .Akron
15-17 . . . . . .Harrisburg
18-20 . . . . at Richmond
22-24 . . . . . at Harrisburg
26-28 . . . . . .Richmond
29-30 . . . . Erie

MAY
1 . . . . Erie
2-5 . . . . at Richmond
6-8 . . . . .Bowie
10-12 . . . . Erie
13-15 . . . .at Binghamton
16-19 . . . . . . .Harrisburg
21-23 . . at New Hampshire
24-27 . . . . . at Portland
28-30 . . . . . .at Trenton
31 . . . . . New Hampshire

JUNE
1-2 . . . . New Hampshire
3-5 . . . . at Erie
7-9 . . . . .Akron
11-13 . . . . . Portland
14-16 . . . .at Binghamton
17-19 . . . . . .Harrisburg

21-23 . . . . . . at Hartford
24-26 . . . . . at Richmond
27-30 . . . . . Binghamton

JULY
1-3 . . . . .at Akron
4-7 . . . . Erie
11-14 . . . . at Erie
15-17 . . . . Trenton
18-21 . . . . . . .at Bowie
22-24 . . . . Erie
25-28 . . . . . .Richmond
30-31 . . . . . .at Trenton

AUGUST
1 . . . . .at Trenton
2-4 . . . . .at Reading
5-8 . . . . . . .Richmond
9-11 . . . . Reading
13-15 . . . . . at Harrisburg
16-18 . . . . .Bowie
19-21 . . . . . . Hartford
22-25 . . . . . . at Bowie
26-29 . . . . .Akron
30-31 . . . . . at Harrisburg

SEPTEMBER
1-2 . . . . . . at Harrisburg

BINGHAMTON RUMBLE PONIES

APRIL
4-7 . . . . at New Hampshire
8-10 . . . . at Portland
11-14 . . . . Erie
15-17 . . . . New Hampshire
18-20 . . . . at Erie

22-24 . . . . at Akron
25-28 . . . . Portland
29-30 . . . . .Akron

MAY
1 . . . . .Akron

BOWIE BAYSOX

APRIL
4-7 . . . . at Harrisburg
8-10 . . . . . . at Richmond
11-14 . . . . .Harrisburg
15-17 . . . . Erie
18-20 . . . . . . at Akron
22-24 . . . . . . at Erie
25-28 . . . . .Akron
29-30 . . . . . .Richmond

MAY
1 . . . . .Richmond
2-5 . . . . at Erie
6-8 . . . . . .at Altoona
10-12 . . . . . .Richmond
13-15 . . . . at Akron
16-19 . . . . Erie
20-22 . . . . Binghamton
24-27 . . . . at Erie
28-30 . . . . .Akron
31 . . . . Hartford

JUNE
1-2 . . . . Hartford
4-6 . . . . at New Hampshire
7-9 . . . . at Portland
11-13 . . . . New Hampshire
14-16 . . . . Trenton

18-20 . . . . . at Hartford
21-23 . . . . . at Harrisburg
24-26 . . . . . Hartford
27-30 . . . . .Akron

JULY
1-3 . . . . at Hartford
4-7 . . . . .Harrisburg
11-14 . . . . . . at Akron
15-17 . . . . . .Harrisburg
18-21 . . . . Altoona
22-24 . . . . at Richmond
25-28 . . . .at Binghamton
29-31 . . . . Reading

AUGUST
2-4 . . . . Portland
6-8 . . . . at Trenton
9-11 . . . . . at Richmond
13-15 . . . . . .Richmond
16-18 . . . . .at Altoona
19-21 . . . . . Binghamton
22-25 . . . . Altoona
26-29 . . . .at Reading
30-31 . . . . . at Richmond

SEPTEMBER
1-2 . . . . at Richmond

ERIE SEAWOLVES

APRIL
5-7 . . . . Trenton
8-10 . . . . Altoona
11-14 . . . .at Binghamton
15-17 . . . . at Bowie
18-20 . . . . . Binghamton
22-24 . . . . .Bowie
26-28 . . . . . at Trenton
29-30 . . . . .at Altoona

MAY
1 . . . . .at Altoona
2-5 . . . . .Bowie
7-9 . . . . .Akron
10-12 . . . . . . .at Altoona
13-15 . . . . . . .Richmond
16-19 . . . . . . at Bowie

20-22 . . . . . . at Hartford
24-27 . . . . .Bowie
28-30 . . . . .at Reading
31 . . . . .Akron

JUNE
1-2 . . . . .Akron
3-5 . . . . Altoona
7-10 . . . . . . at Trenton
11-13 . . . . . .at Reading
14-16 . . . . . . Hartford
17-19 . . . . . . Portland
21-23 . . . . . at Akron
24-26 . . . .at Binghamton
27-30 . . . . . . .Harrisburg

JULY
1-3 . . . . Binghamton

4-7 . . . . .at Altoona
11-14 . . . . Altoona
15-17 . . . . .Akron
18-21 . . . . . . at Richmond
22-24 . . . . . .at Altoona
25-29 . . . . Trenton
30-31 . . . . .at Binghamton

AUGUST

1 . . . . . . .at Binghamton
2-4 . . . . . . New Hampshire

HARRISBURG SENATORS

APRIL

4-7 . . . . .Bowie
8-10 . . . . Hartford
11-14 . . . . at Bowie
15-17 . . . . . . .at Altoona
18-20 . . . . Reading
22-24 . . . . Altoona
25-28 . . . . . at Hartford
29-30 . . . . . at Reading

MAY

1 . . . . .at Reading
2-5 . . . . Trenton
7-9 . . . . . . Binghamton
10-12 . . . . at Hartford
13-15 . . . . Trenton
16-19 . . . . .at Altoona
21-23 . . . . . at Akron
24-27 . . . . Reading
28-30 . . . New Hampshire
31 . . . . . . .at Trenton

JUNE

1-2 . . . . .at Trenton
4-6 . . . . . . Binghamton
7-9 . . . . . . .at Reading
11-13 . . . . . at Richmond
14-16 . . . . . . Reading

HARTFORD YARD GOATS

APRIL

4-7 . . . . . . at Richmond
8-10 . . . . . at Harrisburg
11-14 . . . New Hampshire
15-17 . . . . . . .Richmond
18-20 . . at New Hampshire
22-24 . . . . . at Portland
25-28 . . . . . .Harrisburg
29-30 . . . . . . Portland

MAY

1 . . . . Portland
2-5 . . . . at New Hampshire
7-9 . . . . .at Reading
10-12 . . . . . .Harrisburg
13-15 . . . . at Portland
16-19 . . . New Hampshire
20-22 . . . . Erie
24-27 . . at New Hampshire
28-30 . . . . Portland
31 . . . . at Bowie

JUNE

1-2 . . . . at Bowie
4-6 . . . . Trenton
7-9 . . . . . . Binghamton
11-13 . . . . . at Akron
14-16 . . . . Erie

6-8 . . . . at Portland
9-11 . . . at New Hampshire
13-15 . . . . Reading
16-18 . . . . .Akron
19-21 . . . . at Richmond
22-25 . . . at Harrisburg
26-29 . . . . . . .Richmond
30-31 . . . . . at Akron

SEPTEMBER

1-2 . . . . at Akron

17-19 . . . . . . .at Altoona
21-23 . . . . .Bowie
24-26 . . . . . . .Akron
27-30 . . . . . at Erie

JULY

1-3 . . . . .Richmond
4-7 . . . . at Bowie
11-14 . . . . . . .Richmond
15-17 . . . . . . at Bowie
18-21 . . . . Portland
22-24 . . at New Hampshire
25-28 . . . . at Portland
30-31 . . . . . . Hartford

AUGUST

1 . . . . Hartford
2-4 . . . . .Richmond
6-8 . . . . . .at Binghamton
9-11 . . . . at Trenton
13-15 . . . . . . Altoona
16-18 . . . . at Richmond
19-21 . . . . . at Akron
22-25 . . . . Erie
26-29 . . . . at Hartford
30-31 . . . . Altoona

SEPTEMBER

1-2 . . . . Altoona

18-20 . . . . . . .Bowie
21-23 . . . . Altoona
24-26 . . . . . . at Bowie
27-30 . . . . at Richmond

JULY

1-3 . . . . .Bowie
4-7 . . . . .at Trenton
11-14 . . . New Hampshire
15-17 . . . . . . .Richmond
18-21 . . . . . at Trenton
22-24 . . . . at Portland
25-28 . . . . .Akron
30-31 . . . . . at Harrisburg

AUGUST

1 . . . . .at Harrisburg
2-4 . . . . Trenton
6-8 . . . . . . .at Reading
9-11 . . . . . . Binghamton
13-15 . . . . Portland
16-18 . . . .at Binghamton
19-21 . . . . . .at Altoona
22-25 . . . . Reading
26-29 . . . . . . .Harrisburg
30-31 . . . .at Binghamton

SEPTEMBER

1-2 . . . . . .at Binghamton

NEW HAMPSHIRE FISHER CATS

APRIL

4-7 . . . . Binghamton
8-10 . . . . Reading
11-14 . . . . . at Hartford
15-17 . . . .at Binghamton
18-20 . . . . . . Hartford
22-24 . . . . . . Trenton
25-28 . . . .at Reading
29-30 . . . . . . at Trenton

MAY

1 . . . . .at Trenton
2-5 . . . . Hartford
7-9 . . . . . . at Portland
10-12 . . . at Binghamton
13-15 . . . . . . Reading
16-19 . . . . . at Hartford
21-23 . . . . . . Altoona
24-27 . . . . . . Hartford
28-30 . . . :at Harrisburg
31 . . . . . . .at Altoona

JUNE

1-2 . . . . .at Altoona
4-6 . . . . .Bowie
7-9 . . . . . . .Richmond
11-13 . . . . . .at Bowie
14-16 . . . . at Richmond

18-20 . . . . . Binghamton
21-23 . . . . Trenton
24-26 . . . . at Portland
27-30 . . . . .at Trenton

JULY

1-3 . . . . .at Reading
4-7 . . . . Portland
11-14 . . . . at Hartford
15-17 . . . . . . Portland
18-21 . . . . .at Reading
22-24 . . . . . .Harrisburg
25-28 . . . . Reading
30-31 . . . . . at Akron

AUGUST

1 . . . . at Akron
2-4 . . . . at Erie
6-8 . . . . .Akron
9-11 . . . . Erie
13-15 . . .at Binghamton
16-18 . . . . . . Portland
19-21 . . . . . at Trenton
22-25 . . . Binghamton
26-29 . . . . . . Trenton
30-31 . . . . at Portland

SEPTEMBER

1-2 . . . . . . at Portland

PORTLAND SEA DOGS

APRIL

4-7 . . . . Reading
8-10 . . . . . . Binghamton
12-14 . . . . . at Trenton
15-17 . . . .at Reading
18-20 . . . . . Trenton
22-24 . . . . . Hartford
25-28 . . .at Binghamton
29-30 . . . . at Hartford

MAY

1 . . . . at Hartford
2-5 . . . . . . Binghamton
7-9 . . . . . New Hampshire
10-12 . . . . at Trenton
13-15 . . . . Hartford
16-19 . . . .at Reading
20-23 . . . at Trenton
24-27 . . . . Altoona
28-30 . . . . at Hartford
31 . . . .at Binghamton

JUNE

1-2 . . . . .at Binghamton
4-6 . . . . .Richmond
7-9 . . . . .Bowie
11-13 . . . .at Altoona
14-16 . . . . . at Akron

READING FIGHTIN PHILS

APRIL

4-7 . . . . . . at Portland
8-10 . . at New Hampshire
12-14 . . . . .Richmond
15-17 . . . . . Portland
18-20 . . . . at Harrisburg
22-24 . . . . at Richmond
25-28 . . . New Hampshire
29-30 . . . . . . .Harrisburg

MAY

1 . . . . .Harrisburg
2-5 . . . . at Akron

17-19 . . . . . . at Erie
21-23 . . . . Reading
24-26 . . . New Hampshire
27-30 . . . . .at Reading

JULY

1-3 . . . . Trenton
4-7 . . . at New Hampshire
11-14 . . . Binghamton
15-17 . . at New Hampshire
18-21 . . . . . at Harrisburg
22-24 . . . . . . Hartford
25-28 . . . . . .Harrisburg
30-31 . . . . at Richmond

AUGUST

1 . . . . at Richmond
2-4 . . . . at Bowie
6-8 . . . . Erie
9-11 . . . . . . .Akron
13-15 . . . . at Hartford
16-18 . . at New Hampshire
19-21 . . . . . . Reading
22-25 . . . . . Trenton
26-29 . . . at Binghamton
30-31 . . . New Hampshire

SEPTEMBER

1-2 . . . . . New Hampshire

7-9 . . . . Hartford
10-12 . . . . . . .Akron
13-15 . . at New Hampshire
16-19 . . . . . Portland
21-23 . . . . at Richmond
24-27 . . . . at Harrisburg
28-30 . . . . Erie
31 . . . . .Richmond

JUNE

1-3 . . . . .Richmond
4-6 . . . . at Akron
7-9 . . . . . . .Harrisburg

11-13 . . . . Erie	29-31 . . . . at Bowie
14-16 . . . . . at Harrisburg	**AUGUST**
18-20 . . . . Akron	2-4 . . . . Altoona
21-23 . . . . . . at Portland	6-8 . . . . Hartford
24-26 . . . . . . at Trenton	9-11 . . . . . . at Altoona
27-30 . . . . Portland	13-15 . . . . at Erie
JULY	16-18 . . . . Trenton
1-3 . . . . . New Hampshire	19-21 . . . . . at Portland
4-7 . . . . . . at Richmond	22-25 . . . . . at Hartford
11-14 . . . . Trenton	26-29 . . . . .Bowie
15-17 . . . .at Binghamton	30-31 . . . . . . at Trenton
18-21 . . . . New Hampshire	**SEPTEMBER**
22-24 . . . . . Binghamton	1-2 . . . . at Trenton
25-28 . . at New Hampshire	

RICHMOND FLYING SQUIRRELS

APRIL	18-20 . . . . at Trenton
4-7 . . . . Hartford	21-23 . . . .at Binghamton
8-10 . . . . .Bowie	24-26 . . . . Altoona
12-14 . . . . . .at Reading	27-30 . . . . Hartford
15-17 . . . . . at Hartford	**JULY**
18-20 . . . . Altoona	1-3 . . . . . . at Harrisburg
22-24 . . . . Reading	4-7 . . . . Reading
26-28 . . . . . .at Altoona	11-14 . . . at Harrisburg
29-30 . . . . at Bowie	15-17 . . . . at Hartford
MAY	18-21 . . . . Erie
1 . . . . .at Bowie	22-24 . . . . .Bowie
2-5 . . . . Altoona	25-28 . . . . .at Altoona
6-8 . . . . Trenton	30-31 . . . . Portland
10-12 . . . . . . .at Bowie	**AUGUST**
13-15 . . . . at Erie	1 . . . . Portland
16-19 . . . . .Akron	2-4 . . . . . at Harrisburg
21-23 . . . . Reading	5-8 . . . . . . .at Altoona
24-27 . . . . . . at Akron	9-11 . . . . .Bowie
28-30 . . . . . Binghamton	13-15 . . . . . at Bowie
31 . . . . .at Reading	16-18 . . . . .Harrisburg
JUNE	19-21 . . . . Erie
1-3 . . . . .at Reading	22-25 . . . . . at Akron
4-6 . . . . .at Portland	26-29 . . . . . at Erie
7-9 . . . . at New Hampshire	30-31 . . . . .Bowie
11-13 . . . . . .Harrisburg	**SEPTEMBER**
14-16 . . . . New Hampshire	1-2 . . . . .Bowie

TRENTON THUNDER

APRIL	21-23 . . at New Hampshire
5-7 . . . . at Erie	24-26 . . . . Reading
8-10 . . . . at Akron	27-30 . . . . New Hampshire
12-14 . . . . Portland	**JULY**
15-17 . . . . .Akron	1-3 . . . . at Portland
18-20 . . . . . . at Portland	4-7 . . . . Hartford
22-24 . . at New Hampshire	11-14 . . . . . .at Reading
26-28 . . . . Erie	15-17 . . . . .at Altoona
29-30 . . . . New Hampshire	18-21 . . . . Hartford
MAY	22-24 . . . . .Akron
1 . . . . New Hampshire	25-29 . . . . . . at Erie
2-5 . . . . . . at Harrisburg	30-31 . . . . Altoona
6-8 . . . . . . at Richmond	**AUGUST**
10-12 . . . . Portland	1 . . . . Altoona
13-15 . . . . at Harrisburg	2-4 . . . . . . at Hartford
16-19 . . . . . Binghamton	6-8 . . . . .Bowie
20-23 . . . . Portland	9-11 . . . . . . .Harrisburg
24-27 . . . .at Binghamton	13-15 . . . . . . .at Akron
28-30 . . . . Altoona	16-18 . . . . . .at Reading
31 . . . . .Harrisburg	19-21 . . . New Hampshire
JUNE	22-25 . . . . . at Portland
1-2 . . . . .Harrisburg	26-29 . . at New Hampshire
4-6 . . . . at Hartford	30-31 . . . . Reading
7-10 . . . . Erie	**SEPTEMBER**
11-13 . . . .at Binghamton	1-2 . . . . Reading
14-16 . . . . .at Bowie	
18-20 . . . . .Richmond	

SOUTHERN LEAGUE

BILOXI SHUCKERS

APRIL	25-29 . . . . . at Pensacola
4-8 . . . . Birmingham	30 . . . . Mobile
10-14 . . . . at Montgomery	**JULY**
15-19 . . . . Pensacola	1-3 . . . . Mobile
20-24 . . . . . Jacksonville	4-9 . . . . . . at Mississippi
25-29 . . . at Chattanooga	11-16 . . . . Chattanooga
MAY	18-21 . . . . . . at Mobile
1-5 . . . . . . at Pensacola	22-26 . . . at Jacksonville
6-10 . . . . . Montgomery	27-31 . . . . Jackson
11-15 . . . at Jacksonville	**AUGUST**
16-20 . . . . . Chattanooga	1-5 . . . . .Jacksonville
22-26 . . . . . at Mobile	7-11 . . . . . at Tennessee
28-31 . . . . . .Tennessee	13-17 . . . . Mobile
JUNE	18-22 . . . at Montgomery
1 . . . . .Tennessee	23-27 . . . . . .Mississippi
2-6 . . . . . at Mississippi	29-31 . . .at Birmingham
7-11 . . . . Pensacola	**SEPTEMBER**
12-16 . . . . . . at Jackson	1-2 . . . . . .at Birmingham
20-24 . . . . .Mississippi	

BIRMINGHAM BARONS

APRIL	25-29 . . . . Mobile
4-8 . . . . at Biloxi	30 . . . . . at Tennessee
10-14 . . . . . Tennessee	**JULY**
15-19 . . . at Jacksonville	1-3 . . . . . at Tennessee
20-24 . . . . Jackson	4-9 . . . . Pensacola
25-29 . . . at Montgomery	11-16 . . . . . . .at Jackson
MAY	18-21 . . . . . .Tennessee
1-5 . . . . . . Chattanooga	22-26 . . . . . Chattanooga
6-10 . . . . . . .at Jackson	27-31 . . . at Montgomery
11-15 . . . . at Tennessee	**AUGUST**
16-20 . . . . .Mississippi	1-5 . . . . . . at Pensacola
22-26 . . . at Chattanooga	7-11 . . . . . . Montgomery
28-31 . . . . Montgomery	13-17 . . . . at Mississippi
JUNE	18-22 . . . . .Jacksonville
1 . . . . Montgomery	23-27 . . . . at Tennessee
2-6 . . . . Jackson	29-31 . . . . Biloxi
7-11 . . . . at Mobile	**SEPTEMBER**
12-16 . . . .Jacksonville	1-2 . . . . Biloxi
20-24 . . . at Chattanooga	

CHATTANOOGA LOOKOUTS

APRIL	25-29 . . . . . .Tennessee
4-8 . . . . Montgomery	30 . . . . . at Jacksonville
10-14 . . . . . . .at Jackson	**JULY**
15-19 . . . . . . .Mississippi	1-3 . . . . . at Jacksonville
20-24 . . . . at Tennessee	4-9 . . . . Jackson
25-29 . . . . Biloxi	11-16 . . . . . . at Biloxi
MAY	18-21 . . . . .Jacksonville
1-5 . . . .at Birmingham	22-26 . . .at Birmingham
6-10 . . . . . .Tennessee	27-31 . . . . . .Tennessee
11-15 . . . . . Pensacola	**AUGUST**
16-20 . . . . . . at Biloxi	1-5 . . . . . at Montgomery
22-26 . . . . . Birmingham	7-11 . . . . Jackson
28-31 . . . . . . at Jackson	13-17 . . . . at Pensacola
JUNE	18-22 . . . . . . at Mobile
1 . . . . at Jackson	23-27 . . . . .Montgomery
2-6 . . . . Mobile	29-31 . . . .at Mississippi
7-11 . . . . . at Tennessee	**SEPTEMBER**
12-16 . . . at Montgomery	1-2 . . . . . . .at Mississippi
20-24 . . . . . Birmingham	

JACKSON GENERALS

APRIL
4-8 . . . . . . at Jacksonville
10-14 . . . . . Chattanooga
15-19 . . . . . at Tennessee
20-24 . . . at Birmingham
25-29 . . . . . Pensacola
MAY
1-5 . . . . . at Tennessee
6-10 . . . . . Birmingham
11-15 . . . . at Mobile
16-20 . . . . . Tennessee
22-26 . . . . at Montgomery
28-31 . . . . . Chattanooga
JUNE
1 . . . . Chattanooga
2-6 . . . . at Birmingham
7-11 . . . . . Mississippi
12-16 . . . . Biloxi
20-24 . . . . . at Mobile
25-29 . . . . . at Mississippi
30 . . . . Montgomery
JULY
1-3 . . . . . . Montgomery
4-9 . . . . at Chattanooga
11-16 . . . . . Birmingham
18-21 . . . . at Montgomery
22-26 . . . . . Mississippi
27-31 . . . . . at Biloxi
AUGUST
1-5 . . . . Mobile
7-11 . . . . at Chattanooga
13-17 . . . . . Montgomery
18-22 . . . . . Tennessee
23-27 . . . at Pensacola
29-31 . . . . Jacksonville
SEPTEMBER
1-2 . . . . . . Jacksonville

JACKSONVILLE JUMBO SHRIMP

APRIL
4-8 . . . . Jackson
10-14 . . . . at Pensacola
15-19 . . . . . Birmingham
20-24 . . . . at Biloxi
25-29 . . . . . Tennessee
MAY
1-5 . . . at Mississippi
6-10 . . . . at Mobile
11-15 . . . . . Biloxi
16-20 . . . . Montgomery
22-26 . . . at Mississippi
28-31 . . . . . Mobile
JUNE
1 . . . . Mobile
2-6 . . . . . . at Pensacola
7-11 . . . . Montgomery
12-16 . . . at Birmingham
20-24 . . . . . Pensacola
25-29 . . . at Montgomery
30 . . . . Chattanooga
JULY
1-3 . . . . . . Chattanooga
4-9 . . . . at Mobile
11-16 . . . . Mississippi
18-21 . . . at Chattanooga
22-26 . . . . . . Biloxi
27-31 . . . . . Pensacola
AUGUST
1-5 . . . . . . at Biloxi
7-11 . . . . Mississippi
13-17 . . . at Tennessee
18-22 . . . at Birmingham
23-27 . . . . . Mobile
29-31 . . . at Jackson
SEPTEMBER
1-2 . . . . . . at Jackson

MISSISSIPPI BRAVES

APRIL
4-8 . . . . . at Tennessee
10-14 . . . . Mobile
15-19 . . at Chattanooga
20-24 . . . . . Montgomery
25-29 . . . . at Mobile
MAY
1-5 . . . . . Jacksonville
6-10 . . . . . . Pensacola
11-15 . . at Montgomery
16-20 . . at Birmingham
22-26 . . Jacksonville
28-31 . . at Pensacola
JUNE
1 . . . . . . at Pensacola
2-6 . . . . Biloxi
7-11 . . . . at Jackson
12-16 . . . . Mobile
20-24 . . . . at Biloxi
25-29 . . . . . Jackson
30 . . . . . . at Pensacola
JULY
1-3 . . . . . at Pensacola
4-9 . . . . Biloxi
11-16 . . . at Jacksonville
18-21 . . . . Pensacola
22-26 . . . at Jackson
27-31 . . . at Mobile
AUGUST
1-5 . . . . . . Tennessee
7-11 . . . at Jacksonville
13-17 . . . Birmingham
18-22 . . . . Pensacola
23-27 . . . . at Biloxi
29-31 . . . Chattanooga
SEPTEMBER
1-2 . . . . . Chattanooga

MOBILE BAYBEARS

APRIL
4-8 . . . . Pensacola
10-14 . . . . at Mississippi
15-19 . . . . Montgomery
20-24 . . . . . at Pensacola
25-29 . . . . . . Mississippi
MAY
1-5 . . . . . at Montgomery
6-10 . . . . . . Jacksonville
11-15 . . . . . Jackson
16-20 . . . . at Pensacola
22-26 . . . . . . Biloxi
28-31 . . . . at Jacksonville
JUNE
1 . . . . . at Jacksonville
2-6 . . . . . at Chattanooga
7-11 . . . . . Birmingham
12-16 . . . . at Mississippi
20-24 . . . . . Jackson
25-29 . . at Birmingham
30 . . . . at Biloxi
JULY
1-3 . . . . at Biloxi
4-9 . . . . Jacksonville
11-16 . . . . at Tennessee
18-21 . . . . . Biloxi
22-26 . . . at Pensacola
27-31 . . . . . Mississippi
AUGUST
1-5 . . . . at Jackson
7-11 . . . . . . Pensacola
13-17 . . . . at Biloxi
18-22 . . . Chattanooga
23-27 . . . at Jacksonville
29-31 . . . . . Tennessee
SEPTEMBER
1-2 . . . . Tennessee

MONTGOMERY BISCUITS

APRIL
4-8 . . . . . at Chattanooga
10-14 . . . . . Biloxi
15-19 . . . . . at Mobile
20-24 . . . at Mississippi
25-29 . . . . Birmingham
MAY
1-5 . . . . Mobile
6-10 . . . . . at Biloxi
11-15 . . . Mississippi
16-20 . . at Jacksonville
22-26 . . . . . Jackson
28-31 . . . at Birmingham
JUNE
1 . . . . . at Birmingham
2-6 . . . . . . Tennessee
7-11 . . . . at Jacksonville
12-16 . . . . Chattanooga
20-24 . . . at Tennessee
JULY
1-3 . . . . . . at Jackson
4-9 . . . . . . Tennessee
11-16 . . . at Pensacola
18-21 . . . . . Jackson
22-26 . . . at Tennessee
27-31 . . . . Birmingham
AUGUST
1-5 . . . . . . Chattanooga
7-11 . . . at Birmingham
13-17 . . . at Jackson
18-22 . . . . . Biloxi
23-27 . . . at Chattanooga
29-31 . . . . Pensacola
SEPTEMBER
1-2 . . . . Pensacola

25-29 . . . . . Jacksonville
30 . . . . at Jackson

PENSACOLA BLUE WAHOOS

APRIL
4-8 . . . . at Mobile
10-14 . . . . . Jacksonville
15-19 . . . . . at Biloxi
20-24 . . . . . . Mobile
25-29 . . . . . at Jackson
MAY
1-5 . . . . Biloxi
6-10 . . . . . at Mississippi
11-15 . . . at Chattanooga
16-20 . . . . . . Mobile
22-26 . . . . at Tennessee
28-31 . . . . . Mississippi
JUNE
1 . . . . Mississippi
2-6 . . . . . Jacksonville
7-11 . . . . at Biloxi
12-16 . . . . . Tennessee
20-24 . . . . at Jacksonville
25-29 . . . . Biloxi
30 . . . . Mississippi
JULY
1-3 . . . . Mississippi
4-9 . . . . . at Birmingham
11-16 . . . . . Montgomery
18-21 . . . at Mississippi
22-26 . . . . . . Mobile
27-31 . . . . at Jacksonville
AUGUST
1-5 . . . . . . Birmingham
7-11 . . . . . . at Mobile
13-17 . . . . Chattanooga
18-22 . . . at Mississippi
23-27 . . . . . . Jackson
29-31 . . . at Montgomery
SEPTEMBER
1-2 . . . . . at Montgomery

TENNESSEE SMOKIES

APRIL
4-8 . . . . Mississippi
10-14 . . . . at Birmingham
15-19 . . . . Jackson
20-24 . . . . . Chattanooga
25-29 . . . . at Jacksonville
MAY
1-5 . . . . Jackson
6-10 . . . . at Chattanooga
11-15 . . . . . Birmingham
16-20 . . . . at Jackson
22-26 . . . . Pensacola
28-31 . . . . . . at Biloxi

JUNE
1 . . . . at Biloxi
2-6 . . . . . . at Montgomery
7-11 . . . . Chattanooga
12-16 . . . . . at Pensacola
20-24 . . . . . Montgomery
25-29 . . . at Chattanooga
30 . . . . Birmingham

JULY
1-3 . . . . Birmingham
4-9 . . . . . at Montgomery
11-16 . . . . Mobile

TEXAS LEAGUE

AMARILLO SOD POODLES

APRIL
4-7 . . . . . at Corpus Christi
8-10 . . . . Midland
11-14 . . . . . Corpus Christi
15-17 . . . . . . at Midland
18-20 . . . . . Corpus Christi
22-25 . . . at Springfield
26-29 . . . . at Arkansas

MAY
1-3 . . . . Springfield
4-7 . . . . Arkansas
9-12 . . . at Corpus Christi
13-15 . . . . Midland
16-19 . . . . . . at Frisco
20-22 . . . . . Corpus Christi
23-26 . . . . Midland
28-30 . . . . . at Frisco
31 . . . . at Midland

JUNE
1-2 . . . . . . at Midland
3-5 . . . . Frisco
6-9 . . . at Corpus Christi
11-13 . . . NW Arkansas
14-16 . . . . Tulsa
17-19 . . at NW Arkansas

ARKANSAS TRAVELERS

APRIL
4-7 . . . . at Tulsa
8-10 . . . . at NW Arkansas
11-14 . . . . Tulsa
15-17 . . . . . NW Arkansas
18-20 . . . . at Tulsa
22-25 . . . . Frisco
26-29 . . . . Amarillo

MAY
1-3 . . . . at Frisco
4-7 . . . . . . at Amarillo
9-12 . . . . Tulsa
13-15 . . . at Springfield
16-19 . . . . . . at Tulsa
20-22 . . . . . NW Arkansas
23-26 . . . . . Springfield
28-30 . . . at NW Arkansas
31 . . . . Tulsa

JUNE
1-2 . . . . Tulsa
3-5 . . . . at NW Arkansas
6-9 . . . . at Tulsa
11-13 . . . . Corpus Christi
14-16 . . . . . . Midland
17-19 . . at Corpus Christi
20-23 . . . . . . at Midland
27-30 . . . . Tulsa

18-21 . . . . . at Birmingham
22-26 . . . . . Montgomery
27-31 . . . at Chattanooga

AUGUST
1-5 . . . . at Mississippi
7-11 . . . . Biloxi
13-17 . . . Jacksonville
18-22 . . . . at Jackson
23-27 . . . . Birmingham
29-31 . . . . . . at Mobile

SEPTEMBER
1-2 . . . . at Mobile

JULY
20-23 . . . . at Tulsa
27-30 . . . . Corpus Christi

JULY
1-3 . . . . at Midland
4-7 . . . . Frisco
8-10 . . . . . at Midland
11-14 . . . . . at Frisco
16-18 . . . . . Springfield
19-22 . . . NW Arkansas
24-26 . . . at Springfield
27-30 . . . at NW Arkansas

AUGUST
1-4 . . . . Frisco
5-7 . . . . . at Midland
8-11 . . . . at Frisco
12-15 . . . . . . Midland
16-18 . . . . Frisco
20-22 . . . . . . at Tulsa
23-25 . . . at Arkansas
26-29 . . . . . Tulsa
30-31 . . . . . Arkansas

SEPTEMBER
1-2 . . . . Arkansas

JULY
1-3 . . . . at NW Arkansas
4-7 . . . . Springfield
8-10 . . . . . NW Arkansas
11-14 . . . at Springfield
16-18 . . . . . . Midland
19-22 . . . . . . Frisco
24-26 . . . . at Midland
27-30 . . . at Frisco

AUGUST
1-4 . . . . Springfield
5-7 . . . . . NW Arkansas
8-11 . . . . . at Springfield
12-15 . . . . NW Arkansas
16-18 . . . at Springfield
20-22 . . . Corpus Christi
23-25 . . . . . . Amarillo
26-29 . . . at Corpus Christi
30-31 . . . . at Amarillo

SEPTEMBER
1-2 . . . . at Amarillo

CORPUS CHRISTI HOOKS

APRIL
4-7 . . . . Amarillo
8-10 . . . . at Frisco
11-14 . . . . at Amarillo
15-17 . . . . Frisco
18-20 . . . . at Amarillo
22-25 . . . NW Arkansas
26-29 . . . . Tulsa

MAY
1-3 . . . . at NW Arkansas
4-7 . . . . . . at Tulsa
9-12 . . . . . Amarillo
13-15 . . . . . Frisco
16-19 . . . . at Midland
20-22 . . . . at Amarillo
23-26 . . . . . Frisco
28-30 . . . . at Midland
31 . . . . at Frisco

JUNE
1-2 . . . . . at Frisco
3-5 . . . . . Midland
6-9 . . . . . Amarillo
11-13 . . . . at Arkansas
14-16 . . . at Springfield
17-19 . . . . . Arkansas

20-23 . . . . . Springfield
27-30 . . . . at Amarillo

JULY
1-3 . . . . at Frisco
4-7 . . . . . Midland
8-10 . . . . . at Frisco
11-14 . . . at Midland
16-18 . . . NW Arkansas
19-22 . . . Springfield
24-26 . . at NW Arkansas
27-30 . . at Springfield

AUGUST
1-4 . . . . . Midland
5-7 . . . . at Frisco
8-11 . . . at Midland
12-15 . . . Frisco
16-18 . . . . Midland
20-22 . . at Arkansas
23-25 . . at Tulsa
26-29 . . . . Arkansas
30-31 . . . Tulsa

SEPTEMBER
1-2 . . . . . . Tulsa

FRISCO ROUGHRIDERS

APRIL
4-7 . . . . . . Midland
8-10 . . . . Corpus Christi
11-14 . . . . at Midland
15-17 . . at Corpus Christi
18-20 . . . . . Midland
22-25 . . . . at Arkansas
26-29 . . . at Springfield

MAY
1-3 . . . . Arkansas
4-7 . . . . . Springfield
9-12 . . . . at Midland
13-15 . . at Corpus Christi
16-19 . . . . Amarillo
20-22 . . . . Midland
23-26 . . at Corpus Christi
28-30 . . . Amarillo
31 . . . . Corpus Christi

JUNE
1-2 . . . . Corpus Christi
3-5 . . . . at Amarillo
6-9 . . . . at Midland
11-13 . . . . . . Tulsa
14-16 . . . NW Arkansas
17-19 . . . . at Tulsa

20-23 . . . at NW Arkansas
27-30 . . . . Midland

JULY
1-3 . . . . Corpus Christi
4-7 . . . . at Amarillo
8-10 . . . Corpus Christi
11-14 . . . Amarillo
16-18 . . . at Tulsa
19-22 . . . at Arkansas
24-26 . . . Tulsa
27-30 . . . Arkansas

AUGUST
1-4 . . . . at Amarillo
5-7 . . . . Corpus Christi
8-11 . . . . Amarillo
12-15 . . at Corpus Christi
16-18 . . . at Amarillo
20-22 . . . Springfield
23-25 . . . NW Arkansas
26-29 . . at Springfield
30-31 . . at NW Arkansas

SEPTEMBER
1-2 . . . . at NW Arkansas

MIDLAND ROCKHOUNDS

APRIL
4-7 . . . . at Frisco
8-10 . . . at Amarillo
11-14 . . . Frisco
15-17 . . . Amarillo
18-20 . . . at Frisco
22-25 . . . Tulsa
26-29 . . NW Arkansas

MAY
1-3 . . . . . at Tulsa
4-7 . . . at NW Arkansas
9-12 . . . . Frisco
13-15 . . . at Amarillo
16-19 . . . Corpus Christi

20-22 . . . at Frisco
23-26 . . . at Amarillo
28-30 . . . Corpus Christi
31 . . . . . Amarillo

JUNE
1-2 . . . . . Amarillo
3-5 . . . at Corpus Christi
6-9 . . . . Frisco
11-13 . . . at Springfield
14-16 . . . at Arkansas
17-19 . . . Springfield
20-23 . . . Arkansas
27-30 . . . at Frisco

JULY
1-3	Amarillo
4-7	at Corpus Christi
8-10	Amarillo
11-14	Corpus Christi
16-18	at Arkansas
19-22	at Tulsa
24-26	Arkansas
27-30	Tulsa

AUGUST
1-4	at Corpus Christi

5-7	Amarillo
8-11	Corpus Christi
12-15	at Amarillo
16-18	at Corpus Christi
20-22	NW Arkansas
23-25	Springfield
26-29	at NW Arkansas
30-31	at Springfield

SEPTEMBER
1-2	at Springfield

NORTHWEST ARKANSAS NATURALS

APRIL
4-7	Springfield
8-10	Arkansas
11-14	at Springfield
15-17	at Arkansas
18-20	Springfield
22-25	at Corpus Christi
26-29	at Midland

MAY
1-3	Corpus Christi
4-7	Midland
9-12	at Springfield
13-15	Tulsa
16-19	Springfield
20-22	at Arkansas
23-26	at Tulsa
28-30	Arkansas
31	at Springfield

JUNE
1-2	at Springfield
3-5	Arkansas
6-9	Springfield
11-13	at Amarillo
14-16	at Frisco
17-19	Amarillo

20-23	Frisco
27-30	at Springfield

JULY
1-3	Arkansas
4-7	at Tulsa
8-10	at Arkansas
11-14	Tulsa
16-18	at Corpus Christi
19-22	at Amarillo
24-26	Corpus Christi
27-30	Amarillo

AUGUST
1-4	at Tulsa
5-7	at Arkansas
8-11	Tulsa
12-15	at Arkansas
16-18	Tulsa
20-22	at Midland
23-25	at Frisco
26-29	Midland
30-31	Frisco

SEPTEMBER
1-2	Frisco

SPRINGFIELD CARDINALS

APRIL
4-7	at NW Arkansas
8-10	at Tulsa
11-14	NW Arkansas
15-17	Tulsa
18-20	at NW Arkansas

22-25	Amarillo
26-29	Frisco

MAY
1-3	at Amarillo
4-7	at Frisco
9-12	NW Arkansas

13-15	Arkansas
16-19	at NW Arkansas
20-22	Tulsa
23-26	at Arkansas
28-30	Tulsa
31	NW Arkansas

JUNE
1-2	NW Arkansas
3-5	at Tulsa
6-9	at NW Arkansas
11-13	Midland
14-16	Corpus Christi
17-19	at Midland
20-23	at Corpus Christi
27-30	NW Arkansas

JULY
1-3	Tulsa
4-7	at Arkansas

TULSA DRILLERS

APRIL
4-7	Arkansas
8-10	Springfield
11-14	at Arkansas
15-17	at Springfield
18-20	Arkansas
22-25	at Midland
26-29	at Corpus Christi

MAY
1-3	Midland
4-7	Corpus Christi
9-12	at Arkansas
13-15	at NW Arkansas
16-19	Arkansas
20-22	at Springfield
23-26	NW Arkansas
28-30	at Springfield
31	at Arkansas

JUNE
1-2	at Arkansas
3-5	Springfield
6-9	Arkansas
11-13	at Frisco
14-16	at Amarillo
17-19	Frisco

20-23	Amarillo
27-30	at Arkansas

JULY
1-3	at Springfield
4-7	NW Arkansas
8-10	Springfield
11-14	at NW Arkansas
16-18	Frisco
19-22	Midland
24-26	at Frisco
27-30	at Midland

AUGUST
1-4	NW Arkansas
5-7	Springfield
8-11	at NW Arkansas
12-15	Springfield
16-18	at NW Arkansas
20-22	Amarillo
23-25	Corpus Christi
26-29	at Amarillo
30-31	at Corpus Christi

SEPTEMBER
1-2	at Corpus Christi

HIGH CLASS A

CALIFORNIA LEAGUE

INLAND EMPIRE 66ERS

APRIL
4-7	Lake Elsinore
8-10	Modesto
11-14	at Lake Elsinore
15-17	at Lancaster
18-20	Lake Elsinore
22-25	Rancho Cucamonga
26-28	at Lake Elsinore
29-30	San Jose

MAY
1-2	San Jose
3-5	at Visalia
7-9	at Rancho Cucamonga

10-12	Stockton
13-16	at San Jose
17-19	at Stockton
21-23	Lancaster
24-26	Stockton
27-29	at Visalia
30-31	at Rancho Cucamonga

JUNE
1-2	at Rancho Cucamonga
4-6	Lake Elsinore
7-11	Rancho Cucamonga
12-16	at Lancaster
20-23	at Lake Elsinore

24-26	Lancaster
27-30	Lake Elsinore

JULY
1-3	at Lancaster
4-6	Rancho Cucamonga
7-9	Lancaster
10-12	at Visalia
13-15	at Modesto
17-19	Visalia
20-22	Modesto
23-25	at Rancho Cucamonga
26-28	at Lake Elsinore
30-31	Visalia

AUGUST
1	Visalia
2-4	San Jose
6-8	at Modesto
9-11	Lake Elsinore
13-15	at Stockton
16-18	at San Jose
20-22	Lancaster
23-26	Rancho Cucamonga
27-29	at Lancaster
30-31	at Rancho Cucamonga

SEPTEMBER
1-2	at Rancho Cucamonga

LAKE ELSINORE STORM

APRIL
4-7	at Inland Empire

8-10	at Lancaster
11-14	Inland Empire

15-17 . Rancho Cucamonga
18-20 . . . .at Inland Empire
22-25 . . . . Lancaster
26-28 . . . . . . Inland Empire
29-30 at Rancho Cucamonga

MAY
1-2 . .at Rancho Cucamonga
3-5 . . . . . . .at Lancaster
7-9 . . . . Visalia
10-12 . . . . San Jose
13-16 . . . . . at Stockton
17-19 . . . . . at San Jose
21-23 . . . . . . Stockton
24-26 . . . . . at Modesto
27-29 . Rancho Cucamonga
30-31 . . . . . . San Jose

JUNE
1-2 . . . . San Jose
4-6 . . . .at Inland Empire
7-11 . . . . . . Lancaster
12-16 at Rancho Cucamonga
20-23 . . . . Inland Empire
24-26 . Rancho Cucamonga
27-30 . . . .at Inland Empire

JULY
1-3 . .at Rancho Cucamonga
4-6 . . . . Lancaster
7-9 . . Rancho Cucamonga
10-12 . . . . . . at Modesto
13-15 . . . . at Visalia
17-19 . . . . . . .Modesto
20-22 . . . . Visalia
23-25 . . . . . .at Lancaster
26-28 . . . . . Inland Empire
30-31 . . . . at San Jose

AUGUST
1 . . . . at San Jose
2-4 . . . . at Stockton
5-7 . . . . San Jose
9-11 . . .at Inland Empire
13-15 . . . . . .at Lancaster
16-18 . . . . . . .Stockton
20-22 . Rancho Cucamonga
23-26 . . . . . .at Lancaster
27-29 at Rancho Cucamonga
30-31 . . . . . . Lancaster

SEPTEMBER
1-2 . . . . Lancaster

LANCASTER JETHAWKS

APRIL
4-7 . . . . .Modesto
8-10 . . . . . . Lake Elsinore
11-14 at Rancho Cucamonga
15-17 . . . . Inland Empire
18-20 . . . . . . at Visalia
22-25 . . . at Lake Elsinore
26-28 . . . . . . Visalia
29-30 . . . . at Modesto

MAY
1-2 . . . . . . at Modesto
3-5 . . . . . . Lake Elsinore
7-9 . . . . .Stockton
10-12 . . . . at Modesto
13-16 . Rancho Cucamonga
17-19 . . . . .at Visalia
21-23 . . . at Inland Empire
24-26 . Rancho Cucamonga
27-29 . . . . at San Jose
30-31 . . . . . . .Stockton

JUNE
1-2 . . . . . . .Stockton
4-6 . .at Rancho Cucamonga
7-11 . . . . at Lake Elsinore
12-16 . . . Inland Empire
20-23 . Rancho Cucamonga
24-26 . . . .at Inland Empire

27-30 at Rancho Cucamonga

JULY
1-3 . . . . . . Inland Empire
4-6 . . . . at Lake Elsinore
7-9 . . . . .at Inland Empire
10-12 . . . . . . .Stockton
13-15 . . . . . . San Jose
17-19 . . . . at Stockton
20-22 . . . . at San Jose
23-25 . . . . Lake Elsinore
26-28 . . . . . .at Visalia
30-31 . Rancho Cucamonga

AUGUST
1 . . . . Rancho Cucamonga
2-4 . . . . .Modesto
6-8 . .at Rancho Cucamonga
9-11 . . . . Visalia
13-15 . . . . . Lake Elsinore
16-18 . . . . . at Modesto
20-22 . . . at Inland Empire
23-26 . . . . . Lake Elsinore
27-29 . . . . Inland Empire
30-31 . . . . at Lake Elsinore

SEPTEMBER
1-2 . . . . . at Lake Elsinore

MODESTO NUTS

APRIL
4-7 . . . . .at Lancaster
8-10 . . . .at Inland Empire
11-14 . . . . . . .Stockton
15-17 . . . . Visalia
18-20 . . . . at Stockton
22-25 . . . at San Jose
26-28 . Rancho Cucamonga
29-30 . . . . . . Lancaster

MAY
1-2 . . . . Lancaster
3-5 . . . . at Stockton
7-9 . . . . . . San Jose
10-12 . . . . . . Lancaster
13-16 . . . . . .at Visalia
17-19 at Rancho Cucamonga
21-23 . . . . San Jose
24-26 . . . . . Lake Elsinore
27-29 . . . . . . at Stockton
30-31 . . . . Visalia

JUNE
1-2 . . . . Visalia
4-6 . . . . at San Jose
7-11 . . . . . at Visalia
12-16 . . . . .Stockton
20-23 . . . . . .at Visalia
24-26 . . . . at San Jose
27-30 . . . . . . Visalia

JULY
1-3 . . . . San Jose
4-6 . . . . at Stockton
7-9 . . . . at San Jose
10-12 . . . . Lake Elsinore
13-15 . . . . Inland Empire
17-19 . . . at Lake Elsinore
20-22 . . .at Inland Empire
23-25 . . . . . . .Stockton
26-28 . . . . . San Jose
30-31 . . . . . at Stockton

AUGUST
1 . . . . at Stockton
2-4 . . . . . . .at Lancaster
6-8 . . . . . . Inland Empire
9-11 . . . . . . at San Jose
13-15 at Rancho Cucamonga
16-18 . . . . . . Lancaster
20-22 . . . . . . San Jose
23-26 . . . . . .at Visalia
27-29 . . . . . .Stockton
30-31 . . . . Visalia

SEPTEMBER
1-2 . . . . Visalia

RANCHO CUCAMONGA QUAKES

APRIL
4-7 . . . . at Stockton
8-10 . . . . at Visalia
11-14 . . . . . . Lancaster
15-17 . . at Lake Elsinore
18-20 . . . . . San Jose
22-25 . . .at Inland Empire
26-28 . . . . at Modesto
29-30 . . . . Lake Elsinore

MAY
1-2 . . . . . . Lake Elsinore
3-5 . . . . at San Jose
7-9 . . . . . Inland Empire
10-12 . . . . Visalia
13-16 . . . .at Lancaster
17-19 . . . . . .Modesto
21-23 . . . . Visalia
24-26 . . . .at Lancaster
27-29 . . at Lake Elsinore
30-31 . . . . Inland Empire

JUNE
1-2 . . . . Inland Empire
4-6 . . . . Lancaster
7-11 . . . .at Inland Empire
12-16 . . . Lake Elsinore
20-23 . . . . .at Lancaster
24-26 . . . . at Lake Elsinore
27-30 . . . . . Lancaster

JULY
1-3 . . . . . . Lake Elsinore
4-6 . . . .at Inland Empire
7-9 . . . . . at Lake Elsinore
10-12 . . . . . San Jose
13-15 . . . . . .Stockton
17-19 . . . . at San Jose
20-22 . . . . at Stockton
23-25 . . . . Inland Empire
26-28 . . . . . .Stockton
30-31 . . . .at Lancaster

AUGUST
1 . . . . .at Lancaster
2-4 . . . . at Visalia
6-8 . . . . Lancaster
9-11 . . . . . at Stockton
13-15 . . . . . .Modesto
16-18 . . . . Visalia
20-22 . . . at Lake Elsinore
23-26 . . .at Inland Empire
27-29 . . . . Lake Elsinore
30-31 . . . . Inland Empire

SEPTEMBER
1-2 . . . . . . Inland Empire

SAN JOSE GIANTS

APRIL
4-7 . . . . at Visalia
8-10 . . . . . . at Stockton
11-14 . . . . Visalia
15-17 . . . . . .Stockton
18-20 at Rancho Cucamonga
22-25 . . . . . .Modesto
26-28 . . . . . .Stockton
29-30 . . . .at Inland Empire

MAY
1-2 . . . . .at Inland Empire
3-5 . . . Rancho Cucamonga
7-9 . . . . at Modesto
10-12 . . . at Lake Elsinore
13-16 . . . . Inland Empire
17-19 . . . . Lake Elsinore
21-23 . . . . at Modesto
24-26 . . . . . . .at Visalia
27-29 . . . . . . Lancaster
30-31 . . . at Lake Elsinore

JUNE
1-2 . . . . at Lake Elsinore
4-6 . . . . Modesto
7-11 . . . . . at Stockton
12-16 . . . . . Visalia
20-23 . . . . at Stockton
24-26 . . . . .Modesto
27-30 . . . . . . .Stockton

JULY
1-3 . . . . at Modesto
4-6 . . . . Visalia
7-9 . . . . .Modesto
10-12 at Rancho Cucamonga
13-15 . . . .at Lancaster
17-19 . Rancho Cucamonga
20-22 . . . . . . Lancaster
23-25 . . . . . . .at Visalia
26-28 . . . . . at Modesto
30-31 . . . . . Lake Elsinore

AUGUST
1 . . . . Lake Elsinore
2-4 . . . . .at Inland Empire
5-7 . . . . at Lake Elsinore
9-11 . . . . .Modesto
13-15 . . . . . . .at Visalia
16-18 . . . . Inland Empire
20-22 . . . . . at Modesto
23-26 . . . . . at Stockton
27-29 . . . . Visalia
30-31 . . . . . . .Stockton

SEPTEMBER
1-2 . . . . .Stockton

STOCKTON PORTS

APRIL
4-7. . . Rancho Cucamonga
8-10 . . . . San Jose
11-14 . . . . . . at Modesto
15-17 . . . . . at San Jose
18-20 . . . . Modesto
22-25 . . . . . . at Visalia
26-28 . . . . at San Jose
29-30 . . . . Visalia

MAY
1-2. . . . . Visalia
3-5. . . . . Modesto
7-9. . . . . . .at Lancaster
10-12 . . .at Inland Empire
13-16 . . . . . Lake Elsinore
17-19 . . . . Inland Empire
21-23 . . at Lake Elsinore
24-26 . . . .at Inland Empire
27-29 . . . . . . Modesto
30-31 . . . . .at Lancaster

JUNE
1-2. . . . . . .at Lancaster
3-5. . . . . Visalia
7-11 . . . . . . San Jose
12-16 . . . . . at Modesto
20-23 . . . . . . San Jose

24-26 . . . . Visalia
27-30 . . . . . . at San Jose

JULY
1-3. . . . . at Visalia
4-6. . . . . .Modesto
7-9. . . . . Visalia
10-12 . . . .at Lancaster
13-15 at Rancho Cucamonga
17-19 . . . . . . Lancaster
20-22 . Rancho Cucamonga
23-25 . . . . . at Modesto
26-28 at Rancho Cucamonga
30-31 . . . . . .Modesto

AUGUST
1 . . . . .Modesto
2-4. . . . . Lake Elsinore
6-8. . . . . . . at Visalia
9-11 . . Rancho Cucamonga
13-15 . . . . Inland Empire
16-18 . . at Lake Elsinore
19-21 . . . . . at Visalia
23-26 . . . . . . San Jose
27-29 . . . . at Modesto
30-31 . . . . at San Jose

SEPTEMBER
1-2. . . . . at San Jose

VISALIA RAWHIDE

APRIL
4-7. . . . . San Jose
8-10 . . Rancho Cucamonga
11-14 . . . . at San Jose
15-17 . . . . at Modesto
18-20 . . . . . Lancaster
22-25 . . . . . . Stockton
26-28 . . . .at Lancaster
29-30 . . . . at Stockton

MAY
1-2. . . . . . at Stockton
3-5. . . . . Inland Empire
7-9. . . . at Lake Elsinore
10-12 at Rancho Cucamonga
13-16 . . . . Modesto
17-19 . . . . . Lancaster
21-23 at Rancho Cucamonga
24-26 . . . . San Jose
27-29 . . . . Inland Empire
30-31 . . . . . at Modesto

JUNE
1-2. . . . . . . at Modesto
3-5. . . . . . .at Stockton
7-11 . . . . .Modesto
12-16 . . . . at San Jose
20-23 . . . . . . .Modesto

24-26 . . . . . . at Stockton
27-30 . . . . . at Modesto

JULY
1-3. . . . . .Stockton
4-6. . . . . . at San Jose
7-9. . . . . . at Stockton
10-12 . . . . Inland Empire
13-15 . . . Lake Elsinore
17-19 . . .at Inland Empire
20-22 . . at Lake Elsinore
23-25 . . . . . . San Jose
26-28 . . . . . . Lancaster
30-31 . . . .at Inland Empire

AUGUST
1 . . . . . .at Inland Empire
2-4. . . Rancho Cucamonga
6-8. . . . . Stockton
9-11 . . . .at Lancaster
13-15 . . . . . San Jose
16-18 at Rancho Cucamonga
19-21 . . . . . Stockton
23-26 . . . . . . Modesto
27-29 . . . . at San Jose
30-31 . . . . . at Modesto

SEPTEMBER
1-2. . . . . . . at Modesto

CAROLINA LEAGUE

CAROLINA MUDCATS

APRIL
4-7. . . . . at Down East
8-10 . . . . . . at Potomac
11-14 . . . . . .Wilmington
15-17 . . . . . Fayetteville
18-21 . . . . at Fayetteville
23-25 . . . at Myrtle Beach
26-28 . . . . . .Potomac
29-30 . . . . at Salem

MAY
1-2. . . . . at Salem
3-5. . . . . at Wilmington
7-9. . . . . . . Fayetteville
10-12 . . . Myrtle Beach
13-16 . . . . at Lynchburg
17-19 . . . at Fayetteville
20-23 . . . . . .Lynchburg
24-27 . . . . .Down East

29-31 . . . at Winston-Salem

JUNE
1 . . . . . at Winston-Salem
2-4. . . . . . . .Frederick
6-9. . . . . .Salem
10-12 . . . at Frederick
13-16 . . . .Winston-Salem
20-23 . . . . at Potomac
24-26 . . . .Down East
27-30 . . . . . .Potomac

JULY
1-3. . . . at Myrtle Beach
4-6. . . . . . . .Frederick
7-9. . . . . . . .Lynchburg
10-12 . . . at Frederick
13-15 . . . . at Wilmington
17-19 . . . Myrtle Beach

DOWN EAST WOOD DUCKS

APRIL
4-7. . . . . Carolina
8-10 . . . . Myrtle Beach
11-14 . . . . .Lynchburg
15-17 . . . . . at Salem
18-21 . . . . at Wilmington
23-25 . . . . .Lynchburg
26-28 . . . . Fayetteville
29-30 . . . at Myrtle Beach

MAY
1-2. . . . . at Myrtle Beach
3-5. . . . . at Fayetteville
7-9. . . . . Myrtle Beach
10-12 . . . at Winston-Salem
13-16 . . . . at Potomac
17-19 . .Winston-Salem
20-23 . . . . . . .Potomac
24-27 . . . .at Carolina
29-31 . . . . .Salem

JUNE
1 . . . . .Salem
2-4. . . .at Lynchburg
6-9. . . . . . . .Frederick
10-12 . . . . at Potomac
13-16 . . at Myrtle Beach
20-23 . . . . .Salem

24-26 . . . . . .at Carolina
27-30 . . . . .at Lynchburg

JULY
1-3. . . . . .Winston-Salem
4-6. . . . . . . at Salem
7-9. . . . . at Myrtle Beach
10-12 . . . . . .Lynchburg
13-15 . . . .Winston-Salem
17-19 . . . . . . at Salem
20-22 . . . at Winston-Salem
23-25 . . . . . . Carolina
26-28 . . . . . . Wilmington
30-31 . . . . . . .at Carolina

AUGUST
1. . . . . .at Carolina
2-4. . . . . .Frederick
6-8. . . . . Carolina
9-11 . . . . . at Frederick
13-15 . . . . at Fayetteville
16-18 . . . . .Wilmington
20-22 . . . . . Fayetteville
23-25 . . . . at Wilmington
26-29 . . . . . . .Frederick
30-31 . . . at Fayetteville

SEPTEMBER
1-2. . . . . . . at Fayetteville

FAYETTEVILLE WOODPECKERS

APRIL
4-7. . . . . . . at Potomac
8-10 . . . . . . .at Frederick
11-14 . . at Myrtle Beach
15-17 . . . . . .at Carolina
18-21 . . . . . . Carolina
23-25 . . . . .Frederick
26-28 . . . . at Down East
29-30 . . . .Lynchburg

MAY
1-2. . . . . .Lynchburg
3-5. . . . . . . .Down East
7-9. . . . . . .at Carolina
10-12 . . . . at Frederick
13-16 . . . . .Salem
17-19 . . . . Carolina
20-23 . . . at Winston-Salem
24-27 . . . at Lynchburg
29-31 . . . .Wilmington

JUNE
1 . . . . Wilmington
2-4. . . . .Winston-Salem
6-9. . . . . . at Wilmington

10-12 . . . . . Myrtle Beach
13-16 . . . . .Potomac
20-23 . . . . at Myrtle Beach
24-26 . . . . at Salem
27-30 . . . Myrtle Beach

JULY
1-3. . . . . .Salem
4-6. . . . . at Winston-Salem
7-9. . . . . at Potomac
10-12 . . . .Winston-Salem
13-15 . . . . .Potomac
17-19 . . . . at Lynchburg
20-22 . . . . at Potomac
23-25 . . . . . .Lynchburg
26-28 . . . . Carolina
30-31 . . . at Wilmington

AUGUST
1. . . . . at Wilmington
2-4. . . . . . . Myrtle Beach
6-8. . . . . .Wilmington
9-11 . . . . at Winston-Salem
13-15 . . . . . .Down East
16-18 . . . . . . .at Frederick

20-22 . . . . . . at Down East
23-25 . . . . . . .Frederick
26-29 . . . . . . .at Carolina

FREDERICK KEYS

APRIL
4-7 . . . . . .Winston-Salem
8-10 . . . . . . Fayetteville
11-14 . . . . at Salem
15-17 . . . . at Myrtle Beach
18-21 . . . . .Salem
23-25 . . . . at Fayetteville
26-28 . . . at Winston-Salem
29-30 . . . . . . Wilmington

MAY
1-2 . . . . Wilmington
3-5 . . . . . . at Lynchburg
7-9 . . . . .Potomac
10-12 . . . . . . Fayetteville
13-16 . . . . . at Wilmington
17-19 . . . . .Salem
20-23 . . . . . Myrtle Beach
24-27 . . . . . at Potomac
29-31 . . . . . . .Lynchburg

JUNE
1 . . . . .Lynchburg
2-4 . . . . .at Carolina
6-9 . . . . at Down East
10-12 . . . . Carolina
13-16 . . . . at Salem
20-23 . . . . . at Wilmington

LYNCHBURG HILLCATS

APRIL
4-7 . . . . at Myrtle Beach
8-10 . . . . .Salem
11-14 . . . . . at Down East
15-17 . . . . Potomac
18-21 . . . . . Myrtle Beach
23-25 . . . . at Down East
26-28 . . . . . Wilmington
29-30 . . . . at Fayetteville

MAY
1-2 . . . . . at Fayetteville
3-5 . . . . .Frederick
7-9 . . . . at Winston-Salem
10-12 . . . . .Salem
13-16 . . . . Carolina
17-19 . . . . . Myrtle Beach
20-23 . . . .at Carolina
24-27 . . . . . Fayetteville
29-31 . . . . . at Frederick

JUNE
1 . . . . at Frederick
2-4 . . . . .Down East
6-9 . . . . at Potomac
10-12 . . . . at Wilmington
13-16 . . . . . Wilmington
20-23 . . . at Winston-Salem

MYRTLE BEACH PELICANS

APRIL
4-7 . . . . . . .Lynchburg
8-10 . . . . . at Down East
11-14 . . . . . Fayetteville
15-17 . . . . . . .Frederick
18-21 . . . . . at Lynchburg
23-25 . . . . Carolina
26-28 . . . . at Salem

30-31 . . . . . . .Down East
SEPTEMBER
1-2 . . . . .Down East

24-26 . . . . . at Lynchburg
27-30 . . . . . . Wilmington
JULY
1-3 . . . . . . .Lynchburg
4-6 . . . . . .at Carolina
7-9 . . . . at Winston-Salem
10-12 . . . . . . Carolina
13-15 . . . . Salem
17-19 . . . . . . at Potomac
20-22 . . . . at Lynchburg
23-25 . . . Myrtle Beach
26-28 . . . . . .Potomac
30-31 . . . at Myrtle Beach

AUGUST
1 . . . . . at Myrtle Beach
2-4 . . . . at Down East
6-8 . . . . .Potomac
9-11 . . . . .Down East
13-15 . . . . . . .at Salem
16-18 . . . . . . Fayetteville
20-22 . . . . Potomac
23-25 . . . at Fayetteville
26-29 . . . . at Down East
30-31 . . . . .Potomac

SEPTEMBER
1-2 . . . . .Potomac

24-26 . . . . . . .Frederick
27-30 . . . . . . .Down East
JULY
1-3 . . . . at Frederick
4-6 . . . . . Myrtle Beach
7-9 . . . . . .at Carolina
10-12 . . . . . at Down East
13-15 . . . at Myrtle Beach
17-19 . . . . . . Fayetteville
20-22 . . . . . . .Frederick
23-25 . . . at Fayetteville
26-28 . . . . Winston-Salem
30-31 . . . at Winston-Salem

AUGUST
1 . . . . . at Winston-Salem
2-8 . . . . at Salem
9-11 . . . . . . at Potomac
13-15 . . . . at Wilmington
16-18 . . . . Carolina
20-22 . . . . Winston-Salem
23-25 . . . . . at Carolina
26-29 . . . . . Wilmington
30-31 . . . . Winston-Salem

SEPTEMBER
1-2 . . . . . .Winston-Salem

29-30 . . . . . . .Down East
MAY
1-2 . . . . .Down East
3-5 . . . . .Salem
7-9 . . . . at Down East
10-12 . . . . .at Carolina
13-16 . . . . .Winston-Salem

17-19 . . . . . at Lynchburg
20-23 . . . . . . at Frederick
24-27 . . . . at Wilmington
29-31 . . . . Potomac

JUNE
1 . . . . .Potomac
2-4 . . . . Wilmington
6-9 . . . . at Winston-Salem
10-12 . . . at Fayetteville
13-16 . . . . . . .Down East
20-23 . . . . . . Fayetteville
24-26 . . . at Winston-Salem
27-30 . . . . at Fayetteville

JULY
1-3 . . . . Carolina
4-6 . . . . . at Lynchburg
7-9 . . . . . . .Down East
10-12 . . . . . . .Potomac
13-15 . . . . . . .Lynchburg

POTOMAC NATIONALS

APRIL
4-7 . . . . Fayetteville
8-10 . . . . Carolina
11-14 . . . at Winston-Salem
15-17 . . . . . at Lynchburg
18-21 . . . .Winston-Salem
23-25 . . . . .Salem
26-28 . . . . . .at Carolina
29-30 . . . at Winston-Salem

MAY
1-2 . . . . at Winston-Salem
3-5 . . . . . .Winston-Salem
7-9 . . . . . . at Frederick
10-12 . . . . at Wilmington
13-16 . . . . . .Down East
17-19 . . . . Wilmington
20-23 . . . at Down East
24-27 . . . . . . .Frederick
29-31 . . . at Myrtle Beach

JUNE
1 . . . . . at Myrtle Beach
2-4 . . . . at Salem
6-9 . . . . .Lynchburg
10-12 . . . . . .Down East
13-16 . . . at Fayetteville
20-23 . . . . Carolina

SALEM RED SOX

APRIL
4-7 . . . . . . at Wilmington
8-10 . . . . . at Lynchburg
11-14 . . . . . . .Frederick
15-17 . . . . . .Down East
18-21 . . . . . at Frederick
23-25 . . . . . at Potomac
26-28 . . . . Myrtle Beach
29-30 . . . . Carolina

MAY
1-2 . . . . Carolina
3-5 . . . . at Myrtle Beach
7-9 . . . . Wilmington
10-12 . . . . at Lynchburg
13-16 . . . . at Fayetteville
17-19 . . . . at Frederick
20-23 . . . . . Wilmington
24-27 . . . .Winston-Salem
29-31 . . . . at Down East

JUNE
1 . . . . . at Down East

17-19 . . . . .at Carolina
20-22 . . . . .Salem
23-25 . . . . at Frederick
26-28 . . . . . . at Salem
30-31 . . . . . . .Frederick

AUGUST
1 . . . . .Frederick
2-4 . . . . . . at Fayetteville
6-8 . . . . . .Winston-Salem
9-11 . . . . Wilmington
13-15 . . . . . . at Potomac
16-18 . . . . .Salem
20-22 . . . . . . Carolina
23-25 . . . . . . at Salem
26-29 . . . . . at Potomac
30-31 . . . . at Wilmington

SEPTEMBER
1-2 . . . . . . at Wilmington

24-26 . . . . . . Wilmington
27-30 . . . . . .at Carolina
JULY
1-3 . . . . . . at Wilmington
4-6 . . . . Wilmington
7-9 . . . . . . Fayetteville
10-12 . . . . at Myrtle Beach
13-15 . . . . at Fayetteville
17-19 . . . . .Frederick
20-22 . . . . . . Fayetteville
23-25 . . . . at Wilmington
26-28 . . . . . at Frederick
30-31 . . . . .Salem

AUGUST
1 . . . . .Salem
2-4 . . . . . at Wilmington
6-8 . . . . at Frederick
9-11 . . . . .Lynchburg
13-15 . . . . . Myrtle Beach
16-18 . . . at Winston-Salem
20-22 . . . . . at Frederick
23-25 . . . . .Winston-Salem
26-29 . . . . Myrtle Beach
30-31 . . . . . at Frederick

SEPTEMBER
1-2 . . . . at Frederick

2-4 . . . . .Potomac
6-9 . . . . at Carolina
10-12 . . . at Winston-Salem
13-16 . . . . . . .Frederick
20-23 . . . . at Down East
24-26 . . . . Fayetteville
27-30 . . . .Winston-Salem

JULY
1-3 . . . . at Fayetteville
4-6 . . . . .Down East
7-8 . . . . Wilmington
10-12 . . . . at Wilmington
13-15 . . . . . at Frederick
17-19 . . . . . .Down East
20-22 . . . . at Myrtle Beach
23-25 . . . .Winston-Salem
26-28 . . . . Myrtle Beach
30-31 . . . . . at Potomac

AUGUST
1 . . . . at Potomac
2-8 . . . . .Lynchburg

9-11 . . . . .at Carolina
13-15 . . . . .Frederick
16-18 . . . at Myrtle Beach
20-22 . . . . at Wilmington
23-25 . . . . . Myrtle Beach

26-29 . . . at Winston-Salem
30-31 . . . . Carolina

SEPTEMBER
1-2. . . . . Carolina

WILMINGTON BLUE ROCKS

APRIL	
4-7. . . . . .Salem	
8-10 . . . . .Winston-Salem	
11-14 . . . . .at Carolina	
15-17 . . at Winston-Salem	
18-21 . . . . . . .Down East	
22-24 . . . . .Winston-Salem	
26-28 . . . . at Lynchburg	
29-30 . . . . . at Frederick	

MAY	
1-2. . . . . at Frederick	
3-5. . . . . Carolina	
7-9. . . . . at Salem	
10-12 . . . . .Potomac	
13-16 . . . . .Frederick	
17-19 . . . . . . at Potomac	
20-23 . . . . . . at Salem	
24-27 . . . . . Myrtle Beach	
29-31 . . . . at Fayetteville	

JUNE	
1 . . . . . . at Fayetteville	
2-4. . . . at Myrtle Beach	
6-9. . . . . . . Fayetteville	
10-12 . . . . . .Lynchburg	
13-16 . . . . .at Lynchburg	
20-23 . . . . .Frederick	

24-26 . . . . . . at Potomac
27-30 . . . . . .at Frederick

JULY
1-3. . . . . Potomac
4-6. . . . . at Potomac
7-8. . . . . at Salem
10-12 . . . . .Salem
13-15 . . . . . . Carolina
17-19 . . at Winston-Salem
20-22 . . . . . . .at Carolina
23-25 . . . . .Potomac
26-28 . . . . . at Down East
30-31 . . . . . Fayetteville

AUGUST
1 . . . . Fayetteville
2-4. . . . . .Potomac
6-8. . . . . at Fayetteville
9-11 . . . at Myrtle Beach
13-15 . . . . . . .Lynchburg
16-18 . . . . at Down East
20-22 . . . . .Salem
23-25 . . . . . .Down East
26-29 . . . . at Lynchburg
30-31 . . . . Myrtle Beach

SEPTEMBER
1-2. . . . . . Myrtle Beach

WINSTON-SALEM DASH

APRIL	
4-7. . . . . at Frederick	
8-10 . . . . . at Wilmington	
11-14 . . . . .Potomac	
15-17 . . . . Wilmington	
18-21 . . . . . at Potomac	
22-24 . . . . at Wilmington	
26-28 . . . . . . .Frederick	
29-30 . . . . .Potomac	

MAY	
1-2. . . . . .Potomac	
3-5. . . . . . . at Potomac	
7-9. . . . . .Lynchburg	
10-12 . . . . . .Down East	
13-16 . . . . at Myrtle Beach	
17-19 . . . .at Down East	
20-23 . . . . . . Fayetteville	
24-27 . . . . .at Salem	
29-31 . . . . Carolina	

JUNE	
1 . . . . Carolina	
2-4. . . . . at Fayetteville	
6-9. . . . . Myrtle Beach	
10-12 . . . . .Salem	
13-16 . . . . .at Carolina	
20-23 . . . . . . .Lynchburg	

24-26 . . . . . Myrtle Beach
27-30 . . . . . . at Salem

JULY
1-3. . . . . . at Down East
4-6. . . . . . . Fayetteville
7-9. . . . . .Frederick
10-12 . . . . at Fayetteville
13-15 . . . . . at Down East
17-19 . . . . Wilmington
20-22 . . . . . . .Down East
23-25 . . . . at Salem
26-28 . . . . at Lynchburg
30-31 . . . . . . .Lynchburg

AUGUST
1 . . . . .Lynchburg
2-4. . . . . Carolina
6-8. . . . . at Myrtle Beach
9-11 . . . . . . Fayetteville
13-15 . . . . . .at Carolina
16-18 . . . . Potomac
20-22 . . . . at Lynchburg
23-25 . . . . at Potomac
26-29 . . . . .Salem
30-31 . . . . at Lynchburg

SEPTEMBER
1-2. . . . . at Lynchburg

FLORIDA STATE LEAGUE
BRADENTON MARAUDERS

APRIL	
4-5. . . . . at St. Lucie	
6-7. . . . . St. Lucie	

8-9. . . . . . . .at Charlotte
10-11 . . . . Charlotte
12-14 . . . . . . .at Dunedin

15-17 . . . . .at Tampa
18-20 . . . . Jupiter
22-24 . . . . . .Fort Myers
25-28 . . . . . . at Daytona
30 . . . . at Jupiter

MAY
1-2. . . . . at Jupiter
3-5. . . . . .Lakeland
6-8. . . . . . at Clearwater
9-11 . . . . . . Palm Beach
13 . . . . at Fort Myers
14-16 . . . . . .Fort Myers
17-19 . . . at Palm Beach
20-21 . . . . at Fort Myers
22 . . . . .Fort Myers
23-26 . . . . Tampa
28-30 . . . . .Lakeland
31 . . . . .at Tampa

JUNE
1-2. . . . . .at Tampa
3-6. . . . . at Daytona
7-9. . . . . Dunedin
10-11 . . . . .at Charlotte
12-13 . . . . Charlotte
17-19 . . . . . Clearwater
20-23 . . . . Tampa

CHARLOTTE STONE CRABS

APRIL	
4-5. . . . . . at Fort Myers	
6-7. . . . . . . .Fort Myers	
8-9. . . . . .Bradenton	
10-11 . . . . . at Bradenton	
12-14 . . . . . Palm Beach	
15-17 . . . . .Dunedin	
18-20 . . . . at Fort Myers	
22-24 . . . . Tampa	
25-28 . . . . . . at Lakeland	
30 . . . . .at Tampa	

MAY	
1-2. . . . . .at Tampa	
3-5. . . . . Jupiter	
6-7. . . . . . . .Fort Myers	
8 . . . . at Fort Myers	
9-11 . . . . . at St. Lucie	
13-16 . . . . . . Daytona	
17-19 . . .at Clearwater	
20-22 . . . . . . at Jupiter	
23-26 . . . . . Palm Beach	
28-30 . . . . . Clearwater	
31 . . . . St. Lucie	

JUNE	
1-2. . . . . St. Lucie	
3-6. . . . . . at Dunedin	
7-9. . . . . . at Palm Beach	
10-11 . . . . . .Bradenton	
12-13 . . . . at Bradenton	
17 . . . . . at Fort Myers	

18 . . . . .Fort Myers
19 . . . . at Fort Myers
20-23 . . . . .Lakeland
25-26 . . . . . .Fort Myers
27 . . . . . . at Fort Myers
28-30 . . . . at Palm Beach

JULY
1-3. . . . . St. Lucie
4-7. . . . . at Jupiter
8-11 . . . . at Florida
12-14 . . . . Tampa
16-18 . . . . . at St. Lucie
19-21 . . . . Dunedin
22-24 . . . . Jupiter
25-28 . . .at Clearwater
30-31 . . . . . at Bradenton

AUGUST
1 . . . . at Bradenton
2-4. . . . . . . Palm Beach
5-7. . . . . .Bradenton
8-11 . . . . .at Tampa
12-15 . . . . . at Daytona
16-18 . . . . St. Lucie
20 . . . . .Fort Myers
21-22 . . . . at Fort Myers
23-25 . . . . . Clearwater
26-29 . . . . Florida
30-31 . . . . . at Dunedin

SEPTEMBER
1 . . . . at Dunedin

CLEARWATER THRESHERS

APRIL	
4 . . . . at Dunedin	
5-6. . . . . Dunedin	
7 . . . . at Dunedin	
8-11 . . . . . . at Lakeland	
12-14 . . . . . .Fort Myers	
15-17 . . . . . . at Florida	
18-20 . . . . . . Tampa	
22-24 . . . . Florida	
25-28 . . . . . . .at Tampa	
30 . . . . at Fort Myers	

MAY	
1-2. . . . . . . at Fort Myers	
3-5. . . . . Daytona	
6-8. . . . . .Bradenton	
9-11 . . . . . . at Dunedin	
13-16 . . . . . . .Lakeland	
17-19 . . . . . Charlotte	
20-22 . . . . at Daytona	
23-26 . . . . . . at Jupiter	
28-30 . . . . at Charlotte	
31 . . . . Dunedin	

JUNE
1-2 . . . . Dunedin
3-6 . . . . Jupiter
7-9 . . . . . at Daytona
10-13 . . . . . St. Lucie
17-19 . . . . at Bradenton
20-23 . . . . . Daytona
25-27 . . . . at Lakeland
28-30 . . . . at St. Lucie

JULY
1-3 . . . . Fort Myers
4-7 . . . . at Tampa
8-11 . . . . . Palm Beach
12-14 . . . . . Florida
16-18 . . . . at Bradenton
19-21 . . . . at St. Lucie
22-24 . . . . Bradenton
25-28 . . . . Charlotte

30-31 . . . . at Florida

AUGUST
1 . . . . at Florida
2-4 . . . . Tampa
5 . . . . at Dunedin
6 . . . . Dunedin
7 . . . . at Dunedin
8-11 . . . . . at Palm Beach
12 . . . . at Dunedin
13-15 . . . . Dunedin
16-18 . . . . Florida
20-22 . . . . . at St. Lucie
23-25 . . . . at Charlotte
26-29 . . . . . . Lakeland
30-31 . . . . at Fort Myers

SEPTEMBER
1 . . . . at Fort Myers

DAYTONA TORTUGAS

APRIL
4-5 . . . . Florida
6-7 . . . . at Florida
8-11 . . . at Palm Beach
12-14 . . . . Tampa
15-17 . . . . . at Jupiter
18-20 . . . . . at Florida
22-24 . . . . . . Dunedin
25-28 . . . . . Bradenton
30 . . . . at Dunedin

MAY
1-2 . . . . . at Dunedin
3-5 . . . . at Clearwater
6-8 . . . . . Palm Beach
9-11 . . . . . . Lakeland
13-16 . . . . at Charlotte
17-19 . . . . . at Tampa
20-22 . . . . Clearwater
23-26 . . . . Fort Myers
28-30 . . . at Palm Beach
31 . . . . at Jupiter

JUNE
1-2 . . . . at Jupiter
3-6 . . . . Bradenton
7-9 . . . . Clearwater
10-13 . . . . at Lakeland
17-19 . . . . Florida
20-23 . . . . at Clearwater

25-27 . . . . Tampa
28-30 . . . . Dunedin

JULY
1-3 . . . . Tampa
4-7 . . . . . . at St. Lucie
8-11 . . . at Fort Myers
12-14 . . . . . . Lakeland
16-18 . . . . . . Jupiter
19-21 . . . . at Lakeland
22-24 . . . . . . at Tampa
25-28 . . . . . at Florida
30-31 . . . . . at Jupiter

AUGUST
1 . . . . at Jupiter
2-4 . . . . St. Lucie
5-7 . . . . Florida
8-11 . . . . . . at St. Lucie
12-15 . . . . . . Charlotte
16-18 . . . . Palm Beach
20-22 . . . . at Dunedin
23-25 . . . . at Bradenton
26-29 . . . . . St. Lucie
30-31 . . . . Jupiter

SEPTEMBER
1 . . . . Jupiter

DUNEDIN BLUE JAYS

APRIL
4 . . . . Clearwater
5-6 . . . . . at Clearwater
7 . . . . Clearwater
8-11 . . . . . at Fort Myers
12-14 . . . . . . Bradenton
15-17 . . . . at Charlotte
18-19 . . . . . Lakeland
20 . . . . at Lakeland
22-24 . . . . . at Daytona
25-28 . . . . . at Jupiter
30 . . . . Daytona

MAY
1-2 . . . . Daytona
3-5 . . . . St. Lucie
6-8 . . . . at Tampa
9-11 . . . . . . Clearwater
13-16 . . . . Jupiter
17-18 . . . . at Lakeland
19 . . . . Lakeland
20-22 . . . . at St. Lucie
23-26 . . . . Florida
28-30 . . . . Tampa
31 . . . . . at Clearwater

JUNE
1-2 . . . . . at Clearwater
3-6 . . . . Charlotte
7-9 . . . . . at Bradenton
10-13 . . . . . . at Florida
17-19 . . . . Tampa
20-23 . . . . Palm Beach
25-27 . . . . . at St. Lucie
28-30 . . . . . at Daytona

JULY
1-3 . . . . Florida
4-7 . . . . . . at Lakeland
8-11 . . . . . . at Tampa
12-14 . . . . . . St. Lucie
16-18 . . . . . . Lakeland
19-21 . . . . at Charlotte
22-24 . . . . . Fort Myers
25-28 . . . . at Palm Beach
30-31 . . . at Fort Myers

AUGUST
1 . . . . at Fort Myers
2-4 . . . . Bradenton
5 . . . . Clearwater
6 . . . . at Clearwater
7 . . . . Clearwater
8-11 . . . . . at Bradenton
12 . . . . Clearwater
13-15 . . . at Clearwater
16-18 . . . . Tampa
20-22 . . . . Daytona
23-25 . . . . . . at Florida
26-29 . . . . . . Fort Myers
30-31 . . . . . . Charlotte

SEPTEMBER
1 . . . . Charlotte

FLORIDA FIRE FROGS

APRIL
4-5 . . . . at Daytona
6-7 . . . . Daytona
8-11 . . . . Jupiter
12-14 . . . . . at St. Lucie
15-17 . . . . . Clearwater
18-20 . . . . Daytona
22-24 . . . . at Clearwater
25-28 . . . . . at St. Lucie
30 . . . . Lakeland

MAY
1-2 . . . . Lakeland
3-5 . . . . Tampa
6-8 . . . . . at Lakeland
9-11 . . . . . . at Jupiter
13-16 . . . . . . St. Lucie
17-19 . . . . Jupiter
20-22 . . . . . . at Tampa
23-26 . . . . . at Dunedin
28-30 . . . . . Fort Myers
31 . . . . Palm Beach

JUNE
1-2 . . . . Palm Beach
3-6 . . . . . at Fort Myers
7-9 . . . . at Tampa
10-13 . . . . Dunedin
17-19 . . . . . at Daytona
20-23 . . . . St. Lucie
25-27 . . . . Palm Beach
28-30 . . . . at Tampa

JULY
1-3 . . . . at Dunedin
4-7 . . . . . . at Bradenton
8-11 . . . . Charlotte
12-14 . . . . at Clearwater
16-18 . . . . at Palm Beach
19-21 . . . . . . Fort Myers
22-24 . . . . at Lakeland
25-28 . . . . . . Daytona
30-31 . . . . . Clearwater

AUGUST
1 . . . . Clearwater
2-4 . . . . at Jupiter
5-7 . . . . . . at Daytona
8-11 . . . . Lakeland
12-15 . . . . . Bradenton
16-18 . . . at Clearwater
20-22 . . . . Tampa
23-25 . . . . Dunedin
26-29 . . . . at Charlotte
30-31 . . . at Palm Beach

SEPTEMBER
1 . . . . . . at Palm Beach

FORT MYERS MIRACLE

APRIL
4-5 . . . . Charlotte
6-7 . . . . . . at Charlotte
8-11 . . . . Dunedin
12-14 . . . at Clearwater
15-17 . . . . . at St. Lucie
18-20 . . . . . Charlotte
22-24 . . . . at Bradenton
25-28 . . . . Palm Beach
30 . . . . Clearwater

MAY
1-2 . . . . Clearwater
3-5 . . . at Palm Beach
6-7 . . . . . at Charlotte
8 . . . . Charlotte
9-11 . . . . Tampa
13 . . . . Bradenton
14-16 . . . . at Bradenton
17-19 . . . . . . St. Lucie
20-21 . . . . . Bradenton
22 . . . . . . at Bradenton
23-26 . . . . . at Daytona
28-30 . . . . . at Florida
31 . . . . . . at Lakeland

JUNE
1-2 . . . . . at Lakeland
3-6 . . . . Florida
7-9 . . . . Jupiter
10-13 . . . . . at Tampa
17 . . . . Charlotte
18 . . . . . . at Charlotte
19 . . . . Charlotte
20-23 . . . . . at Jupiter
25-26 . . . . at Charlotte
27 . . . . Charlotte
28-30 . . . . . Bradenton

JULY
1-3 . . . . . . at Clearwater
4-7 . . . . . . Palm Beach
8-11 . . . . Daytona
12-14 . . . . at Bradenton
16-18 . . . . Tampa
19-21 . . . . . at Florida
22-24 . . . . at Dunedin
25-28 . . . . . Lakeland
30-31 . . . . . . Dunedin

AUGUST
1 . . . . Dunedin
2-4 . . . . at Lakeland
5-7 . . . . . . at St. Lucie
8-11 . . . . Jupiter
12-15 . . . . . St. Lucie
16-18 . . . . . at Jupiter
20 . . . . . . at Charlotte
21-22 . . . . . Charlotte
23-25 . . . at Palm Beach
26-29 . . . . at Dunedin
30-31 . . . . . Clearwater

SEPTEMBER
1 . . . . Clearwater

JUPITER HAMMERHEADS

APRIL
4-5 . . . . . . at Palm Beach
6-7 . . . . . Palm Beach
8-11 . . . . at Florida
12-14 . . . . . . .Lakeland
15-17 . . . . Daytona
18-20 . . . . at Bradenton
22-24 . . . . at Palm Beach
25-28 . . . . Dunedin
30 . . . . . . .Bradenton

MAY
1-2 . . . . .Bradenton
3-5 . . . . at Charlotte
6-8 . . . . St. Lucie
9-11 . . . . Florida
13-16 . . . . . . at Dunedin
17-19 . . . . . at Florida
20-22 . . . . . . Charlotte
23-26 . . . . . Clearwater
28-30 . . . . at St. Lucie
31 . . . . Daytona

JUNE
1-2 . . . . Daytona
3-6 . . . . . .at Clearwater
7-9 . . . . . . at Fort Myers
10-13 . . . .Palm Beach
17-19 . . . . at Palm Beach

20-23 . . . . . . .Fort Myers
25-27 . . . . . . .Bradenton
28-30 . . . . . . at Lakeland

JULY
1-3 . . . . at Bradenton
4-7 . . . . Charlotte
8-11 . . . . St. Lucie
12-14 . . . . at Palm Beach
16-18 . . . . . at Daytona
19-21 . . . . . Palm Beach
22-24 . . . . . .at Charlotte
25-28 . . . . . .at Tampa
30-31 . . . . . Daytona

AUGUST
1 . . . . Daytona
2-4 . . . . Florida
5-7 . . . . at Palm Beach
8-11 . . . . at Fort Myers
12-15 . . . . . . .Lakeland
16-18 . . . . . .Fort Myers
20-22 . . . . . at Lakeland
23-25 . . . . . at St. Lucie
26-29 . . . . Tampa
30-31 . . . . . at Daytona

SEPTEMBER
1 . . . . at Daytona

LAKELAND FLYING TIGERS

APRIL
4-5 . . . . Tampa
6-7 . . . . .at Tampa
8-11 . . . . Clearwater
12-14 . . . . at Jupiter
15-17 . . . . . Palm Beach
18-19 . . . . at Dunedin
20 . . . . Dunedin
22-24 . . . . . St. Lucie
25-28 . . . . . Charlotte
30 . . . . at Florida

MAY
1-2 . . . . at Florida
3-5 . . . . . . at Bradenton
6-8 . . . . Florida
9-11 . . . . . . at Daytona
13-16 . . . .at Clearwater
17-18 . . . . . . .Dunedin
19 . . . . . . at Dunedin
20-22 . . . . . Palm Beach
23-26 . . . . . at St. Lucie
28-30 . . . . at Bradenton
31 . . . . .Fort Myers

JUNE
1-2 . . . . .Fort Myers
3-6 . . . . at Palm Beach
7-9 . . . . St. Lucie
10-13 . . . . Daytona

17-19 . . . . . . at St. Lucie
20-23 . . . . .at Charlotte
25-27 . . . . . Clearwater
28-30 . . . . . . Jupiter

JULY
1-3 . . . . . . at Palm Beach
4-7 . . . . Dunedin
8-11 . . . . .Bradenton
12-14 . . . . . at Daytona
16-18 . . . . at Dunedin
19-21 . . . . . . Daytona
22-24 . . . . Florida
25-28 . . . at Fort Myers
30-31 . . . . . . .at Tampa

AUGUST
1 . . . . .at Tampa
2-4 . . . . .Fort Myers
5-7 . . . . Tampa
8-11 . . . . . at Florida
12-15 . . . . . at Jupiter
16-18 . . . . . .Bradenton
20-22 . . . . Jupiter
23-25 . . . . . . .at Tampa
26-29 . . . at Clearwater
30-31 . . . . Tampa

SEPTEMBER
1 . . . . Tampa

PALM BEACH CARDINALS

APRIL
4-5 . . . . Jupiter
6-7 . . . . at Jupiter
8-11 . . . . Daytona
12-14 . . . . . .at Charlotte
15-17 . . . . at Lakeland
18-20 . . . . . St. Lucie
22-24 . . . . . . Jupiter
25-28 . . . at Fort Myers
30 . . . . . . at St. Lucie

MAY
1-2 . . . . at St. Lucie
3-5 . . . . .Fort Myers
6-8 . . . . at Daytona
9-11 . . . . at Bradenton
13-16 . . . . Tampa
17-19 . . . . . . .Bradenton
20-22 . . . . at Lakeland
23-26 . . . .at Charlotte
28-30 . . . . Daytona

31 . . . . at Florida

JUNE
1-2 . . . . at Florida
3-6 . . . . . . .Lakeland
7-9 . . . . Charlotte
10-13 . . . . at Jupiter
17-19 . . . . Jupiter
20-23 . . . at Dunedin
25-27 . . . . at Florida
28-30 . . . . Charlotte

JULY
1-3 . . . . . . .Lakeland
4-7 . . . . . . at Fort Myers
8-11 . . . .at Clearwater
12-14 . . . . . . Jupiter
16-18 . . . . . . Florida
19-21 . . . . at Jupiter

ST. LUCIE METS

APRIL
4-5 . . . . .Bradenton
6-7 . . . . . . at Bradenton
8-11 . . . . . . .at Tampa
12-14 . . . . . . Florida
15-17 . . . . .Fort Myers
18-20 . . at Palm Beach
22-24 . . . . at Lakeland
25-28 . . . . Florida
30 . . . . . . Palm Beach

MAY
1-2 . . . . Palm Beach
3-5 . . . . . . at Dunedin
6-8 . . . . . . at Jupiter
9-11 . . . . Charlotte
13-16 . . . . . . at Florida
17-19 . . . at Fort Myers
20-22 . . . . . Dunedin
23-26 . . . . . Lakeland
28-30 . . . . Jupiter
31 . . . . .at Charlotte

JUNE
1-2 . . . . . at Charlotte
3-6 . . . . Tampa
7-9 . . . . . at Lakeland
10-13 . . . . .at Clearwater
17-19 . . . . . .Lakeland

20-23 . . . . . at Florida
25-27 . . . . . Dunedin
28-30 . . . . Clearwater

JULY
1-3 . . . . . .at Charlotte
4-7 . . . . Daytona
8-11 . . . . . at Jupiter
12-14 . . . . at Dunedin
16-18 . . . . Charlotte
19-21 . . . . . Clearwater
22-24 . . . . at Palm Beach
25-28 . . . . at Bradenton
30-31 . . . . Palm Beach

AUGUST
1 . . . . Palm Beach
2-4 . . . . at Daytona
5-7 . . . . . . .Fort Myers
8-11 . . . . Daytona
12-15 . . . . at Fort Myers
16-18 . . . . .at Charlotte
20-22 . . . . Clearwater
23-25 . . . . . . Jupiter
26-29 . . . . at Daytona
30-31 . . . . .Bradenton

SEPTEMBER
1 . . . . .Bradenton

TAMPA TARPONS

APRIL
4-5 . . . . at Lakeland
6-7 . . . . .Lakeland
8-11 . . . . St. Lucie
12-14 . . . . . at Daytona
15-17 . . . . . .Bradenton
18-20 . . . at Clearwater
22-24 . . . . .at Charlotte
25-28 . . . . Clearwater
30 . . . . Charlotte

MAY
1-2 . . . . Charlotte
3-5 . . . . . . at Florida
6-8 . . . . Dunedin
9-11 . . . . at Fort Myers
13-16 . . . . at Palm Beach
17-19 . . . . . . Daytona
20-22 . . . . Florida
23-26 . . . . at Bradenton
28-30 . . . . at Dunedin
31 . . . . . .Bradenton

JUNE
1-2 . . . . .Bradenton
3-6 . . . . . at St. Lucie
7-9 . . . . Florida
10-13 . . . .Fort Myers
17-19 . . . . at Dunedin

20-23 . . . . . at Bradenton
25-27 . . . . . at Daytona
28-30 . . . . . Florida

JULY
1-3 . . . . at Daytona
4-7 . . . . Clearwater
8-11 . . . . Dunedin
12-14 . . . .at Charlotte
16-18 . . . . at Fort Myers
19-21 . . . . . .Bradenton
22-24 . . . . . Daytona
25-28 . . . . . Jupiter
30-31 . . . . . .Lakeland

AUGUST
1 . . . . .Lakeland
2-4 . . . . . . at Clearwater
5-7 . . . . . . at Lakeland
8-11 . . . . . Charlotte
12-15 . . . . Palm Beach
16-18 . . . . at Dunedin
20-22 . . . . . at Florida
23-25 . . . . . Lakeland
26-29 . . . . . at Jupiter
30-31 . . . . at Lakeland

SEPTEMBER
1 . . . . at Lakeland

LOW CLASS A

MIDWEST LEAGUE

BELOIT SNAPPERS

APRIL	
4-5	. . . . Wisconsin
6-7	. . . . at Peoria
8-11	. . . . . . at Burlington
12-14	. . . . Clinton
15-17	. . . . Wisconsin
18-20	. . . at Cedar Rapids
22-24	. . . . at Clinton
25-28	. . . . Peoria
30	. . . . . at Great Lakes

MAY	
1-2	. . . . . at Great Lakes
3-5	. . . . at Lansing
6-8	. . . . . . Lake County
9-11	. . . . . . Fort Wayne
13-15	. . . . at Peoria
16-19	. . . . . Kane County
20-23	. . . . Clinton
24-27	. . . at Kane County
28-30	. . . . at Quad Cities
31	. . . . . . Cedar Rapids

JUNE	
1-2	. . . . . . Cedar Rapids
4-6	. . . . Burlington
7-10	. . . . . at Wisconsin
11-13	. . . . . Quad Cities
14-16	. . . at Kane County
20-23	. . . . . Quad Cities

25-28	. . . at Kane County
29-30	. . . . . . Wisconsin

JULY	
1	. . . . Wisconsin
2-3	. . . . Clinton
4-5	. . . . at Quad Cities
6-8	. . . . . . at Wisconsin
10-12	. . at Bowling Green
13-15	. . . . . . at Dayton
17-19	. . . West Michigan
20-22	. . . . . South Bend
24-26	. . . . at Burlington
27-29	. . . . . Quad Cities
30-31	. . . . . Cedar Rapids

AUGUST	
1-2	. . . . . . Cedar Rapids
3-6	. . . . at Clinton
7-9	. . . . Peoria
10-12	. . at Cedar Rapids
14-16	. . . at Quad Cities
17-20	. . . . . . Burlington
21-23	. . . . . Kane County
24-27	. . . . at Burlington
28-30	. . . . at Peoria
31	. . . . . . Cedar Rapids

SEPTEMBER	
1-2	. . . . . Cedar Rapids

BOWLING GREEN HOT RODS

APRIL	
4-5	. . . . at Dayton
6-7	. . . . Dayton
8-11	. . . at Lake County
12-14	. . . . . . Fort Wayne
15-17	. . . . Lake County
18-20	. . . at Great Lakes
22-24	. . . . . at Fort Wayne
25-28	. . . . Lansing
30	. . . . . at Cedar Rapids

MAY	
1-2	. . . . . at Cedar Rapids
3-5	. . . . at Peoria
6-8	. . . . Burlington
9-11	. . . . Clinton
13-15	. . . . . South Bend
16-19	. . . at Lake County
20-23	. . at West Michigan
24-27	. . . . Dayton
28-30	. . . . Great Lakes
31	. . . . at Lansing

JUNE	
1-2	. . . . at Lansing
4-6	. . . . at South Bend
7-10	. . . . . West Michigan
11-13	. . . . Fort Wayne
14-16	. . . . at Lansing
20-23	. . . at South Bend

25-28	. . . . . . Great Lakes
29-30	. . . . at Lansing

JULY	
1	. . . . at Lansing
2-3	. . . . at Dayton
4-5	. . . . Dayton
6-8	. . . . West Michigan
10-12	. . . . Beloit
13-15	. . . . Wisconsin
17-19	. . at Kane County
20-22	. . . . at Quad Cities
24-26	. . . . . Fort Wayne
27-29	. . . . Lake County
30-31	. . . . . . at Dayton

AUGUST	
1-2	. . . . at Dayton
3-6	. . . . Lansing
7-9	. . . at West Michigan
10-12	. . at Great Lakes
14-16	. . . . Dayton
17-20	. . at Fort Wayne
21-23	. . at Lake County
24-27	. . . . . South Bend
28-30	. . . . Lake County
31	. . . . . at South Bend

SEPTEMBER	
1-2	. . . . . at South Bend

BURLINGTON BEES

APRIL	
4-5	. . . . at Quad Cities

6-7	. . . . Quad Cities
8-11	. . . . Beloit

12-14	. . . at Cedar Rapids
15-17	. . . at Kane County
18-20	. . . . Peoria
22-24	. . . . . Kane County
25-28	. . . . . at Wisconsin
30	. . . . South Bend

MAY	
1-2	. . . . . . South Bend
3-5	. . . . . West Michigan
6-8	. . . at Bowling Green
9-11	. . . . . . at Dayton
13-15	. . . . Clinton
16-19	. . . . . Wisconsin
20-23	. . at Cedar Rapids
24-27	. . . . . at Clinton
28-30	. . . . Cedar Rapids
31	. . . . . Quad Cities

JUNE	
1-2	. . . . . Quad Cities
4-6	. . . . . . at Beloit
7-10	. . . . Clinton
11-13	. at Kane County
14-16	. . . . at Peoria
20-23	. . . Kane County
25-26	. . . . Quad Cities
27-28	. . at Quad Cities

CEDAR RAPIDS KERNELS

APRIL	
4-5	. . . . Peoria
6-7	. . . . . . at Wisconsin
8-11	. . . . . Kane County
12-14	. . . . . . Burlington
15-17	. . . at Quad Cities
18-20	. . . . Beloit
22-24	. . . . at Wisconsin
25-28	. . . at Kane County
30	. . . . . Bowling Green

MAY	
1-2	. . . . . Bowling Green
3-5	. . . . Dayton
6-8	. . . . at South Bend
9-11	. . . at West Michigan
13-15	. . . . Quad Cities
16-19	. . . . . at Clinton
20-23	. . . . . . Burlington
24-27	. . . . Peoria
28-30	. . at Burlington
31	. . . . at Beloit

JUNE	
1-2	. . . . at Beloit
4-6	. . . . . . at Clinton
7-10	. . . . . at Peoria
11-13	. . . . . Wisconsin
14-16	. . . . Clinton
20-23	. . . . . at Peoria

25-28	. . . . . . Wisconsin
29-30	. . . . Kane County

JULY	
1	. . . . Kane County
2-3	. . . . . . at Burlington
4-5	. . . . Burlington
6-8	. . . . . at Quad Cities
10-12	. . . . Great Lakes
13-15	. . . . Lansing
17-19	. . . at Lake County
20-22	. . . at Fort Wayne
24-26	. . . . . Wisconsin
27-29	. . . . . . Clinton
30-31	. . . . . . at Beloit

AUGUST	
1-2	. . . . at Beloit
3-6	. . . . Burlington
7-9	. . . at Kane County
10-12	. . . . Beloit
14-16	. . . at Wisconsin
17-20	. . at Quad Cities
21-23	. . . . . at Clinton
24-27	. . . . Peoria
28-30	. . . Quad Cities
31	. . . . at Beloit

SEPTEMBER	
1-2	. . . . at Beloit

CLINTON LUMBERKINGS

APRIL	
4-5	. . . at Kane County
6-7	. . . . . . Kane County
8-11	. . . . . Quad Cities
12-14	. . . . at Beloit
15-17	. . . . . . at Peoria
18-20	. . . . . . Wisconsin
22-24	. . . . Beloit
25-28	. . . at Quad Cities
30	. . . . . West Michigan

MAY	
1-2	. . . . . West Michigan
3-5	. . . . . . South Bend
6-8	. . . . at Dayton
9-11	. . . at Bowling Green
13-15	. . . at Burlington
16-19	. . . . . Cedar Rapids
20-23	. . . . . . at Beloit
24-27	. . . . . . Burlington

28-30 . . . . . at Wisconsin
31 . . . . Kane County

JUNE
1-2 . . . . . . Kane County
4-6 . . . . Cedar Rapids
7-10 . . . . . . at Burlington
11-13 . . . . Peoria
14-16 . . . . at Cedar Rapids
20-23 . . . . . at Wisconsin
25-28 . . . . Peoria
29-30 . . . . Quad Cities

JULY
1 . . . . Quad Cities
2-3 . . . . at Beloit
4-5 . . . . Peoria
6-8 . . . . . at Kane County
10-12 . . . . . Lake County
13-15 . . . . . Fort Wayne

DAYTON DRAGONS

APRIL
4-5 . . . . . . Bowling Green
6-7 . . . . at Bowling Green
8-11 . . . . . at Fort Wayne
12-14 . . . . . Lake County
15-17 . . . . . Fort Wayne
18-20 . . . . . at Lansing
22-24 . . . at Lake County
25-28 . . . . . Great Lakes
30 . . . . at Peoria

MAY
1-2 . . . . at Peoria
3-5 . . . . at Cedar Rapids
6-8 . . . . Clinton
9-11 . . . . Burlington
13-15 . . . . at Great Lakes
16-19 . . . . at South Bend
20-23 . . . . . Lake County
24-27 . . at Bowling Green
28-30 . . . . Lansing
31 . . . . South Bend

JUNE
1-2 . . . . South Bend
4-6 . . . . at West Michigan
7-10 . . . . Fort Wayne
11-13 . . . West Michigan
14-16 . . . . at Great Lakes
20-23 . . . . Lansing

FORT WAYNE TINCAPS

APRIL
4-5 . . . . Lansing
6-7 . . . . at Lansing
8-11 . . . . Dayton
12-14 . . at Bowling Green
15-17 . . . . . at Dayton
18-20 . . . . West Michigan
22-24 . . . . Bowling Green
25-28 . . . at South Bend
30 . . . . Kane County

MAY
1-2 . . . . . . Kane County
3-5 . . . . . . Quad Cities
6-8 . . . . . . at Wisconsin
9-11 . . . . at Beloit
13-15 . . . at Lake County
16-19 . . . . . . Lansing
20-23 . . . . . . South Bend
24-27 . . . . at Great Lakes
28-30 . . at West Michigan

17-19 . . . . . at Great Lakes
20-22 . . . . at Lansing
24-26 . . . . . Kane County
27-29 . . . at Cedar Rapids
30-31 . . . . . at Wisconsin

AUGUST
1-2 . . . . . . at Wisconsin
3-6 . . . . Beloit
7-9 . . . . . at Quad Cities
10-12 . . . . . at Peoria
14-16 . . . . . . Burlington
17-20 . . . . at Kane County
21-23 . . . . . Cedar Rapids
24-27 . . . . . . Wisconsin
28-30 . . . at Burlington
31 . . . . Peoria

SEPTEMBER
1-2 . . . . Peoria

25-28 . . . at West Michigan
29-30 . . . . . at South Bend

JULY
1 . . . . . . at South Bend
2-3 . . . . . . Bowling Green
4-5 . . . . . at Bowling Green
6-8 . . . . . . South Bend
10-12 . . . . Wisconsin
13-15 . . . . Beloit
17-19 . . . . at Quad Cities
20-22 . . . . at Kane County
24-26 . . . . . Great Lakes
27-29 . . . . at Fort Wayne
30-31 . . . . . Bowling Green

AUGUST
1-2 . . . . . . Bowling Green
3-6 . . . . Lake County
7-9 . . . . . . at Fort Wayne
10-12 . . . . Lansing
14-16 . . . at Bowling Green
17-20 . . . . at Lansing
21-23 . . . . . . Fort Wayne
24-27 . . . . at Lake County
28-30 . . . . at Great Lakes
31 . . . . . . West Michigan

SEPTEMBER
1-2 . . . . . . West Michigan

31 . . . . Great Lakes

JUNE
1-2 . . . . Great Lakes
4-6 . . . . . . Lake County
7-10 . . . . . . at Dayton
11-13 . . at Bowling Green
14-16 . . . . . Lake County
20-23 . . . . at Great Lakes
25-28 . . . . . . South Bend
29-30 . . . . . Great Lakes

JULY
1 . . . . Great Lakes
2-3 . . . . at Lake County
4-5 . . . . . Lake County
6-8 . . . . at Great Lakes
10-12 . . . at Burlington
13-15 . . . . at Clinton
17-19 . . . . Peoria
20-22 . . . . . Cedar Rapids
24-26 . . . at Bowling Green

27-29 . . . . Dayton
30-31 . . . . . at Great Lakes

AUGUST
1-2 . . . . . . at Great Lakes
3-6 . . . . . . West Michigan
7-9 . . . . Dayton
10-12 . . . . at South Bend
14-16 . . . . . at Lansing

GREAT LAKES LOONS

APRIL
4-5 . . . . . at Lake County
6-7 . . . . . Lake County
8-11 . . . . . . South Bend
12-14 . . at West Michigan
15-17 . . . at South Bend
18-20 . . . . Bowling Green
22-24 . . . . West Michigan
25-28 . . . . . at Dayton
30 . . . . Beloit

MAY
1-2 . . . . Beloit
3-5 . . . . Wisconsin
6-8 . . . . . at Kane County
9-11 . . . . at Quad Cities
13-15 . . . . Dayton
16-19 . . . at West Michigan
20-23 . . . . . . at Lansing
24-27 . . . . . Fort Wayne
28-30 . . . at Bowling Green
31 . . . . . at Fort Wayne

JUNE
1-2 . . . . at Fort Wayne
4-6 . . . . Lansing
7-10 . . . . . . South Bend
11-13 . . at Lake County
14-16 . . . . Dayton
20-23 . . . . . Fort Wayne

KANE COUNTY COUGARS

APRIL
4-5 . . . . Clinton
6-7 . . . . at Clinton
8-11 . . . . . at Cedar Rapids
12-14 . . . . Peoria
15-17 . . . . . . Burlington
18-20 . . . . at Quad Cities
22-24 . . . . . at Burlington
25-28 . . . . . Cedar Rapids
30 . . . . at Fort Wayne

MAY
1-2 . . . . at Fort Wayne
3-5 . . . . at Lake County
6-8 . . . . . . Great Lakes
9-11 . . . . . . Lansing
13-15 . . . at Wisconsin
16-19 . . . . . at Beloit
20-23 . . . . . Quad Cities
24-27 . . . . Beloit
28-30 . . . . . . at Peoria
31 . . . . . . at Clinton

JUNE
1-2 . . . . . . at Clinton
4-6 . . . . Wisconsin
7-10 . . . . . at Quad Cities
11-13 . . . . . . Burlington
14-16 . . . . . . Beloit
20-23 . . . . at Burlington

17-20 . . . . . Bowling Green
21-23 . . . . . at Dayton
24-27 . . . at West Michigan
28-30 . . . . . . South Bend
31 . . . . Lansing

SEPTEMBER
1-2 . . . . Lansing

25-28 . . . at Bowling Green
29-30 . . . . . at Fort Wayne

JULY
1 . . . . at Fort Wayne
2-3 . . . . Lansing
4-5 . . . . at Lansing
6-8 . . . . Fort Wayne
10-12 . . . . at Cedar Rapids
13-15 . . . . . at Peoria
17-19 . . . . Clinton
20-22 . . . . . . Burlington
24-26 . . . . . . at Dayton
27-29 . . . at West Michigan
30-31 . . . . . . Fort Wayne

AUGUST
1-2 . . . . . . Fort Wayne
3-6 . . . . . . at South Bend
7-9 . . . . . . Lake County
10-12 . . . Bowling Green
14-16 . . . at West Michigan
17-20 . . . . . South Bend
21-23 . . . West Michigan
24-27 . . . . at Lansing
28-30 . . . . . . Dayton
31 . . . . . . at Lake County

SEPTEMBER
1-2 . . . . . at Lake County

25-28 . . . . Beloit
29-30 . . . . at Cedar Rapids

JULY
1 . . . . . . at Cedar Rapids
2-3 . . . . at Peoria
4-5 . . . . Wisconsin
6-8 . . . . Clinton
10-12 . . . . . at South Bend
13-15 . . . at West Michigan
17-19 . . . . . Bowling Green
20-22 . . . . Dayton
24-26 . . . . at Clinton
27-29 . . . . Wisconsin
30-31 . . . . at Peoria

AUGUST
1-2 . . . . at Peoria
3-6 . . . . Quad Cities
7-9 . . . . Cedar Rapids
10-12 . . . . . at Burlington
14-16 . . . . Peoria
17-20 . . . . Clinton
21-23 . . . . at Beloit
24-27 . . . at Quad Cities
28-30 . . . . . at Wisconsin
31 . . . . Burlington

SEPTEMBER
1-2 . . . . Burlington

LAKE COUNTY CAPTAINS

APRIL
4-5 . . . . Great Lakes
6-7 . . . . . . at Great Lakes
8-11 . . . . . Bowling Green
12-14 . . . . at Dayton
15-17 . . at Bowling Green
18-20 . . . . . . South Bend
22-24 . . . . Dayton
25-28 . . at West Michigan
30 . . . . Quad Cities

MAY
1-2 . . . . Quad Cities
3-5 . . . . Kane County
6-8 . . . . at Beloit
9-11 . . . . . . at Wisconsin
13-15 . . . . . . Fort Wayne
16-19 . . . . Bowling Green
20-23 . . . . at Dayton
24-27 . . . . . . at Lansing
28-30 . . . . . at South Bend
31 . . . . . West Michigan

JUNE
1-2 . . . . . West Michigan
4-6 . . . . . . at Fort Wayne
7-10 . . . . Lansing
11-13 . . . . . Great Lakes
14-16 . . . . at Fort Wayne
20-23 . . . . West Michigan

25-28 . . . . at Lansing
29-30 . . . at West Michigan

JULY
1 . . . . . . at West Michigan
2-3 . . . . Fort Wayne
4-5 . . . . . . .at Fort Wayne
6-8 . . . . Lansing
10-12 . . . . . . at Clinton
13-15 . . . . at Burlington
17-19 . . . . Cedar Rapids
20-22 . . . . Peoria
24-26 . . . . at South Bend
27-29 . . at Bowling Green
30-31 . . . . Lansing

AUGUST
1-2 . . . . Lansing
3-6 . . . . at Dayton
7-9 . . . . . at Great Lakes
10-12 . . . West Michigan
14-16 . . . . . South Bend
17-20 . . at West Michigan
21-23 . . . . Bowling Green
24-27 . . . . Dayton
28-30 . . at Bowling Green
31 . . . . Great Lakes

SEPTEMBER
1-2 . . . . Great Lakes

LANSING LUGNUTS

APRIL
4-5 . . . . . . .at Fort Wayne
6-7 . . . . Fort Wayne
8-11 . . . . . West Michigan
12-14 . . . . . at South Bend
15-17 . . at West Michigan
18-20 . . . . .Dayton
22-24 . . . . . South Bend
25-28 . . at Bowling Green
30 . . . . Wisconsin

MAY
1-2 . . . . Wisconsin
3-5 . . . . Beloit
6-8 . . . . at Quad Cities
9-11 . . . . at Kane County
13-15 . . . . West Michigan
16-19 . . . .at Fort Wayne
20-23 . . . . . Great Lakes
24-27 . . . . . Lake County
28-30 . . . . . . at Dayton
31 . . . . . Bowling Green

JUNE
1-2 . . . . . Bowling Green
4-6 . . . . . at Great Lakes
7-10 . . . .at Lake County
11-13 . . . . at South Bend
14-16 . . . .Bowling Green
20-23 . . . . . . at Dayton

25-28 . . . . . Lake County
29-30 . . . . Bowling Green

JULY
1 . . . . Bowling Green
2-3 . . . . . at Great Lakes
4-5 . . . . Great Lakes
6-8 . . . .at Lake County
10-12 . . . . . . at Peoria
13-15 . . . . at Cedar Rapids
17-19 . . . . . .Burlington
20-22 . . . . Clinton
24-26 . . at West Michigan
27-29 . . . . . South Bend
30-31 . . .at Lake County

AUGUST
1-2 . . . . . .at Lake County
3-6 . . . at Bowling Green
7-9 . . . . . . South Bend
10-12 . . . . . . at Dayton
14-16 . . . . . Fort Wayne
17-20 . . . . .Dayton
21-23 . . . . at South Bend
24-27 . . . . . Great Lakes
28-30 . . . . West Michigan
31 . . . . .at Fort Wayne

SEPTEMBER
1-2 . . . . . . .at Fort Wayne

PEORIA CHIEFS

APRIL
4-5 . . . . . at Cedar Rapids
6-7 . . . . Beloit
8-11 . . . . Wisconsin
12-14 . . . . at Kane County
15-17 . . . . . . .Clinton
18-20 . . . . . at Burlington
22-24 . . . . . Quad Cities

25-28 . . . . at Beloit
30 . . . . Dayton

MAY
1-2 . . . . .Dayton
3-5 . . . . . .Bowling Green
6-8 . . . . at West Michigan
9-11 . . . . . at South Bend
13-15 . . . . Beloit

16-19 . . . . . . Quad Cities
20-23 . . . . . at Wisconsin
24-27 . . . at Cedar Rapids
28-30 . . . . Kane County
31 . . . . at Wisconsin

JUNE
1-2 . . . . at Wisconsin
4-6 . . . . . . at Quad Cities
7-10 . . . . . Cedar Rapids
11-13 . . . . . . at Clinton
14-16 . . . .Burlington
20-23 . . . . Cedar Rapids
25-28 . . . . . at Clinton
29-30 . . . . .Burlington

JULY
1 . . . . .Burlington
2-3 . . . . . Kane County
4-5 . . . . at Clinton
6-8 . . . . at Burlington
10-12 . . . . . . Lansing

QUAD CITIES RIVER BANDITS

APRIL
4-5 . . . . .Burlington
6-7 . . . . . . at Burlington
8-11 . . . . . . at Clinton
12-14 . . . . at Wisconsin
15-17 . . . Cedar Rapids
18-20 . . . . . Kane County
22-24 . . . . . . at Peoria
25-28 . . . . .Clinton
30 . . . . . .at Lake County

MAY
1-2 . . . . .at Lake County
3-5 . . . . . .at Fort Wayne
6-8 . . . . Lansing
9-11 . . . . . . Great Lakes
13-15 . . . at Cedar Rapids
16-19 . . . . . . .at Peoria
20-23 . . . at Kane County
24-27 . . . . Wisconsin
28-30 . . . . .Beloit
31 . . . . at Burlington

JUNE
1-2 . . . . at Burlington
4-6 . . . . Peoria
7-10 . . . . Kane County
11-13 . . . . . . at Beloit
14-16 . . . . . Wisconsin
20-23 . . . . at Beloit
25-26 . . . . at Burlington

SOUTH BEND CUBS

APRIL
4-5 . . . . . . West Michigan
6-7 . . . . at West Michigan
8-11 . . . . . at Great Lakes
12-14 . . . . Lansing
15-17 . . . . Great Lakes
18-20 . . .at Lake County
22-24 . . . . . . .at Lansing
25-28 . . . . . Fort Wayne
30 . . . . . . at Burlington

MAY
1-2 . . . . at Burlington
3-5 . . . . . . at Clinton
6-8 . . . . . Cedar Rapids
9-11 . . . . Peoria
13-15 . . at Bowling Green
16-19 . . . . .Dayton
20-23 . . .at Fort Wayne

27-28 . . . . . . .Burlington
29-30 . . . . at Clinton

JULY
1 . . . . at Clinton
2-3 . . . . at Wisconsin
4-5 . . . . Beloit
6-8 . . . . . . Cedar Rapids
10-12 . . . at West Michigan
13-15 . . . . at South Bend
17-19 . . . . .Dayton
20-22 . . . . Bowling Green
24-26 . . . . Peoria
27-29 . . . . . . at Beloit
30-31 . . . . .Burlington

AUGUST
1-2 . . . . at Burlington
3-6 . . . . at Kane County
7-9 . . . . Clinton
10-12 . . . . at Wisconsin
14-16 . . . . .Beloit
17-20 . . . . Cedar Rapids
21-23 . . . . . . .at Peoria
24-27 . . . . Kane County
28-30 . . at Cedar Rapids
31 . . . . Wisconsin

SEPTEMBER
1-2 . . . . Wisconsin

24-27 . . . . West Michigan
28-30 . . . Lake County
31 . . . . at Dayton

JUNE
1-2 . . . . at Dayton
4-6 . . . . . . Bowling Green
7-10 . . . at Great Lakes
11-13 . . . . . . Lansing
14-16 . . at West Michigan
20-23 . . . Bowling Green
25-28 . . . . .at Fort Wayne
29-30 . . . . .Dayton

JULY
1 . . . . .Dayton
2-3 . . . . . . West Michigan
4-5 . . . . at West Michigan
6-8 . . . . at Dayton
10-12 . . . . . Kane County

13-15 . . . . . . Quad Cities
17-19 . . . . . at Wisconsin
20-22 . . . . at Beloit
24-26 . . . . . Lake County
27-29 . . . . at Lansing
30-31 . . . West Michigan
AUGUST
1-2 . . . . . . West Michigan
3-6 . . . . Great Lakes
7-9 . . . . at Lansing

WEST MICHIGAN WHITECAPS

APRIL
4-5 . . . . . . at South Bend
6-7 . . . . South Bend
8-11 . . . . at Lansing
12-14 . . . . . . Great Lakes
15-17 . . . . Lansing
18-20 . . . . . at Fort Wayne
22-24 . . . . . at Great Lakes
25-28 . . . . . Lake County
30 . . . . at Clinton
MAY
1-2 . . . . at Clinton
3-5 . . . . . . at Burlington
6-8 . . . . Peoria
9-11 . . . . . . Cedar Rapids
13-15 . . . . at Lansing
16-19 . . . . . . Great Lakes
20-23 . . . . Bowling Green
24-27 . . . . at South Bend
28-30 . . . . . Fort Wayne
31 . . . . . . at Lake County
JUNE
1-2 . . . . . at Lake County
4-6 . . . . Dayton
7-10 . . at Bowling Green
11-13 . . . . at Dayton
14-16 . . . . . South Bend
20-23 . . . . at Lake County

25-28 . . . . Dayton
29-30 . . . . . Lake County
JULY
1 . . . . Lake County
2-3 . . . . at South Bend
4-5 . . . . South Bend
6-8 . . . at Bowling Green
10-12 . . . . Quad Cities
13-15 . . . . Kane County
17-19 . . . . at Beloit
20-22 . . . . . at Wisconsin
24-26 . . . . Lansing
27-29 . . . . . Great Lakes
30-31 . . . . at South Bend
AUGUST
1-2 . . . . . at South Bend
3-6 . . . . . . at Fort Wayne
7-9 . . . . . Bowling Green
10-12 . . . at Lake County
14-16 . . . . . Great Lakes
17-20 . . . . Lake County
21-23 . . . . at Great Lakes
24-27 . . . . . Fort Wayne
28-30 . . . . . . at Lansing
31 . . . . at Dayton
SEPTEMBER
1-2 . . . . at Dayton

WISCONSIN TIMBER RATTLERS

APRIL
4-5 . . . . at Beloit
6-7 . . . . Cedar Rapids
8-11 . . . . at Peoria
12-14 . . . . . Quad Cities
15-17 . . . . . . at Beloit
18-20 . . . . . . at Clinton
22-24 . . . . . Cedar Rapids
25-28 . . . . Burlington
30 . . . . at Lansing
MAY
1-2 . . . . at Lansing
3-5 . . . . . at Great Lakes
6-8 . . . . Fort Wayne
9-11 . . . . . . Lake County
13-15 . . . . Kane County
16-19 . . . . . at Burlington
20-23 . . . . Peoria
24-27 . . . . at Quad Cities
28-30 . . . . Clinton
31 . . . . Peoria
JUNE
1-2 . . . . Peoria
4-6 . . . . . at Kane County
7-10 . . . . Beloit
11-13 . . at Cedar Rapids
14-16 . . . . at Quad Cities
20-23 . . . . Clinton

25-28 . . . . at Cedar Rapids
29-30 . . . . at Beloit
JULY
1 . . . . at Beloit
2-3 . . . . . . Quad Cities
4-5 . . . . . at Kane County
6-8 . . . . Beloit
10-12 . . . . at Dayton
13-15 . . at Bowling Green
17-19 . . . . . South Bend
20-22 . . . . West Michigan
24-26 . . . . at Cedar Rapids
27-29 . . . . at Kane County
30-31 . . . . Clinton
AUGUST
1-2 . . . . Clinton
3-6 . . . . Peoria
7-9 . . . . . . at Burlington
10-12 . . . . . Quad Cities
14-16 . . . . Cedar Rapids
17-20 . . . . . . at Peoria
21-23 . . . . Burlington
24-27 . . . . . at Clinton
28-30 . . . . Kane County
31 . . . . . . at Quad Cities
SEPTEMBER
1-2 . . . . . at Quad Cities

SOUTH ATLANTIC LEAGUE

ASHEVILLE TOURISTS

APRIL
4-7 . . . . Augusta
8-10 . . . . Charleston
11-14 . . . . at Hagerstown
15-17 . . . . . . at Hickory
18-20 . . . . West Virginia
22-24 . . . . at Delmarva
25-28 . . at West Virginia
30 . . . . Hagerstown
MAY
1-2 . . . . Hagerstown
3-6 . . . . Delmarva
8-10 . . . . at Hickory
11-13 . . . . . . Greenville
14-16 . . . . . . at Rome
17-20 . . . at Lexington
21-24 . . . . . Charleston
25-28 . . . . . . at Rome
30-31 . . . . West Virginia
JUNE
1-2 . . . . . . West Virginia
3-5 . . . . Augusta
6-9 . . . . . at Charleston
10-12 . . . at Columbia
13-16 . . . . . . Lakewood

20-23 . . . . Columbia
24-26 . . . . . . at Augusta
27-30 . . . . . at Charleston
JULY
1-3 . . . . Lexington
4-7 . . . . at Rome
9-11 . . . . Greenville
12-14 . . . . Augusta
15-17 . . . . at Greenville
18-21 . . . . Rome
23-25 . . . . at Greensboro
26-29 . . . . . at Hickory
31 . . . . Lexington
AUGUST
1-2 . . . . Lexington
3-6 . . . . Lakewood
8-11 . . . . at Greensboro
12-14 . . . . Rome
15-18 . . . . . Charleston
20-22 . . . . . at Augusta
23-25 . . . . at Greenville
26-29 . . . . . Charleston
30-31 . . . . . . at Rome
SEPTEMBER
1-2 . . . . at Rome

AUGUSTA GREENJACKETS

APRIL
4-7 . . . . at Asheville
8-10 . . . . . at Greenville
11-14 . . . at West Virginia
15-17 . . . . Greensboro
18-20 . . . . . Charleston
22-24 . . . . . at Hickory
25-28 . . . . at Delmarva
30 . . . . Lexington
MAY
1-2 . . . . Lexington
3-6 . . . . Hagerstown
8-10 . . . at West Virginia
11-13 . . . . . at Lexington
14-16 . . . . . Columbia
17-20 . . . . at Charleston
21-24 . . . . Rome
25-28 . . . . . Greenville
30-31 . . . . at Columbia
JUNE
1-2 . . . . . at Columbia
3-5 . . . . . at Asheville
6-9 . . . . Kannapolis
10-12 . . . at Lexington
13-16 . . . . Rome

20-23 . . . . . at Kannapolis
24-26 . . . . Asheville
27-30 . . . . . . Lexington
JULY
1-3 . . . . . . at Charleston
4-7 . . . . Kannapolis
9-11 . . . . . at Columbia
12-14 . . . . at Asheville
15-17 . . . . . Charleston
18-21 . . . . . Greensboro
23-25 . . . at Columbia
26-29 . . . . at Lexington
31 . . . . Lakewood
AUGUST
1-2 . . . . Lakewood
3-6 . . . . Hickory
8-11 . . . . . . at Rome
12-14 . . . . . Greenville
15-18 . . . . at Greensboro
20-22 . . . . . . Asheville
23-25 . . . . . Lexington
26-29 . . . at Greenville
30-31 . . . . . . Columbia
SEPTEMBER
1-2 . . . . Columbia

CHARLESTON RIVERDOGS

APRIL
4-7 . . . . at Columbia
8-10 . . . . . at Asheville
11-14 . . . | . . . Greensboro
15-17 . . . . . Greenville
18-20 . . . . at Augusta
22-24 . . . . . Kannapolis
25-28 . . . . . Columbia
30 . . . . . at Kannapolis
MAY
1-2 . . . . . at Kannapolis

3-6 . . . . at Greenville
8-10 . . . . Columbia
11-13 . . . . . . at Hickory
14-16 . . . . . West Virginia
17-20 . . . . . . Augusta
21-24 . . . . at Asheville
25-28 . . . . . Columbia
30-31 . . . . at Lexington
JUNE
1-2 . . . . . . at Lexington
3-5 . . . . . at Greensboro

6-9 . . . . .Asheville
10-12 . . . . at Rome
13-16 . . . . Greenville
20-23 . . . . at Hickory
24-26 . . . . at Rome
27-30 . . . . .Asheville

JULY
1-3 . . . . Augusta
4-7 . . . . at Greenville
9-11 . . . . .Rome
12-14 . . . . . .at Columbia
15-17 . . . . . at Augusta
18-21 . . . . . . Lexington
23-25 . . . . . at Lakewood

COLUMBIA FIREFLIES

APRIL
4-7 . . . . Charleston
8-10 . . . . .Rome
11-14 . . . . . at Lexington
15-17 . . . . . . at Rome
18-20 . . . . .Hickory
22-24 . . . . . at West Virginia
25-28 . . . . .at Charleston
30 . . . . Delmarva

MAY
1-2 . . . . Delmarva
3-6 . . . . Lexington
8-10 . . . .at Charleston
11-13 . . . . .Rome
14-16 . . . . . at Augusta
17-20 . . . . at Rome
21-24 . . . . . Greenville
25-28 . . . .at Charleston
30-31 . . . . . . Augusta

JUNE
1-2 . . . . Augusta
3-5 . . . . .Rome
6-9 . . . . . . at Hickory
10-12 . . . . . .Asheville
13-16 . . . . . . Lexington

DELMARVA SHOREBIRDS

APRIL
4-7 . . . . at Lexington
8-10 . . . . . .at Kannapolis
11-14 . . . . . .Lakewood
15-17 . . . . . . Kannapolis
18-20 . . at Greensboro
22-24 . . . . . . .Asheville
25-28 . . . . . Augusta
30 . . . . . . .at Columbia

MAY
1-2 . . . . .at Columbia
3-6 . . . . . . at Asheville
8-10 . . . . . Greensboro
11-13 . . . . . .Hagerstown
14-16 . . . . at Greensboro
17-20 . . . . .at Kannapolis
21-24 . . . . . .Lakewood
25-28 . . . . . .Hagerstown
30-31 . . . at Greenville

JUNE
1-2 . . . . at Greenville
3-5 . . . .at Kannapolis
6-9 . . . . . . .Hagerstown
10-12 . . . . at West Virginia
13-16 . . . . .Hickory

26-29 . . . . . .at Delmarva
31 . . . . .Hickory

AUGUST
1-2 . . . . .Hickory
3-6 . . . . Delmarva
8-11 . . . . . . at Hickory
12-14 . . . . . . Columbia
15-18 . . . . . at Asheville
20-22 . . . . . West Virginia
23-25 . . . . . Kannapolis
26-29 . . . . . at Asheville
30-31 . . . . . . Greenville

SEPTEMBER
1-2 . . . . Greenville

20-23 . . . . . . at Asheville
24-26 . . . . . at Lexington
27-30 . . . . . .Hickory

JULY
1-3 . . . . Greenville
4-7 . . . . at Hickory
9-11 . . . . Augusta
12-14 . . . . . . Charleston
15-17 . . at West Virginia
18-21 . . . . . at Greenville
23-25 . . . . . . Augusta
26-29 . . . .Hagerstown
31 . . . . . . at Kannapolis

AUGUST
1-2 . . . . . .at Kannapolis
3-6 . . . at Hagerstown
8-11 . . . . . . Greenville
12-14 . . . at Charleston
15-18 . . . . .Rome
20-22 . . . . . at Hickory
23-25 . . . . . at Rome
26-29 . . . . . . .Hickory
30-31 . . . . at Augusta

SEPTEMBER
1-2 . . . . . at Augusta

20-23 . . . . at Greensboro
24-26 . . . . . . .Lakewood
27-30 . . . . . at Hagerstown

JULY
1-3 . . . . at Lakewood
4-7 . . . . .Hagerstown
9-11 . . . . at West Virginia
12-14 . . . . . . .Hickory
15-17 . . . . . . Lakewood
18-21 . . . at West Virginia
23-25 . . . . . . Greenville
26-29 . . . . . Charleston
31 . . . . . . at Greenville

AUGUST
1-2 . . . . . . at Greenville
3-6 . . . . at Charleston
8-11 . . . . . . Kannapolis
12-14 . . . . . West Virginia
15-18 . . . . at Lakewood
20-22 . . . . . .Greensboro
23-25 . . . . at Hagerstown
26-29 . . . . at Lakewood
30-31 . . . . . . Kannapolis

SEPTEMBER
1-2 . . . . . . Kannapolis

GREENSBORO GRASSHOPPERS

APRIL
4-7 . . . . . . .Hagerstown
8-10 . . . . .Hickory
11-14 . . . .at Charleston
15-17 . . . . . . at Augusta
18-20 . . . . . Delmarva
22-24 . . . at Lexington
25-28 . . . at Hagerstown
30 . . . . .Rome

MAY
1-2 . . . . .Rome
3-6 . . . . . West Virginia
8-10 . . . .at Delmarva
11-13 . . . . at Lakewood
14-16 . . . . . . Delmarva
17-20 . . . . . .Lakewood
21-24 . . . at West Virginia
25-28 . . . . at Hickory
30-31 . . . . . .Lakewood

JUNE
1-2 . . . . . . .Lakewood
3-5 . . . . . . Charleston
6-9 . . . . at Lakewood
10-12 . . . . .Hickory
13-16 . . . .at Kannapolis

20-23 . . . . Delmarva
24-26 . . . . . West Virginia
27-30 . . . . . at Lakewood

JULY
1-3 . . . . . at Hagerstown
4-7 . . . . .Lakewood
9-11 . . . .at Hagerstown
12-14 . . . . . West Virginia
15-17 . . . . . .Hagerstown
18-21 . . . . . at Augusta
23-25 . . . . . . .Asheville
26-29 . . . . . Kannapolis
31 . . . . . . at West Virginia

AUGUST
1-2 . . . . . at West Virginia
3-6 . . . . . at Greenville
8-11 . . . . . . .Asheville
12-14 . . . .at Kannapolis
15-18 . . . . . . Augusta
20-22 . . .at Delmarva
23-25 . . . . . at Hickory
26-29 . . . . .Rome
30-31 . . . at West Virginia

SEPTEMBER
1-2 . . . . . at West Virginia

GREENVILLE DRIVE

APRIL
4-7 . . . . . . West Virginia
8-10 . . . . Augusta
11-14 . . . . at Rome
15-17 . . .at Charleston
18-20 . . . . . . .Rome
22-24 . . . at Hagerstown
25-28 . . . . . at Lexington
30 . . . . .Hickory

MAY
1-2 . . . . .Hickory
3-6 . . . . Charleston
8-10 . . . . . at Rome
11-13 . . . . . at Asheville
14-16 . . . . . . .Hickory
17-20 . . . . West Virginia
21-24 . . . .at Columbia
25-28 . . . . at Augusta
30-31 . . . . . Delmarva

JUNE
1-2 . . . . Delmarva
3-5 . . . . Lexington
6-9 . . . . at West Virginia
10-12 . . . . . Kannapolis
13-16 . . . at Charleston

20-23 . . . . . at Lexington
24-26 . . . . . Kannapolis
27-30 . . . . . . .Rome

JULY
1-3 . . . . .at Columbia
4-7 . . . . Charleston
9-11 . . . . . at Asheville
12-14 . . . . at Lexington
15-17 . . . . . .Asheville
18-21 . . . . . . Columbia
23-25 . . . .at Delmarva
26-29 . . . at Lakewood
31 . . . . . . Delmarva

AUGUST
1-2 . . . . Delmarva
3-6 . . . . . . .Greensboro
8-11 . . . .at Columbia
12-14 . . . . at Augusta
15-18 . . . . . . .Hickory
20-22 . . . at Hagerstown
23-25 . . . . . . .Asheville
26-29 . . . . . Augusta
30-31 . . . .at Charleston

SEPTEMBER
1-2 . . . . . at Charleston

HAGERSTOWN SUNS

APRIL
4-7 . . . . . at Greensboro
8-10 . . . . at Lakewood
11-14 . . . . . .Asheville
15-17 . . . . . Lexington
18-20 . . .at Kannapolis
22-24 . . . . . Greenville
25-28 . . . . Greensboro
30 . . . . . . at Asheville

MAY
1-2 . . . . . . at Asheville
3-6 . . . . at Augusta
8-10 . . . . Lakewood

11-13 . . . . .at Delmarva
14-16 . . . at Lakewood
17-20 . . . . . . .Hickory
21-24 . . . . . Kannapolis
25-28 . . . .at Delmarva
30-31 . . . . .Rome

JUNE
1-2 . . . . .Rome
3-5 . . . . at Lakewood
6-9 . . . . . . .at Delmarva
10-12 . . . . . .Lakewood
13-16 . . . . West Virginia
20-23 . . . . at Rome

24-26 . . . . at Hickory
27-30 . . . . Delmarva

JULY
1-3 . . . . Greensboro
4-7 . . . . .at Delmarva
9-11 . . . . Lexington
12-14 . . . . at Lakewood
15-17 . . . at Greensboro
18-21 . . . . .Hickory
23-25 . . . . . . at Rome
26-29 . . . . . .at Columbia
31 . . . . Rome

HICKORY CRAWDADS

APRIL
4-7 . . . . . . at Lakewood
8-10 . . . . at Greensboro
11-14 . . . . . . Kannapolis
15-17 . . . . .Asheville
18-20 . . . .at Columbia
22-24 . . . . Augusta
25-28 . . . . . . Lakewood
30 . . . . at Greenville

MAY
1-2 . . . . . . at Greenville
3-6 . . . .at Kannapolis
8-10 . . . . .Asheville
11-13 . . . . . Charleston
14-16 . . . . at Greenville
17-20 . . . at Hagerstown
21-24 . . . . . . Lexington
25-28 . . . . . Greensboro
30-31 . . . . .at Kannapolis

JUNE
1-2 . . . . . .at Kannapolis
3-5 . . . . . . West Virginia
6-9 . . . . Columbia
10-12 . . . at Greensboro
13-16 . . . .at Delmarva

KANNAPOLIS INTIMIDATORS

APRIL
4-7 . . . . .Rome
8-10 . . . . Delmarva
11-14 . . . . at Hickory
15-17 . . . .at Delmarva
18-20 . . . . . .Hagerstown
22-24 . . . .at Charleston
25-28 . . . . at Rome
30 . . . . Charleston

MAY
1-2 . . . . Charleston
3-6 . . . . .Hickory
8-10 . . . . . at Lexington
11-13 . . . . at West Virginia
14-16 . . . . Lexington
17-20 . . . . . . Delmarva
21-24 . . . . at Hagerstown
25-28 . . . . at Lakewood
30-31 . . . . .Hickory

JUNE
1-2 . . . . .Hickory
3-5 . . . . Delmarva
6-9 . . . . at Augusta
10-12 . . . . at Greenville
13-16 . . . . Greensboro

20-23 . . . . . Charleston
24-26 . . . . . .Hagerstown
27-30 . . . .at Columbia

JULY
1-3 . . . . . at West Virginia
4-7 . . . . . . Columbia
9-11 . . . . at Lakewood
12-14 . . . .at Delmarva
15-17 . . . . Kannapolis
18-21 . . . at Hagerstown
23-25 . . . . West Virginia
26-29 . . . . .Asheville
31 . . . . . .at Charleston

AUGUST
1-2 . . . . . . at Charleston
3-6 . . . . at Augusta
8-11 . . . . . . Charleston
12-14 . . . . at Lexington
15-18 . . . at Greenville
20-22 . . . . Columbia
23-25 . . . . . . Greensboro
26-29 . . . .at Columbia
30-31 . . . . Lexington

SEPTEMBER
1-2 . . . . Lexington

20-23 . . . . Augusta
24-26 . . . . . . at Greenville
27-30 . . . at West Virginia

JULY
1-3 . . . . .Rome
4-7 . . . . . . at Augusta
9-11 . . . . . . Greensboro
12-14 . . . . .Rome
15-17 . . . . . at Hickory
18-21 . . . . . . Lakewood
23-25 . . . at Lexington
26-29 . . . at Greensboro
31 . . . . Columbia

AUGUST
1-2 . . . . Columbia
3-6 . . . . Lexington
8-11 . . . . . .at Delmarva
12-14 . . . . . Greensboro
15-18 . . . . . Lexington
20-22 . . . . . . at Rome
23-25 . . . .at Charleston
26-29 . . . . . .Hagerstown
30-31 . . . .at Delmarva

SEPTEMBER
1-2 . . . . .at Delmarva

LAKEWOOD BLUECLAWS

APRIL
4-7 . . . . .Hickory
8-10 . . . . . .Hagerstown
11-14 . . . .at Delmarva
15-17 . . . at West Virginia
18-20 . . . . . Lexington
22-24 . . . . . at Rome
25-28 . . . . .at Hickory
30 . . . . . . West Virginia

MAY
1-2 . . . . . . West Virginia
3-6 . . . . .Rome
8-10 . . . . . at Hagerstown
11-13 . . . . . Greensboro
14-16 . . . . .Hagerstown
17-20 . . . at Greensboro
21-24 . . . .at Delmarva
25-28 . . . . Kannapolis
30-31 . . . at Greensboro

JUNE
1-2 . . . . . at Greensboro
3-5 . . . . . . .Hagerstown
6-9 . . . . Greensboro
10-12 . . . at Hagerstown
13-16 . . . . at Asheville

LEXINGTON LEGENDS

APRIL
4-7 . . . . Delmarva
8-10 . . . . . West Virginia
11-14 . . . . Columbia
15-17 . . . at Hagerstown
18-20 . . . . at Lakewood
22-24 . . . . . Greensboro
25-28 . . . . . Greenville
30 . . . . at Augusta

MAY
1-2 . . . . at Augusta
3-6 . . . . . .at Columbia
8-10 . . . . Kannapolis
11-13 . . . . Augusta
14-16 . . . . .at Kannapolis
17-20 . . . . . . .Asheville
21-24 . . . . . at Hickory
25-28 . . . at West Virginia
30-31 . . . . . Charleston

JUNE
1-2 . . . . Charleston
3-5 . . . . . . at Greenville
6-9 . . . . at Rome
10-12 . . . . Augusta
13-16 . . . .at Columbia

20-23 . . . . West Virginia
24-26 . . . . . .at Delmarva
27-30 . . . . . . .Greensboro

JULY
1-3 . . . . Delmarva
4-7 . . . , . . . at Greensboro
9-11 . . . . .Hickory
12-14 . . . . . .Hagerstown
15-17 . . . . .at Delmarva
18-21 . . . . .at Kannapolis
23-25 . . . . . Charleston
26-29 . . . . . Greenville
31 . . . . at Augusta

AUGUST
1-2 . . . . at Augusta
3-6 . . . . at Asheville
8-11 . . . . . West Virginia
12-14 . . . at Hagerstown
15-18 . . . . . Delmarva
20-22 . . . . at Lexington
23-25 . . . at West Virginia
26-29 . . . . . Delmarva
30-31 . . . at Hagerstown

SEPTEMBER
1-2 . . . . . . at Hagerstown

20-23 . . . . Greenville
24-26 . . . . . . Columbia
27-30 . . . . . at Augusta

JULY
1-3 . . . . at Asheville
4-7 . . . . . . West Virginia
9-11 . . . at Hagerstown
12-14 . . . . . . Greenville
15-17 . . . . at Rome
18-21 . . . .at Charleston
23-25 . . . . Kannapolis
26-29 . . . . . . Augusta
31 . . . . at Asheville

AUGUST
1-2 . . . . at Asheville
3-6 . . . . .at Kannapolis
8-11 . . . . .Hagerstown
12-14 . . . . . . .Hickory
15-18 . . . .at Kannapolis
20-22 . . . . . .Lakewood
23-25 . . . . at Augusta
26-29 . . . West Virginia
30-31 . . . . . . at Hickory

SEPTEMBER
1-2 . . . . at Hickory

ROME BRAVES

APRIL
4-7 . . . . . .at Kannapolis
8-10 . . . . .at Columbia
11-14 . . . . . Greenville
15-17 . . . . . . Columbia
18-20 . . . at Greenville
22-24 . . . . . .Lakewood
25-28 . . . . . . Kannapolis
30 . . . . . at Greensboro

MAY
1-2 . . . . . . at Greensboro
3-6 . . . . . . at Lakewood
8-10 . . . . Greenville

11-13 . . . . . .at Columbia
14-16 . . . . .Asheville
17-20 . . . . Columbia
21-24 . . . . . at Augusta
25-28 . . . . .Asheville
30-31 . . . at Hagerstown

JUNE
1-2 . . . . . at Hagerstown
3-5 . . . . .at Columbia
6-9 . . . . Lexington
10-12 . . . . Charleston
13-16 . . . . . . at Augusta
20-23 . . . . . .Hagerstown

| 24-26 . . . . Charleston |
| 27-30 . . . . . . at Greenville |

JULY

| 1-3 . . . . .at Kannapolis |
| 4-7 . . . . .Asheville |
| 9-11 . . . . . . at Charleston |
| 12-14 . . . . . .at Kannapolis |
| 15-17 . . . . Lexington |
| 18-21 . . . . . . at Asheville |
| 23-25 . . . . . .Hagerstown |
| 26-29 . . . . West Virginia |
| 31 . . . . . . at Hagerstown |

WEST VIRGINIA POWER

APRIL

| 4-7 . . . . at Greenville |
| 8-10 . . . . . . at Lexington |
| 11-14 . . . . Augusta |
| 15-17 . . . . . . .Lakewood |

AUGUST

| 1-2 . . . . . . at Hagerstown |
| 3-6 . . . . . . at West Virginia |
| 8-11 . . . . Augusta |
| 12-14 . . . . . . at Asheville |
| 15-18 . . . . . .at Columbia |
| 20-22 . . . . . Kannapolis |
| 23-25 . . . . Columbia |
| 26-29 . . . . at Greensboro |
| 30-31 . . . . .Asheville |

SEPTEMBER

| 1-2 . . . . .Asheville |

| 18-20 . . . . . . at Asheville |
| 22-24 . . . . . Columbia |
| 25-28 . . . . Asheville |
| 30 . . . . . at Lakewood |

MAY

| 1-2 . . . . . . at Lakewood |
| 3-6 . . . . . . at Greensboro |
| 8-10 . . . . Augusta |
| 11-13 . . . . . Kannapolis |
| 14-16 . . . . .at Charleston |
| 17-20 . . . . . at Greenville |
| 21-24 . . . . . . Greensboro |
| 25-28 . . . . . . Lexington |
| 30-31 . . . . . . at Asheville |

JUNE

| 1-2 . . . . at Asheville |
| 3-5 . . . . at Hickory |
| 6-9 . . . . Greenville |
| 10-12 . . . . Delmarva |
| 13-16 . . . . .at Hagerstown |
| 20-23 . . . . . at Lakewood |
| 24-26 . . . . at Greensboro |
| 27-30 . . . . . . Kannapolis |

JULY

| 1-3 . . . . .Hickory |

| 4-7 . . . . at Lexington |
| 9-11 . . . . Delmarva |
| 12-14 . . . at Greensboro |
| 15-17 . . . . . . Columbia |
| 18-21 . . . . . Delmarva |
| 23-25 . . . . . at Hickory |
| 26-29 . . . . . at Rome |
| 31 . . . . . .Greensboro |

AUGUST

| 1-2 . . . . .Greensboro |
| 3-6 . . . . .Rome |
| 8-11 . . . . . at Lakewood |
| 12-14 . . . .at Delmarva |
| 15-18 . . . .Hagerstown |
| 20-22 . . . .at Charleston |
| 23-25 . . . . . . .Lakewood |
| 26-29 . . . . at Lexington |
| 30-31 . . . .Greensboro |

SEPTEMBER

| 1-2 . . . . .Greensboro |

SHORT SEASON

NEW YORK-PENN LEAGUE

ABERDEEN IRONBIRDS

JUNE

| 14-15 . . . . . Hudson Valley |
| 16-17 . . . . . at Brooklyn |
| 18-20 . . . . Tri-City |
| 21-23 . . .at Hudson Valley |
| 25-27 . . . . . .Brooklyn |
| 28-30 . . . . . at Tri-City |

JULY

| 1-3 . . . . .Connecticut |
| 4-6 . . . . . . at Brooklyn |
| 7-9 . . . . Lowell |
| 10-12 . . . at West Virginia |
| 13-15 . . . . . Williamsport |
| 17-19 . . . .Connecticut |
| 20-22 . . . . at Staten Island |
| 23-25 . . . . Lowell |

AUBURN DOUBLEDAYS

JUNE

| 14-15 . . . . at Batavia |
| 16-17 . . . . State College |
| 18-19 . . . . at Batavia |
| 20 . . . . Batavia |
| 21-23 . . at Mahoning Valley |
| 25-27 . . . . . Williamsport |
| 28-30 . . . . at State College |

JULY

| 1-3 . . . . West Virginia |
| 4-6 . . . . Batavia |
| 7-9 . . . . . at West Virginia |
| 10-12 . . . . .Connecticut |
| 13-15 . . . . .at Lowell |
| 17-18 . . . . . at Batavia |
| 19 . . . . Batavia |
| 20-22 . . . . West Virginia |
| 23-25 . . . . .at Williamsport |

BATAVIA MUCKDOGS

JUNE

| 14-15 . . . . .Auburn |

| 20 . . . . at Auburn |
| 21-23 . . . .at Williamsport |
| 25-27 . . . . West Virginia |
| 28-30 . . at Mahoning Valley |

JULY

| 1-3 . . . . State College |
| 4-6 . . . . at Auburn |
| 7-9 . . . . at State College |
| 10-12 . . . . Lowell |
| 13-15 . . . . . at Vermont |
| 17-18 . . . . at Auburn |
| 19 . . . . at Auburn |
| 20-22 . . .Mahoning Valley |
| 23-25 . . . at West Virginia |
| 26-28 . . . . Williamsport |
| 30-31 . . . . . at Tri-City |

| 26-28 . . . . . Hudson Valley |
| 30-31 . . at Mahoning Valley |

AUGUST

| 1 . . . . at Mahoning Valley |
| 2-4 . . . . Vermont |
| 5-7 . . . . at Connecticut |
| 8-10 . . . . . . Staten Island |
| 11-13 . . . . . at Vermont |
| 14-16 . . . . at Tri-City |
| 17-19 . . . . Vermont |
| 22-24 . . . at Staten Island |
| 25-27 . . . . .at Lowell |
| 28-30 . . . . . . .Brooklyn |
| 31 . . . . .at Hudson Valley |

SEPTEMBER

| 1-2 . . . . . .at Hudson Valley |

| 26-28 . . . .Mahoning Valley |
| 30-31 . . .at Hudson Valley |

AUGUST

| 1 . . . . . .at Hudson Valley |
| 2-4 . . . . Tri-City |
| 5-7 . . . . State College |
| 8-10 . . at Mahoning Valley |
| 11-13 . . . . at West Virginia |
| 14-16 . . . . . . Williamsport |
| 17-19 . . . at State College |
| 22-24 . . . . . West Virginia |
| 25-27 . . . .Mahoning Valley |
| 28-30 . . . .at Williamsport |
| 31 . . . . at Batavia |

SEPTEMBER

| 1 . . . . at Batavia |
| 2 . . . . Batavia |

| 16-17 . . at Mahoning Valley |
| 18-19 . . . . .Auburn |

BROOKLYN CYCLONES

JUNE

| 14 . . . . Staten Island |
| 15 . . . . . at Staten Island |
| 16-17 . . . . Aberdeen |
| 18-20 . . . . .at Lowell |
| 21 . . . . Staten Island |
| 22 . . . . . at Staten Island |
| 23 . . . . Staten Island |
| 25-27 . . . . . at Aberdeen |
| 28-30 . . . . Lowell |

JULY

| 1-3 . . . . .at Hudson Valley |
| 4-6 . . . . Aberdeen |
| 7-9 . . . . at Tri-City |
| 10-12 . . .Mahoning Valley |
| 13-15 . . . . . West Virginia |
| 17-19 . . at Hudson Valley |
| 20-22 . . .at Connecticut |
| 23-25 . . . . Tri-City |

CONNECTICUT TIGERS

JUNE

| 14-15 . . . . .at Lowell |
| 16-17 . . . . Vermont |
| 18-20 . . . at Staten Island |
| 21-23 . . . . Lowell |
| 25-27 . . . . . at Vermont |

| 26-28 . . . . . . at Vermont |
| 30-31 . . . . Lowell |

AUGUST

| 1 . . . . Lowell |
| 2-4 . . . . . .at Williamsport |
| 5-7 . . . . . . Hudson Valley |
| 8-10 . . . . . . .Connecticut |
| 11 . . . . . at Staten Island |
| 12 . . . . . . Staten Island |
| 13 . . . . . at Staten Island |
| 14-16 . . . . . . at Vermont |
| 17-19 . . . . Tri-City |
| 22-24 . . . at Connecticut |
| 25-27 . . . . .Vermont |
| 28-30 . . . . . at Aberdeen |
| 31 . . . . . . Staten Island |

SEPTEMBER

| 1 . . . . at Staten Island |
| 2 . . . . . . Staten Island |

| 28-30 . . . . . Hudson Valley |

JULY

| 1-3 . . . . at Aberdeen |
| 4-6 . . . . Vermont |
| 7-9 . . . . at Staten Island |
| 10-12 . . . . . . at Auburn |

13-15 . . . . Tri-City	8-10 . . . . . . at Brooklyn
17-19 . . . . . at Aberdeen	11-13 . . . . Tri-City
20-22 . . . . Brooklyn	14-16 . . . . Hudson Valley
23-25 . . . . . Staten Island	17-19 . . . . . . .at Lowell
26-28 . . . . . . at Tri-City	22-24 . . . . . . .Brooklyn
30-31 . . . . . Williamsport	25-27 . . .at Hudson Valley
AUGUST	28-30 . . . . . at Vermont
1 . . . . Williamsport	31 . . . . Lowell
2-4 . . . . at Batavia	**SEPTEMBER**
5-7 . . . . Aberdeen	1-2 . . . . Lowell

HUDSON VALLEY RENEGADES

JUNE	26-28 . . . . . at Aberdeen
14-15 . . . . . at Aberdeen	30-31 . . . . .Auburn
16-17 . . . . Lowell	**AUGUST**
18-20 . . . . . at Vermont	1 . . . . .Auburn
21-23 . . . . . . Aberdeen	2-4 . . . . . . West Virginia
25-27 . . at Staten Island	5-7 . . . . . . at Brooklyn
28-30 . . . at Connecticut	8-10 . . . . Tri-City
JULY	11-13 . . . . . . .at Lowell
1-3 . . . . Brooklyn	14-16 . . . at Connecticut
4 . . . . at Tri-City	17-19 . . . Staten Island
5-6 . . . . Tri-City	22-23 . . . . . at Tri-City
7-9 . . . . . . at Vermont	24 . . . . Tri-City
10-12 . . . Staten Island	25-27 . . . . . .Connecticut
13-15 . at Mahoning Valley	28-30 . . . at Staten Island
17-19 . . . . . . Brooklyn	31 . . . . Aberdeen
20-22 . . . . . .at Lowell	**SEPTEMBER**
23-25 . . . . . Vermont	1-2 . . . . Aberdeen

LOWELL SPINNERS

JUNE	26-28 . . . . at Staten Island
14-15 . . . . . .Connecticut	30-31 . . . . . . at Brooklyn
16-17 . . .at Hudson Valley	**AUGUST**
18-20 . . . . Brooklyn	1 . . . . at Brooklyn
21-23 . . . at Connecticut	2-4 . . . . State College
25-27 . . . . Tri-City	5-7 . . . . . . at Tri-City
28-30 . . . . . at Brooklyn	8-10 . . . . . . .Vermont
JULY	11-13 . . . . Hudson Valley
1-3 . . . . Vermont	14-16 . . . at Staten Island
4-6 . . . . . Staten Island	17-19 . . . . .Connecticut
7-9 . . . . . at Aberdeen	22-24 . . . . . at Vermont
10-12 . . . . . . at Batavia	25-27 . . . . . Aberdeen
13-15 . . . . .Auburn	28-30 . . . . . . Tri-City
17-19 . . . . at Tri-City	31 . . . . . . at Connecticut
20-22 . . . . Hudson Valley	**SEPTEMBER**
23-25 . . . . . at Aberdeen	1-2 . . . . . .at Connecticut

MAHONING VALLEY SCRAPPERS

JUNE	26-28 . . . . at Auburn
14-15 . . . . at West Virginia	30-31 . . . . Aberdeen
16-17 . . . . Batavia	**AUGUST**
18-20 . . . . at West Virginia	1 . . . . Aberdeen
21-23 . . . . .Auburn	2-4 . . . . . at Staten Island
25-27 . . . at State College	5-7 . . . . . . West Virginia
28-30 . . . . Batavia	8-10 . . . . .Auburn
JULY	11-13 . . . . . at Batavia
1-3 . . . .at Williamsport	14-16 . . . at State College
4-6 . . . . . . State College	17-19 . . . . Batavia
7-9 . . . . . . Williamsport	22-24 . . . .at Williamsport
10-12 . . . . . at Brooklyn	25-27 . . . . . . at Auburn
13-15 . . . . Hudson Valley	28-30 . . . . State College
17-19 . . . .at Williamsport	31 . . . . . . West Virginia
20-22 . . . . . at Batavia	**SEPTEMBER**
23-25 . . . . . State College	1-2 . . . . West Virginia

STATE COLLEGE SPIKES

JUNE	26-28 . . . . . West Virginia
14 . . . . .at Williamsport	30-31 . . . . Vermont
15 . . . . . . Williamsport	**AUGUST**
16-17 . . . . . at Auburn	1 . . . . .Vermont
18 . . .at Williamsport	2-4 . . . . .at Lowell
19-20 . . . Williamsport	5-7 . . . . . . at Auburn
21-23 . . . at West Virginia	8-10 . . . . . . .Batavia
25-27 . . .Mahoning Valley	11-12 . . . .at Williamsport
28-30 . . . . .Auburn	13 . . . . . . Williamsport
JULY	14-16 . . .Mahoning Valley
1-3 . . . . at Batavia	17-19 . . . . . . .Auburn
4-6 . . . at Mahoning Valley	22-24 . . . . . at Batavia
7-9 . . . . Batavia	25-27 . . . West Virginia
10-12 . . . . . at Tri-City	28-30 . at Mahoning Valley
13-15 . . . . Staten Island	31 . . . . . .at Williamsport
17-19 . . . at West Virginia	**SEPTEMBER**
20-22 . . . Williamsport	1 . . . . Williamsport
23-25 . . Mahoning Valley	2 . . . . . .at Williamsport

STATEN ISLAND YANKEES

JUNE	26-28 . . . . Lowell
14 . . . . . . at Brooklyn	30-31 . . . at West Virginia
15 . . . . Brooklyn	**AUGUST**
16-17 . . . . at Tri-City	1 . . . . . . at West Virginia
18-20 . . . . .Connecticut	2-4 . . . . .Mahoning Valley
21 . . . . at Brooklyn	5-7 . . . . . at Vermont
22 . . . . Brooklyn	8-10 . . . . . at Aberdeen
23 . . . . Brooklyn	11 . . . . .Brooklyn
25-27 . . . Hudson Valley	12 . . . . . at Brooklyn
28-30 . . . . . at Vermont	13 . . . . .Brooklyn
JULY	14-16 . . . . Lowell
1-3 . . . . Tri-City	17-19 . . .at Hudson Valley
4-6 . . . . .at Lowell	22-24 . . . . . Aberdeen
7-9 . . . . .Connecticut	25-27 . . . . . at Tri-City
10-12 . . .at Hudson Valley	28-30 . . . Hudson Valley
13-15 . . . at State College	31 . . . . . . at Brooklyn
17-19 . . . . . Vermont	**SEPTEMBER**
20-22 . . . . . Aberdeen	1 . . . . .Brooklyn
23-25 . . . . .at Connecticut	2 . . . . . . at Brooklyn

TRI-CITY VALLEYCATS

JUNE	26-28 . . . . . .Connecticut
14-15 . . . . . . at Vermont	30-31 . . . . Batavia
16-17 . . . . Staten Island	**AUGUST**
18-20 . . . . at Aberdeen	1 . . . . Batavia
21-23 . . . . Vermont	2-4 . . . . . . at Auburn
25-27 . . . . . .at Lowell	5-7 . . . . Lowell
28-30 . . . . . Aberdeen	8-10 . . .at Hudson Valley
JULY	11-13 . . . at Connecticut
1-3 . . . . at Staten Island	14-16 . . . . . Aberdeen
4 . . . . Hudson Valley	17-19 . . . . at Brooklyn
5-6 . . . . .at Hudson Valley	22-23 . . . Hudson Valley
7-9 . . . . Brooklyn	24 . . . . .at Hudson Valley
10-12 . . . . State College	25-27 . . . . Staten Island
13-15 . . .at Connecticut	28-30 . . . . .at Lowell
17-19 . . . . . Lowell	31 . . . . .Vermont
20-22 . . . . . at Vermont	**SEPTEMBER**
23-25 . . . at Brooklyn	1-2 . . . . Vermont

VERMONT LAKE MONSTERS

JUNE	25-27 . . . . . .Connecticut
14-15 . . . . Tri-City	28-30 . . . . . Staten Island
16-17 . . . .at Connecticut	**JULY**
18-20 . . . Hudson Valley	1-3 . . . . .at Lowell
21-23 . . . . . at Tri-City	4-6 . . . . . .at Connecticut

7-9 . . . . . . Hudson Valley	5-7 . . . . Staten Island
10-12 . . . . .at Williamsport	8-10 . . . . .at Lowell
13-15 . . . . .Batavia	11-13 . . . . .Aberdeen
17-19 . . . . at Staten Island	14-16 . . . . .Brooklyn
20-22 . . . . Tri-City	17-19 . . . . at Aberdeen
23-25 . . .at Hudson Valley	22-24 . . . . Lowell
26-28 . . . . .Brooklyn	25-27 . . . . at Brooklyn
30-31 . . . . at State College	28-30 . . . . . .Connecticut
AUGUST	31 . . . . at Tri-City
1 . . . . . . at State College	**SEPTEMBER**
2-4 . . . . at Aberdeen	1-2 . . . . at Tri-City

WEST VIRGINIA BLACK BEARS

JUNE	26-28 . . . . at State College
14-15 . . .Mahoning Valley	30-31 . . . . . . Staten Island
16-17 . . . . at Williamsport	**AUGUST**
18-20 . . . .Mahoning Valley	1 . . . . Staten Island
21-23 . . . . . State College	2-4 . . . .at Hudson Valley
25-27 . . . . . . at Batavia	5-7 . . . at Mahoning Valley
28-30 . . . . . Williamsport	8-10 . . . . . . Williamsport
JULY	11-13 . . . . .Auburn
1-3 . . . . at Auburn	14-16 . . . . . . at Batavia
4-6 . . . . . .at Williamsport	17-19 . . . . . Williamsport
7-9 . . . . .Auburn	22-24 . . . . . at Auburn
10-12 . . . . Aberdeen	25-27 . . . at State College
13-15 . . . . . at Brooklyn	28-30 . . . . . Batavia
17-19 . . . . . State College	31 . . . . at Mahoning Valley
20-22 . . . . . . at Auburn	**SEPTEMBER**
23-25 . . . . .Batavia	1-2 . . . at Mahoning Valley

WILLIAMSPORT CROSSCUTTERS

JUNE	26-28 . . . . at Batavia
14 . . . . State College	30-31 . . . . .at Connecticut
15 . . . . . at State College	**AUGUST**
16-17 . . . . . West Virginia	1 . . . . .at Connecticut
18 . . . . . at State College	2-4 . . . . .Brooklyn
19-20 . . . at State College	5-7 . . . . .Batavia
21-23 . . . . .Batavia	8-10 . . . . at West Virginia
25-27 . . . . . . at Auburn	11-12 . . . . . State College
28-30 . . . . at West Virginia	13 . . . . . at State College
JULY	14-16 . . . . at Auburn
1-3 . . . . .Mahoning Valley	17-19 . . . . at West Virginia
4-6 . . . . West Virginia	22-24 . . . .Mahoning Valley
7-9 . . at Mahoning Valley	25-27 . . . . at Batavia
10-12 . . . . .Vermont	28-30 . . . . .Auburn
13-15 . . . . . at Aberdeen	31 . . . . State College
17-19 . . . .Mahoning Valley	**SEPTEMBER**
20-22 . . at State College	1 . . . . . . at State College
23-25 . . . . .Auburn	2 . . . . State College

NORTHWEST LEAGUE

BOISE HAWKS

JUNE	26-28 . . . . .Hillsboro
14-16 . . . . at Salem-Keizer	29-31 . . . . . . .Vancouver
17-20 . . . . Everett	**AUGUST**
21-24 . . . . . . at Spokane	1 . . . . .Vancouver
25-27 . . . . .Eugene	2-4 . . . . at Eugene
28-30 . . . . . Salem-Keizer	8-10 . . . . .Eugene
JULY	11-13 . . . . .Spokane
1-3 . . . . at Everett	14-16 . . . . . . at Hillsboro
4-6 . . . . Tri-City	17-19 . . . . at Vancouver
7-9 . . . . . . at Hillsboro	20-22 . . . at Salem-Keizer
11-13 . . . . . . .Hillsboro	23-26 . . . . at Tri-City
14-16 . . . . . . .Eugene	28-30 . . . . . at Hillsboro
17-19 . . at Salem-Keizer	31 . . . . .Hillsboro
20-22 . . . . Salem-Keizer	**SEPTEMBER**
23-25 . . . . at Eugene	1-2 . . . . .Hillsboro

EUGENE EMERALDS

JUNE	26-28 . . . . at Salem-Keizer
14-16 . . . . .Hillsboro	29-31 . . . . Spokane
17-20 . . . . . at Vancouver	**AUGUST**
21-24 . . . . . . Tri-City	1 . . . . Spokane
25-27 . . . . at Boise	2-4 . . . . Boise
28-30 . . . . at Hillsboro	8-10 . . . . at Boise
JULY	11-13 . . . . . . .Vancouver
1-3 . . . . at Tri-City	14-16 . . . . . Salem-Keizer
4-6 . . . . .Everett	17-19 . . . . . at Spokane
7-8 . . . . . . Salem-Keizer	20-22 . . . . .Hillsboro
10-13 . . . at Salem-Keizer	23-26 . . . . . . at Everett
14-16 . . . . . . at Boise	28-31 . . . . Salem-Keizer
17-19 . . . . . . .Hillsboro	**SEPTEMBER**
20-22 . . . . at Hillsboro	1-2 . . . . . at Salem-Keizer
23-25 . . . . Boise	

EVERETT AQUASOX

JUNE	26-28 . . . . Tri-City
14-16 . . . . at Tri-City	29-31 . . . . . . at Hillsboro
17-20 . . . . . . at Boise	**AUGUST**
21-24 . . . . Salem-Keizer	1 . . . . at Hillsboro
25-27 . . . .Vancouver	2-4 . . . . .Spokane
28-30 . . . . at Tri-City	8-10 . . . . at Vancouver
JULY	11-13 . . . . . . .Hillsboro
1-3 . . . . Boise	14-16 . . . . Tri-City
4-6 . . . . at Eugene	17-19 . . . at Salem-Keizer
7-9 . . . . . . at Vancouver	20-22 . . . . .Spokane
11-13 . . . . . .Vancouver	23-26 . . . . .Eugene
14-16 . . . . at Spokane	28-30 . . . . . at Spokane
17-19 . . . . . at Tri-City	31 . . . . .Vancouver
20-22 . . . . .Spokane	**SEPTEMBER**
23-25 . . . . at Vancouver	1-2 . . . . .Vancouver

HILLSBORO HOPS

JUNE	26-28 . . . . at Boise
14-16 . . . . at Eugene	29-31 . . . . Everett
17-20 . . . . at Tri-City	**AUGUST**
21-24 . . . . .Vancouver	1 . . . . Everett
25-27 . . . at Salem-Keizer	2-4 . . . . . . Salem-Keizer
28-30 . . . . . . .Eugene	8-10 . . . at Salem-Keizer
JULY	11-13 . . . . at Everett
1-3 . . . . at Vancouver	14-16 . . . . Boise
4-6 . . . . .Spokane	17-19 . . . . Tri-City
7-9 . . . . Boise	20-22 . . . . . at Eugene
11-13 . . . . at Boise	23-26 . . . . . at Spokane
14-16 . . . . . Salem-Keizer	28-30 . . . . Boise
17-19 . . . . . at Eugene	31 . . . . at Boise
20-22 . . . . . . .Eugene	**SEPTEMBER**
23-25 . . . . . Salem-Keizer	1-2 . . . . at Boise

SALEM-KEIZER VOLCANOES

JUNE	23-25 . . . . . . at Hillsboro
14-16 . . . . Boise	26-28 . . . . .Eugene
17-20 . . . . Spokane	29-31 . . . . Tri-City
21-24 . . . . at Everett	**AUGUST**
25-27 . . . . . .Hillsboro	1 . . . . Tri-City
28-30 . . . . at Boise	2-4 . . . . at Hillsboro
JULY	8-10 . . . . .Hillsboro
1-3 . . . . at Spokane	11-13 . . . . at Tri-City
4-6 . . . . .Vancouver	14-16 . . . . . . at Everett
7-8 . . . . at Eugene	17-19 . . . . Everett
10-13 . . . . . . .Eugene	20-22 . . . . Boise
14-16 . . . . . at Hillsboro	23-26 . . . . at Vancouver
17-19 . . . . Boise	28-31 . . . . . at Eugene
20-22 . . . . . . at Boise	**SEPTEMBER**
	1-2 . . . . .Eugene

SPOKANE INDIANS

JUNE
14-16 . . . . . at Vancouver
17-20 . . . . at Salem-Keizer
21-24 . . . . Boise
25-27 . . . . Tri-City
28-30 . . . . . at Vancouver

JULY
1-3 . . . . . Salem-Keizer
4-6 . . . . at Hillsboro
7-9 . . . . Tri-City
11-13 . . . . . at Tri-City
14-16 . . . . Everett
17-19 . . . . . . .Vancouver
20-22 . . . . . at Everett
23-25 . . . . . at Tri-City

26-28 . . . . . . .Vancouver
29-31 . . . . . . at Eugene

AUGUST
1 . . . . at Eugene
2-4 . . . . at Everett
8-10 . . . . Tri-City
11-13 . . . . at Boise
14-16 . . . . . . .Vancouver
17-19 . . . . .Eugene
20-22 . . . . . . at Everett
23-26 . . . . .Hillsboro
28-30 . . . . Everett
31 . . . . at Tri-City

SEPTEMBER
1-2 . . . . at Tri-City

TRI-CITY DUST DEVILS

JUNE
14-16 . . . . Everett
17-20 . . . . . . .Hillsboro
21-24 . . . . at Eugene
25-27 . . . . . at Spokane
28-30 . . . . Everett

JULY
1-3 . . . . .Eugene
4-6 . . . . at Boise
7-9 . . . . . at Spokane
11-13 . . . . Spokane
14-16 . . . . . at Vancouver
17-19 . . . . Everett

20-22 . . . . . at Vancouver
23-25 . . . . Spokane
26-28 . . . . . . at Everett
29-31 . . . at Salem-Keizer

AUGUST
1 . . . . . at Salem-Keizer
2-4 . . . . .Vancouver
8-10 . . . . at Spokane
11-13 . . . . . Salem-Keizer

VANCOUVER CANADIANS

JUNE
14-16 . . . . Spokane
17-20 . . . . .Eugene
21-24 . . . . at Hillsboro
25-27 . . . . . at Everett
28-30 . . . . Spokane

JULY
1-3 . . . . .Hillsboro
4-6 . . . . . at Salem-Keizer
7-9 . . . . Everett
11-13 . . . . . at Everett
14-16 . . . . Tri-City
17-19 . . . at Spokane
20-22 . . . . Tri-City
23-25 . . . . Everett

14-16 . . . . at Everett
17-19 . . . . at Hillsboro
20-22 . . . . . . .Vancouver
23-26 . . . . Boise
28-30 . . . . . at Vancouver
31 . . . . .Spokane

SEPTEMBER
1-2 . . . . Spokane

26-28 . . . . . . at Spokane
29-31 . . . . at Boise

AUGUST
1 . . . . at Boise
2-4 . . . . . at Tri-City
8-10 . . . . Everett
11-13 . . . . . . at Eugene
14-16 . . . . at Spokane
17-19 . . . . Boise
20-22 . . . . at Tri-City
23-26 . . . . . Salem-Keizer
28-30 . . . . . . Tri-City
31 . . . . at Everett

SEPTEMBER
1-2 . . . . at Everett

ROOKIE

APPALACHIAN LEAGUE

BLUEFIELD BLUE JAYS

JUNE
18-20 . . . . .at Elizabethton
21-23 . . . . at Pulaski
25-27 . . . . Danville
28-30 . . . . . . .Burlington

JULY
1-3 . . . . .at Danville
4-6 . . . . Johnson City
7-8 . . . . . .at Princeton
10-12 . . . . . . at Pulaski
13-16 . . . . . . Princeton
17-19 . . . . at Burlington
20-22 . . . . . Elizabethton

23-25 . . . . Pulaski
26-28 . . . . . .at Danville
30-31 . . . . Kingsport

AUGUST
1 . . . . Kingsport
2-4 . . . . at Johnson City
5-7 . . . . . .at Greeneville
8-10 . . . . Princeton
11-13 . . . . at Bristol
15-17 . . . . . Greeneville
18-20 . . . . Bristol
21-22 . . . . .at Princeton
23-25 . . . . . at Kingsport
26-28 . . . . . . .Burlington

BRISTOL PIRATES

JUNE
18-20 . . . . . .Burlington
21-23 . . . . . . Greeneville
25-27 . . . .at Elizabethton
28-30 . . . . . . Princeton

JULY
1-3 . . . . at Kingsport
4-6 . . . . . . .at Greeneville
7-8 . . . . Pulaski
10-12 . . . . . Johnson City
13-16 . . . . . . at Pulaski
17-19 . . . . at Johnson City
20-22 . . . . Kingsport

23-25 . . . . . at Burlington
26-28 . . . . . Elizabethton
30-31 . . . . . . Greeneville

AUGUST
1 . . . . Greeneville
2-4 . . . . .at Elizabethton
5-7 . . . . . .at Danville
8-10 . . . . . . Kingsport
11-13 . . . . . . .Bluefield
15-17 . . . . .at Princeton
18-20 . . . . at Bluefield
21-22 . . . . Pulaski
23-25 . . . . at Johnson City
26-28 . . . . Danville

BURLINGTON ROYALS

JUNE
18-20 . . . . .at Bristol
21-23 . . . . . .at Princeton
24-26 . . . . Kingsport
28-30 . . . . at Bluefield

JULY
1-3 . . . . Princeton
4-6 . . . . Pulaski
7-8 . . . . . . .at Danville
10-12 . . . at Elizabethton
13-16 . . . . Danville
17-19 . . . . . . .Bluefield
20-22 . . . . . . at Pulaski

23-25 . . . . Bristol
26-28 . . . .at Princeton
29-31 . . . . . Elizabethton

AUGUST
2-4 . . . . at Kingsport
5-7 . . . . at Johnson City
8-10 . . . . Danville
11-13 . . . .at Greeneville
15-17 . . . . Johnson City
18-20 . . . . . . Greeneville
21-22 . . . .at Danville
23-25 . . . . Pulaski
26-28 . . . . . at Bluefield

DANVILLE BRAVES

JUNE
18-20 . . . . Princeton
21-23 . . . . . . Johnson City
25-27 . . . . . at Bluefield
28-30 . . . . . at Pulaski

JULY
1-3 . . . . .Bluefield
4-6 . . . . . .at Princeton
7-8 . . . . .Burlington
10-12 . . . . . . Greeneville
13-16 . . . . at Burlington
17-19 . . . . Pulaski
20-22 . . . . at Johnson City

23-25 . . . . .at Greeneville
26-28 . . . . . . .Bluefield
30-31 . . . . at Pulaski

AUGUST
1 . . . . at Pulaski
2-4 . . . . Princeton
5-7 . . . . Bristol
8-10 . . . . . at Burlington
12-14 . . . . . at Kingsport
15-17 . . . . . Elizabethton
18-20 . . . . . Kingsport
21-22 . . . . . .Burlington
23-25 . . . .at Elizabethton
26-28 . . . . .at Bristol

ELIZABETHTON TWINS

JUNE	
18-20	Bluefield
21-23	at Kingsport
25-27	Bristol
28-30	at Greeneville

JULY	
1-3	at Pulaski
4-6	Kingsport
7	Johnson City
8	at Johnson City
10-12	Burlington
13-16	Johnson City
17-19	at Greeneville
20-22	at Bluefield

23-25	Princeton
26-28	at Bristol
29-31	at Burlington

AUGUST	
2-4	Bristol
5-7	at Kingsport
8	at Johnson City
9-10	Johnson City
11-13	Pulaski
15-17	at Danville
18-20	at Princeton
21-22	at Johnson City
23-25	Danville
26-28	Greeneville

GREENEVILLE REDS

JUNE	
18-19	Kingsport
20	at Kingsport
21-23	at Bristol
25-27	Johnson City
28-30	Elizabethton

JULY	
1-3	at Johnson City
4-6	Bristol
7-8	Kingsport
10-12	at Danville
13-14	at Kingsport
15	Kingsport
16	at Kingsport
17-19	Elizabethton

20-22	at Princeton
23-25	Danville
26-28	at Johnson City
30-31	at Bristol

AUGUST	
1	at Bristol
2-4	Pulaski
5-7	Bluefield
8-10	at Pulaski
11-13	Burlington
15-17	at Bluefield
18-20	at Burlington
21-22	Kingsport
23-25	Princeton
26-28	at Elizabethton

JOHNSON CITY CARDINALS

JUNE	
18-20	Pulaski
21-23	at Danville
25-27	at Greeneville
28-30	Kingsport

JULY	
1-3	Greeneville
4-6	at Bluefield
7	at Elizabethton
8	Elizabethton
10-12	at Bristol
13-16	at Elizabethton
17-19	Bristol
20-22	Danville
23-25	at Kingsport

26-28	Greeneville
30-31	at Princeton

AUGUST	
1	at Princeton
2-4	Bluefield
5-7	Burlington
8	Elizabethton
9-10	at Elizabethton
11-13	Princeton
15-17	at Burlington
18-20	at Pulaski
21-22	Elizabethton
23-25	Bristol
26-28	at Kingsport

KINGSPORT METS

JUNE	
18-19	at Greeneville
20	Greeneville
21-23	Elizabethton
24-26	at Burlington
28-30	at Johnson City

JULY	
1-3	Bristol
4-6	at Elizabethton
7-8	at Greeneville
10-12	Princeton
13-14	Greeneville
15	at Greeneville
16	Greeneville
17-19	at Princeton

20-22	at Bristol
23-25	Johnson City
26-28	Pulaski
30-31	at Bluefield

AUGUST	
1	at Bluefield
2-4	Burlington
5-7	Elizabethton
8-10	at Bristol
12-14	Danville
15-17	at Pulaski
18-20	at Danville
21-22	at Greeneville
23-25	Bluefield
26-28	Johnson City

PRINCETON RAYS

JUNE	
18-20	at Danville
21-23	Burlington
25-26	Pulaski
27	at Pulaski
28-30	at Bristol

JULY	
1-3	at Burlington
4-6	Danville
7-8	Bluefield
10-12	at Kingsport
13-16	at Bluefield
17-19	Kingsport
20-22	Greeneville

23-25	at Elizabethton
26-28	Burlington
30-31	Johnson City

AUGUST	
1	Johnson City
2-4	at Danville
5-7	Pulaski
8-10	at Bluefield
11-13	at Johnson City
15-17	Bristol
18-20	Elizabethton
21-22	Bluefield
23-25	at Greeneville
26-27	at Pulaski
28	Pulaski

PULASKI YANKEES

JUNE	
18-20	at Johnson City
21-23	Bluefield
25-26	at Princeton
27	Princeton
28-30	Danville

JULY	
1-3	Elizabethton
4-6	at Burlington
7-8	at Bristol
10-12	Bluefield
13-16	Bristol
17-19	at Danville
20-22	Burlington

23-25	at Bluefield
26-28	at Kingsport
30-31	Danville

AUGUST	
1	Danville
2-4	at Greeneville
5-7	at Princeton
8-10	Greeneville
11-13	at Elizabethton
15-17	Kingsport
18-20	Johnson City
21-22	at Bristol
23-25	at Burlington
26-27	Princeton
28	at Princeton

PIONEER LEAGUE

BILLINGS MUSTANGS

JUNE	
14-16	Idaho Falls
18-20	Great Falls
21-23	at Idaho Falls
24-26	at Missoula
27-29	Missoula

JULY	
1-2	Great Falls
3-5	at Great Falls
6-8	Missoula
10-13	at Rocky Mountain
14-17	at Grand Junction
19-21	Idaho Falls
22-24	Great Falls

25-28	at Missoula
29-31	at Great Falls

AUGUST	
1-3	at Idaho Falls
8-11	Rocky Mountain
12-15	Grand Junction
16-19	at Idaho Falls
20-21	Great Falls
22-25	Idaho Falls
27-29	at Missoula
30-31	at Great Falls

SEPTEMBER	
1-2	at Great Falls
4-7	Missoula

GRAND JUNCTION ROCKIES

JUNE	
14-17	at Ogden
18-19	Rocky Mountain
21-23	at Rocky Mountain
25-26	Orem
27-29	Ogden
30	at Rocky Mountain

JULY	
1	at Rocky Mountain
2-3	Rocky Mountain
4-5	Orem
6-8	at Orem
10-13	Great Falls
14-17	Billings

18-20	at Orem
22-24	at Ogden
25-27	Rocky Mountain
29-31	Ogden

AUGUST	
1-2	Orem
3-4	at Orem
8-11	at Great Falls
12-15	at Billings
17-20	Orem
21-24	Ogden
26-27	at Orem
28-30	at Ogden
31	Rocky Mountain

SEPTEMBER		
1-2 . . . . . Rocky Mountain	2-5 . . . . Orem	6-7 . . . . at Orem
3-7 . . . at Rocky Mountain		

GREAT FALLS VOYAGERS

JUNE	
14-16 . . . . Missoula	25-28 . . . . Idaho Falls
18-20 . . . . at Billings	29-31 . . . . Billings
21-23 . . . . . at Missoula	**AUGUST**
25-27 . . . . . . Idaho Falls	1-3 . . . . at Missoula
28-30 . . . at Idaho Falls	8-11 . . . . Grand Junction
JULY	12-15 . . . . Rocky Mountain
1-2 . . . . at Billings	16-19 . . . . at Missoula
3-5 . . . . Billings	20-21 . . . . . at Billings
6-8 . . . . . . Idaho Falls	22-25 . . . . . . Missoula
10-13 . . at Grand Junction	27-29 . . . at Idaho Falls
14-17 . . at Rocky Mountain	30-31 . . . . Billings
19-21 . . . . Missoula	**SEPTEMBER**
22-24 . . . . . . at Billings	1-2 . . . . Billings
	4-7 . . . . . . at Idaho Falls

IDAHO FALLS CHUKARS

JUNE	
14-16 . . . . at Billings	25-28 . . . . . at Great Falls
17-19 . . . . Missoula	29-31 . . . . Missoula
21-23 . . . . Billings	**AUGUST**
25-27 . . . . at Great Falls	1-3 . . . . Billings
28-30 . . . . . . Great Falls	8-11 . . . . at Ogden
JULY	12-15 . . . . . at Orem
1-3 . . . . . . at Missoula	16-19 . . . . Billings
4-5 . . . . Missoula	20-21 . . . . at Missoula
6-8 . . . . at Great Falls	22-25 . . . . . at Billings
10-13 . . . . Ogden	27-29 . . . . . Great Falls
14-17 . . . . Orem	30-31 . . . . at Missoula
19-21 . . . . . at Billings	**SEPTEMBER**
22-24 . . . . at Missoula	2-3 . . . . Missoula
	4-7 . . . . Great Falls

MISSOULA OSPREY

JUNE	
14-16 . . . . . at Great Falls	25-28 . . . . Billings
17-19 . . . . at Idaho Falls	29-31 . . . . . at Idaho Falls
21-23 . . . . . . Great Falls	**AUGUST**
24-26 . . . . Billings	1-3 . . . . . . Great Falls
27-29 . . . . . at Billings	8-11 . . . . at Orem
JULY	12-15 . . . . . at Ogden
1-3 . . . . Idaho Falls	16-19 . . . . . Great Falls
4-5 . . . . . at Idaho Falls	20-21 . . . . . Idaho Falls
6-8 . . . . . at Billings	22-25 . . . at Great Falls
10-13 . . . . Orem	27-29 . . . . . . Billings
14-17 . . . . Ogden	30-31 . . . . . Idaho Falls
19-21 . . at Great Falls	**SEPTEMBER**
22-24 . . . . . Idaho Falls	2-3 . . . . . at Idaho Falls
	4-7 . . . . at Billings

OGDEN RAPTORS

JUNE	
14-17 . . . Grand Junction	26-27 . . . . Orem
18-19 . . . . . . at Orem	29-31 . . at Grand Junction
20-23 . . . . Orem	**AUGUST**
25-26 . . at Rocky Mountain	1-4 . . . at Rocky Mountain
27-29 . . at Grand Junction	8-11 . . . . . Idaho Falls
JULY	12-15 . . . . . . Missoula
1-3 . . . . . . at Orem	17-20 . . at Rocky Mountain
4-8 . . . . . Rocky Mountain	21-24 . . at Grand Junction
10-13 . . . . at Idaho Falls	26-27 . . . Rocky Mountain
14-17 . . . . at Missoula	28-30 . . . Grand Junction
19-21 . . . Rocky Mountain	31 . . . . . . at Orem
22-24 . . . Grand Junction	**SEPTEMBER**
25 . . . . . . at Orem	1 . . . . at Orem

OREM OWLZ

JUNE	
14-17 . . . Rocky Mountain	29-31 . . at Rocky Mountain
18-19 . . . . . . Ogden	**AUGUST**
20-23 . . . . . at Ogden	1-2 . . . at Grand Junction
25-26 . . at Grand Junction	3-4 . . . . Grand Junction
27-29 . . at Rocky Mountain	8-11 . . . . . Missoula
JULY	12-15 . . . . Idaho Falls
1-3 . . . . Ogden	17-20 . . at Grand Junction
4-5 . . . at Grand Junction	21-24 . . at Rocky Mountain
6-8 . . . . Grand Junction	26-27 . . . Grand Junction
10-13 . . . . at Missoula	28-30 . . . Rocky Mountain
14-17 . . . at Idaho Falls	31 . . . . Ogden
18-20 . . . . Grand Junction	**SEPTEMBER**
22-24 . . . Rocky Mountain	1 . . . . Ogden
25 . . . . Ogden	2-5 . . . . at Ogden
26-27 . . . . . at Ogden	6-7 . . . . Ogden

ROCKY MOUNTAIN VIBES

JUNE	
14-17 . . . . at Orem	25-27 . . . at Grand Junction
18-19 . . at Grand Junction	29-31 . . . . Orem
21-23 . . . Grand Junction	**AUGUST**
25-26 . . . . Ogden	1-4 . . . . Ogden
27-29 . . . . Orem	8-11 . . . . . . at Billings
30 . . . . . Grand Junction	12-15 . . . . at Great Falls
JULY	17-20 . . . . Ogden
1 . . . . . . Grand Junction	21-24 . . . . Orem
2-3 . . . at Grand Junction	26-27 . . . . . at Ogden
4-8 . . . . . at Ogden	28-30 . . . . . at Orem
10-13 . . . . Billings	31 . . . at Grand Junction
14-17 . . . . . Great Falls	**SEPTEMBER**
19-21 . . . . . at Ogden	1-2 . . . . at Grand Junction
22-24 . . . . . . at Orem	3-7 . . . . . Grand Junction

ARIZONA LEAGUE

AZL ANGELS
Home Games Only

JUNE	
19 . . . . Cubs 2	22 . . . . Indians Blue
22 . . . . Cubs 1	25 . . . . Royals
25 . . . . Padres 2	28 . . . . Cubs 1
27 . . . . . Giants Orange	31 . . . . . Athletics Green
29 . . . . Mariners	**AUGUST**
30 . . . . . . Brewers Blue	2 . . . . Giants Orange
JULY	4 . . . . Dodgers 2
6 . . . . Dodgers 1	5 . . . . Padres 1
7-10 . . . . Athletics Green	11 . . . . . Giants Orange
13 . . . . D-backs	12-14 . . . . Athletics Green
15 . . . . . Giants Black	17 . . . . D-backs
16 . . . . Padres 1	19 . . . . Giants Black
21 . . . . . . Indians Red	20 . . . . Reds
	25 . . . . . . Brewers Gold
	26 . . . . Padres 2

AZL ATHLETICS GOLD

JUNE	
19 . . . . . Giants Orange	7 . . . . Mariners
21 . . . . . Athletics Green	12 . . . . . Giants Black
26 . . . . Dodgers 1	13 . . . . Cubs 1
27 . . . . Cubs 2	15 . . . . Rangers
29 . . . . Royals	18 . . . . Angels
JULY	20 . . . . Cubs 2
1 . . . . Dodgers 2	21 . . . . D-backs
5 . . . . . Brewers Blue	25 . . . . Padres 1
	27 . . . . . Athletics Green

AUGUST	
1	Cubs 1
2	White Sox
4	D-backs
6	Indians Red
10	Indians Blue

12	Brewers Gold
16	Giants Black
17	Cubs 1
19	Mariners
22	Angels
24	Padres 2
25	Indians Red

5	Padres 1
7	Dodgers 2
10	Giants Orange
12	Cubs 2
17	Giants Orange
18	Athletics Green
20	Giants Black
21	Brewers Blue
25	D-backs
26	Athletics Green
30	Padres 1

AUGUST	
2	Brewers Gold
5	Indians Red
7	Dodgers 2
10	White Sox
12	Reds
14	Giants Orange
16	Angels
21	Padres 2
22	Athletics Green
24	Giants Black
25	Cubs 2

AZL ATHLETICS GREEN

JUNE	
17	Cubs 1
20	Padres 2
22	Dodgers 1
24	Giants Orange
25	Indians Blue
30	Padres 1
JULY	
2	Dodgers 2
4	Giants Black
6	Royals
10	Cubs 2
11	Angels
16	D-backs
17	Athletics Green
22	Reds

23	Cubs 1
26	Brewers Gold
28	Rangers
30	Giants Orange
31	Cubs 1
AUGUST	
5	White Sox
7	Angels
9	Giants Black
11	Brewers Blue
14	Cubs 2
15	Angels
20	D-backs
21	Athletics Green
26	Mariners

AZL CUBS 2

JUNE	
17	Athletics Green
21	Giants Orange
22	Rangers
25	D-backs
26	Indians Red
29	Athletics Green
JULY	
1	Padres 2
4	Angels
6	Mariners
11	Athletics Green
13	White Sox
15	Royals
16	Cubs 1

22	Giants Black
23	Reds
27	Giants Orange
28	Dodgers 1
31	D-backs
AUGUST	
1	Angels
4	Cubs 1
6	Athletics Green
9	Angels
11	Padres 1
15	Athletics Green
17	Giants Orange
19	Rangers
20	Cubs 1
26	Giants Black

AZL BREWERS BLUE

JUNE	
17	Dodgers 1
20	White Sox
23	Royals
27	Rangers
28	Padres 1
JULY	
1	Brewers Gold
2	Athletics Green
7	Giants Black
8	D-backs
11	Rangers
14	Indians Red
16	Reds
17	Padres 2

22	Mariners
23	Dodgers 1
26	Angels
29	Royals
AUGUST	
2	Dodgers 2
3	Padres 1
6	Cubs 1
7	Giants Orange
12	Cubs 2
13	Brewers Gold
15	Rangers
18	Indians Red
20	Athletics Green
21	Indians Blue
25	Athletics Green

AZL BREWERS GOLD

JUNE	
18	Mariners
21	Dodgers 2
22	Athletics Green
25	White Sox
26	Angels
30	Reds
JULY	
3	Indians Blue
5	Athletics Green
6	Padres 1
12	Padres 2
13	Brewers Blue
18	Dodgers 1
19	Rangers

21	Cubs 2
24	Giants Orange
27	Cubs 1
28	Indians Red
31	White Sox
AUGUST	
1	Giants Black
5	Reds
8	Indians Blue
10	Brewers Blue
11	Indians Red
16	Padres 2
17	Dodgers 1
23	D-backs
23	Dodgers 2
26	Dodgers 2

AZL CUBS 1

JUNE	
19	D-backs
20	Athletics Green
24	Angels

27	Indians Blue
30	Royals
JULY	
2	Rangers

AZL D-BACKS

JUNE	
17	Giants Black
20	Cubs 2
22	Brewers Blue
23	Indians Blue
27	White Sox
30	Athletics Green
JULY	
3	Mariners
4	Padres 2
7	Brewers Gold
11	Cubs 1
14	Giants Orange
15	Athletics Green
19	Indians Red
20	Angels

23	Giants Black
26	Cubs 2
28	Giants Black
29	Indians Blue
AUGUST	
2	Rangers
5	Athletics Green
8	Reds
9	Dodgers 1
12	Dodgers 2
15	Cubs 1
18	Giants Orange
19	Athletics Green
23	Royals
24	Angels

AZL DODGERS 1

JUNE	
18	Rangers
21	Indians Red
24	Padres 1
27	Dodgers 2
29	Giants Orange
JULY	
1	Cubs 1
2	D-backs
7	Reds
8	Giants Black
12	Angels
14	Royals
19	Brewers Blue
20	Mariners
22	Brewers Gold

24	Rangers
27	Indians Red
30	Cubs 2
AUGUST	
2	Indians Blue
4	Athletics Green
6	Padres 2
7	Athletics Green
12	Mariners
13	White Sox
16	Brewers Blue
18	Royals
23	Rangers
24	Mariners
26	Indians Blue

AZL DODGERS 2

JUNE	
17 . . . . .Indians Blue	23 . . . . . . Brewers Gold
19 . . . . . Athletics Green	25 . . . . Rangers
22 . . . . Mariners	28 . . . . Brewers Blue
23 . . . . Reds	29 . . . . Reds
26 . . . . Padres 2	**AUGUST**
28 . . . .Giants Black	1 . . . . Padres 2
JULY	3 . . . . .Giants Black
3 . . . . .Reds	8 . . . . White Sox
4 . . . . Royals	9 . . . . Cubs 1
6 . . . . Indians Red	11 . . . . . Athletics Green
10 . . . . White Sox	14 . . . . White Sox
13 . . . . .Indians Blue	17 . . . . .Indians Blue
15 . . . . .Dodgers 1	19 . . . . .Dodgers 1
17 . . . . Brewers Gold	21 . . . . Cubs 2
18 . . . . D-backs	22 . . . . Indians Red

AZL GIANTS BLACK

JUNE	
18 . . . . D-backs	19 . . . . . . Giants Orange
19 . . . . Padres 1	24 . . . . D-backs
21 . . . . Angels	25 . . . . . . Giants Orange
24 . . . . . Athletics Green	27 . . . . Angels
27 . . . . . . Brewers Gold	30 . . . . . Athletics Green
29 . . . . .Dodgers 2	**AUGUST**
JULY	2 . . . . Cubs 2
1 . . . . Indians Red	4 . . . . Mariners
2 . . . . Cubs 2	6 . . . . . . Giants Orange
6 . . . . Cubs 1	7 . . . . Cubs 2
10 . . . . Royals	11 . . . . .Dodgers 1
13 . . . . . Athletics Green	14 . . . . Padres 2
14 . . . . White Sox	17 . . . . . Athletics Green
17 . . . . Reds	18 . . . . Reds
	21 . . . . Brewers Gold
	23 . . . . Brewers Blue

AZL GIANTS ORANGE

JUNE	
17 . . . . Angels	22 . . . . . Athletics Green
22 . . . . Indians Red	23 . . . . Angels
23 . . . . .Giants Black	28 . . . . . Athletics Green
26 . . . . . Athletics Green	29 . . . . . .Giants Black
28 . . . . D-backs	**AUGUST**
JULY	1 . . . . . Athletics Green
3 . . . . White Sox	3 . . . . Rangers
4 . . . . .Dodgers 1	8 . . . . Padres 2
7 . . . . Cubs 2	9 . . . . Royals
8 . . . . .Indians Blue	12 . . . . . .Giants Black
12 . . . . . . Brewers Blue	13 . . . . D-backs
15 . . . . Cubs 1	16 . . . . Cubs 2
18 . . . . Mariners	19 . . . . Cubs 1
20 . . . . .Dodgers 2	22 . . . . Cubs 2
	24-26 . . . . Athletics Green

AZL INDIANS BLUE

JUNE	
18 . . . . . . Giants Orange	18 . . . . Brewers Blue
21 . . . . Reds	19 . . . . .Dodgers 2
22 . . . . White Sox	21 . . . . Padres 1
26 . . . . . .Giants Black	24 . . . . Mariners
28 . . . . Rangers	27 . . . . Reds
30 . . . . Cubs 2	28 . . . . White Sox
JULY	**AUGUST**
1 . . . . Angels	1 . . . . .Dodgers 1
6 . . . . . Athletics Green	3 . . . . D-backs
7 . . . . Indians Red	5 . . . . Royals
11 . . . . Brewers Gold	6 . . . . Angels
14 . . . . Padres 2	11 . . . . Cubs 1
	12 . . . . Rangers

AZL INDIANS RED

JUNE	
15 . . . . Brewers Gold	23 . . . . Indians Red
18 . . . . Padres 2	25 . . . . Padres 1
22 . . . . .Dodgers 1	

JUNE	
17 . . . . . . .Brewers Gold	22 . . . . Padres 2
20 . . . . Royals	23 . . . . White Sox
23 . . . . Padres 1	26 . . . . Royals
25 . . . . Brewers Blue	29 . . . . Padres 1
27 . . . . . Athletics Green	31 . . . . Brewers Blue
JULY	**AUGUST**
2 . . . . . . Giants Orange	2 . . . . Reds
3 . . . . .Dodgers 1	7 . . . . Rangers
5 . . . . Cubs 2	8 . . . . .Dodgers 1
8 . . . . .Dodgers 2	10 . . . . D-backs
12 . . . . . . .Indians Blue	13 . . . . . .Giants Black
13 . . . . Mariners	16 . . . . . Athletics Green
16 . . . . Rangers	17 . . . . Mariners
17 . . . . Angels	20 . . . . Rangers
	21 . . . . Angels
	26 . . . . Cubs 1

AZL MARINERS

JUNE	
17 . . . . White Sox	19 . . . . Padres 1
19 . . . . .Dodgers 1	23 . . . . .Indians Blue
21 . . . . Brewers Blue	25 . . . . .Dodgers 1
24 . . . . Rangers	27 . . . Brewers Blue
27 . . . . Reds	30 . . . . Rangers
28 . . . . Indians Red	**AUGUST**
JULY	2 . . . . . Athletics Green
2 . . . . Angels	3 . . . . Indians Red
4 . . . . Cubs 1	7 . . . . D-backs
8 . . . . . . Brewers Gold	9 . . . . . Athletics Green
10 . . . . Padres 2	13 . . . . Reds
12 . . . . Royals	14-16 . . . . Royals
14 . . . . .Dodgers 2	18 . . . . White Sox
17 . . . . Cubs 2	21 . . . . . . Giants Orange
	23 . . . . Padres 1

AZL PADRES 1

JUNE	
18 . . . . Indians Red	22 . . . . .Dodgers 2
20 . . . . . . Brewers Gold	24 . . . . Indians Red
25 . . . . Royals	26 . . . . White Sox
26 . . . . . . Brewers Blue	31 . . . . Royals
29 . . . . Cubs 1	**AUGUST**
JULY	1 . . . . Brewers Blue
1 . . . . Mariners	4 . . . . . . Giants Orange
3 . . . . .Giants Black	6-8 . . . . Mariners
4 . . . . Rangers	9 . . . . Rangers
10 . . . . D-backs	14 . . . . D-backs
12 . . . . . Athletics Green	16 . . . . .Indians Blue
14 . . . . Reds	18 . . . . Brewers Gold
17 . . . . .Dodgers 1	21 . . . . .Dodgers 1
20 . . . . Padres 2	24 . . . . Cubs 2
	26 . . . . Reds

AZL PADRES 2

JUNE	
19	Rangers
21	Cubs 1
23	Dodgers 1
24	Dodgers 2
28	Brewers Gold
30	Indians Red

JULY	
5	D-backs
6	Giants Orange
8	White Sox
11	Reds
15	Padres 1
16	Indians Blue
19	Royals

21	White Sox
25	Athletics Green
27	Dodgers 2
29	Brewers Gold
30	Dodgers 2

AUGUST	
3	Brewers Gold
5	Brewers Blue
10	Cubs 2
11	Mariners
13	Indians Blue
15	Reds
19	Padres 1
20	Indians Blue
23	Giants Orange
25	White Sox

AZL RANGERS

JUNE	
17	Reds
20	Angels
23	Mariners
25	Cubs 1
29	D-backs
30	White Sox

JULY	
3	Brewers Blue
5	Indians Blue
8	Padres 1
10	Dodgers 1
13	Giants Orange
14	Brewers Gold
18	Indians Red

20	Royals
23	Athletics Green
26	Padres 2
29	Mariners
31	Padres 2

AUGUST	
4	Royals
5	Cubs 2
8	Brewers Blue
10	Athletics Green
13	Padres 1
14	Dodgers 1
17	Brewers Blue
18	Dodgers 2
22	Giants Black
24	Royals

AZL REDS

JUNE	
18	Padres 2
20	Indians Blue
22	Giants Black
25	Athletics Green
26	Cubs 1

JULY	
1	Giants Orange
2	Brewers Gold
5	Angels
6	Brewers Blue
12	Dodgers 2
13	Dodgers 1
18	Cubs 2
19	White Sox

21	Athletics Green
24	Padres 2
26	Indians Blue
28	Mariners
31	Indians Blue

AUGUST	
1	Indians Red
6	Dodgers 2
7	Brewers Gold
10	Padres 1
11	Royals
16	Dodgers 2
17	White Sox
22	Mariners
23	White Sox
25	D-backs

AZL ROYALS

JUNE	
18	Brewers Blue
21	Padres 1
24	Cubs 2
26	Mariners
28	Dodgers 1

JULY	
1	Athletics Green
3	Padres 2
5	White Sox
8	Reds
11	Indians Red
16	Athletics Green

17	Indians Blue
21	Rangers
22	Cubs 1
24	Brewers Blue
27	Padres 1
30	D-backs

AUGUST	
1	Mariners
3	Dodgers 1
6	Brewers Gold
8	Giants Black
10	Angels
13	Dodgers 2

15	Indians Red
20	Padres 1
21	Reds

AZL WHITE SOX

JUNE	
18	Dodgers 2
19	Royals
23	Brewers Gold
24	D-backs
28	Reds
29	Padres 2

JULY	
2	Indians Blue
4	Athletics Green
7	Rangers
11	Padres 1
15	Mariners
16	Brewers Gold
18	Giants Black
20	Athletics Green

24	Dodgers 2
25	Cubs 2
29	Dodgers 1
30	Angels

AUGUST	
3	Reds
4	Padres 2
7	Indians Blue
9	Padres 2
12	Indians Red
15	Padres 1
19	Royals
20	Brewers Gold
22	Brewers Blue
24	Dodgers 2

GULF COAST LEAGUE

GCL ASTROS

Home Games Only

JUNE	
26	Mets
29	Marlins
30	Nationals

JULY	
2	Cardinals
6	Mets
9	Marlins
10	Nationals
12	Cardinals
16	Mets
19	Marlins
20	Nationals
22	Cardinals
26	Mets

29	Marlins
30	Nationals

AUGUST	
1	Cardinals
5	Mets
8	Marlins
9	Nationals
11	Cardinals
15	Mets
18	Marlins
19	Nationals
21	Cardinals
25	Mets
28	Marlins
29	Nationals
31	Cardinals

GCL BLUE JAYS

JUNE	
24	Tigers West
27	Phillies West
29	Yankees East

JULY	
3	Phillies East
4	Yankees West
10	Tigers West
13	Phillies West
15	Tigers East
16	Yankees East
19	Phillies West
20	Yankees West
23	Tigers East

26	Tigers West
30	Phillies West

AUGUST	
1	Yankees East
5	Phillies East
6	Yankees West
8	Tigers East
12	Tigers West
15	Phillies West
17	Yankees East
21	Phillies East
22	Yankees East
24	Tigers East
28	Tigers West
31	Phillies West

GCL BRAVES

JUNE	
25	Orioles
29	Rays

JULY	
2	Pirates
4	Twins

5	Rays
8	Orioles
10	Red Sox
13	Rays
15	Pirates
17	Twins
19	Rays

23 . . . . Orioles	10 . . . . Rays
25 . . . . Red Sox	12 . . . . Pirates
27 . . . . Rays	14 . . . . Twins
30 . . . . Pirates	15 . . . . Twins

AUGUST	16 . . . . Rays
1 . . . . Twins	20 . . . . Orioles
2 . . . . Rays	22 . . . . Red Sox
5 . . . . Orioles	24 . . . . Rays
7 . . . . Red Sox	27 . . . . Pirates
	30 . . . . Rays

GCL CARDINALS

JUNE	29 . . . . Nationals
27 . . . . .Astros	30 . . . . Mets
29 . . . . Nationals	**AUGUST**
30 . . . . Mets	2 . . . . .Marlins

JULY	6 . . . . .Astros
3 . . . . .Marlins	8 . . . . Nationals
7 . . . . .Astros	9 . . . . Mets
9 . . . . Nationals	12 . . . . .Marlins
10 . . . . Mets	16 . . . . .Astros
13 . . . . .Marlins	18 . . . . Nationals
17 . . . . .Astros	19 . . . . Mets
19 . . . . Nationals	22 . . . . .Marlins
20 . . . . Mets	26 . . . . .Astros
23 . . . . .Marlins	28 . . . . Nationals
27 . . . . .Astros	29 . . . . Mets

GCL MARLINS

JUNE	26 . . . . Nationals
24 . . . . .Astros	28 . . . . .Cardinals
26 . . . . Nationals	**AUGUST**
28 . . . . .Cardinals	1 . . . . Mets

JULY	3 . . . . .Astros
2 . . . . Mets	5 . . . . Nationals
4 . . . . .Astros	7 . . . . .Cardinals
6 . . . . Nationals	11 . . . . Mets
8 . . . . .Cardinals	13 . . . . .Astros
12 . . . . Mets	15 . . . . Nationals
14 . . . . .Astros	17 . . . . .Cardinals
16 . . . . Nationals	21 . . . . Mets
18 . . . . .Cardinals	23 . . . . .Astros
22 . . . . Mets	25 . . . . Nationals
24 . . . . .Astros	27 . . . . .Cardinals
	31 . . . . Mets

GCL METS

JUNE	27 . . . . .Marlins
25 . . . . .Cardinals	31 . . . . .Astros
27 . . . . .Marlins	**AUGUST**

JULY	2 . . . . Nationals
1 . . . . .Astros	4 . . . . .Cardinals
3 . . . . Nationals	6 . . . . .Marlins
5 . . . . .Cardinals	10 . . . . .Astros
7 . . . . .Marlins	12 . . . . Nationals
11 . . . . .Astros	14 . . . . .Cardinals
13 . . . . Nationals	16 . . . . .Marlins
15 . . . . .Cardinals	20 . . . . .Astros
17 . . . . .Marlins	22 . . . . Nationals
21 . . . . .Astros	24 . . . . .Cardinals
23 . . . . Nationals	26 . . . . .Marlins
25 . . . . .Cardinals	30 . . . . .Astros

GCL NATIONALS

JUNE	**JULY**
24 . . . . .Cardinals	1 . . . . .Marlins
25 . . . . .Astros	4 . . . . .Cardinals
28 . . . . Mets	5 . . . . .Astros
	8 . . . . Mets

11 . . . . .Marlins	4 . . . . .Astros
14 . . . . .Cardinals	7 . . . . Mets
15 . . . . .Astros	10 . . . . .Marlins
18 . . . . Mets	13 . . . . .Cardinals
21 . . . . .Marlins	14 . . . . .Astros
24 . . . . .Cardinals	17 . . . . Mets
25 . . . . .Astros	20 . . . . .Marlins
28 . . . . Mets	23 . . . . .Cardinals
31 . . . . .Marlins	24 . . . . .Astros

AUGUST	27 . . . . Mets
3 . . . . .Cardinals	30 . . . . .Marlins

GCL ORIOLES

JUNE	24 . . . . Twins
26 . . . . Twins	26 . . . . Pirates
24 . . . . Braves	30 . . . . Red Sox
28 . . . . Pirates	**AUGUST**

JULY	1 . . . . Rays
2 . . . . Red Sox	3 . . . . Pirates
4 . . . . .Rays	6 . . . . Braves
6 . . . . Pirates	9 . . . . Pirates
9 . . . . Braves	12 . . . . Red Sox
11 . . . . Twins	14 . . . . .Rays
12 . . . . Pirates	17 . . . . Pirates
15 . . . . Red Sox	19 . . . . Braves
17 . . . . .Rays	21 . . . . Twins
20 . . . . Pirates	23 . . . . Pirates
22 . . . . Braves	27 . . . . Red Sox
	31 . . . . Pirates

GCL PHILLIES EAST

JUNE	27 . . . . .Blue Jays
25 . . . . . . .Blue Jays	30 . . . . Tigers West
27 . . . . . . Tigers West	31 . . . . . . Yankees East
28 . . . . . Yankees East	**AUGUST**

JULY	2 . . . . . . .Yankees West
1 . . . . . . .Yankees West	3 . . . . Tigers East
2 . . . . . . .Tigers East	6 . . . . Phillies West
4 . . . . . Phillies West	13 . . . . .Blue Jays
6 . . . . . . Yankees East	15 . . . . Tigers West
11 . . . . . . .Blue Jays	16 . . . . . . Yankees East
13 . . . . . Tigers West	19 . . . . . .Yankees West
17 . . . . .Yankees West	20 . . . . . . .Tigers East
18 . . . . . . .Tigers East	22 . . . . . . Phillies West
20 . . . . . Phillies West	29 . . . . . . .Blue Jays
	31 . . . . Tigers West

GCL PHILLIES WEST

JUNE	26 . . . . Yankees East
24 . . . . . Yankees East	29 . . . . Phillies East
26 . . . . . . Phillies East	**AUGUST**

JULY	5 . . . . Tigers West
3 . . . . Tigers West	7 . . . . .Blue Jays
5 . . . . . . .Blue Jays	9 . . . . . . .Yankees West
8 . . . . . . Yankees West	10 . . . . .Tigers East
9 . . . . . . .Tigers East	12 . . . . . . Yankees East
10 . . . . . . Yankees East	14 . . . . Phillies East
12 . . . . . . Phillies East	21 . . . . Tigers West
19 . . . . . . Tigers West	23 . . . . .Blue Jays
22 . . . . . . .Blue Jays	26 . . . . . .Yankees West
24 . . . . . Yankees West	27 . . . . .Tigers East
25 . . . . . .Tigers East	28 . . . . . . Yankees East
	30 . . . . Phillies East

GCL PIRATES

JUNE	
25	Twins
29	Orioles

JULY	
1	Braves
3	Red Sox
5	Orioles
8	Twins
10	Rays
13	Orioles
16	Braves
19	Orioles
23	Twins
25	Rays
27	Orioles
29	Braves
31	Red Sox

AUGUST	
2	Orioles
5	Twins
7	Rays
10	Orioles
13	Braves
15	Red Sox
16	Orioles
20	Twins
22	Rays
24	Orioles
26	Braves
28	Red Sox
30	Orioles

GCL RAYS

JUNE	
24	Red Sox
26	Pirates
28	Braves

JULY	
1	Twins
3	Orioles
6	Braves
9	Red Sox
11	Pirates
12	Braves
16	Twins
20	Braves
22	Red Sox
24	Pirates
26	Braves
29	Twins
31	Orioles

AUGUST	
3	Braves
6	Red Sox
9	Braves
13	Twins
15	Orioles
17	Braves
19	Red Sox
21	Pirates
23	Braves
26	Twins
28	Orioles
31	Braves

GCL RED SOX

JUNE	
25	Rays
26	Braves
29	Twins

JULY	
1	Orioles
4	Pirates
5	Twins
8	Rays
11	Braves
13	Twins
16	Orioles
17	Pirates
19	Twins
23	Rays
24	Braves
27	Twins
29	Orioles

AUGUST	
26	Orioles
30	Twins

GCL TIGERS EAST

JUNE	
24	Phillies East
26	Yankees East
28	Blue Jays

JULY	
1	Phillies West
3	Yankees West
6	Blue Jays
8	Tigers West
10	Phillies East
12	Yankees East
17	Phillies West
19	Yankees West
24	Tigers West
26	Phillies East
29	Yankees East
31	Blue Jays

AUGUST	
2	Phillies West
5	Yankees West
9	Tigers West
12	Phillies East
14	Yankees East
16	Blue Jays
19	Phillies West
21	Yankees West
26	Tigers West
28	Phillies East
30	Yankees East

GCL TIGERS WEST

JUNE	
25	Phillies West
29	Tigers East

JULY	
2	Blue Jays
5	Phillies East
9	Yankees East
11	Phillies West
15	Yankees West
16	Tigers East
18	Blue Jays
22	Phillies East
23	Yankees West
25	Yankees East
27	Phillies West

AUGUST	
1	Tigers East
3	Blue Jays
7	Phillies East
8	Yankees West
10	Yankees East
13	Phillies West
17	Tigers East
20	Blue Jays
23	Phillies East
24	Yankees West
27	Yankees East
29	Phillies West

GCL TWINS

JUNE	
24	Pirates
28	Red Sox

JULY	
2	Rays
3	Braves
6	Red Sox
9	Pirates
10	Orioles
12	Red Sox
15	Rays
20	Red Sox
22	Pirates
25	Orioles
26	Red Sox
30	Rays
31	Braves

AUGUST	
3	Red Sox
6	Pirates
7	Orioles
9	Red Sox
12	Rays
17	Red Sox
19	Pirates
22	Orioles
23	Red Sox
27	Rays
28	Braves
31	Red Sox

GCL YANKEES EAST

JUNE	
27	Yankees West

JULY	
1	Tigers West
2	Phillies West
4	Tigers East
8	Blue Jays
13	Yankees West
15	Phillies East
17	Tigers West
18	Phillies West
20	Tigers East
23	Phillies East
24	Blue Jays
30	Yankees West

AUGUST	
2	Tigers West
3	Phillies West
6	Tigers East
8	Phillies East
9	Blue Jays
15	Yankees West
19	Tigers West
20	Phillies West
22	Tigers East
24	Phillies East
26	Blue Jays
31	Yankees West

GCL YANKEES WEST

JUNE	
25	Tigers East
26	Blue Jays
28	Tigers West
29	Phillies West

JULY	
5	Yankees East
6	Tigers East
9	Phillies East
11	Tigers East
12	Blue Jays
16	Phillies West
22	Yankees East
25	Phillies East
27	Tigers East
29	Blue Jays
31	Tigers West

AUGUST	
1	Phillies West
7	Yankees East
10	Phillies East
13	Tigers East
14	Blue Jays
16	Tigers West
17	Phillies West
23	Yankees East
27	Phillies East
29	Tigers East
30	Blue Jays

INDEPENDENT

AMERICAN ASSOCIATION

CLEBURNE

MAY		JULY	
16-19	Sioux Falls	2-4	Chicago
20-22	Winnipeg	5-7	Gary SouthShore
28-30	Fargo-Moorhead	16-18	Lincoln
31	St. Paul	19-21	Milwaukee

JUNE		AUGUST	
1-2	St. Paul	3-5	Sioux Falls
11-13	Kansas City	6-8	Kansas City
14-17	Sioux City	15-17	Sioux City
18-20	Texas	24-26	Texas
25-27	Cleburne		

FARGO-MOORHEAD

MAY		9-11	Sioux City
20-23	Fargo-Moorhead	12-13	Lincoln
24-26	Texas	19-21	St. Paul
JUNE		30-31	Chicago
3-5	Lincoln	AUGUST	
18-20	Gary SouthShore	15-17	Sioux Falls
21-23	Chicago	18-20	Gary SouthShore
28-30	St. Paul	24-26	Winnipeg
JULY		31	Cleburne
4	Lincoln	SEPTEMBER	
5-7	Milwaukee	1-2	Cleburne

GARY SOUTHSHORE

MAY		19-21	Chicago
21-23	Sioux City	30-31	Winnipeg
24-26	Sioux Falls	AUGUST	
JUNE		1	Winnipeg
3-6	Chicago	2-4	Milwaukee
11-13	Winnipeg	6-8	Fargo-Moorhead
14-16	St. Paul	12-14	Texas
28-30	Kansas City	15-17	Milwaukee
JULY		21-23	St. Paul
12-14	Cleburne	31	Lincoln
15-18	Fargo-Moorhead	SEPTEMBER	
		1-2	Lincoln

LINCOLN

MAY		9-11	Winnipeg
23-26	Cleburne	24-26	Fargo-Moorhead
27-29	St. Paul	30-31	Sioux City
JUNE		AUGUST	
6-9	Texas	1	Sioux City
18-20	Milwaukee	2-4	Kansas City
21-23	Texas	9-11	Sioux Falls
28-30	Sioux City	12-14	Chicago
JULY		15-17	St. Paul
5-7	Kansas City	25-26	Gary SouthShore
		28-30	Cleburne

MILWAUKEE

MAY		3-6	Kansas City
24-26	Chicago	11-13	Sioux Falls
31	Lincoln	14-16	Winnipeg
JUNE		24-27	Gary SouthShore
1-2	Lincoln		

JULY		12-14	Fargo-Moorhead
9-11	Cleburne	18-20	Chicago
12-14	Sioux City	21-23	Fargo-Moorhead
27-29	Gary SouthShore	24-26	Sioux Falls
30-31	St. Paul	31	Texas
AUGUST		SEPTEMBER	
1	St. Paul	1-2	Texas
9-11	Winnipeg		

ST. PAUL

MAY		12-14	Winnipeg
16-19	Milwaukee	16-18	Kansas City
21-23	Chicago	24-26	Cleburne
24-26	Sioux City	28-29	Kansas City
JUNE		AUGUST	
7-9	Milwaukee	9-11	Gary SouthShore
11-13	Fargo-Moorhead	12-14	Winnipeg
21-23	Gary SouthShore	24-27	Chicago
24-26	Texas	28-30	Fargo-Moorhead
JULY		SEPTEMBER	
1-3	Lincoln	1-2	Cleburne

SIOUX CITY

MAY		15-17	Chicago
16-19	Lincoln	19-21	Sioux Falls
28-30	Texas	24-26	Gary SouthShore
JUNE		27-29	Texas
7-9	Fargo-Moorhead	AUGUST	
10-13	Lincoln	6-8	St. Paul
21-23	Sioux Falls	9-11	Cleburne
25-27	Winnipeg	19-20	Kansas City
JULY		21-23	Cleburne
2-4	Milwaukee	24-26	Kansas City

SIOUX FALLS

MAY		JULY	
31	Winnipeg	5-7	Sioux City
JUNE		8-11	Texas
1-2	Winnipeg	12-14	Chicago
3-6	Cleburne	24-26	Kansas City
7-9	Fargo-Moorhead	27-29	Lincoln
14-16	Lincoln	AUGUST	
17-20	St. Paul	12-13	Sioux City
24-27	Fargo-Moorhead	18-20	Cleburne
28-30	Milwaukee	21-23	Texas
		27-29	Sioux City

TEXAS

MAY		2-4	Gary SouthShore
16-19	Winnipeg	5-7	Chicago
20-22	Sioux Falls	16-18	Milwaukee
31	Fargo-Moorhead	19-21	Lincoln
JUNE		31	Cleburne
1-2	Fargo-Moorhead	AUGUST	
3-5	St. Paul	1-2	Cleburne
14-16	Kansas City	3-5	Sioux City
28-30	Cleburne	6-8	Sioux Falls
JULY		16-17	Kansas City
1	Cleburne	18-20	Lincoln
		27-29	Kansas City

WINNIPEG

MAY	
24-26	Kansas City
28-30	Gary SouthShore

JUNE	
3-6	Sioux City
7-9	Cleburne
18-20	Chicago
21-23	Milwaukee

JULY	
1-3	Fargo-Moorhead
4-8	St Paul

16-18	Sioux Falls
24-26	Texas
27-28	Fargo-Moorhead

AUGUST	
6-8	Lincoln
15-17	Chicago
18-19	St. Paul
27-29	Gary SouthShore
30-31	Sioux Falls

SEPTEMBER	
1-2	Sioux Falls

ATLANTIC LEAGUE

HIGH POINT ROCKERS

MAY	
2-5	Sugar Land
6-8	New Britain
17-19	Southern Maryland
21-23	Long Island
31	New Britain

JUNE	
1-2	New Britain
3-6	York
14-16	Long Island
18-20	Lancaster

JULY	
1-4	Lancaster
5-7	Somerset

19-21	Somerset
25-28	Sugar Land
29-31	Southern Maryland

AUGUST	
1	Southern Maryland
6-8	Sugar Land
9-11	York
16-18	Long Island
23-25	York
27-29	New Britain

SEPTEMBER	
1-5	Southern Maryland
11-12	Lancaster
13-16	Somerset

LANCASTER BARNSTORMERS

APRIL	
26-28	High Point
29-30	Long Island

MAY	
1-2	Long Island
7-8	Sugar Land
17-19	Somerset
21-23	New Britain
31	Southern Maryland

JUNE	
1-2	Southern Maryland
4-6	Sugar Land
14-16	York
25-27	Somerset
28-30	Southern Maryland

JULY	
5-7	York
16-18	High Point
23-25	Somerset
26-28	Southern Maryland

AUGUST	
6-8	New Britain
9-11	Long Island
19-22	High Point
23-25	Sugar Land
30-31	New Britain

SEPTEMBER	
1	New Britain
2-5	Long Island
13-15	York

LONG ISLAND DUCKS

MAY	
3-5	York
7-9	Southern Maryland
17-19	New Britain
24-26	Sugar Land
27-30	Lancaster

JUNE	
7-9	High Point
11-13	Somerset
21-23	Lancaster
25-27	New Britain

JULY	
1-4	Sugar Land

5-7	Southern Maryland
19-21	Lancaster
22-25	New Britain

AUGUST	
2-4	High Point
13-15	York
19-22	Somerset
26-29	Southern Maryland
30-31	Somerset

SEPTEMBER	
1	Somerset
6-8	Sugar Land
9-12	York
20-22	High Point

NEW BRITAIN BEES

MAY	
3-5	Somerset
14-16	Lancaster
24-26	High Point
28-30	York

JUNE	
3-6	Long Island
7-9	Lancaster
18-20	Southern Maryland
21-23	Sugar Land

JULY	
1-4	Somerset
5-7	Sugar Land

16-18	Southern Maryland
19-21	York
30-31	Long Island

AUGUST	
1	Long Island
2-4	York
9-11	Southern Maryland
12-15	High Point
23-25	Long Island

SEPTEMBER	
2-5	Somerset
6-8	Lancaster
13-16	Sugar Land
17-19	High Point

SOMERSET PATRIOTS

APRIL	
26-28	New Britain
29-30	High Point

MAY	
1	High Point
9-12	Lancaster
14-16	High Point
21-23	Sugar Land

JUNE	
4-6	Southern Maryland
7-9	York
14-16	Southern Maryland
18-20	Long Island
28-30	Long Island

JULY	
12-14	New Britain
15-18	York
26-28	Long Island
30-31	York

AUGUST	
1	York
9-11	Sugar Land
13-15	Lancaster
23-25	Southern Maryland
26-29	Lancaster

SEPTEMBER	
6-8	High Point
10-12	Sugar Land
20-22	New Britain

SOUTHERN MARYLAND

MAY	
3-5	Lancaster
10-12	New Britain
13-16	Long Island
24-26	Somerset
27-30	High Point

JUNE	
7-9	Sugar Land
10-13	New Britain
21-23	High Point
24-26	York

JULY	
2-4	York
12-14	Lancaster

19-21	Sugar Land
22-24	High Point

AUGUST	
2-4	Somerset
5-8	Long Island
12-15	Sugar Land
16-18	Somerset
30-31	York

SEPTEMBER	
1	York
10-12	New Britain
13-15	Long Island
16-19	Lancaster

SUGAR LAND

APRIL	
25-30	Southern Maryland

MAY	
1	Southern Maryland
10-12	Long Island
13-19	York
27-31	Somerset

JUNE	
1-2	Somerset
10-13	Lancaster
14-17	New Britain
25-30	High Point

JULY	
12-17	Long Island
29-31	Lancaster

AUGUST	
1-4	Lancaster
16-22	New Britain
30-31	High Point

SEPTEMBER	
1	High Point
3-5	York
17-19	Somerset
20-22	Southern Maryland

YORK

APRIL	
26-28	Long Island

30	New Britain

MAY		JULY	
1-2	New Britain	12-14	High Point
6-8	Somerset	22-24	Sugar Land
9-12	High Point	26-28	New Britain
20-23	Southern Maryland	**AUGUST**	
24-26	Lancaster	5-8	Somerset
31	Long Island	16-18	Lancaster
JUNE		19-22	Southern Maryland
1-2	Long Island	26-29	Sugar Land
10-13	High Point	**SEPTEMBER**	
18-20	Sugar Land	6-8	Southern Maryland
21-23	Somerset	16-19	Long Island
28-30	New Britain	20-22	Lancaster

AMERICAN ASSOCIATION

CHICAGO

MAY		24-26	Milwaukee
17-19	Gary	27-29	Cleburne
27-29	Sioux Falls	**AUGUST**	
31	Sioux City	2-4	St. Paul
JUNE		6-8	Milwaukee
1-2	Sioux City	9-11	Fargo-Moorhead
10-12	Texas	21-23	Winnipeg
14-16	Fargo-Moorhead	28-30	Milwaukee
24-27	Kansas City	31	St. Paul
28-30	Winnipeg	**SEPTEMBER**	
JULY		1-2	St. Paul
9-11	Gary		

CLEBURNE

MAY		JULY	
16-19	Sioux Falls	2-4	Chicago
20-22	Winnipeg	5-7	Gary
28-30	Fargo-Moorhead	16-18	Lincoln
31	St. Paul	19-21	Milwaukee
JUNE		**AUGUST**	
1-2	St Paul	3-5	Sioux Falls
11-13	Kansas City	6-8	Kansas City
14-17	Sioux City	15-17	Sioux City
18-20	Texas	24-26	Texas
25-27	Lincoln		

CAN-AM LEAGUE

NEW JERSEY

MAY		17-18	Sussex County
24-27	Trois-Rivieres	19-21	Trois-Rivieres
28-30	Quebec	24	Sussex County
JUNE		31	Rockland
7-9	Rockland	**AUGUST**	
11-13	Sussex County	1	Rockland
18-20	Ottawa	2-4	Ottawa
21-23	International-1	7	Rockland
28-30	International-2	9-10	Sussex County
JULY		20-23	Rockland
1-3	Quebec	23-25	Ottawa
11-14	Quebec	29	Sussex County

OTTAWA

MAY		11-13	Quebec
17-20	New Jersey	14-16	International
28-30	Rockland	21-23	Quebec
31	Trois-Rivieres	25-27	New Jersey
JUNE		**JULY**	
1-2	Trois-Rivieres	1-4	International

15-17	Rockland	16-18	New Jersey
26-28	Sussex County	27-29	Rockland
AUGUST		30-31	Quebec
6-8	Sussex County	**SEPTEMBER**	
9-11	Trois-Rivieres	1-2	Quebec

ROCKLAND

MAY		5-7	New Jersey
16	Sussex County	19-21	Sussex County
18	Sussex County	23-25	Ottawa
21-23	Ottawa	26-28	Quebec
31	Quebec	30	New Jersey
JUNE		**AUGUST**	
1-2	Quebec	6	New Jersey
4-6	Sussex County	8	New Jersey
14-16	New Jersey	9-11	Quebec
18-20	International	16-18	Sussex County
25-27	International	23-25	Trois-Rivieres
30	Sussex County	30	Sussex County
JULY		**SEPTEMBER**	
2-4	Trois-Rivieres	1	Sussex County

QUEBEC

MAY		JULY	
21-23	New Jersey	5-7	Sussex County
24-27	Rockland	19-21	Ottawa
JUNE		23-25	Trois-Rivieres
4-6	Ottawa	**AUGUST**	
14-16	Trois-Rivieres	2-4	Rockland
18-20	International-2	6-8	Trois-Rivieres
25-27	Sussex County	12-15	New Jersey
28-30	International-1	20-22	Ottawa
		23-25	Sussex County
		27-29	Trois-Rivieres

SUSSEX COUNTY

MAY		JULY	
17	Rockland	1-4	International-2
19	Rockland	11-14	Ottawa
22-23	Trois-Rivieres	23	New Jersey
24-27	Ottawa	25	New Jersey
31	New Jersey	30-31	Quebec
JUNE		**AUGUST**	
1-2	New Jersey	1	Quebec
7-9	Quebec	2-4	Trois-Rivieres
14-16	International-1	11	New Jersey
18-20	Trois-Rivieres	13-15	Ottawa
21-23	Rockland	27-28	New Jersey
28-29	Rockland	31	Rockland
		SEPTEMBER	
		2	Rockland

TROIS-RIVIERES

MAY		16-18	Quebec
17-20	Quebec	26-28	New Jersey
28-29	Sussex County	30-31	Ottawa
JUNE		**AUGUST**	
4-6	New Jersey	1	August
7-9	Ottawa	13-15	Rockland
11-13	Rockland	16-18	Quebec
21-23	International	19-22	Sussex County
25-27	International	30-31	New Jersey
28-30	Ottawa	**SEPTEMBER**	
JULY		1-2	New Jersey
11-14	Rockland		

FRONTIER LEAGUE

EVANSVILLE

MAY	
10-12	Southern Illinois
17-19	Florence
28-30	Washington

JUNE	
11-13	Windy City
14-16	Schaumburg
25-27	Schaumburg
28-30	River City

JULY	
12-14	Lake Erie
16-18	Joliet
26-28	Windy City

AUGUST	
2-4	Southern Illinois
6-8	Lake Erie
13-15	River City
16-18	Gateway
23-25	Florence
27-29	Gateway

FLORENCE

MAY	
9	Lake Erie
10-12	Joliet
15-16	River City
24-26	Southern Illinois
31	Evansville

JUNE	
1-2	Evansville
5-6	Windy City
11-13	Schaumburg
14-16	Lake Erie
21-24	Gateway

JULY	
2-4	Southern Illinois
5-6	Lake Erie
19-21	Evansville
31	Gateway

AUGUST	
1	Gateway
2-4	Washington
16-18	River City
21-22	Washington
27-29	Joliet

GATEWAY

MAY	
10-12	Schaumburg
21-23	Evansville
28-30	Florence
31	Washington

JUNE	
1-2	Washington
11-13	River City
14-16	Windy City
28-30	Southern Illinois

JULY	
2-4	Evansville

12-14	Florence
23-25	Lake Erie
26-28	Joliet

AUGUST	
6-8	Southern Illinois
9-11	Windy City
20-22	Schaumburg
23-25	River City
30-31	Washington

SEPTEMBER	
1	Washington

JOLIET

MAY	
9	Windy City
14-16	Gateway
17-19	Schaumburg
28-29	Windy City

JUNE	
4-6	Evansville
11-13	Lake Erie
14-16	Washington
21-23	River City
25-27	Florence

JULY	
2-4	River City
5-7	Windy City
19-21	Gateway
23-25	Evansville

AUGUST	
2-4	Schaumburg
13-15	Washington
16-18	Southern Illinois
30-31	Lake Erie

SEPTEMBER	
1	Lake Erie

LAKE ERIE

MAY	
10-12	Windy City
14-16	Southern Illinois
28-30	Schaumburg

JUNE	
1-2	Joliet
7-9	Southern Illinois

18-20	Gateway
21-23	Evansville

JULY	
2-4	Washington
16-18	Florence
19-21	Washington
30-31	Evansville

RIVER CITY

MAY	
9-12	Washington
17-19	Gateway
21-23	Southern Illinois
24-26	Evansville

JUNE	
5-6	Lake Erie
7-9	Joliet
18-20	Florence
26-27	Gateway

JULY	
5-7	Evansville
17-18	Schaumburg
19-21	Southern Illinois
26-28	Lake Erie

AUGUST	
7-8	Windy City
9-11	Florence
21-22	Joliet
28-29	Washington

AUGUST	
1	Evansville
2-4	River City

9-11	Joliet
13-15	Gateway
20-22	Windy City
23-25	Schaumburg

SCHAUMBURG

MAY	
14-16	Washington
21-23	Lake Erie
24-27	Joliet

JUNE	
4-6	Gateway
7-9	Evansville
19-20	Joliet
21-23	Southern Illinois
28-30	Florence

JULY	
2-4	Windy City
12-14	Washington
19-21	Windy City
23-25	Southern Illinois
29-31	River City

AUGUST	
1	River City
6-8	Florence
16-18	Lake Erie
30-31	River City

SOUTHERN ILLINOIS

MAY	
17-19	Windy City
28-30	River City
31	Schaumburg

JUNE	
1-2	Schaumburg
11-13	Washington
14-16	River City
25-27	Windy City

JULY	
5-7	Gateway
12-14	Joliet

16-17	Gateway
26-27	Florence
30-31	Joliet

AUGUST	
1	Joliet
9-11	Schaumburg
13-15	Florence
20-22	Evansville
27-29	Lake Erie
30-31	Evansville

SEPTEMBER	
1	Evansville

WASHINGTON

MAY	
17-19	Lake Erie
22-23	Florence
24-26	Gateway

JUNE	
4-6	Southern Illinois
7-9	Florence
18-20	Evansville
25-27	Lake Erie
28-30	Joliet

JULY	
5-7	Schaumburg
16-18	Windy City
23-25	River City
26-28	Schaumburg

AUGUST	
6-8	Joliet
9-11	Evansville
16-18	Windy City
23-25	Southern Illinois

WINDY CITY

MAY	
14-16	Evansville
21-23	Joliet
24-26	Lake Erie
31	River City

JUNE	
1-2	River City
7-9	Gateway
18-20	Southern Illinois
21-23	Washington
28-30	Lake Erie

JULY	
12-14	River City
23-25	Florence
30-31	Washington

AUGUST	
1	Washington
2-4	Gateway
13-15	Schaumburg
23-25	Joliet
27-29	Schaumburg
30-31	Florence

INDEPENDENT
LEAGUES

AMERICAN ASSOCIATION

Mailing and Street Address: 935 37th Ave S, Suite 128, Moorhead, MN 56560.
Telephone: (218) 359-3599.
Email: info@aaipb.com
Website: www.americanassociationbaseball.com.
Year Founded: 2005.
Executive Director: Josh Buchholz. **Director of Umpires:** Ron Teague. **Media Relations Manager:** Brady Drake.
Directors: Jim Abel, John Ehlert, Daryn Eudaly, Marv Goldklang, Shawn Hunter, Sam Katz, Donnie Nelson, Mark Ogren, John Roost, Patrick Salvi, Bruce Thom and Mike Zimmerman.
Opening Date: May 16. **Closing Date:** September 2.
Regular Season: 100 games.
Division Structure: North—Chicago Dogs, Gary SouthShore RailCats, Fargo-Moorhead RedHawks, Milwaukee Milkmen, St. Paul Saints, Winnipeg Goldeyes. **South**—Cleburne Railroaders, Kansas City T-Bones, Lincoln Saltdogs, Sioux City Explorers, Sioux Falls Canaries, Texas AirHogs.
Playoff Format: Top two teams in each division play in best-of-five series. Winners play in best-of-five American Association Championship.
Roster Limit: 23.
Player Eligibility Rule: Minimum of five first-year players; maximum of five veterans (at least six or more years of professional service).
Brand of Baseball: Rawlings.
Statistician: Pointstreak.com, 602-1595 16th Avenue, Richmond Hill, ON Canada L4B 3N9.

STADIUM INFORMATION

Club	Stadium	Opened	Dimensions LF	CF	RF	Capacity	2018 Att.
Chicago	Impact Field	2018	313	389	294	6,300	138,155
Cleburne	The Depot at Cleburne Station	2017	335	400	320	3,750	64,226
Fargo-Moorhead	Newman Outdoor Field	1996	314	408	318	4,172	166,717
Gary SouthShore	U.S. Steel Yard	2002	320	400	335	6,139	167,152
Kansas City	T-Bones Stadium	2003	300	396	328	6,270	189,981
Lincoln	Haymarket Park	2001	335	403	325	4,500	160,124
Milwaukee	Routine Field	2019	330	408	330	4,000	N/A
St. Paul	CHS Field	2015	330	396	320	7,140	408,921
Sioux City	Mercy Field at Lewis and Clark Park	1993	330	400	330	3,800	63,498
Sioux Falls	Sioux Falls Stadium	1964	313	410	312	4,462	124,127
Texas	AirHogs Stadium	2008	330	400	330	4,500	80,196
Winnipeg	Shaw Park	1999	325	400	325	7,481	219,370

CHICAGO DOGS

Office Address: 9800 Balmoral Avenue, Rosemont, IL, 60018
Telephone: 847.636.5450.
E-mail: info@thechicagodogs.com. **Website:** www.thechicagodogs.com.
Owners: Shawn Hunter, Steven Gluckstern
Field Manager: Butch Hobson

GAME INFORMATION
Stadium Name: Impact Field, 9800 Balmoral Avenue, Rosemont, IL 60018.
Standard Game Times: Mon.-Sat., 7:05 pm; Sun., 1:05 pm (May-June), 3:05 pm (July-Sept.)

CLEBURNE RAILROADERS

Office Address: 1906 Brazzle Boulevard, Cleburne, TX 76033
Telephone: (817) 945-8705
Email address: info@railroaderbaseball.com. **Website:** www.railroaderbaseball.com
President/Co-Owner: John Junker. **Co-Owner:** Daryn Eudaly.
Director of Baseball Operations: Josh Robertson. **Director of Business Operations:** Bill Adams. **Director of Corporate Sales:** Jennifer Forrester. **Community Relations and Group Sales Manager:** Janice Nickell. **Production Manager:** Douglas Fenyes. **Ticket Office Manager:** Patty Hicks. **Facility and Maintenance Manager:** Jon Starke. **Director of Broadcasting and Media Relations:** Brad Allred. **Broadcasting and Media Relations Manager:** Denning Gerig. **Clubhouse Manager:** Cleo Welch. **Field Manager:** Brent Clevlen. **Pitching Coach:** Mike Jeffcoat. **Hitting Coach:** John Rodriguez. **Athletic Trainer:** Rachel Pryor.

GAME INFORMATION

Broadcasters: Brad Allred and Denning Gerig. **No. of Games Broadcast:** 100. **Webcast Address:** www.953khits. com. **Stadium Name:** The Depot at Cleburne Station. **Capacity:** 3,020. **Directions:** From Chisholm Trail Parkway (toll road) continue south across US HWY 67, turn left onto Cleburne Station Boulevard. From US HWY 67 South, exit Nolan River Road, turn left onto Nolan River Road, turn left onto Cleburne Station Boulevard. From US HWY 67 North, exit Nolan River Road, turn right onto Nolan River Road, turn left onto Cleburne Station Boulevard. **Standard Game Times:** Mon.-Sat., 7:06 pm, Sun., 6:05 pm

FARGO-MOORHEAD REDHAWKS

Office Address: 1515 15th Ave N, Fargo, ND 58102.
Telephone: (701) 235-6161. **Fax:** (701) 297-9247.
Email Address: redhawks@fmredhawks.com. **Website:** www.fmredhawks.com.
Operated by: Fargo Baseball LLC.
Chairman of the Board: Bruce Thom. **President & CEO:** Brad Thom. **General Manager:** Matt Rau.
Director, Accounting: Rick Larson. **Assistant General Manager:** Karl Hoium. **Director, Ticket Operations:** Isaac Olson. **Director, Communications:** Chad Ekren. **Coordinator, Group Sales:** Cole Milberger. **Director, Stadium Operations:** Michael Stark. **Director, Food and Beverage:** Derek Wang. **Field Manager:** Michael Schlact. **Coaches:** Chris Coste, Anthony Renz, Robbie Lopez. **Athletic Trainer:** Matt McManus. **Clubhouse Manager:** Chris "Bambino" Krick. **Player Personnel Consultant:** Jeff Bittiger.

GAME INFORMATION

Radio Announcers: Jack Michaels, Chase Miller. **No. of Games Broadcast:** 100. **Flagship Station:** 740-AM The FAN (KNFL-AM). **Stadium Name:** Newman Outdoor Field. **Location:** I-29 North to exit 67, east on 19th Ave North, right on Albrecht Boulevard. **Standard Game Times:** Mon.-Fri., 7:02 pm, Sat., 6:00 pm, Sun., 1:00 pm.

GARY SOUTHSHORE RAILCATS

Office Address: One Stadium Plaza, Gary, IN 46402.
Telephone: (219) 882-2255. **Fax:** (219) 882-2259.
Email Address: info@railcatsbaseball.com. **Website:** www.railcatsbaseball.com.
Operated by: Salvi Sports Enterprises.
Owner/CEO: Pat Salvi. **Owner:** Lindy Salvi.
President, Salvi Sports Enterprises: Brian Lyter. **General Manager:** Brian Flenner. **Director of Sales:** Daniel Faulkner. **Director, Marketing/Promotions:** David Kerr. **Manager, Box Office/Account Executive:** Hisham Abad. **Marketing Consultant:** Renee Connelly. **Senior Director of Operations/Head Groundskeeper:** Noah Simmons. **Community Relations Coordinator:** Ashley Nylen. **Field Manager:** Greg Tagert. **Pitching Coach:** Alain Quijano. **Hitting Coach:** Mike Habas.

GAME INFORMATION

Broadcaster: Jared Shlensky. **No. of Games Broadcast:** 100. **Flagship Station:** WEFM 95.9-FM. **Stadium Name:** US Steel Yard. **Location:** Take I-65 North to end of highway at U.S. 12/20 (Dunes Highway). Turn left on U.S. 12/20 heading west for 1.5 miles (three stop lights). Stadium is on left side. **Standard Game Times:** Mon.-Tues., Thurs.-Fri., 7:10 pm, Wed,, 6:45 pm, Sat., 6:10 pm, Sun., 2:10 pm.

KANSAS CITY T-BONES

Office Address: 1800 Village West Parkway, Kansas City, KS 66111.
Telephone: (913) 328-5618. **Fax:** (913) 328-5674.
Email Address: tickets@tbonesbaseball.com.
Website: www.tbonesbaseball.com.
Operated By: T-Bones Baseball Club, LLC; Ehlert Development.
Owner: John Ehlert. **President:** Adam Ehlert.
VP/General Manager: Chris Browne. **VP, Corporate Sponsorships/Sales:** Scott Steckly. **Director, Group Sales:** Nick Restivo **Director, Marketing/Promotions:** Morgan Kolenda. **Director, Ticket Sales/Merchandise:** Kacy Muller. **Account Executive/Group Sales:** Daniel Portillo. **Director Stadium Operations:** Kyle Disney. **Head Groundskeeper:** Nathan Miller. **Field Manager:** Joe Calfapietra. **Coaches:** Frank White, Bill Sobbe. **Equipment Manager:** John West.

GAME INFORMATION

Radio Announcer: Dan Vaughan. **No. of Games Broadcast:** 100. **Flagship Station:** tbonesbaseball.com. **Stadium Name:** T-Bones Stadium. **Location:** State Avenue West off I-435 and State Avenue. **Standard Game Times:** Mon.-Sat., 7:05 pm, Sun., 1:05 pm.

LINCOLN SALTDOGS

Office Address: 403 Line Drive Circle, Suite A, Lincoln, NE 68508.
Telephone: (402) 474-2255. **Fax:** (402) 474-2254.
Email Address: info@saltdogs.com. **Website:** www.saltdogs.com.
Chairman: Jim Abel. **President/GM:** Charlie Meyer.
Director, Marketing: Bret Beer. **Director, Broadcasting/Communications:** Michael
Dixon. **Director, Stadium Operations:** Dave Aschwege. **Director, Sales:** Steve Zoucha. Director, **Merchandise &
Promotions:** Alex Hanus. **Director, Video Production:** Cade McFadden. **Assistant Director, Stadium Operations:** Dan
Busch. **Manager, Ticket Sales:** Colter Clarke, Daniel Thomas. **Turf Manager:** Jeremy Johnson. **Assistant Turf Manager:**
Jen Roeber. **Office Manager:** Kaydra Brodine. **Field Manager:** Bobby Brown. **Coaches:** Tom Carcione, Dan Reichert.
Athletic Trainers: Corey Courtney.

GAME INFORMATION
Radio Announcer: Unavailable. **No. of Games Broadcast:** 100. **Flagship Station:** KLMS 1480AM & ESPN101.5
FM. **Webcast Address:** www.americanassociationbaseball.com. **Stadium Name:** Haymarket Park. **Location:** I-80 to
Cornhusker Highway West, left on First Street, right on Sun Valley Boulevard, left on Line Drive. **Standard Game Times:**
Mon.-Sat., 7:05 pm, Sun., 5:05 pm.

MILWAUKEE MILKMEN

Website: www.milwaukeemilkmen.com
Owner: Michael Zimmerman.
Vice President, Corporate Partnerships: Joe Zimmerman. **Vice President of Ticket
Sales & Service:** Trish Rasberry. **Entertainment & Events:** Jim Rinelli. **On Field Host &
Director of Fun:** Van McNeil. **Finance:** Tom Johns. **Administration:** Mike Doyle. **Head
Team Physician:** Dr. Damian Kosempa. **Manager:** Unavailable.

GAME INFORMATION
Ballpark: Routine Field. **Location:** 9625 S 54th St, Franklin, WI 53132.
Standard Game Time: Mon.-Fri., 7:05 pm. Sat., 6:05 pm. Sun., 1:05 pm.

ST. PAUL SAINTS

Office Address: 360 Broadway Street, St. Paul, MN 55101.
Telephone: (651) 644-3517. **Fax:** (651) 644-1627.
Email Address: funisgood@saintsbaseball.com.
Website: www.saintsbaseball.com.
Principal Owners: Marv Goldklang, Jeff Goldklang, Gerald Goldklang, Mike Goldklang, Bill Murray, Mike Veeck, Larr
Eagel, Tom Whaley, Alton Phillips. **Chairman:** Marv Goldklang. **President:** Jeff Goldklang.
Executive VP/General Manager: Derek Sharrer. **Executive VP:** Tom Whaley. **Senior VP/Assistant GM:** Chris Schwab.
Business Manager: Krista Schnelle. **Vice President/Director, Broadcast/Media Relations:** Sean Aronson. **Director,
Promotions/Marketing:** Sierra Bailey. **Director, Corporate Partnerships:** Tyson Jeffers. **Director of Sales:** Zane
Heinselman. **Ticket Sales Executive:** Abbie Farrell. **Ticket Sales Executive:** Brian Silva. **Ticket Office Manager:** Aaron
Boettger. **Director, Operations:** Curtis Nachtsheim. **Manager, Marketing Services:** Kelly Hagenson. **Director, Digital
Media and Video Production:** Jordan Lynn. **Office Manager:** Gina Kray. **Events Manager:** Anna Gutknecht. **Director,
Food/Beverage:** Justin Grandstaff, Gregg Kraly. **Head Groundskeeper:** Marcus Campbell. **Director, Community
Partnerships/Fan Services:** Eddie Coblentz. **Field Manager:** George Tsamis. **Coaches:** Kerry Ligtenberg, Ole Sheldon.
Athletic Trainer: Jason Ellenbecker.

GAME INFORMATION
Radio Announcer: Sean Aronson. **No. of Games Broadcast:** 100. **Flagship Station:** KFAN+ 96.7 FM. **Webcast
Address:** www.saintsbaseball.com. **Stadium Name:** CHS Field. **Location:** From the west take I-94 to the 7th St. Exit and
head south to 5th & Broadway. From the east take I-94 to the Mounds Blvd/US-61N exit. Turn left on Kellogg and a right
on Broadway until you reach 5th St. **Standard Game Times:** Mon.-Sat., 7:05 pm, Sun., 5:05 pm.

SIOUX CITY EXPLORERS

Office Address: 3400 Line Drive, Sioux City, IA 51106.
Telephone: (712) 277-9467. **Fax:** (712) 277-9406.
Email Address: promotions@xsbaseball.com. **Website:** www.xsbaseball.com.
President: Matt Adamski. **VP/General Manager:** Shane M Tritz.
Director, Marketing: Tyler Hinker. **Director, Ticketing:** Connor Ryan. **Groundskeeper/Director, Stadium Operations:** Brent Recker. **Manager, Promotions/Community Relations:** Julie Targy. **Field Manager:** Steve Montgomery. **Coaches:** Bobby Post, Matt Passerelle.

GAME INFORMATION
Radio Announcer: Connor Ryan. **No. of Games Broadcast:** 100. **Flagship Station:** KSCJ 1360-AM. **Webcast Address:** www.xsbaseball.com. **Stadium Name:** Mercy Field at Lewis and Clark Park. **Location:** I-29 to Singing Hills Blvd, North, right on Line Drive. **Standard Game Times:** Mon.-Fri., 7:12 pm, Sat., 6:05 pm, Sun., 4:02 pm.

SIOUX FALLS CANARIES

Office Address: 1001 N West Ave, Sioux Falls, SD 57104.
Telephone: (605) 336-6060.
Email Address: info@sfcanaries.com. **Website:** www.sfcanaries.com.
Operated by: Canaries Baseball, LLC. **CEO/Managing Partner:** Tom Garrity.
General Manager: Duell Higbe. **Sales:** Caleb Nowicki.
Field Manager: Mike Meyer. **Coach:** Ben Moore, Mitch Glasser.

GAME INFORMATION
Radio Announcer: Carter Woodiel. **No. of Games Broadcast:** 100. **Flagship Station:** KWSN 1230-AM. **Webcast Address:** www.kwsn.com. **Stadium Name:** Sioux Falls Stadium. **Location:** I-29 to Russell Street, east one mile, south on West Avenue. **Standard Game Times:** Mon.-Fri., 7:05 pm, Sat., 6:05 pm, Sun., 1:05 pm.

TEXAS AIRHOGS

Office Address: 1600 Lone Star Parkway, Grand Prairie, TX 75050.
Telephone: (972) 504-9383. **Fax:** (972) 504-2288.
Website: www.airhogsbaseball.com. **Email:** info@airhogsbaseball.com.
President/General Manager: J.T. Onyett.
VP of Hospitality: Nate Gutierrez. **Directors, Business Development:** Tim Costello, Jason Anderson, Justin Terry, Matt Smith. **Coordinator, Digital Marketing:** Molly Onyett. **Field Manager:** John McLaren

GAME INFORMATION
Broadcaster: Tim Costello. **No of Games Broadcast:** 100. **Webcast:** www.airhogsbaseball.com. **Stadium Name:** AirHogs Stadium. **Location:** From I-30, take Beltline Road exit going north, take Lone Star Park entrance towards the stadium. **Standard Game Times:** Mon.-Sat., 7:05 pm, Sun., 2:05 pm (May-June), 6:05 pm (July-September).

WINNIPEG GOLDEYES

Office Address: One Portage Ave E, Winnipeg, Manitoba R3B 3N3.
Telephone: (204) 982-2273. **Fax:** (204) 982-2274.
Email Address: goldeyes@goldeyes.com. **Website:** www.goldeyes.com.
Operated by: Winnipeg Goldeyes Baseball Club, Inc.
Principal Owner/President: Sam Katz. **General Manager:** Andrew Collier. **Vice President & COO:** Regan Katz. **CFO:** Jason McRae-King. **Director, Sales/Marketing:** Dan Chase. **Manager, Box Office:** Paul Duque. **Coordinator, Food/Beverage:** Melissa Schlichting. **Account Executive:** Steve Schuster. **Suite Manager/Sales & Marketing:** Angela Sanche. **Media Coordinator:** Nigel Batchelor. **Manager, Retail:** Kendra Gibson. **Controller:** Kim Saito. **Facility Manager:** Don Ferguson. **Executive Assistant:** Sherri Rheubottom. **Administrative Assistant:** Bonnie Benson. **Manager/Director, Player Procurement:** Rick Forney. **Coach:** Tom Vaeth. **Clubhouse Manager:** Jamie Samson.

GAME INFORMATION
Radio Announcer: Steve Schuster. **No. of Games Broadcast:** 100. **Flagship Station:** CJNU 93.7 FM. **Stadium Name:** Shaw Park. **Location:** North on Pembina Highway to Broadway, East on Broadway to Main Street, North on Main Street to Water Avenue, East on Water Avenue to Westbrook Street, North on Westbrook Street to Lombard Avenue, East on Lombard Avenue to Mill Street, South on Mill Street to ballpark. **Standard Game Times:** Mon.-Fri., 7:00 pm, Sat., 6:00 pm, Sun., 1:00 pm.

ATLANTIC LEAGUE

Mailing Address: PO Box 5190, Lancaster, Pa., 17606.
Telephone: (720) 389-6992 or (978) 790-5421
Email Address: info@atlanticleague.com. **Website:** www.atlanticleague.com.
Year Founded: 1998.
Founder/Chairman: Frank Boulton.
Senior Vice Presidents/Executive Committee: Frank Boulton, Bill Shipley, Bob Zlotnik.
President: Rick White. **League Administrator:** Emily Merrill.
Division Structure: Freedom—Lancaster, Southern Maryland, Sugar Land, York.
Liberty—High Point, Long Island, New Britain, Somerset.
Regular Season: 126 games (split-schedule).
2019 Opening Date: April 25. **Closing Date:** Sept. 22. **All-Star Game:** July 10, at York.
Playoff Format: First-half division winners meet second-half winners in best-of-five series; Winners meet in best-of-five final for league championship.
Roster Limit: 25. Teams may keep 27 players from start of season until May 31. **Eligibility Rule:** No restrictions; MLB and MiLB suspensions honored.
Brand of Baseball: Rawlings. **Statistical Service:** Pointstreak.

STADIUM INFORMATION

Club	Stadium	Opened	Dimensions LF	CF	RF	Capacity	2018 Att.
High Point Rockers	BB&T Point	2019	336	400	339	4,024	NA
Lancaster	Clipper Magazine Stadium	2005	372	400	300	6,000	249,792
Long Island	Bethpage Ballpark	2000	325	400	325	6,002	349,058
New Britain	New Britain Stadium	1996	330	400	330	6,146	183,147
Somerset	TD Bank Ballpark	1999	317	402	315	6,100	352,603
So. Maryland	Regency Furniture Stadium	2008	305	400	320	6,000	205,947
Sugar Land	Constellation Field	2012	348	405	325	7,500	328,491
York	PeoplesBank Park	2007	300	400	325	5,000	180,807

HIGH POINT ROCKERS

Office Address: 214 Lindsay Street, High Point, NC 27262
Telephone: (336) 888-1000
E-Mail Address: info@highpointrockers.com.
Website: www.highpointrockers.com
Owner: High Point Baseball, Inc.
President: Ken Lehner. **Assistant General Manager:** Christian Heimall. **Director of Ticket Sales:** Susan Ormond. **Ticket Operations Manager:** Leighton Foster. **Facilities Operations Manager:** Shane Poling. **Office & Retail Manager:** Ashley Kearns. **Account Executive:** Matthew Scott. **Account Executive:** Brittany Llewellan. **Corporate Sales Manager:** David Martin. **Field Manager:** Jamie Keefe. **Pitching Coach:** Frank Viola. **Bench Coach & Player Procurement:** Billy Horn.

GAME INFORMATION
No. of Games Broadcast: 140. **Flagship Station:** www.highpointrockers.com. **Stadium Name:** BB&T Point.
Location: 214 Lindsay Street, High Point, NC 27262. **Standard Game Times:** Mon.-Thur., Sat., 6:35 pm, Fri., 7:05 pm, Sun., 2:05 pm. **Visiting Club Hotel:** Red Lion Hotel. 135 S. Main Street, High Point, NC 27262.

LANCASTER BARNSTORMERS

Office Address: 650 North Prince Street, Lancaster, PA 17603
Telephone: (717) 509-4487
Website: www.lancasterbarnstormers.com.
General Manager: Michael Reynolds. **VP, Marketing:** Kristen Simon. **Director of Finance:** Phil Soto-Ortiz. **Corporate Sales Manager:** John Erisman. **Corporate Sales Manager:** Melissa Tucker. **Director of Community Relationships:** Maureen Wheeler. **Director, Media Relations/Broadcasting:** Dave Collins. **Vice President of Stadium Operations:** Mike Logan. **Director, Ticket Operations:** Michael Kalchick. **Human Resource Generalist:** Tania Atkinson. **Director of Special Events and Promotions:** Alex Einhorn. **Business Development Specialist, Groups:** Adam Smith. **Business Development Specialist, Groups:** Brett Snyder. **Promotions & Sponsorship Fulfillment Manager:** Alexandra Bunn. **Business Development Specialist, Groups:** Andrew Spanos. **Operations Manager:** Tim Snyder. **Box Office Manager:** Doug Condran. **Business Development Specialist, Groups:** Kyle Witman. **Senior Staffing and Mascot Coordinator:** Lori Krchnar. **Cleaning Services Supervisor:** Miggy Rosado. **Creative Services Coordinator:** Ryan Cortazzo. **Group Sales Manager:** Samantha Biastre. **Corporate Sales**

Representative: Alison Kelser. **Director of Marketing:** Debra MacDonald. **Business Development Specialist, Season Tickets:** Christopher Heal. **Business Development Specialist, Season Tickets:** Taylor Gunden. **Business Development Specialist, Season Tickets:** Erica Giuliani. **Business Development Specialist, Season Tickets:** PJ McClane. **Client Relations Representative:** Yvette Ramos. **Manager:** Ross Peeples. **Baseball Operations Manager:** Troy Steffy.

GAME INFORMATION
Stadium: Clipper Magazine Stadium. **Location:** 650 North Prince Street, Lancaster, PA 17603. **Standard Game Times:** Mon.-Fri., 7:00 pm, Sat., 6:00 pm, Sun., 1:00 pm.

LONG ISLAND DUCKS

Mailing Address: 3 Court House Dr, Central Islip, NY 11722.
Telephone: (631) 940-3825. **Fax:** (631) 940-3800.
Email Address: info@liducks.com. **Website:** www.liducks.com.
Operated by: Long Island Ducks Professional Baseball Club, LLC.
Founder/CEO: Frank Boulton. **Owner/Chairman:** Seth Waugh. **Owner/Senior Vice President, Baseball Operations:** Bud Harrelson. **President/General Manager:** Michael Pfaff. **Assistant GM/Senior VP, Sales:** Doug Cohen. **Senior Director, Administration:** Gerry Anderson. **VP, Sales/Operations:** John Wolff. **Director, Season Sales:** Brad Kallman. **Manager, Box Office:** Ben Harper. **Director, Media Relations/Broadcasting:** Michael Polak. **Director, Marketing/Promotions:** Jordan Schiff. **Staff Accountant:** Annmarie DeMasi. **Manager, Group Sales:** Sean Smith. **Manager, Merchandise/Client Services:** Katelyn Paquette. **Manager, Stadium Operations:** DJ Bornschein. **Coordinator, Administration:** Michelle Jensen. **Account Executives:** Camilo Paez, Anthony Fiorelli. **Head Groundskeeper:** Brett Franklin. **Field Manager:** Wally Backman. **Coaches:** Ed Lynch, Lew Ford. **Coordinator, Medical Services:** Tony Amin. **Head Trainer:** Dotty Pitchford.

GAME INFORMATION
Radio Announcers: Michael Polak, Chris King, David Weiss. **No. of Games Broadcast:** 140 on LIDucks.com, Facebook Live and YouTube. **PA Announcer:** Bob Ottone. **Official Scorer:** Michael Polak.

NEW BRITAIN BEES

Office Address: 230 John Karbonic Way, New Britain, CT 06051
Telephone: (860) 826-2337.
Email Address: info@nbbees.com. **Website:** www.nbbees.com.
Operated by: Hard Hittin' Professional Baseball, LLC.
Principal Owner: Anthony Iacovone. **Partner:** Frank Boulton, Michael Pfaff. **General Manager:** Brad Smith.
Assistant GM: Paul Herrmann. **Business Manager:** Bret DeRosa. **Box Office Manager:** Cory Cohen. **Sales Director:** Tony Gionfriddo. **Account Executive:** Sal Scarpati. **Account Executive:** Tim Moro. **Field Manager:** Mauro Gozzo.

GAME INFORMATION
Stadium Name: New Britain Stadium. **Location:** 230 John Karbonic Way, New Britain, CT 06051. **Directions:** From Route 9, take the ramp left towards New Britain, Merge onto CT-571 via exit 24 on left toward CT-71/CT-371/Kensington. Take the CT-71 ramp toward Kensington, and then make slight left onto John Karbonic Way. **Standard Game Times:** Mon.-Sat., 6:35 pm, Sun., 1:35 pm.

SOMERSET PATRIOTS

Office Address: One Patriots Park, Bridgewater, NJ 08807.
Telephone: (908) 252-0700. **Fax:** (908) 252-0776.
Website: www.somersetpatriots.com.
Operated by: Somerset Baseball Partners, LLC. **Principal Owners:** Steve Kalafer, Josh Kalafer, Jonathan Kalafer. **Chairman Emeritus:** Steve Kalafer. **Chairmen:** Josh Kalafer and Jonathan Kalafer. **President/General Manager:** Patrick McVerry. **Senior Vice President, Marketing:** Dave Marek. **VP, Public Relations:** Marc Russinoff. **VP, Operations:** Bryan Iwicki. **VP, Ticket Operations:** Matt Kopas. **Senior Director, Merchandise:** Rob Crossman. **Director, Tickets:** Nick Cherrillo. **Director, Broadcasting & Media Relations:** Marc Schwartz. **Director, Marketing:** Hal Hansen. **Corporate Sales Manager:** Ken Smith. **Group Sales Managers:** Matt Hayden, Zach Keller, Nick Izzo, Mike Seppi. **Ticket Office, Manager:** Tim O'Leary. **Executive Assistant to GM:** Michele DaCosta. **Senior VP/Treasurer:** Ron Schulz. **Accountant:** Stephanie DePass. **GM, HomePlate Catering/Hospitality:** Mike McDermott. **Operations Manager, HomePlate Catering/Hospitality:** Jimmy Search. **Head Groundskeeper:** Dan Purner. **Field Manager:** Brett Jodie. **Hitting/Third Base Coach:** Glen Barker. **Pitching Coach/Director, Baseball Operations:** Jon Hunton. **Athletic Trainer:** Phil Lee. **Manager Emeritus:** Sparky Lyle.

GAME INFORMATION
Radio Announcer: Marc Schwartz. **No. of Games Broadcast:** Home-70, Away-70. **Flagship Station:** WCTC 1450-AM. **Video Streams:** SPN.tv. **Ballpark Name:** TD Bank Ballpark. **Standard Game Times:** Mon.-Sat., 7:05 pm, Sun., 1:05 pm.

SOUTHERN MARYLAND
BLUE CRABS

Office Address: 11765 St. Linus Drive, Waldorf, Maryland 20602.
Telephone: (301) 638-9788.
Principal Owners: Crabs On Deck LLC.
General Manager: Courtney Knichel. **Marketing Manager:** Hayley Bingham.
Director, Sales: Tom Fink. **Box Office Manager:** Devin Monahan. **Sales Executive:** Mario Pietroluongo. **Sales Executive:** Seth Distler. **Director of Operations:** Tim Lillis. **Operations Assistant:** Michael McPherson. **Field Manager:** Stan Cliburn. **Hitting Coach:** Kash Beauchamp

GAME INFORMATION

Radio Announcer: Andrew Bandstra. **Stadium Name:** Blue Crabs Stadium.
Standard Game Times: Mon.-Sat., 6:35 pm; Sun. 2:05 pm.

SUGAR LAND SKEETERS

Office Address: 1 Stadium Drive, Sugar Land, Texas, 77498.
Telephone: (281) 240-4487.
Owners: Bob, Kevin and Marcie Zlotnik. **Special Advisor:** Deacon Jones.
General Manager: Tyler Stamm. **Senior Vice President, Sales and Marketing:** Bob Merril. **Vice President, Community:** Kyle Dawson. **Executive Administrator:** Kailee Kubicek. **Director, Finances:** Greg Hodges. **Vice President, Sales:** Scott Podsim. **Director, Ticket Sales:** Jennifer Schwarz. **Box Office Manager:** Kaitlin Klinchock. **Operations Director:** Clayton Lemke. **Head Groundskeeper:** Brad Detmore. **Assistant Groundskeeper:** Robert Croteau. **Vice President, Events:** Matt Thompson. **Special Events Manager:** Eddy Juarez. **Event Operations Manager:** Russell Wohldmann. **Event Operations Manager:** Douglas Failing. **Senior Sales Managers:** Sunny Okpon. **Sales Managers:** Daniel Linan, Ashley Richter, Dolores Townley. **Vice President, Customer Service:** Adam Mettler. **Vice President, Sponsorship Sales:** Chris Parsons. **Marketing/Digital Media Coordinator:** Megan Murnane. **Media Relations Coordinator/Broadcaster:** Ryan Posner. **Community Relations Manager:** Sallie Weir. **Video Production Coordinator:** Troy Young. **Graphics Coordinator:** Shay Villarreal. **Mascot Coordinator:** Megan Brown. **Legends General Manager:** Greg Hernandez. **Legends Events Manager:** Jay Lero. **Legends Accountant:** Andrea Jennings. **Legends Operations Manager:** Ginavieve Strickland. **Executive Chef:** Eric Robison. **Field Manager:** Pete Incaviglia. **Team Doctor:** Dr. Bhojani. **Athletic Trainer:** Max Mahaffey.

GAME INFORMATION

Radio Announcer: Ryan Posner. **No. of Games Broadcast:** 70. **Flagship Streaming Station:** YouTube. **Standard Game Times:** Mon.-Fri., 7:05 pm, Sat., 6:05 pm, Sun., 2:05 pm. **Visiting Club Hotel:** Sugar Land Marriott Town Square. **Telephone:** (281) 275-8400.

YORK REVOLUTION

Office Address: 5 Brooks Robinson Way, York, PA 17401.
Telephone: (717) 801-4487. **Fax:** (717) 801-4499.
Email Address: info@yorkrevolution.com. **Website:** www.yorkrevolution.com.
Operated by: York Professional Baseball Club, LLC. **Principal Owners:** York Professional Baseball Club, LLC.
President: Eric Menzer. **General Manager/Vice President, Operations:** John Gibson. **VP, Business Development:** Nate Tile. **Finance Coordinator:** Jen Martin. **Finance Assistant:** Mike Allen. **Director, Ticketing:** Cindy Brown. **Box Office Manager:** Bob Gibson. **Director, Marketing/Communications:** Doug Eppler. **Director, Fan Engagement:** Reed Gunderson. **Creative Director:** Cody Bannon. **Marketing Manager:** Sarah Dailey. **Senior Account Executives:** Mary Beth Ching, Brandon Tesluk. **Account Executives:** Brett Pietrzak, Allyson Stough. **Season Ticket Account Executive:** Jordan Haidle. **Director, Client Services:** Tylor Toll. **Director, Operations:** David Dicce. **Director, Special Events:** Adam Nugent. **Revolution Hospitality GM:** Rob Wilson. **Revolution Hospitality Catering Manager:** Kate Hammond. **Revolution Hospitality Chef:** Tiffany Livering. **Revolution Hospitality Concessions Manager:** Amanda Shusko. **Revolution Retail Manager:** Kelsey Dorner. **Field Manager:** Mark Mason. **Pitching Coach:** Paul Fletcher. **Bench/Third Base Coach:** Enohel Polanco.

GAME INFORMATION

WOYK GM/Broadcaster: Darrell Henry. **No. of Games Broadcast:** 140. **Flagship Station:** WOYK 1350 AM. **Official Scorer:** Brian Wisler. **Stadium Name:** PeoplesBank Park. **Standard Game Times:** Mon.-Sat., 6:30 pm, Sun., 1:00 pm. **Visiting Club Hotel:** Wyndham Garden York, 2000 Loucks Road, York, PA 17408. **Telephone:** (717) 846-9500.

CAN-AM LEAGUE

Office Address: 610 Yount Dr. Dayton OH 45433.
Telephone: (862) 283-5935. **Fax:** (919) 401-8152.
Website: www.canamleague.com.
Year Founded: 2005.
Executive Director: Kevin Winn.
Regular Season: 100 games. **2019 Opening Date:** May 16. **Closing Date:** Sept. 2.
All-Star Game: Can-Am vs. Frontier League, July 10 at Rockland.
Playoff Format: Top four teams meet in best-of-five semifinals; winners meet in best-of-five finals.
Roster Limit: 22. **Eligibility Rule:** Minimum of five and maximum of eight first-year players; minimum of five players must be an LS-4 or higher; a maximum of four may be veterans.
Brand of Baseball: Rawlings.
Statistician: Pointstreak.com.

STADIUM INFORMATION

Club	Stadium	Opened	Dimensions LF	CF	RF	Capacity	2018 Att.
New Jersey	Yogi Berra Stadium	1998	308	398	308	3,784	83,610
Ottawa	RCGT Park	1993	325	404	325	10,332	93,395
Quebec	Stade Canac de Québec	1938	315	385	315	4,500	126,483
Rockland	Provident Bank Park	2011	323	403	313	4,750	129,599
Sussex County	Skylands Stadium	1994	330	392	330	4,200	74,827
Trois-Rivieres	Stade Stereo+	1938	342	372	342	4,500	91,605

NEW JERSEY JACKALS

Office Address: 8 Yogi Berra Drive, Little Falls, NJ 07424. **Telephone:** (973) 746-7434.
Email Address: contact@jackals.com. **Website:** www.jackals.com.
Owner/President: Al Dorso. **President, Baseball Operations:** Gregory Lockard.
Sr. Vice President, Operations: Al Dorso Jr. **Vice President, Marketing:** Mike Dorso.
Coordinator, Group Sales: Kristopher Jones. **Director, Creative Services:** Dennis Mark.
Public Relations: Steven Solomon. **Field Manager:** Brooks Carey.

GAME INFORMATION

Webcast Announcer: Alex Cammarata. **No. of Games Broadcast:** 100. **Webcast Address:** www.jackals.com.
Stadium Name: Yogi Berra Stadium. **Location:** On the campus of Montclair State University; Route 80 or Garden State Parkway to Route 46, take Valley Road exit to Montclair State University. **Standard Game Times:** Mon.-Fri., 7:05 pm, Sat., 6:05 pm., Sun., 2:05 pm.

OTTAWA CHAMPIONS

Office Address: 300 Coventry Road, Ottawa, ON K1K 4P5.
Telephone: (613) 745-2255. **Fax:** (613) 745-3289.
Email Address: info@ottawachampions.com. **Website:** www.ottawachampions.com.
Owner: Miles Wolff. **Assistant General Manager:** Davyd Balloch. **Director, Business Operations and Ticketing:** Ian Hooper. **Director of Communications:** Michael Nellis. **Director of Game Ops/Promotions:** Martin Boyce. **Director of Player Procurement:** Doug Simunic. **Field Manager:** Sebastien Boucher.
Coaches: Jared Lemieux, Phillippe Aumont.

GAME INFORMATION

Broadcaster—English: Mike Nellis. **Broadcaster—French:** Dominic Murray. **Webcast—English/French. Webcast Address:** www.ckdj.net. **Stadium Name:** Raymond Chabot Grant Thornton Park. **Location:** From Hwy #417 (Queensway), take Vanier Parkway (Exit #117). Turn right on to Coventry Road. Raymond Chabot Grant Thornton Park is at your immediate right. **Standard Game Times:** Mon-Sat., 7:05 pm, Sun., 1:35 pm.

QUEBEC CAPITALES

Owners: Jean Tremblay, Pierre Tremblay, Marie-Pierre Simard.
President: Michel Laplante. **General Manager:** Bobby Baril. **Administrative Coordinator:** Julie Lefrancois. **Marketing:** Anne-Pier Couture. **Communications Manager:** Jean Grignon-Francke. **Souvenir Shop:** Jean-Philippe Otis. **Baseball Operations:** Charles Demers. **Victoria Baseball Complex:** Alexandre Harvey. **Graphic Consultant:** Frederic Gariépy. **Administrative Officer:** Francine Gendron.

Ticketing: Émilie Grenier. **Field Manager:** Patrick Scalabrini. **Pitching Coach:** Karl Gelinas. **Coach:** Jean-Philippe Roy.

GAME INFORMATION

Stadium Name: Stade Canac de Québec. **Location:** Highway 40 to Highway 173 (Centre-Ville) exit 2 to Parc Victoria. **Standard Game Times:** Mon.-Fri., 7:05 pm, Sat., 6:05 pm, Sun., 1:05 pm.

ROCKLAND BOULDERS

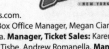

Office Address: 1 Palisades Credit Union Park Drive, Pomona, NY 10970.
Telephone: (845) 364-0009. **Fax:** (845) 364-0001.
E-Mail Address: info@rocklandboulders.com. **Website:** rocklandboulders.com.
President/General Manager: Shawn Reilly. Assistant General Manager, Box Office Manager, Megan Ciampo.
Director of Finance: Michele Almash. **Manager, Retail Store:** Deidra Verona. **Manager, Ticket Sales:** Karen McCombs.
Assistant Manager, Ticket Sales: Courtney Vardi. **Account Executives:** Joe Tisbe, Andrew Romanella. **Manager, Promotions and Entertainment:** Julie Trainor. **Coordinator, Facilities and Operations:** Bobby Nodelman. **Director, Public Relations and Media:** Steve Balsan. **Director, Educational Outreach:** Gail Gultz. **Director, Community Relations:** Vanessa Mauriello. **Manager, Concessions:** Danyel Del Rosario-Alvarado. **Director, Security:** Jeff Rinaldi. **Audio/Visual Specialist:** Jim Houston. **Assistant, Audio/Video Specialist:** Brad Sarno. **Field Manager:** Kevin Baez. **Athletic Trainer:** Lori Rahaim. **Director of Player Development and Scouting:** Kevin Tuve

GAME INFORMATION

Broadcaster: Marc Ernay. **No. of Games Broadcast:** 55. **Flagship Station:** WRCR 1700-AM. TV – Eleven Sports. **Webcast Address:** www.canamleague.tv. **Stadium Name:** Palisades Credit Union Park. **Location:** Take Palisades Parkway Exit 12 towards Route 45, make left at stop sign on Conklin Road, make left on Route 45, turn right on Pomona Road, take 1st right on Fireman's Memorial Drive. **Standard Game Times:** Mon.-Sat., 6:30 pm, Sun., 1:35 pm (May-June), 5:00 pm (July-August).

SUSSEX COUNTY MINERS

Owner, President: Al Dorso Sr.
President, Baseball Operations: Greg Lockard. **Vice President, Operations:** Al Dorso Jr. **Vice President, Marketing:** Mike Dorso. **Gemela Manager:** Justin Ferrarella.
Director, Creative Services: Dennis Mark. **Director, Broadcasting and Media Relations:** Bret Leuthner. **Manager, Corporate Partnerships:** Joann Ciancitto. **Concessions Manager:** Scott Goriscak. **Group Sales Coordinator:** Marina Agacinski. **Youth Programs Coordinator:** Adrienne Lina. **Senior Graphic Design:** Will Romano. **Graphic Design:** Georgina Fakhoury. **Field Manager/Director of Baseball Operations:** Bobby Jones. **Bench Coach:** Vladimir Fontalvo Jr. **Assistant Coach:** Simon Walters. **Athletic Trainer:** Steven Chen.

GAME INFORMATION

Broadcaster: Bret Leuthner. **No. of Games Broadcast:** 100. **Webcast Address:** www.scminers.com. **Stadium Name:** Skylands Stadium. **Location:** In New Jersey, I-80 to exit 34B (Route 15 North) to Route 565 North; From Pennsylvania, I-84 to Route 6 (Matamoras) to Route 206 North to Route 565 North. **Standard Game Times:** Mon.-Fri., 7:05 pm, Sat., 6:05 pm, Sun., 2:05 pm (May-June, Sept.), 4:05 pm (July-August).

TROIS-RIVIÈRES AIGLES

Office Address: 1760 Avenue Gilles-Villeneuve, Trois-Rivières, QC G9A 5K8.
Telephone: (819) 379-0404. **Email Address:** info@lesaiglestr.com.
Website: www.lesaiglestr.com
President: Marc-André Bergeron. **General Manager:** René Martin.
Director, Marketing: Zoé Labranche-Newbury. **Director, Communications :** Zoé Labranche-Newbury.
Box Office/Accounting: Frédérik Bélanger. **Field Manager:** T.J. Stanton. **Coaches:** Matthew Rusch, Chris Torres.

GAME INFORMATION

Broadcaster: Simon Laliberté. **No. of Games Broadcast:** 65. **Webcast Address:** www.cfou.ca/direct.php **Stadium Name:** Stade de Trois-Rivières. **Location:** Take Hwy 40 West, exit Boul. des Forges/Centre-ville, keep right, turn right at light, turn right at stop sign. **Standard Game Times:** Mon.-Fri., 7:05 pm., Sat.-Sun., 1:05 pm.

FRONTIER LEAGUE

Office Address: 2041 Goose Lake Rd Suite 2A, Sauget, IL 62206.
Telephone: (618) 215-4134. **Fax:** (618) 332-2115.
Email Address: office@frontierleague.com. **Website:** www.frontierleague.com.
Year Founded: 1993.
Commissioner: Bill Lee.
Deputy Commissioner: Steve Tahsler.
President: Rich Sauget (Gateway). **Vice President, Operations:** Tom Kramig (Lake Erie).
Vice President, Marketing: John Stanley (Evansville)
Board of Directors: Kim Brown (Florence), Nick Semaca (Joliet), Dan Dial (River City),
Brian Lyter (Schaumburg), Mike Pinto (Southern Illinois), Stu Williams (Washington), Al Oremus (Windy City).
Division Structure: East—Joliet, Lake Erie, Schaumburg, Washington,
Windy City. **West**—Evansville, Florence, Gateway, River City, Southern Illinois.
Regular Season: 96 games. **2019 Opening Date:** May 9. **Closing Date:** Sept 1.
All-Star Game: Wednesday, July 10 vs. Can-Am League at Rockland
Playoff Format: Two division winners and next two best records; two best-of-five rounds.
Roster Limit: 24. **Eligibility Rule:** Minimum of twelve Rookie 1/Rookie 2 players. No player may be 27 prior to Oct. 1
of current season with one exemption. **Brand of Baseball:** Rawlings.
Statistician: Pointstreak/Stack Sports, 5360 Legacy Drive, Suite #150, Plano, TX 75024.

STADIUM INFORMATION

Club	Stadium	Opened	Dimensions LF	CF	RF	Capacity	2018 Att.
Evansville	Bosse Field	1915	315	415	315	5,110	94,498
Florence	UC Health Stadium	2004	325	395	325	4,200	105,805
Gateway	GCS Ballpark	2002	318	395	325	5,500	125,536
Joliet	Joliet Route 66 Stadium	2002	330	400	327	6,229	88,198
Lake Erie	Sprenger Stadium	2009	325	400	325	5,000	101,229
River City	CarShield Field	1999	320	382	299	4,989	85,036
Schaumburg	Schaumburg Stadium	1999	355	400	353	8,107	149,255
So. Illinois	Rent One Park	2007	325	400	330	4,500	109,691
Washington	Wild Things Park	2002	325	400	325	3,200	87,534
Windy City	Standard Bank Stadium	1999	335	390	335	2,598	78,177

EVANSVILLE OTTERS

Mailing Address: 23 Don Mattingly Way, Evansville, IN 47711.
Telephone: (812) 435-8686. **Website:** www.evansvilleotters.com.
Facebook—Evansville Otters, **Twitter**—@EvilleOtters, **Instagram**—@evansvilleotters
Operated by: Evansville Baseball, LLC. **Owner:** Bussing family. **President:** John Stanley.
Vice President, Sales: Joel Padfield. **Assistant General Manager:** Josh Hack Wilson. **Director of Marketing/
Community Relations:** Elspeth Urbina. **Director of Communications:** Preston Leinenbach. **PA Announcer:** Zane
Clodfelter. **Gift Shop Manager:** Rhonda Trail. **Account Executive:** Keith Millikan, Zoe Urbina. **Sports Turf Manager:**
Lance Adler. **Field Manager:** Andy McCauley.

GAME INFORMATION

No. of Games Broadcast: Home-48, Away-48. **Radio/Video Stream:** evansvilleotters.com (Otters Digital Network).
Stadium Name: Bosse Field (Opened in 1915). **Directions:** US 41 to Lloyd Expressway West (IN-62), Main St Exit, Right
on Main St, ahead 1 mile to Bosse Field. **Standard Game Times:** Mon.-Sat., 6:35 pm, Sun., 12:35, 5:05. **Doubleheaders:**
5:35 p.m. **Visiting Club Hotel:** Clarion Inn & Suites, 5538 E Indiana St., Evansville, IN 47715. **Phone:** (812) 477-6663.

FLORENCE FREEDOM

Office Address: 7950 Freedom Way, Florence, KY, 41042.
Telephone: (859) 594-4487. **Fax:** (859) 594-3194.
Email Address: info@florencefreedom.com.
Operated by: Canterbury Baseball, LLC.
President/GM of Operations: Kim Brown. **VP/General Manager:** Josh Anderson.
Assistant GM of Premium Ticket Sales: Amanda Sipple. **Director of Corporate Partnerships:** Knicko Hartung.
Box Office Manager: Eric Cox. **Director of PR & Promotions:** Hannah Siefert. **Account Executive:** Aaron Luken.
Director of Amateur Baseball & Stadium Operations: Morgan Dougherty. **Bookkeeper:** Max Johnson. **Group Sales
Executive:** Eric Quallen. **Field Manager:** Dennis Pelfrey. **Pitching Coach:** Unavailable. **Hitting Coach:** Unavailable.

GAME INFORMATION

Official Scorer: Unavailable. **Stadium:** UC Health Stadium. **Location:** I-71/75 South to exit 180, left onto US 42, right on Freedom Way; I-71/75 North to exit 180. **Standard Game Times:** Mon.-Thurs., 6:35 pm, Fri., 7:05 pm, Sat.-Sun., 6:05 pm. **Visiting Club Hotel:** Microtel Inn & Suites, Florence, KY

GATEWAY GRIZZLIES

Telephone: (618) 337-3000. **Fax:** (618) 332-3625.
Email Address: info@gatewaygrizzlies.com. **Website:** www.gatewaygrizzlies.com
Operated by: Gateway Baseball, LLC. **Managing Officer:** Rich Sauget.
General Manager: Steven Gomric. **Assistant General Manager, Director of Stadium Operations and Events:** Kurt Ringkamp. **Assistant General Manager, Director of Sales & Marketing:** James Caldwell. **Radio & Media Broadcaster:** Nate Gatter. **Director of Community Relations:** Gayle Lymer. **Box Office & Business Manager:** Brett Helfrich. **Director of New Media & In-Game Entertainment:** Brody Bence. **Marketing Director:** Collin Vieth. **Director of Promotions and Fan Engagement:** Brady Huber. **Operations & Events Assistants:** Jacob Vantrees and Brenndon Tindall. **Assistant Box Office Manager:** Justin Dettmann. **Assistant Marketing Manager:** Kaylee Roskowski. **Field Manager:** Phil Warren. **Athletic Trainer:** Geof Manzo.

GAME INFORMATION

Radio Announcer: Nate Gatter. **No. of Games Broadcast:** Home-50, Away-48. **PA Announcer:** Tom Calhoun. **Stadium Name:** GCS Ballpark. **Location:** I-255 at exit 15 (Mousette Lane). **Standard Game Times:** Mon.-Sat., 7:05 pm, Sun., 6:05 pm.

JOLIET SLAMMERS

Office Address: 1 Mayor Art Schultz Dr, Joliet, IL 60432
Telephone: (815) 722-2287
E-Mail Address: info@jolietslammers.com. **Website:** www.jolietslammers.com
Owner: Joliet Community Baseball & Entertainment, LLC.
General Manager: Heather Mills. **VP of Sales & Marketing:** John Wilson. **Director of Food/Beverage:** Tom Fremarek. **Director, Community Relations:** Ken Miller. **Director, Tournaments & Special Events:** Cor Herbert. **Group Sales Manager:** Lauren Rhodes. **Account Executive:** TJ Propp. **Corporate Sales and Service Manager:** Alisa Lerario. **Inside Sales Representatives:** Casey Bucz, Christine Bialbok, Niko Daniello. **Field Manager:** Jeff Isom.

GAME INFORMATION

No. of Games Broadcast: 96. **Flagship Station:** www.jolietslammers.com. **Official Scorer:** Dave Laketa. **Stadium Name:** Joliet Route 66 Stadium. **Location:** 1 Mayor Art Schultz Drive, Joliet, IL 60432. **Standard Game Times:** Mon.-Fri., 7:05 pm, Sat., 6:05 pm., Sun., 1:05 pm. **Visiting Club Hotel:** Harrah's Casino Joliet & Joliet Super 8.

LAKE ERIE CRUSHERS

Address: 2009 Baseball Boulevard. Avon, Ohio 44011.
Telephone: 440-934-3636. **Website:** www.lakeeriecrushers.com.
Operated by: Blue Dog Baseball, LLC. **Managing Officer:** Tom Kramig.
VP Operations: Paul Siegwarth. **Accountant:** DJ Saylor. **Box Office Manager:** Collin DeJong, Allison Albers. **Director, Concessions/Catering:** Greg Kobunski. **Digital Marketing Manager & Promotions:** Catie Graf. Shelly Carandang. **Promotions Manager:** Kelly Scott. **Director of Ticketing:** Jay Miller. **Account Executive:** Matt Moos, Mike Mays. Chris Meyer, Ryan Acus, Kyle Wagoner. **Director, Broadcasting:** Andy Barch. **Field Manager:** Cam Roth

GAME INFORMATION
Stadium Name: Sprenger Health Care Stadium. **Location:** Intersection of I-90 and Colorado Ave in Avon, OH.
Standard Game Times: Mon.-Sat., 7:05 pm, Sun., 2:05 pm.

RIVER CITY RASCALS

Office Address: 900 TR Hughes Blvd, O'Fallon, MO 63366.
Telephone: (636) 240-2287. **Fax:** (636) 240-7313.
Email Address: info@rivercityrascals.com. **Website:** www.rivercityrascals.com.
Operated by: PS and J Professional Baseball Club LLC.
Owners: Tim Hoeksema, Jan Hoeksema, Fred Stratton, Anne Stratton, Pam Malliet, Steve Malliet, Michael Veeck, Greg Wendt. **President:** Dan Dial. **General Manager:** David Schmoll. **Director of Tickets:** Nicole Anderson. **Director of Stadium Operations:** Tom Bauer. **Group Sales & Box Office Manager:** Kyle Lewis. **Director of Entertainment:** Jacey Clemens. **Sr. Director of Business Operations:** Carrie Green. **Field Manager:** Steve Brook. **Bench Coach:** Alex Ferguson, Josh Lundy.

GAME INFORMATION
No. of Games Broadcast: Home-48, Away-48. **PA Announcer:** Mike Kromer. **Stadium Name:** CarShield Field.
Location: I-70 to exit 219, north on TR Hughes Road, follow signs to ballpark. **Standard Game Times:** Mon.-Sat., 6:35 pm, Sun., 5:05 pm. **Visiting Club Hotel:** America's Best Value Inn 1310 Bass Pro Drive St Charles, MO. **Telephone:** (636) 947-5900.

SCHAUMBURG BOOMERS

Office Address: 1999 Springinsguth Road, Schaumburg, IL 60193
Email Address: info@boomersbaseball.com. **Website:** www.boomersbaseball.com
Owned by: Pat and Lindy Salvi. **General Manager:** Michael Larson. **Business Manager:** Todd Fulk. **Director of Facilities:** Mike Tlusty. **Director Food/Beverage:** Devin Maney.
Broadcaster: Tim Calderwood. **Box Office Manager:** Anthony Giammanco. **Director of Promotions:** Riley Anderson. **Director of Community Relations:** Peter Long. **Director of Stadium Operations:** Collin Cunningham. **Account Executive:** Hanna Olson. **Baseball Operations & Account Executive:** Drew Winter. **Account Executive:** Allyson Jefferson. **Field Manager:** Jamie Bennett.

GAME INFORMATION
Broadcaster: Tim Calderwood. **No. of Games Broadcast:** Home-48, Away-48. **Flagship Station:** WRMN 1410 AM Elgin. **Stadium:** Schaumburg Boomers Stadium. **Location:** I-290 to Thorndale Ave Exit, head West on Elgin-O'Hare Expressway until Springinsguth Road Exit, second left at Springinsguth Road (shared parking lot with Schaumburg Metra Station). **Visiting Club Hotel:** AmericInn Hotel & Suites, 1300 East Higgins Road, Schaumburg IL 60173.

SOUTHERN ILLINOIS MINERS

Office Address: Rent One Park, 1000 Miners Drive, Marion, IL 62959.
Telephone: (618) 998-8499. **Fax:** (618) 969-8550.
Email Address: info@southernillinoisminers.com. **Website:** southernillinoisminers.com.
Operated by: Southern Illinois Baseball Group. **Owner:** Jayne Simmons.
Chief Operating Officer: Mike Pinto. **General Manager:** Cathy Perry. **Assistant General Manager:** Will Niermann. **Stadium Operations:** Joe Klinger. **Director, Ticket Operations:** Zach Smith. **Director, Video Production/Creative Services:** Unavailable. **Director, Promotions:** Katie Basil. **Director, Radio Broadcasting/Media Relations:** Jason Guerette. **Sponsorship/Group Coordinator:** Pat McCarthy. **Account Executives:** Landon Rhodes, Client Service Manager, Doug Hexamer. **Field Manager:** Mike Pinto. **Hitting Coach:** Steve Marino. **Pitching Coach:** Tyler Martin. **Instructor:** Ralph Santana. **Strength & Conditioning Coordinator:** Chris Stone.

GAME INFORMATION
No. of Games Broadcast: 96. **Flagship Station:** 97.7 WHET-FM. **Stadium Name:** Rent One Park. **Location:** US 57 to Route 13 East, right at Halfway Road to Fairmont Drive. **Standard Game Times:** Mon-Fri., 7:05 pm, Sat., 6:05 pm, Sun., 5:05 pm. **Visiting Club Hotel:** EconoLodge, 1806 Bittle Place, Marion, IL 62959 618-993-1644

WASHINGTON WILD THINGS

Office Address: One Washington Federal Way, Washington, PA 15301.
Telephone: (724) 250-9555. **Fax:** (724) 250-2333.
Email Address: info@washingtonwildthings.com. **Website:** washingtonwildthings.com.
Owned by: Sports Facility, LLC. **Operated by:** Washington Frontier League Baseball, LLC.
President/Chief Executive Officer: Stuart Williams.
Managing Partner: Francine W. Williams. **Vice President & General Manager:** Steven Zavacky.
Assistant GM: Tony Buccilli. Director of Marketing/**Communications/Corporate Relations:** Christine Blaine.
Corporate Account Executive: Debra Lavelle. **Ticket Manager:** Austin Snodgrass. **Ticket Account Executive:** Edwin Valentin, Austin Weekly. **Controller:** JJ Heider. **Creative Services:** Craig Lion. **Field Manager:** Gregg Langbehn.

GAME INFORMATION
Stadium Name: Wild Things Park. **Location:** I-70 to exit 15 (Chestnut. Street), right on Chestnut Street to Washington Crown Center Mall, right at mall entrance, right on to Mall Drive to stadium. **Standard Game Times:** Mon.-Sat., 7:05 pm, Sun., 5:35 pm. **Visiting Club Hotel:** Red Roof Inn.

WINDY CITY THUNDERBOLTS

Office Address: 14011 South Kenton Avenue, Crestwood, IL 60418
Telephone: (708) 489-2255. **Fax:** (708) 489-2999.
Email Address: info@wcthunderbolts.com. **Website:** www.wcthunderbolts.com.
Owned by: Crestwood Professional Baseball, LLC.
General Manager: Mike Lucas. **Assistant GM:** Mike VerSchave. **Senior Sales Executive:** Bill Waliewski.
Director, Community Relations: Johnny Sole. **Director, Group Sales:** Kenny Thorne. **Field Manager:** Brian Smith.

GAME INFORMATION
Radio Announcer: Terry Bonadonna. **No. of Games Broadcast:** 96. **Flagship Station:** WXAV, 88.3 FM. **Official Scorer:** Chris Gbur. **Stadium Name:** Standard Bank Stadium. **Location:** I-294 to South Cicero Ave, exit (Route 50), south for 1 1/2 miles, left at Midlothian Turnpike, right on Kenton Ave; I-57 to 147th Street, west on 147th to Cicero, north on Cicero, right on Midlothian Turnpike, right on Kenton. **Standard Game Times:** Mon.-Fri., 7:05 pm, Sat., 6:05 pm, Sun., 2:05 pm. **Visiting Club Hotel:** Georgio's Quality Inn & Suites, 8800 W 159th St, Orland Park, IL 60462. **Telephone:** (708) 403-1100.

ADDITIONAL LEAGUES

PACIFIC ASSOCIATION

Mailing address: 117 W Napa St Suite F, Sonoma, CA 95476
Telephone: (707) 857-1780 or (925) 588-3047
Year Founded: 2013.
Teams: San Rafael Pacifics, Sonoma Stompers, Vallejo Admirals and Pittsburg Diamonds, Martinez Clippers, Napa Silverados.
Roster Limit: 23. **Eligibility Rules:** None.
2019 Start Date: May 29
Playoff Format: Top four advance. One-game semifinals. One-game final.
2019 Playoff Start Date: Aug. 30.
Brand of Baseball: Rawlings.
Statistician: Pointstreak.

PECOS LEAGUE

Website: www.PecosLeague.com.
Address: PO Box 271489, Houston, TX 77277.
Telephone: 575-680-2212.
E-mail: info@pecosleague.com
Commissioner: Andrew Dunn.
Teams: Mountain—Alpine Cowboys, Alpine, Texas; Garden City Wind, Garden City, Kan.; Santa Fe Fuego, Santa Fe, N.M.; Trinidad Triggers, Trinidad, Colo.; Roswell Invaders, Roswell, N.M.; White Sands Pupfish, Alamogordo, N.M. **Pacific**—Bakersfield Train Robbers, Bakersfield, Calif.; California City Whiptails, California City, Calif; High Desert Yardbirds, Adelanto, Calif; Monterey Amberjacks, Monterey, Calif. Tucson Saguaros, Tucson, Ariz.; Wasco Reserves, Wasco Calif.
Year Founded: 2010.
Regular Season: 64 games. **Start Date:** May 30.
Playoff Format: First round—Best-of-three. **Second round**—Best-of-three. **Finals**—Best-of-three.
Roster Limit: 22 (no designated hitter).
Eligibility Rules: 25 and under.
Brand of Baseball: Rawlings-National League.

UNITED SHORE PROFESSIONAL BASEBALL LEAGUE

Location: Jimmy Johns Field. 7171 Auburn Rd, Utica MI.
Telephone: (248) 327-4829.
Email: baseballoperations@uspbl.com. **Website:** www.uspbl.com.
Ownership Group: General Sports & Entertainment.
CEO: Andrew D. Appelby. **COO:** Dana L. Schmitt. **VP of Corporate Sponsorship:** Matthew J. Schul. **VP of Marketing and Public Relations:** Scott MacDonald. **Director of Premium Sales and Services:** Nicole Pazzi. **VP of Groups Sales & Events:** Theresa Doan. **Director of Client Services:** Jeremiah Hergott. **Director of Ballpark Operations:** Dillon Dubois. **Promotions and Marketing Coordinator:** Katie Page. **Director of Food & Beverage:** Nathan Liska. **Director of Baseball Operations:** Justin Orenduff. **Director of Baseball Administration:** Mike Zielinski. **Fielding Coordinator:** Paul Niggebrugge. **Pitching Coordinator:** Shane McCatty. **Assistant Pitching Coordinator:** Alan Oaks.
Teams: Birmingham-Bloomfield Beavers, Eastside Diamond Hoppers, Utica Unicorns, Westside Woolly Mammoths.
Managers: Birmingham-Bloomfield Beavers—Chris Newell. **Eastside Diamond Hoppers**—Paul Noce. **Utica Unicorns**—Jim Essian. **Westside Woolly Mammoths**—Mark Weidemaier.
Roster Limit: 20. **Eligibility Rules:** Players must be between 18 and 26-years-old.
2019 Start Date: May 11th. **Season length:** 50 games per team.
Playoff Format: Single-game elimination.

INTERNATIONAL

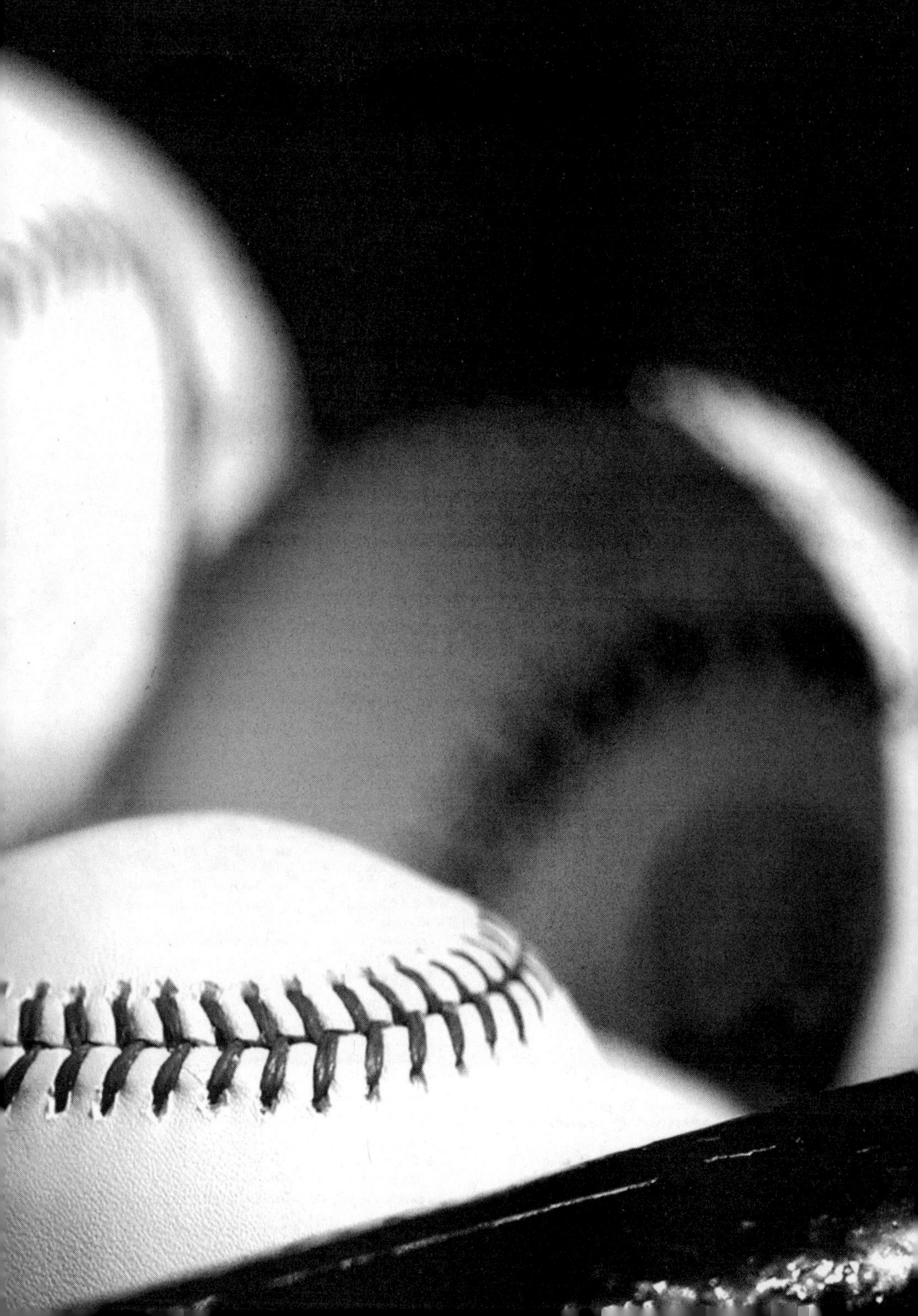

AMERICAS

MEXICO

MEXICAN LEAGUE

MEMBER, NATIONAL ASSOCIATION

NOTE: The Mexican League is a member of the National Association of Professional Baseball Leagues and has a Triple-A classification. However, its member clubs operate largely independent of the 30 major league teams, and for that reason the league is listed in the international section.

Address: Av Insurgentes Sur #797 3er. piso. Col. Napoles. C.P. 03810, Benito Juarez, Mexico, D.F. **Telephone:** 52-55-5557-1007. **Fax:** 52-55-5395-2454. **E-Mail Address:** oficina@lmb.com.mx. **Website:** www.lmb.com.mx.

Years League Active: 1955-.
President: Javier Salinas Hernandez. **Director, Administration:** Oscar Neri Rojas Salazar.
Division Structure: North—Durango, Mexico City, Monclova, Monterrey, Saltillo, Tijuana. **South**—Campeche, Laredo, Oaxaca, Quintana Roo, Tabasco, Yucatan.
Regular Season: 114 games (split-schedule). **2019 Opening Date:** First week of April. **Closing Date:** Last week of September.
All-Star Game: Not Available.
Playoff Format: Eight teams qualify, including the top three teams in each division. The fourth and fifth place teams in each division will hold a wild-card elimination game, as long as they are separated by no more than three games.
Roster Limit: 28. **Roster Limit, Imports:** 7.

CAMPECHE PIRATAS

Office Address: Calle Filiberto Qui Farfan No. 2, Col. Camino Real, CP 24020, Campeche, Campeche. **Telephone:** (52) 981-827-4759. **Fax:** (52) 981-827-4767. **E-Mail Address:** piratas@prodigy.net.mx. **Website:** www. piratasdecampeche.mx.
President: Gabriel Escalante Castillo. **General Manager:** Gabriel Lozano Berron.
Manager: Romulo Martinez.

DURANGO GENERALES

Office Address: De Los Deportes, Unidad Deportiva, 98065_00 Zacatecas, ZAC. **Telephone:** (52) 496-105-3940. **E-Mail Address:** contacto@generalesbeisbol .com.mx. **Website:** http://generales.mx
President: Virgilio Ruiz Isassi.
Manager: Matias Carrillo.

LAREDO TECOLOTES

Office Address: Lib. de Nuevo Laredo 20, Tamaulipas. **Website:** http://www.facebook.com/TecolotesNvoLdo.
President: Jose Antonio Mansur Beltran. **General Manager:** Grimaldo Martinez Gonzalez.
Manager: Eddy Castro.

MEXICO CITY DIABLOS ROJOS

Office Address: Av Cuauhtemoc #451-101, Col Narvarte, CP 03020, Mexico DF. **Telephone:** (56) 398-722-9722. **E-Mail Address:** contacto@diablos-rojos.com. **Website:** www.diablos.com.mx.
President: Alfredo Harp Helu. **General Manager:** Diego Patricio Perez Ochoa
Manager: Victor Bojorquez.

MONCLOVA ACEREROS

Office Address: Cuauhtemoc #299, Col Ciudad Deportiva, CP 25750, Monclova, Coahuila. **Telephone:** (52) 866-636-2650. **Fax:** (52) 866-636-2688. **E-Mail Address:** contacto@acereros.com.mx. **Website:** www. acereros.com.mx.
President: Gerardo Benavides Pape. **General Manager:** Sergio Atwell Vielleden.
Manager: Pedro Mere

MONTERREY SULTANES

Office Address: Av Manuel Barragan s/n, Estadio Monterrey, Apartado Postal 870, Monterrey, Nuevo Leon, CP 66460. **Telephone:** (52) 81-2270-2000. **Fax:** (52) 81-8351-8022. **E-Mail Address:** sultanes@sultanes .com.mx. **Website:** www.sultanes.com.mx.
President: José Maiz Garcia. **General Manager:** Miguel Flores.
Manager: Roberto Kelly.

OAXACA GUERREROS

Office Address: M Bravo 417 Col Centro 68000, Oaxaca, Oaxaca. **Telephone:** (52) 951-515-5522. **Fax:** (52) 951-515-4966. **E-Mail Address:** oaxacaguerreros@gmail. com. **Website:** www.guerreros.mx.
President: Lorenzo Peón Escalante. **General Manager:** Guillermo Spindola Morales.
Manager: Jose Luis Sandoval.

QUINTANA ROO TIGRES

Office Address: SM 21, 21, 77500 Cancún, Quintana Roo. **Telephone:** (52) 998-887-3108. **Fax:** (52) 998-887-1313. **E-Mail Address:** medios@tigresqroo.com. **Website:** www.tigresqroo.com.
President: Carlos Peralta Quintero. **General Manager:** Francisco Minjarez Garcia.
Manager: Raul Sanchez.

SALTILLO SARAPEROS

Office Address: Blvd Nazario Ortiz Esquina con Blvd Jesus Sanchez, CP 25280, Saltillo, Coahuila. **Telephone:** (52) 844-416-9455. **Fax:** (52) 844-439-1330. **E-Mail Address:** aley@grupoley.com. **Website:** www.saraperos. com.mx.
President: Alvaro Ley Lopez. **General Manager:** Eduardo Valenzuela Guajardo.
Manager: Len Picota.

TABASCO OLMECAS

Office Address: Avenida Velodromo de la Ciudad Deportiva S/N, Atasta, 86100 Villahermosa, Tabasco. **Telephone:** (52) 993-352-2787. **Fax:** (52) 993-352-2788. **E-Mail Address:** hola@olmecastasco.mx. **Website:** www. olmecastabasco.net.
President: Ángel Solis Carballo. **General Manager:** Felix Zulueta García.
Manager: Eddy Castro.

TIJUANA TOROS

Office Address: Blvd Agua Caliente #11720, Col Hipodromo 22020, Tijuana, BC. **Telephone:** (52) 664-635-5600. **E-Mail Address:** contacto@torosdetijuana.com. **Website:** www.torosdetijuana.com.
General Manager: Antonio Cano.
Manager: Oscar Robles.

YUCATAN LEONES

Office Address: Edificio Vector 50, Calle 50 #402-D x 31 y 33 Col. Jesús Carranza, Mérida, Yucatán. C.P. 97109. **Telephone:** (01999) 926 3022. **Fax:** (52) 999-926-3631.

E-Mail Addresses: contacto@leones.mx. **Website:** www.leones.mx.

President: Erick Ernesto Arellano Hernández. **General Manager:** Alejandro Orozco Garcia.

Manager: Roberto Vizcarra.

MEXICAN ACADEMY

Rookie Classification

Mailing Address: Ubicación: Av. El Fundador #100, Col. San Miguel, El Carmen N.L., C.P. 66550. **Telephone:** (81) 8158-7900. **Fax:** (52) 555-395-2454. **E-Mail Address:** pgarza@academia-lmb.com. **Website:** www.academia-lmb.com.

President: C.P. Plinio Escalante Bolio. **Director General:** Salvador Viera Higuera.

Regular Season: 50 games. **Opening Date:** Not available. **Closing Date:** Not available.

DOMINICAN REPUBLIC

DOMINICAN SUMMER LEAGUE

Member, National Association
Rookie Classification

Mailing Address: Calle Segunda No 64, Reparto Antilla, Santo Domingo, Dominican Republic. **Telephone/Fax:** (809) 532-3619. **Website:** www.dominicansummer

league.com. **E-Mail Address:** ligadeverano@codetel.net.do.

Years League Active: 1985-.

President: Orlando Diaz.

Member Clubs/Division Structure: North—Cubs1, Dodgers Guerrero, Indians, Indians/Brewers, Pirates, Rangers1, Rays2, Red Sox2. **South—Angels,** Cardinals Blue, Mets1, Nationals, Phillies Red, Rockies, Twins, Yankees. **Northwest—**Astros, Athletics, Braves, Dodgers Robinson, Marlins, Rays1, Red Sox1, Royals1. **Baseball City—**Blue Jays, D-backs1, Orioles, Padres, Reds, White Sox. **San Pedro de Macoris—**Brewers, Cardinals Red, Cubs2, D-backs2, Mets2, Phillies White, Rangers, Tigers1. **Northeast—**Colorado, Giants, Mariners, Pirates2, Royals2, Tigers2.

Regular Season: 72 games. **Opening Date:** Unavailable. **Closing Date:** Unavailable.

Playoff Format: Six teams qualify for playoffs, including four division winners and two wild-card teams. Teams with two best records receive a bye to the semifinals; four other playoff teams play best-of-three series. Winners advance to best-of-three semifinals. Winners advance to best-of-five championship series.

Roster Limit: 35 active. **Player Eligibility Rule:** No player may have four or more years of prior minor league service. No draft-eligible player from the U.S. or Canada (not including players from Puerto Rico) may participate in the DSL. No age limits apply.

ASIA

JAPAN

Mailing Address: Mita Bellju Building, 11th Floor, 5-36-7 Shiba, Minato-ku, Tokyo 108-0014. **Telephone:** 03-6400-1189. **Fax:** 03-6400-1190.

Website: www.npb.or.jp, www.npb.or.jp/eng

Commissioner: Atsushi Saito.

Executive Secretary: Atsushi Ihara. **Executive Director, Baseball Operations:** Minoru Hata. **Executive Director, NPB Rules & Labor:** Nobuhisa "Nobby" Ito.

Executive Director, Central League Operations: Kazuhide Kinefuchi. **Executive Director, Pacific League Operations:** Kazuo Nakano.

Nippon Series: Best-of-seven series between Central and Pacific League champions, begins Oct 27.

All-Star Series: July 13 at Kyocera Dome; July 14 at Fujisaki Prefectural Baseball Stadium.

Roster Limit: 70 per organization (one major league club, one minor league club). Major league club is permitted to register 28 players at a time, though just 25 may be available for each game.

Roster Limit, Imports: Four in majors (no more than three position players or pitchers); unlimited in minors.

CENTRAL LEAGUE

Regular Season: 143 games.

2017 Opening Date: March 31. **Closing Date:** Oct. 1.

Playoff Format: Second-place team meets third-place team in best-of-three series. Winner meets first-place team in best-of-seven series to determine representative in Japan Series (first-place team has one-game advantage to begin series).

CHUNICHI DRAGONS

Mailing Address: Chunichi Bldg 6F, 4-1-1 Sakae, Naka-ku, Nagoya 460-0008. **Telephone:** 052-261-8811. **Chairman:** Bungo Shirai. **President:** Takao Sasaki. **Field

Manager: Shigekazu Mori.

HANSHIN TIGERS

Mailing Address: 2-33 Koshien-cho, Nishinomiya-shi, Hyogo-ken 663-8152. **Telephone:** 0798-46-1515. **Chairman:** Shinya Sakai. **President:** Keiichiro Yotsufuji. **Field Manager:** Tomoaki Kanemoto.

HIROSHIMA TOYO CARP

Mailing Address: 2-3-1 Minami Kaniya, Minami-ku, Hiroshima 732-8501. **Telephone:** 082-554-1000. **President:** Hajime Matsuda. **General Manager:** Kiyoaki Suzuki. **Field Manager:** Koichi Ogata.

TOKYO YAKULT SWALLOWS

Mailing Address: Seizan Bldg, 4F, 2-12-28 Kita Aoyama, Minato-ku, Tokyo 107-0061. **Telephone:** 03-3405-8960.

Chairman: Sumiya Hori. **President:** Tsuyoshi Klnugasa. **Senior Director:** Junji Ogawa. **Field Manager:** Mitsuru Manaka.

YOKOHAMA DENA BAYSTARS

Mailing Address: Kannai Arai Bldg, 7F, 1-8 Onoe-cho, Naka-ku, Yokohama 231-0015. **Telephone:** 045-681-0811.

Chairman: Makoto Haruta. **President:** Shingo Okamura. **General Manager:** Shigeru Takada. **Field Manager:** Alex Ramirez.

YOMIURI GIANTS

Mailing Address: Yomiuri Shimbun Bldg, 26F, 1-7-1 Otemachi, Chiyoda-ku, Tokyo 100-8151. **Telephone:** 03-3246-7733. **Fax:** 03-3246-2726.

Chairman: Kojiro Shiraishi. **President:** Hiroshi Kubo. **General Manager:** Tatsuyoshi Tsutsumi. **Field Manager:** Yoshinobu Takahashi.

PACIFIC LEAGUE

Regular Season: 143 games.

2017 Opening Date: March 31. **Closing Date:** Oct. 5.

Playoff Format: Second-place team meets third-place team in best-of-three series. Winner meets first-place team in best-of-seven series to determine league's representative in Japan Series (first-place team has one-game advantage to begin series).

CHIBA LOTTE MARINES

Mailing Address: 1 Mihama, Mihama-ku, Chiba-shi, Chiba-ken 261-8587. **Telephone:** 03-5682-6341.

Chairman: Takeo Shigemitsu. **President:** Shinya Yamamuro. **Field Manager:** Tsutomu Ito.

FUKUOKA SOFTBANK HAWKS

Mailing Address: Fukuoka Yahuoku Japan Dome, Hawks Town, 2-2-2 Jigyohama, Chuo-ku, Fukuoka 810-0065. **Telephone:** 092-847-1006. **Owner:** Masayoshi Son. **Chairman:** Sadaharu Oh. **President:** Yoshimitsu Goto. **Field Manager:** Kimiyasu Kudo.

HOKKAIDO NIPPON HAM FIGHTERS

Mailing Address: 1 Hitsujigaoka, Toyohira-ku, Sapporo 062-8655. **Telephone:** 011-857-3939.

Chairman: Juichi Suezawa. **President:** Kenso Takeda. **General Manager:** Hiroshi Yoshimura. **Field Manager:** Hideki Kuriyama.

ORIX BUFFALOES

Mailing Address: 3-Kita-2-30 Chiyozaki, Nishi-ku, Osaka 550-0023. **Telephone:** 06-6586-0221. **Fax:** 06-6586-0240.

Chairman: Yoshihiko Miyauchi. **President:** Hiroaki Nishina. **General Manager:** Hiroyuki Nagamura. **Field Manager:** Junichi Fukura.

SAITAMA SEIBU LIONS

Mailing Address: 2135 Kami-Yamaguchi, Tokorozawa-shi, Saitama-ken 359-1189. **Telephone:** 04-2924-1155. **Fax:** 04-2928-1919.

President: Hajime Igo. **Field Manager:** Hatsuhiko Tsuji.

TOHOKU RAKUTEN GOLDEN EAGLES

Mailing Address: 2-11-6 Miyagino, Miyagino-ku, Sendai-shi, Miyagi-ken 983-0045. **Telephone:** 022-298-5300. **Fax:** 022-298-5360.

Chairman: Hiroshi Mikitani. **President:** Yozo Tachibana. **Field Manager:** Masataka Nashida.

KOREA

KOREA BASEBALL ORGANIZATION

Mailing Address: 946-16 Dokokdong, Kangnam-gu, Seoul, Korea. **Telephone:** (02) 3460-4600. **Fax:** (02) 3460-4639.

Years League Active: 1982-.

Website: www.koreabaseball.com.

Commissioner: Koo Bon-Neung. **Secretary General:** Yang Hae-Young.

Member Clubs: Doosan Bears, Hanwha Eagles, Kia Tigers, KT Wiz, LG Twins, Lotte Giants, NC Dinos, Nexen Heroes, Samsung Lions, SK Wyverns.

Regular Season: 128 games. **2018 Opening Date:** April 1.

Playoffs: Third- and fourth-place teams meet in best-of-three series; winner advances to meet second-place team in best-of-five series; winner meets first-place team in best-of-seven Korean Series for league championship.

Roster Limit: 26 active through Sept 1, when rosters expand to 31. **Imports:** Two active.

TAIWAN

CHINESE PROFESSIONAL BASEBALL LEAGUE

Mailing Address: 2F, No 32, Pateh Road, Sec 3, Taipei, Taiwan 10559. **Telephone:** 886-2-2577-6992. **Fax:** 886-2-2577-2606. **Website:** www.cpbl.com.tw.

Years League Active: 1990-.

Commissioner: Jenn-Tai Hwang. **Deputy Secretary General:** Hueimin Wang. **E-Mail Address:** richard.wang@cpbl.com.tw.

Member Clubs: Chinatrust Brothers, Fubon Guardians, Lamigo Monkeys, Uni-President 7-Eleven Lions.

Regular Season: 120 games. Each team plays 60 games in the first and second halves of the season. **2018 Opening Date:** Not available. **Playoffs:** Half-season winners are eligible for the postseason. If a non-half-season winner team possesses a higher overall winning percentage than any other half-season winner, then this team gains a wild card and will play a best-of-five series against the half-season winner with the lower winning percentage. The winner of the playoff series advances to Taiwan Series (best-of-seven). If the same team clinches both first- and second-half seasons, then that team is awarded one win to start the Taiwan Series.

EUROPE

NETHERLANDS
DUTCH MAJOR LEAGUE

Mailing Address: Koninklijke Nederlandse Baseball en Softball Bond (Royal Dutch Baseball and Softball Association), Postbus 2650, 3430 GB Nieuwegein, Holland. **Telephone:** 31-30-751-3650. **Fax:** 31-30-751-3651. **Website:** www.knbsb.nl.
Member Clubs: Curacao Neptunus, De Glaskoning Twins, DSS, HCAW, Hoofddorp Pioniers, L&D Amsterdam, Pickles UVV.
Regular season: 42 games.
President: Bob Bergkamp.

ITALY
ITALIAN BASEBALL LEAGUE

Mailing Address: Federazione Italiana Baseball Softball, Viale Tiziano 74, 00196 Roma, Italy. **Telephone:** 39-06-32297201. **Fax:** 39-06-36858201. **Website:** www. fibs.it.
Member Clubs: Bologna, Nettuno, Novara, Parma, Padulo. Rimini, San Marino, Tomassin. **President:** Riccardo Fraccari.
Regular season: 34 games.
Playoffs: Top four teams advance to best-of-five semi-finals. Semifinal winners play best-of-five Italian Series.

WINTER BASEBALL

CARIBBEAN BASEBALL CONFEDERATION
Mailing Address: Frank Feliz Miranda No 1 Naco, Santo Domingo, Dominican Republic. **Telephone:** (809) 381-2643. **Fax:** (809) 565-4654.
Commissioner: Juan Francisco Puello. **Secretary:** Benny Agosto.
Member Countries: Cuba, Colombia, Dominican Republic, Mexico, Nicaragua, Panama, Puerto Rico, Venezuela.
2020 Caribbean Series: Puerto Rico, February.

DOMINICAN LEAGUE

Office Address: Ave. Tiradentes, Ensanche La Fé, Estadio Quisqueya, Santo Domingo, Dominican Republic. **Telephone:** (809) 567-6371. **Fax:** (809) 567-5720. **E-Mail Address:** ligadom@hotmail.com. **Website:** www.lidom. com.
Years League Active: 1951-.
President: Vitelio Mejía Ortiz. **Vice President:** Winston Llenas Davila.
Member Clubs: Aguilas Cibaenas, Estrellas de Oriente, Gigantes del Cibao, Leones del Escogido, Tigres del Licey, Toros del Este.
Regular Season: 50 games.
Playoff Format: Top four teams meet in 18-game round-robin. Top two teams advance to best-of-nine series for league championship. Winner advances to Caribbean Series.
Roster Limit: 30. **Imports:** 7.

MEXICAN PACIFIC LEAGUE

Mailing Address: Ave. Américas No. 1905, 5to. Piso, Col. Colomos Providencia, Guadalajara, Jalisco. **Telephone:** (52) 662-310-9714. **Fax:** (52) 662-310-9715. **E-Mail Address:** medios@lmp.mx. **Website:** www.lmp. mx.
Years League Active: 1958-.
President: Omar Canizales Soto. **General Manager:** Christian Veliz Valencia.
Member Clubs: Culiacan Tomateros, Hermosillo Naranjeros, Jalisco Charros, Los Mochis Caneros, Mazatlan Venados, Mexicali Aguilas, Navojoa Mayos, Obregon Yaquis.

Regular Season: 68 games.
Playoff Format: Six teams advance to best-of-seven quarterfinals. Three winners and losing team with best record advance to best-of-seven semifinals. Winners meet in best-of-seven series for league championship. Winner advances to Caribbean Series.
Roster Limit: 30. **Imports:** 5.

PUERTO RICAN LEAGUE

Office Address: Avenida Munoz Rivera 1056, Edificio First Federal, Suite 501, Rio Piedras, PR 00925. **Mailing Address:** PO Box 191852, San Juan, PR 00019. **Telephone:** (786) 244-1146. **Fax:** (787) 767-3028. **Website:** www.ligapr.com. **E-mail address:** info@ligapr .com
Years League Active: 1938-2007; 2008-
President: Juan Flores Galarza. **Operations Director:** Carlos J. Berroa Puertas. **Press Director:** Karla Pacheco.
Member Clubs: Caguas Criollos, Carolina Gigantes, Mayaguez Indios, Santurce Cangrejeros.
Regular Season: 40 games.
Playoff Format: Top three teams meet in round robin series, with top two teams advancing to best-of-seven final. Winner advances to Caribbean Series.
Roster Limit: 30. **Imports:** 5.

VENEZUELAN LEAGUE

Mailing Address: Avenida Casanova, Centro Comercial "El Recreo," Torre Sur, Piso 3, Oficinas 6 y 7, Sabana Grande, Caracas, Venezuela. **Telephone:** (58) 212-761-6408. **Fax:** (58) 212-761-7661. **Website:** www. lvbp.com.
Years League Active: 1946-.
President: Juan Jose Avila. **Vice Presidents:** Esteban Palacios Lozada, Domingo Santander. **General Manager:** Domingo Alvarez.
Member Clubs: Anzoategui Caribes, Aragua Tigres, Caracas Leones, La Guaira Tiburones, Lara Cardenales, Magallanes Navegantes, Margarita Bravos, Zulia Aguilas.
Regular Season: 64 games.
Playoff Format: Top two teams in each division, plus a wild-card team, meet in 16-game round-robin series. Top two finishers meet in best-of-seven series for league championship. Winner advances to Caribbean Series.
Roster Limit: 26. **Imports:** 7.

COLOMBIAN LEAGUE

Office/Mailing Address: Hotel Eslait Cra 53 No. 72-27 2do piso, Baranquilla. **Telephone:** (57) 368-6561. **E-mail Address:** lcpbcolombia@gmail.com. **Website:** www.lcbp.com.co.

President: Edinson Renteria. **Director, Operations:** Harold Herrera. **Director, Communications:** Gabriel Chavez.

Member Clubs: Barranquilla Caimanes, Cartagena Tigres, Monteria Leones, Sincelejo Toros.

Regular season: 42 games.

Playoff Format: Top three teams play eight-game round robin. Top two teams meet in best-of-seven finals for league championship.

AUSTRALIA

AUSTRALIAN BASEBALL LEAGUE

Street Address: Suite 5/65-67 Thomas Drive Chevron Island QLD 4217. **Postal Address:** PO Box 218 Chevron Island QLD 4217. **Telephone:** (07) 5510 6800. **Fax:** (07) 5510 6855. **E-mail Address:** abfadmin@baseball.org.au. **Website:** web.theabl.com.au.

CEO: Cam Vale. **General Manager:** Ben Foster.

Teams: Adelaide Bite, Auckland Tuatara, Brisbane Bandits, Canberra Cavalry, Geelong-Korea, Melbourne Aces, Perth Heat, Sydney Blue Sox.

2019 Opening Date: Unavailable. Play usually opens in November with playoffs in February.

Playoff Format: The teams with the best four records qualify for the playoffs. Teams are seeded 1-4, with the top two seeds hosting all three games of the best-of-three semifinal series. Winners advance to a best-of-three championship series.

DOMESTIC LEAGUE

ARIZONA FALL LEAGUE

Mailing Address: Scottsdale Stadium, 7408 E. Osborn, Scottsdale, AZ 85251. **Telephone:** (480)-990-1005. **Fax:** (602) 281-7313. **E-Mail Address:** afl@mlb.com. **Website:** mlb.mlb.com/mlb/events/afl/.

Years League Active: 1992-.

Operated by: Major League Baseball.

Executive Director: Steve Cobb. **Administrator:** Darlene Emert. **Communications:** Paul Jensen.

Teams: Glendale Desert Dogs, Mesa Solar Sox, Peoria Javelinas, Salt River Rafters, Scottsdale Scorpions, Surprise Saguaros.

Regular season: 32 games. **2019 Opening Date:** Unavailable. Play usually opens in mid-October. **Playoff Format:** Division champions meet in one-game championship.

Roster Limit: 35 players per team plus a "taxi squad" of reserve players. Each major-league organization is required to provide seven players. Triple-A and Double-A players are eligible provided they are on Double-A or Triple-A rosters no later than August 15. Each organization is permitted to send two high Class A level players and two players below high Class A. No players with more than one year active or two years total of credited major-league service as of August 31 (including major league disabled list time) are eligible. Each team is allotted 20 pitchers but only 15 are designated "active" each game day.

COLLEGES

COLLEGE ORGANIZATIONS

NATIONAL COLLEGIATE ATHLETIC ASSOCIATION

Mailing Address: 700 W. Washington Street, PO Box 6222, Indianapolis, IN 46206. **Telephone:** (317) 917-6222. **Fax:** (317) 917-6826 (championships), (317) 917-6710 (baseball).

E-mail Addresses: Division I Championship: aholman@ncaa.org (Anthony Holman), rlburhr@ncaa.org (Randy Buhr), ctolliver@ncaa.org (Chad Tolliver), thalpin@ncaa.org (Ty Halpin), jhamilton@ncaa.org (JD Hamilton), kgiles@ncaa.org (Kim Giles). **Division II Championship:** ebreece@ncaa.org (Eric Breece). **Division III:** jpwilliams@ncaa.org (J.P. Williams).

Websites: www.ncaa.org, www.ncaa.com.

President: Dr. Mark Emmert. **Managing director, Division I Championships/Alliances:** Anthony Holman. **Director, Division I Championships/Alliances:** Randy Buhr. **Associate Director, Championships/Alliances:** Chad Tolliver. **Division II Assistant Director, Championshps/Alliances:** Eric Breece. **Division III Assistant Director, Championships/Alliances:** J.P. Williams. **Media Contact, Division I Championships, Alliances/College World Series:** J.D. Hamilton. **Playing Rules Contact:** Ty Halpin. **Statistics Contacts:** Jeff Williams (Division I and RPI); Mark Bedics (Division II); Sean Straziscar (Division III).

Chairman, Division I Baseball Committee: Ray Tanner (Director of Athletics, South Carolina).

Division I Baseball Committee: Jeff Altier (Director of Athletics, Stetson); David Blank (Director of Athletics, Elon); Mike Bobinski (Director of Athletics, Purdue); Mike Buddie (Director of Athletics, Furman); Christopher Del Conte (Director of Athletics, Texas); Joe Karlgaard (Director of Athletics, Rice); Benjamin Shove (Assistant Commissioner, Northeast Conference); Ray Tanner (Director of Athletics, South Carolina); Marianne Vydra (Deputy Athletics Director, Oregon State).

Chairman, Division II Baseball Committee: Sue Willey (Director of Athletics, Indianapolis). **Chairman, Division III Baseball Committee:** Paul F. Murphy (Associate Director of Athletics, Gwynedd Mercy, Pa.).

2019 National Convention: Jan. 22-25 at Anaheim.

2019 CHAMPIONSHIP TOURNAMENTS

NCAA DIVISION I
College World Series: Omaha, Neb., June 15-25/26
Super Regionals (8): Campus sites, June 7-10
Regionals (16): Campus sites, May 31-June 3

NCAA DIVISION II
World Series: USA Baseball National Training Complex, Cary, N.C. June 1-8

NCAA DIVISION III
World Series: Veterans Memorial Stadium, Cedar Rapids, Iowa, May 31-June 5

NATIONAL JUNIOR COLLEGE ATHLETIC ASSOCIATION

Mailing Address: 1631 Mesa Ave., Suite B, Colorado Springs, CO 80906. **Telephone:** (719) 590-9788. **Fax:** (719) 590-7324. **E-Mail Address:** rwebster@njcaa.org. **Website:** www.njcaa.org.

Executive Director: Christopher Parker. **Director, Division I Baseball Tournament:** Jamie Hamilton. **Director, Division II Baseball Tournament:** Billy Mayberry. **Director, Division III Baseball Tournament:** Bill Ellis. **Director, Media Relations:** Ricky Webster.

2019 CHAMPIONSHIP TOURNAMENTS

DIVISION I
World Series: Grand Junction, CO, May 25-May 31/June 1

DIVISION II
World Series: Enid, OK, May 25-May 31/June 1

DIVISION III
World Series: Greeneville, TN, May 25-May 29/30

CALIFORNIA COMMUNITY COLLEGE ATHLETIC ASSOCIATION

Mailing Address: 2017 O St., Sacramento, CA 95811. **Telephone:** (916) 444-1600. **Fax:** (916) 444-2616. **E-Mail Addresses:** ccarter@cccaasports.org, jboggs@cccaasports.org. **Website:** www.cccaasports.org.

Executive Director: Carlyle Carter. **Director, Membership Services:** Jennifer Cardone. **Director, Championships:** George Mategakis. **Buisness Operations Specialist:** Rina Kasim, rkasim@cccaasports.org. **Administrative Assistant:** Rima Trotter, rtrotter@cccaasports.org.

2019 CHAMPIONSHIP TOURNAMENT

State Championship: Fresno, CA, May 25-27.

NORTHWEST ATHLETIC CONFERENCE

Mailing Address: Clark College TGB 121, 1933 Fort Vancouver Way, Vancouver, WA 98663. **Telephone:** (360) 992-2833. **Fax:** (360) 696-6210. **E-Mail Address:** nwaacc@clark.edu. **Website:** www.nwacsports.org.

Executive Director: Marco Azurdia. **Executive Assistant:** Donna Hays. **Sports Information Director:** Tracy Swisher. **Director, Operations:** Alli Young.

2019 CHAMPIONSHIP TOURNAMENT

NWAC Championship: Lower Columbia College, Longview, WA, May 23-27.

AMERICAN BASEBALL COACHES ASSOCIATION

Office Address: 4101 Piedmont Parkway, Suite C, Greensboro, NC 27410. **Telephone:** (336) 821-3140. **Fax:** (336) 886-0000. **E-Mail Address:** abca@abca.org. **Website:** www.abca.org.

Executive Director: Craig Keilitz. **Director, Exhibits/Branding:** Juahn Clark. **Communications/Business Coordinator:** Jon Litchfield. **Membership/Convention Coordinator:** Zach Haile.

Chairman: Mark Johnson. **President:** John Kolasinski (Siena Heights, Mich.).

2020 National Convention: Jan. 2-5 in Nashville.

NCAA DIVISION I CONFERENCES

AMERICA EAST CONFERENCE

Mailing Address: 451 D Street, Suite 702, Boston, MA 02127. **Telephone:** (617) 695-6369. **Fax:** (617) 695-6380.
E-Mail Address: hager@americaeast.com.
Website: www.americaeast.com.
Baseball Members (First Year): Albany (2002), Binghamton (2002), Hartford (1990), Maine (1990), Maryland-Baltimore County (2004), Massachusetts-Lowell (2014), Stony Brook (2002). **Director, Strategic Media/ Baseball Contact:** Jared Hager. **2019 Tournament:** Six teams, double-elimination, May 22-25 at Bearcat Baseball Complex, Vestal, N.Y.

AMERICAN ATHLETIC CONFERENCE

Mailing Address: 15 Park Row West, Providence, RI 02903. **Telephone:** (401) 453-0660. **Fax:** (401) 751-8540.
E-Mail Address: csullivan@theamerican.org.
Website: www.theamerican.org.
Baseball Members (First Year): Central Florida (2014), Cincinnati (2014), Connecticut (2014), East Carolina (2015), Houston (2014), Memphis (2014), South Florida (2014), Tulane (2015), Wichita State (2018). **Director, Communications:** Chuck Sullivan. **2019 Tournament:** Eight teams, double-elimination until the final, May 21-26 at Spectrum Field, Clearwater, Fla.

ATLANTIC COAST CONFERENCE

Mailing Address: 4512 Weybridge Ln., Greensboro, NC 27407. **Telephone:** (336) 851-6062. **Fax:** (336) 854-8797.
E-Mail Address: sphillips@theacc.org.
Website: www.theacc.com.
Baseball Members (First Year): Boston College (2006), Clemson (1954), Duke (1954), Florida State (1992), Georgia Tech (1980), Maryland (1954), Miami (2005), North Carolina (1954), North Carolina State (1954), Notre Dame (2014), Pittsburgh (2014), Virginia (1955), Virginia Tech (2005), Wake Forest (1954). **Associate Director, Communications:** Steve Phillips. **2019 Tournament:** 12 teams, group play followed by single-elimination semifinals and finals. May 21-26 at Durham Bulls Athletic Park, Durham.

ATLANTIC SUN CONFERENCE

Mailing Address: 3370 Vineville Ave., Suite 108-B, Macon, GA 31204. **Telephone:** (478) 474-3394. **Fax:** (478) 474-4272.
E-Mail Addresses: pmccoy@atlanticsun.org.
Website: www.atlanticsun.org.
Baseball Members (First Year): Florida Gulf Coast (2008), Jacksonville (1999), Kennesaw State (2006), Liberty (2019), Lipscomb (2004), New Jersey Tech (2016), North Alabama (2019), North Florida (2006), Stetson (1986). **Director, Sports Information:** Patrick McCoy. **2019 Tournament:** Eight teams, double-elimination. May 22-25 at Melching Field, DeLand, Fla.

ATLANTIC 10 CONFERENCE

Mailing Address: 11827 Canon Blvd., Suite 200, Newport News, VA 23606. **Telephone:** (757) 706-3059. **Fax:** (757) 706-3042.
E-Mail Address: ddickerson@atlantic10.org.
Website: www.atlantic10.com.
Baseball Members (First Year): Davidson (2015), Dayton (1996), Fordham (1996), George Mason (2014), George Washington (1977), La Salle (1996), Massachu-

setts (1977), Rhode Island (1981), Richmond (2002), St. Bonaventure (1980), Saint Joseph's (1983), Saint Louis (2006), Virginia Commonwealth (2013). **Commissioner:** Bernadette V. McGlade. **Director, Communications:** Drew Dickerson. **2019 Tournament:** Seven teams, double elimination. May 22-25 at Houlihan Park, Bronx, N.Y.

BIG EAST CONFERENCE

Mailing Address: BIG EAST Conference, 655 3rd Avenue, 7th Floor, New York, NY 10017. **Telephone:** (212) 969-3181. **Fax:** (212) 969-2900.
E-Mail Address: kquinn@bigeast.com.
Website: www.bigeast.com.
Baseball Members (First Year): Butler (2014), Creighton (2014), Georgetown (1985), St. John's (1985), Seton Hall (1985), Villanova (1985), Xavier (2014). **Assistant Commissioner, Olympic Sports/Marketing Communications:** Kristin Quinn. **2019 Tournament:** Four teams, modified double-elimination. May 23-26 at Prasco Park, Mason, Ohio.

BIG SOUTH CONFERENCE

Mailing Address: 7233 Pineville-Matthews Rd., Suite 100, Charlotte, NC 28226. **Telephone:** (704) 341-7990. **Fax:** (704) 341-7991.
E-Mail Address: brandonm@bigsouth.org.
Website: www.bigsouthsports.com.
Baseball Members (First Year): Campbell (2012), Charleston Southern (1983), Gardner-Webb (2009), High Point (1999), Longwood (2013), UNC Asheville (1985), Presbyterian (2009), Radford (1983), South Carolina-Upstate (2019), Winthrop (1983). **Assistant Director, Public Relations/Baseball Contact:** Brandon McGinnis. **2019 Tournament:** Eight teams, double-elimination. May 21-25, at Fayetteville Ballpark, Fayetteville, N.C.

BIG TEN CONFERENCE

Mailing Address: 5440 Park Place, Rosemont, IL 60018. **Telephone:** (847) 696-1010. **Fax:** (847) 696-1110.
E-Mail Addresses: kkane@bigten.org.
Website: www.bigten.org.
Baseball Members (First Year): Illinois (1896), Indiana (1906), Iowa (1906), Maryland (2015), Michigan (1896), Michigan State (1950), Minnesota (1906), Nebraska (2012), Northwestern (1898), Ohio State (1913), Penn State (1992), Purdue (1906), Rutgers (2015). **2019 Tournament:** Eight teams, double-elimination. May 22-26 at TD Ameritrade Park, Omaha.

BIG 12 CONFERENCE

Mailing Address: 400 E. John Carpenter Freeway, Irving, TX 75062. **Telephone:** (469) 524-1009.
E-Mail Address: russell@big12sports.com.
Website: www.big12sports.com.
Baseball Members (First Year): Baylor (1997), Kansas (1997), Kansas State (1997), Oklahoma (1997), Oklahoma State (1997), Texas Christian (2013), Texas (1997), Texas Tech (1997), West Virginia (2013). **Assistant Director, Media Relations:** Russell Luna. **2019 Tournament:** Eight teams, double-elimination. May 22-26 at Chickasaw Bricktown Ballpark, Oklahoma City.

BIG WEST CONFERENCE

Mailing Address: 2 Corporate Park, Suite 206, Irvine, CA 92606. **Telephone:** (949) 261-2525. **Fax:** (949) 261-2528.
E-Mail Address: jstcyr@bigwest.org.

Website: www.bigwest.org.
Baseball Members (First Year): Cal Poly (1997), UC Davis (2008), UC Irvine (2002), UC Riverside (2002), UC Santa Barbara (1970), Cal State Fullerton (1975), Cal State Northridge (2001), Hawaii (2013), Long Beach State (1970). **Director, Communications:** Julie St. Cyr. **2019 Tournament:** None.

COLONIAL ATHLETIC ASSOCIATION

Mailing Address: 8625 Patterson Ave., Richmond, VA 23229. **Telephone:** (804) 754-1616. **Fax:** (804) 754-1973.
E-Mail Address: rwashburn@caasports.com.
Website: www.caasports.com.
Baseball Members (First Year): College of Charleston (2014), Delaware (2002), Elon (2015), Hofstra (2002), James Madison (1986), UNC Wilmington (1986), Northeastern (2006), Towson (2002), William & Mary (1986). **Associate Commissioner/Communications:** Rob Washburn. **2019 Tournament:** Six teams, double-elimination. May 22-25 at Eagle Field at Veterans Memorial Park, Harrisonburg, Va.

CONFERENCE USA

Mailing Address: 5201 N. O'Connor Blvd., Suite 300, Irving, TX 75039. **Telephone:** (214) 774-1300. **Fax:** (214) 496-0055.
E-Mail Address: rdanderson@c-usa.org.
Website: www.conferenceusa.com.
Baseball Members (First Year): Alabama-Birmingham (1996), Charlotte (2014), Florida Atlantic (2014), Florida International (2014), Louisiana Tech (2014), Marshall (2006), Middle Tennessee State (2014), Old Dominion (2014), Rice (2006), Southern Mississippi (1996), Texas-San Antonio (2014), Western Kentucky (2015). **Assistant Commissioner, Baseball Operations:** Russell Anderson. **2019 Tournament:** Eight teams, double-elimination. May 22-26 at MGM Park, Biloxi, Miss.

HORIZON LEAGUE

Mailing Address: 201 S. Capitol Ave., Suite 500, Indianapolis, IN 46225. **Telephone:** (317) 237-5604. **Fax:** (317) 237-5620.
E-Mail Address: dgliot@horizonleague.org.
Website: www.horizonleague.org.
Baseball Members (First Year): Illinois-Chicago (1994), Northern Kentucky (2016), Oakland (2014), Wright State (1994), Wisconsin-Milwaukee (1994), Youngstown State (2002). **Director, Communications and Digital Media Strategy:** Dan Gliot. **2019 Tournament:** Six teams, modified double-elimination. May 22-25, hosted by No. 1 seed.

IVY LEAGUE

Mailing Address: 228 Alexander Rd., Second Floor, Princeton, NJ 08544. **Telephone:** (609) 258-6426. **Fax:** (609) 258-1690.
E-Mail Address: trevor@ivyleaguesports.com.
Website: www.ivyleaguesports.com.
Baseball Members (First Year): Rolfe—Brown (1948), Dartmouth (1930), Harvard (1948), Yale (1930). Gehrig—Columbia (1930), Cornell (1930), Pennsylvania (1930), Princeton (1930). **Assistant Executive Director, Communications/Championships:** Trevor Rutledge-Leverenz. **2019 Tournament:** Best-of-three series between division champions. Team with best Ivy League record hosts. May 19-20.

METRO ATLANTIC ATHLETIC CONFERENCE

Mailing Address: 712 Amboy Ave., Edison, NJ 08837. **Telephone:** (732) 738-5455.
E-Mail Address: phil.paquette@maac.org.
Website: www.maacsports.com.
Baseball Members (First Year): Canisius (1990), Fairfield (1982), Iona (1982), Manhattan (1982), Marist (1998), Monmouth (2014), Niagara (1990), Quinnipiac (2014), Rider (1998), Saint Peter's (1982), Siena (1990). **Director, New Media:** Phil Paquette. **2019 Tournament:** Six teams, double-elimination. May 22-25 at Richmond County Bank Ballpark, Staten Island, N.Y.

MID-AMERICAN CONFERENCE

Mailing Address: 24 Public Square, 15th Floor, Cleveland, OH 44113. **Telephone:** (216) 566-4622. **Fax:** (216) 858-9622.
E-Mail Address: jguy@mac-sports.com.
Website: www.mac-sports.com.
Baseball Members (First Year): Ball State (1973), Bowling Green State (1952), Central Michigan (1971), Eastern Michigan (1971), Kent State (1951), Miami (1947), Northern Illinois (1997), Ohio (1946), Toledo (1950), Western Michigan (1947). **Assistant Commissioner, Communications and Social Media:** Jeremy Guy. **2019 Tournament:** Eight teams, double-elimination. May 22-26 at Springer Stadium, Avon, Ohio.

MID-EASTERN ATHLETIC CONFERENCE

Mailing Address: 2730 Ellsmere Ave., Norfolk, VA 23513. **Telephone:** (757) 951-2055. **Fax:** (757) 951-2077.
E-Mail Address: cunninghamj@themeac.com; porterp@themeac.com.
Website: www.meacsports.com.
Baseball Members (First Year): Bethune-Cookman (1979), Coppin State (1985), Delaware State (1970), Florida A&M (1979), Maryland Eastern Shore (1970), Norfolk State (1998), North Carolina A&T (1970), North Carolina Central (2012), Savannah State (2012). **Assistant Director, Media Relations:** Jeff Cunningham. **2019 Tournament:** six-teams, double-elimination. May 15-18 at Jackie Robinson Stadium, Daytona Beach, Fla.

MISSOURI VALLEY CONFERENCE

Mailing Address: 1818 Chouteau Ave., St. Louis, MO 63103. **Telephone:** (314) 444-4300. **Fax:** (314) 444-4333.
E-Mail Address: davis@mvc.org.
Website: www.mvc-sports.com.
Baseball Members (First Year): Bradley (1955), Dallas Baptist (2014), Evansville (1994), Illinois State (1980), Indiana State (1976), Missouri State (1990), Southern Illinois (1974), Valparaiso (2019). **Assistant Commissioner, Communications:** Ryan Davis. **2019 Tournament:** Eight-teams, double-elimination. May 21-25 at Duffy Bass Field, Normal, Ill.

MOUNTAIN WEST CONFERENCE

Mailing Address: 10807 New Allegiance Dr., Suite 250, Colorado Springs, CO 80921. **Telephone:** (719) 488-4052. **Fax:** (719) 487-7241.
E-Mail Address: sbuchanan@themw.com.
Website: www.themw.com.
Baseball Members (First Year): Air Force (2000), Fresno State (2013), Nevada (2013), Nevada-Las Vegas (2000), New Mexico (2000), San Diego State (2000), San Jose State (2013). **Director, Strategic Communication:** Stuart Buchanan. **2019 Tournament:** Four teams, double-elimination. May 23-26 at Peccole Park, Reno, Nev.

NORTHEAST CONFERENCE

Mailing Address: 200 Cottontail Lane, Vantage Court South, Somerset, NJ 08873. **Telephone:** (732) 469-0440. **Fax:** (732) 469-0744.

E-Mail Address: rventre@northeast conference.org.
Website: www.northeastconference.org.
Baseball Members (First Year): Bryant (2010), Central Connecticut State (1999), Fairleigh Dickinson (1981), Long Island -Brooklyn (1981), Mount St. Mary's (1989), Sacred Heart (2000), Wagner (1981). **Director, Communications/ Social Media:** Ralph Ventre. **2019 Tournament:** Four teams, double-elimination. May 23-26 at Dodd Stadium, Norwich, Conn.

OHIO VALLEY CONFERENCE

Mailing Address: 215 Centerview Dr., Suite 115, Brentwood, TN 37027. **Telephone:** (615) 371-1698. **Fax:** (615) 891-1682.

E-Mail Address: kschwartz@ovc.org.
Website: www.ovcsports.com.
Baseball Members (First Year): Austin Peay State (1962), Belmont (2013), Eastern Illinois (1996), Eastern Kentucky (1948), Jacksonville State (2003), Morehead State (1948), Murray State (1948), Southeast Missouri State (1991), Southern Illinois-Edwardsville (2012), Tennessee-Martin (1992), Tennessee Tech (1949). **Assistant Commissioner:** Kyle Schwartz. **2019 Tournament:** Eight teams. May 21-26 at Marion, Ill.

PACIFIC-12 CONFERENCE

Mailing Address: Pac-12 Conference 360 3rd Street, 3rd Floor San Francisco, CA 94107. **Telephone:** (415) 580-4200. **Fax:** (415)549-2828.

E-Mail Address: jolivero@pac-12.org.
Website: www.pac-12.com.
Baseball Members (First Year): Arizona (1979), Arizona State (1979), California (1916), UCLA (1928), Oregon (2009) Oregon State (1916), Southern California (1923), Stanford (1918), Utah (2012), Washington (1916), Washington State (1919). **Public Relations Contact:** Jon Olivero. **2019 Tournament:** None.

PATRIOT LEAGUE

Mailing Address: 3773 Corporate Pkwy., Suite 190, Center Valley, PA 18034. **Telephone:** (610) 289-1950. **Fax:** (610) 289-1951.

E-Mail Address: rsakamoto@patriotleague.com.
Website: www.patriotleague.org.
Baseball Members (First Year): Army (1993), Bucknell (1991), Holy Cross (1991), Lafayette (1991), Lehigh (1991), Navy (1993). **Assistant Commissioner, Communications:** Ryan Sakamoto. **2019 Tournament:** Four teams, best-of-three semifinals May 11-12 and best-of-three finals May 17-19 at higher seeds.

SOUTHEASTERN CONFERENCE

Mailing Address: 2201 Richard Arrington Blvd. N., Birmingham, AL 35203. **Telephone:** (205) 458-3000. **Fax:** (205) 458-3030.

E-Mail Address: scartell@sec.org.
Website: www.secsports.com.
Baseball Members (First Year): East Division— Florida (1933), Georgia (1933), Kentucky (1933), Missouri (2013), South Carolina (1992), Tennessee (1933), Vanderbilt (1933). **West Division—**Alabama (1933), Arkansas (1992), Auburn (1933), Louisiana State (1933), Mississippi (1933), Mississippi State (1933), Texas A&M (2013). **Direc-**

tor, Communications: Chuck Dunlap. **2019 Tournament:** 12 teams, modified single/double-elimination. May 21-26 at Hoover Metropolitan Stadium, Hoover, Ala.

SOUTHERN CONFERENCE

Mailing Address: 702 N. Pine St., Spartanburg, SC 29303. **Telephone:** (864) 591-5100. **Fax:** (864) 591-3448.

E-Mail Address: hsimmons@socon.org.
Website: www.soconsports.com.
Baseball Members (First Year): The Citadel (1937), East Tennessee State (1979-2005, 2015), Furman (1937), Mercer (2015), UNC Greensboro (1998), Samford (2009), VMI (1925-2003, 2015), Western Carolina (1977), Wofford (1998). **Media Relations Assistant:** Hannah Simmons. **2019 Tournament:** Nine teams, single-game play-in for bottom two seeds, followed by double-elimination bracket play. May 21-26 at Fluor Field, Greenville, S.C.

SOUTHLAND CONFERENCE

Mailing Address: 2600 Network Blvd, Suite 150, Frisco, Texas 75034. **Telephone:** (972) 422-9500. **Fax:** (972) 422-9225.

E-Mail Address: gstieren@southland.org
Website: southland.org.
Baseball Members (First Year): Abilene Christian (2014), Central Arkansas (2007), Houston Baptist (2014), Incarnate Word (2014), Lamar (1999), McNeese State (1973), New Orleans (2014), Nicholls State (1992), Northwestern State (1988), Sam Houston State (1988), Southeastern Louisiana (1998), Stephen F. Austin State (2006), Texas A&M-Corpus Christi (2007). **Associate Commissioner, Strategic Communications:** George Stieren. **2019 Tournament:** Two four-team brackets, double-elimination. May 22-25 at Constellation Field, Sugar Land, Texas.

SOUTHWESTERN ATHLETIC CONFERENCE

Mailing Address: 2101 6th Ave. North, Suite 700, Birmingham, AL 35203. **Telephone:** (205) 251-7573. **Fax:** (205) 297-9820.

E-Mail Address: a.roberts@swac.org.
Website: www.swac.org.
Baseball Members (First Year): East Division—Alabama A&M (2000), Alabama State (1982), Alcorn State (1962), Jackson State (1958), Mississippi Valley State (1968). **West Division—**Arkansas-Pine Bluff (1999), Grambling State (1958), Prairie View A&M (1920), Southern (1934), Texas Southern (1954). **Assistant Commissioner, Communications:** Andrew Roberts. **2019 Tournament:** Eight teams, double-elimination. May 15-19 at Wesley Barrow Stadium, New Orleans, La.

SUMMIT LEAGUE

Mailing Address: 340 W. Butterfield Rd., Suite 3D, Elmhurst, IL 60126. **Telephone:** (630) 516-0661. **Fax:** (630) 516-0673.

E-Mail Address: powell@thesummitleague.org.
Website: www.thesummitleague.org.
Baseball Members (First Year): IPFW (2008), Nebraska-Omaha (2013), North Dakota State (2008), Oral Roberts (1998), South Dakota State (2008), Western Illinois (1984). **Associate Commissioner, Communications:** Ryan Powell. **2019 Tournament:** Four teams, double-elimination. May 22-25 at J.L. Johnson Stadium, Tulsa, Okla.

SUN BELT CONFERENCE

Mailing Address: 1500 Sugar Bowl Dr., New Orleans, LA 70112. **Telephone:** (504) 556-0884. **Fax:** (504) 299-9068. **E-Mail Address:** nunez@sunbeltsports.org. **Website:** www.sunbeltsports.org.
Baseball Members (First Year): East Division—Appalachian State (2015), Coastal Carolina (2017), Georgia Southern, (2015), Georgia State (2014), South Alabama (1976), Troy (2006). **West Division**—Arkansas-Little Rock (1991), Arkansas State (1991), Louisiana-Lafayette (1991), Louisiana-Monroe (2007), Texas-Arlington (2014), Texas State (2014). **Assistant Commissioner, Digital & Creative Services:** Keith Nunez. **2019 Tournament:** Eight teams, double-elimination. May 21-26 at Springs Brooks Field, Conway, S.C.

WESTERN ATHLETIC CONFERENCE

Mailing Address: 9250 East Costilla Ave., Suite 300, Englewood, CO 80112. **Telephone:** (303) 799-9221. **Fax:** (303) 799-3888.
E-Mail Address: cthompson@wac.org.
Website: www.wacsports.com.
Baseball Members (First Year): California Baptist (2019), Cal State Bakersfield (2013), Chicago State (2014), Grand Canyon (2014), New Mexico State (2006), Northern Colorado (2014), Sacramento State (2006), Seattle (2013), Texas-Rio Grande Valley (2014), Utah Valley (2014). **Director, Media Relations:** Chris Thompson. **2019 Tournament:** Six teams, double-elimination, May 22-25/26 at Hohokam Stadium, Mesa, Ariz.

WEST COAST CONFERENCE

Mailing Address: 1111 Bayhill Dr., Suite 405, San Bruno, CA 94066. **Telephone:** (650) 873-8622. **Fax:** (650) 873-7846. **E-Mail Addresses:** rmccrary@westcoast.org.
Website: www.wccsports.com.
Baseball Members (First Year): Brigham Young (2012), Gonzaga (1996), Loyola Marymount (1968), Pacific (2014), Pepperdine (1968), Portland (1996), Saint Mary's (1968), San Diego (1979), San Francisco (1968), Santa Clara (1968). **Assistant Commissioner, Communications:** Ryan McCrary. **2019 Tournament:** Four teams, May 23-25 at Banner Island Ballpark, Stockton, Calif.

NCAA DIVISION I TEAMS

* Denotes recruiting coordinator

ABILENE CHRISTIAN WILDCATS

Conference: Southland. **Mailing Address:** 1201 E Ambler Ave., Abilene, TX, 79601. **Website:** www.acusports.com. **Head Coach:** Rick McCarty. **Telephone:** (325) 674-2325. **Baseball SID:** Chris Macaluso. **Telephone:** (325) 674-6171. **Assistant Coaches:** *Blaze Lambert, Craig Parry. **Telephone:** (325) 674-2817. **Home Field:** Crutcher Scott Field. **Seating Capacity:** 4000. **Outfield Dimension: LF**—334, **CF**—400, **RF**—334. **Press Box Telephone:** (325) 674-6934.

AIR FORCE FALCONS

Conference: Mountain West. **Mailing Address:** 2169 Field House Drive, USAF Academy, CO 80840.
Website: www.goairforcefalcons.com.
Head Coach: Mike Kazlausky (Maj. Retired).
Telephone: (719) 333-0835. **Baseball SID:** Dan

Whitaker. **Telephone:** (719) 333-3950. **Assistant Coaches:** Ryan Forrest, C.J. Gillman. **Telephone:** (719) 333-7539. **Home Field:** Falcon Field. **Seating Capacity:** 1,000. **Outfield Dimension: LF**—349, **CF**—400, **RF**—315.

ALABAMA CRIMSON TIDE

Conference: Southeastern. **Mailing Address:** Sewell-Thomas Stadium, 1201 Coliseum Drive, Tuscaloosa, AL 35487. **Website:** www.RollTide.com. **Head Coach:** Brad Bohannon. **Telephone:** (205) 348-4029. **Baseball SID:** Alexander Thompson. **Telephone:** (205) 348-6084. **Assistant Coaches:** Jason Jackson, *Jerry Zulli. **Telephone:** (205) 348-4029. **Home Field:** Sewell-Thomas Stadium. **Seating Capacity:** 5,867+. **Outfield Dimension: LF**—320, **CF**—390, **RF**—320.

ALABAMA A&M BULLDOGS

Conference: Southwestern Athletic. **Mailing Address:** 4900 Meridian Street, PO Box 1597, Normal, AL 35762. **Website:** www.aamusports.com. **Head Coach:** Mitch Hill. **Telephone:** (256) 372-4004. **Baseball SID:** Bud McLaughlin. **Telephone:** (256) 372-4005. **Assistant Coaches:** Manny Lora. **Telephone:** (256) 372-7213. **Home Field:** Bulldog Baseball Field. **Seating Capacity:** 500. **Outfield Dimension: LF**—330, **CF**—402, **RF**—318.

ALABAMA STATE HORNETS

Conference: Southwestern Athletic. **Mailing Address:** 905 S Jackson St., Montgomery, AL 36104. **Website:** www.bamastatesports.com. **Head Coach:** Jose Vazquez. **Telephone:** (334) 229-5600. **Baseball SID:** Travis Jarome. **Telephone:** (334) 832-2632. **Assistant Coaches:** *Drew Clark, Matt Crane. **Telephone:** (334) 229-5607. **Home Field:** Wheeler-Watkins Ballpark. **Seating Capacity:** 500. **Outfield Dimension: LF**—330, **CF**—400, **RF**—330.

ALABAMA-BIRMINGHAM BLAZERS

Conference: Conference USA. **Mailing Address:** 617 13th Street South Birmingham, AL, 35294. **Website:** www.uabsports.com. **Head Coach:** Brian Shoop. **Telephone:** (205) 934-5181. **Baseball SID:** Abby Vinson. **Telephone:** (205) 934-0722. **Assistant Coaches:** Ron Polk, *Perry Roth. **Telephone:** (205) 934-5182. **Home Field:** Young Memorial Field. **Seating Capacity:** 1000. **Outfield Dimension: LF**—330, **CF**—400, **RF**—330.

ALBANY GREAT DANES

Conference: America East. **Mailing Address:** 1400 Washington Avenue Albany, NY 12222. **Website:** ualbanysports.com. **Head Coach:** Jon Mueller. **Telephone:** (518) 442-3337. **Baseball SID:** Aly Greene. **Telephone:** (518) 442-3072. **Assistant Coaches:** *Jeff Kaier, Jordan Tabakman. **Telephone:** (518) 442-3337. **Home Field:** Varsity Field. **Outfield Dimension: LF**—330, **CF**—400, **RF**—330.

ALCORN STATE BRAVES

Conference: Southwestern Athletic. **Mailing Address:** 1000 ASU Drive #510, Lorman, MS 39096. **Website:** www.alcornsports.com. **Head Coach:** Bretton Richardson. **Telephone:** (601) 877-4090. **Baseball SID:** Robbie Kleinmuntz. **Telephone:** (601) 877-2322. **Assistant Coaches:** Tristan Toorie, Cedric Bell. **Home Field:** Foster Baseball Field at McGowan Stadium.

APPALACHIAN STATE MOUNTAINEERS

Conference: Sun Belt. **Mailing Address:** 225 Broyhill Inn Ln Boone NC, 28607. **Website:** www.appstatesports.com. **Head Coach:** Kermit Smith. **Telephone:** (828) 262-6097. **Baseball SID:** Bret Strelow. **Telephone:** (828) 262-7162. **Assistant Coaches:** Justin Aspegren, *Britt Johnson. **Telephone:** (828)-262-8664. **Home Field:** Jim and Bettie Smith Stadium. **Seating Capacity:** 1100. **Outfield Dimension: LF**—335, **CF**—405, **RF**—330.

ARIZONA WILDCATS

Conference: Pac-12. **Mailing Address:** 1 National Championship Drive Tucson, AZ 85721. **Website:** www.arizonawildcats.com. **Head Coach:** Jay Johnson. **Telephone:** (520) 621-4102. **Baseball SID:** Brett Gleason. **Telephone:** (520) 621-4163. **Assistant Coaches:** *Sergio Brown, Dave Lawn. **Telephone:** (520) 621-4714. **Home Field:** Hi Corbett Field. **Seating Capacity:** 8,400. **Outfield Dimension: LF**—366, **CF**—395, **RF**—349.

ARIZONA STATE SUN DEVILS

Conference: Pac-12. **Mailing Address:** PO Box 872505 Tempe AZ 85287. **Website:** thesundevils.com. **Head Coach:** Tracy Smith. **Telephone:** (480) 965-1904. **Baseball SID:** Jeremy Hawkes. **Telephone:** (480) 965-9544. **Assistant Coaches:** Mike Cather, *Ben Greenspan. **Telephone:** (480) 965-5060. **Home Field:** Phoenix Municipal Stadium. **Seating Capacity:** 8,775. **Outfield Dimension: LF**—345, **CF**—410, **RF**—345.

ARKANSAS RAZORBACKS

Conference: Southeastern. **Mailing Address:** University of Arkansas Department of Athletics, Broyles Athletic Center, P.O. Box 7777, Fayetteville, AR, 72702. **Website:** ArkansasRazorbacks.com. **Head Coach:** Dave Van Horn. **Telephone:** (479) 575-3655. **Baseball SID:** John Thomas. **Telephone:** (479) 575-7430. **Fax:** .**Assistant Coaches:** Matt Hobbs, *Nate Thompson. **Telephone:** (479) 575-3552. **Home Field:** Baum Stadium. **Seating Capacity:** 10,737. **Outfield Dimension: LF**—320, **CF**—400, **RF**—320. **Press Box Telephone:** (479) 313-2564.

ARKANSAS STATE RED WOLVES

Conference: Sun Belt. **Mailing Address:** 228 Broyles Center, PO Box 7777, Fayetteville, AR 72701. **Website:** www.astateredwolves.com. **Head Coach:** Tommy Raffo. **Telephone:** (870) 972-2700. **Baseball SID:** Dennen Cuthbertson. **Telephone:** (870) 972-3383. **Assistant Coaches:** *Rick Guarno, Rowdy Hardy, Craig Massoni. **Telephone:** (870) 680-4338. **Home Field:** Tomlinson Stadium-Kell Field. **Seating Capacity:** 1,200. **Outfield Dimension: LF**—335, **CF**—400, **RF**—335.

ARKANSAS-LITTLE ROCK TROJANS

Conference: Sun Belt. **Mailing Address:** 2801 South University Ave. Little Rock, AR 72204. **Website:** www.ualrtrojans.com. **Head Coach:** Chris Curry. **Telephone:** (501) 519-2452. **Baseball SID:** Jeff Rebello. **Telephone:** (501) 569-3403. **Assistant Coaches:** *Noah Sanders, R.D. Spiehs. **Telephone:** (501) 690-2516. **Home Field:** Gary Hogan Field. **Seating Capacity:** 2000. **Outfield Dimension: LF**—325, **CF**—390, **RF**—305.

ARKANSAS-PINE BLUFF GOLDEN LIONS

Conference: Southwestern Athletic. **Website:** www.uapblionsroar.com. **Head Coach:** Carlos James. **Telephone:** (870) 575-8995. **Baseball SID:** Habtom Keleta. **Telephone:** (870) 575-7949. **Assistant Coaches:** Cory Bonner, *Roger Mallison. **Telephone:** (870) 575-8995. **Home Field:** Torii Hunter Baseball Complex. **Seating Capacity:** 1,500. **Outfield Dimension: LF**—330, **CF**—400, **RF**—330.

ARMY BLACK KNIGHTS

Conference: Patriot. **Mailing Address:** 639 Howard Road, West Point, N.Y., 10996. **Website:** GoArmyWestPoint.com. **Head Coach:** Jim Foster. **Telephone:** (845) 938-4938. **Baseball SID:** Kat Castner. **Telephone:** (845) 938-7197. **Assistant Coaches:** John Murphy, *Jamie Pinzino. **Telephone:** (845) 938-4929. **Home Field:** Johnson Stadium at Doubleday Field. **Seating Capacity:** 880. **Outfield Dimension: LF**—327, **CF**—400, **RF**—327.

AUBURN TIGERS

Conference: Southeastern. **Mailing Address:** Auburn Athletics Complex, 392 S Donahue Drive, Auburn, AL 36849. **Website:** auburntigers.com. **Head Coach:** Butch Thompson. **Telephone:** (334) 844-4990. **Baseball SID:** George Nunnelley. **Telephone:** (502) 609-9982. **Assistant Coaches:** Gabe Gross, *Karl Nonemaker. **Telephone:** (334) 844-4990. **Home Field:** Hitchcock Field at Plainsman Park. **Seating Capacity:** 4096. **Outfield Dimension: LF**—315, **CF**—385, **RF**—331. **Press Box Telephone:** (334) 844-4138.

AUSTIN PEAY STATE GOVERNORS

Conference: Ohio Valley. **Mailing Address:** 601 College Street, Clarksville, TN 37044. **Website:** www.letsgopeay.com. **Head Coach:** Travis Janssen. **Telephone:** (931) 221-6266. **Baseball SID:** Cody Bush. **Telephone:** (931) 221-7561. **Assistant Coaches:** Greg Byron, *David Weber. **Telephone:** (931) 221-6392. **Home Field:** Raymond C. Hand Park. **Seating Capacity:** 777. **Outfield Dimension: LF**—319, **CF**—392, **RF**—327.

BALL STATE CARDINALS

Conference: Mid-American. **Mailing Address:** 2000 University Ave, Muncie IN 47304. **Website:** www.bsu.edu. **Head Coach:** Rich Maloney. **Telephone:** (765) 285-1425. **Baseball SID:** Mike Clark. **Telephone:** (765) 285-8904. **Assistant Coaches:** *Blake Beemer, Dustin Glant. **Telephone:** (765) 285-2862. **Home Field:** Ball Diamond at First Merchants Ballpark Complex. **Seating Capacity:** 1500. **Outfield Dimension: LF**—325, **CF**—394, **RF**—325.

BAYLOR BEARS

Conference: Big 12. **Mailing Address:** 1612 S. University Parks Dr., Waco, TX 76706. **Website:** www.baylorbears.com. **Head Coach:** Steve Rodriguez. **Telephone:** (254) 710-3029. **Baseball SID:** Rachel Caton. **Telephone:** (254) 710-3784. **Assistant Coaches:** Jon Strauss, *Mike Taylor. **Telephone:** (254) 710-3044. **Home Field:** Baylor Ballpark. **Seating Capacity:** 5000. **Outfield Dimension: LF**—330, **CF**—400, **RF**—330.

BELMONT BRUINS

Conference: Ohio Valley. **Mailing Address:** 1900 Belmont Blvd. Nashville, TN 37212. **Website:** www.belmontbruins.com. **Head Coach:** Dave Jarvis. **Telephone:** (615) 460-6166. **Baseball SID:** Hannah Jo Riley. **Telephone:** (615) 460-8023. **Assistant Coaches:** Caleb Longshore, *Aaron Smith. **Telephone:** (615) 460-5586. **Home Field:** E.S. Rose Park. **Seating Capacity:** 500. **Outfield Dimension: LF**—330, **CF**—400, **RF**—330.

BETHUNE-COOKMAN WILDCATS

Conference: Mid-Eastern. **Mailing Address:** 640 Dr. Mary McLeod Bethune Blvd.; Daytona Beach, FL 32114. **Website:** www.bcuathletics.com. **Head Coach:** Jonathan Hernandez. **Telephone:** (386) 481-2224. **Baseball SID:** Bryan J. Harvey. **Telephone:** (386) 481-2206. **Assistant Coaches:** *Keith Zuniga. **Telephone:** (386) 481-2242. **Home Field:** Jackie Robinson Ballpark. **Seating Capacity:** 4200. **Outfield Dimension: LF**—317, **CF**—400, **RF**—325.

BINGHAMTON BEARCATS

Conference: America East. **Mailing Address:** 4400 Vestal Parkway East, Binghamton, NY 13902. **Website:** www.bubearcats.com. **Head Coach:** Tim Sinicki. **Telephone:** (607) 777-2525. **Baseball SID:** John Hartrick. **Telephone:** (607) 777-6800. **Assistant Coaches:** Mike Folli, *Ryan Hurba. **Telephone:** (607) 777-2525. **Home Field:** Baseball Complex. **Seating Capacity:** 464 plus lawn seating. **Outfield Dimension: LF**—325, **CF**—390, **RF**—325.

BOSTON COLLEGE EAGLES

Conference: Atlantic Coast. **Mailing Address:** 412 Conte Forum 140 Commonwealth Ave. Chestnut Hill MA, 02467. **Website:** www.bceagles.com. **Head Coach:** Mike Gambino. **Telephone:** (617) 552-2674. **Baseball SID:** Zanna Ollove. **Telephone:** (617) 552-2004. **Assistant Coaches:** *Greg Sullivan, Alex Trezza. **Telephone:** (617) 552-1131. **Home Field:** Brighton Field. **Seating Capacity:** 2,500. **Outfield Dimension: LF**—330, **CF**—403, **RF**—330.

BOWLING GREEN STATE FALCONS

Conference: Mid-American. **Mailing Address:** 1610 Stadium Drive, Bowling Green Ohio 43403. **Website:** www.bgsufalcons.com. **Head Coach:** Danny Schmitz. **Telephone:** (419) 372-7065. **Baseball SID:** James Nahikian. **Telephone:** (419) 372-7105. **Assistant Coaches:** Kyle Hallock, Ryan Shay. **Telephone:** (419) 372-7641. **Home Field:** Warren E. Steller. **Seating Capacity:** 1,100. **Outfield Dimension: LF**—340, **CF**—400, **RF**—340.

BRADLEY BRAVES

Conference: Missouri Valley. **Mailing Address:** 1600 W Main St. Peoria, Il. **Website:** bradleybraves.com. **Head Coach:** Elvis Dominguez. **Telephone:** (309) 677-2684. **Baseball SID:** Bobby Parker. **Telephone:** (309) 677-2624. **Assistant Coaches:** *Larry Scully, Kyle Trewyn. **Telephone:** (309) 677-4996. **Home Field:** Dozer Park. **Seating Capacity:** 7500. **Outfield Dimension: LF**—310, **CF**—400, **RF**—310.

BRIGHAM YOUNG COUGARS

Conference: West Coast. **Mailing Address:** 111 Miller Park, Provo UT 84602. **Website:** www.byucougars.com. **Head Coach:** Mike Littlewood. **Telephone:** (801) 422-5049. **Baseball SID:** Ralph Zobell.

Telephone: (801) 422-9769. **Assistant Coaches:** *Brent Haring, Trent Pratt. **Telephone:** (801) 422-5064. **Home Field:** Miller Park. **Seating Capacity:** 2,500. **Outfield Dimension: LF**—345, **CF**—400, **RF**—345.

BROWN BEARS

Conference: Ivy League. **Mailing Address:** 235 Hope St. Box 1932, Providence, RI 02912. **Website:** www.brownbears.com. **Head Coach:** Grant Achilles. **Telephone:** (401) 863-3090. **Baseball SID:** Eric Peterson. **Telephone:** (401) 863-7014. **Assistant Coaches:** Jonathan Grosse, *Mike McCormack. **Telephone:** (401) 863-2032. **Home Field:** Murray Stadium. **Seating Capacity:** 1,500. **Outfield Dimension: LF**—330, **CF**—415, **RF**—320.

BRYANT BULLDOGS

Conference: Northeast. **Mailing Address:** 1150 Douglas Pike Smithfield, RI 02917. **Website:** bryantbulldogs.com. **Head Coach:** Steve Owens. **Telephone:** (401) 232-6397. **Baseball SID:** Tristan Hobbes. **Telephone:** (401) 232-6558. **Assistant Coaches:** *Brendan Monaghan, Kyle Pettoruto. **Telephone:** (401) 232-6967. **Home Field:** Conaty Park. **Seating Capacity:** 300. **Outfield Dimension: LF**—330, **CF**—400, **RF**—330.

BUCKNELL BISON

Conference: Patriot. **Mailing Address:** 700 Moore Avenue Lewisburg, Pa. 17837. **Website:** bucknellbison.com. **Head Coach:** Scott Heather. **Telephone:** (570) 577-3593. **Baseball SID:** Cole Cloonan. **Telephone:** (570) 577-1227. **Assistant Coaches:** Jason Neitz. **Telephone:** (570) 577-1059. **Home Field:** Depew Field. **Seating Capacity:** 1000. **Outfield Dimension: LF**—330, **CF**—400, **RF**—330.

BUTLER BULLDOGS

Conference: Big East. **Mailing Address:** 4600 Sunset Avenue, Indianapolis, IN 46208. **Website:** www.butlersports.com. **Head Coach:** Dave Schrage. **Telephone:** (317) 940-9721. **Baseball SID:** Kit Stetzel. **Telephone:** (317) 940-9994. **Assistant Coaches:** Ben Norton, *Andy Pascoe. **Telephone:** (317) 940-6536. **Home Field:** Bulldog Park. **Seating Capacity:** 500. **Outfield Dimension: LF**—330, **CF**—400, **RF**—300.

CALIFORNIA GOLDEN BEARS

Conference: Pac-12. **Mailing Address:** Haas Pavilion #4422, Berkeley, CA 94720-4422. **Website:** www.calbears.com. **Head Coach:** Mike Neu. **Telephone:** (510) 643-6006. **Baseball SID:** Ben Enos. **Telephone:** (510) 642-5363. **Assistant Coaches:** *Noah Jackson, Damon Lessler. **Telephone:** (510) 643-6006. **Home Field:** Evans Diamond. **Seating Capacity:** 3500. **Outfield Dimension: LF**—320, **CF**—410, **RF**—320.

CALIFORNIA BAPTIST LANCERS

Conference: Western Athletic. **Mailing Address:** 8432 Magnolia Ave., Riverside, CA 92504. **Website:** www.cbulancers.com. **Head Coach:** Gary Adcock. **Telephone:** (951) 343-4382 . **Baseball SID:** Andrew Shortall. **Telephone:** (951) 343-4779 . **Assistant Coaches:** Andrew Brasington, Jesse Zepeda. **Telephone:** (951) 343-4581. **Home Field:** Totman Stadium. **Seating Capacity:** 800.

CAL POLY MUSTANGS

Conference: Big West. **Mailing Address:** 1 Grand Avenue, San Luis Obispo, CA 93407-0388. **Website:** www.

gopoly.com. **Head Coach:** Larry Lee. **Telephone:** (805) 756-6367. **Baseball SID:** Eric Burdick. **Telephone:** (805) 756-6550. **Assistant Coaches:** Chal Fanning, *Teddy Warrecker. **Telephone:** (805) 756-1201. **Home Field:** Baggett Stadium. **Seating Capacity:** 3,138. **Outfield Dimension:** LF—335, CF—405, RF—335. **Press Box Telephone:** (805) 756-7456.

CAL STATE BAKERSFIELD ROADRUNNERS

Conference: Western Athletic. **Mailing Address:** 90001 Stockdale Hwy, 8 Gym, Bakersfield, CA 93311. **Website:** gorunners.com. **Head Coach:** Jeremy Beard. **Telephone:** (661) 654-2678. **Baseball SID:** Lou Groce. **Telephone:** (661) 654-6071. **Assistant Coaches:** Jonathan Johnson. **Telephone:** (661) 654-2678. **Home Field:** Hardt Field. **Seating Capacity:** 750. **Outfield Dimension:** LF—325, CF—390, RF—325.

CAL STATE FULLERTON TITANS

Conference: Big West. **Mailing Address:** 800 N. State College Blvd Fullerton, CA 92834. **Website:** www.fullertontitans.com. **Head Coach:** Rick Vanderhook. **Telephone:** (657) 278-3039. **Baseball SID:** Bryant Freese. **Telephone:** (657) 278-7083. **Assistant Coaches:** *Chad Baum, Steve Rousey. **Telephone:** (657) 278-2492. **Home Field:** Goodwin Field. **Seating Capacity:** 4000. **Outfield Dimension:** LF—330, CF—395, RF—330.

CAL STATE NORTHRIDGE MATADORS

Conference: Big West. **Mailing Address:** 18111 Nordhoff St., Northridge, CA 91330. **Website:** www.gomatadors.com. **Head Coach:** Greg Moore. **Telephone:** (818) 677-7055. **Baseball SID:** Nick Bocanegra. **Telephone:** (818) 677-7188. **Assistant Coaches:** *Tony Asaro, Jordon Twohig. **Telephone:** (818) 677-3218. **Home Field:** Matador Field. **Seating Capacity:** 1000. **Outfield Dimension:** LF—325, CF—390, RF—325.

CAMPBELL CAMELS

Conference: Big South. **Mailing Address:** 79 Upchurch Ln, Buies Creek, NC 27506. **Website:** www.gocamels.com. **Head Coach:** Justin Haire. **Telephone:** (910) 893-1338. **Baseball SID:** Eric Ortiz. **Telephone:** (910) 893-1529. **Assistant Coaches:** *Chris Marx, Tyler Robinson. **Telephone:** (910) 814-5510. **Home Field:** Jim Perry Stadium. **Seating Capacity:** 1,500. **Outfield Dimension:** LF—337, CF—395, RF—328.

CANISIUS GOLDEN GRIFFINS

Conference: Metro Atlantic. **Mailing Address:** 2001 Main St. **Website:** GoGriffs.com. **Head Coach:** Matt Mazurek. **Telephone:** (716) 888-8479. **Baseball SID:** Marshal Filipowicz. **Telephone:** (716) 888-8266. **Assistant Coaches:** Brandon Bielecki, *Matt Mazurek. **Telephone:** (716) 888-8485. **Home Field:** Demske Sports Complex. **Seating Capacity:** 1000. **Outfield Dimension:** LF—327, CF—346, RF—330.

CENTRAL ARKANSAS BEARS

Conference: Southland. **Mailing Address:** 201 Donaghey Ave, Conway, AR 72035. **Website:** www.uca-sports.com. **Head Coach:** Allen Gum. **Telephone:** (501) 499-1707. **Baseball SID:** Steve East. **Telephone:** (501) 450-5743. **Fax:** (501) 450-3151. **Assistant Coaches:** Nick Harlan, Justin Cunningham. **Telephone:** (402) 366-5948. **Home Field:** Bear Stadium. **Seating Capacity:** 1,500. **Outfield Dimension:** LF—330, CF—400, RF—330.

CENTRAL CONNECTICUT STATE BLUE DEVILS

Conference: Northeast. **Mailing Address:** 1615 Stanley St, New Britain, CT 06050. **Website:** www.CCSUBlueDevils. **Head Coach:** Charlie Hickey. **Telephone:** (860) 832-3074. **Baseball SID:** Jeff Mead. **Telephone:** (860) 832-3057. **Assistant Coaches:** *Pat Hall, Jim Ziogas. **Telephone:** (860) 832-3075. **Home Field:** CCSU Baseball Field. **Seating Capacity:** 1000. **Outfield Dimension:** LF—330, CF—400, RF—315.

CENTRAL FLORIDA KNIGHTS

Conference: American Athletic. **Mailing Address:** 4465 Knights Victory Way, Orlando, FL, 32816. **Website:** UCFKnights.com. **Head Coach:** Greg Lovelady. **Telephone:**. (407) 823-4869. **Baseball SID:** Ian MacDougall. **Telephone:** (407) 823-5395. **Assistant Coaches:** *Ryan Klosterman, Nick Otte. **Telephone:** (407) 823-5265. **Home Field:** John Euliano Park. **Seating Capacity:** 3841. **Outfield Dimension:** LF—320, CF—390, RF—320.

CENTRAL MICHIGAN CHIPPEWAS

Conference: Mid-American. **Mailing Address:** 100 Rose Center, Mount Pleasant, MI 48859. **Website:** cmuchippewas.com. **Head Coach:** Jordan Bischel. **Telephone:** (989) 774-4392. **Baseball SID:** Cullen Maksimowski. **Telephone:** (989) 774-3277. **Assistant Coaches:** Tony Jandron, *Kyle Schroeder. **Telephone:** (989) 774-1484. **Home Field:** Theunissen Stadium. **Seating Capacity:** 2046. **Outfield Dimension:** LF—330, CF—400, RF—330.

CHARLESTON SOUTHERN BUCCANEERS

Conference: Big South. **Mailing Address:** 9200 University Boulevard Charleston, S.C. 29406. **Website:** www.csusports.com. **Head Coach:** Adam Ward. **Telephone:** (843) 863-7832. **Baseball SID:** Derrick Bennington. **Telephone:** (843) 863-7433. **Assistant Coaches:** George Schaefer. **Telephone:** (843) **863-7832.** **Home Field:** Nielsen Field at CSU Ballpark. **Seating Capacity:** 1000. **Outfield Dimension:** LF—330, CF—400, RF—330.

CHARLOTTE 49ERS

Conference: Conference USA. **Mailing Address:** 9201 University City Blvd, Charlotte, NC, 28223. **Website:** Charlotte49ers.com. **Head Coach:** Loren Hibbs. **Telephone:** (704) 687-0726. **Baseball SID:** Sean Fox. **Telephone:** (704) 687-1023. **Assistant Coaches:** Shohn Doty, *Bo Robinson. **Telephone:** (704) 687-0727. **Home Field:** Hayes Stadium. **Seating Capacity:** 1200. **Outfield Dimension:** LF—335, CF—290, RF—315.

CHICAGO STATE COUGARS

Conference: Western Athletic. **Mailing Address:** JCC 1502, 9501 South King Drive, Chicago, IL 60628. **Website:** www.gocsucougars.com. **Head Coach:** Steve Joslyn. **Telephone:** (773) 995-3637. **Baseball SID:** TBA. **Assistant Coaches:** Mitch Glass, David Harden, Matt Schmidt. **Home Field:** Cougar Stadium. **Seating Capacity:** 200. **Outfield Dimension:** LF—330, CF—400, RF—330.

CINCINNATI BEARCATS

Conference: American Athletic. **Mailing Address:** 2751 O'Varsity Way, Cincinnati, OH 45221. **Website:** www.gobearcats.com. **Head Coach:** Scott

Googins. **Telephone:** (513) 556-0566. **Baseball SID:** Mollie Radzinski. **Telephone:** (513) 556-0667. **Assistant Coaches:** *JD Heilmann, Kyle Sprague. **Telephone:** (513) 556-0565. **Home Field:** Marge Schott Stadium. **Seating Capacity:** 3,085. **Outfield Dimension: LF**—325, **CF**—400, **RF**—325.

CITADEL BULLDOGS

Conference: Southern. **Mailing Address:** 171 Moultrie St., Charleston, SC, 29409. **Website:** www.citadelsports. com. **Head Coach:** Tony Skole. **Baseball SID:** John Brush. **Telephone:** (843) 953-6795. **Assistant Coaches:** Blake Cooper, *Aaron Gershenfeld. **Home Field:** Joseph. P Riley Park. **Seating Capacity:** 6,000. **Outfield Dimension: LF**—337, **CF**—398, **RF**—337.

CLEMSON TIGERS

Conference: Atlantic Coast. **Mailing Address:** Clemson, SC 29634. **Website:** ClemsonTigers.com. **Head Coach:** Monte Lee. **Telephone:** (864) 656-1947. **Baseball SID:** Brian Hennessy. **Telephone:** (864) 656-1921. **Assistant Coaches:** *Bradley LeCroy, Andrew See. **Telephone:** (864) 656-1948. **Home Field:** Doug Kingsmore Stadium. **Seating Capacity:** 6272. **Outfield Dimension: LF**—310, **CF**—390, **RF**—320. **Press Box Telephone:** (864) 656-7731.

COASTAL CAROLINA CHANTICLEERS

Conference: Sun Belt. **Mailing Address:** 100 Chanticleer Dr. E, Conway, S.C. 29528. **Website:** www. GoCCUSports.com. **Head Coach:** Gary Gilmore. **Telephone:** (843) 349-2524. **Baseball SID:** Kevin Davis. **Telephone:** (843) 349-2822. **Assistant Coaches:** *Kevin Schnall, Drew Thomas. **Telephone:** (843) 349-2849. **Home Field:** Springs Brooks Stadium. **Seating Capacity:** 5400. **Outfield Dimension: LF**—320, **CF**—390, **RF**—320. **Press Box Telephone:** (843) 234-3472.

COLLEGE OF CHARLESTON COUGARS

Conference: Colonial. **Mailing Address:** 301 Meeting St. Charleston, SC 29401. **Website:** cofcsports.com. **Head Coach:** Chad Holbrook. **Telephone:** (843) 953-5961. **Baseball SID:** Whitney Noble. **Telephone:** (843) 953-3683. **Assistant Coaches:** Will Dorton, *Kevin Nichols. **Telephone:** (843) 953-7013. **Home Field:** Patriots Point. **Seating Capacity:** 2,000. **Outfield Dimension: LF**—300, **CF**—400, **RF**—330.

COLUMBIA LIONS

Conference: Ivy League. **Mailing Address:** Dodge Physical Fitness Center 3030 Broadway New York, N.Y. 10027. **Website:** www.gocolumbialions.com. **Head Coach:** Brett Boretti. **Telephone:** (212) 854-8448. **Baseball SID:** Mike Kowalsky. **Telephone: :** (212) 854-7064. **Assistant Coaches:** Erik Supplee, *Dan Tischler. **Telephone:**(212) 854-7772. **Home Field:** Robertson Field at Satow Stadium. **Seating Capacity:** 600.

CONNECTICUT HUSKIES

Conference: American Athletic. **Mailing Address:** 2095 Hillside Road Unit 1173, Storrs, CT 06269. **Website:** uconnhuskies.com. **Head Coach:** Jim Penders. **Telephone:** (860) 486-4089. **Baseball SID:** Chris Jones. **Telephone:** (860) 486-4707. **Assistant Coaches:** Jeffrey Hourigan, Joshua McDonald. **Telephone:** (860) 465-6088. **Home Field:** J.O.Christian Field. **Seating Capacity:** 2,000. **Outfield Dimension: LF**—337, **CF**—400, **RF**—325.

COPPIN STATE EAGLES

Conference: Mid-Eastern. **Mailing Address:** 2500 W. North Avenue. **Website:** coppinstatesports.com. **Head Coach:** Sherman Reed Sr. **Telephone:** (410) 951-3723. **Baseball SID:** Steve Kramer. **Telephone:** (410) 951-3729. **Assistant Coaches:** *Matthew Greely, Lyndon Watkins. **Telephone:** (410) 951-6941. **Home Field:** Joe Cannon Stadium. **Seating Capacity:** 1500. **Outfield Dimension: LF**—325, **CF**—410, **RF**—325. **Press Box Telephone:** (410) 222-6652.

CORNELL BIG RED

Conference: Ivy League. **Mailing Address:** Teagle Hall, Campus Rd. Ithaca, NY 14853. **Website:** www.cornellbigred.com. **Head Coach:** Dan Pepicelli. **Telephone:** (607) 255-3812. **Baseball SID:** Brandon Thomas. **Telephone:** (607) 255-5627. **Assistant Coaches:** Tom Ford, *Frank Hager. **Telephone:** (607) 255-6604. **Home Field:** Hoy Field. **Seating Capacity:** 1,000. **Outfield Dimension: LF**—315, **CF**—405, **RF**—325.

CREIGHTON BLUEJAYS

Conference: Big East. **Mailing Address:** 2500 California Plaza, Athletic Department, Omaha, NE 68178. **Website:** www.gocreighton.com. **Head Coach:** Ed Servais. **Telephone:** (402) 280-2483. **Baseball SID:** Glen Sisk. **Telephone:** (402) 280-2433. **Assistant Coaches:** *Connor Gandossy, Eric Wordekemper, Paul Weidner. **Telephone:** (402) 280-5545. **Home Field:** TD Ameritrade Park Omaha. **Seating Capacity:** 24,000. **Outfield Dimension: LF**—335, **CF**—408, **RF**—335.

DALLAS BAPTIST PATRIOTS

Conference: Missouri Valley. **Mailing Address:** 3000 Mountain Creek Pkwy. Dallas, TX 75211. **Website:** www. dbupatriots.com. **Head Coach:** Dan Heefner. **Telephone:** (214) 333-5324. **Baseball SID:** Reagan Ratcliff. **Telephone:** (214) 333-6957. **Assistant Coaches:** *Dan Fitzgerald, Josh Hopper. **Telephone:** (214) 333-6987. **Home Field:** Horner Ballpark. **Seating Capacity:** 2000. **Outfield Dimension: LF**—330, **CF**—390, **RF**—330.

DARTMOUTH BIG GREEN

Conference: Ivy League. **Mailing Address:** 6083 Alumni Gym, Hanover, NH 03755. **Website:** www.dartmouthsports.com. **Head Coach:** Bob Whalen. **Telephone:** (603) 646-2477. **Baseball SID:** Rick Bender. **Telephone:** (603) 646-1030. **Fax:** (603) 646-3348. **Assistant Coaches:** *Jonathan Anderson, Andy Revell. **Telephone:** (603) 646-9775. **Home Field:** Red Rolfe Field at Biondi Park. **Seating Capacity:** 2,000. **Outfield Dimension: LF**—324, **CF**—403, **RF**—342.

DAVIDSON WILDCATS

Conference: Atlantic 10. **Mailing Address:** Box 7158 Davidson, NC 28035. **Website:** davidsonwildcats.com. **Head Coach:** Rucker Taylor. **Telephone:** (704) 892-2772. **Baseball SID:** Justin Parker. **Telephone:** (704) 894-2931. **Assistant Coaches:** Parker Bangs, *Ryan Munger. **Telephone:** (704) 892-2772. **Home Field:** Wilson Field. **Seating Capacity:** 1000. **Outfield Dimension: LF**—325, **CF**—390, **RF**—330.

DAYTON FLYERS

Conference: Atlantic 10. **Mailing Address:** 300 College Park Dayton OH 45469. **Website:** www.daytonflyers.com. **Head Coach:** Jayson King. **Telephone:** (603) 381-1279. **Baseball SID:** Jay Kafer. **Telephone:** (630) 301-0017. **Assistant Coaches:** *Tommy Chase, Travis Ferrick. **Telephone:** (540) 903-4967. **Home Field:** Woerner Field. **Seating Capacity:** 2,000. **Outfield Dimension:** LF—330, **CF**—400, **RF**—330.

DELAWARE BLUE HENS

Conference: Colonial. **Mailing Address:** 631 S. College Ave, Newark, Del. 19716. **Website:** www.blue-hens.com. **Head Coach:** Jim Sherman. **Telephone:** (302) 831-8596. **Baseball SID:** Mike Scholze. **Telephone:** (302) 831-6519. **Fax:** (302) 831-7206. **Assistant Coaches:** Dan Hammer, Juan Pimentel. **Telephone:** (302) 831-3097. **Home Field:** Bob Hannah Stadium. **Seating Capacity:** 1300. **Outfield Dimension:** LF—320, **CF**—400, **RF**—330.

DELAWARE STATE HORNETS

Conference: Mid-Eastern Athletic. **Mailing Address:** 1200 North DuPont Highway, Dover, DE 19901. **Website:** www.dsuhornets.com. **Head Coach:** J.P. Blandin. **Telephone:** (302) 857-6035. **Baseball SID:** Derrick Slayton. **Telephone:** (302) 857-6239. **Assistant Coaches:** Matt Domian, Geoff Kimmel. **Telephone:** (302) 857-7809. **Home Field:** Soldier Field. **Seating Capacity:** 500. **Outfield Dimension:** LF-320-, **CF**—380, **RF**—320.

DUKE BLUE DEVILS

Conference: Atlantic Coast. **Mailing Address:** Duke University Athletics PO Box 90555 Durham, NC 27708. **Website:** goduke.com. **Head Coach:** Chris Pollard. **Telephone:** (919) 668-0255. **Baseball SID:** Ashley Wolf. **Telephone:** (919) 668-4393. **Assistant Coaches:** *Josh Jordan, Jason Stein. **Home Field:** Durham Bulls Athletic Park. **Seating Capacity:** 10000. **Outfield Dimension:** **LF**—305, **CF**—400, **RF**—325.

EAST CAROLINA PIRATES

Conference: American Athletic. **Mailing Address:** 102 Clark-LeClair Stadium Greenville, NC 27858. **Website:** www.ecupirates.com. **Head Coach:** Cliff Godwin. **Telephone:** (252) 737-1985. **Baseball SID:** Malcolm Gray. **Telephone:** (252) 737-4523. **Fax:** (252) 737-1988. **Assistant Coaches:** *Jeff Palumbo, Dan Roszel. **Telephone:** (252) 737-1985. **Home Field:** Clark-LeClair Stadium. **Seating Capacity:** 5500. **Outfield Dimension:** **LF**—320, **CF**—400, **RF**—320.

EAST TENNESSEE STATE BUCCANEERS

Conference: Southern. **Mailing Address:** 1081 John Robert Bell Dr., Johnson City, TN 37601. **Website:** ETSUBucs.com. **Head Coach:** Joe Pennucci. **Telephone:** (423) 439-4496. **Baseball SID:** Mike Ezekiel. **Telephone:** (423) 439-8212. **Assistant Coaches:** *Ross Oeder, Micah Posey. **Telephone:** (423) 439-5727. **Home Field:** Thomas Stadium. **Seating Capacity:** 1000. **Outfield Dimension:** **LF**—325, **CF**—400, **RF**—325.

EASTERN ILLINOIS PANTHERS

Conference: Ohio Valley. **Mailing Address:** 600 Lincoln Ave., Charleston, IL 61920. **Website:** eiupanthers.com. **Head Coach:** Jason Anderson. **Telephone:** (217) 581-7283. **Baseball SID:** Thomas Manzello. **Telephone:** (217) 581-6408. **Assistant Coaches:** Andy Lasher, *Julio Godinez. **Telephone:** (217) 581-8510. **Home Field:** Coaches Stadium. **Seating Capacity:** 550. **Outfield Dimension:** LF—340, **CF**—390, **RF**—340.

EASTERN KENTUCKY COLONELS

Conference: Ohio Valley. **Mailing Address:** 115 Alumni Coliseum. **Website:** www.ekusports.com. **Head Coach:** Edwin Thompson. **Telephone:** (859) 622-2128. **Baseball SID:** Chris Wells. **Telephone:** (859) 893-9417. **Assistant Coaches:** Shaun Cole, *Julius McDougal. **Telephone:** (859) 622-4996. **Home Field:** Earle Combs Stadium. **Outfield Dimension:** LF—340 ft, **CF**—410 ft, **RF**—330 ft.

EASTERN MICHIGAN EAGLES

Conference: Mid-American. **Mailing Address:** 200 Bowen Field House, Ypsilanti MI 48197. **Website:** emueagles.com. **Head Coach:** Eric Roof. **Telephone:** (734) 487-1985. **Baseball SID:** Greg Steiner. **Telephone:** (734) 487-0318. **Assistant Coaches:** A.J. Achter, Jonathan Roof. **Telephone:** (734) 487-8660. **Home Field:** Oestrike Stadium. **Seating Capacity:** 1,200. **Outfield Dimension:** LF—325, **CF**—390, **RF**—325.

ELON PHOENIX

Conference: Colonial. **Mailing Address:** 100 Campus Drive, Elon, NC, 27244. **Website:** elonphoenix.com. **Head Coach:** Mike Kennedy. **Telephone:** (336) 278-6741. **Baseball SID:** Pierce Yarberry. **Telephone:** (336) 278-6712. **Assistant Coaches:** *Robbie Huffstetler, Sean McGrath. **Telephone:** (336) 278-6708. **Home Field:** Latham Park. **Seating Capacity:** 5100. **Outfield Dimension:** LF—325, **CF**—385, **RF**—325.

EVANSVILLE PURPLE ACES

Conference: Missouri Valley. **Mailing Address:** 1800 Lincoln Ave., Evansville, IN 47222. **Website:** www.gopurpleaces.com. **Head Coach:** Wes Carroll. **Telephone:** (812) 488-2059. **Baseball SID:** Joe Downs. **Telephone:** (812) 488-2394. **Assistant Coaches:** A.J. Gaura, Jake Mahon. **Telephone:** (812) 488-2764 . **Home Field:** Charles H. Braun Stadium. **Seating Capacity:** 1,200. **Outfield Dimension:** LF—330, **CF**—400, **RF**—330.

FAIRFIELD STAGS

Conference: Metro Atlantic. **Mailing Address:** 1076 North Benson Road, Fairfield CT. **Website:** fairfield-stags.com. **Head Coach:** Bill Currier. **Telephone:** (203) 254-4000. **Baseball SID:** Ivey Speight. **Telephone:** (203) 254-4000. **Assistant Coaches:** *Ted Hurvul, Kyle Nisson. **Telephone:** (203) 254-4000 ext. 3178. **Home Field:** Alumni Diamond. **Outfield Dimension:** LF—320, **CF**—400, **RF**—325.

FAIRLEIGH DICKINSON KNIGHTS

Conference: Northeast. **Mailing Address:** 1000 River Road, Athletic Department, Teaneck, NJ 007666. **Website:** www.fduknights.com. **Head Coach:** Justin McKay. **Telephone:** (201) 692-2245. **Baseball SID:** Bryan Jackson. **Telephone:** (201) 692-2149. **Assistant Coaches:** Eric Anderson, Bryan Radziewski. **Telephone:** (201) 692-2245. **Home Field:** Naimoli Family Baseball Complex. **Seating Capacity:** 1,000. **Outfield Dimension:** LF— 320, **CF**—365, **RF**— 320.

COLLEGE

FLORIDA GATORS

Conference: Southeastern. **Mailing Address:** 157 Gale Lemerand Dr, Gainesville, FL. **Website:** FloridaGators.com. **Head Coach:** Kevin O'Sullivan. **Telephone:** (352) 375-4683, ext. 4457. **Baseball SID:** Dan Apple. **Telephone:** (352) 375-4683 ext. 6199. **Assistant Coaches:** *Craig Bell, Brad Weitzel. **Telephone:**(352) 375-4683 ext. 4457. **Home Field:** McKethan Stadium. **Seating Capacity:** 5500. **Outfield Dimension:** LF—326, CF—404, RF—321.

FLORIDA A&M RATTLERS

Conference: Mid-Eastern. **Mailing Address:** Baseball Offices 1800 Wahnish Way Tallahassee, FL 32307. **Website:** www.famuathletics.com. **Head Coach:** Jamey Shouppe. **Telephone:** (850) 599-3202. **Baseball SID:** Vaughn Wilson. **Telephone:** (850) 599-3200. **Assistant Coaches:** *Bryan Henry, Anthony Robinson. **Telephone:** (850) 556-0769. **Home Field:** Moore-Kittles Field. **Seating Capacity:** 500. **Outfield Dimension:** LF—335, CF—400, RF—335.

FLORIDA ATLANTIC OWLS

Conference: Conference USA. **Mailing Address:** 777 Glades Road, Boca Raton, Fla. 33431. **Website:** www.FAUSports.com. **Head Coach:** John McCormack. **Telephone:** (561) 297-1055. **Baseball SID:** Jonathan Fraysure. **Telephone:** (561) 430-7148. **Assistant Coaches:** David Kopp, *Greg Mamula. **Telephone:** (561) **297-3956.** **Home Field:** FAU Baseball Stadium. **Seating Capacity:** 1718. **Outfield Dimension:** LF—330, CF—400, RF—330.

FLORIDA GULF COAST EAGLES

Conference: Atlantic Sun. **Mailing Address:** 10501 FGCU Blvd. South, Fort Myers, FL 33965. **Website:** www.fgcuathletics.com. **Head Coach:** Dave Tollett. **Telephone:** (239) 590-7051. **Baseball SID:** Matt Fischer. **Telephone:** (239) 590-1327. **Assistant Coaches:** Matt Reid, *Brandon Romans. **Telephone:** (239) 590-7058. **Home Field:** Swanson Stadium. **Seating Capacity:** 1,500. **Outfield Dimension:** LF—325, CF—400, RF—325.

FLORIDA INTERNATIONAL PANTHERS

Conference: Conference USA. **Mailing Address:** 11200 SW 8th St., Miami, FL 33199. **Website:** www.fiusports.com. **Head Coach:** Mervyl Melendez. **Telephone:** (305) 348-3166. **Baseball SID:** Tyler Brain. **Telephone:** (305) 348-2084. **Fax:** (305) 348-1357. **Assistant Coaches:** *Jered Goodwin, Dax Norris. **Telephone:** (305) 348-3168. **Home Field:** Panther Stadium. **Seating Capacity:** 2,000. **Outfield Dimension:** LF—325, CF—405, RF—325.

FLORIDA STATE SEMINOLES

Conference: Atlantic Coast. **Mailing Address:** 403 W. Stadium Dr., Tallahasse, FL. **Website:** www.seminoles.com. **Head Coach:** Mike Martin. **Telephone:** (850) 644-1073. **Baseball SID:** Steven McCartney. **Telephone:** (850) 644-3920. **Assistant Coaches:** Clyde Keller, *Mike Martin. **Telephone:** (850) 644-1073. **Home Field:** Dick Howser Stadium. **Seating Capacity:** 6700. **Outfield Dimension:** LF—320, CF—400, RF—340.

FORDHAM RAMS

Conference: Atlantic 10. **Mailing Address:** 441 East Fordham Road Bronx, NY 10458. **Website:** www.fordhamsports.com. **Head Coach:** Kevin Leighton. **Telephone:** (718) 817-4292. **Baseball SID:** Scott Kwiatkowski.

Telephone: (718) 817-4219. **Assistant Coaches:** *Rob DiToma, Peter Larson. **Telephone:** (718) 817-4290. **Home Field:** Houlihan Park. **Seating Capacity:** 500. **Outfield Dimension:** LF—339, CF—390, RF—325.

FRESNO STATE BULLDOGS

Conference: Mountain West. **Mailing Address:** 1620 East Bulldog Lane OF 87 Fresno, CA 93740. **Website:** gobulldogs.com. **Head Coach:** Mike Batesole. **Telephone:** (559) 278-2178. **Baseball SID:** Travis Blanshan. **Telephone:** (559) 278-4547. **Assistant Coaches:** Jermaine Clark, Rynaln Overland. **Telephone:** (559) 278-2178. **Home Field:** Beiden Field. **Seating Capacity:** 3,575. **Outfield Dimension:** LF—330, CF—400, RF—330.

FURMAN PALADINS

Conference: Southern. **Mailing Address:** 3300 Pointsett Highway, Greenville, SC 29613. **Website:** www.furmanpaladins.com. **Head Coach:** Brett Harker. **Telephone:** (864) 294-2243. **Baseball SID:** Hunter Reid. **Telephone:** (864) 294-2061. **Assistant Coaches:** Andrew Cox, Kaleb Davis, *Taylor Harbin. **Telephone:** (864) 449-1162. **Home Field:** Latham Stadium. **Seating Capacity:** 2,000. **Outfield Dimension:** LF— 330, CF— 393, RF— 330.

GARDNER-WEBB RUNNIN' BULLDOGS

Conference: Big South. **Mailing Address:** 110 S. Main St. Boiling Springs, NC 28017. **Website:** GWUSports.com. **Head Coach:** Rusty Stroupe. **Telephone:** (704) 406-4421. **Baseball SID:** Ryan Bridges. **Telephone:** (704) 406-3523. **Assistant Coaches:** Conner Scarbrough, *Ross Steedley. **Telephone:** (704) 406-3557. **Home Field:** John Henry Moss Stadium. **Seating Capacity:** 550. **Outfield Dimension:** LF—340, CF—395, RF—340.

GEORGE MASON PATRIOTS

Conference: Atlantic 10. **Mailing Address:** 4400 University Drive Fairfax, Va. 22030. **Website:** GoMason.com. **Head Coach:** Bill Brown. **Telephone:** (703) 993-3282. **Baseball SID:** Steve Kolbe. **Telephone:** (703) 993-3268. **Assistant Coaches:** *Tag Montague, Brain Pugh. **Telephone:** (703) 993-3328. **Home Field:** Spuhler Field. **Seating Capacity:** 900. **Outfield Dimension:** LF—320, CF—400, RF—320.

GEORGE WASHINGTON COLONIALS

Conference: Atlantic 10. **Mailing Address:** 600 22nd St NW, Washington, D.C. **Website:** GWsports.com. **Head Coach:** Gregg Ritchie. **Telephone:** (202) 994-7399. **Baseball SID:** Kevin Burke. **Telephone:** (202) 994-5666. **Assistant Coaches:** *Dave Lorber, Rick Oliveri. **Telephone:** (202) 994-5933. **Home Field:** Tucker Field at Barcroft Park. **Seating Capacity:** 500. **Outfield Dimension:** LF—330, CF—380, RF—330.

GEORGETOWN HOYAS

Conference: Big East. **Mailing Address:** 3700 O St. NW, Washington, DC 20057. **Website:** guhoyas.com. **Head Coach:** Pete Wilk. **Telephone:** (202) 687-2462. **Baseball SID:** Brendan Thomas. **Telephone:** (202) 687-6783. **Assistant Coaches:** Eric Niesen, *Ryan Wood. **Telephone:** (202) 687-6406. **Home Field:** Shirley Povich Field. **Seating Capacity:** 1,500. **Outfield Dimension:** LF—330, CF—375, RF—330.

GEORGIA BULLDOGS

Conference: SEC. **Mailing Address:** P.O. Box 1472, Athens, Ga. **Website:** georgiadogs.com. **Head Coach:** Scott Stricklin. **Telephone:** (706) 542-7971. **Baseball SID:** Christopher Lakos. **Telephone:** (706) 542-7994. **Assistant Coaches:** *Scott Daeley, Sean Kenny. **Telephone:** (706) 542-7971. **Home Field:** Foley Field. **Seating Capacity:** 3,291. **Outfield Dimension:** LF—350, CF—404, RF—314.

GEORGIA SOUTHERN EAGLES

Conference: Sun Belt. **Mailing Address:** Box 8095 Statesboro, GA 30460. **Website:** www.gseagles.com. **Head Coach:** Rodney Hennon. **Telephone:** (912) 478-7360. **Baseball SID:** AJ Henderson. **Telephone:** (912) 478-5071. **Assistant Coaches:** Alan Beck, *BJ Green. **Telephone:** (912) 478-1366. **Home Field:** JI Clements Stadium/Jack Stallings Field. **Seating Capacity:** 3200. **Outfield Dimension:** LF—335, CF—390, RF—329.

GEORGIA STATE PANTHERS

Conference: Sun Belt. **Mailing Address:** P.O. Box 3875, Atlanta, GA 30302-3975. **Website:** GeorgiaStateSports.com. **Head Coach:** Greg Frady. **Telephone:** (404) 413-4077. **Baseball SID:** Allison George. **Telephone:** (404) 413-4032. **Assistant Coaches:** *Brock Bennett, Josh Davis. **Telephone:** (404) 413-4077. **Home Field:** GSU Baseball Complex. **Seating Capacity:** 1500. **Outfield Dimension:** LF—334, CF—385, RF—338.

GEORGIA TECH YELLOW JACKETS

Conference: Atlantic Coast. **Mailing Address:** 150 Bobby Dodd Way NW Atlanta, Ga. 30338. **Website:** www.ramblinwreck.com. **Head Coach:** Danny Hall. **Telephone:** (404) 894-5445. **Baseball SID:** Andrew Clausen. **Telephone:** (404) 894-5445. **Assistant Coaches:** *Jason Howell, James Ramsey. **Telephone:** (404) 894-5081. **Home Field:** Russ Chandler Stadium. **Seating Capacity:** 4157. **Outfield Dimension:** LF—329, CF—390, RF—334.

GONZAGA BULLDOGS

Conference: West Coast. **Mailing Address:** 502 E. Boone. **Website:** GoZags.com. **Head Coach:** Mark Machtolf. **Telephone:** (509) 313-4209. **Baseball SID:** Todd Zeidler. **Telephone:** (509) 313-6373. **Assistant Coaches:** *Danny Evans, Brandon Harmon. **Telephone:** (509) 313-3597. **Home Field:** Patterson Baseball Complex and Steve Hertz Field. **Seating Capacity:** 1500. **Outfield Dimension:** LF—328, CF—398, RF—328.

GRAMBLING STATE

Conference: West Coast. **Mailing Address:** Gonzaga University 502 E Boone Ave., Spokane, WA 99258-0066. **Website:** www.gozags.com. **Head Coach:** Mark Machtolf. **Telephone:** (509) 313-4209. **Baseball SID:** Barrett Henderson **Telephone:** (509) 313-4288. **Assistant Coaches:** *Danny Evans, Brandon Harmon. **Telephone:** (509) 313-3597. **Home Field:** Patterson Baseball Complex & Washington Trust Field. **Seating Capacity:** 1,500. **Outfield Dimension:** LF—328, CF—400, RF—328.

GRAND CANYON LOPES

Conference: Western Athletic. **Mailing Address:** 3300 W Camelback Road, Phoenix, AZ 85017. **Website:** gcu-lopes.com. **Head Coach:** Andy Stankiewicz. **Telephone:** (602) 639-6042. **Baseball SID:** Josh Hauser. **Telephone:** (602) 639-8328. **Assistant Coaches:** Rich Dorman, *Gregg Wallis. **Telephone:** (602) 639-8416. **Home Field:** Brazell Field at GCU Ballpark. **Seating Capacity:** 4000. **Outfield Dimension:** LF—320, CF—375, RF—330.

HARTFORD HAWKS

Conference: America East. **Mailing Address:** 200 Bloomfield Ave, West Hartford, CT 06117. **Website:** hartfordhawks.com. **Head Coach:** Justin Blood. **Telephone:** (860) 768-5760. **Baseball SID:** Casey McGarvey. **Telephone:** (860) 768-4501. **Assistant Coaches:** Elliot Glynn, *Steve Malinowski. **Telephone:** (860) 768-4972. **Home Field:** Fiondella Field. **Seating Capacity:** 1000. **Outfield Dimension:** LF—325, CF—400, RF—325.

HARVARD CRIMSON TIDE

Conference: Ivy League. **Mailing Address:** 65 North Harvard Street, Boston, MA 02163. **Website:** gocrimson.com. **Head Coach:** Bill Decker. **Telephone:** (617) 495-2629. **Baseball SID:** Devan Horahan. **Telephone:** (617) 495-2206. **Assistant Coaches:** Brady Kirkpatrick, *Bryan Stark. **Telephone:** (617) 495-1435. **Home Field:** O'Donnell Field. **Seating Capacity:** 1,600. **Outfield Dimension:** LF—340, CF—415, RF—340.

HAWAII RAINBOW WARRIORS

Conference: Big West. **Mailing Address:** 1337 Lower Campus Rd, Honolulu, HI 96822. **Website:** hawaiiathletics.com. **Head Coach:** Mike Trapasso. **Telephone:** (808) 956-6247. **Baseball SID:** Gavin Nevill. **Telephone:** (808) 956-4480. **Assistant Coaches:** *Mike Brown, Carl Fraticelli. **Telephone:** (808) 956-6247. **Home Field:** Les Murakami Stadium. **Seating Capacity:** 4312. **Outfield Dimension:** LF—325, CF—385, RF—325.

HIGH POINT PANTHERS

Conference: Big South. **Mailing Address:** 1 University Parkway, High Point, NC 27268. **Website:** www.highpointpanthers.com. **Head Coach:** Craig Cozart. **Telephone:** (336) 841-9190. **Baseball SID:** Kevin Burke. **Telephone:** (336) 841-4638. **Assistant Coaches:** *Jason Laws, Rick Marlin. **Telephone:** (336) 841-4614. **Home Field:** Williard Stadium. **Seating Capacity:** 550. **Outfield Dimension:** LF—325, CF—400, RF—330.

HOFSTRA PRIDE

Conference: Colonial Athletic. **Mailing Address:** 230 Hofstra University, PEC Room 233, Hempstead, NY 11549. **Website:** www.gohofstra.com. **Head Coach:** John Russo. **Telephone:** (516) 463-3759. **Baseball SID:** Len Skoros. **Telephone:** (516) 463-4602. **Assistant Coaches:** Blake Nation, Matt Wessinger. **Telephone:** (516) 463-5065. **Home Field:** University Field. **Outfield Dimension:** LF—322, CF—382, RF—337.

HOLY CROSS CRUSADERS

Conference: Patriot. **Mailing Address:** 1 College St. Worcester, MA 01610. **Website:** goholycross.com. **Head Coach:** Greg DiCenzo. **Telephone:** (508) 793-2753. **Baseball SID:** Sarah Kirkpatrick. **Telephone:** (508) 793-2780. **Assistant Coaches:** Jason Falcon, *Ed Kahovec. **Telephone:** (508) 793-2753. **Home Field:** Fitton Field. **Seating Capacity:** 3000. **Outfield Dimension:** LF—332, CF—400, RF—330.

HOUSTON COUGARS

Conference: American Athletic. **Mailing Address:** 3204 Cullen Blvd., Houston, TX 77204. **Website:** www.uhcougars.com. **Head Coach:** Todd Whitting. **Telephone:** (713) 743-9396. **Baseball SID:** Kyle Rogers. **Telephone:** (713) 743-9406. **Assistant Coaches:** *Terry Rooney, Ryan Shotzberger, Caleb Barker. **Telephone:** (713) 743-9396. **Home Field:** Schroeder Park. **Seating Capacity:** 3,500. **Outfield Dimension: LF**—330, **CF**—390, **RF**—330.

HOUSTON BAPTIST HUSKIES

Conference: Southland. **Mailing Address:** 7502 Fondren Rd., Houston, TX 77074. **Website:** hbuhuskies.com. **Head Coach:** Jared Moon. **Telephone:** (281) 649-3332. **Baseball SID:** Russ Reneau. **Telephone:** (281) 649-3098. **Fax:** (281) 649-3496. **Assistant Coaches:** *Xavier Hernandez, Russell Stockton. **Telephone:** (281) 649-3264. **Home Field:** Husky Field. **Seating Capacity:** 500. **Outfield Dimension: LF**—330, **CF**—405, **RF**—330.

ILLINOIS FIGHTING ILLINI

Conference: Big Ten. **Mailing Address:** 1700 S. Fourth Street Champaign, IL 61820 217-333-3631. **Website:** fightingillini.com. **Head Coach:** Dan Hartleb. **Telephone:** (217) 244-8144. **Baseball SID:** Brett Moore. **Telephone:** (309) 212-6367. **Assistant Coaches:** *Adam Christ, Drew Dickinson. **Telephone:** (217) 300-2220. **Home Field:** Illinois Field. **Seating Capacity:** 1500. **Outfield Dimension: LF**—330, **CF**—400, **RF**—300.

ILLINOIS STATE REDBIRDS

Conference: Missouri Valley. **Mailing Address:** 100 N University St, Normal, IL 61761. **Website:** goredbirds.com. **Head Coach:** Steve Holm. **Telephone:** (309) 438-4458. **Baseball SID:** Matthew Gocken. **Telephone:** (309) 438-5746. **Assistant Coaches:** *Wally Crancer, Dane Fujinaka. **Telephone:** (309) 438-3338. **Home Field:** Duffy Bass Field. **Seating Capacity:** 1500+. **Outfield Dimension: LF**—330, **CF**—400, **RF**—330.

ILLINOIS-CHICAGO FLAMES

Conference: Horizon. **Mailing Address:** 839 West Roosevelt Road, Chicago, IL 60608. **Website:** uicflames.com. **Head Coach:** Mike Dee. **Telephone:** (312) 996-8645. **Baseball SID:** Dan Yopchick. **Telephone:** (312) 413-9340. **Assistant Coaches:** *John Flood, Sean McDermott. **Telephone:** (312) 355-1757. **Home Field:** Curtis Granderson Stadium. **Seating Capacity:** 1785. **Outfield Dimension: LF**—324, **CF**—399, **RF**—329.

INCARNATE WORD CARDINALS

Conference: Southland. **Mailing Address:** 4301 Broadway St. San Antonio, TX 78209. **Website:** uiwcardinals.com. **Head Coach:** Patrick Hallmark. **Baseball SID:** Cari Gold. **Telephone:** (210) 829-6041. **Assistant Coaches:** *Ryan Aguayo, Scott Shepperd. **Telephone:** (562) 665-8714. **Home Field:** Sullivan Field. **Seating Capacity:** 1500. **Outfield Dimension: LF**—330, **CF**—400, **RF**—330.

INDIANA HOOSIERS

Conference: Big Ten. **Mailing Address:** 1001 E. 17th Street. **Website:** iuhoosiers.com. **Head Coach:** Jeff Mercer. **Telephone:** (812) 855-9155. **Baseball SID:** Greg Kincaid. **Telephone:** (812) 855-4770. **Assistant Coaches:** *Dan Held, Justin Parker. **Telephone:** (812) 855-9155.

Home Field: Bart Kaufman Field. **Seating Capacity:** 2500. **Outfield Dimension: LF**—330, **CF**—400, **RF**—330.

INDIANA STATE SYCAMORES

Conference: Missouri Valley. **Mailing Address:** 401 N. 4th St, Terre Haute, IN. **Website:** gosycamores.com. **Head Coach:** Mitch Hannahs. **Telephone:** (812) 237-4051. **Baseball SID:** Tim McCaughan. **Telephone:** (812) 237-4159. **Fax:** (812) 237-4041. **Assistant Coaches:** *Brian Smiley, Jordan Tiegs. **Telephone:** (812) 237-4630. **Home Field:** Bob Warn Field. **Seating Capacity:** 2000. **Outfield Dimension: LF**—340, **CF**—402, **RF**—340.

IONA GAELS

Conference: Metro Atlantic Athletic. **Mailing Address:** Hynes Center, 715 North Ave., New Rochelle, NY 10801. **Website:** www.icgaels.com. **Head Coach:** Paul Panik. **Telephone:** (914) 633-2319. **Baseball SID:** Pat McWalters. **Telephone:** (914) 633-2334. **Assistant Coaches:** *Andrew Pezzuto, Adam Cornwell, JT Genovese. **Telephone:** (914) 633-2319. **Home Field:** City Park.

IOWA HAWKEYES

Conference: Big Ten. **Mailing Address:** N 411 CHA, Iowa City, IA 52242. **Website:** hawkeyesports.com. **Head Coach:** Rick Heller. **Telephone:** (319) 335-9390. **Baseball SID:** James Allan. **Telephone:** (319) 335-6439. **Assistant Coaches:** Desi Druschel, *Marty Sutherland. **Telephone:** (319) 384-1719. **Home Field:** Duane Banks Field. **Seating Capacity:** 3000. **Outfield Dimension: LF**—329, **CF**—395, **RF**—329.

IPFW FORT WAYNE MASTODONS

Conference: Summit. **Mailing Address:** 2101 E. Coliseum Blvd. Fort Wayne, IN 46805. **Website:** www.gomastodons.com. **Head Coach:** Bobby Pierce. **Telephone:** (260) 481-5480. **Baseball SID:** Derrick Sloboda. **Telephone:** (260) 481-0729. **Assistant Coaches:** *Grant Birely, Connor Lawhead. **Telephone:** (260) 481-5455. **Home Field:** Mastodon Field. **Seating Capacity:** 200. **Outfield Dimension: LF**—330, **CF**—405, **RF**—330.

JACKSON STATE TIGERS

Conference: Southwestern Athletic. **Mailing Address:** 1400 John R. Lynch Street Jackson, MS 39217. **Website:** www.gojsutigers.com. **Head Coach:** Omar Johnson. **Telephone:** (601) 979-3930. **Baseball SID:** Dennis Driscoll. **Telephone:** (601) 979-0857. **Assistant Coaches:** *Christopher Crenshaw, Chadwick Hall. **Telephone:** (601) 979-3928. **Home Field:** Robert "Bob" Braddy Field. **Seating Capacity:** 2000. **Outfield Dimension: LF**—325, **CF**—401, **RF**—325.

JACKSONVILLE DOLPHINS

Conference: Atlantic Sun. **Mailing Address:** 2800 University Blvd N, Jacksonville, FL, 32211. **Website:** judolphins.com. **Head Coach:** Chris Hayes. **Telephone:** (904) 256-7476. **Baseball SID:** Scott Manze. **Telephone:** (904) 256-7444. **Assistant Coaches:** Mark Guerra, *Rich Wallace. **Telephone:** (904) 256-7414. **Home Field:** John Sessions Stadium. **Seating Capacity:** 2000. **Outfield Dimension: LF**—340, **CF**—405, **RF**—340.

JACKSONVILLE STATE GAMECOCKS

Conference: Ohio Valley. **Mailing Address:** 700

Pelham Rd N, Jacksonville, AL 36265. **Website:** www.jsugamecocks.com. **Head Coach:** Jim Case. **Telephone:** (256) 782-5367. **Baseball SID:** Tony Schmidt. **Telephone:** (256) 782-5377. **Assistant Coaches:** *Evan Bush, Mike Murphree. **Telephone:** (256) 782-8141. **Home Field:** Rudy Abbott Field at Jim Case Stadium. **Outfield Dimension:** LF—300, CF—400, RF—335.

JAMES MADISON DUKES

Conference: Colonial. **Mailing Address:** 395 S High Street Harrisonburg Va 22807. **Website:** https://jmusports.com. **Head Coach:** Marlin Ikenberry. **Telephone:** (540) 568-3932. **Baseball SID:** Aaron Socha. **Telephone:** (540) 568-6155. **Assistant Coaches:** *Alex Guerra, Jimmy Jackson. **Telephone:** (540) 568-6516. **Home Field:** Eagle Field at Veterans Memorial Park. **Seating Capacity:** 3,500. **Outfield Dimension:** LF— 330, CF—400, RF—320.

KANSAS JAYHAWKS

Conference: Big 12. **Mailing Address:** 1651 Naismith Drive. **Website:** kuathletics.com. **Head Coach:** Ritch Price. **Telephone:** (785) 864-4196. **Baseball SID:** D.J. Haurin. **Telephone:** (785) 864-3575. **Assistant Coaches:** Ryan Graves, *Ritchie Price Jr. **Telephone:** (785) 864-7908. **Home Field:** Hoglund Ballpark. **Seating Capacity:** 2200. **Outfield Dimension:** LF—330, CF—395, RF—330.

KANSAS STATE WILDCATS

Conference: Big 12. **Mailing Address:** 1800 College Ave, Manhattan, KS 66502. **Website:** kstatesports.com. **Head Coach:** Pete Hughes. **Telephone:** (785) 532-5723. **Baseball SID:** Chris Brown. **Telephone:** (785) 532-7976. **Assistant Coaches:** Shane Conlon, *Ryan Connolly. **Telephone:** (785) 532-7968. **Home Field:** Tointon Family Stadium. **Seating Capacity:** 2,331. **Outfield Dimension:** LF—340, CF—400, RF—325.

KENNESAW STATE OWLS

Conference: Atlantic Sun. **Mailing Address:** 590 Cobb Ave MD #0201 Kennesaw, GA 30144. **Website:** ksuowls.com. **Head Coach:** Mike Sansing. **Telephone:** (470) 578-6264. **Baseball SID:** Aury St. Germain. **Telephone:** (470) 578-7789. **Assistant Coaches:** Kevin Erminio, *Trey Fowler. **Telephone:** (470) 578-2099. **Home Field:** Stillwell Stadium. **Seating Capacity:** 1200. **Outfield Dimension:** LF—330, CF—400, RF—330.

KENT STATE GOLDEN FLASHES

Conference: Mid-American. **Mailing Address:** 234 MAC Center P.O. Box 5190 Kent, OH 44242. **Website:** kentstatesports.com. **Head Coach:** Jeff Duncan. **Telephone:** (330) 672-8432. **Baseball SID:** Sarah Klopfer. **Telephone:** (330) 672-8419. **Assistant Coaches:** Mike Birkbeck, *Derek Simmons. **Telephone:** (330) 672-8433. **Home Field:** Schoonover Stadium. **Seating Capacity:** 500. **Outfield Dimension:** LF—320, CF—415, RF—320.

KENTUCKY WILDCATS

Conference: Southeastern. **Mailing Address:** 510 Wildcat Ct., Lexington, KY 40506. **Website:** UKathletics.com. **Head Coach:** Nick Mingione. **Telephone:** (859) 257-8052. **Baseball SID:** Matt May. **Telephone:** (859) 257-8504. **Assistant Coaches:** Jim Belanger, *Roland Fanning. **Telephone:** (859) 257-8052. **Home Field:** Kentucky Proud Park. **Seating Capacity:** 4000. **Outfield Dimension:** LF—335, CF—400, RF—320.

LA SALLE EXPLORERS

Conference: Atlantic 10. **Mailing Address:** 1900 W Olney Ave. Philadelphia, PA 19141. **Website:** goexplorers.com. **Head Coach:** David Miller. **Telephone:** (215) 280-7646. **Baseball SID:** Dan Lobacz. **Telephone:** (215) 951-1932. **Assistant Coaches:** *Andrew Amaro, Jim Gulden. **Telephone:** (215) 951-1141. **Home Field:** Hank Da Vincent Field. **Seating Capacity:** 1000. **Outfield Dimension:** LF—310, CF—450, RF—310.

LAFAYETTE LEOPARDS

Conference: Patriot. **Mailing Address:** 730 High St. Easton, PA 18042. **Website:** goleopards.com. **Head Coach:** Joe Kinney. **Telephone:** (610) 330-5476. **Baseball SID:** Eric Oakley. **Telephone:** (610) 330-5518. **Assistant Coaches:** Andrew Dickson, *Tim Reilly. **Telephone:** (610) 330-3257. **Home Field:** Hilton Rahn Field at Kamine Stadium. **Seating Capacity:** 500. **Outfield Dimension:** LF—332, CF—403, RF—335.

LAMAR CARDINALS

Conference: Southland. **Mailing Address:** Jim Gilligan Way, Beaumont, TX 77705. **Website:** lamarcardinals.com. **Head Coach:** Will Davis. **Telephone:** (409) 880-8974. **Baseball SID:** Cooper Welch. **Telephone:** (409) 880-7845. **Assistant Coaches:** Scott Hatten, Sean Snedeker. **Telephone:** (409) 880-8135. **Home Field:** Vincent-Beck Stadium. **Seating Capacity:** 3,500. **Outfield Dimension:** LF—325, CF—380, RF—325.

LEHIGH MOUNTAIN HAWKS

Conference: Patriot. **Mailing Address:** 641 Taylor Street Bethlehem PA 18015. **Website:** lehighsports.com. **Head Coach:** Sean Leary. **Telephone:** (610) 758-4315. **Baseball SID:** Josh Liddick. **Telephone:** (610) 758-5043. **Assistant Coaches:** Dan Gusovsky, *AJ Miller. **Telephone:** (610) 758-4315. **Home Field:** J. David Walker Field at Legacy Park. **Seating Capacity:** 370+. **Outfield Dimension:** LF—320, CF—400, RF—320.

LIBERTY FLAMES

Conference: Atlantic Sun. **Mailing Address:** 1971 University Blvd. Lynchburg, VA 24515. **Website:** LibertyFlames.com. **Head Coach:** Scott Jackson. **Telephone:** (434) 582-2101. **Baseball SID:** Ryan Bomberger. **Telephone:** (434) 582-2292. **Assistant Coaches:** *Tyler Cannon, Bryant Gaines. **Telephone:** (434) 582-2101. **Home Field:** Liberty Baseball Stadium. **Seating Capacity:** 2500. **Outfield Dimension:** LF—325, CF—395, RF—325.

LIPSCOMB BISONS

Conference: Atlantic Sun. **Mailing Address:** 1 University Park Dr., Nashville, TN 37204. **Website:** www.lipscombsports.com. **Head Coach:** Jeff Forehand. **Telephone:** (615) 966-5716. **Baseball SID:** Kirk Downs. **Telephone:** (615) 966-5457. **Fax:** (615) 966-1806. **Assistant Coaches:** Brad Coon. **Telephone:** (615) 966-5149. **Home Field:** Ken Dugan Field at Stephen L. Marsh Stadium. **Seating Capacity:** 750. **Outfield Dimension:** LF—330, CF—405, RF—330.

LONG BEACH STATE DIRTBAGS

Conference: Big West. **Mailing Address:** 1250 Bellflower Blvd. Long Beach, CA 90840. **Website:** longbeachstate.com. **Head Coach:** Troy Buckley. **Telephone:**

(562) 985-4661. **Baseball SID:** Tyler Hendrickson. **Telephone:** (562) 985-7797. **Assistant Coaches:** *Greg Bergeron, Dan Ricabal. **Telephone:** (562) 985-7548. **Home Field:** Bohl Diamond at Blair Field. **Capacity:** 3000. **Outfield Dimension:** LF—335, CF—393, RF—330.

LONG ISLAND-BROOKLYN BLACKBIRDS

Conference: Northeast. **Mailing Address:** 1 University Plaza. **Website:** liuathletics.com. **Head Coach:** Dan Pirillo. **Telephone:** (718) 488-1538. **Baseball SID:** Brian Duane. **Telephone:** (718) 488-1420. **Assistant Coaches:** *Tom Carty, John Ziznewski. **Telephone:** (718) 780-6059. **Home Field:** "The Birdcage". **Seating Capacity:** 200. **Outfield Dimension:** LF—300, CF—390, RF—285.

LONGWOOD LANCERS

Conference: Big South. **Mailing Address:** 201 High St., Farmville, VA 23909. **Website:** longwoodlancers. com. **Head Coach:** Ryan Mau. **Telephone:** (434) 395-2843. **Baseball SID:** Sam Hovan. **Telephone:** (434) 395-2345. **Assistant Coaches:** C.J. Rhodes, *Daniel Wood. **Telephone:** (434) 395-2351. **Home Field:** Buddy Bolding Stadium. **Seating Capacity:** 500. **Outfield Dimension:** LF—335, CF—400, RF—335.

LOUISIANA STATE TIGERS

Conference: SEC. **Mailing Address:** Nicholson Dr. @ N. Stadium Dr. Baton Rouge, LA 70803. **Website:** LSUsports.net. **Head Coach:** Paul Mainieri. **Telephone:** (225) 578-4148. **Baseball SID:** Bill Franques. **Telephone:** (225) 578-8226. **Assistant Coaches:** *Nolan Cain, Alan Dunn. **Telephone:** (225) 578-4148. **Home Field:** Alex Box Stadium, Skip Bertman Field. **Seating Capacity:** 10326. **Outfield Dimension:** LF—330, CF—405, RF—330.

LOUISIANA TECH BULLDOGS

Conference: Conference USA. **Mailing Address:** 1600 W. Alabama Ave, Ruston, LA, 71272. **Website:** www.latechsports.com. **Head Coach:** Lane Burroughs. **Telephone:** (318) 257-5318. **Baseball SID:** Brock McKee. **Telephone:** (318) 257-5305. **Fax:** (318) 257-3757. **Assistant Coaches:** Austin McKnight, Mike Silva, *Travis Creel. **Telephone:** (318) 257-5220. **Home Field:** J.C. Love Field at Pat Patterson Park. **Seating Capacity:** 2,000. **Outfield Dimension:** LF—315, CF—385, RF—325.

LOUISIANA-LAFAYETTE RAGIN' CAJUNS

Conference: Sun Belt. **Mailing Address:** 201 Reinhardt Dr., Lafayette, LA 70506. **Website:** www.ragin-cajuns.com. **Head Coach:** Tony Robichaux. **Telephone:** (337) 262-5189. **Baseball SID:** Josh Brunner. **Telephone:** (205) 568-6559. **Fax:** (337) 482-1041. **Assistant Coaches:** Anthony Babineaux, *Jeremy Talbot, Jake Wells, Daniel Freeman. **Telephone:** (337) 262-5189. **Home Field:** M.L. "Tigue" Moore Field at Russo Park. **Seating Capacity:** 4,650. **Outfield Dimension:** LF—330, CF—400, RF—330.

LOUISIANA-MONROE WARHAWKS

Conference: Sun Belt. **Mailing Address:** 308 Warhawk Way, Monroe, LA 71209. **Website:** ULMWarhawks.com. **Head Coach:** Michael Federico. **Telephone:** (318) 342-3591. **Baseball SID:** Mike Hammett. **Telephone:** (318) 342-7925. **Assistant Coaches:** *Jake Carlson, Matt Collins. **Telephone:** (318) 342-3589. **Home Field:** Warhawk Field. **Seating Capacity:** 1800. **Outfield Dimension:** LF—330, CF—400, RF—330.

LOUISVILLE CARDINALS

Conference: Atlantic Coast. **Mailing Address:** 215 Cardinal Station, Room 101, Louisville, KY 40292. **Website:** GoCards.com. **Head Coach:** Dan McDonnell. **Telephone:** (502) 852-0103. **Baseball SID:** Garett Wall. **Telephone:** (502) 852-3088. **Assistant Coaches:** *Eric Snider, Roger Williams. **Telephone:** (502) 852-3929. **Home Field:** Jim Patterson Stadium. **Seating Capacity:** 4000. **Outfield Dimension:** LF—330, CF—402, RF—330.

LOYOLA MARYMOUNT LIONS

Conference: West Coast. **Mailing Address:** 1 LMU Dr., Los Angees, CA 90045. **Website:** www.lmulions. com. **Head Coach:** Jason Gill. **Telephone:** (310) 338-2949. **Baseball SID:** Steven Esparza. **Telephone:** (310) 338-7638. **Assistant Coaches:** Bobby Andrews, Nathan Choate. **Telephone:** (310) 338-4511. **Home Field:** Page Stadium. **Seating Capacity:** 600. **Outfield Dimension:** LF—326, CF—406, RF—321.

MAINE BLACK BEARS

Conference: America East. **Mailing Address:** 5747 Memorial Gym Orono, ME 04469. **Website:** goblackbears. com. **Head Coach:** Nick Derba. **Telephone:** (207) 581-1090. **Baseball SID:** Ryan Long. **Telephone:** (207) 581-4849. **Assistant Coaches:** *Conor Burke, John Schiffner. **Telephone:** (207) 581-1097. **Home Field:** Mahaney Diamond. **Seating Capacity:** 3000. **Outfield Dimension:** LF—330, CF—400, RF—330.

MANHATTAN JASPERS

Conference: Metro Atlantic. **Mailing Address:** 4513 Manhattan College Parkway, Riverdale, NY. **Website:** www.gojaspers.com. **Head Coach:** Mike Colege. **Telephone:** (718) 862-7821. **Baseball SID:** Kevin Ross. **Telephone:** (718) 862-7228. **Assistant Coaches:** Chris Cody, Pat Porter. **Telephone:** (718) 862-7218. **Home Field:** Dutchess Stadium. **Seating Capacity:** 4500. **Outfield Dimension:** LF—330, CF—405, RF—330.

MARIST RED FOXES

Conference: Metro Atlantic. **Mailing Address:** 3399 North Rd., Poughkeepsie, NY 12601. **Website:** www.goredfoxes.com. **Head Coach:** Chris Tracz. **Telephone:** (845) 575-2570. **Baseball SID:** Peter Fagan. **Telephone:** (845) 575-2441. **Assistant Coaches:** *Eric Pelletier, Trey Stover. **Telephone:** (845) 575-7583. **Home Field:** McCann Field. **Outfield Dimension:** LF—320, CF—390, RF—320.

MARSHALL THUNDERING HERD

Conference: Conference USA. **Mailing Address:** 1801 Third Ave., Huntington, WV 25703. **Website:** www. herdzone.com. **Head Coach:** Jeff Waggoner. **Telephone:** (304) 696-6454. **Baseball SID:** Cody Linn. **Telephone:** (304) 696-2418. **Fax:** (304) 696-2325. **Assistant Coaches:** *Joe Renner, Brian Karlet, Chris O'Neill. **Telephone:** (304) 696-7146. **Home Field:** Appalachian Power Park. **Seating Capacity:** 4,500. **Outfield Dimension:** LF—330, CF—400, RF—320.

MARYLAND TERRAPINS

Conference: Big Ten. **Mailing Address:** 8500 Paint Branch Dr. College Park, MD 20742. **Website:** umterps. com. **Head Coach:** Rob Vaughn. **Telephone:** (301) 314-1845. **Baseball SID:** Taylor Smyth. **Telephone:** (301) 314-8052. **Assistant Coaches:** Corey Muscara, *Matt

Swope. **Telephone:** (301) 314-9772. **Home Field:** Bob "Turtle" Smith Stadium. **Seating Capacity:** 2500. **Outfield Dimension:** LF—320, CF—385, RF—325.

MARYLAND–BALTIMORE COUNTY RETRIEVERS

Conference: America East. **Mailing Address:** 1000 Hilltop Circle Baltimore, MD 21250. **Website:** www.umb-cretrievers.com. **Head Coach:** Bob Mumma. **Telephone:** (410) 455-2239. **Baseball SID:** David Castellanos. **Telephone:** (410) 455-2639. **Assistant Coaches:** *Liam Bowen, Ryan Terrill. **Home Field:** Alumni Field. **Seating Capacity:** 500. **Outfield Dimension:** LF—330, CF—360, RF—340.

MARYLAND–EASTERN SHORE

Conference: Mid-Eastern. **Mailing Address:** 1 Backbone Road, Princess Anne, MD 21853. **Website:** easternshorehawks.com. **Head Coach:** Brian Hollamon. **Telephone:** (410) 651-7864. **Baseball SID:** Matt McCann. **Telephone:** (410) 621-2354. **Assistant Coaches:** Ben Kirk. **Telephone:** (410) 621-7014. **Home Field:** Arthur W. Perdue Stadium. **Seating Capacity:** 6000. **Outfield Dimension:** LF—309, CF—402, RF—309.

MASSACHUSETTS MINUTEMEN

Conference: Atlantic 10. **Mailing Address:** 131 Commonwealth Ave. Amherst, MA 01003. **Website:** umassathletics.com. **Head Coach:** Matt Reynolds. **Telephone:** (413) 545-3120. **Baseball SID:** Ryan Gallant. **Telephone:** (413) 687-3793. **Assistant Coaches:** *Nathan Cole, Mark Royer. **Telephone:** (413) 545-3766. **Home Field:** Earl Lorden Field. **Seating Capacity:** 1500. **Outfield Dimension:** LF—330, CF—400, RF—301.

MASSACHUSETTS–LOWELL RIVER HAWKS

Conference: America East. **Mailing Address:** 1 University Avenue Lowell, Mass. 01854. **Website:** www.goriverhawks.com. **Head Coach:** Ken Harring. **Telephone:** (978) 943-2344. **Baseball SID:** Tommy Coyle. **Telephone:** (978) 934-6748. **Assistant Coaches:** *Jerod Edmondson, Matt Perper. **Telephone:** (978) 934-2564. **Home Field:** LeLacheur Park. **Seating Capacity:** 5,030. **Outfield Dimension:** LF—337, CF—400, RF—301.

McNEESE STATE COWBOYS

Conference: Southland. **Mailing Address:** 700 E. McNeese St., Lake Charles, LA 70609. **Website:** www.mcneesesports.com. **Head Coach:** Justin Hill. **Telephone:** (337) 475-5484. **Baseball SID:** Matthew Bonnette. **Telephone:** (337) 475-5207. **Assistant Coaches:** Jimmy Ricklefsen, *Nick Zaleski, Will Fox. **Telephone:** (337) 475-5904. **Home Field:** Joe Miller Ballpark. **Seating Capacity:** 2,000. **Outfield Dimension:** LF—330, CF—400, RF—330.

MEMPHIS TIGERS

Conference: American Athletic. **Mailing Address:** 3720 Alumni Ave Memphis TN 38152. **Website:** www.gotigersgo.com. **Head Coach:** Daron Schoenrock. **Telephone:** (901) 678-5041. **Baseball SID:** Kevin Rodriguez. **Telephone:** (901) 678-5108. **Assistant Coaches:** *Clay Greene, Russ Mcnicklr. **Telephone:** (901) 678-5041. **Home Field:** Fed Ex Park. **Seating Capacity:** 2000. **Outfield Dimension:** LF—318, CF—380, RF—317.

MERCER BEARS

Conference: Southern. **Mailing Address:** 1501 Mercer University Drive, University Center, Macon, GA 31207. **Website:** www.mercerbears.com. **Head Coach:** Craig Gibson. **Telephone:** (478) 301-2396. **Baseball SID:** Gerrit Van Genderen. **Telephone:** (478) 301-5209.

Assistant Coaches: *Brent Shade, Willie Stewart. **Telephone:** (478) 301-2738. **Home Field:** OrthoGeorgia Park at Claude Smith Field. **Seating Capacity:** 1,500. **Outfield Dimension:** LF—330, CF—400, RF—320.

MIAMI HURRICANES

Conference: Atlantic Coast. **Mailing Address:** 6201 San Amaro Dr., Coral Gables, FL 33146. **Website:** www.hurricanesports.com. **Head Coach:** Gino DiMare. **Telephone:** (305) 284-4171. **Baseball SID:** David Villavicencio. **Telephone:** (305) 284-3244. **Assistant Coaches:** J.D. Arteaga, *Norberto Lopez. **Telephone:** (305) 284-4171. **Home Field:** Mark Light Field at Alex Rodriguez Park. **Seating Capacity:** 5,000. **Outfield Dimension:** LF—330, CF—400, RF—330.

MIAMI (OHIO) REDHAWKS

Conference: Mid-American. **Mailing Address:** 550 E. Withrow St., Oxford, OH 45056. **Website:** miamiredhawks.com. **Head Coach:** Danny Hayden. **Telephone:** (513) 529-6631. **Baseball SID:** Mike Roth. **Telephone:** (513) 529-7092. **Assistant Coaches:** Matt Davis, Justin Dedman, Matt Passauer. **Telephone:** (513) 529-7293. **Home Field:** McKie Field at Hayden Park. **Seating Capacity:** 2,000. **Outfield Dimension:** LF—332, CF—400, RF—343.

MICHIGAN WOLVERINES

Conference: Big Ten. **Mailing Address:** 1000 S. State St. Ann Arbor, MI 48109. **Website:** mgoblue.com. **Head Coach:** Erik Bakich. **Telephone:** (734) 763-1957. **Baseball SID:** Katie Hewitt, Kurt Svoboda. **Telephone:** (813) 748-5293, (617) 872-6111. **Assistant Coaches:** Chris Fetter, *Nick Schnabel. **Telephone:** (734) 615-0010. **Home Field:** Ray Fisher Stadium. **Seating Capacity:** 3500. **Outfield Dimension:** LF—312, CF—395, RF—320.

MICHIGAN STATE SPARTANS

Conference: Big Ten. **Website:** www.msuspartans.com. **Head Coach:** Jake Boss. **Telephone:** (517) 355-4486. **Baseball SID:** Zack Fisher. **Telephone:** (517) 355-2271. **Assistant Coaches:** *Graham Sikes, Mark VanAmeyde. **Telephone:** (517) 355-0259. **Home Field:** Kobs Field at McLane Stadium. **Seating Capacity:** 3000. **Outfield Dimension:** LF—330, CF—403, RF—302.

MIDDLE TENNESSEE STATE BLUE RAIDERS

Conference: Conference USA. **Mailing Address:** 1301 E Main St, Murfreesboro, TN 37132. **Website:** gobluer-aiders.com. **Head Coach:** Jim Toman. **Telephone:** (615) 898-2961. **Baseball SID:** Tony Stinnett. **Telephone:** (615) 898-5270. **Fax:** (615) 898-5626. **Assistant Coaches:** Kyle Bunn. **Home Field:** Reese Smith Jr. Field. **Seating Capacity:** 2600. **Outfield Dimension:** LF—330, CF—390, RF—330.

MINNESOTA GOLDEN GOPHERS

Conference: Big Ten. **Mailing Address:** 200 Gibson Nagurski Football Building 600 15th Ave SE. **Website:** www.gophersports.com. **Head Coach:** John Anderson. **Telephone:** (612) 625-1060. **Baseball SID:** Joe Hansen. **Telephone:** (612) 625-4090. **Assistant Coaches:** *Patrick Casey, Ty McDevitt. **Telephone:** (612) 625-3568. **Home Field:** Siebert Field. **Seating Capacity:** 1420. **Outfield Dimension:** LF—330, CF—390, RF—330.

MISSISSIPPI REBELS

Conference: Southeastern. **Mailing Address:** 400 University Place, University, MS 38677. **Website:** OleMissSports.com. **Head Coach:** Mike Bianco. **Telephone:** (662) 915-6643. **Baseball SID:** Alex Sims. **Telephone:** (662) 915-1083. **Assistant Coaches:** Mike Clement, *Carl Lafferty. **Telephone:** (662) 915-7556. **Home Field:** Swayze Field. **Seating Capacity:** 10715. **Outfield Dimension:** LF—330, CF—390, RF—330.

MISSISSIPPI STATE BULLDOGS

Conference: Southeastern. **Mailing Address:** P.O. Box 5327, Mississippi State, MS 39762. **Website:** hailstate. com. **Head Coach:** Chris Lemonis. **Telephone:** (662) 325-3597. **Baseball SID:** Greg Campbell. **Telephone:** (662) 325-0972. **Assistant Coaches:** Scott Foxhall, *Jake Gautreau. **Telephone:** (662) 325-3597. **Home Field:** Dudy Noble Field. **Seating Capacity:** N/A. **Outfield Dimension:** LF—330, CF—400, RF—305.

MISSISSIPPI VALLEY STATE DELTA DEVILS

Conference: Southwestern Athletic. **Mailing Address:** 14000 Hwy. 82 W. #7246, Itta Bena, MS 38941. **Website:** www.mvsusports.com. **Head Coach:** Aaron Stevens. **Telephone:** (662) 254-3834. **Baseball SID:** Jason Pompey. **Telephone:** (662) 254-3011. **Assistant Coaches:** Terrance Steele. **Telephone:** (662) 254-3834. **Home Field:** Magnolia Field. **Seating Capacity:** 3006. **Outfield Dimension:** LF—315, CF—395, RF—315.

MISSOURI TIGERS

Conference: Southeastern. **Mailing Address:** 100 MATC Columbia, MO 65211. **Website:** mutigers.com. **Head Coach:** Steve Bieser. **Telephone:** (573) 884-6428. **Baseball SID:** Andy Oldenberg. **Telephone:** (573) 882-1645. **Assistant Coaches:** Fred Corral, *Lance Rhodes. **Telephone:** (573) 884-4783. **Home Field:** Taylor Stadium. **Seating Capacity:** 3,031. **Outfield Dimension:** LF—333, CF—390, RF—339.

MISSOURI STATE BEARS

Conference: Missouri Valley. **Mailing Address:** 901 S. National Ave., Springfield MO 65897. **Website:** missouristatebears.com. **Head Coach:** Keith Guttin. **Telephone:** (417) 836-4497. **Baseball SID:** Eric Doennig. **Telephone:** (417) 836-4586. **Assistant Coaches:** Paul Evans, *Matt Lawson. **Telephone:** (417) 836-4496. **Home Field:** Hammons Field. **Seating Capacity:** 8,000. **Outfield Dimension:** LF—315, CF—400, RF—330.

MONMOUTH HAWKS

Conference: Metro Atlantic. **Mailing Address:** 400 Cedar Ave., West Long Branch, NJ 07764. **Website:** www. monmouthhawks.com. **Head Coach:** Dean Ehehalt. **Telephone:** (732) 263-5186. **Baseball SID:** Gary Kowal. **Telephone:** (732) 263-5557. **Assistant Coaches:** *Chris Collazo, Brady Kirkpatrick. **Telephone:** (732) 263-5347. **Home Field:** MU Baseball Field. **Seating Capacity:** 2,100. **Outfield Dimension:** LF—325, CF—395, RF—320.

MOREHEAD STATE EAGLES

Conference: Ohio Valley. **Mailing Address:** 195 AAC Morehead, KY 40351. **Website:** msueagles.com. **Head Coach:** Mike McGuire. **Telephone:** (606) 783-2882. **Baseball SID:** Matt Schabert. **Telephone:** (606) 783-2556. **Assistant Coaches:** *Adam Brown, Kane Sweeney. **Telephone:** (606) 783-2881. **Home Field:** Allen Field. **Seating Capacity:** 1000. **Outfield Dimension:** LF—320, CF—380, RF—315.

MOUNT ST. MARY'S

Conference: Northeast. **Mailing Address:** 16300 Old Emmitsburg Rd., Emmitsburg, MD 21727. **Website:** www.mountathletics.com. **Head Coach:** Scott Thompson. **Telephone:** (301) 447-3806. **Baseball SID:** Zach Kenworthy. **Telephone:** (301) 447-5384. **Assistant Coaches:** Ivor Hodgson, Kyle Kane, Jeff Gergic. **Telephone:** (301) 447-3806. **Home Field:** E.T. Straw Family Stadium. **Seating Capacity:** 500.

MURRAY STATE RACERS

Conference: Ohio Valley. **Mailing Address:** 102 Curris Center, Murray, KY 42071. **Website:** goracers.com. **Head Coach:** Dan Skirka. **Telephone:** (270) 809-4892. **Baseball SID:** Adam Grossman. **Telephone:** (270) 809-7044. **Assistant Coaches:** Tanner Gordon, *Kent Rollins. **Home Field:** Johnny Reagan Field. **Seating Capacity:** 800. **Outfield Dimension:** LF—330, CF—400, RF—330.

NAVY MIDSHIPMEN

Conference: Patriot. **Mailing Address:** 566 Brownson Road, Annapolis, MD, 21402. **Website:** navysports.com. **Head Coach:** Paul Kostacopoulos. **Telephone:** (410) 293-5571. **Baseball SID:** David Gerhart. **Telephone:** (410) 293-8787. **Assistant Coaches:** Bobby Applegate, *Jeff Kane. **Telephone:** (410) 293-8946. **Home Field:** Terwilliger Brothers Field at Max Bishop Stadium. **Seating Capacity:** 1500. **Outfield Dimension:** LF—322, CF—397, RF—304.

NEBRASKA CORNHUSKERS

Conference: Big Ten. **Mailing Address:** One Memorial Stadium, 800 Stadium Dr., Lincoln, NE 68588. **Website:** www.huskers.com. **Head Coach:** Darin Erstad. **Telephone:** (402) 472-9166. **Baseball SID:** Connor Stange. **Telephone:** (402) 472-6684. **Assistant Coaches:** Mike Kirby, *Ted Silva. **Telephone:** (402) 472-1445. **Home Field:** Hawks Field at Haymarket Park. **Seating Capacity:** 8486. **Outfield Dimension:** LF—335, CF—395, RF—325.

NEBRASKA-OMAHA MAVERICKS

Conference: Summit. **Mailing Address:** Sapp Fieldhouse, 6001 Dodge St., Omaha, NE 68182. **Website:** www.omavs.com. **Head Coach:** Evan Porter. **Telephone:** (402) 554-2141. **Baseball SID:** Zack Kirby. **Telephone:** (402) 554-2140. **Assistant Coaches:** Chris Gadsden, Brian Strawn. **Telephone:** (402) 554-2141. **Home Field:** Ballpark at Boys Town. **Outfield Dimension:** LF—335, CF—410, RF—335.

NEVADA WOLF PACK

Conference: Mountain West. **Mailing Address:** 1664 N Virginia St, Reno, NV 89557. **Website:** www.nevada-wolfpack.com. **Head Coach:** TJ Bruce. **Telephone:** (775) 682-6978. **Baseball SID:** Jack Kuestermeyer. **Telephone:** (775) 682-6984. **Fax:** (775) 784-4386. **Assistant Coaches:** Steven Bennett, *Jake Silverman. **Telephone:** (775) 682-6942. **Home Field:** Peccole Park. **Seating Capacity:** 3000. **Outfield Dimension:** LF—340, CF—401, RF—340.

NEVADA-LAS VEGAS REBELS

Conference: Mountain West. **Mailing Address:** 4505 S. Maryland Parkway Las Vegas, Nevada 89154. **Website:** unlvrebels.com. **Head Coach:** Stan Stolte. **Telephone:** (702) 895-3499. **Baseball SID:** Jeff Seals. **Telephone:** (702) 895-3134. **Assistant Coaches:** *Patrick Armstrong, Kevin Higgins. **Telephone:** (702) 895-3835. **Home Field:** Earl E Wilson Stadium. **Seating Capacity:** 3000. **Outfield Dimension:** LF—335, CF—400, RF—335.

NEW JERSEY TECH HIGHLANDERS

Conference: Atlantic Sun. **Mailing Address:** 80 Lock St, Newark NJ. **Website:** njithighlanders.com. **Head Coach:** Robbie McClellan. **Telephone:** (973) 596-8396. **Baseball SID:** Stephanie Pillari. **Telephone:** (973) 596-8324. **Assistant Coaches:** Anthony Deleo, *Giuseppe Papaccio. **Telephone:** (973) 596-5827. **Home Field:** Riverfront Stadium. **Seating Capacity:** 6,500. **Outfield Dimension:** LF—305, CF—396, RF—315.

NEW MEXICO LOBOS

Conference: Mountain West. **Mailing Address:** 1715 University SE, Albuquerque, NM. **Website:** golobos. com. **Head Coach:** Ray Birmingham. **Telephone:** (505) 925-5720. **Baseball SID:** Daniel Gallegos. **Telephone:** (501) 442-2930. **Assistant Coaches:** *Jon Coyne, Brandon Higelin. **Telephone:** (505) 925-5720. **Home Field:** Santa Ana Star Field. **Seating Capacity:** 1000. **Outfield Dimension:** LF—340, CF—420, RF—340.

NEW MEXICO STATE AGGIES

Conference: Western Athletic. **Mailing Address:** 1815 Wells Street Las Cruces, NM 88003. **Website:** www.nmstatesports.com. **Head Coach:** Brian Green. **Telephone:** (575) 646-7693. **Baseball SID:** Chris Kennedy. **Telephone:** (575) 646-3269. **Assistant Coaches:** Anthony Claggett, *Terry Davis. **Telephone:** (575) 616-7693. **Home Field:** Presley Askew Field. **Seating Capacity:** 1000. **Outfield Dimension:** LF—345, CF—400, RF—345.

NEW ORLEANS PRIVATEERS

Conference: Southland. **Mailing Address:** 2000 Lakeshore Dr. New Orleans, LA 70148. **Website:** www. unoprivateers.com. **Head Coach:** Blake Dean. **Telephone:** (504) 280-3879. **Baseball SID:** Kelvin Queliz. **Telephone:** (504) 280-6284. **Assistant Coaches:** Rudy Darrow, *Brett Stewart, Dylan Belanger. **Telephone:** (504) 280-3879. **Home Field:** Maestri Field. **Seating Capacity:** 2900. **Outfield Dimension:** LF—330, CF—405, RF—330.

NIAGARA PURPLE EAGLES

Conference: Metro Atlantic Athletic. **Mailing Address:** Upper Level Gallagher Center, P.O. Box 2009, Niagara University, NY 14109. **Website:** www.purpleeagles.com. **Head Coach:** Rob McCoy. **Telephone:** (716) 286-7361. **Baseball SID:** Breanna Jacobs. **Telephone:** (716) 286-

8586. **Assistant Coaches:** *Matt Spatafora, Sean Stacy. **Telephone:** (716) 286-8624. **Home Field:** Bobo Field.

NICHOLLS STATE COLONELS

Conference: Southland. **Mailing Address:** 906 East 1st St. Thibodaux, LA 70301. **Website:** geauxcolonels. com. **Head Coach:** Seth Thibodeaux. **Telephone:** (985) 449-7149. **Baseball SID:** Jordan Bergeron. **Telephone:** (985) 448-4282. **Assistant Coaches:** Zach Butler, *Walt Jones. **Telephone:** (985) 448-4807.
Home Field: Ray E. Didier Field. **Seating Capacity:** 3500. **Outfield Dimension:** LF—330, CF—400, RF—315.

NORFOLK STATE SPARTANS

Conference: Mid-Eastern Athletic. **Mailing Address:** 700 Park Ave., Norfolk, VA 23504. **Website:** nsuspartans. com. **Head Coach:** Keith Shumate. **Telephone:** (757) 823-8196. **Baseball SID:** Matt Michalec. **Telephone:** (757) 823-2628. **Assistant Coaches:** Matt Mitchell, Brian Beard. **Telephone:** (757) 823-8196. **Home Field:** Marty L. Miller Field. **Seating Capacity:** 1,500. **Outfield Dimension:** LF—330, CF—404, RF—318.

NORTH ALABAMA LIONS

Conference: Atlantic Sun. **Mailing Address:** UNA Box 5071, Florence, AL 35632. **Website:** roarlions.com. **Head Coach:** Mike Keehn. **Telephone:** (256) 765-4635. **Baseball SID:** Jeff Hodges. **Telephone:** (256) 765-4595. **Assistant Coaches:** Anthony DeCicco, Nick McGregor. **Telephone:** (256) 765-5065. **Home Field:** Lane Field. **Outfield Dimension:** LF—330, CF—385, RF—320.

NORTH CAROLINA TAR HEELS

Conference: Atlantic Coast. **Mailing Address:** 235 Ridge Road, Chapel Hill NC 27599. **Website:** GoHeels. com. **Head Coach:** Mike Fox. **Telephone:** (919) 962-2351. **Baseball SID:** TJ Scholl. **Telephone:** (919) 962-2123. **Assistant Coaches:** *Scott Forbes, Robert Woodard, Jesse Wierzbicki. **Telephone:** (919) 962-7006. **Home Field:** Boshamer Stadium. **Seating Capacity:** 5000. **Outfield Dimension:** LF—335, CF—400, RF—340.

NORTH CAROLINA A&T AGGIES

Conference: Mid-Eastern Athletic. **Mailing Address:** 1601 E. Market St., Greensboro, NC 27411. **Website:** www.ncataggies.com. **Head Coach:** Ben Hall. **Telephone:** (336) 285-4272. **Baseball SID:** Brian Holloway. **Telephone:** (336) 285-3608. **Assistant Coaches:** Stefan Jordan, Jamie Serber. **Telephone:** (336) 285-4272. **Home Field:** War Memorial Stadium. **Seating Capacity:** 2000. **Outfield Dimension:** LF—327, CF—401, RF—327.

NORTH CAROLINA CENTRAL EAGLES

Conference: Mid-Eastern Athletic. **Mailing Address:** 1801 Fayetteville St., Durham, NC 27707. **Website:** www.nccueaglepride.com. **Head Coach:** Jim Koerner. **Telephone:** (919) 530-6273. **Baseball SID:** Jonathan Duren. **Telephone:** (919) 530-6892. **Assistant Coaches:** A.J. Battisto, Neal Henry. **Telephone:** (919) 530-5439. **Home Field:** Durham Athletic Park. **Seating Capacity:** 2,000. **Outfield Dimension:** LF—327, CF—398, RF—290.

NORTH CAROLINA STATE WOLFPACK

Conference: Atlantic Coast. **Mailing Address:** 1081 Varsity Dr., Raleigh, NC 27606. **Website:** gopack.com. **Head Coach:** Elliott Avent. **Telephone:** (919) 515-3613.

Baseball SID: Justin Wilson. Telephone: (919) 746-8438. Assistant Coaches: Clint Chrysler, *Chris Hart. Telephone: (919) 515-3613. Home Field: Doak Field at Dail Park. Seating Capacity: 3100. Outfield Dimension: LF—325, CF—400, RF—330.

NORTH DAKOTA STATE BISON

Conference: Summit. Mailing Address: NDSU Dept 1200 PO Box 6050, Fargo, ND 58108-6050. Website: www.gobison.com. Head Coach: Tod Brown. Telephone: (701) 231-8853. Baseball SID: Ryan Workman. Telephone: (701) 231-5591. Assistant Coaches: Jeff Ditch, *Tyler Oakes. Telephone: (701) 231-7817. Home Field: Newman Outdoor Field. Seating Capacity: 4419. Outfield Dimension: LF—318, CF—408, RF—314.

NORTH FLORIDA OSPREY

Conference: Atlantic Sun. Mailing Address: 1 UNF Drive, Jacksonville, FL 32224. Website: unfospreys.com. Head Coach: Tim Parenton. Telephone: (904) 620-1556. Baseball SID: Brock Borgeson. Telephone: (904) 420-2596. Assistant Coaches: *Tommy Boss, Andrew Hannon. Telephone: (904) 620-2586. Home Field: Harmon Stadium. Seating Capacity: 1000. Outfield Dimension: LF—325, CF—400, RF—325.

NORTHEASTERN HUSKIES

Conference: Colonial. Mailing Address: 360 Huntington Ave., 219 Cabot Center, Boston MA 02420. Website: nuhuskies.com. Head Coach: Mike Glavine. Telephone: (617) 373-3657. Baseball SID: Mike Skovan. Telephone: (617) 373-7931. Assistant Coaches: *Kevin Cobb, Nick Puccio. Telephone: (617) 373-5256. Home Field: Friedman Diamond. Seating Capacity: 1000. Outfield Dimension: LF—326, CF—415, RF—342.

NORTHERN COLORADO BEARS

Conference: Western Athletic. Mailing Address: 270D Butler-Hancock Athletic Center Greeley, CO 80639. Website: uncbears.com. Head Coach: Carl Iwasaki. Telephone: (970) 351-1714. Baseball SID: Ryan Ronan. Telephone: (970) 351-1065. Assistant Coaches: Nick Childs, *Nate Rasmussen. Telephone: (970) 351-1203. Home Field: Jackson Field. Seating Capacity: 1,500. Outfield Dimension: LF—345, CF—407, RF—356.

NORTHERN ILLINOIS HUSKIES

Conference: Mid-American. Mailing Address: 1525 W. Lincoln HWY, DeKalb, IL 60115. Website: niuhuskies.com. Head Coach: Mike Kunigonis. Telephone: (815) 753-0147. Baseball SID: Mike Haase. Telephone: (815) 753-9538. Assistant Coaches: *Andrew Maki, Luke Stewart. Telephone: (815) 753-0147. Home Field: Ralph McKinzie Field. Seating Capacity: . Outfield Dimension: LF—312, CF—395, RF—322.

NORTHERN KENTUCKY NORSE

Conference: Horizon. Mailing Address: 500 Nunn Drive Highland Heights, KY 41099. Website: nkunorse.com. Head Coach: Todd Asalon. Telephone: (859) 572-6474. Baseball SID: Ryan Wilker. Telephone: (859) 572-7850. Assistant Coaches: Dizzy Peyton. Telephone: (859) 572-5940. Home Field: Bill Aker Baseball Complex. Seating Capacity: 500. Outfield Dimension: LF—320, CF—395, RF—320.

NORTHWESTERN WILDCATS

Conference: Big Ten. Mailing Address: 1501 Central St. Evanston, IL 60201. Website: nusports.com. Head Coach: Spencer Allen. Telephone: (847) 644-1427. Baseball SID: Preston Michelson. Telephone: (847) 467-3274. Assistant Coaches: Dusty Napoleon, *Josh Reynolds. Telephone: (773) 790-5777. Home Field: Rocky & Berenice Miller Park. Seating Capacity: 720. Outfield Dimension: LF—326, CF—408, RF—310.

NORTHWESTERN STATE DEMONS

Conference: Southland. Mailing Address: 468 Caspari Drive, Natchitoches, LA 71497. Website: www.NSUDemons.com. Head Coach: Bobby Barbier. Telephone: (318) 357-4139. Baseball SID: Jason Pugh. Telephone: (318) 357-6467. Assistant Coaches: *Chris Bertrand, Taylor Dugas. Telephone: (318) 357-4176. Home Field: Brown-Stroud Field. Seating Capacity: 1200. Outfield Dimension: LF—320, CF—400, RF—340. Press Box Telephone: (318) 663-5701.

NOTRE DAME FIGHTING IRISH

Conference: Atlantic Coast. Mailing Address: 113 Joyce Center Notre Dame, IN 46556. Website: und.com. Head Coach: Mik Aoki. Telephone: (574) 485-4844. Baseball SID: Matt Paras. Telephone: (574) 631-9471. Assistant Coaches: Adam Pavkovich, *Chuck Ristano. Telephone: (574) 631-4840. Home Field: Frank Eck Stadium. Seating Capacity: 2500. Outfield Dimension: LF—330, CF—400, RF—330.

OAKLAND GOLDEN GRIZZLIES

Conference: Horizon. Mailing Address: 569 Pioneer Drive, Rochester, MI, 48309. Website: goldengrizzlies.com. Co-Head Coach: Colin Kaline, Jacke Healey. Telephone: (248) 370-4059. Baseball SID: Mekye Phelps. Telephone: (248) 370-2933. Assistant Coaches: Justin Karn. Home Field: Oakland Baseball Field. Seating Capacity: 500. Outfield Dimension: LF—330, CF—380, RF—320.

OHIO BOBCATS

Conference: Mid-American. Mailing Address: Bob Wren Stadium, Athens, OH 45701. Website: www.ohiobobcats.com. Head Coach: Rob Smith. Telephone: (740) 593-1180. Baseball SID: Mike Ashcraft. Telephone: (740) 593-1299. Assistant Coaches: Craig Moore, *C.J. Wamsley. Telephone: (740) 593-1954. Home Field: Bob Wren Stadium. Seating Capacity: 4000. Outfield Dimension: LF—340, CF—400, RF—340.

OHIO STATE BUCKEYES

Conference: Big Ten. Mailing Address: 560 Borror Dr, Columbus, OH 43210. Website: ohiostatebuckeyes.com. Head Coach: Greg Beals. Telephone: (614) 292-1075. Baseball SID: Alex Morando. Telephone: (614) 292-1389. Assistant Coaches: *Matt Angle, Mike Stafford. Telephone: (614) 292-1075. Home Field: Bill Davis Stadium. Seating Capacity: 4450. Outfield Dimension: LF—330, CF—400, RF—330.

OKLAHOMA SOONERS

Conference: Big 12. Mailing Address: 401 Imhoff Rd, Norman, OK 73072. Website: SoonerSports.com. Head Coach: Skip Johnson. Telephone: (405) 325-8354.

Baseball SID: Eric Hollier. **Telephone:** (405) 325-6449. **Assistant Coaches:** Clay Overcash, Clay Van Hook. **Telephone:** (405) 325-8354. **Home Field:** L. Dale Mitchell Park. **Seating Capacity:** 3,180. **Outfield Dimension:** **LF**—330, **CF**—410, **RF**—330.

OKLAHOMA STATE COWBOYS

Conference: Big 12. **Mailing Address:** 598 N Duck Street, Stillwater, OK 74078. **Website:** okstate.com. **Head Coach:** Josh Holliday. **Telephone:** (405) 744-7141. **Baseball SID:** Wade McWhorter. **Telephone:** (405) 744-7714. **Assistant Coaches:** *James Vilade, Rob Walton. **Telephone:** (405) 744-7141. **Home Field:** Allie P. Reynolds Stadium. **Seating Capacity:** 4000. **Outfield Dimension:** **LF**—330, **CF**—398, **RF**—330.

OLD DOMINION MONARCHS

Conference: Conference USA. **Mailing Address:** Jim Jarrett Athletic Admin. Building, Norfolk, VA 23529. **Website:** www.odusports.com. **Head Coach:** Chris Finwood. **Telephone:** (757) 683-4230. **Baseball SID:** Tim Wentz. **Telephone:** (757) 683-5581. **Assistant Coaches:** Mike Marron, *Logan Robbins. **Telephone:** (757) 683-4331. **Home Field:** Bud Metheny Baseball Complex. **Seating Capacity:** 2,500. **Outfield Dimension:** **LF**—325, **CF**—395, **RF**—325.

ORAL ROBERTS GOLDEN EAGLES

Conference: Summit. **Mailing Address:** 7777 S Lewis Ave, Tulsa, OK 74171. **Website:** www.ORUAthletics.com. **Head Coach:** Ryan Folmar. **Telephone:** (918) 495-7639. **Baseball SID:** Scott Slarks. **Telephone:** (918) 495-6646. **Assistant Coaches:** Wes Davis, *Ryan Neill. **Telephone:** (918) 495-7206. **Home Field:** J.L. Johnson Stadium. **Seating Capacity:** 2418. **Outfield Dimension:** **LF**—330, **CF**—400, **RF**—330.

OREGON DUCKS

Conference: Pac-12. **Mailing Address:** 2727 Leo Harris Parkway, Eugene, OR 97401. **Website:** goducks.com. **Head Coach:** George Horton. **Telephone:** (541) 346-5776. **Baseball SID:** Todd Miles. **Telephone:** (541) 346-0962. **Assistant Coaches:** *Jason Dietrich, Jay Uhlman. **Telephone:** (541) 346-5768. **Home Field:** PK Park. **Seating Capacity:** 4000. **Outfield Dimension:** **LF**—335, **CF**—400, **RF**—325.

OREGON STATE BEAVERS

Conference: Pac-12. **Mailing Address:** 114 Gill Coliseum, Corvallis, OR 97331. **Website:** OSUBeavers.com. **Head Coach:** Pat Bailey. **Telephone:** (541) 737-0598. **Baseball SID:** Hank Hager. **Telephone:** (541) 737-3720. **Assistant Coaches:** Andy Jenkins, *Nate Yeskie, Ryan Gipson. **Telephone:** (541) 737-0598. **Home Field:** Goss Stadium at Coleman Field. **Seating Capacity:** 3315. **Outfield Dimension:** **LF**—335, **CF**—400, **RF**—335.

PACIFIC TIGERS

Conference: West Coast. **Mailing Address:** 3601 Pacific Ave, Stockton, CA 95211. **Website:** pacifictigers.com. **Head Coach:** Ryan Garko. **Telephone:** (209) 946-3177. **Baseball SID:** Tony McDaniel. **Telephone:** (209) 946-2479. **Assistant Coaches:** Joey Centanni, Michael Reuvekamp. **Telephone:** (209) 946-2386. **Home Field:** Klein Family Field. **Seating Capacity:** 2500. **Outfield Dimension:** **LF**—317, **CF**—405, **RF**—317.

PENN STATE NITTANY LIONS

Conference: Big Ten. **Mailing Address:** Medlar Field at Lubrano Park State College, PA 16801. **Website:** gopsusports.com. **Head Coach:** Rob Cooper. **Telephone:** (814) 863-0230. **Baseball SID:** Mark Brumbaugh. **Telephone:** (814) 863-1377. **Assistant Coaches:** Andre Butler, *Josh Newman, Dallas Burke. **Telephone:** (814) 865-8605. **Home Field:** Medlar Field at Lubrano Park. **Seating Capacity:** 5406. **Outfield Dimension:** **LF**—325, **CF**—399, **RF**—320.

PENNSYLVANIA QUAKERS

Conference: Ivy League. **Mailing Address:** 233 S. 33rd St., Philadelphia, PA 19104. **Website:** pennathletics.com. **Head Coach:** John Yurkow. **Telephone:** (215) 898-6282. **Baseball SID:** Greg Mays. **Telephone:** (803) 431-6663. **Assistant Coaches:** *Mike Santello, Josh Schwartz, Will Kaufman. **Telephone:** (215) 746-2325. **Home Field:** Meiklejohn Stadium. **Seating Capacity:** 1,000. **Outfield Dimension:** **LF**—325, **CF**—390, **RF**—325.

PEPPERDINE WAVES

Conference: West Coast. **Mailing Address:** 24255 Pacific Coast Highway, Malibu, CA 90263. **Website:** pepperdinewaves.com. **Head Coach:** Rick Hirtensteiner. **Telephone:** (310) 506-4404. **Baseball SID:** Ricky Davis. **Telephone:** (310) 506-4333. **Assistant Coaches:** *Rolando Garza, Danny Worth. **Telephone:** (310) 506-4199. **Home Field:** Eddy D. Field Stadium. **Seating Capacity:** 1,800. **Outfield Dimension:** **LF**—330, **CF**—400, **RF**—330.

PITTSBURGH PANTHERS

Conference: Atlantic Coast. **Mailing Address:** University of Pitt Department of Athletics 3719 Terrace St, Pittsburgh, PA 15261. **Website:** pittsburghpanthers.com. **Head Coach:** Mike Bell. **Telephone:** Unavailable. **Baseball SID:** Kelly Dumrauf. **Telephone:** (412) 228-2561. **Assistant Coaches:** *Ty Megahee, Jerry Oakes. **Telephone:** (412) 648-8556. **Home Field:** Charles L. Cost Field. **Seating Capacity:** 900. **Outfield Dimension:** **LF**—325, **CF**—405, **RF**—330.

PORTLAND PILOTS

Conference: West Coast. **Mailing Address:** 5000 N. Willamette Blvd. Portland, OR 97203. **Website:** portlandpilots.com. **Head Coach:** Geoff Loomis. **Telephone:** (503) 943-7707. **Baseball SID:** Adam "The Rock" Linnman. **Telephone:** (503) 943-7731. **Assistant Coaches:** Connor Lambert, *Jake Valentine. **Telephone:** (503) 943-7745. **Home Field:** Joe Etzel Field. **Seating Capacity:** 1300. **Outfield Dimension:** **LF**—325, **CF**—390, **RF**—325.

PRAIRIE VIEW A&M PANTHERS

Conference: Southwestern Athletic. **Mailing Address:** PVAMU Athletics Department, P.O. Box 519, MS 1500, Prairie View, TX 77446. **Website:** www.pvpanthers.com. **Head Coach:** Auntwan Riggins. **Telephone:** (936) 261-3955. **Baseball SID:** Duane Lewis. **Telephone:** (936) 261-3950. **Assistant Coaches:** John Sheehan, Brian White. **Telephone:** (936) 261-3955. **Home Field:** Tankersley Field. **Seating Capacity:** 512.

PRESBYTERIAN BLUE HOSE

Conference: Big South. **Mailing Address:** 105 Ashland Ave., Clinton, SC 29325. **Website:** gobluehose.com.

com. **Head Coach:** Elton Pollock. **Telephone:** (864) 833-8236. **Baseball SID:** Greg Hartlage. **Telephone:** (864) 833-7095. **Assistant Coaches:** Blake Miller, Gil Walker. **Telephone:** (205) 566-1470. **Home Field:** Presbyterian College Baseball Complex. **Seating Capacity:** 500. **Outfield Dimension:** LF—325, CF—400, RF—325.

PRINCETON TIGERS

Conference: Ivy League. **Mailing Address:** Jadwin Gymnasium. **Website:** goprincetontigers.com. **Head Coach:** Scott Bradley. **Telephone:** (609) 258-5059. **Baseball SID:** Warren Croxton. **Telephone:** (609) 258-2630. **Assistant Coaches:** *Lloyd Brewer, Mike Russo. **Telephone:** (609) 258-5684. **Home Field:** Clarke Field. **Seating Capacity:** 850. **Outfield Dimension:** LF—325, CF—400, RF—315.

PURDUE BOILERMAKERS

Conference: Big Ten. **Mailing Address:** 900 John R. Wooden Dr, West Lafayette, IN 47907. **Website:** www.purduesports.com. **Head Coach:** Mark Wasikowski. **Telephone:** (765) 494-3998. **Baseball SID:** Ben Turner. **Telephone:** (765) 494-3198. **Assistant Coaches:** Elliott Cribby, Cooper Fouts. **Telephone:** (765) 494-9360. **Home Field:** Alexander Field. **Seating Capacity:** 2000. **Outfield Dimension:** LF—340, CF—408, RF—330.

QUINNIPIAC BOBCATS

Conference: Metro Atlantic. **Mailing Address:** 275 Mount Carmel Ave, Hamden, CT, 06518. **Website:** quinnipiacbobcats.com. **Head Coach:** John Delaney. **Telephone:** (203) 582-6546. **Baseball SID:** Kevin Noonan. **Telephone:** (203) 582-5387. **Assistant Coaches:** *Pat Egan, Corey Keane. **Telephone:** (203) 582-6571. **Home Field:** QU Baseball Field. **Seating Capacity:** 1,000. **Outfield Dimension:** LF—340, CF—400, RF—325.

RADFORD HIGHLANDERS

Conference: Big South. **Mailing Address:** P.O. Box 6913, Radford, VA 24142. **Website:** radfordathletics.com. **Head Coach:** Joe Raccuia. **Telephone:** (540) 831-5881. **Baseball SID:** David Gansell. **Telephone:** (540) 831-5211. **Assistant Coaches:** Matt Rein. **Telephone:** (540) 831-6578. **Home Field:** Sherman Carter Memorial Stadium. **Seating Capacity:** 800. **Outfield Dimension:** LF—330, CF—400, RF—330.

RHODE ISLAND RAMS

Conference: Atlantic 10. **Mailing Address:** 3 Keaney Rd Suite One. Kingston, RI. **Website:** www.gorhody.com. **Head Coach:** Raphael Cerrato. **Telephone:** (401) 874-4550. **Baseball SID:** Jodi Pontbriand. **Telephone:** (401) 874-5356. **Assistant Coaches:** *Sean O'Brien, Kevin Vance. **Telephone:** (401) 874-4880. **Home Field:** Bill Beck Field. **Seating Capacity:** 500. **Outfield Dimension:** LF—330, CF—400, RF—330.

RICE OWLS

Conference: Conference USA. **Mailing Address:** 6100 Main St., Houston, TX. **Website:** RiceOwls.com. **Head Coach:** Matt Bragga. **Telephone:** (713) 348-8864. **Baseball SID:** John Sullivan. **Telephone:** (713) 348-5636. **Assistant Coaches:** *Cory Barton, Paul Janish. **Telephone:** (713) 348-8859. **Home Field:** Reckling Park. **Seating Capacity:** 6193. **Outfield Dimension:** LF—335, CF—400, RF—335. **Telephone:** (713) 348-4931.

RICHMOND SPIDERS

Conference: Atlantic 10. **Mailing Address:** Robins Center, University of Richmond, Va. 23173. **Website:** richmondspiders.com. **Head Coach:** Tracy Woodson. **Telephone:** (804) 289-8391. **Baseball SID:** Dan Wacker. **Telephone:** (804) 289-8365. **Assistant Coaches:** *Nate Mulberg, RJ Thomas. **Telephone:** (804) 289-8391. **Home Field:** Pitt Field. **Seating Capacity:** 600. **Outfield Dimension:** LF—328, CF—390, RF—328.

RIDER BRONCS

Conference: Metro Atlantic. **Mailing Address:** 2083 Lawrenceville Rd., Lawrenceville, NJ 08648. **Website:** www.gobroncs.com. **Head Coach:** Barry Davis. **Telephone:** (609) 896-5055. **Baseball SID:** Steve Cunha. **Telephone:** (609) 896-5135. **Fax:** (609) 896-0341. **Assistant Coaches:** *John Crane, Lee Lipinski. **Telephone:** (609) 895-5703. **Home Field:** Sonny Pittaro Field. **Seating Capacity:** 400. **Outfield Dimension:** LF—330, CF—405, RF—330.

RUTGERS SCARLET KNIGHTS

Conference: Big Ten. **Mailing Address:** 83 Rockafeller Road, Piscataway, NJ 08854. **Website:** ScarletKnights.com. **Head Coach:** Joe Litterio. **Telephone:** (732) 445-7834. **Baseball SID:** Jimmy Gill. **Telephone:** (732) 445-8103. **Assistant Coaches:** Phil Cundari, *Jim Duffy. **Telephone:** (732) 445-7834. **Home Field:** Bainton Field. **Seating Capacity:** 1500. **Outfield Dimension:** LF—330, CF—410, RF—320.

SACRAMENTO STATE HORNETS

Conference: Western Athletic. **Mailing Address:** 6000 J Street Sacramento, CA 95819. **Website:** www.hornetsports.com. **Head Coach:** Reggie Christiansen. **Telephone:** (916) 278-4036. **Baseball SID:** Robert Barsanti. **Telephone:** (916) 278-6896. **Assistant Coaches:** *Jake Angier, Tim Wheeler. **Telephone:** (916) 278-2018. **Home Field:** John Smith Field. **Seating Capacity:** 1250. **Outfield Dimension:** LF—330, CF—395, RF—330.

SACRED HEART PIONEERS

Conference: Northeast. **Mailing Address:** 5151 Park Ave., Fairfield, CT 06825. **Website:** www.shubigred.com. **Head Coach:** Nick Restaino. **Telephone:** (203) 365-7632. **Baseball SID:** Tyrell Walden-Martin. **Telephone:** (203) 396-8127. **Assistant Coaches:** T.K. Kiernan, *Wayne Mazzoni. **Telephone:** (203) 365-4469. **Home Field:** The Ballpark at Harbor Yard. **Seating Capacity:** 5,300. **Outfield Dimension:** LF—325, CF—405, RF—325.

SAINT LOUIS BILLIKENS

Conference: Atlantic 10. **Mailing Address:** 3330 Laclede Ave St Louis MO 63103. **Website:** slubillikens.com. **Head Coach:** Darin Hendrickson. **Telephone:** (314) 977-3172. **Baseball SID:** Nick Rettig. **Telephone:** (314) 977-2524. **Assistant Coaches:** *William Bradley, Joey Hawkins. **Telephone:** (314) 977-3260. **Home Field:** Billiken Sports Center. **Seating Capacity:** 500. **Outfield Dimension:** LF—330, CF—403, RF—330.

SAM HOUSTON STATE BEARKATS

Conference: Southland. **Mailing Address:** 620 Bowers Blvd Huntsville, TX 77341. **Website:** gobearkats.com. **Head Coach:** Matt Deggs. **Telephone:** (936) 294-1731. **Baseball SID:** Ben Rikard. **Telephone:** (936) 294-

1764. **Assistant Coaches:** *Lance Harvell, Jay Sirianni. **Telephone:** (936) 294-2580. **Home Field:** Don Sanders Stadium. **Outfield Dimension: LF**—330, **CF**—400, **RF**—330.

SAMFORD BULLDOGS

Conference: Southern. **Mailing Address:** 800 Lakeshore Dr., Birmingham, AL 35229. **Website:** www.samfordsports.com. **Head Coach:** Casey Dunn. **Telephone:** (205) 726-2134. **Baseball SID:** Joey Mullins. **Telephone:** (205) 726-2799. **Assistant Coaches:** Tony David, *Tyler Shrout. **Telephone:** (205) 726-4294. **Home Field:** Joe Lee Griffin Field. **Seating Capacity:** 1,000. **Outfield Dimension: LF**—330, **CF**—390, **RF**—335.

SAN DIEGO TOREROS

Conference: West Coast. **Mailing Address:** 5998 Alcala Park, San Diego, CA 92110. **Website:** usdtoreros. com. **Head Coach:** Rich Hill. **Telephone:** (619) 260-5953. **Baseball SID:** Rose McPherson. **Telephone:** (619) 260-4745. **Assistant Coaches:** Matthew Florer, *Brock Ungricht. **Telephone:** Unavailable. **Home Field:** Fowler Park. **Seating Capacity:** 3000. **Outfield Dimension: LF**—312, **CF**—391, **RF**—327.

SAN DIEGO STATE AZTECS

Conference: Mountain West. **Mailing Address:** 5500 Campanile Rd. San Diego, CA 92182. **Website:** www. goaztecs.com. **Head Coach:** Mark Martinez. **Telephone:** (619) 594-6889. **Baseball SID:** Martin Foley. **Telephone:** (619) 594-6889. **Assistant Coaches:** *Joe Oliveira, Sam Peraza. **Telephone:** (619) 594-6889. **Home Field:** Tony Gwynn Stadium. **Seating Capacity:** 3500. **Outfield Dimension: LF**—340, **CF**—410, **RF**—340.

SAN FRANCISCO DONS

Conference: West Coast. **Mailing Address:** 2130 Fulton St. G20 San Francisco, CA 94117. **Website:** usf-dons.com. **Head Coach:** Nino Giarratano. **Telephone:** (415) 422-2934. **Baseball SID:** Mark Rivera. **Assistant Coaches:** *Troy Nakamura, Matt Hiserman. **Home Field:** Benedetti Diamond at Ulrich Field. **Seating Capacity:** 1000. **Outfield Dimension: LF**—330, **CF**—420, **RF**—300.

SAN JOSE STATE SPARTANS

Conference: Mountain West. **Mailing Address:** 1 Washington Square, San Jose, CA 95192. **Website:** www.sjuspartans.com. **Head Coach:** Brad SanFilippo. **Telephone:** (408) 924-1287. **Baseball SID:** Matt Penland. **Telephone:** (408) 924-1208. **Assistant Coaches:** Tyler LaTorre, Eddie Cornejo. **Telephone:** (408) 924-1467. **Home Field:** Municipal Stadium. **Seating Capacity:** 5,200. **Outfield Dimension: LF**—320, **CF**—390, **RF**—320.

SANTA CLARA BRONCOS

Conference: West Coast. **Mailing Address:** 500 El Camino Real, Santa Clara, CA 95053. **Website:** www. santaclarabroncos.com. **Head Coach:** Rusty Filter. **Telephone:** (408) 554-4882. **Baseball SID:** Dean Obara. **Telephone:** (408) 554-4690. **Assistant Coaches:** *Jon Karcich, B.K. Santy, Greg Gonzalez. **Telephone:** (408) 554-4151. **Home Field:** Stephen Schott Stadium. **Seating Capacity:** 1,500. **Outfield Dimension: LF**—340, **CF**—402, RF 335.

SAVANNAH STATE TIGERS

Conference: Mid-Eastern. **Mailing Address:** 3219 College Street/PO Box 20271/Baseball Office/Savannah, GA 31404. **Website:** ssuathletics.com. **Head Coach:** Carlton Hardy. **Telephone:** (912) 358-3082. **Baseball SID:** Opio Mashariki. **Telephone:** (912) 358-3430. **Assistant Coaches:** Eric McCombie. **Telephone:** (912) 358-3093. **Home Field:** Tiger Field. **Seating Capacity:** 800. **Outfield Dimension: LF**—330, **CF**—400, **RF**—330.

SEATTLE REDHAWKS

Conference: Western Athletic. **Mailing Address:** 901 12th Ave., Seattle, WA 98122. **Website:** goseattleu.com. **Head Coach:** Donny Harrel. **Telephone:** (206) 398-4399. **Baseball SID:** Sarah Finney. **Telephone:** (206) 295-5915. **Assistant Coaches:** *Greg Goetz, Wes Long. **Telephone:** (206) 398-4397. **Home Field:** Bannerwood Park. **Seating Capacity:** 1,500. **Outfield Dimension: LF**—325, **CF**—405, **RF**—325.

SETON HALL PIRATES

Conference: Big East. **Mailing Address:** 400 South Orange Ave., South Orange, NJ 07079. **Website:** www.SHUpirates.com. **Head Coach:** Rob Sheppard. **Telephone:** (973) 761-9557. **Baseball SID:** Matt Sweeney. **Telephone:** (973) 761-9493. **Assistant Coaches:** *Mark Pappas, Pat Pinkman. **Telephone:** (973) 761-9557. **Home Field:** Owen T. Carroll Field. **Seating Capacity:** 1000. **Outfield Dimension: LF**—318, **CF**—400, **RF**—325.

SIENA SAINTS

Conference: Metro Atlantic. **Mailing Address:** Siena College. **Website:** www.sienasaints.com. **Head Coach:** Tony Rossi. **Telephone:** (518) 786-5044. **Baseball SID:** Mike Demos. **Telephone:** (518) 783-2377. **Assistant Coaches:** *Steve Adkins, Dave Yamane. **Telephone:** (518) 782-6875. **Home Field:** Connors Field. **Seating Capacity:** 1000. **Outfield Dimension: LF**—300, **CF**—400, **RF**—325. **Press Box Telephone:** (336) 675-7374.

SOUTH ALABAMA JAGUARS

Conference: Sun Belt. **Mailing Address:** 70 Stadium Boulevard; Mobile, AL 36608. **Website:** usajaguars.com. **Head Coach:** Mark Calvi. **Telephone:** (251) 414-8243. **Baseball SID:** Charlie Nicholls. **Telephone:** (251) 414-8017. **Assistant Coaches:** Alan Luckie, Brad Phillips, *Chris Prothro. **Telephone:** (251) 460-6970. **Home Field:** Stanky Field. **Seating Capacity:** 3775. **Outfield Dimension: LF**—330, **CF**—400, **RF**—330.

SOUTH CAROLINA GAMECOCKS

Conference: Southeastern. **Mailing Address:** 1304 Heyward Street, Columbia, SC 29208. **Website:** GamecocksOnline.com. **Head Coach:** Mark Kingston. **Telephone:** (803) 777-7808. **Baseball SID:** Kent Reichert. **Telephone:** (803) 777-5257. **Assistant Coaches:** *Mike Current. **Telephone:** (803) 777-7808. **Home Field:** Founders Park. **Seating Capacity:** 8248. **Outfield Dimension: LF**—325, **CF**—400, **RF**—325.

SOUTH CAROLINA-UPSTATE

Conference: Big South. **Mailing Address:** 800 Unviersity Way Spartanburg, SC 29303. **Website:** www. upstatespartans.com. **Head Coach:** Matt Fincher. **Telephone:** (864) 503-5135. **Baseball SID:** Wesley

Herring. **Telephone:** (864) 503-5152. **Assistant Coaches:** Tim Brown, *Tyler Cook. **Telephone:** (864) 503-5164. **Home Field:** Harley Park. **Seating Capacity:** 500. **Outfield Dimension:** LF—335, CF—402, RF—335.

SOUTH DAKOTA STATE JACKRABBITS

Conference: Summit. **Mailing Address:** 2820 Marshall Center Brookings, SD 57007. **Website:** www.gojacks.com. **Head Coach:** Rob Bishop. **Telephone:** (605) 688-5625. **Baseball SID:** Jason Hove. **Telephone:** (605) 688-4623. **Assistant Coaches:** *Brian Grunzke, Mitch Mormann. **Telephone:** (605) 688-5625. **Home Field:** Erv Huether Stadium. **Seating Capacity:** 500. **Outfield Dimension:** LF—325, CF—395, RF—320.

SOUTH FLORIDA BULLS

Conference: American Athletic. **Mailing Address:** 4202 E Fowler Ave, Tampa, FL 33620. **Website:** gousfbulls.com. **Head Coach:** Billy Mohl. **Telephone:** (813) 974-2504. **Baseball SID:** Patrick Puzzo. **Telephone:** (813) 974-4087. **Assistant Coaches:** Chris Cates, *Chuck Jeroloman. **Telephone:** (813) 974-0567. **Home Field:** USF Baseball Stadium. **Seating Capacity:** 3211. **Outfield Dimension:** LF—325, CF—400, RF—330.

SOUTHEAST MISSOURI STATE

Conference: Ohio Valley. **Mailing Address:** 1 University Plaza, Cape Girardeau, MO 63701. **Website:** www.gosoutheast.com. **Head Coach:** Andy Sawyers. **Telephone:** (573) 986-6002. **Baseball SID:** Morgan Harding. **Telephone:** (573) 651-2294. **Assistant Coaches:** *Curt Dixon, Craig Ringe. **Telephone:** (573) 986-6002. **Home Field:** Alumni Field. **Seating Capacity:** 2,000. **Outfield Dimension:** LF—330, CF—400, RF—330.

SOUTHEASTERN LOUISIANA LIONS

Conference: Southland. **Mailing Address:** 800 Galloway Drive, Hammond, La. 70402. **Website:** www.LionSports.net. **Head Coach:** Matt Riser. **Telephone:** (985) 549-5130. **Baseball SID:** Damon Sunde. **Telephone:** (985) 549-3774. **Assistant Coaches:** *Tim Donnelly, Andrew Gipson. **Telephone:** (985) 549-5130. **Home Field:** Pat Kenelly Diamond at Alumni Field. **Seating Capacity:** 2000. **Outfield Dimension:** LF—330, CF—400, RF—300.

SOUTHERN JAGUARS

Conference: Southwestern Athletic. **Mailing Address:** 801 Harding Blvd. Baton Rouge, 70813. **Website:** gojagsports.com. **Head Coach:** Kerrick Jackson. **Telephone:** (225) 771-2513. **Baseball SID:** Chris Jones. **Telephone:** (225) 771-3495. **Assistant Coaches:** Stephanos Stroop. **Telephone:** (225) 771-3882. **Home Field:** Lee-Hines Stadium. **Seating Capacity:** 2,500. **Outfield Dimension:** LF—360, CF—400, RF—325.

SOUTHERN CALIFORNIA TROJANS

Conference: Pac-12. **Mailing Address:** 1021 Childs Way, Los Angeles, CA 90089. **Website:** usctrojans.com. **Head Coach:** Dan Hubbs. **Telephone:** (213) 740-8446. **Baseball SID:** Jacob Breems. **Telephone:** (213) 740-3809. **Assistant Coaches:** *Gabe Alvarez, Matt Curtis. **Telephone:** (213) 740-8447. **Home Field:** Dedeaux Field. **Seating Capacity:** 2500. **Outfield Dimension:** LF—330, CF—400, RF—330.

SOUTHERN ILLINOIS SALUKIS

Conference: Missouri Valley. **Mailing Address:** 425 Saluki Dr., Carbondale, IL 62901. **Website:** www.siusalukis.com. **Head Coach:** Ken Henderson. **Telephone:** (618) 453-3794. **Baseball SID:** John Lock. **Telephone:** (618) 453-7102. **Assistant Coaches:** P.J. Finigan, Seth LaRue. **Telephone:** (618) 453-2802. **Home Field:** Itchy Jones Stadium. **Seating Capacity:** 2,000. **Outfield Dimension:** LF—330, CF—390, RF—330.

SOUTHERN ILLINOIS-EDWARDSVILLE COUGARS

Conference: Ohio Valley. **Mailing Address:** 35 Circle Dr., Edwardsville, IL 62026. **Website:** www.siuecougars.com. **Head Coach:** Sean Lyons. **Telephone:** (618) 650-2032. **Baseball SID:** Joe Pott. **Telephone:** (618) 650-3608. **Assistant Coaches:** Tyler Hancock, Brandon Scott. **Telephone:** (618) 650-2032. **Home Field:** Simmons Complex. **Seating Capacity:** 1,300. **Outfield Dimension:** LF—330, CF—390, RF—330.

SOUTHERN MISSISSIPPI GOLDEN EAGLES

Conference: Conference USA. **Mailing Address:** 118 College Dr., Box 5017, Hattiesburg, MS 39406. **Website:** www.southernmiss.com. **Head Coach:** Scott Berry. **Telephone:** (601) 266-6542. **Baseball SID:** Jack Duggan. **Telephone:** (601) 266-5947. **Fax:** (601) 266-4507. **Assistant Coaches:** *Chad Caillet, Christian Ostrander. **Telephone:** (601) 266-6542. **Home Field:** Pete Taylor Park at Hill Denson Field. **Seating Capacity:** 4,200. **Outfield Dimension:** LF—340, CF—400, RF—340.

ST. BONAVENTURE BONNIES

Conference: Atlantic 10. **Mailing Address:** P.O. Box G, Reilly Center, St. Bonaventure, NY 14778. **Website:** www.gobonnies.sbu.edu. **Head Coach:** Larry Sudbrook. **Telephone:** (716) 375-2641. **Baseball SID:** Scott Eddy. **Telephone:** (716) 375-4019. **Assistant Coaches:** B.J. Salerno. **Telephone:** (716) 375-2699. **Home Field:** Fred Handler Park. **Seating Capacity:** 500. **Outfield Dimension:** LF—330, CF—403, RF—330.

ST. JOHN'S RED STORM

Conference: Big East. **Mailing Address:** 8000 Utopia Parkway, Queens, NY 11439. **Website:** RedStormSports.com. **Head Coach:** Ed Blankmeyer. **Telephone:** (718) 990-6148. **Baseball SID:** Andrew O'Connell. **Telephone:** (718) 990-1522. **Assistant Coaches:** George Brown, *Mike Hampton. **Telephone:** (718) 990-7523. **Home Field:** Jack Kaiser Stadium. **Seating Capacity:** 3500. **Outfield Dimension:** LF—325, CF—390, RF—325.

ST. JOSEPH'S HAWKS

Conference: Atlantic 10. **Mailing Address:** 5600 City Avenue Philadelphia, PA 19131. **Website:** www.sjuhawks.com. **Head Coach:** Fritz Hamburg. **Telephone:** (610) 660-1718. **Baseball SID:** Joe Greenwich. **Telephone:** (610) 660-1738. **Assistant Coaches:** Pete O'Hara, *Ryan Wheeler. **Telephone:** (610) 660-1704. **Home Field:** Smithson Field. **Seating Capacity:** 400. **Outfield Dimension:** LF—330, CF—400, RF—330.

ST. MARY'S GAELS

Conference: West Coast. **Mailing Address:** 1928 Saint Mary's Rd. Moraga CA, 94575. **Website:** smcgaels.com. **Head Coach:** Eric Valenzuela. **Telephone:** (925) 631-4637. **Baseball SID:** Stephen Ellis. **Telephone:** (925) 631-4950.

Assistant Coaches: *Daniel Costanza. Telephone: (925) 631-4658. Home Field: Louis Guisto Field. Outfield Dimension: LF—330, CF—400, RF—330.

ST. PETER'S PEACOCKS

Conference: Metro Atlantic. Mailing Address: 2641 Kennedy Blvd., Jersey City, NJ 07306. Website: www. saintpeterspeacocks.com. Head Coach: Danny Ramirez. Telephone: (201) 761-7319. Baseball SID: Hamilton Cook. Telephone: (201) 761-7316. Assistant Coaches: Richie Benes, Dan Prigge. Telephone: Unavailable. Home Field: Jaroshack Field. Outfield Dimension: LF—318, CF—405, RF—310.

STANFORD CARDINAL

Conference: Pac-12. Mailing Address: 641 E Campus Dr. Stanford, CA. 94305. Website: gostanford.com. Head Coach: David Esquer. Telephone: (650) 723-4528. Baseball SID: Nick Sako. Telephone: (650) 224-0979. Assistant Coaches: Thomas Eager, Tommy Nicholson. Telephone: (650) 725-9528. Home Field: Klein Field. Seating Capacity: 4,000. Outfield Dimension: LF—335, CF—400, RF—335.

STEPHEN F. AUSTIN STATE LUMBERJACKS

Conference: Southland. Mailing Address: 172 Hayter Street Nacogdoches, TX 75962. Website: SFAJacks.com. Head Coach: Johnny Cardenas. Telephone: Unavailable. Baseball SID: Charlie Hurley. Telephone: (936) 468-2606. Assistant Coaches: Caleb Clowers, *Mike Haynes. Telephone: (936) 468-7796. Home Field: Jaycees Field. Seating Capacity: 1000. Outfield Dimension: LF—320, CF—390, RF—320.

STETSON HATTERS

Conference: Atlantic Sun. Mailing Address: 421 N. Woodland Blvd., DeLand, FL 32723. Website: www. gohatters.com. Head Coach: Steve Trimper. Telephone: (386) 822-8100. Baseball SID: Ricky Hazel. Telephone: (386) 822-8130. Fax: (386) 822-7486. Assistant Coaches: *Joe Mercadante, Dave Therneau. Telephone: (386) 822-8733. Home Field: Melching Field at Conrad Park. Seating Capacity: 2,500. Outfield Dimension: LF—335, CF—403, RF—335.

STONY BROOK SEAWOLVES

Conference: America East. Mailing Address: 100 Circle Road, Stony Brook, NY 11794. Website: www. stonybrookathletics.com. Head Coach: Matt Senk. Telephone: (631) 632-9226. Baseball SID: Cameron Boon. Telephone: (631) 632-7289. Assistant Coaches: Jim Martin. Telephone: (631) 632-4672. Home Field: Joe Nathan Field. Seating Capacity: 1000. Outfield Dimension: LF—330, CF—390, RF—330.

TENNESSEE VOLUNTEERS

Conference: Southeastern. Mailing Address: 1511 Pat Summitt Dr., Knoxville, TN, 37996. Website: UTSports. com. Head Coach: Tony Vitello. Telephone: (865) 974-2057. Baseball SID: Sean Barows. Telephone: (865) 974-7478. Assistant Coaches: Frank Anderson, *Josh Elander. Telephone: (865) 974-2057. Home Field: Lindsey Nelson Stadium. Seating Capacity: 4283. Outfield Dimension: LF—320, CF—390, RF—320.

TENNESSEE TECH GOLDEN EAGLES

Conference: Ohio Valley. Mailing Address: 1100 McGee Blvd. Cookeville, TN 38501. Website: ttusports. com. Head Coach: Justin Holmes. Telephone: (931) 372-3925. Baseball SID: Mike Lehman. Telephone: (931) 372-3088. Assistant Coaches: Jimmy Redovian, *Mitchell Wright. Telephone: (931) 372-3853. Home Field: Quillen Field at Bush Stadium at the Averitt Express Baseball Complex. Seating Capacity: 1100. Outfield Dimension: LF—329, CF—405, RF—330.

TENNESSEE-MARTIN SKYHAWKS

Conference: Ohio Valley. Mailing Address: 1022 Elam Center, 15 Mt. Pelia Rd., Martin, TN 38238. Website: www.utmsports.com. Head Coach: Ryan Jenkins. Telephone: (731) 881-3691. Baseball SID: Jake Rogers. Telephone: (731) 881-7694. Assistant Coaches: Matt Heath, Hunter Morris. Telephone: (731) 881-3691. Home Field: Skyhawk Park. Seating Capacity: 1,000. Outfield Dimension: LF—325, CF—394, RF—325.

TEXAS LONGHORNS

Conference: Big 12. Mailing Address: 1300 E. MLK Austin, TX 78722. Website: www.texassports.com. Head Coach: David Pierce. Telephone: (512) 471-5732. Baseball SID: TBA. Telephone: (512) 471-2078. Assistant Coaches: *Sean Allen, Philip Miller. Telephone: (512) 471-5732. Home Field: UFCU Disch-Falk Field. Seating Capacity: 6,985. Outfield Dimension: LF—340, CF—400, RF—325.

TEXAS A&M AGGIES

Conference: Southeastern. Mailing Address: 301 Olsen Blvd, College Station, TX 77840. Website: www.12thman.com. Head Coach: Rob Childress. Telephone: (979) 845-4810. Baseball SID: Thomas Dick. Telephone: (979) 845-4810. Assistant Coaches: Will Bolt, *Justin Seely. Telephone: (979) 845-4810. Home Field: Olsen Field at Blue Bell Park. Seating Capacity: 6100. Outfield Dimension: LF—330, CF—400, RF—330.

TEXAS A&M-CORPUS CHRISTI ISLANDERS

Conference: Southland. Mailing Address: 6300 Ocean Dr., Unit 5719, Corpus Christi, TX 78412. Website: www.goislanders.com. Head Coach: Scott Malone. Telephone: (361) 825-3413. Baseball SID: James Sullivan. Telephone: (210) 683-7717. Assistant Coaches: Nick Magnifico, Marty Smith. Telephone: (361) 825-3720. Home Field: Chapman Field. Seating Capacity: 700. Outfield Dimension: LF—330, CF—404, RF—330.

TEXAS CHRISTIAN HORNED FROGS

Conference: Big 12. Mailing Address: 2900 Stadium Dr., Fort Worth, TX 76129. Website: www.gofrogs. com. Head Coach: Jim Schlossnagle. Telephone: (817) 257-5354. Baseball SID: Brandie Davidson. Telephone: (817) 257-7479. Assistant Coaches: Bill Mosiello, *Kirk Saarloos. Telephone: (817) 257-5155. Home Field: Lupton Stadium. Seating Capacity: 4,500. Outfield Dimension: LF—330, CF—395, RF—330.

TEXAS SOUTHERN TIGERS

Conference: Southwestern Athletic. **Mailing Address:** 3100 Cleburne St., Houston, TX 77004. **Website:** www.tsusports.com. **Head Coach:** Michael Robertson. **Telephone:** (713) 313-4315. **Baseball SID:** Alan Wiederhold-Sohn. **Telephone:** (713) 313-6829. **Assistant Coaches:** Aaron Gilbreath. **Telephone:** (713) 313-7993. **Home Field:** MacGregor Park. **Outfield Dimension:** LF—315, CF—395, RF—315.

TEXAS STATE BOBCATS

Conference: Sun Belt. **Mailing Address:** 601 University Dr, San Marcos, TX 78666. **Website:** txstatebobcats.com. **Head Coach:** Ty Harrington. **Telephone:** (512) 245-3383. **Baseball SID:** Phillip Pongratz. **Telephone:** (512) 245-4692. **Assistant Coaches:** Chad Massengale, *Steven Trout. **Telephone:** (512) 245-3383. **Home Field:** Bobcat Ballpark. **Seating Capacity:** 2000. **Outfield Dimension:** LF—330, CF—405, RF—330.

TEXAS TECH RED RAIDERS

Conference: Big 12. **Mailing Address:** 2901 Drive of Champions Ste. 200 Lubbock, TX 79409. **Website:** www.texastech.com. **Head Coach:** Tim Tadlock. **Telephone:** (806) 834-4646. **Baseball SID:** Ty Parker. **Telephone:** (806) 834-2769. **Assistant Coaches:** Matt Gardner, *J-Bob Thomas. **Telephone:** (806) 834-4583. **Home Field:** Dan Law Field at Rip Griffin Park. **Seating Capacity:** 4818. **Outfield Dimension:** LF—327, CF—402, RF—327.

TEXAS-ARLINGTON MAVERICKS

Conference: Sun Belt. **Mailing Address:** 1309 West Mitchell Street Arlington, TX 76019. **Website:** www.uta-mavs.com. **Head Coach:** Darin Thomas. **Telephone:** (817) 272-9744. **Baseball SID:** Michael Hill. **Telephone:** (817) 272-2212. **Assistant Coaches:** *Fuller Smith, Jon Wente. **Telephone:** (817) 272-9744. **Home Field:** Clay Gould Ballpark. **Seating Capacity:** 1500. **Outfield Dimension:** LF—330, CF—400, RF—330.

TEXAS-RIO GRANDE VALLEY VAQUEROS

Conference: Western Athletic. **Mailing Address:** 1201 W. University Dr. Edinburg, TX 78539. **Website:** www.goutrgv.com. **Head Coach:** Derek Matlock. **Telephone:** (956) 665-2235. **Baseball SID:** Jonah Goldberg. **Telephone:** (956) 665-2240. **Assistant Coaches:** Josh Blakley, *Russell Raley. **Telephone:** (956) 665-2891. **Home Field:** UTRGV Baseball Stadium. **Seating Capacity:** 5000. **Outfield Dimension:** LF—325, CF—410, RF—325.

TEXAS-SAN ANTONIO ROADRUNNERS

Conference: Conference USA. **Mailing Address:** 1 UTSA Circle, San Antonio, TX 78249. **Website:** goutsa.com. **Head Coach:** Jason Marshall. **Telephone:** (210) 458-4811. **Baseball SID:** Brent Ingram. **Telephone:** (210) 845-8651. **Assistant Coaches:** Jim Blair, Jake Carlson. **Telephone:** (210) 458-4805. **Home Field:** Roadrunner Field. **Seating Capacity:** 800. **Outfield Dimension:** LF—335, CF—405, RF—340.

TOLEDO ROCKETS

Conference: Mid-American. **Mailing Address:** 2801 West Bancroft St., Toledo, OH 43606. **Website:** utrockets.com. **Head Coach:** Cory Mee. **Telephone:** (419) 530-6263. **Baseball SID:** Chris Cullum. **Telephone:** (419) 530-4913. **Assistant Coaches:** *Josh Bradford, Nick McIntyre.

Telephone: (419) 530-3097. **Home Field:** Scott Park. **Seating Capacity:** 1000. **Outfield Dimension:** LF—330, CF—400, RF—330.

TOWSON TIGERS

Conference: Colonial. **Mailing Address:** 8000 York Road, Towson, MD 21252. **Website:** www.towsontigers.com. **Head Coach:** Matt Tyner. **Telephone:**(410) 704-3775. **Baseball SID:** Joshua McIntosh. **Telephone:** (410) 704-2737. **Assistant Coaches:** Tanner Biagini, *Miles Miller. **Telephone:** (410) 704-2646. **Home Field:** Schuerholz Park. **Seating Capacity:** 500. **Outfield Dimension:** LF—312, CF—424, RF—302.

TROY TROJANS

Conference: Sun Belt. **Mailing Address:** Tine Davis Field House, Troy, AL 36082. **Website:** www.troytrojans.com. **Head Coach:** Mark Smartt. **Telephone:** (334) 670-5945. **Baseball SID:** Jace Sanders. **Telephone:** (334) 670-5654. **Assistant Coaches:** *Shane Gierke, Matt Hancock. **Telephone:** (334) 670-5705. **Home Field:** Riddle Pace Field. **Seating Capacity:** 2,000. **Outfield Dimension:** LF—312, CF—404, RF—301.

TULANE GREEN WAVE

Conference: American Athletic. **Mailing Address:** 333 James W Wilson Jr. Center Ben Weiner Drive New Orleans, LA 70118. **Website:** tulanegreenwave.com. **Head Coach:** Travis Jewett. **Telephone:** (504) 862-8216. **Baseball SID:** Clyde Verdin. **Telephone:** (504) 314-7271. **Assistant Coaches:** Daniel Latham, *Eddie Smith, Brian Harris. **Telephone:** (504) 314-7202. **Home Field:** Greer Field at Turchin Stadium. **Seating Capacity:** 5000. **Outfield Dimension:** LF—325, CF—400, RF—325.

UC DAVIS AGGIES

Conference: Big West. **Mailing Address:** One Shields Avenue, Davis, CA 95616. **Website:** www.ucdavisaggies.com. **Head Coach:** Matt Vaughn. **Telephone:** (530) 752-7513. **Baseball SID:** Bryn Lutz. **Telephone:** (760) 707-4094. **Assistant Coaches:** *Lloyd Acosta, Brett Lindgren. **Telephone:** (503) 752-7513. **Home Field:** Phil Swimley Field at Dobbins Stadium. **Seating Capacity:** 3500. **Outfield Dimension:** LF—385, CF—410, RF—385.

UC IRVINE ANTEATERS

Conference: Big West. **Mailing Address:** 625 Humanities Quad, Irvine, CA 92697. **Website:** www.ucirvinesports.com. **Head Coach:** Ben Orloff. **Telephone:** (949) 824-6033. **Baseball SID:** Alex Croteau. **Telephone:** (949) 824-5814. **Assistant Coaches:** Danny Bibona, J.T. Bloodworth. **Telephone:** (949) 824-1154. **Home Field:** Cicerone Field at Anteater Ballpark. **Seating Capacity:** 1,500. **Outfield Dimension:** LF—335, CF—408, RF—335.

UC RIVERSIDE HIGHLANDERS

Conference: Big West. **Mailing Address:** 3401 Watkins Dr., Riverside, CA 92521. **Website:** gohighlanders.com. **Head Coach:** Troy Percival. **Telephone:** (951) 827-5441. **Baseball SID:** Quinn Roberts. **Telephone:** (951) 827-5438. **Assistant Coaches:** *Justin Johnson, Curtis Smith. **Telephone:** (951) 827-5441. **Home Field:** Riverside Sports Complex "The Plex". **Seating Capacity:** 2500. **Outfield Dimension:** LF—330, CF—400, RF—330.

UC SANTA BARBARA GAUCHOS

Conference: Big West. **Mailing Address:** UCSB Intercollegiate Athletics Department ICA Building Santa Barbara, CA 93106-5200. **Website:** UCSBgauchos.com. **Head Coach:** Andrew Checketts. **Telephone:** (805) 893-3690. **Baseball SID:** Matthew McClenathen. **Telephone:** (805) 893-8603. **Assistant Coaches:** Donegal Fergus, *Matt Fonteno. **Telephone:** (206) 330-6733. **Home Field:** Caesar Uyesaka Stadium. **Seating Capacity:** 1000. **Outfield Dimension: LF**—335, **CF**—400, **RF**—335.

UCLA BRUINS

Conference: Pac-12. **Mailing Address:** 325 Westwood Plaza, Los Angeles, 90095. **Website:** UCLABruins.com. **Head Coach:** John Savage. **Telephone:** (310) 794-8210. **Baseball SID:** Andrew Wagner. **Telephone:** (310) 206-4008. **Assistant Coaches:** Rex Peters, *Bryant Ward. **Telephone:** (310) 204-2473. **Home Field:** Jackie Robinson Stadium. **Seating Capacity:** 1820. **Outfield Dimension: LF**—330, **CF**—390, **RF**—330.

UNC-ASHEVILLE BULLDOGS

Conference: Big South. **Mailing Address:** 1 University Heights, CPO #2600, Asheville, NC 28804. **Website:** www.uncabulldogs.com. **Head Coach:** Scott Friedholm. **Telephone:** (828) 251-6920. **Baseball SID:** Mitchell Miegel. **Telephone:** (828) 251-6931. **Assistant Coaches:** Chris Bresnahan, Kyle Ward, Pete Guy. **Telephone:** (828) 250-2309. **Home Field:** Greenwood Field. **Seating Capacity:** 750. **Outfield Dimension: LF**—324, **CF**—395, **RF**—335.

UNC GREENSBORO SPARTANS

Conference: Southern. **Mailing Address:** 1509 Walker Ave. Greensboro, NC 27412. **Website:** uncgspartans.com. **Head Coach:** Link Jarrett. **Telephone:** (336) 334-3247. **Baseball SID:** Will Toman. **Telephone:** (614) 327-0306. **Assistant Coaches:** Jerry Edwards, *Joey Holcomb. **Telephone:** (336) 334-3247. **Home Field:** UNCG Baseball Stadium. **Seating Capacity:** 3500. **Outfield Dimension: LF**—340, **CF**—410, **RF**—340.

UNC WILMINGTON SEAHAWKS

Conference: Colonial. **Mailing Address:** 601 South College Road, Wilmington, NC 28403. **Website:** UNCWSports.com. **Head Coach:** Mark Scalf. **Telephone:** (910) 962-3570. **Baseball SID:** Tom Riordan. **Telephone:** (910) 962-4099. **Assistant Coaches:** *Randy Hood, Matt Myers. **Telephone:** (910) 962-7471. **Home Field:** Brooks Field. **Seating Capacity:** 3500. **Outfield Dimension: LF**—340, **CF**—380, **RF**—340.

UTAH UTES

Conference: Pac-12. **Mailing Address:** 1825 E. South Campus Dr.. **Website:** utahutes.com. **Head Coach:** Bill Kinnerberg. **Telephone:** (801) 581-3526. **Baseball SID:** Joseph Feldman. **Telephone:** (801) 585-1295. **Assistant Coaches:** Jay Brossman, *Mike Crawford. **Telephone:** (801) 585-6779. **Home Field:** Smith's Ball Park. **Seating Capacity:** 14511. **Outfield Dimension: LF**—345, **CF**—420, **RF**—315.

UTAH VALLEY WOLVERINES.

Conference: Western Athletic. **Mailing Address:** 800 W University Parkway, Orem, UT 84058. **Website:** www.gouvu. **Head Coach:** Eric Madsen. **Telephone:** (801) 863-

6509. **Baseball SID:** James Warnick. **Telephone:** (801) 863-6231. **Fax:** (801) 863-8813. **Assistant Coaches:** David Carter. **Telephone:** (801) 863-8647. **Home Field:** UCCU Ballpark. **Seating Capacity:** 5,000. **Outfield Dimension: LF**—312, **CF**—408, **RF**—315.

VALPARAISO CRUSADERS

Conference: Missouri Valley. **Mailing Address:** 1009 Union Street, Valparaiso, IN. 46383. **Website:** www.valpoathletics.com. **Head Coach:** Brian Schmack. **Telephone:** (219) 464-6117. **Baseball SID:** Brandon Vickrey. **Telephone:** (219) 464-5396. **Assistant Coaches:** Casey Fletcher, *Kory Winter. **Telephone:** (219) 465-7961. **Home Field:** Emory G. Bauer Field. **Seating Capacity:** 1000. **Outfield Dimension: LF**—330, **CF**—400, **RF**—330.

VANDERBILT COMMODORES

Conference: Southeastern. **Mailing Address:** 2601 Jess Neely Drive. **Website:** vucommodores.com. **Head Coach:** Tim Corbin. **Telephone:** (615) 322-3716. **Baseball SID:** Andrew Pate. **Telephone:** (615) 343-6811. **Assistant Coaches:** *Mike Baxter, Scott Brown. **Telephone:** (615) 322-3716. **Home Field:** Hawkins Field. **Seating Capacity:** 3626. **Outfield Dimension: LF**—310, **CF**—400, **RF**—330.

VILLANOVA WILDCATS

Conference: Big East. **Mailing Address:** 800 Lancaster Ave., Villanova, PA 19085. **Website:** www.villanova.com. **Head Coach:** Kevin Mulvey. **Telephone:** (610) 519-4529. **Baseball SID:** David Berman. **Telephone:** (610) 519-4122. **Assistant Coaches:** Eddie Brown, Rob Delaney. **Telephone:** (610) 519-5520. **Home Field:** Villanova Ballpark at Plymouth. **Seating Capacity:** 750. **Outfield Dimension: LF**—330, **CF**—410, **RF**—330.

VIRGINIA CAVALIERS

Conference: Atlantic Coast. **Mailing Address:** University Hall, P.O. Box 400839, Charlottesville, VA 22904. **Website:** www.virginiasports.com. **Head Coach:** Brian O'Connor. **Telephone:** (434) 243-5114. **Baseball SID:** Scott Fitzgerald. **Telephone:** (434) 982-5500. **Assistant Coaches:** Karl Kuhn, *Kevin McMullan, Matt Kirby. **Telephone:** (434) 243-5114. **Home Field:** Davenport Field. **Seating Capacity:** 5,025. **Outfield Dimension: LF**—332, **CF**—404, **RF**—332.

VIRGINIA COMMONWEALTH RAMS

Conference: Atlantic 10. **Mailing Address:** 1300 W. Broad St., Richmond, VA 23284. **Website:** vcuathletics.com. **Head Coach:** Shawn Stiffler. **Telephone:** (804) 828-4822. **Baseball SID:** Chris Kowalczyk. **Telephone:** (804) 828-8818. **Assistant Coaches:** Mike McRae, Rich Witten, Josh Tutwiler. **Telephone:** (804) 828-4821. **Home Field:** The Diamond. **Seating Capacity:** 9,560. **Outfield Dimension: LF**—330, **CF**—402, **RF**—330.

VIRGINIA MILITARY INSTITUTE KEYDETS

Conference: Southern. **Mailing Address:** Cameron Hall, Lexington, VA 24450. **Website:** vmikeydets.com. **Head Coach:** Jonathan Hadra. **Telephone:** (540) 464-7601. **Baseball SID:** Mike Carpenter. **Telephone:** (540) 464-7015. **Assistant Coaches:** *Geoffrey Murphy, Sam Roberts. **Telephone:** (540) 464-7609. **Home Field:** Gray-Minor Stadium. **Seating Capacity:** 1,000. **Outfield Dimension: LF**—330, **CF**—395, **RF**—330.

VIRGINIA TECH HOKIES

Conference: Atlantic Coast. **Mailing Address:** 25 Beamer Way, Blacksburg, VA 24061. **Website:** www.hokiesports.com. **Head Coach:** John Szefc. **Telephone:** (540) 231-5906. **Baseball SID:** Marc Mullen. **Telephone:** (540) 231-1894. **Assistant Coaches:** *Kurt Elbin, Ryan Fecteau, Tyler Hanson. **Telephone:** (540) 231-5906. **Home Field:** English Field at Union Park. **Seating Capacity:** 4,000. **Outfield Dimension:** LF—330, CF—400, RF—330.

WAGNER SEAHAWKS

Conference: Northeast. **Mailing Address:** 1 Campus Rd., Staten Island, NY 10301. **Website:** wagnerathletics.com. **Head Coach:** Jim Carone. **Telephone:** (718) 390-3154. **Baseball SID:** Brian Morales. **Telephone:** (718) 390-3215. **Assistant Coaches:** Paul Piccolino, *Craig Noto. **Telephone:** (718) 420-4121. **Home Field:** Richmond County Bank Ballpark. **Seating Capacity:** 7,171. **Outfield Dimension:** LF—320, CF—390, RF—318.

WAKE FOREST DEMON DEACONS

Conference: Atlantic Coast. **Mailing Address:** 401 Deacon Blvd., Winston-Salem, NC 27106. **Website:** www.wakeforestsports.com. **Head Coach:** Tom Walter. **Telephone:** (336) 758-5570. **Baseball SID:** Jay Garneau. **Telephone:** (336) 758-3229. **Assistant Coaches:** *Bill Cilento, Matt Hobbs. **Telephone:** (336) 758-4208. **Home Field:** David F. Couch Ballpark. **Seating Capacity:** 3,823. **Outfield Dimension:** LF—310, CF—400, RF—300.

WASHINGTON HUSKIES

Conference: Pac-12. **Mailing Address:** Box 354070. **Website:** www.gohuskies.com. **Head Coach:** Lindsay Meggs. **Telephone:** (206) 616-4335. **Baseball SID:** Brian Tom. **Telephone:** (206) 897-1742. **Assistant Coaches:** *Jason Kelly, Ronnie Prettyman. **Telephone:** (206) 543-2919. **Home Field:** Husky Ballpark. **Seating Capacity:** 3000. **Outfield Dimension:** LF—327, CF—395, RF—317.

WASHINGTON STATE COUGARS

Conference: Pac-12. **Mailing Address:** Bohler Athletic Complex, Washington State University, Pullman, WA, 99163. **Website:** www.wsucougars.com. **Head Coach:** Marty Lees. **Telephone:** (509) 335-0311. **Baseball SID:** Bobby Alworth. **Telephone:** (509) 335-5785. **Assistant Coaches:** *Marty Lees, Dan Spencer. **Telephone:** (509) 335-0311. **Home Field:** Bailey-Brayton Field. **Seating Capacity:** 3500. **Outfield Dimension:** LF—330, CF—400, RF—330.

WEST VIRGINIA MOUNTAINEERS

Conference: Big 12. **Mailing Address:** 3450 Monongahela Blvd. Morgantown WV 26507. **Website:** WVUsports.com. **Head Coach:** Randy Mazey. **Telephone:** (304) 293-4740. **Baseball SID:** Charlie Healy. **Telephone:** (304) 293-2821. **Assistant Coaches:** Mark Ginther, *Steve Sabins. **Telephone:** (304) 293-9880. **Home Field:** Monongalia County Ballpark. **Seating Capacity:** 3500. **Outfield Dimension:** LF—325, CF—400, RF—325.

WESTERN CAROLINA CATAMOUNTS

Conference: Southern. **Mailing Address:** Ramsey Center Athletics; 92 Catamount Rd.; Cullowhee, NC 28723. **Website:** www.CatamountSports.com. **Head Coach:** Bobby Moranda. **Telephone:** (828) 227-2021. **Baseball SID:** Daniel Hooker. **Telephone:** (828) 227-2339.

Assistant Coaches: David Garcia, *Taylor Sandefur. **Telephone:** (828) 227-2510. **Home Field:** Childress Field at Hennon Stadium. **Seating Capacity:** 1500. **Outfield Dimension:** LF—325, CF—395, RF—325.

WESTERN ILLINOIS LEATHERNECKS

Conference: Summit. **Mailing Address:** Western Hall 209, 1 University Circle, Macomb, IL 61455. **Website:** www.goleathernecks.com. **Head Coach:** Ryan Brownlee. **Telephone:** (309) 298-1521. **Baseball SID:** Monyae Williamson. **Telephone:** (309) 298-1133. **Assistant Coaches:** Parker Osborne, *Matt Risdon. **Telephone:** (309) 298-1521. **Home Field:** Al Boyer Stadium. **Seating Capacity:** 1500. **Outfield Dimension:** LF—330, CF—395, RF—330.

WESTERN KENTUCKY HILLTOPPERS

Conference: Conference USA. **Mailing Address:** 1605 Avenue of Champions. **Website:** wkusports.com. **Head Coach:** John Pawlowski. **Telephone:** (270) 745-2277. **Baseball SID:** Bryan Fyalkowski. **Telephone:** (270) 745-5388. **Assistant Coaches:** *Rob Reinstetle, Ben Wolgamot. **Telephone:** (270) 745-2276. **Home Field:** Nick Denes Field. **Seating Capacity:** 1500. **Outfield Dimension:** LF—330, CF—400, RF—330.

WESTERN MICHIGAN BRONCOS

Conference: Mid-American. **Mailing Address:** 1903 W Michigan Ave, Kalamazoo, MI 49008. **Website:** www.wmubroncos.com. **Head Coach:** Billy Gernon. **Telephone:** (269) 276-3205. **Baseball SID:** Nathan Palcowski. **Telephone:** (269) 387-4138. **Assistant Coaches:** Will Nimke, *Adam Piotrowicz. **Telephone:** (269) 276-3208. **Home Field:** Robert J Bobb Stadium at Hyames Field. **Seating Capacity:** 1200. **Outfield Dimension:** LF—310, CF—400, RF—330.

WICHITA STATE SHOCKERS

Conference: American Athletic. **Mailing Address:** 1845 Fairmont Dr., Wichita, KS 67260. **Website:** www.goshockers.com. **Head Coach:** Todd Butler. **Telephone:** (316) 978-3636. **Baseball SID:** Tami Cutler. **Telephone:** (316) 978-5559. **Assistant Coaches:** *Sammy Esposito, Mike Pelfrey. **Telephone:** (316) 978-3636. **Home Field:** Eck Stadium. **Seating Capacity:** 7,851. **Outfield Dimension:** LF—330, CF—390, RF—330.

WILLIAM & MARY TRIBE

Conference: Colonial. **Mailing Address:** 751 Ukrop Way, Williamsburg, VA, 23185. **Website:** tribeathletics.com. **Head Coach:** Brian Murphy. **Telephone:** (757) 221-3492. **Baseball SID:** Jordan Williams. **Telephone:** (757) 221-3344. **Assistant Coaches:** *Brian Casey, Pat McKenna. **Telephone:** (757) 221-3399. **Home Field:** Plumeri Park. **Seating Capacity:** 1200. **Outfield Dimension:** LF—325, CF—400, RF—325.

WINTHROP EAGLES

Conference: Big South. **Mailing Address:** 1162 Eden Terrace, Rock Hill, SC 29733. **Website:** winthropeagles.com. **Head Coach:** Thomas Riginos. **Telephone:** (864) 903-9796. **Baseball SID:** Brett Redden. **Telephone:** (803) 323-2129 ext. 6246. **Assistant Coaches:** *Austin Hill, Robbie Monday. **Telephone:** (252) 294-4409. **Home Field:** Winthrop Ballpark. **Seating Capacity:** 1900. **Outfield Dimension:** LF—325, CF—390, RF—325.

WISCONSIN-MILWAUKEE PANTHERS

Conference: Horizon. **Mailing Address:** 3409 N. Downer Ave., Milwaukee 53211. **Website:** www.mkepanthers.com. **Head Coach:** Scott Doffek. **Telephone:** (414) 229-5670. **Baseball SID:** Ashley Steltenpohl. **Telephone:** (414) 435-8118. **Assistant Coaches:** Cory Bigler, Shaun Wegner. **Telephone:** (414) 229-2433. **Home Field:** Henry Aaron Field. **Seating Capacity:** 500. **Outfield Dimension: LF**—320, **CF**—390, **RF**—320.

WOFFORD TERRIERS

Conference: Southern. **Mailing Address:** 429 N. Church Street, Spartanburg, SC 29303. **Website:** www.woffordterriers.com. **Head Coach:** Todd Interdonato. **Telephone:** (864) 597-4497. **Baseball SID:** Brent Williamson. **Telephone:** (864) 597-4093. **Assistant Coaches:** Seth Cutler-Voltz, *JJ Edwards. **Telephone:** (864) 597-4126. **Home Field:** Russell C. King Field. **Seating Capacity:** 2500. **Outfield Dimension: LF**—325, **CF**—395, **RF**—325.

WRIGHT STATE RAIDERS

Conference: Horizon. **Mailing Address:** 3640 Colonel Glenn Hwy., Dayton, OH 45435. **Website:** www.wsuraiders.com. **Head Coach:** Alex Sogard. **Telephone:** (937) 775-3668. **Baseball SID:** Bob Noss. **Telephone:** (937) 775-2816. **Assistant Coaches:** *Nate Metzger, Matt Talarico, Matt Reed. **Telephone:** (937) 775-4188. **Home Field:** Nischwitz Stadium. **Seating Capacity:** 750. **Outfield Dimension: LF**—330, **CF**—400, **RF**—330.

XAVIER MUSKETEERS

Conference: Big East. **Mailing Address:** 3800 Victory Parkway CIncinnati OH 45207. **Website:** goxavier.com. **Head Coach:** Billy O'Conner. **Telephone:** (513) 745-2890. **Baseball SID:** Brendan Bergen. **Telephone:** (513) 745-3388. **Assistant Coaches:** Austin Cousino, *Brian Furlong. **Telephone:** (513) 745-1962. **Home Field:** Hayden Field. **Seating Capacity:** 500. **Outfield Dimension: LF**—310, **CF**—380, **RF**—310.

YALE BULLDOGS

Conference: Ivy League. **Mailing Address:** PO Box 208216, New Haven, CT 06520. **Website:** yalebulldogs.com. **Head Coach:** John Stuper. **Telephone:** (203) 432-1466. **Baseball SID:** Sam Rubin. **Telephone:** (203) 432-1455. **Assistant Coaches:** Tucker Frawley, *Josh Schulman. **Telephone:** (203) 432-1467. **Home Field:** Yale Field. **Seating Capacity:** 5,000. **Outfield Dimension: LF**—330, **CF**—405, **RF**—315.

YOUNGSTOWN STATE PENGUINS

Conference: Horizon. **Mailing Address:** 1 University Plaza, Youngstown, OH 44555. **Website:** www.ysusports.com. **Head Coach:** Dan Bertolini. **Baseball SID:** Drae Smith. **Telephone:** (330) 941-1480. **Assistant Coaches:** Josh Merrigan, *Eric Smith. **Home Field:** Eastwood Field. **Seating Capacity:** 6,300. **Outfield Dimension: LF**—335, **CF**—405, **RF**—335.

AMATEUR
& YOUTH

INTERNATIONAL ORGANIZATIONS

WORLD BASEBALL SOFTBALL CONFEDERATION

Headquarters: Maison du Sport International—54, Avenue de Rhodanie, 1007 Lausanne, Switzerland.
Telephone: (+41-21) 318-82-40. **Fax:** (41-21) 318-82-41. **Website:** www.wbsc.org. **E-Mail:** office@wbsc.org. **Year Founded:** 1938.

President: Riccardo Fraccari (Italy). **Secretary General:** Beng Choo Low (Japan). **Vice President Baseball:** Willi Kaltschmitt Luján (Guam). **Vice President Softball:** Beatrice Allen (Gambia). **Softball Executive VP:** Craig Cress (USA). **Baseball Executive VP:** Tom Peng (Taiwan). **Treasurer:** Angelo Vicini (San Marino). **Members At-Large:** Ron Finlay (Australia), Paul Seiler (USA). Taeki Utsugi (Japan), Tommy Velázquez (Puerto Rico). **Athlete Representative For Baseball:** Justin Huber (Austrailia). **Athlete Representative For Softball:** María José Soto Gil (Venezuela). **Global Ambassador:** Antonio Castro Soto del Valle (Cuba), Meliton Sanchez Rivas (Panama). **Executive Director:** Michael Schmidt. **Softball Director:** Ron Radigonda. **Assistant to the President:** Giovanni Pantaleoni. **Marketing/Tournament Manager:** Masaru Yokoo, Laurie Gouthro. **Public Relations Officer:** Oscar Lopez, Lori Nolan. **National Federation Relations:** Francesca Fabretto, Brian Glauser, Aki Huang, Amy Park. **Antidoping Officer:** Victor Isola. **Administration/Finance:** Sandrine Pennone, Laetitia Barbey.

CONTINENTAL ASSOCIATIONS

CONFEDERATION PAN AMERICANA DE BEISBOL (COPABE)

Mailing Address: Calle 3, Francisco Filos, Vista Hermosa, Edificio 74, Planta Baja Local No. 1, Panama City, Panama. **Telephone:** (507) 229-8684. **Website:** www.copabe.net. **E-Mail:** copabe@sinfo.net.

Chairman: Eduardo De Bello (Panama). **Secretary General:** Hector Pereyra (Dominican Republic).

AFRICA BASEBALL SOFTBALL ASSOCIATION (ABSA)

Office Address: Paiko Road, Chanchaga, Minna, Niger State, Nigeria.
Mailing Address: P.M.B. 150, Minna, Niger State, Nigeria.
Telephone: (234) 8037188491. **E-mail:** absasecretariat@yahoo.com

President: Sabeur Jlajla. **Vice President Baseball:** Etienne N'Guessan. **Vice President Softball:** Fridah Shiroya. **Secretary General:** Ibrahim N'Diaye. **Treasurer:** Moira Dempsey. **Executive Director:** Lieutenant Colonel (rtd) Friday Ichide. **Deputy Executive Director:** Francoise Kameni-Lele.

BASEBALL FEDERATION OF ASIA

Mailing Address: 9F. -3, No. 288, Sec 6 Civic Blvd.,Xinyi Dist., Taipei City, Taiwan (R.O.C.). **Telephone:** 886-2-27473368. **E-Mail Address:** bfa@baseballasia.org

President: Tom Peng. **Vice Presidents:** Suzuki Yoshinobu, Chen Xu, Hae Young Yang. **Secretary General:** Hua-Wei Lin. **Executive Director:** Richard Lin. **Members At Large:** Allan Mak, Alfonso Martin Eizmendi, Syed Khawar Shah. **Senior Advisor:** Kazuhiro Tawa. **China Baseball Development Executive Director:** Tian Yuan. **West Asia Baseball Development Executive Director:** Syed Khawar Shah.

EUROPEAN BASEBALL CONFEDERATION

Mailing Address: Savska cesta 137, 10 000 Zagreb, Croatia. **Telephone/Fax:** +385 1 561 5227. **E-Mail Address:** office@baseballeurope.com. **Website:** baseballeurope.com.

President: Didier Seminet (France). **1st Vice President:** Petr Ditrich (Czech Republic). **2nd Vice President:** Jürgen Elsishans (Germany). **3rd Vice President:** Rainer Husty (Austria). **Secretary General:** Krunoslav Karin (Croatia) **Treasurer:** Rene Laforce (Belgium). **Vocals:** Roderick Balk (Netherlands), Marco Mannucci (Italy), Oleg Boyko (Ukraine).

BASEBALL CONFEDERATION OF OCEANIA

Mailing Address: 48 Partridge Way, Mooroolbark, Victoria 3138, Australia. **Telephone:** +613 9727 1779. **Fax:** 613 9727 5959. **E-Mail Address:** bcosecgeneral@baseballoceania.com.

President: Bob Steffy (Guam). **1st Vice President:** Laurent Cassier (New Caledonia). **2nd Vice President:** Victor Langkilde (American Samoa). **Secretary General:** Chet Gray (Australia). **Executive Committee:** Rose Igitol (CNMI), Temmy Shmull (Palau), Innoke Niubalavu (Fiji).

INTERNATIONAL GOODWILL SERIES, INC.

Mailing Address: 981 Slate Drive, Santa Rosa, CA 95405. **Telephone:** (707) 538-0777. **E-Mail Address:** goodwillseries24@gmail.com.
Website: www.goodwillseries.org.
President, Goodwill Series, Inc.: Bob Williams.

ISG BASEBALL

Mailing Address: 3829 S Oakbrook Dr. Greenfield, WI 53228. **Telephone:** 414-704-5467. **E-Mail Address:** isgbaseball14@gmail.com. **Website:** www.isgbaseball.com. **President:** Tom O'Connell. **Vice President:** Peter Caliendo. **Secretary/Treasurer:** Randy Town. **Board Members:** Jim Jones, Rick Steen, Bill Mathews, Pat Doyle, John Vodenlich.

NATIONAL ORGANIZATIONS

USA BASEBALL

Mailing Address, Corporate Headquarters: 1030 Swabia Court Suite 201, Durham, NC 27703
Telephone: (919) 474-8721.
Fax: (855) 420-5910.
E-mail Address: info@usabaseball.com.
Website: www.usabaseball.com.
President: Mike Gaski.
Treasurer: Jason Dobis.
Board of Directors: Mike Gaski (President), Jason Dobis (Treasurer), Jenny Dalton-Hill (Secretary);
Members: Willie Bloomquist, Steve Cloud, John Gall, George Grande, Abraham Key, Chris Marinak, John McHale Jr., Richard Neely, Davis Whitfield.
National Members Organizations: Amateur Athletic Union (AAU); American Amateur Baseball Congress (AABC); American Baseball Coaches Association (ABCA); American Legion Baseball, Babe Ruth Baseball, Dixie Baseball, Little League Baseball, National Amateur Baseball Federation (NABF); National Association of Intercollegiate Athletics (NAIA); National Baseball Congress (NBC); National Collegiate Athletic Association (NCAA); National Federation of State High School Athletic Associations, National High School Baseball Coaches Association (BCA); National Junior College Athletic Association (NJCAA); Police Athletic League (PAL); PONY Baseball, T-Ball USA, United States Specialty Sports Association (USSSA).
Events: www.usabaseball.com/events/schedule.jsp.

STAFF
Executive Director/Chief Executive Officer: Paul Seiler. **Assistant Director, Marketing:** Brittany Allen. **Senior Director, Retail:** Carrington Austin. **Graphic Designer:** Taylor Banner. **Assistant Director, Prospect Development Pipeline:** Bailey Beck. **Senior Director, Baseball Operations:** Ashley Bratcher. **Senior Director, Player Development:** Scott Brosius. **General Manager, National Teams:** Eric Campbell. **Director, Youth Programs:** Tyler Collins. **Director, Youth Programs:** Tyler Collins. **Director, Baseball Operations:** Brett Curll. **Chief Finance Officer:** Ray Darwin. **Assistant Director, Media Relations:** Emily Fedewa. **Director, Travel Services:** Monica Garza. **Assistant Director, Retail:** Tayler Gainer. **Assistant Director, Travel Services:** Allison Gupton. **Director, USABat Program:** Russell Hartford. **Assistant Director, SafeSport & Compliance:** Jenny Haskill. **Assistant Director, Baseball Administration:** Carter Hicks. **Graphic Designer:**

Jenna Hiscock. **Director, Prospect Development Pipeline:** Jules Johnson. **Director, Creative Services:** Kevin Jones. **Director, Retail Services:** Megan Kane. **Director, Baseball Operations:** Ben Kelley. **Assistant Director, Finance & Accounting:** Alex Kerr. **Director, Baseball Operations:** Charles Lane. **Assistant Director, Baseball Operations:** Jacob Larson. **Senior Director, SafeSport & Compliance:** Kyle Lubrano. **Director, Finance & Accounting:** Cicely Mclaughlin. **Assistant Director, Prospect Development Pipeline:** Matt Pajak. **Chief Operating Officer:** David Perkins. **Assistant Director, Media Relations:** Chris Pharis. **Director, Educational Resources:** Lauren Rhyne. **Chief Development Officer:** Rick Riccobono. **Assistant Director, Baseball Operations:** Ann Claire Roberson. **Director, 12U National Team:** Will Schworer. **Director, NTC Operations:** James Vick. **Director, Media Relations:** Brad Young.

BASEBALL CANADA

Mailing Address: 2212 Gladwin Cres., Suite A7, Ottawa, Ontario K1B 5N1. **Telephone:** (613) 748-5606. **Fax:** (613) 748-5767. **E-mail Address:** info@baseball.ca. **Website:** www.baseball.ca.
Director General: Jim Baba. **Head Coach/Director, National Teams:** Greg Hamilton. **Business/Sport Development Director/Women's National Team Manager:** Andre Lachance. **Program Coordinator:** Kelsey McIntosh. **Media/PR Coordinator:** Adam Morissette. **Administrative Coordinator:** June Sterling. **Administrative Assistant:** Penny Baba.

NATIONAL BASEBALL CONGRESS

Mailing Address: 111 S. Main, Suite 600, Wichita, KS 67202. **Telephone:** (316) 977-9400. **Fax:** (316) 462-4506. **Website:** www.nbcbaseball.com.
Year Founded: 1931.

ATHLETES IN ACTION

Mailing Address: 651 Taylor Dr., Xenia, OH 45385. **Telephone:** (937) 352-1000. **Fax:** (937) 352-1245. **E-mail Address:** baseball@athletesinaction.org. **Website:** www.aiabaseball.org. **Director, AIA Baseball:** Chris Beck. **General Manager, Alaska:** Chris Beck. **General Manager, Great Lakes:** Dave Gnau. **International Teams Director:** John McLaughlin. **Youth Baseball Director:** Dave Gnau.

SUMMER COLLEGE LEAGUES

NATIONAL ALLIANCE OF COLLEGE SUMMER BASEBALL

Telephone: (321) 206-9714 **E-Mail Address:** RSitz@FloridaLeague.com. **Website:** www.nacsb.org
Executive Director: Rob Sitz (Florida League) **Assistant Executive Director:** Bobby Bennett (Sunbelt Baseball League), Jeff Carter (Southern Collegiate Baseball League). **Treasurer:** Jason Woodward (Cal Ripken Collegiate Baseball League). **Director, Marketing & PR:** Stefano

Foggi (Florida Collegiate Summer League). **Compliance Officer:** Paul Galop (Cape Cod Baseball League).
Member Leagues: Atlantic Collegiate Baseball League, California Collegiate League, Cal Ripken Collegiate Baseball League, Cape Cod Baseball League, Florida Collegiate Summer League, Great Lakes Summer Collegiate League, New England Collegiate Baseball League, Hamptons Collegiate Baseball League, New York Collegiate Baseball League, Southern Collegiate Baseball League, Sunbelt Baseball League, Valley Baseball League.

ALASKA BASEBALL LEAGUE

League Mailing Address: 435 W. 10th Avenue, Ste. B, Anchorage, AK, 99501. 5 teams, 44 league games and approximately 5 non league games. Season begins play June 5 and ends Aug. 1. **Commissioner**: Jim Posey. **Email**: commissionerposeyabl@gmail.com.

MAT-SU MINERS

General Manager: Pete Christopher.
Mailing Address: P.O. Box 2690 Palmer, AK 99645.
Telephone: 907-746-4914/907-745-6401. **Fax:** 907-746-5068. **E-Mail:** gmminers@gci.net. **Fax:** 907-561-2920. **Website:** www.matsuminers.org.
Head Coach: Ben Taylor, Chandler-Gilbert (Ariz.) CC.
Field: Hermon Brothers, Grass, No Lights.

ANCHORAGE BUCS

General Manager: Shawn Maltby
Mailing Address: 435 W. 10th Avenue Suite B, Anchorage, AK 99501. **Office:** 907-561-2827. **Fax:** 907-561-2920. **E-Mail:** shawn@anchoragebucs.com.
Website: www.anchoragebucs.com
Head Coach: Grant Palmer, El Camino CC (Calif.)
Field: Mulcahy Field -Turf Infield, Grass Outfield, Lights

ANCHORAGE GLACIER PILOTS

General Manager: Mike Hinshaw
Mailing Address: 435 W. 10th Avenue, Suite A, Anchorage, Alaska 99501. **Office:** 907-274-3627.
Fax: 907-274-3628. **E-Mail:** gpilots@alaska.net.
Website: www.glacierpilots.com.
Head Coach: Jeff Pritchard, Cabrillo CC.
Field: Mulcahy Field -Turf Infield, Grass Outfield, Lights

CHUGIAK-EAGLE RIVER CHINOOKS

General Manager: Chris Beck
Mailing Address: 651 Taylor Drive, Xenia, Ohio 45385.
Office: 937-352-1237. **Fax:** 937-352-1001.
E-Mail: Chris.beck@athletesinaction.org.
Website: www.cerchinooks.com.
Head Coach: Jon Groth, Tyler (Texas) CC
Field: Lee Jordan Field-Turf Infield, Grass Outfield, No Lights

PENINSULA OILERS

General Manager: Tory Smith.
Mailing Address: 601 S. Main St., Kenai, Alaska 99611.
Office: 907-283-7133. **Fax:** 907-283-3390.
E-Mail: tory@oilersbaseball.com.
Website: www.oilersbaseball.com
Head Coach: Kyle Brown, Southwestern College
Field: Coral Seymour Memorial Park-Grass , No Lights

ATLANTIC COLLEGIATE BASEBALL LEAGUE

Mailing Address: 1760 Joanne Drive, Quakertown, PA 18951.
Telephone: (215) 536-5777. **Fax:** (215) 536-5777.
E-Mail: tbonekemper@verizon.net.
Website: www.acbl-online.com.
Year Founded: 1967.
Commissioner: Ralph Addonizio.
President: Tom Bonekemper.
Acting Secretary: Mike Kalb. **Vice President:** Angelo Fiore, Doug Cinella. **Treasurer:** Bob Hoffman.

Regular Season: 40 games. **Opening Date:** June 1.
Closing Date: August 4. **All-Star Game:** July 8, Yogi Berra Stadium. **Roster Limit:** 26.

ALLENTOWN RAILERS

Mailing Address: Suite 202, 1801 Union Blvd, Allentown, PA 18109. **E-Mail Address:** ddando@lehigh-valleybaseballacademy.com. **Field Manager:** Dylan Dando.

JERSEY PILOTS

Mailing Address: 11 Danemar Drive, Middletown, NJ 07748. **Telephone:** (732) 939-0627. **E-Mail Address:** baseball@jerseypilots.com. **General Manager:** Mike Kalb. **Field Manager:** Zac Dreher.

NORTH JERSEY EAGLES

Mailing Address: 12 Wright Way, Oakland NJ 07436.
General Manager: Brian Casey. **Field Manager:** Chris Buser.

OCEAN GULLS

General Manager: Angelo Fiore, afiore@fioreservice group.com. **Field Manager:** Rich Gawlak

QUAKERTOWN BLAZERS

Telephone: (215) 679-5072. **E-Mail Address:** gbonekemper@yahoo.com.
Website: www.quakertownblazers.com. **General Manager:** George Bonekemper. **Field Manager:** Chris Ray.

TRENTON GENERALS

E-Mail Address: mrolsh@msn.com. **General Manager:** Michael Olshin. **Field Manager:** Kevin Snyder.

CALIFORNIA COLLEGIATE LEAGUE

Mailing Address: 806 W Pedregosa St, Santa Barbara, CA 93101. **Telephone:** (805) 680-1047. **Fax:** (805) 684-8596. **E-Mail Address:** burns@calsummerball.com. **Website:** www.calsummerball.com.
Founded: 1993.
Commissioner: Pat Burns.

ACADEMY BARONS

Address: 901 E. Artesia Blvd, Compton, CA 90221.
Telephone: (424) 209-5727. **Website:** calsummerball.com/academy-barons-roster. **E-Mail Address:** darrell.miller@mlb.com. **Contact:** Natalia Reynoso, director.
Field manager: Kenny Landreaux.

ARROYO SECO SAINTS

Telephone: (626) 695-6903. **Website:** http://calsummerball.com/arroyo-seco-saints-roster. **E-mail Address:** amilam@arroyosecobaseball.com. **General Manager:** Aaron Milam. **Field Manager:** Sean Buller.

CONEJO OAKS

Address: 1710 N. Moorpark Rd., #106, Thousand Oaks, CA 91360. **Telephone:** 805-304-0126.
Website: calsummerball.com/conejo-oaks-roster/.
E-Mail Address: oaksbaseball@yahoo.com. **Field Manager:** David Soliz. **General Manager:** Randy Riley.

HEALDSBURG PRUNE PACKERS

Telephone: (707) 280-6693. **E-mail Address:** jgg21@aol.com. **Field Manager:** Joey Gomes.

ORANGE COUNTY RIPTIDE

Address: 14 Calendula Rancho, Santa Margarita, CA 92688. **Telephone:** (949) 228-7676. **Website:** ocriptide.com. **E-Mail Address:** ocriptidebaseball@gmail.com. **Field Manager:** Tyger Pederson. **General Manager:** Moe Geohagen. **Head Coach:** Clemente Bonilla.

SAN LUIS OBISPO BLUES

Address: 3442 Empresa Drive, Ste. #B, San Luis Obispo, CA 93401. **Telephone:** (805) 704-4388. **Website:** calsummerball.com/san-luis-obispo-blues/. **E-Mail Address:** adam@bluesbaseball.com. **General Manager:** Adam Stowe. **Field Manager:** Dan Marple.

SANTA BARBARA FORESTERS

Address: 4299 Carpinteria Ave., Suite 201, Carpinteria, CA 93013. **Telephone:** (805) 684-0657. **Website:** cal summerball.com/santa-barbara-foresters-roster/. **E-Mail Address:** pintard@earthlink.net. **Field Manager:** Bill Pintard.

SOUTHERN CALIFORNIA CATCH

Telephone (GM): (562) 686-8262. **Website:** calsummerball.com/socal-catch-roster/. **E-mail Address (GM):** borr@fca.org. **General Manager:** Ben Orr. **Field Manager:** Dan Peters.

VENTURA COUNTY PIRATES

Website: calsummerball.com/ventura-county-pirates-affiliated-team-2018-roster/. **E-mail Address (GM):** gvranau.pirates@gmail.com. **General Manager:** George Vranau.

CAL RIPKEN COLLEGIATE LEAGUE

Address: 24219 Hawkins Landing Drive, Gaithersburg, MD 20882. **Telephone:** (301) 693-2577. **E-Mail:** jason_d_woodward@mcpsmd.org. **Website:** www.calripkenleague.org.

Year Founded: 2005.

Commissioner: Jason Woodward. **League President:** Brad Rifkin. **Deputy Commissioner:** Jerry Wargo.

Regular Season: 40 games. **Playoff Format:** Top two teams from each division plus two remaining teams with best records qualify. Teams play best of three series, winners advance to best of three series for league championship. **Roster Limit:** 35 (college-eligible players 22 and under).

ALEXANDRIA ACES

Address: 221 9th Street, S.E. Washington, DC 20003. **Telephone:** (202) 255-1683. **E-Mail:** cberset21@gmail.com. **Website:** www.alexandriaaces.org. **Chairman/CEO:** Donald Dinan. **General Manager:** TBD. **Head Coach:** Chris Berset. **Ballpark:** Frank Mann Field at Four Mile Run Park.

BALTIMORE DODGERS

Address: 17 Sunrise Court Randallstown, MD 21133. **Telephone:** (443) 834-3500. **Email:** juan.waters@verizon.net. **Website:** www.baltimoredodgers.org. **President:** Juan Waters. **Head Coach:** Derek Brown. **Ballpark:** Joe Cannon Stadium at Harmans Park.

BETHESDA BIG TRAIN

Address: 6400 Goldsboro Road Suite 220 Bethesda, MD 20817. **Telephone:** 301-229-1854. **Fax:** 301-229-8362. **E-Mail:** faninfo@bigtrain.org. **Website:** www.bigtrain.org. **General Manager:** David Schneider. **Head Coach:** Sal Colangelo. **Ballpark:** Shirley Povich Field.

D.C. GRAYS

Address: 1800 M Street NW, 500 South Tower, Washington, DC 20036. **Telephone:** (202) 492-6226. **Website:** www.dcgrays.com. **E-Mail Address:** barbera@acg-consultants.com. **President:** Mike Barbera. **General Manager:** Antonio Scott. **Head Coach:** Reggie Terry. **Ballpark:** Washington Nationals Youth Academy.

GAITHERSBURG GIANTS

Address: 18221A Flower Hill Way, Gaithersburg, MD 20879. **Telephone:** (240) 888-6810. **E-Mail:** alriley13@gmail.com. **Website:** www.gaithersburggiants.org. **General Manager:** Alfie Riley. **Head Coach:** Jeff Rabberman. **Ballpark:** Criswell Automotive Field.

FCA BRAVES

Address: 8925 Leesburg Pike, Vienna, VA 22182. **Telephone:** (702) 909-2750. **Fax:** (703) 783-1319. **E-Mail:** fcabraves@gmail.com. **Website:** www.fcabraves.com. **President/General Manager:** Todd Burger. **Head Coach:** Chris Warren. **Ballpark:** Annandale High School.

SILVER SPRING-TAKOMA T-BOLTS

Address: 906 Glaizewood Court, Takoma Park, MD 20912. **Telephone:** 301-983-1358. **E-Mail:** tboltsbaseball@gmail.com. **Website:** www.tbolts.org. **General Manager:** Brian Brewer. **Head Coach:** Doug Remer. **Ballpark:** Blair Stadium at Montgomery Blair High School.

CAPE COD BASEBALL LEAGUE

Mailing Address: PO Box 266, Harwich Port, MA 02646. **Telephone:** (508) 432-6909.

E-Mail: info@capecodbaseball.org.

Website: www.capecodbaseball.org.

Year Founded: 1885.

Commissioner: Eric Zmuda. **President:** Chuck Sturtevant. **Treasurer:** Steve Wilson. **Secretary:** Paula Tufts. **Senior VP:** Bill Bussiere. **VP:** Tom Gay, Mary Henderson. **Senior Deputy Commissioner/Umpire-In-Chief:** Sol Yas. **Deputy Commissioner, West:** Mike Carrier. **Deputy Commissioner, East:** Peter Hall. **Director Public Relations:** Kyla Costa. **DIrector Broadcasting:** John Garner. **Director, Communications:** Jim McGonigle. **Division Structure: East**—Brewster, Chatham, Harwich, Orleans, Yarmouth-Dennis. **West**—Bourne, Cotuit, Falmouth, Hyannis, Wareham.

Regular Season: 44 games. **All-Star Game:** July 21. **Playoff Format:** Top four teams in each division qualify for three rounds of best-of-three series.

Roster Limit: 30 (college-eligible players only).

BOURNE BRAVES

Mailing Address: PO Box 895, Monument Beach, MA 02553. **Telephone:** (508) 868-8378. **E-Mail Address:** nnorkevicius@yahoo.com. **Website:** www.bournebraves.org.

President: Nicole Norkevicius. **General Manager:** Darin Weeks. **Head Coach:** Harvey Shapiro.

BREWSTER WHITECAPS

Mailing Address: PO Box 2349, Brewster, MA 02631. **Telephone:** (508) 896-8500, ext. 147. **Fax:** (508) 896-9845.
E-Mail Address: ckenney@brewsterwhitecaps.com.
Website: www.brewsterwhitecaps.com.
President: Chris Kenney. **General Manager:** Ned Monthie.

CHATHAM ANGLERS

Mailing Address: PO Box 428, Chatham, MA 02633.
Website: www.chathamas.com. **President:** Steve West.
General Manager: Mike Geylin. **Email:** mgeylin@kgpr.com. **Head Coach:** Tom Holliday.

COTUIT KETTLEERS

Mailing Address: PO Box 411, Cotuit, MA 02635.
Telephone: (508) 428-3358. **E-Mail Address:** bmurpf cape@aol.com. **Website:** www.kettleers.org. **President:** Andy Bonacker. **General Manager:** Bruce Murphy. **Head Coach:** Mike Roberts.

FALMOUTH COMMODORES

Mailing Address: PO Box 808 Falmouth, MA 02541.
Telephone: (508) 566-4988. **Website:** www.falmouth commodores.org. **President:** Mark Kasprzyk. **General Manager:** Eric Zmuda. **Head Coach:** Jeff Trundy.

HARWICH MARINERS

Mailing Address: PO Box 201, Harwich Port, MA 02646. **Telephone:** (508) 432-2000. **Fax:** (508) 432-5357.
E-Mail Address: mehendy@comcast.net. **Website:** www.harwichmariners.org.
President: Mary Henderson. **General Manager:** Ben Layton. **Head Coach:** Steve Englert.

HYANNIS HARBOR HAWKS

Mailing Address: PO Box 832, West Hyannis Port, MA 02672. **Telephone:** (508) 737-5890. **Fax:** (877) 822-2703.
E-Mail Address: brpfeifer@aol.com. **Website:** www.harborhawks.org.
President: Brad Pfeifer. **General Manager:** Tino DiGiovanni. **Head Coach:** Chad Gassman.

ORLEANS FIREBIRDS

Mailing Address: PO Box 504, Orleans, MA 02653.
Telephone: (508) 255-0793. **Fax:** (508) 255-2237. **E-Mail Address:** bodonnell15@gmail.com. **Website:** www.orleansfirebirds.com.
President: Bob O'Donnell. **General Manager:** Sue Horton. **Head Coach:** Kelly Nicholson.

WAREHAM GATEMEN

Mailing Address: PO Box 287, Wareham, MA 02571.
Telephone: (508) 748-0287. **Fax:** (508) 880-2602. **E-Mail Address:** alang.gatemen@gmail.com.
Website: www.gatemen.org. **President:** Tom Gay.
General Manager: Andrew Lang. **Head Coach:** Jerry Weinstein.

YARMOUTH-DENNIS RED SOX

Mailing Address: PO Box 78 Yarmouth Port, MA 02675. **Telephone:** (508) 889-8721. **E-Mail Address:** sfaucher64@gmail.com. **Website:** www.ydredsox.org.
President: Ed Pereira. **General Manager:** Steve Faucher.
Head Coach: Scott Pickler.

CENTRAL VALLEY COLLEGIATE LEAGUE

Mailing Address: P.O. Box 561, Fowler, CA 93625.
E-mail: j_scot25@hotmail.com, jcederquist@aol.com.
Website: www.cvclbaseball.webs.com. **Twitter:** @CVCL1.
Year Founded: 2013. **President:**Jon Scott. **Regular Season:** 30 games. **2019 Opening Date:** May 31.
Closing Date: July 26. **All-Star Game:** July 15, Fresno, Calif. **Roster Limit:** 30

BAKERSFIELD BRAVES

Mailing Address: PO Box 20760, Bakersfield, CA, 93390. **Website:** eteamz.com/bakersfieldbraves. **Field Manager:** Bobby Maitia.

CALIFORNIA EXPOS

Mailing Address: P.O. Box 561, Fowler, CA 93625.
E-mail: exposcv@aol.com. **Website:** www.calibaseball.com. **Twitter:** @cvexpos. **Field Manager:** Thomas Raymundo.

CALIFORNIA PILOTS

Mailing Address: PO Box 561 Fowler, CA 93625.
E-mail: valleystormbaseball@aol.com. **Website:** www.calibaseball.com. **Twitter:** @calistorm1. **Field Manager:** Kenny Corona.

CALIFORNIA STORM

Mailing Address: PO Box 561 Fowler, CA 93625.
E-mail: valleystormbaseball@aol.com. **Website:** www.calibaseball.com. **Twitter:** @calistorm1. **Field Manager:** Kolton Cabral.

SANTA MARIA PACKERS

Mailing Address: P.O. Box 144, Kingsburg, CA 93631.
E-mail: j_scot25@hotmail.com. **Website:** www.cvipers.webs.com. **Twitter:** @SouthcountryV. **Field Manager:** Jon Scott.

SOUTH COUNTY VIPERS

Mailing Address: P.O. Box 144, Kingsburg, CA 93631.
E-mail: j_scot25@hotmail.com. **Website:** www.cvipers.webs.com. **Twitter:** @SouthcountryV. **Field Manager:** Jon Scott.

COASTAL PLAIN LEAGUE

Mailing Address: 112 N. Main St., Holly Springs, NC 27540. **Telephone:** (919) 852-1960. **Fax:** (919) 516-0852.
Email Address: justins@coastalplain.com. **Website:** www.coastalplain.com. **Year Founded:** 1997. **Chairman/CEO:** Jerry Petitt. **COO/Commissioner:** Justin Sel lers.
Director of Media Relations: Shelby Hilliard. **Director of Operations & Sponsorships:** Catherine Roth.
Division Structure: East— Fayetteville, Holly Springs, Morehead City, Wilmington. **West—**Asheboro, Gastonia, High Point-Thomasville, Forest City. **North—**Edenton, Martinsville, Peninsula, Wilson. **South—**Florence,

Lexington County, Macon, Savannah
Regular Season: 52 games (split schedule). **Playoff Format:** Three rounds. **Rd 1/2:** One game, **Rd 3:** Best of three.
Roster Limit: 32 (college-eligible players and graduated seniors only).

ASHEBORO COPPERHEADS

Mailing Address: PO Box 4036, Asheboro, NC 27204. **Telephone:** (336) 460-7018. **Fax:** (336) 629-2651. **E-Mail Address:** info@teamcopperhead.com. **Website:** www. teamcopperhead.com. **Owners:** Ronnie Pugh, Steve Pugh, Doug Pugh, Mike Pugh. **General Manager:** Max Kaufmann. **Head Coach:** Keith Ritsche

EDENTON STEAMERS

Mailing Address: PO Box 86, Edenton, NC 27932. **Telephone:** (252) 482-4080. **Fax:** (252) 482-1717. **E-Mail Address:** edentonsteamers@hotmail.com. **Website:** www.edentonsteamers.com. **Owner:** Frank Burke. **General Manager:** Tyler Russell. **Head Coach:** Russ Burroughs.

FAYETTEVILLE SWAMPDOGS

Mailing Address: 2823 Legion Road, Fayetteville, NC 28306.**Telephone:** (910) 426-5900. **E-Mail Address:** info@goswampdogs.com. **Website:** www.goswampdogs. com. **Owner:** Lew Handelsman. **General Manager:** Jeremy Aagard. **Head Coach:** Matt Hollod

FLORENCE REDWOLVES

Mailing Address: PO Box 809, Florence, SC 29503. **Telephone:** (843) 629-0700. **Fax:** (843) 629-0703. **E-Mail Address:** barbara@florenceredwolves.com. **Website:** www.florenceredwolves.com. **Owners:** Kevin Barth, Donna Barth. **General Manager:** Barbara Osborne. **Head Coach:** Ryan Vruggink.

FOREST CITY OWLS

Mailing Address: 214 McNair Field Drive, Forest City, NC 28043. **Telephone:** (828) 245-0000. **Fax:** (828) 245-6666. **E-Mail Address:** info@forestcitybaseball.com. **Website:** www.forestcitybaseball.com. **Owners:** Phil & Becky Dangel. **General Manager:** Kiva Fuller. **Head Coach:** Matt Reed.

GASTONIA GRIZZLIES

Mailing Address: 1001 Dr. Martin Luther King Jr. Way, Gastonia, NC 28054. **Telephone:** (704) 866-8622. **Fax:** (704) 864-6122. **E-Mail Address:** jesse@gastoniagrizzlies .com. **Website:** www.gastoniagrizzlies.com. **Owners:** Matt Perry. **General Manager:** David McDonald. **Head Coach:** Charles Bradley.

HIGH POINT-THOMASVILLE HI-TOMS

Mailing Address: 7003 Ballpark Road, Thomasville, NC 27360. **Telephone:** (336) 472-8667. **Fax:** (336) 472-7198. **E-Mail Address:** info@hitoms.com. **Website:** www. hitoms.com. **Owner:** Richard Holland. **President:** Greg Suire. **Head Coach:** Brian Rountree.

HOLLY SPRINGS SALAMANDERS

Mailing Address: 101 Tennis Court, Holly Springs, NC 27540. **Telephone:** 919-249-7322. **Email Address:** info@ salamandersbaseball.com. **Website:** www.salamanders baseball.com. **Owner:** Jerry Petitt. **General Manager:** Peter Wallace. **Head Coach:** Dustin Coffman.

LEXINGTON COUNTY BLOWFISH

Mailing Address: 101 E. Main St. Lexington, SC 29072. **Telephone:** (803) 254-3474. **E-Mail Address:** info@blow fishbaseball.com. **Website:** www.goblowfishbaseball. com. **Owner:** Bill & Vicki Shanahan. **General Manager:** Theo Bacot. **Head Coach:** Marshall McDonald.

MACON BACON

Mailing Address: 225 Willie Smokey Glover Drive, Macon, GA. **Telephone:** 478-803-1795. **E-Mail Address:** info@maconbaconbaseball.com **Website:** www.macon baconbaseball.com. **Owner:** SRO Partners (Jon Spoelstra & Steve DeLay). **President:** Brandon Raphael. **Head Coach:** Danny Higginbotham.

MOREHEAD CITY MARLINS

Mailing Address: PO Box 460, New Bern, NC 28563. **Telephone:** (252) 269-9767. **Fax:** (252) 637-2721. **E-Mail Address:** mcmarlins@gmail.com. **Website:** www.mhc marlins.com. **General Manager:** Buddy Bengel. **Head Coach:** Jesse Lancaster.

PENINSULA PILOTS

Mailing Address: 1889 W. Pembroke Ave., Hampton, VA 23661. **Telephone:** (757) 245-2222. **Fax:** (757) 245-8030. **E-Mail Address:** info@peninsulapilots.com. **Website:** www.peninsulapilots.com. **Owner:** Henry Morgan. **General Manager:** Jason Cantone. **Head Coach/Vice President:** Hank Morgan.

SAVANNAH BANANAS

Mailing Address: 1401 E. Victory Drive, Savannah, GA 31404. **Telephone:** 912-712-2482. **E-Mail Address:** jared@thesavannahbananas.com. **Website:** www.the savannahbananas.com. **Owner:** Fans First Entertainment (Jesse & Emily Cole). **President:** Jared Orton. **Head Coach:** Tyler Gillum

WILMINGTON SHARKS

Mailing Address: 2149 Carolina Beach Road, Wilmington, NC 28401. **Telephone:** (910) 343-5621. **Fax:** (910) 343-8932. **E-Mail Address:** media@wilmington sharks.com. **Website:** www.wilmingtonsharks.com. **Owners:** Smith Family Baseball Wilmington, LLC. **General Manager:** Carson Bowen. **Head Coach:** Tyler Jackson

WILSON TOBS

Mailing Address: 300 Stadium St. SW., Wilson, NC 27893. **Telephone:** (252) 291-8627. **Fax:** (252) 291-1224. **E-Mail Address:** mike@wilsontobs.com. **Website:** www. wilsontobs.com. **Owner:** Richard Holland. **President:** Greg Suire. **General Manager:** Mike Bell. **Head Coach:** Bryan Hill.

FLORIDA COLLEGIATE SUMMER LEAGUE

Mailing Address: 250 National Place, Unit #152, Longwood, FL 32750. **Telephone:** (321) 206-9174. **Fax:** (407) 574-7926. **E-Mail Address:** info@floridaleague.com. **Website:** www.floridaleague.com.

Year Founded: 2004.

President: Stefano Foggi. **League Operations Director:** Phil Chinnery.

Regular Season: 45 games. **2019 Opening Date:** May 30. **All-Star Game:** July 6. **Playoffs Begin:** July 30. **Playoff Format:** Five teams qualify; No. 4 and No. 5 seeds meet in one-game playoff. Remaining four teams play best-of-three series. Winners play best-of-three series for league championship.

Roster Limit: 28 (college-eligible players only). High school grads allowed with MLB approval. Part of the National Alliance of College Summer Baseball.

DELAND SUNS

Operated by the league office. **E-Mail Address:** suns@floridaleague.com. **Head Coach:** Rick Hall.

LEESBURG LIGHTNING

E-Mail Address: lightning@floridaleague.com. **Head Coach:** Rich Billings.

SANFORD RIVER RATS

Operated by the league office. **E-Mail Address:** rats@floridaleague.com. **Head Coach:** Josh Montero.

SEMINOLE COUNTY SCORPIONS

Operated by the league office. **E-Mail Address:** scorpions@floridaleague.com. **Head Coach:** Bob Rikeman.

WINTER GARDEN SQUEEZE

Operated by the league office. **Email Address:** squeeze@floridaleague.com. **Head Coach:** Terry Abbott. **General Manager:** Adam Bates.

WINTER PARK DIAMOND DAWGS

E-Mail Address: dawgs@floridaleague.com. **Head Coach:** Chuck Schall.

FUTURES COLLEGIATE LEAGUE OF NEW ENGLAND

Mailing Address: 46 Chestnut Hill Rd, Chelmsford, MA 01824. **Telephone:** (617) 593-2112. **E-Mail Address:** futuresleague@yahoo.com

Website: www.thefuturesleague.com.

Year Founded: 2010.

Commissioner: Chris Hall.

Teams (Contact): Bristol Blues (www.bristolbluesbaseball.com) (**Brian Rooney:** gm@bristolblues.com); Brockton Rox (**Todd Marlin:** tmarlin@brocktonrox.com); Martha's Vineyard Sharks (**Russ Curran:** russ.curran@mvsharks.com); Nashua Silver Knights (**Rick Muntean:** rick@nashuasilverknights.com); North Shore Navigators (**Bill Terlecky:** navigatorsgm@gmail.com); Pittsfield Suns (**Kristen Huss:** kristen@pittsfieldsuns.com); Worcester Bravehearts (**Dave Peterson:** dave@worcesterbravhearts.com)

Regular Season: 56 games; 28 home, 28 away.

Playoff Format: Six teams qualify. First round consists of two single elimination play-in games (3 seed vs. 6 seed and 4 seed vs 5 seed), two remaining teams play a best of three semifinal round followed by a best-of- three championship round to determine league champion. Extra-inning Games are determined by Home Run Derby!!

Roster Limit: 35. 10 must be from New England or play collegiately at a New England college.

GREAT LAKES SUMMER COLLEGIATE LEAGUE

Mailing Address: PO Box 666, Troy, OH 45373. **Telephone:** (937) 308-1536. **E-Mail:** glsclcommish@gmail.com.

Website: www.greatlakesleague.org.

Year Founded: 1986.

President: Jim DeSana. **Commissioner:** Deron Brown.

Regular Season: 42 games. **Playoff Format:** Top six teams meet in playoffs. **Roster Limit:** 30 (college-eligible players only).

Teams: (15 Teams)—Cincinnati Steam (Cincinnati, OH); Galion Graders (Galion, OH); Grand Lake Mariners (Celina, OH); Grand River Loggers (Grand Haven, MI); Hamilton Joes (Hamilton, OH); Lake Erie Monarchs (Flat Rock, MI); Licking County Settlers (Newark, OH); Lima Locos (Lima, OH); Lorain County Ironmen (Lorain, OH); Muskegon Clippers (Muskegon, MI); Richmond Jazz (Richmond, IN); Saint Clair Green Giants (Tecumseh, ON); Southern Ohio Copperheads (Athens, OH); Xenia Scouts (Xenia, OH).

METROPOLITAN COLLEGIATE BASEBALL LEAGUE

Mailing Address: 78 Knollwood Drive, Paramus NJ 07652

President: Brian Casey 374-545-1991

Website: www.metropolitanbaseball.com

Email: mcbl@metropolitanbaseball.com

MIDWEST COLLEGIATE LEAGUE

Mailing Address: PO Box 172, Flossmoor, IL 60422. **E-Mail Address:** commissioner@midwestcollegiateleague.com. **Website:** www.midwestcollegiateleague.com.

Year Founded: 2010.

President/Commissioner: Don Popravak.

Regular Season: 52 games. **Playoff Format:** Top four teams meet in best of three series. Winners meet in best of three championship series.

Roster Limit: 30

Teams: Bloomington Bobcats, Crestwood Panthers, DuPage County Hounds, Joliet Admirals, NWI Oilmen, Southland Vikings.

M.I.N.K. LEAGUE

(Missouri, Iowa, Nebraska, Kansas)

Mailing Address: PO Box 367, Nevada, MO 64772. **Telephone:** (417) 667-6159. Fax: (417) 667- 4210.

Email Address: jpost@morrisonpost.com. **Website:** www.minkleaguebaseball.com

Year Founded: 1995.

Commissioner: Bob Steinkamp. **President:** Jeff Post. **Vice President:** Jud Kindle. **Secretary:** Edwina Rains.

Regular season: 44 games.

Playoff Format: The top three teams from each division will qualify for the playoffs. The second and third place finishers in each division will play a "Wild Card" one-game playoff. The winner of those games will play the regular season division winner from each division in a one game playoff. The winner of each division will then play a two out of three series to determine the MINK

League Champion. Championship starts on July 25.
Opening day: June 1st.
All-Star Game: June 26th.

CHILLICOTHE MUDCATS

Mailing Address: 426 E Jackson, Chillicothe, MO 64601. **Telephone:** (660) 247-1504. **Fax:** (660) 646-6933. **E-Mail Address:** doughty@greenhills.net. **Website:** www.chillicothemudcats.com. **General Manager:** Doug Doughty.

CLARINDA A'S

Mailing Address: 225 East Lincoln, Clarinda, IA 51632. **Telephone:** (712) 542-4272. **E-Mail Address:** m.everly@mchsi.com. **Website:** www.clarindaiowa-as-baseball.org. **General Managers:** Ryan Eberly, Rodney J. Eberly. **Head Coach:** Ryan Eberly.

JOPLIN OUTLAWS

Mailing Address: 5860 North Pearl, Joplin, MO 64801. **Telephone:** (417) 825-4218. **E-Mail Address:** merains@mchsi.com. **Website:** www.joplinoutlaws.com. **President/General Manager:** Mark Rains.

NEVADA GRIFFONS

Mailing Address: PO Box 601, Nevada, MO 64772. **Telephone:** (417) 667-6159. **E-Mail Address:** Ryan.Mansfield@mcckc.edu. **Website:** www.nevadagriffons.org. **President:** Dan Keller. **General Manager:** Ryan Mansfield. **Head Coach:** Ryan Mansfield.

OZARK GENERALS

Mailing Address: 1336 W Farm Road 182, Springfield, MO 65810. **Telephone:** (417) 832-8830. **Fax:** (417) 877-4625. **E-Mail Address:** rda160@yahoo.com. **Website:** www.generalsbaseballclub.com. **General Manager/Head Coach:** Rusty Aton.

ST. JOSEPH MUSTANGS

Mailing Address: 2600 SW Parkway, St. Joseph, MO 64503. **Telephone:** (816) 279-7856. **Fax:** (816) 749-4082. **E-Mail Address:** kyturner@stjoemustangs.com. **Website:** www.stjoemustangs.com. **President:** Dan Gerson. **General Manager:** Ky Turner. **Manager/Director**, **Player Personnel:** Johnny Coy.

SEDALIA BOMBERS

Mailing Address: 2205 S Grand, Sedalia, MO 65301. **Telephone:** (660) 287-4722. **E-Mail Address:** eric@sedaliabombers.com. **Website:** www.sedaliabombers.com. **President/General Manager/Head Coach:** Jud Kindle. **Vice President:** Ross Dey.

JEFFERSON CITY RENEGADES

Telephone: 630-781-7247 **E-Mail Address:** jcrenegades@gmail.com. **Website:** www.jcrenegades.com. **President/General Manager:** Steve Dullard. **Head Coach:** Mike DeMilia.

NEW ENGLAND COLLEGIATE LEAGUE

Mailing Address: 122 Mass Moca Way, North Adams, MA 01247. **Telephone:** (413) 652-1031. **Fax:** (413) 473-0012. **E-Mail Address:** smcgrath@necbl.com. **Website:** www.necbl.com. **Year founded:** 1993. **President:** John DeRosa. **Commissioner:** Sean McGrath. **Deputy**

Commissioner: Gregg Hunt. **Secretary:** Max Pinto. **Treasurer:** Tim Porter. **Regular Season:** 44 games. **2019 Opening Date:** June 5. **Closing Date:** Aug. 1. **All-Star Game:** July 28. **Roster Limit:** 33 (college players only).

DANBURY WESTERNERS

Mailing Address: PO Box 3828, Danbury, CT 06813. **Telephone:** (203) 502-9167. **E-Mail Address:** jspitser@msn.com. **Website:** www.danburywesterners.com. **President:** Jon Pitser. **General Manager:** Chris Nathanson. **Field Manager:** Josh Parrow.

VALLEY BLUE SOX

Mailing Address: 100 Congress St, Springfield, MA 01104. **Telephone:** 860-305-1684. **E-Mail Address:** hunter@valleybluesox.com. **Website:** www.valleybluesox.com. **President:** Clark Eckhoff. **General Manager:** Hunter Golden. **Field Manager:** John Raiola.

KEENE SWAMP BATS

Mailing Address: 303 Park Ave., Keene, NH 03431. **Telephone:** 603-731-5240. **E-Mail Address:** swampbatsribby@gmail.com. **Website:** www.swampbats.com. **President:** Kevin Watterson. **Field Manager:** Gary Calhoun.

WINNIPESAUKEE MUSKRATS

Mailing Address: 97 Ashley Drive, Laconia, NH 03246. **Telephone:** 603-303-7806. **E-Mail Address:** kristian@muskratsbaseball.com. **Website:** www.winnipesaukeemuskrats.com. **President:** Mike Smith. **General Manager:** Kristian Svindland. **Field Manager:** Mike Miller.

MYSTIC SCHOONERS

Mailing Address: PO Box 432, Mystic, CT 06355. **Telephone:** (860) 608-3287. **E-Mail Address:** dlong@mysticbaseball.org. **Website:** www.mysticbaseball.org. **Executive Director:** Don Benoit. **General Manager:** Dennis Long. **Field Manager:** Rob Bono.

NEW BEDFORD BAY SOX

Mailing Address: 309 Princeton St., New Bedford, MA 02740. **Telephone:** 508-985-3052. **E-Mail Address:** tsilveira17@gmail.com. **Website:** www.nbbaysox.com. **President:** Stephen King. **General Manager:** Tammy Silveira. **Field Manager:** Chris Cabe.

NEWPORT GULLS

Mailing Address: PO Box 777, Newport, RI 02840. **Telephone:** (401) 845-6832. **E-Mail Address:** gm@newportgulls.com. **Website:** www.newportgulls.com. **President/General Manager:** Chuck Paiva. **Executive VP of Baseball Operations:** Chris Patsos. **Director of Baseball Operations:** Mike Falcone. **Field Manager:** Kevin Winterrowd.

NORTH ADAMS STEEPLECATS

Mailing Address: PO Box 540, North Adams, MA 01247. **Telephone:** 413-896-3153. **E-Mail Address:** matt.tora@steeplecats.org. **Website:** www.steeplecats.org. **President:** TBA. **General Manager:** Matt Tora. **Field Manager:** Mike Dailey.

OCEAN STATE WAVES

Mailing Address: 1174 Kingstown Rd, Wakefield, RI 02879. **Telephone:** (401) 360-2977. **E-Mail Address:** matt@oceanstatewaves.com. **Website:** www. oceanstatewaves.com. **President/General Manager:** Matt Finlayson. **Field Manager:** Jim Sauro.

PLYMOUTH PILGRIMS

Mailing Address: 111 Camelot Drive, Plymouth, MA 02360. **Telephone:** 617-694-2658.. **E-Mail Address:** KPlant@pilgrimsbaseball.com. **Website:** www.pilgrims baseball.com. **President:** Peter Plant. **General Manager:** Kevin Plant. **Field Manager:** Greg Zackrison.

SANFORD MARINERS

Field Address: Goodall Park, 38m Roberts Street, Sanford, ME 04073. **Telephone:** (207) 650-1902. **E-Mail:** aizaryk@bridgtonacademy.org. **General Manager:** Aaron Izaryk. **Field Manager:** Chris Morris.

VERMONT MOUNTAINEERS

Mailing Address: PO Box 57, East Montpelier, VT 05651. **Telephone:** (802) 272-8728. **E-Mail Address:** gmvtm@comcast.net. **Website:** www.thevermont mountaineers.com. **General Manager:** Brian Gallagher. **Field Manager:** Charlie Barbieri.

UPPER VALLEY NIGHTHAWKS

Mailing Address: 134 Stevens Road Lebanon, NH 03766. **Telephone:** 864-380-2873 **E-Mail Address:** noah@uppervalleynighthawks.com. **Website:** upper valleybaseball.pointstreaksites.com. **President:** Jonathan Crane. **General Manager:** TBA. **Field Manager:** Jason Szafarski.

NEW YORK COLLEGIATE BASEBALL LEAGUE

Mailing Address: 398 East Dyke St. Wellsville, NY 14895. **Telephone:** (585) 455-2345. **Website:** www.nycbl. com. **Year founded:** 1978. **President:** Bill McConnell. **Commissioner:** Joe Brown. **Vice President:** Brian McConnell Jr. **Senior Marketing Director:** Dave Meluni. **Treasurer:** Dennis Duffy. **Secretary:** Steven Ackley. **Franchises: Eastern Division:** Cortland Crush, Onondaga Flames, Rome Generals, Sherrill Silversmiths, Syracuse Spartans, Saratoga Revolution. **Western Division:** Genesee Rapids, Hornell Dodgers, Niagara Power, Olean Oilers, Rochester Ridgemen, Wellsville Nitros. **Playoff Format:** six teams qualify and play a 1 game playoff and then two rounds of best of three series. **Roster Limit:** Unlimited (college-eligible players only).

CORTLAND CRUSH

Mailing Address: 2745 Summer Ridge Rd, LaFayette, NY 13084. **Telephone:** 315-391-8167. **Email Address:** wmmac4@aol.com. **Website:** www.cortlandcrush. com. **President:** Gary VanGorder. **Field Manager:** Bill McConnell.

GENESEE RAPIDS

Mailing Address: 9726 Rt. 19 Houghton, NY 14474. **Telephone:** 716-969-0688. **Email Address:** rkerr@ frontiernet.net. **President:** Ralph Kerr. **Field Manager:** Joe Mesa.

HORNELL DODGERS

Mailing Address: PO Box 235, Hornell, NY 14843. **Telephone:** (607) 661-4173. **Fax:** (607) 661-4173. **E-Mail Address:** gm@hornelldodgers.com. **Website:** hornelldodgers.com. **General Manager:** Paul Welker. **Field Manager:** Justin Oney.

MANSFIELD DESTROYERS

Mailing Address: Mansfield Destroyers, 508 Gaines Street, Elmira, NY 14901. **Telephone:** (570) 335-9575. **E-Mail Address:** info@mansfielddestroyers.com. **President:** Don Lewis. **General Manager:** TBA. **Field Manager:** Brian Hill.

NIAGARA POWER

Mailing Address: P.O. Box 2012, Niagara University, NY 14109. **Telephone:** (716) 286-8653. **E-Mail Address:** ptutka@niagara.edu. **Website:** www.niagarapowerbase ball.com. **President:** Dr. Patrick Tutka. **Field Manager:** Unavailable.

OLEAN OILERS

Mailing Address: 126 N 10th, Olean, NY 14760. **Telephone:** 716-378-0641. **E-Mail Address:** Brian@ oconnelllaw.net. **President:** Brian O'Connell. **Field Manager:** Unavailable.

ROCHESTER RIDGEMEN

Mailing Address: 651 Taylor Dr, Xenia, OH 45385. **Telephone:** (937) 352-1225. **E-Mail Addresses:** baseball @athletesinaction.org. **Website:** www.rochesterridgemen .org. **President:** Jason Jipson. **Field Manager:** John Byington.

ROME GENERALS

Email Address: Romegenerals@gmail.com. **Telephone:** (315) 542-0675. **Website:** www.rome generals.com. **Baseball Director:** Ray DiBrango. **Field Manager:** Unavailable.

SHERRILL SILVERSMITHS

Mailing Address: PO Box 111, Sherrill, NY 13440. **Telephone:** (315) 264-4334. **E-Mail Address:** Djduffy316@gmail.com. **Website:** www.leaguelineup. com/silversmiths. **President:** Dennis Duffy & Mike Sherlock. **Field Manager:** Tim Bailey.

SYRACUSE SALT CATS

Mailing Address: 208 Lakeland Ave, Syracuse, NY 13209. **Telephone:** (315) 727-9220. **Fax:** (315) 488-1750. **E-Mail Address:** mmarti6044@yahoo.com. **Website:** www.leaguelineup.com/saltcats. **President:** Mike Martinez. **Field Manager:** Mike Martinez.

SYRACUSE SPARTANS

Mailing Address: 4155 Tommy's Trail. Liverpool, NY 13090. **Telephone:** (315) 720-4251. **Website:** www. syracusespartans.com. **General Manager:** JJ Potrikus. **Field Manager:** Brian Burns.

WELLSVILLE NITROS

Mailing Address: 2848 O'Donnell Rd, Wellsville, NY 14895. **Telephone:** 585-596-9523. **Fax:** 585-593-5260.

E-Mail Address: nitros04@gmail.com. **Website:** www.nitrosbaseball.com. **President:** Steven J. Ackley. **Field Manager:** Tucker Hughes.

NORTHWOODS LEAGUE

Office Address: 2900 4th St SW, Rochester, MN 55902. **Telephone:** (507) 536-4579. **Fax:** (507) 536-4597. **E-Mail Address:** info@northwoodsleague.com.

Website: www.northwoodsleague.com.

Year Founded: 1994.

Chairman: Dick Radatz, Jr. **President:** Gary Hoover. **Vice President, Business Development:** Matt Bomberg. **Vice President, Operations:** Glen Showalter. **Vice President, Licensing/Technology:** Tina Coil. **Vice President, Technology Development:** Greg Goodwin. **Division Structure: East**—Kokomo Jackrabbits, Traverse City, Rockford Rivets, Kalamazoo Growlers, Battle Creek Bombers. **West**—Fond du Lac Dock Spiders, Green Bay Booyah, Madison Mallards, Wisconsin Rapids Rafters, Lakeshore Chinooks. **Great Plains Division: East** – Duluth Huskies, Eau Claire Express, Waterloo Bucks, Thunder Bay Border Cats, La Crosse Loggers. **West**—Bismarck Larks, Mankato MoonDogs, Willmar Stingers, St. Cloud Rox, Rochester Honkers.

Regular Season: 72 games (split schedule). **2019 Opening Date:** May 28. **Closing Date:** August 11. **All-Star Game:** July 16.

Playoff Format: First and second half sub-divisional winners are eligible for the playoffs. The two-playoff eligible teams in each sub-division will compete in a best of three sub-divisional series. The two sub-divisional series winners will play in a one-game divisional championship game. The two divisional game winners will play in a one-game league championship.

Roster Limit: 30 (college-eligible players only).

BATTLE CREEK BOMBERS

Mailing Address: 189 Bridge Street, Battle Creek, MI 49017. **Telephone:** (269) 962-0735. **Fax:** (269) 962-0741. **Email Address:** info@battlecreekbombers.com. **Website:** www.battlecreekbombers.com. **General Manager:** Tyler Shore. **Field Manager:** Josh Rebandt. **Field:** C.O. Brown Stadium**.**

BISMARCK LARKS

Mailing Address: 300 N 4th Street, Suite 103, Bismarck, ND 58501. **Telephone:** (701) 557-7600. **Email Address:** info@larksbaseball.com. **Website:** www.larks baseball.com. **General Manager:** John Bollinger. **Field Manager:** Brian Solemsaas. **Field:** Bismarck Municipal.

DULUTH HUSKIES

Mailing Address: PO Box 16231, Duluth, MN 55816. **Telephone:** (218) 786-9909.

Fax: (218) 786-9001. **E-Mail Address:** huskies@duluth huskies.com. **Website:** www.duluthhuskies.com. **Owner:** Michael Rosenzweig. **General Manager:** Greg Culver. **Field Manager:** Tyger Pederson. **Field:** Wade Stadium.

EAU CLAIRE EXPRESS

Mailing Address: 108 E Grand Ave, Eau Claire, WI 54701. **Telephone:** (715) 839-7788. **Fax:** (715) 839-7676. **E-Mail Address:** info@eauclaireexpress.com. **Website:** www.eauclaireexpress.com. **Owner:** Bill Rowlett. **Assistant Managing Director:** Andy Neborak. **General Manager:** Jacob Servais. **Director of Operations/Field Manager:** Dale Varsho. **Field:** Carson Park.

FOND DU LAC DOCK SPIDERS

Mailing Address: 254 Winnebago Dr., Fond du Lac, WI 54935. **Telephone:** (920) 907-9833. **Email Address:** info@dockspiders.com **Website:** www.dockspiders.com. **President:** Rob Zerjav. **General Manager:** Ryan Moede. **Field Manager:** Zac Charbonneau. **Field:** Herr-Baker Field

GREEN BAY BOOYAH

Mailing Address: 2325 Holgrem Way Suite, Green Bay, WI 54303. **Telephone:** (920) 497-7225. **Fax:** (920) 437-3551. **Email Address:** info@booyahbaseball.com. **Website:** www.booyahbaseball.com. **General Manager:** Sieeria Vieaux. **Field Manager:** TBA. **Field:** Capital Credit Union Park.

KALAMAZOO GROWLERS

Mailing Address: 251 Mills St, Kalamazoo, MI 49048. **Telephone:** (269) 492-9966.

Website: www.growlersbaseball.com. **General Manager:** Brian Colopy. **Field Manager:** Cody Piechocki. **Field:** Homer Stryker Field.

KENOSHA KINGFISH

Mailing Address: 7817 Sheridan Rd, Kenosha, WI 53143. **Telephone:** (262) 653-0900. **Website:** www.king fishbaseball.com. **General Manager:** Doug Cole. **Field Manager:** Duffy Dyer. **Field:** Simmons Field.

LA CROSSE LOGGERS

Mailing Address: 1223 Caledonia St, La Crosse, WI 54603. **Telephone:** (608) 796-9553. **Fax:** (608) 796-9032. **E-Mail Address:** info@lacrosseloggers.com. **Website:** www.lacrosseloggers.com. **Owner:** Dan Kapanke. **General Manager:** Chris Goodell. **Assistant General Manager:** Ben Kapanke. **Field Manager:** Brian Lewis. **Field:** Copeland Park.

LAKESHORE CHINOOKS

Mailing Address: 995 Badger Circle, Grafton, WI 53024. **Telephone:** (262) 618-4659. **Fax:** (262) 618-4362. **E-Mail Address:** info@lakeshorechinooks.com. **Website:** www.lakeshorechinooks.com. **Owner:** Jim Kacmarcik. **General Manager:** Shawn Kison. **Field Manager:** Travis Akre. **Field:** Kapco Park.

MADISON MALLARDS

Mailing Address: 2920 N Sherman Ave, Madison, WI 53704. **Telephone:** (608) 246-4277. **Fax:** (608) 246-4163. **E-Mail Address:** info@mallardsbaseball.com. **Website:** www.mallardsbaseball.com. **Owner:** Steve Schmitt. **President:** Vern Stenman. **General Manager:** Tyler Isham. **Field Manager:** Donnie Scott. **Field:** Warner Park.

MANKATO MOONDOGS

Mailing Address: 1221 Caledonia Street, Mankato, MN 56001. **Telephone:** (507) 625-7047. **Fax:** (507) 625-7059. **E-Mail Address:** office@mankatomoondogs.com. **Website:** www.mankatomoondogs.com. **General Manager:** Austin Link. **Field Manager:** Matt Wollenzin. **Field:** Franklin Rogers Park.

ROCHESTER HONKERS

Mailing Address: 307 E Center St, Rochester, MN 55904. **Telephone:** (507) 289-1170. **Fax:** (507) 289-1866. **E-Mail Address:** honkersbaseball@gmail.com. **Website:** www.rochesterhonkers.com. **Owner General Manager:** Dan Litzinger/Kim Archer. **Field Manager:** Thomas Walker. **Field:** Mayo Field.

ROCKFORD RIVETS

Mailing Address: 4503 Interstate Blvd., Loves Park, IL 61111. **Telephone:** 815-240-4159. **E-Mail Address:** info@rockfordrivets.com. **Website:** www.rockfordrivets.com. **General Manager:** Chad Bauer. **Field Manager:** Josh Keim. **Field:** Rivets Stadium.

ST. CLOUD ROX

Mailing Address: 5001 8th St N, St. Cloud, MN 56303. **Telephone:** (320) 240-9798. **Fax:** (320) 255-5228. **E-Mail Address:** info@stcloudrox.com. **Website:** www.stcloudrox.com. **President:** Gary Posch. **Vice President:** Scott Schreiner. **General Manager:** Mike Johnson. **Field Manager:** Augie Rodriguez. **Field:** Joe Faber Field.

ST. CROIX RIVER HOUNDS

Mailing Address: PO Box 10, Hudson, WI 54016. **Telephon:** (651) 272-7483. **E-Mail Address:** info@scriverhounds.com. **Owners:** Klint Klaas, Robb Quinlan, Tom Quinlan, Andy Persby, Kevin McMann, Steve Fleischhacker. **President/General Manager:** Bill Fanning. **Field Manager:** TBA.

THUNDER BAY BORDER CATS

Mailing Address: PO Box 29105 Thunder Bay, Ontario P7B 6P9. **Telephone:** (807) 766-2287. **General Manager:** Dan Grant. **Field Manager:** Eric Vasquez. **Field:** Port Arthur Stadium.

TRAVERSE CITY PIT SPITTERS

E-Mail Address: info@traversecitybaseball.com. **General Manager:** TBA. **Field Manager:** Josh Rebandt.

WATERLOO BUCKS

Mailing Address: PO Box 4124, Waterloo, IA 50704. **Telephone:** (319) 232-0500. **Fax:** (319) 232-0700. **E-Mail Address:** waterloobucks@waterloobucks.com. **Website:** www.waterloobucks.com. **General Manager:** Dan Corbin. **Field Manager:** Casey Harms. **Field:** Riverfront Stadium.

WILLMAR STINGERS

Mailing Address: PO Box 201, Willmar, MN, 56201. **Telephone:** (320) 222-2010. **E-Mail Address:** ryan@willmarstingers.com. **Website:** www.willmarstingers.com. **Owners:** Marc Jerzak, Ryan Voz. **General Manager:** Nick McCallum. **Field Manager:** Bo Henning. **Field:** Taunton Stadium.

WISCONSIN RAPIDS RAFTERS

Mailing Address: 521 Lincoln St, Wisconsin Rapids, WI 54494. **Telephone:** (715) 424-5400. **E-Mail Address:** info@raftersbaseball.com. **Website:** www.raftersbaseball.com. **Owner:** Vern Stenman. **General Manager:** Andy Francis. **Field Manager:** Craig Noto. **Field:** Witter Field.

WISCONSIN WOODCHUCKS

Mailing Address: PO Box 6157, Wausau, WI 54402. **Telephone:** (715) 845-5055. **Fax:** (715) 845-5015. **E-Mail Address:** info@woodchucks.com. **Website:** www.woodchucks.com. **Owner:** Mark Macdonald. **General Manager:** Ryan Treu. **Field Manager:** Andrew Fabian. **Field:** Athletic Park.

PACIFIC INTERNATIONAL LEAGUE

Mailing Address: 4400 26th Ave W, Seattle, WA 98199. **Telephone:** (206) 623-8844. **Fax:** (206) 623-8361. **E-Mail Address:** spotter@potterprinting.com. **Website:** www.pacificinternationalleague.com.

Year Founded: 1992.

President: Al Oremus. **Vice President:** Martin Lawrence. **Commissioner:** Terry Howard. **Secretary:** Steve Potter. **Treasurer:** Mark Dow. **Member Clubs:** Northwest Honkers, Everett Merchants, Seattle Studs, Highline Bears, Redmond Dudes, North Sound Emeralds. **Regular Season:** 20 league games. **Playoff Format:** Top team is invited to National Baseball Congress World Series.

Roster Limit: 30; 25 eligible for games (players must be at least 18 years old).

PERFECT GAME COLLEGIATE LEAGUE

Mailing Address: 8 Michaels Lane, Old Brookville, NY 11545. **Telephone:** (516) 521-0206. **Fax:** (516) 801-0818.

E-Mail Address: valkun@aol.com.

Website: www.pgcbl.com.

Year Founded: 2010.

President: Jeffrey Kunion.

Director of Communications: Travis Larner

Executive Committee: Bob Ohmann (Newark Pilots), Paul Samulski (Albany Dutchmen). Robbie Nichols (Elmira Pioneers), George Deak (Utica Blue Sox), Kevin Hinchey (Saugerties Stallions)

Teams: East—Albany Dutchmen, Amsterdam Mohawks, Glens Falls Dragons, Mohawk Valley DiamondDawgs, Oneonta Outlaws, Saugerties Stallions, Utica Blue Sox. **West**—Adirondack Trail Blazers, Elmira Pioneers, Geneva Red Wings, Jamestown Jammers, Newark Pilots, Onondaga Flames

Regular Season: 50. **Playoff Format:** Top four teams in each division qualify for one-game playoff; next two series are best of three. **Roster Limit:** 35 (maximum of two graduated high school players per team).

ADIRONDACK TRAIL BLAZERS

President: Bobby Miller. **Head Coach:** Bobby McLaughlin. **Telephone:** (315) 542-0675. **Field:** Robert Smith Sports Complex.

ALBANY DUTCHMEN

Mailing Address: PO Box 72, Saratoga Springs, N.Y. 12866. **President:** Paul Samulski. **General Manager:** Jason Brinkman. **E-Mail:** jbrinkma@gmail.com. **Telephone:** 518-210-8383. **Head Coach:** Nick Davey. **Field:** Siena Field.

AMSTERDAM MOHAWKS

Mailing Address: P.O. Box 334, Amsterdam, N.Y., 12010. **President:** Brian Spagnola. **Head Coach:** Keith Griffin. **E-Mail Address:** gm@amsterdammohawks.com. **Telephone:** (607) 222-4086. **Field:** Shuttlesworth Park.

ELMIRA PIONEERS

Mailing Address: 546 Luce Street, Elmira, N.Y. 14904. **Owners:** Nellie Franco-Nichols, Donald Lewis, Robbie Nichols. **Head Coach:** Matt Burch. **Telephone:** (607) 734-2690. **E-Mail Address:** donspioneers@gmail.com. Field: Dunn Field.

GENEVA RED WINGS

Mailing Address: N/A. **Owners:** Bob Ohmann, Lesilie Ohmann, Bill Kohlberger. **Head Coach:** Dan Shwam. **Email:** info@genevaredwings.com. **Telephone:** (919) 422-4323. **Field:** McDonough Park.

GLENS FALLS DRAGONS

Mailing Address: PO Box 897, Glens Falls, N.Y. 12801. **President:** Ben Bernard. **Head Coach:** Cameron Curler. **Telephone:** (518) 361-5316. **E-Mail Address:** ben bernard1@yahoo.com. **Field:** East Field Stadium.

JAMESTOWN JAMMERS

Owner: Mike Zimmerman. **President:** Dan Kuenzi. **Head Coach:** Anthony Barone. **Telephone:** (716) 720-4465. **E-Mail Address:** dkuenzi@mkesports.com. **Field:** Russell E. Diethrick Jr. Park.

MOHAWK VALLEY DIAMONDDAWGS

Mailing Address: PO Box 902, Little Falls, N.Y. 13365. **Owner:** Travis Heiser. **Head Coach:** Cory Haggerty. **Telephone:** (315) 985-0692. **E-Mail Address:** travis@ mydiamonddawgs.com. **Field:** Veterans Memorial Park.

NEWARK PILOTS

Mailing Address: 65 Williams Street, Lyons, N.Y. 14489. **Owner:** Bob Ohmann, Leslie Ohmann. **Head Coach:** Matt Colbert. **Telephone:** (315) 576-6710. **E-Mail Address:** newarkpilots@gmail.com. **Field:** Colburn Park.

ONEONTA OUTLAWS

Mailing Address: 291 Chestnut Street, Oneonta, N.Y., 13280. **Owner:** Gary Laing. **General Manager:** Joe Hughes. **Head Coach:** Joe Hughes. **Telephone:** (607) 432-6326. **E-Mail Address:** joehughes@oneontaoutlaws.com. **Field:** Damaschke Field.

SAUGERTIES STALLIONS

Mailing Address: 645 Rte 212, Saugerties, NY 12477. **Owner:** Kevin Hinchey. **Head Coach:** Collin Martin. **Telephone:** (845) 707-0265. **E-Mail Address:** the saugertiesstallions@gmail.com. **Field:** Cantine Field.

UTICA BLUE SOX

Mailing Address: PO Box 7, Marcy, N.Y. 13403. **Owner:** George Deak. **General Manager:** Butch Russo. **Head Coach:** Doug Delett. **Telephone:** (315) 855-5013. **E-Mail Address:** George@globalgraphicsny.com. **Field:** Donovan Stadium at Murnane Field.

WATERTOWN RAPIDS

Mailing Address: PO Box 6250, Watertown, N.Y. 13601. **Owners:** Michael Schell, Paul Velte. **General Manager:** Brandon Noble. **Field Manager:** Dave Anderson. **Telephone:** (315) 836-1545. **E-Mail Address:** rapidsgm@gmail.com. **Field:** Alex T. Duffy Fairgrounds.

PROSPECT LEAGUE

Mailing Address: PO Box 84, Elkville, IL 62932. **Telephone:** (618) 559-1343. **E-Mail Address:** commissioner@prospectleague.com. **Website:** www.prospectleague.com.

Year Founded: 1963 as Central Illinois Collegiate League; known as Prospect League since 2009.

Commissioner: Dennis Bastien.

Regular Season: 60 games. **2019 Opening Date:** May 30. **Closing Date:** Aug. 6. **All-Star Series:** July 22-23. **Championship Series:** Aug. 6-13. **Roster Limit:** 32.

CHAMPION CITY KINGS

Mailing Address: 1301 Mitchell Blvd., Springfield, OH 45503. **Telephone:** (937) 342-0320. **Fax:** (937) 342-0320. **E-Mail Address:** cckings@gmail.com. **Website:** www.championcitykings.com. **General Manager:** Ginger Fulton. **Field Manager:** John Jeanes.

CHILLICOTHE PAINTS

Mailing Address: 59 North Paint Street, Chillicothe, OH 45601. **Telephone:** (740) 773-8326. **Fax:** (740) 773-8338. **E-Mail Address:** paints@bright.net. **Website:** www.chillicothepaints.com. **General Manager:** Bryan Wickline. **Field Manager:** Brian Bigam.

DANVILLE DANS

Mailing Address: 4 Maywood, Danville, IL 61832. **Telephone:** (217) 918-3401. **Fax:** (217) 446-9995. **E-Mail Address:** danvilledans@comcast.net. **Website:** www.danvilledans.com. **League Director:** Jeanie Cooke. **Co-General Managers:** Jeanie Cooke. **Field Manager:** Eric Coleman.

HANNIBAL HOOTS

Telephone: 573-629-2018. **Team President:** Rick DeStefane. **General Manager:** Matt Stembridge. **Field Manager:** Clayton Hicks.

KOKOMO JACKRABBITS

Mailing Address: 400 S Union St, Kokomo, IN 46901. **Telephone:** (414)-224-9283. **Fax:** (414) 224-9290. **E-Mail Address:** johnp@kokomojackrabbits.com. **Website:** www.kokomojackrabbits.com. **Owner:** Mike Zimmerman. **League Director:** Dan Kuenzi. **Field Manager:** Gary McClure.

LAFAYETTE AVIATORS

Mailing Address: PO Box 6494, Lafayette, IN 47904. **Telephone:** (414) 224-9283. **Fax:** (414) 224-9290. **E-Mail Address:** zchartrand@lafayettebaseball.com. **Website:** www.lafayettebaseball.com. **President:** Sean Churchill. **General Manager:** Zach Chartrand. **League Director:** Dan Kuenzi. **Field Manager:** Brent McNeil.

QUINCY GEMS

Mailing Address: 1400 N. 30th St., Suite 1, Quincy, IL 62301. **Telephone:** (217) 214-7436. **Fax:** (217) 214-7436. **E-Mail Address:** quincygems@yahoo.com. **Website:** www.quincygems.com. **League Director/General Manager:** Jimmie/Julie Louthan. **Field Manager:** Pat Robles.

SPRINGFIELD SLIDERS

Mailing Address: 1415 North Grand Avenue East, Suite B, Springfield, IL 62702. **Telephone:** (217) 679-3511. **Fax:** (217) 679-3512. **E-Mail Address:** slidersfun@spring fieldsliders.com. **Website:** www.springfieldsliders.com. **League Director/General Manager:** Todd Miller. **Field Manager:** Steve Leonetti.

TERRE HAUTE REX

Mailing Address:111 North 3rd St, Terre Haute, IN 47807. **Telephone:** (812) 478-3817. **Fax:** (812) 232-5353. **E-mail Address:** frontoffice@rexbaseball.com. **Website:** www.rexbaseball.com. **League Director/General Manager:** Bruce Rosselli. **Field Manager:**Tyler Wampler.

WEST VIRGINIA MINERS

Mailing Address: 476 Ragland Road, Suite 2, Beckley, WV 25801. **Telephone:** (304) 252-7233. **Fax:** (304) 253-1998. **E-mail Address:** wvminers@wvminersbaseball .com. **Website:** www.wvminersbaseball.com. **President:** Doug Epling. **League Director/General Manager/Field Manager::** Tim Epling.

SOUTHERN COLLEGIATE BASEBALL LEAGUE

Mailing Address: 9723 Northcross Center Court, Huntersville, NC 28078. **Telephone:** (704) 635-7126. **Cell:** (704) 906-7776. **E-Mail Address:** hhampton@scbl.org. **Website:** www.scbl.org.
Year Founded: 1999.
Chairman: Bill Capps, **Commissioner:** Harold Hampton. **President:** Jeff Carter. **Treasurer:** Brenda Templin. **Umpire in Chief:** Gary Swanson.
Regular Season: 42 games. **Playoff Format:** Six-team single-elimination tournament with best of three championship series between final two teams.
Roster Limit: 35 (College-eligible players only).

CHARLOTTE GALAXY

Mailing Address: 7209 East WT Harris Blvd, Suite J #245, Charlotte, NC 28227. **Telephone:** (704) 668-9167. **Email Address:** baseballnbeyond@aol.com. **General Manager:** David "Doc" Booth. **Head Coach:** Addison Rouse.

CONCORD ATHLETICS

Mailing Address: 366 George Lyles Parkway, Suite 125, Concord, NC 28027. **Telephone:** (704) 786-2255. **Email Address:** playconcordathletics@gmail.com. **General Manager:** David Darwin. **Head Coach:** Charles Weber

LAKE NORMAN COPPERHEADS

Mailing Address: 16405 Northcross Drive, Suite A Huntersville, NC 28078. **Telephone:** (704) 305-3649. **Email Address:** dshoe@copperheadsports.org. **General Manager:** Derek Shoe. **Head Coach:** Jeremy Johnson.

PIEDMONT PRIDE

Mailing Address: 1524 Summit View Drive, Rock Hill, SC 29732. **Telephone:** (803) 412-7982. **E-Mail Address:** joe@pridebaseball.net. **General Manager:** Logan Hudak. **Head Coach:** Joe Hudak.

CAROLINA VIPERS

Mailing Address: 12104 Copper Way, Suite 200, Charlotte NC 28277. **Telephone:** 980-256-5346. **E-Mail Address:** bnichols@goviperbaseball.com. **President:** Mike Polito. **General Manager:** Blaine Nichols. **Head Coach:** Aaron Bray.

MOORSVILLE SPINNERS

Mailing Address: 2643 N Hwy 16 Denver, NC 28037. **Telephone:** (704) 491-4112. **E-Mail Address:** ploftin@ mooresvillespinners.com. **General Manager:** Phillip Loftin. **Head Coach:** David Newcomer

LINOIRE OILERS

Mailing Address: PO Box 1113 Icard NC 28666. **Telephone** 828-455-1289. **E-Mail Address:** LenoirOilers@ gmail.com. **General Manager** Sara Wert. **Head Coach:** Ivan Acuna.

TEXAS COLLEGIATE LEAGUE

Mailing Address: 735 Plaza Blvd, Suite 200, Coppell, TX 75019. **Telephone:** (979) 985-5198. **Fax:** (979) 779-2398. **E-Mail Address:** info@tclbaseball.com.
Website: www.texascollegiateleague.com.
Year Founded: 2004.
President: Uri Geva.
Roster Limit: 30 (College-eligible players only)

ACADIANA CANE CUTTERS

Mailing Address: 221 La Neuville, Youngsville, LA 70592. **Telephone:** (337) 451-6582. **E-Mail Address:** info@cane cuttersbaseball.com. **Website:** www.canecuttersbaseball. com. **Owners:** Richard Chalmers, Sandi Chalmers. **General Manager:** Richard Haifley.

BRAZOS VALLEY BOMBERS

Mailing Address: 405 Mitchell St, Bryan, TX 77801. **Telephone:** (979) 799-7529. **Fax:** (979) 779-2398. **E-Mail Address:** info@bvbombers.com. **Website:** www.bv bombers.com. **Owners:** Uri Geva. **General Manger:** Chris Clark. **Field Manager:** Curt Dixon.

TEXAS MARSHALS

Mailing Address: 7920 Beltline Rd, 8th Floor Suite 860 Dallas, TX 75254. **Telephone:** (855) 808-7529. **E-Mail Address:** info@texasmarshals.com. **Website:** www.texas marshals.com. **Owner:** Marc Landry. **General Manager:** Kenderick Moore. **Field Manager:** Brent Lavallee.

TEXARKANA TWINS

Ballpark: George Dobson Field, 4303 N Park Rd, Texarkana, TX 75503. **Telephone:** (903) 294-7529. **Head Coach:** Bill Clay.

VICTORIA GENERALS

Mailing Address: 1307 E Airline Road, Suite H, Victoria, TX 77901. **Telephone:** (361) 485-9522. **Fax:** (361) 485-0936. **E-Mail Address:** info@baseballinvictoria.com, tkyoung@victoriagenerals.com. **Website:** www.victoria generals.com. **President:** Tracy Young. **VP/General Manager:** Mike Yokum.

VALLEY BASEBALL LEAGUE

Mailing Address: Valley Baseball League, PO Box 1127, New Market, VA 22844. **Telephone:** (540) 810-9194. **Fax:** (540) 435-8453. **E-Mail Addresses:** cbalger@shentel. net. **Website:** www.valleyleaguebaseball.com.

Year Founded: 1897. **President:** C. Bruce Alger. **Assistant to the President:** Steve Shifflett. **Executive Vice President:** Jay Neal. **Media Relations Director:** Jimmy McCumber. **Secretary:** Stacy Locke. **Treasurer:** Ed Yoder. **Regular Season:** 42 games. **Playoff Format:** Eight teams qualify; play three rounds of best of three series. **Roster Limit:** 30 (college eligible players only)

COVINGTON LUMBERJACKS

Mailing Address: PO Box 30, Covington, VA 24426. **Telephone:** (540) 969-9923, (540) 962-1155. **Fax:** (540) 962-7153. **E-Mail Address:** covingtonlumberjacks@valley leaguebaseball.com. **Website:** www.lumberjacksbase ball.com. **President:** Dizzy Garten. **Head Coach:** Alex Kotheimer.

PURCELLVILLE CANNONS

Mailing Address: P.O. Box 114, Purcellville, VA 20132. **Telephone:** (540) 303-9673. **Fax:** (304) 856-1619. **E-Mail Address:** info@purcellvillecannons.com. **Website:** www.purcellvillecannons.com. President/**Recruiting Coordinator/Head Coach:** Brett Fuller. **General Manager:** Ridge Fuller.

CHARLOTTESVILLE TOM SOX

Mailing Address: P. O. Box 4836, Virginia 22905. **Telephone:** (703)282-4425. **E-Mail:** mpad71@gmail. com. **Website:** www.TomSox.com. **President:** Greg Allen. **General Manager:** Mike Paduano. **Head Coach:** Cory Hunt.

FRONT ROYAL CARDINALS

Mailing Address: 382 Morgans Ridge Road, Front Royal, VA 22630. **Telephone:** (703) 244-6662, (540) 631-9201. **E-Mail Address:** DonnaSettle@centurylink.net. frontroyalcardinals@valleyleaguebaseball.com. **Website:** www.valleyleaguebaseball.com. **President:** Donna Settle. **Head Coach:** Zeke Mitchem.

HARRISONBURG TURKS

Mailing Address: 1489 S Main St, Harrisonburg, VA 22801. **Telephone:** (540) 434-5919. **Fax:** (540) 434-5919. **E-Mail Address:** turksbaseball@hotmail.com. **Website:** www.harrisonburgturks.com. **Operations Manager:** Teresa Wease. **General Manager/Head Coach:** Bob Wease.

NEW MARKET REBELS

Mailing Address: PO Box 902, New Market, VA 22844. **Telephone:** (540) 435-8453. **Fax:** (540) 740-9486. **E-Mail Address:** nmrebels@shentel.net. **Website:** www.new marketrebels.com. **President/General Manager:** Bruce Alger. **Head Coach:** Matt Schaeffer.

STAUNTON BRAVES

Mailing Address: PO Box 428, Stuarts Draft, VA 24447. **Telephone:** (540) 886-0987. **Fax:** (540) 886-0905. **E-Mail Address:** sbraves@hotmail.com. **Website:** www. stauntonbravesbaseball.com. **General Manager:** Steve Cox. **Head Coach:** Lukas Ray.

STRASBURG EXPRESS

Mailing Address: PO Box 417, Strasburg, VA 22657. **Telephone:** (540) 325-5677, (540) 459-4041. **Fax:** (540) 459-3398. **E-Mail Address:** neallaw@shentel.net, strasburgxpress@gmail.com. **Website:** www.strasburg express.com. **General Manager:** Jay Neal. **Head coach:** Anthony Goncalves.

WAYNESBORO GENERALS

Mailing Address: 3144 Village Drive, Waynesboro, VA 22980. **Telephone:** (540) 932-2300. **Fax:** (540) 932-2322. **E-Mail Address:** contact@waynesborogenerals.net. **Website:** www.waynesborogenerals.com. **Chairman:** Brent Ward. **General Manager:** Tyler Hoffman. **Head Coach:** John Jeanes.

WINCHESTER ROYALS

Mailing Address: PO Box 2485, Winchester, VA 22604. **Telephone:** (540) 974-4104, (540) 664-3978. **Fax:** (540) 662-1434. **E-Mail Addresses:** winchesterroyals@gmail. com, info@winchesterroyals.org. **Website:** www. winchesterroyals.com. **President:** Donna Turrill. **Operations Director:** Jimmie Shipp. **Coach:** Mike Smith.

WOODSTOCK RIVER BANDITS

Mailing Address: P.O. Box 227, Woodstock, VA 22664. **Telephone:** (540) 481-0525. **Fax:** (540) 459-2093. **E-Mail Address:** woodstockriverbandits@valleyleaguebaseball. com. **Website:** www.woodstockriverbandits.org. **General Manager:** R.W. Bowman Jr. **Head Coach:** Greg Keaton.

WEST COAST LEAGUE

Mailing Address: PO Box 10771, Portland OR 97296. **Telephone:** 503-233-2490. **E-Mail Address:** info@west coastleague.com. **Website:** www.westcoastleague.com.

Year Founded: 2005.

Commissioner: Rob Neyer. **President:** Tony Bonacci. **Vice President:** Glenn Kirkpatrick. **Secretary:** Jose Oglesby. **Treasurer:** Dan Segel. **Supervisor, Umpires:** Dave Perez. **Division Structure: South—**Bend Elks, Corvallis Knights, Cowlitz Black Bears, Ridgefield Raptors, Walla Walla Sweets. **North—**Bellingham Bells, Kelowna Falcons, Port Angeles Lefties, Victoria Harbourcats, Wenatchee Applesox, Yakima Valley Pippins. **2019 Opening Date:** June 4. **Closing Date:** August 11. **Playoff Format:** Four-team tournament. **Roster Limit:** 35 (college-eligible players only).

BELLINGHAM BELLS

Mailing Address: 1221 Potter Street, Bellingham, WA 98229. **Telephone:** (360) 527-1035. **E-Mail Address:** stephanie@bellinghambells.com. **Website:** www. bellinghambells.com. **Owner:** Glenn Kirkpatrick. **General Manager:** Stephanie Morrell. **Head Coach:** Bob Miller. **Assistant Coaches:** Jim Clem, Jake Whisler, Adam Geaslen.

BEND ELKS

Mailing Address: 70 SW Century Dr Suite 100-373 Bend, Oregon 97702. **Telephone:** (541) 312-9259. **Website:** www.bendelks.com. **Owners:** John and Tami Marick. **Marketing and Sales:** Kelsie Hirko. **General Manager:** Michael Hirko. **Head Coach:** Alan Embree. **Assistant Coaches:** Dylan Jones, Blake Woosley.

CORVALLIS KNIGHTS

Mailing Address: PO Box 1356, Corvallis, OR 97339. **Telephone:** (541) 752-5656. **E-Mail Address:** dan.segel@ corvallisknights.com. **Website:** www.corvallisknights. com. **President:** Dan Segel. **General Manager:** Bre Miller. **Head Coach:** Brooke Knight. **Associate Head Coach/ Pitching Coach:** Ed Knaggs. **Assistant Coach:** Youngjin Yoon, Kellen Camus.

COWLITZ BLACK BEARS

Mailing Address: PO Box 1255, Longview, WA 98632. **Telephone:** (360) 703-3195. **Website:** www.cowlitzblac kbears.com. **Owner/President:** Tony Bonacci. **General Manager:** Jim Appleby. **Head Coach:** Grady Tweit. **Assistant Coaches:** Jason Mackey, Michael Forgione.

KELOWNA FALCONS

Mailing Address: 201-1014 Glenmore Dr, Kelowna, BC, V1Y 4P2. **Telephone:** (250) 763-4100. **Website:** www.kelownafalcons.com. **Owner:** Dan Nonis. **General Manager:** Mark Nonis. **Head Coach:** Bryan Donohue.

PORT ANGELES LEFTIES

Mailing Address: PO Box 2204, Port Angeles, WA 98362. **Phone:** (360) 701-1087. **Website:** www.lefties baseball.com. **E-Mail Address:** matt@leftiesbaseball.com. **Owners:** Matt Acker, Jacob Oppelt. **General Manager:** Ryan Hickey. **Head Coach:** Darren Westergard. **Assistant Coach:** Trevor Podratz.

PORTLAND PICKLES

Address: 5308 SE 92nd Ave. Portland, OR 97266. **Phone:** (503) 775-3080. **Owners:** Alan Miller, Bill Stewart, Jon Ryan, Scott Barchus. **Head Coach:** Justin Barchus. **Hitting Coach:** Mark Magdaleno. **Pitching Coach:** Zach Miller. **Bench Coach:** Jim Hoppel.

RIDGEFIELD RAPTORS

E-Mail Address: info@ridgefieldraptors.com. **General Manager:** Gus Farah.

VICTORIA HARBOURCATS

Mailing Address: 101-1814 Vancouver Street, Victoria, BC, Canada, V8T 5E3. **Telephone:** (778) 265-0327. **Website:** www.harbourcats.com. **Owners:** Rich Harder, Jim Swanson, Ken Swanson, John Wilson. **Managing Partner:** Jim Swanson. **General Manager:** Brad Norris-Jones. **Head Coach:** Brian McRae. **Assistant Coaches:** Ian Sanderson, Todd Haney, Troy Birtwistle, Jason Leone, Curtis Pelletier.

WALLA WALLA SWEETS

Mailing Address: 109 E Main Street, Walla Walla, WA 99362. **Telephone:** (509) 522-2255. **E-Mail Address:** info@wallawallasweets.com. **Website:** www.wallawalla sweets.com. **Owner:** Pacific Baseball Ventures, LLC. **President/COO:** Zachary Fraser. **General Manager:** Dan Ferguson. **Head Coach:** Frank Mutz. **Assistant Coaches:** Raul Camacho, Kyle Wilkerson.

WENATCHEE APPLESOX

Mailing Address: 610 N. Mission St. #204, Wenatchee, WA 98801. **Telephone:** (509) 665-6900. **E-Mail Address:** info@applesox.com. **Website:** www.applesox.com. **Owner/General Manager:** Jose Oglesby. **Owner/ Assistant General Manager:** Ken Osborne. **Head Coach:** Kyle Krustangel.

YAKIMA VALLEY PIPPINS

Mailing Address: 12 S. Secont St., Yakima, WA 98901. **Telephone:** (509) 575-4487. **E-Mail Address:** info@ pippinsbaseball.com. **Website:** www.pippinsbaseball. com. **Owner:** Pacific Baseball Ventures, LLC. **President/ COO:** Zachary Fraser. **General Manager:** Jeff Garretson. **Head Coach:** Marcus McKimmy. **Pitching Coach:** Rob Hippi.

HIGH SCHOOL BASEBALL

NATIONAL FEDERATION OF STATE HIGH SCHOOL ASSOCIATIONS

Mailing Address: PO Box 690, Indianapolis, IN 46206. **Telephone:** (317) 972-6900. **Fax:** (317) 822-5700. **E-Mail Address:** baseball@nfhs.org. **Website:** www.nfhs.org.

Executive Director: Karissa Niehoff. **Chief Operating Officer:** Davis Whitfield. **Director of Sports, Sanctioning and Student Services:** B. Elliot Hopkins. **Director, Publications/Communications:** Bruce Howard.

NATIONAL HIGH SCHOOL BASEBALL COACHES ASSOCIATION

Mailing Address: PO Box 1038, Dublin, OH 43017. **Telephone:** (614) 578-1864. **E-Mail Address:** tsaunders@baseballcoaches.org. **Website:** www.baseball coaches.org. **Executive Director:** Tim Saunders (Dublin Coffman HS, Ohio). **Assistant Executive Director:** Ty Whittaker (Eastern Technical HS, Md.). **Associate Executive Director:** Ray Benjamin (St. Charles HS, Ohio). **Associate Exectuive Director:** Paul Twenge (Minnetonka HS, Minn.). Executive Secretary Robert Colburn. **President:** Tony Perkins (Francis Howell HS, Mo.). **1st VP:** Tim Bordenet (Lafayette Central Catholic HS, Ind.). **2nd VP:** Scott Manahan (Bishop Watterson HS, Ohio). **2019 National Convention:** Dec. 5-8 in Columbus, Ohio.

NATIONAL TOURNAMENTS

IN-SEASON

INTERNATIONAL PAPER CLASSIC
Mailing Address: 4775 Johnson Rd., Georgetown, SC 29440. **Telephone:** (843) 527-9606. **Fax:** (843) 546-8521. **Website:** www.ipclassic.com.
Tournament Director: Alicia Johnson.
2019 Tournament: TBD.

45TH ANNUAL ANAHEIM LIONS CLUB BASEBALL TOURNAMENT
Mailing Address: 8281 Walker Street, La Palma, CA 90623. **Telephone:** (714) 220-4101x27502. **Fax:** (714) 995-1833. **Email:** Pascal_C@AUHSD.US. **Website:** www. anaheimlionstourney.com.
Tournament Director: Chris Pascal.
2019 Tournament: March 23-27 (85 teams).

NATIONAL CLASSIC BASEBALL TOURNAMENT
Mailing Address: 1651 Valencia Ave, Placentia, CA 92870. **Telephone:** (714) 993-2838. **Fax:** (714) 993-5350. **E-Mail Address:** mlucas@pylusd.org. **Website:** www. national-classic.com.
Tournament Director: Matt Lucas.
2019 Tournament: April 1-4.

USA BASEBALL NATIONAL HIGH SCHOOL INVITATIONAL
Mailing Address: 1030 Swabia Ct., Suite 201; Durham, NC 27703. **Telephone:** (919) 474-8721. **Fax:** (919) 474-8822. **Email:** carterhicks@usabaseball.com. **Website:** www.usabaseball.com.
2019 Tournament: April 3-6 at USA Baseball National Training Complex, Cary, NC (16 teams).

POSTSEASON

ALL-STAR GAMES/AWARDS
PERFECT GAME ALL-AMERICAN CLASSIC
Mailing Address: 850 Twixt Town Rd. NE, Cedar Rapids, IA 52402. **Telephone:** (319) 298-2923. Fax (319) 298-2924. **Event Organizer:** Blue Ridge Sports & Entertainment. **VP, Showcases/Scouting:** Greg Sabers.
2019 Game: Aug. 11 at Petco Park, San Diego.

UNDER ARMOUR ALL-AMERICA GAME, POWERED BY BASEBALL FACTORY
Mailing Address: 9212 Berger Rd., Suite 200, Columbia, MD 21046. **Telephone:** (410) 715-5080. **E-mail Address:** jason@factoryathletics.com. **Website:** baseball factory.com/AllAmerica. **Event Organizers:** Baseball Factory, Team One Baseball.
2019 Game: Summer, TBD.

GATORADE CIRCLE OF CHAMPIONS
(National HS Player of the Year Award)
Mailing Address: The Gatorade Company, 321 N. Clark St., Suite 24-3, Chicago, IL, 60610. **Telephone:** (312) 821-1000. **Website:** www.gatorade.com.

SHOWCASE EVENTS

AREA CODE BASEBALL GAMES PRESENTED BY NEW BALANCE

Mailing Address: 23954 Madison Street, Torrance, CA 90505. **Telephone:** (310) 791-1142 x 4426. **E-Mail:** baseball@studentsports.com. **Website:** AreaCodeBaseball.com.
Event Organizer: Kirsten Leetch.
2019 Area Code Games: Aug. 5-9 at Blair Field in Long Beach, Calif.

AREA CODE BASEBALL UNDERCLASS GAMES PRESENTED BY NEW BALANCE

Event Organizer: Kirsten Leetch.
2019 Area Code Games: Aug. 10-12 at MLB Youth Academy in Compton, Calif.

ARIZONA FALL CLASSIC

Mailing Address: 9962 W. Villa Hermosa, Peoria, AZ 85383. **Telephone:** (602) 228-1592.
E-mail Address: azfallclassic@gmail.com.
Website: www.azfallclassic.com.
President: Tracy Heid
Event Director: Trevor Heid,
Information Directors: Tiffini Robinson, Tiana Eves

2019 EVENTS

Four Corner Classic............ Peoria, AZ, May 30-June 2
California Classic Qualifiers:

Freshman..June 7-9
Sophomore...............................May 31-June 2
Junior ....July 19-21
Senior ....June 7-9
SoCal Locations TBA

AZ Freshman
Fall Classic (class of 2023) ....Peoria, AZ, Oct. 17-20

AZ Sophomore
Fall Classic (class of 2022) ....Peoria, AZ, Sept. 26-29

AZ Senior
Fall Classic (class of 2020) ....Peoria, AZ, Oct. 9-13

Senior All Academic Game .... Oct. 10

Junior College All Star Series .... TBD

AZ Junior
Fall Classic (class of 2021) ....Peoria, AZ , Oct. 3-6

Junior All Academic Tryout & Game.................Oct. 3

Universal Fall Classic ....Peoria, AZ, Oct. 24-27

BASEBALL FACTORY

Office Address: 9212 Berger Rd., Suite 200, Columbia, MD 21046. **Telephone:** (800) 641-4487, (410) 715-5080. **Fax:** (410) 715-1975. **E-mail Address:** info@baseballfactory.com. **Website:** www.baseballfactory.com.
Chief Executive Officer/Founder: Steve Sclafani. **President:** Rob Naddelman. **Chief Program Officer:** Jim Gemler. **Executive VP, Baseball Operations/Chairman, Under Armour All-America Game Selection Committee:** Steve Bernhardt. **Senior VP, Player Development:** Dan Forester. **VP, Tournament Division:** Justin Roswell. **VP, Business Development:** Dave Packer. **Chief Marketing Officer:** Tyler Blyleven. **Director,**

Marketing & Partnerships: Catherine Lee. **Executive Director, College Recruiting:** Dan Mooney. **Senior Multimedia Producer:** Brian Johnson. **Senior Director, Web Development:** Wei Xue. **Senior Director, Event Experience:** Ryan Liddle. **Senior Director, Baseball Player Development Events:** Nolan Fuller. **Senior Director, Under Armour Baseball Factory National Tryout:** Patrick Lawrence.
Executive Player Development Coordinator: Steve Nagler. **Senior Player Development Coordinators:** Adam Darvick, John Perko. **Senior Regional Player Development Coordinators:** Chris Brown, Rob Onolfi. **Regional Player Development Coordinators:** Robert Appleby, Ed Bach, Chris Brown, Josh Eldridge, Corson Fidler, Josh Hippensteel, Jane Lukas, David O'Neil, Julia Rice, Jesse Tome, Patrick Wuebben. **Director of College Recruiting:** Matt Richter.
Director, Athlete & Family Experience: Danielle Lawson. **Director, Social Media/Web Content:** Matt Lund. **Director of Player Development at FDI:** Mike Landis. **Director, Retail & Team Sales:** Lindsey Gutridge & Kevin Heinrich. **Director, Factory Athletics Foundation:** Emma Connor.

Under Armour All-America

Pre-Season Tournament...........Jan. 12-14, Mesa, Ariz.
(Sloan Park, Spring Training Home of the Chicago Cubs).

Under Armour

All-America Game.........................Summer, TBD

2018 Under Armour Baseball Factory National Tryouts/College PREP Recruiting Program: Year round at various locations across the country. Open to high school players, ages 14–18, with a separate division for middle school players, ages 12–14. **Full schedule:** www.baseballfactory.com/tryouts.

EAST COAST PROFESSIONAL SHOWCASE

Website: www.eastcoastpro.org. **Mailing Address:** Hoover Met Complex, 100 Ben Chapman Dr, Hoover, AL 25244. **E-mail Address:** info@eastcoastpro.org
Tournament Directors: John Castleberry, Rich Sparks, Sean Gibbs, Arthur McConnehead, Lori Bridges.
2019 Showcase: Aug. 1-4, Hoover Met Complex, 100 Ben Chapman Dr., Hoover, AL 35244.

IMPACT BASEBALL

Mailing Address: P.O. Box 47, Sedalia, NC 27342. **E-mail Address:** impactbaseballstaff@gmail.com. **Website:** impactbaseball.com. **Founder/CEO:** Andy Partin. **2018 Events:** Various dates, May-Aug. 2018.

NORTHWEST CHAMPIONSHIPS

Mailing Address: 9849 Fox Street, Aumsville, OR 97325. **Telephone:** (503) 302-7117. **E-mail Address:** joshuapwarner@gmail.com. **Website:** www.baseballnorthwest.com. **Tournament Organizer:** Josh Warner.

Northwest Championships
Date: August 8-11
Location: Centralia, Wash.
Facility: Borst Park Sports Complex
Grad Classes: 2020-2022

Junior Northwest Championships
Date: August 15-18
Location: Centralia, Wash.
Facility: Borst Park Sports Complex
Grad Classes: 2023-2024

PERFECT GAME USA

(A Division of Perfect Game USA)
Mailing Address: 850 Twixt Town Rd. NE, Cedar Rapids, IA 52402. **Telephone:** (319) 298-2923. **Fax:** (319) 298-2924. **E-mail Address:** pgba@perfectgame.org. **Website:** www.perfectgame.org.
Year Founded: 1995.
President: Jerry Ford. **VP, Operations:** Taylor McCollough. **VP, Showcases/Scouting:** Greg Sabers.

PREP BASEBALL REPORT

Mailing Address: 4750 S. Vernon Ave, McCook, IL 60525. Telephone: 708-387-0500.
President: Sean Duncan. **Vice President of Operations and Multimedia:** Matt Yarber. **National Crosschecker:** Shooter Hunt. **National Supervisor:** Nathan Rode.

PROFESSIONAL BASEBALL INSTRUCTION—BATTERY INVITATIONAL

(for top high school pitchers and catchers)
Mailing Address: 12 Wright Way, Oakland NJ 07436. **Telephone:** (800) 282-4638. **Fax:** (201) 760-8820. **E-mail Address:** info@baseballclinics.com. **Website:** www.baseballclinics.com/battery invitational/
President: Doug Cinnella.
Director of PR/Marketing: Jim Monaghan.
Event Date: Oct. 20, 2019.

SELECTFEST BASEBALL

Mailing Address: P.O. Box 852, Morris Plains, NJ 07950. **E-mail Address:** selectfest@selectfestbaseball.org. **Website:** www.selectfestbaseball.org. **Camp Directors:** Bruce Shatel, Robert Maida.
2019 Showcase: June 21-22.

TEAM ONE BASEBALL

(A division of Baseball Factory)
Office Address: 220 Newport Center Drive, 11418, Newport Beach, CA 92660. **Telephone:** (800) 621-5452. **Fax:** (949) 209-1829. **E-Mail Address:** jroswell@teamonebaseball.com. **Website:** www.teamonebaseball.com.
Executive Director: Justin Roswell. **Chief Program Officer:** Jim Gemler. **Executive VP:** Steve Bernhardt. **Senior VP, Player Development:** Dan Forester.

2019 Under Armour Showcases:

UA West Showcase.................................. TBA
UA South Showcase................................ TBA
UA Texas Showcase .... TBA
UA Florida Showcase............................... TBA
For a full listing of showcases visit www.teamonebaseball.com/showcases.

2019 Under Armour Tournaments:

Under Armour Memorial Day Classic.......... May 24-27
Irvine, CA (Orange County Great Park)

Under Armour Father's Day Classic ....June 14–17
Irvine, CA (Orange County Great Park)

Under Armour 4th of July Classic .... June 28 –July 2
Glendora, CA (Citrus/ELAC)

Under Armour Firecracker Classic.................July 5-9
Jupiter, FL (Roger Dean Sports Complex)

Under Armour
Southwest Championships 16U .... July 19-23
in La Verne, CA (University of La Verne)

Under Armour
Southwest Championships 17U .... July 26 – July 30
La Verne, CA (University of La Verne)

Under Armour Fall Classic ....September 28–29
Jupiter, FL (Roger Dean Sports Complex)

Under Armour SoCal Classic Underclass ...October 18–20
La Verne, CA (University of La Verne)

Under Armour SoCal Classic Upperclass ...October 25-27
La Verne, CA (University of La Verne)

For a full listing of tournaments visit:
www.teamonebaseball.com/tournaments.

TOP 96 COLLEGE COACHES CLINICS

Mailing Address: 2639 Connecticut Avenue NW, Suite 250, Washington, DC 20008. **Telephone:** (202) 313-7385. **E-mail Address:** info@top96.com. **Website:** www.top96.com. **Directors:** Doug Henson, Dave Callum.

YOUTH BASEBALL

ALL AMERICAN AMATEUR BASEBALL ASSOCIATION

Mailing Address: 1101 Flamingo Drive, APT 3106, Altoona, PA 16602.
Cell: (814) 931-8698.
E-Mail Address: aaabaprez@atlanticbb.net.
Website: aaabajohnstown.org
President: Jay Elliot
Executive Director: John Austin
2019 Events: AAABA National Tournament August 5-10 in Johnstown PA.

AMATEUR ATHLETIC UNION OF THE UNITED STATES, INC.

Mailing Address: P.O. Box 22409, Lake Buena Vista, FL 32830. **Telephone:** (407) 828-3459. **Fax:** (407) 934-7242. **E-mail Address:** tmeyer@aausports.org. **Website:** www.aaubaseball.org.
Year Founded: 1982. **Senior Sport Manager, Baseball:** Tim Meyer.

AMERICAN AMATEUR BASEBALL CONGRESS

National Headquarters: 100 West Broadway, Farmington, NM 87401. **Telephone:** (505) 327-3120. **Fax:** (505) 327-3132. **E-mail Address:** info@aabc.us. **Website:** www.aabc.us.
Year Founded: 1935.
President: Richard Neely.

AMERICAN AMATEUR YOUTH BASEBALL ALLIANCE

Mailing Address: 3851 Iris Lane, Bonne Terre, MO 63628. **Telephone:** (314) 650-0028. **E-mail Address:** info@aayba.com. **Website:** www.aayba.com.
President, Baseball Operations: Carroll Wood. President, **Business Operations:** Greg Moore.

AMERICAN LEGION BASEBALL

National Headquarters: American Legion Baseball, 700 N Pennsylvania St., Indianapolis, IN 46204.
Telephone: (317) 630-1213. **Fax:** (317) 630-1369. **E-mail Address:** baseball@legion.org. **Website:** www.legion.org/baseball.
Year Founded: 1925.
Program Coordinator: Steve Cloud.
2019 World Series (19 and under): Aug. 15-20 at Keeter Stadium, Shelby, N.C. 2019 Regional Tournaments (Aug. 7-11): **Northeast**—Shrewsbury, Mass.; Mid-**Atlantic**—Asheboro, N.C.; **Southeast**—Tampa, Fla..; Mid-**South**—Hastings, Neb.; **Great Lakes**—Charleston, Ill.; **Central Plains**—Sioux Falls, S.D.; **Northwest**—Lewiston, Ida.; **West**—Fairfield, Calif.

BABE RUTH BASEBALL

International Headquarters: 1670 Whitehorse-Mercerville Rd., Hamilton, NJ 08619. **Telephone:** (800) 880-3142. **Fax:** (609) 695-2505. **E-mail Address:** info@baberuthleague.org. **Website:** www.baberuthleague.org.
Year Founded: 1951.
President/Chief Executive Officer: Steven Tellefsen.

BASEBALL FOR ALL

Mailing Address: 30745 Pacific Coast Hwy #328 Los Angeles, CA 90265. **E-mail Address:** girlsbaseball@baseballforall.com. **Website:** BaseballForAll.com
Providing baseball programming for girls.

BASEBALL USA

Mailing Address: 2626 West Sam Houston Pkwy. N., Houston, TX 77043. **Telephone:** (713) 690-5564. **E-mail Address:** info@baseballusa.com. **Website:** www.baseballusa.com.
President: Jason Krug.

CALIFORNIA COMPETITIVE YOUTH BASEBALL

Mailing Address: P.O. Box 338, Placentia, CA 92870. **Telephone:** (714) 993-2838. **E-mail Address:** ccybnet@gmail.com. **Website:** www.ccyb.net.
Tournament Director: Todd Rogers.

COCOA EXPO SPORTS CENTER

Mailing Address: 500 Friday Road, Cocoa, FL 32926. **Telephone:** (321) 639-3976. **Fax:** (407) 390-9435. **E-mail Address:** brad@cocoaexpo.com. **Website:** www.cocoaexpo.com.
Activities: Spring training program, spring & fall leagues, instructional camps, team training camps, youth tournaments.

CONTINENTAL AMATEUR BASEBALL ASSOCIATION

Mailing Address: P.O. Box 1684 Mt. Pleasant, SC 29465. **Telephone:** (843) 860-1568. **E-mail Address:** Diamonddevils@aol.com. **Website:** www.cababaseball.com.
Year Founded: 1984.
Chief Executive Officer: Larry Redwine. **President/COO:** John Rhodes. **Executive Vice President:** Fran Pell.

COOPERSTOWN BASEBALL WORLD

Mailing Address: P.O. Box 646, Allenwood, NJ 08720. **Telephone:** (888) CBW-8750. **Fax:** (888) CBW-8720. **E-mail:** cbw@cooperstownbaseballworld.com. **Website:** www.cooperstownbaseballworld.com.
Complex Address: Cooperstown Baseball World, SUNY-Oneonta, Ravine Parkway, Oneonta, NY 13820.
President: Debra Sirianni.
2019 Tournaments (15 Teams Per Week): Open to 12U, 13U, 14U, 15U, 16U

COOPERSTOWN DREAMS PARK

Mailing Address: 330 S. Main St., Salisbury, NC 28144. **Telephone:** (704) 630-0050. **Fax:** (704) 630-0737. **E-mail Address:** info@cooperstowndreamspark.com. **Website:** www.cooperstowndreamspark.com.
Complex Address: 4550 State Highway 28, Milford, NY 13807.
Chief Operating Officer: Mike Walter. Director, **Baseball Operations:** Geoff Davis.
2019 Tournaments: June 1-Aug. 17.

COOPERSTOWN ALL STAR VILLAGE

Mailing Address: P.O. Box 670, Cooperstown, NY 13326. **Telephone:** (800) 327-6790. **Fax:** (607) 432-1076. **E-mail Address:** info@cooperstownallstarvillage.com. **Website:** www.cooperstownallstarvillage.com.

Team Registrations: Hunter Grace. **Hotel Room Reservations:** Tracie Jones. **Presidents:** Martin and Brenda Patton.

DIXIE YOUTH BASEBALL

Mailing Address: P.O. Box 877, Marshall, TX 75671. **Telephone:** (903) 927-2255. **Fax:** (903) 927-1846. **E-mail Address:** dyb@dixie.org. **Website:** youth.dixie.org.

Year Founded: 1955.
Commissioner: Wes Skelton.

DIXIE BOYS BASEBALL

Mailing Address: P.O. Box 8263, Dothan, AL 36304. **Telephone:** (334) 793-3331. **E-mail Address:** jjones29@sw.rr.com. **Website:** http://baseball.dixie.org.
Commissioner/Chief Executive Officer: Sandy Jones.

DIZZY DEAN BASEBALL

Mailing Address: P.O. Box 856, Hernando, MS 38632. **Telephone:** (662) 429-4365. **E-mail Address:** danny phillips637@gmail.com. **Website:** www.dizzydeanbbinc.org.
Year Founded: 1962.
Commissioner: Danny Phillips. **President:** Chris Landry. **VP:** Bobby Dunn. **Secretary:** Joe Chandler. **Treasurer:** Jim Dunn.

HAP DUMONT YOUTH BASEBALL

(A Division of the National Baseball Congress)
E-mail Address: hapdumontbaseball@gmail.com.
Year Founded: 1974.
President: Bruce Pinkall

KC SPORTS TOURNAMENTS

Mailing Address: KC Sports, 6324 N. Chatham Ave., No. 136, Kansas City, MO 64151.
Telephone: (816) 587-4545. **Fax:** (816) 587-4549.
E-mail Address: info@kcsports.org.
Website: www.kcsports.org.
Activities: USSSA Youth tournaments (ages 6-18).

LITTLE LEAGUE BASEBALL

International Headquarters: 539 US Route 15 Hwy, P.O. Box 3485, Williamsport, PA 17701-0485. **Telephone:** (570) 326-1921. **Fax:** (570) 326-1074. **E-Mail Address:** media@littleleague.org. **Website:** www.littleleague.org.
Year Founded: 1939.
Chairman: Hugh E. Tanner.
President/Chief Executive Officer: Stephen D. Keener. **Chief Financial Officer:** David Houseknecht. **Vice President, Operations:** Patrick Wilson. **Treasurer:** Melissa Singer. **Vice President, Marketing and Communications:** Liz Brown.

NATIONS BASEBALL-ARIZONA

Mailing Address: 20230 Cypress Rosehill Road, Tomball, TX 77377. **Telephone:** (877) 259-1150. **Website:** arizona.nations-baseball.com. **E-Mail:** info@nations-baseball.com.

NATIONAL AMATEUR BASEBALL FEDERATION

Mailing Address: P.O. Box 705, Bowie, MD 20718. **Telephone:** (410) 721-4727. **Fax:** (410) 721-4940.
E-mail Address: nabf1914@aol.com.
Website: www.nabf.com.
Year Founded: 1914.
Executive Director: Charles Blackburn.

INSTRUCTIONAL SCHOOLS/ PRIVATE CAMPS

ALL-STAR BASEBALL ACADEMY

Mailing Address: 1475 Phoenixville Pike Suite 12, West Chester, PA 19380. **Telephone:** (484) 770-8325. **Fax:** (484) 770-8336. **E-mail Address:** basba@allstarbaseball academy.com. **Website:** www.allstarbaseballacademy. com. **President/CEO:** Jim Freeman. **Executive Director:** Mike Manning.

AMERICAN BASEBALL FOUNDATION

Mailing Address: 833 Saint Vincent's Drive Suite 205A, Birmingham, AL 35205. **Telephone:** (205) 558-4235. **Fax:** (205) 918-0800. **E-mail Address:** abf@asmi.org. **Website:** www.americanbaseballfoundation.com. **Executive Director:** David Osinski.

ABC BASEBALL CAMPS

Mailing Address: 3020 ISSQ Pine Lake Road #12, Sammamish, WA 98075. **Telephone:** (800) 222-8152. **Fax:** (888) 751-8989. **E-mail Address:** sandi@abcsportscamps. com. **Website:** www./collegebaseballcamps.com/abc-baseball-camps/.

CHAMPIONS BASEBALL ACADEMY

Mailing Address: 5994 Linneman Street, Cincinnati, OH 45230. **Telephone:** (513) 831-8873. **Fax:** (513) 247-0040. **E-mail Address:** championsbaseball@ymail.com. **Website:** www.championsbaseball.net. **Director:** Mike Bricker.

ELEV8 SPORTS INSTITUTE

Mailing Address: 490 Dotterel Road, Delray Beach, FL 33444. **Telephone:** (800) 970-5896. **Fax:** (561) 865-7358. **E-mail Address:** info@elev8si.com. **Website:** http://elev8sportsinstitute.com/

FROZEN ROPES TRAINING CENTERS

Mailing Address: 24 Old Black Meadow Rd., Chester, NY 10918. **Telephone:** (845) 469-7331. **Fax:** (845) 469-6742. **E-mail Address:** info@frozenropes.com. **Website:** www.frozenropes.com.

IMG ACADEMY

Mailing Address: IMG Academy, 5500 34th St. W., Bradenton, FL 34210. **Telephone:** (941) 749-8627. **Fax:** 941-739-7484. **E-mail Address:** colbe.herr@img.com **Website:** www.imgacademy.com

MARK CRESSE BASEBALL SCHOOL

Mailing Address: P.O. Box 1596 Newport Beach, CA 92659. **Telephone:** (714) 892-6145. **Fax:** (714) 890-7017. **E-mail Address:** info@markcresse.com.

Website: www.markcresse.com.
Owner/Founder: Mark Cresse.

US SPORTS CAMPS/NIKE BASEBALL CAMPS

Mailing Address: 1010 B Street Suite 450, San Rafael, CA 94901. **Telephone:** (415) 479-6060. **Fax:** (415) 479-6061. **E-mail Address:** baseball@ussportscamps.com. **Website:** www.ussportscamps.com/baseball/.

MOUNTAIN WEST BASEBALL ACADEMY

Mailing Address: 389 West 10000 South, South Jordan, UT 84095. **Telephone:** (801) 561-1700. **E-mail Address:** kent@utahbaseballacademy.com. **Website:** www.mountainwestbaseball.com. **Director:** Bob Keyes

NORTH CAROLINA BASEBALL ACADEMY

Mailing Address: 1137 Pleasant Ridge Road, Greensboro, NC 27409. **Telephone:** (336) 931-1118. **E-mail Address:** info@ncbaseball.com. **Website:** www.ncbaseball.com.
Owner/Director: Scott Bankhead.

PENNSYLVANIA DIAMOND BUCKS

Mailing Address: 2320 Whitetail Court, Hellertown, PA 18055. **Telephone:** (610) 838-1219, (610) 442-6998. **E-mail Address:** janciganick@yahoo.com. **Camp Director:** Jan Ciganick. **Head of Instruction:** Chuck Ciganick.

PROFESSIONAL BASEBALL INSTRUCTION

Mailing Address: 1300 Route 17 North, Ramsey Square Shopping Center, Ramsey, NJ 07446. **Telephone:** (800) 282-4638. **Fax:** (201) 760-8820. **E-mail Address:** info@baseballclinics.com. **Website:** www.baseballclinics.com. **President:** Doug Cinnella.
2019 Batter Invitational Showcase: October 2019

RIPKEN BASEBALL CAMPS

Mailing Address: 873 Long Drive, Averdeen, MD 21209. **Telephone:** (888) 747-5368. **E-mail Address:** information@ripkenbaseball.com. **Website:** www.ripkenbaseball.com.

SHO-ME BASEBALL CAMP

Mailing Address: P.O. Box 2270, Branson West, MO 65737. **Telephone:** (417) 338-5838. **Fax:** (417) 338-2610. **E-mail Address:** info@shomebaseball.com. **Website:** www.shomebaseball.com.

COLLEGE CAMPS

Almost all of the elite college baseball programs have summer/holiday instructional camps. Please consult the college section for listings.

SENIOR BASEBALL

MEN'S SENIOR BASEBALL LEAGUE

(18+, 25+, 35+, 45+, 55+, 65+)

Mailing Address: One Huntington Quadrangle, Suite 3NO7, Melville, NY 11747. **Telephone:** (631) 753-6725. **Fax:** (631) 753-4031.

President: Steve Sigler. **Vice President:** Gary D'Ambrisi.

E-Mail Address: info@msblnational.com.
Website: www.msblnational.com.

MEN'S ADULT BASEBALL LEAGUE

(18 and Over)

Mailing Address: One Huntington Quadrangle, Suite 3NO7, Melville, NY 11747. **Telephone:** (631) 753-6725. **Fax:** (631) 753-4031.

E-Mail Address: info@msblnational.com. **Website:** www.msblnational.com.

President: Steve Sigler. **Vice President:** Gary D'Ambrisi.

NATIONAL ADULT BASEBALL ASSOCIATION

Mailing Address: 5944 S. Kipling St., Suite 200, Littleton, CO 80127. **Telephone:** (800) 621-6479. **E-Mail:** nabanational@aol.com. **Website:** www.dugout.org.

President: Shane Fugita.

NATIONAL AMATEUR BASEBALL FEDERATION

Mailing Address: P.O. Box 705, Bowie, MD 20718. **Telephone:** (410) 721-4727. **Fax:** (410) 721-4940.

Email Address: nabf1914@aol.com.
Website: www.nabf.com.
Year Founded: 1914.
Executive Director: Charles Blackburn.

ROY HOBBS BASEBALL

Veterans (30 or 35 and Over), Masters (45 and Over), Legends (53 and Over); Classics (60 and Over), Vintage (65 and Over), Timeless (70 and Over), Forever Young (75 and Over).

Mailing Address: 4301-A Edison Ave., Fort Myers, FL 33916. **Telephone:** (330) 923-3400. **E-Mail Address:** rh_bb@royhobbs.com. **Website:** www.royhobbs.com.

CEO: Tom Giffen. **President:** Rob Giffen.

DIRECTORIES

- ■ AGENTS
- ■ SERVICES

AGENT DIRECTORY

BALL PLAYERS AGENCY
132 North Old Woodward Avenue
Birmingham, MI 48009
Phone: 877-TRUST-07
Fax: 248-281-5150
Website: ballplayersagency.com
E-mail: info@ballplayersagency.com
Storm T. Kirschenbaum, Esq. , Michael
Bonanno, Alex Hinz, Esq., Mark Meisner,
Tony Chang

GSE WORLDWIDE
1500 Broadway, Ste. 2501
New York, NY 10036
Phone: 212-334-6880
Fax: 212-334-6895
Website: gseworldwide.com
E-mail: info@gseworldwide.com
Peter E. Greenberg, Esq., Edward L.
Greenberg, Chris Leible, Joe Mizzo, RJ
Hernandez, Joe Brennan

PRO STAR MANAGEMENT, INC.
1600 Scripps Center, 312 Walnut Street
Cincinnati, OH 45202
Phone: 513-762-7676
Fax: 513-721-4628
Website: prostarmanagement.com
E-mail: prostar@fuse.net
Joe Bick, President, Brett Bick, Executive
Vice President

SOSNICK COBBE & KARON
712 Bancroft Rd, #510
Walnut Creek, CA 94598
Phone: 925-890-5283
Fax: 925-476-0130
Website: SosnickCobbeKaron.com
E-mail: info@SosnickCobbeKaron.com
Matt Sosnick, Paul Cobbe, Adam Karon,
Matt Hofer, Jon Einalhori, Tripper Johnson,
John Furmaniak

VERILL DANA SPORTS LAW GROUP
One Portland Square
Portland, ME 04101
Phone: 207-774-4000
Fax: 207-774-7499
Website: verrilldana.com
E-mail: dabramson@verrilldana.com
David S. Abramson, Esq.

SERVICE DIRECTORY

ACCESSORIES

FRANKLIN SPORTS
17 Campanellli Parkway
Stoughton, MA 02072
Phone: 781-344-1111
Fax: 781-341-0333
E-mail: customerservice@franklinsports.com

MIZUNO
4925 Avalon Ridge Parkway
One Jack Curran Way
Norcross, GA 30071
Phone: 800-966-1211
Fax: 770-448-3234
Web: mizunousa.com

RAWLINGS
510 Maryville University Dr., Suite 110
St. Louis, MO 63141
Phone: 866-678-4327
Web: rawlings.com
E-mail: service@rawlings.com

WILSON SPORTING GOODS
1 Prudential Plaza
130 East Randolph Street, Suite 600
Chicago, IL 60601
Phone: 800-800-9936
Web: wilson.com
E-mail: askwilson@wilson.com

APPAREL

DEMARINI
6435 NE Croeni Ave.
Hillsboro, OR 97124
Phone: 800-800-9932
Web: demarini.com

BAGS

DEMARINI
6435 NE Croeni Ave.
Hillsboro, OR 97124
Phone: 800-800-9932
Web: demarini.com

DIAMOND SPORTS
PO BOX 55090
Irvine, CA 92619
Phone: 949-409-9300
Fax: 949-409-9301
Website: diamond-sports.com
E-mail: marketing@diamond-sports.com

GERRY COSBY AND COMPANY
11 Pennsylvania Plaza
New York, NY, 10001
Phone: 877-563-6464
Fax: 212-967-0876
Web: cosbysports.com
Email: gcsmsg@cosbysports.com

LOUISVILLE SLUGGER
1 Prudential Plaza
130 East Randolph Street, Suite 600
Chicago, IL 60601
Phone: 800-800-9935
E-mail: customerservice@slugger.com

MIZUNO
4925 Avalon Ridge Parkway
One Jack Curran Way
Norcross, GA 30071
Phone: 800-966-1211
Fax: 770-448-3234
Web: mizunousa.com

WILSON SPORTING GOODS
1 Prudential Plaza
130 East Randolph Street, Suite 600
Chicago, IL 60601
Phone: 800-800-9936
Web: wilson.com
E-mail: askwilson@wilson.com

BASEBALLS

DIAMOND SPORTS
PO BOX 55090
Irvine, CA 92619
Phone: 949-409-9300
Fax: 949-409-9301
Website: diamond-sports.com
E-mail: marketing@diamond-sports.com

RAWLINGS
510 Maryville University Dr.
Suite 110 St. Louis, MO 63141
Phone: 866-678-4327
Web: rawlings.com
E-mail: service@rawlings.com

WILSON SPORTING GOODS
1 Prudential Plaza
130 East Randolph Street, Suite 600
Chicago, IL 60601
Phone: 800-800-9936
Web: wilson.com
E-mail: askwilson@wilson.com

BASES

C&H BASEBALL
10615 Technology Terrace #100
Lakewood Ranch, FL 34211
Phone: 941-727-1533
Fax: 941-462-3076
Web: chbaseball.com
E-mail: sales@chbaseball.com

BATS

DEMARINI
6435 NE Croeni Ave.
Hillsboro, OR 97124
Phone: 800-800-9932
Web: demarini.com

DIAMOND SPORTS
PO BOX 55090
Irvine, CA 92619
Phone: 949-409-9300
Fax: 949-409-9301
Website: diamond-sports.com
E-mail: marketing@diamond-sports.com

DINGER BATS
PO Box 71, 109 Kimbro St.
Ridgway, IL 62979
Phone: 866-934-6437
Web: dingerbats.com
E-mail: info@dingerbats.com

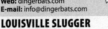
See our ad on the insert!

LOUISVILLE SLUGGER
1 Prudential Plaza
130 East Randolph Street, Suite 600
Chicago, IL 60601
Phone: 800-800-9935
E-mail: customerservice@slugger.com

MIZUNO
4925 Avalon Ridge Parkway
One Jack Curran Way,
Norcross, GA 30071
Phone: 800-966-1211
Fax: 770-448-3234
Web: mizunousa.com

OLD HICKORY
PO Box 588
White House, TN 37188
Phone: 866-PRO-BATS
Fax: 615-285-0512
Web: oldhickorybats.com
Email: mail@oldhickorybats.com

See our ad on page 6!

RAWLINGS
510 Maryville University Dr., Suite 110
St. Louis, MO 63141
Phone: 866-678-4327
Web: rawlings.com
E-mail: service@rawlings.com

BATTING CAGES

C&H BASEBALL
10615 Technology Terrace #100
Lakewood Ranch, FL 34211
Phone: 941-727-1533
Fax: 941-462-3076
Web: chbaseball.com
E-mail: sales@chbaseball.com

WEST COAST NETTING, INC
5075 Flightline Dr.
Kingman, AZ 86401
Phone: 928-692-1144
Fax: 928-692-1501
Website: westcoastnetting.com
E-mail: info@westcoastnetting.com

BATTING GLOVES

DEMARINI
6435 NE Croeni Ave.
Hillsboro, OR 97124
Phone: 800-800-9932
Web: demarini.com

FRANKLIN SPORTS
17 Campanellli Parkway
Stoughton, MA 02072
Phone: 781-344-1111
Fax: 781-341-0333
E-mail: customerservice@franklinsports.com

MIZUNO
4925 Avalon Ridge Parkway
One Jack Curran Way,
Norcross, GA 30071
Phone: 800-966-1211
Fax: 770-448-3234
Web: mizunousa.com

RAWLINGS
510 Maryville University Dr., Suite 110
St. Louis, MO 63141
Phone: 866-678-4327
Web: rawlings.com
E-mail: service@rawlings.com

BUNTING/PLEATED FANS/FLAGS

INDEPENDENCE BUNTING & FLAG CORP
44 West Jefryn Boulevard, Suite T
Deer Park, NY 11729
Phone: 631-761-6007
Fax: 888-824-1060
Website: independence-bunting.com
E-mail: independencebunting@gmail.com

EMBROIDERED SOURCE

THE EMBLEM SOURCE
4575 Westgrove #500
Addison, TX 75001
Phone: 972-248-1909
Fax: 972-248-1615
Website: theemblemsource.com
E-mail: larry@theemblemsource.com

ENGINEERED BACKSTOP DESIGN BUILD

C&H BASEBALL
10615 Technology Terrace #100
Lakewood Ranch, FL 34211
Phone: 941-727-1533
Fax: 941-462-3076
Web: chbaseball.com
E-mail: sales@chbaseball.com

WEST COAST NETTING, INC
5075 Flightline Dr.
Kingman, AZ 86401
Phone: 928-692-1144
Fax: 928-692-1501
Website: westcoastnetting.com
E-mail: info@westcoastnetting.com

FIELD COVERS/TARPS

C&H BASEBALL
10615 Technology Terrace #100
Lakewood Ranch, FL 34211
Phone: 941-727-1533
Fax: 941-462-3076
Web: chbaseball.com
E-mail: sales@chbaseball.com

FIELD WALL PADDING

C&H BASEBALL
10615 Technology Terrace #100
Lakewood Ranch, FL 34211
Phone: 941-727-1533
Fax: 941-462-3076
Web: chbaseball.com
E-mail: sales@chbaseball.com

WEST COAST NETTING, INC
5075 Flightline Dr.
Kingman, AZ 86401
Phone: 928-692-1144
Fax: 928-692-1501
Website: westcoastnetting.com
E-mail: info@westcoastnetting.com

FOOD SERVICE

BUSH'S BEST BEANS
1016 E Weisgarber Rd
Knoxville, TN 37909
Phone: 865-558-5424
E-mail: bcarpenter@bushbros.com

GLOVES

ALL-STAR SPORTING GOODS
17 Leominster Road
Shirley, MA 01464
Phone: 800-777-3810
Web: all-starsports.com
E-mail: weborders@all-starsports.com

See our ad on the inside cover!

DIAMOND SPORTS
PO BOX 55090
Irvine, CA 92619
Phone: 949-409-9300
Fax: 949-409-9301
Website: diamond-sports.com
E-mail: marketing@diamond-sports.com

FORCE3 PRO GEAR
155 New Haven Ave.
Derby, CT 06418
Phone: 315-367-2331
Fax: 866-332-3492
Web: force3progear.com
E-mail: info@force3progear.com

See our ad on the insert!

LOUISVILLE SLUGGER
1 Prudential Plaza
130 East Randolph Street, Suite 600,
Chicago, IL 60601
Phone: 800-800-9935
E-mail: customerservice@slugger.com

MIZUNO
4925 Avalon Ridge Parkway
One Jack Curran Way
Norcross, GA 30071
Phone: 800-966-1211
Fax: 770-448-3234
Web: mizunousa.com

RAWLINGS
510 Maryville University Dr., Suite 110
St. Louis, MO 63141
Phone: 866-678-4327
Web: rawlings.com
E-mail: service@rawlings.com

WILSON SPORTING GOODS
1 Prudential Plaza
130 East Randolph Street, Suite 600,
Chicago, IL 60601
Phone: 800-800-9936
Web: www.wilson.com
E-mail: askwilson@wilson.com

MUSIC/SOUND EFFECTS

SOUND DIRECTOR INC.
2918 SW Royal Way
Gresham, OR 97080
Phone: 503-665-6869
Fax: 503-914-1812
Website: sounddirector.com
E-mail: jj@sounddirector.com

NETTING/POSTS

C&H BASEBALL
10615 Technology Terrace #100
Lakewood Ranch, FL 34211
Phone: 941-727-1533
Fax: 941-462-3076
Web: chbaseball.com
E-mail: sales@chbaseball.com

WEST COAST NETTING, INC
5075 Flightline Dr.
Kingman, AZ 86401
Phone: 928-692-1144
Fax: 928-692-1501
Website: westcoastnetting.com
E-mail: info@westcoastnetting.com

PITCHING MACHINES

ATHLETIC TRAINING EQUIPMENT COMPANY
655 Spice Island Drive
Sparks, NV 89431
Phone: 800-800-9931
Web: atecsports.com
E-mail: askATEC@wilson.com

PLAYING FIELD PRODUCTS

C&H BASEBALL
10615 Technology Terrace #100
Lakewood Ranch, FL 34211
Phone: 941-727-1533
Fax: 941-462-3076

Web: chbaseball.com
E-mail: sales@chbaseball.com

DIAMOND PRO
112 East Copeland Road
Arlington, TX 76011
Phone: 1-800-228-2987
Fax: 1-800-640-6735
Web: diamondpro.com
E-mail: diamondpro@diamondpro.com

WEST COAST NETTING, INC
5075 Flightline Dr.
Kingman, AZ 86401
Phone: 928-692-1144
Fax: 928-692-1501
Website: westcoastnetting.com
E-mail: info@westcoastnetting.com

PROTECTIVE EQUIPMENT

ALL-STAR SPORTING GOODS
17 Leominster Road
Shirley, MA 01464
Phone: 800-777-3810
Web: all-starsports.com
E-mail: weborders@all-starsports.com

See our ad on the inside cover!

C&H BASEBALL
10615 Technology Terrace #100
Lakewood Ranch, FL 34211
Phone: 941-727-1533
Fax: 941-462-3076
Web: chbaseball.com
E-mail: sales@chbaseball.com

DIAMOND SPORTS
PO BOX 55090
Irvine, CA 92619
Phone: 949-409-9300
Fax: 949-409-9301
Website: diamond-sports.com
E-mail: marketing@diamond-sports.com

EVOSHIELD
1 Prudential Plaza
130 East Randolph Street, Suite 600,
Chicago, IL 60601
Phone: 800-800-9934
Web: evoshield.com
E-mail: askwilson@wilson.com

FORCE3 PRO GEAR
155 New Haven Ave.
Derby, CT 06418
Phone: 315-367-2331
Fax: 866-332-3492
Web: force3progear.com
E-mail: info@force3progear.com

See our ad on the insert!

MIZUNO
4925 Avalon Ridge Parkway
One Jack Curran Way
Norcross, GA 30071
Phone: 800-966-1211
Fax: 770-448-3234
Web: mizunousa.com

RAWLINGS
510 Maryville University Dr., Suite 110
St. Louis, MO 63141
Phone: 866-678-4327
Web: rawlings.com
E-mail: service@rawlings.com

WEST COAST NETTING, INC
5075 Flightline Dr.
Kingman, AZ 86401
Phone: 928-692-1144
Fax: 928-692-1501
Website: westcoastnetting.com
E-mail: info@westcoastnetting.com

WILSON SPORTING GOODS
1 Prudential Plaza,
130 East Randolph Street, Suite 600,
Chicago, IL 60601
Phone: 800-800-9936
Web: www.wilson.com
E-mail: askwilson@wilson.com

RADAR EQUIPMENT

POCKET RADAR, INC.
3535 Industrial Dr., Suite A4
Santa Rosa, CA 95403
Phone: 888-381-2672
Fax: 888-381-2672
E-mail: tscaturro@pocketradar.com

STALKER SPORT RADAR
855 E Collins Blvd
Richardson, TX 75081
Phone: 972-398-3780
Website: stalkersportradar.com
E-mail: sales@stalkerradar.com

SCOREBOARD

STALKER SPORT RADAR
855 E Collins Blvd
Richardson, TX 75081
Phone: 972-398-3780
Website: stalkersportradar.com
E-mail: sales@stalkerradar.com

TRAINING EQUIPMENT

ATHLETIC TRAINING EQUIPMENT COMPANY
655 Spice Island Drive
Sparks, NV 89431
Phone: 800-800-9931
Web: atecsports.com
E-mail: askATEC@wilson.com

LOUISVILLE SLUGGER
1 Prudential Plaza,
130 East Randolph Street, Suite 600,
Chicago, IL 60601
Phone: 800-800-9935
E-mail: customerservice@slugger.com

WEST COAST NETTING, INC
5075 Flightline Dr.
Kingman, AZ 86401
Phone: 928-692-1144
Fax: 928-692-1501
Website: westcoastnetting.com
E-mail: info@westcoastnetting.com

UNIFORMS

FRANKLIN SPORTS
17 Campanellli Parkway
Stoughton, MA 02072
Phone: 781-344-1111
Fax: 781-341-0333
E-mail: customerservice@franklinsports.com

MIZUNO
4925 Avalon Ridge Parkway
One Jack Curran Way,
Norcross, GA 30071
Phone: 800-966-1211
Fax: 770-448-3234
Web: mizunousa.com

WILSON SPORTING GOODS
1 Prudential Plaza,
130 East Randolph Street, Suite 600,
Chicago, IL 60601
Phone: 800-800-9936
Web: wilson.com
E-mail: askwilson@wilson.com

WINDSCREENS

C&H BASEBALL
10615 Technology Terrace #100
Lakewood Ranch, FL 34211
Phone: 941-727-1533
Fax: 941-462-3076
Web: chbaseball.com
E-mail: sales@chbaseball.com

WEST COAST NETTING, INC
5075 Flightline Dr.
Kingman, AZ 86401
Phone: 928-692-1144
Fax: 928-692-1501
Website: westcoastnetting.com
E-mail: info@westcoastnetting.com

YOUR NAME HERE
Make sure the baseball
community can find you
in 2019.
Call: 919-213-7924
E-mail: advertising@baseballamerica.com

ED WOLFSTEIN

MAJOR LEAGUE TEAMS

MINOR LEAGUE TEAMS

ANDREW WOOLLEY

MINOR LEAGUE TEAMS, CONT.

INDEPENDENT TEAMS

OTHER ORGANIZATIONS

INDEX